LEGAL ETHICS
FOR PARALEGALS AND
THE LAW OFFICE

LEGAL ETHICS
FOR PARALEGALS AND
THE LAW OFFICE

LAURA L. MORRISON, J.D.

GINA M. DeCIANI, J.D.

DELMAR
CENGAGE Learning™

Australia • Brazil • Japan • Korea • Mexico • Singapore • Spain • United Kingdom • United States

**Legal Ethics for Paralegals
and the Law Office**
Laura L. Morrison,
Gina M. DeCiani

Copy Editor: Cindi Gerber

Text and Cover Designer: Roslyn
Stendahl/Dapper Design

Compositor: Carlisle
Communications, Ltd.

Indexer: Schroeder Indexing
Services

Cover Image: David Chalk,
Chalkmark Graphics

Credits: American Bar Association
Model Code of Professional
Responsibility. Copyright © 1986
American Bar Asssociation. All
Rights Reserved. Reprinted by
permission of the American Bar
Association. American Bar
Association Model Rules of
Professional Conduct. © 1994 by
the American Bar Association. All
Rights Reserved. Reprinted by
permission of the American Bar
Association. Copies of the ABA
Model Code of Professional
Responsibility and the ABA Model
Rules of Professional Conduct are
available from Order Fulfillment,
American Bar Association, 750
North Lake Shore Drive, Chicago,
IL 60611. American Bar
Association, Reprinted by
permission.

For product information and technology assistance, contact us at
Cengage Learning Customer & Sales Support, 1-800-354-9706

For permission to use material from this text or product,
submit all requests online at **www.cengage.com/permissions**
Further permissions questions can be emailed to
permissionrequest@cengage.com

Library of Congress Control Number: 94-27670

ISBN-13: 978-0-314-04173-9

ISBN-10: 0-314-04173-7

Delmar
Executive Woods
5 Maxwell Drive
Clifton Park, NY 12065
USA

Cengage Learning is a leading provider of customized learning solutions with office locations around the globe, including Singapore, the
United Kingdom, Australia, Mexico, Brazil, and Japan. Locate your
local office at **www.cengage.com/global**

Cengage Learning products are represented in Canada by
Nelson Education, Ltd.

To learn more about Delmar, visit **www.cengage.com/delmar**

Purchase any of our products at your local bookstore or at our
preferred online store **www.CengageBrain.com**

Printed in the United States of America
15 16 17 18 19   22 21 20 19 18

DEDICATION

To my husband, Paul Dombrowski, whom I adore.
To my parents, Carol and Bill, and to Paul, Jacqueline M. and Karen L. Kollar, for all their support.

L.M.

To my family and friends.
Without your support, this text would not have been completed.

G.D.

ABOUT THE AUTHORS

LAURA MORRISON

Laura has been committed to the education of paralegals since 1985 when she started teaching in the Paralegal Studies Program at Central Piedmont Community College in Charlotte, North Carolina. Following a move to Chicago, Illinois, she became an instructor and the Academic Director of the Lawyer's Assistant Program at Roosevelt University. She is a graduate of the University of Scranton in Pennsylvania, B.S. 1981, and Saint Louis University School of Law in Missouri, J.D. 1984. Laura has taught numerous college courses including Legal Ethics, Case Analysis, Business Law, Legal Systems, Legal Research and Writing, and Evidence.

Since 1991, Laura has been employed as an Assistant State's Attorney at the Office of the Cook County, Illinois, State's Attorney. She has worked in the Trial, Appellate, and Legal Opinions/Corporate Transactions divisions. In addition, during her time at the state's attorney's office, Laura has developed and implemented a law office skills training course for non-lawyer support staff in the areas of Legal Ethics, Legal Systems, and Legal Research.

Laura is a member of the Chicago Bar Association Professional Responsibility Committee and the American Bar Association Center for Professional Responsibility. She also is a member of the American Association for Paralegal Education and the National Federation of Paralegal Associations. She coauthored an article for the American Bar Association 19th National Conference on Professional Responsibility called "Regulation of Legal Assistants" and served on a panel at the Conference on the topic, "Non Lawyers are People Too."

GINA DeCIANI

Gina DeCiani began her career in paralegal education at Roosevelt University in Chicago, Illinois. At Roosevelt, she held the positions of instructor, Employment Assistance Director, and Acting Director of Education. She is now an adjunct instructor at the American Institute for Paralegal Studies where she teaches legal research and writing.

Gina attended the University of Illinois at Urbana-Champaign, receiving her Bachelor of Science in 1986 and her Juris Doctorate in 1989. She is currently employed as a law clerk at the Appellate Court of Illinois and has clerked for the Tax and Miscellaneous Remedies Division of the Circuit Court of Cook County and for the Supreme Court of Illinois.

Gina is a member of the Chicago Bar Association Professional Responsibility Committee and the American Bar Association Center for Professional Responsibility. She is also a member of the National Association for Legal Assistants, American Association for Paralegal Education, and Professional Legal Assistants. Gina has testified before the American Bar Association Commission on Nonlawyer Practice. Along with Ms. Morrison, she is the coauthor of an article drafted for the American Bar Association 19th National Conference on Professional Responsibility entitled, "Regulation of Legal Assistants."

CONTENTS IN BRIEF

CHAPTER 1   An Introductory History of Paralegals   1

CHAPTER 2   Overview of Legal Ethics   29

CHAPTER 3   The Unauthorized Practice of Law   64

CHAPTER 4   The Duty of Diligence   110

CHAPTER 5   Confidentiality   129

CHAPTER 6   Conflicts of Interest   165

CHAPTER 7   Financial Matters   218

CHAPTER 8   Advertising and Solicitation   248

CHAPTER 9   Reporting Attorney and Paralegal Misconduct   269

CHAPTER 10   Professional Conduct in the Law Office   289

CONTENTS

CHAPTER 1 An Introductory History of Paralegals 1

The Roots of the Paralegal Profession 2
  The Law Clerk-Apprentice 2
  Administrative Agencies 3
  The Legal Secretary 3
  Legal Services Organizations 4
The Development of the Role of the Paralegal 4
  Recognition by the American Bar Association 5
  Development of Educational Programs 8
  National Paralegal Organizations 10
Issues Affecting the Future of the Paralegal 13
  The Freelance Paralegal 14
  Regulation of Legal Assistants 15
FOCUS ON ALICE PENNY 18
CASE In re Opinion No. 24 of the Committee on the Unauthorized Practice of Law 20

CHAPTER 2 Overview of Legal Ethics 29

Principles of Legal Ethics 30
  Attorney Codes of Ethics 31
  Disciplinary Agencies, Case Law, and Ethics Advisory Opinions 34
  Application of Attorney's Codes of Ethics to Legal Assistants 36
  Guidelines for the Utilization of Legal Assistants 42
  Paralegal Codes of Ethics 43
Violations of Ethics Rules 45
  Consequences Resulting to Attorneys 45
  Consequences Resulting to Paralegals 49
  Paralegal Liability for Freelance Work 53

Paralegal Liability for the Actions of the Law Firm 54
Paralegal Liability for the Actions of Corporations 55
FOCUS ON ESTEBAN SANTANA 56
CASE In re Estate of Divine, Lyster et.al. v. Giancola 59

CHAPTER 3 The Unauthorized Practice of Law 64

Historical Analysis of the Unauthorized Practice of Law 65
The Practice of Law 67
The "Practice of Law" in the Law Office 69
  Initial Client Interview 70
  Advising the Client 71
  Drafting Papers and Pleadings 71
  Discovery 72
  Trial Preparation 74
Court Appearances, Criminal Proceedings, and Lay Representation 74
  Criminal Representation 76
Administrative Agency Representation 78
  State Administrative Agencies 79
  Federal Agencies 82
Typing Services and "Do-It-Yourself" Kits 84
Real Estate 92
Disclosure of Nonlawyer Status 93
Consequences of Violating Practice of Law Rules 95
  The Consequences for the Attorney 95
  Sanctions Against the Nonlawyer 97
The Changing Nature of Nonlawyer Practice 98
  The Freelance Paralegal 98
  The American Bar Association Commission on Nonlawyer Practice 100
FOCUS ON INGRID-JOY WARRICK 101
CASE Louisiana State Bar Association v. Edwins 104

CHAPTER 4 The Duty of Diligence   110

The Rule of Zealous Representation   111
  Reasonable Diligence and Promptness   112
  Statutes of Limitation and Filing Dates   113
  Procrastination   115
  What If the Paralegal Has No Experience in a Law Office Setting or Lacks Experience in a Particular Area of the Law?   116
The Duty of Candor   116
  Revealing Adverse Authority   118
  Revealing Nonlawyer Status to the Court   119
***Ex Parte* Communications   120**
  Adverse Parties   120
  Judges and Jurors   121
FOCUS ON REBECCA BIKE   122
CASE IN RE CONDUCT OF BURROWS   125

CHAPTER 5 Confidentiality   129

The General Rule of Confidentiality: An Ethical Obligation   130
  The Purpose of the Rule of Confidentiality   131
  What Is the Rule of Confidentiality?   131
  The Attorney-Client Privilege   132
  The Work Product Doctrine   138
  The Ethical Rules of Confidentiality   140
  Attorney-Client Privilege and Rule of Confidentiality Compared   144
Confidentiality Rules and Legal Assistants   146
Confidentiality and Law Office Practice   152
  Initial Client Visit   152
  Discovery Matters   153
  Internal Documents   155
  Law Office Daily Operations   155
  Trial Testimony   156
The Corporate Paralegal   156
FOCUS ON JANIS SHANE   158
CASE THE SAMARITAN FOUNDATION v. SUPERIOR COURT   161

CHAPTER 6 Conflicts of Interest   165

Conflicts of Interest   166
  Conflict of Interest and the Legal Assistant   167
  Consequences of Violating Conflict of Interest Rules   169
  Determining the Existence of a Conflict   170
Specific Types of Conflicts of Interest   172
  Simultaneous Representation   172
  Prohibited Transactions   178
  Attorney as Witness   191
  Former Clients   193
Imputed Disqualification   195
  Waiving Disqualification   199
  Avoiding Imputed Disqualification through Use of Screening Devices   199
  Screening the Legal Assistant   202
Conflicts Checks   203
  Using Computer Software to Avoid Conflicts   204
FOCUS ON MERLE ISGETT   206
CASE IN RE COMPLEX ASBESTOS LITIGATION   209

CHAPTER 7 Financial Matters   218

Fee Splitting   219
  Nonlawyer Referrals   221
  Business Enterprises between Attorneys and Nonlawyers   221
  Bonuses   223
Billing Practice   224
  Billing Paralegal Time   226
  Padding Billable Hours   227
  Awarding Paralegal Fees to the Prevailing Party   229
  Practical Application of *Missouri v. Jenkins*   231
Commingling Funds   232
  Application to Legal Assistants   234
  Disputed Funds   235

Interest on Accounts 235

Consequences of Commingling Funds 236

Pro Bono Work 239

FOCUS ON KAREN JUDD 241

CASE MISSOURI V. JENKINS 244

CHAPTER 8 Advertising and Solicitation 248

The Rules Regarding Advertising in the Legal Environment 249

Historical Restrictions on the Law Office 251

The Relaxation of Advertising Restrictions 252

Restrictions on the Paralegal 257

Paralegals Handling Attorney Advertising 258

Paralegals on Law Firm Letterhead 259

Paralegals and Business Cards 259

Paralegal Advertisement 260

Paralegal Solicitation 261

FOCUS ON LUCY EBERSOHL 263

CASE IN RE BACHMANN 266

CHAPTER 9 Reporting Attorney and Paralegal Misconduct 269

Attorney Misconduct 270

What Constitutes the Violation 271

To Whom the Violations Are Reported 273

Obligation of the Paralegal to Report Attorney Misconduct 275

What Constitutes the Violation 276

Options for Paralegal Action 277

Particularly Sensitive Areas 279

Special Concerns for the Freelance Paralegal 279

Obligation of the Paralegal to Report Paralegal Misconduct 280

Supervising Paralegal 281

Supervising Attorney 281

Local Paralegal Associations 281

FOCUS ON LAURIE ROSELLE 282

CASE IN RE HIMMEL 285

CHAPTER 10 Professional Conduct in the Law Office 289

Professional Conduct 290

Why Study Professional Behavior? 290

What Is Professional Conduct? 292

Achieving High Standards of Professional Conduct 293

Conduct in the Law Office 294

Interaction with Clients 295

Relationships with Attorneys 298

Conduct toward Paralegals 302

FOCUS ON SHELLEY WIDOFF 304

CASE CASTILLO V. ST. PAUL FIRE & MARINE INSURANCE COMPANY 307

Appendix A   ABA Model Guidelines for the Utilization of Legal Assistant Services   A-1

Appendix B   NFPA Model Code of Ethics and Professional Responsibility   B-1

Appendix C   NALA Model Standards and Guidelines for Utilization of Legal Assistants Annotated   C-1

Appendix D   Code of Ethics and Professional Responsibility of National Association of Legal Assistants, Inc.   D-1

Appendix E   Sample Limited Licensure Legislation   E-1

Table of Cases   T-1

Glossary   G-1

Index   I-1

PREFACE

Legal Ethics for Paralegals and the Law Office is a text which equips students with the tools to face ethical dilemmas on the job. It is not a book about ethics or morals in the philosophical sense. Rather, the comprehensive approach of this book provides a detailed description of attorneys' rules of ethics and how those rules apply to the nonlawyers whom the attorneys supervise.

The features of this text make it unique. Exercises, Highlights, Paralegals in the Spotlight, Tips for the Paralegal, and interviews with accomplished paralegals are colorful devices designed to set the stage for an exciting learning environment. More important, however, the text provides a comprehensive discussion of the ethical obligations of the paralegal. Upon completing this course, students will be familiar with the following topic areas: Unauthorized Practice of Law; Diligence; Confidentiality; Conflicts of Interest; Financial Concerns, including billing practices and client trust fund accounts; Advertising; Reporting Misconduct; and Professionalism. Our hope is that students who use this text will understand their ethical obligations and will enjoy their experience.

However, like any comprehensive overview of a topic area, this book does not seek to and cannot be the definitive source for resolving any and all ethical dilemmas confronting paralegals in the workplace. Rather, this text is a compilation of articles, rules and cases taken from many jurisdictions. These rules may or may not apply in a particular locality. The real-life experiences of the teachers, students and supervising attorneys should provide the final answer when a student is faced with a delicate ethical problem.

CHAPTER FORMAT

Each chapter is presented in a similar style. Chapter features include the following:

- *Chapter Objectives* open each chapter. The objectives are designed to highlight the main concepts of each chapter and to focus student attention on these elements.

- *Opening Exercises* present hypothetical ethical situations and ask students to discuss possible courses of action and the possible consequences of choosing that action. They are designed to pique student interest in the chapter by encouraging them to think about the issues that will be presented.

- *Paralegals in the Spotlight* are summaries of real-life ethical challenges faced by paralegals. They are often taken from periodicals such as *Legal Assistant Today*. For example, Chapter 6 presents the story of Michael Vogel and the problems his conflicts of interest caused his law firm.

- *Key Terminology* is emphasized and reinforced in four ways in the text. Key terms are placed in boldface type and defined in context when they first appear. They are also defined in the margin for easy review. These terms are listed at the end of each chapter and are included in a comprehensive end-of-text glossary.

- *Interplay Boxes* within selected chapters illustrate the interrelationship of various ethical rules. They provide a great instructional tool for discussing the interdependence of ethical rules.

- *Exercises* within the chapter take several forms. Some of the exercises ask students to complete independent research assignments, such as visiting a local library to obtain a copy of that jurisdiction's code of ethics, or to give their opinion concerning a particular contested issue. Other exercises provide short hypothetical situations followed by questions. Students are then asked to apply concepts from the chapter to answer the problem. Additionally, exercises may simply ask students to resolve an ethical dilemma.

- *Tips for the Paralegal* is a list of practical tips for avoiding or dealing with ethical problems that paralegals will face on the job.

- *Focus On . . . features* summarize interviews with accomplished, often well-known, paralegals. Paralegals such as Merle Isgett and Karen Judd discuss their experiences with ethical issues in their working environment and offer sound advice to students concerning how to adhere to the ethical rules.

- *Closing Exercises* end each chapter. They are longer, comprehensive exercises that test student understanding of main concepts discussed in each chapter.

- *Cases* which discuss particular ethical situations often involving paralegals are included at the end of each chapter. *Missouri v. Jenkins* and *In re Complex Asbestos Litigation* are just two of the pivotal court decisions edited for and provided in this text. Questions follow each case to help students focus on the main issues presented.

SUPPORT MATERIAL

This text is accompanied by an extensive teaching and learning package:

- An Instructor's Manual with Test Bank and Transparency Masters by the text authors provide the most extensive teaching support possible. The Instructor's Manual includes sample syllabi for classes of eight weeks', ten weeks', twelve weeks' and fifteen weeks' length. It also includes answers to all exercises included in the text and supplementary information to guide classroom discussion. The comprehensive test bank is designed to provide questions to test student understanding of ethics rules and the application of those rules to legal assistants. True-False, Multiple Choice, Short Answer, Fill-in-the-Blank and Essay Questions are all provided to instructors.

- The "I Never Said I Was A Lawyer" videotape is an excellent tool to stimulate classroom discussion. This tape presents a variety of scenarios to inspire discussion and gives students experience dealing with possible ethical dilemmas arising in the work environment. Topics explored in the tape include the unauthorized practice of law, identification of paralegals as nonlawyers, breaches of confidentiality, and lack of attorney supervision. The tape was created by the Colorado Bar Association Committee on Legal Assistants, but is non–state specific and will be useful in all paralegal programs. The tape is available to adopters of the text.

■ The videotape "Drama of the Law II: Paralegal Issues" is another useful teaching device which accompanies the text. This is a professionally written and prepared tape that presents five hypothetical scenarios involving a fictional law office. The topics explored include ethical situations involving the unauthorized practice of law, strategic information, and client confidentiality. This tape is available to all qualified adopters of the text.

ACKNOWLEDGEMENTS

Thanks and appreciation are extended to the following manuscript reviewers who provided invaluable suggestions and comments:

Susan H. Brewer
  J.S. Reynolds Community College

Katherine A. Currier, J.D.
  Elms College

Diane Dvorak
  Suffolk County Community College

Kimberly Ezzell
  Denver Paralegal Institute

Jean A. Hellman
  Loyola University Chicago

Judge Linda L. Holliday
  Louisiana State University

David C. Jarratt, J.D.
  Concordia University Wisconsin

Dr. Barbara G. Kirkpatrick
  Virginia Intermont College

Jill Martin
  Quinnipiac College

Michelle Migdal, Esq.
  Florida Atlantic University

Robert J. Morrison
  University of Louisville

Diane Pevar
  Manor Junior College

Judge Richard A. Revell
  University of Louisville

Ronald Rotunda
  University of Illinois

Martha Wright Sartoris
  North Hennepin Community College

Camille Stuckey Stell
  Meredith College

Thomas A. Van Horn
  Lakeshore Technical College

Laurel A. Vietzen
  Elgin Community College

Shelley G. Widoff
  Boston University, Metropolitan College

Linda Wilke-Long
  Central Community College

We extend a special thank you to Professor Ronald Rotunda, University of Illinois College of Law, who greatly encouraged us. We also thank our good friends Ed Knuth, Eileen O'Neill, Rob Robertson, and Stephanie Williams for their extensive and unparalleled help and support. Many of our friends have reviewed this book and greatly contributed to its completion. We thank:

retired Illinois Supreme Court Justice Joseph Cunningham, George Doyle, Dean Bruce Schulte of Chicago-Kent College of Law, Alice Penny, Janis Shane, Arlene Conger, Cathy Schweit, the late Judge Mary Conrad, James Grogan of The Attorney Registration and Disciplinary Commission of Illinois. Others who have helped us along the way include: the Cook County Law Library staff, students and faculty at Central Piedmont Community College (especially Ervileen Pridgen), Sandra and Susan DeCiani, Marge Dover, Debbie Bator, and Jay Stein. Our editors at Delmar, Cengage Learning have also provided invaluable support and assistance and we thank: Elizabeth Hannan, Editor; Patty Bryant, Developmental Editor; Poh Lin Khoo, Production Editor, and Amelia Jacobsen, Promotion Manager. These individuals have all greatly contributed to the text before you.

Legal Ethics
for Paralegals and
the Law Office

An Introductory History of Paralegals

CHAPTER OBJECTIVES

After reading this chapter, you should
be able to:

■ Understand the history of the paralegal.

■ Appreciate the role played by the American
Bar Association in the development of the
paralegal.

■ Understand the nature of national paralegal
associations and the role they played in the
acceptance of paralegals as professionals.

■ Recognize issues affecting the future of the
role of the nonlawyer.

The **paralegal** or **legal assistant** profession was born in the 1960s, an era
of rapid social change. During that period, societal forces whittled
away at conventional attitudes and practices. Exchanges about housing
issues, civil rights issues, and criminal procedural issues became standard.
People tested the existence of legal rights which they had never before
asserted. This involved simple legal analysis in some cases, and more complex
legal analysis in others.

Members of the **legal profession** recognized that many of a lawyer's tasks
are routinized. If a lawyer could be free of those tasks, they concluded, he
would be able to devote time to more complex legal problems so a greater
volume of legal problems could be addressed. Members of the legal profession
also recognized that the assistance of paraprofessionals would help to ensure
that simple legal needs, which were going unmet, would be afforded to a
broader base of the population.

This chapter traces the emergence of that new profession—the profession of
the paralegal. Many may feel it is time for the paralegal to step back and
survey the fruits of her struggle to gain acceptance within the legal world.
However, in order to continue growing, to reach the next level of development, it is critical that the paralegal understand the development of his role in
the legal world. Understanding the roots of her profession will help further
define the ever-changing role of the legal assistant.

At the same time, as the unique relationship which **attorneys** and paralegals share develops, it becomes clear that any ethical mistakes of the paralegal
will critically affect the attorney who hires him. These mistakes could
ultimately restrict the growth of this burgeoning profession. Should support
staff error force attorneys to overly concern themselves with possible disciplinary actions, attorneys will become less inclined to hire nonlawyers to
assist them.

It is incumbent on you, as a nonlawyer, to realize the steps to take to avoid
ethical violations. Further development of your profession may depend on it.

PARALEGALS IN THE SPOTLIGHT

Callie Jackson holds a unique place in American history—she is the country's first paralegal.

Jackson was born in November 1875, the granddaughter of a South Carolina runaway slave. She apparently inherited her grandmother's high spirits for at a time when it was difficult for any person to start and maintain a successful business, let alone an African-American woman, Jackson developed a service designed to help others solve their legal problems.

On November 10, 1929, Jackson opened her business, calling it a "Leaning Post," where she served as a legal advocate for those people who would not otherwise have access to the legal system. (In 1932 the name of the business was changed to "The Listening Post.") Jackson helped her customers secure leases, resolve employment claims, prepare wills, and even secure burial rights.

Almost unbelievably, no one interfered with Jackson's work or tried to force her business to close. She was able to continue her work uninterrupted. Jackson believed this was because of the kinds of customers whom she was able to help. Jackson's customers were primarily black and poor Jewish individuals, and she believed very few people were concerned about whether the legal rights of these people were protected.

Callie Jackson lived 105 years. During her time, this amazing woman, who, it could be said, pioneered the entire paralegal movement, was able to help a number of individuals secure their legal rights. She pursued an admirable, enviable existence, and she is owed a debt of gratitude from those who now follow in her footsteps.

Source: Shellie M. Frey, *Callie Jackson: Paralegal Pioneer,* LEGAL ASSISTANT TODAY, Nov.-Dec. 1992, at 30-32.
For more information about Callie Jackson, *see* MR. CHARLIE'S BACK DOOR, written by Callie Jackson's granddaughter, Catherine Jermany. Copyright 1994. James Publishing, Inc. Reprinted with permission from *Legal Assistant Today.* For subscription information, call (714) 755-5450.

THE ROOTS OF THE PARALEGAL PROFESSION

Paralegal/Legal Assistant A nonlawyer, working under the supervision of an attorney, whose work does not involve the exercise of independent legal judgment.

Legal Profession A vocation or occupation requiring special education and skill.

Lawyer/Attorney A legal advisor/counselor who is an officer of the court, educated in the law, and licensed by the jurisdiction in which he engages in his vocation.

The recognition that many of the lawyer's tasks were routinized and standard hastened the development of the role of the paralegal. It was believed that delegating such tasks to nonlawyer personnel would free up the attorney's time, enabling her to focus on solving more complex legal problems. It was presumed that, as a result, more individuals would have access to the legal system.

However, nonlawyers were utilized in many capacities long before the term *paralegal* was coined. Law clerk-apprentices, nonlawyers appearing before administrative agencies, legal secretaries, and those involved in legal services organizations all served to pave the way for the development of the role of the paralegal. (This text uses the terms paralegal and legal assistant interchangeably, as well as the terms lawyer and attorney.)

THE LAW CLERK-APPRENTICE

Long ago a less formal approach was undertaken in learning to become an attorney. Typically, before being allowed to independently practice law, the attorney was made to serve an apprenticeship where he worked as an assistant to a full-fledged attorney.

The apprentice was the attorney's first assistant. Some say the attorney first learned to assign standard, routine tasks to others while the attorney was "training" an apprentice.

In some respects, therefore, the apprentice could logically be called the ancestor of the paralegal. However, it appears that the attorney rarely delegated important work to the apprentice-assistant. The apprentice was most frequently found copying documents in longhand for the attorney for whom he clerked.[1] Obviously, the paralegal's role has extended far beyond that of the apprentice.

ADMINISTRATIVE AGENCIES

Nonlawyers have been allowed to appear before certain **administrative agencies** in some capacity for more than a century.

It appears that, as early as 1874, nonlawyers engaged in the practice of representing others before the patent office. In fact, in *The Telephone Cases*, 126 U.S. 1, 8 S.Ct. 778, 31 L.Ed. 863 (1888), it is shown that one of the inventors of the telephone, a nonlawyer, began distributing cards in 1874, offering his services to others to assist in securing patents.[2]

In 1946 the **Federal Administrative Procedures Act** allowed nonlawyers to appear before administrative bodies in a representative capacity. This Act allows individual agencies to determine whether allowing nonlawyers to practice before them would be in the best interest of the agency. The National Labor Relations Board quickly indicated that this would be a beneficial practice and set about opening itself up to representation by nonlawyers. The U.S. Department of Health, Education and Welfare soon followed suit.

To date, many federal and state administrative agencies have opened their doors to admit practice by nonlawyers. Questions have been raised about the soundness of this practice. (See chapter 3, "The Unauthorized Practice of Law.") However, it has been recognized that practice by nonlawyers before administrative agencies, when controlled by regulation, benefits both the agency and the parties appearing before it. Recognition of this principle has helped the legal assistant in establishing the merits of his career and profession.

THE LEGAL SECRETARY

The role played by the **legal secretary** is perhaps most often recognized as the beginning of the paralegal profession. The legal secretary was the precursor to the legal assistant.

In the early 1960s it became clear that attorneys were spending an inordinate amount of time handling routine matters, and this adversely affected his law firm's income. When the attorney considered alternative ways of organizing his daily schedule to advance the law firm economically, it became obvious that some of the work would have to be delegated.

At that time it was common for an attorney to employ a legal secretary to handle office matters. Therefore, it was a logical step for the attorney to turn over routine tasks, commonly handled by the attorney, to the legal secretary for completion.

Administrative Agency A governmental body that carries out or administers the law.

Federal Administrative Procedures Act A federal law which establishes administrative procedures for use by any person who is handling or involved in matters before any federal administrative agency.

Legal Secretary A nonlawyer working in the law office, who specializes in routine functions like typing, transcribing, and communicating with clients.

---

[1]*See* Brickman, *Expansion of the Lawyering Process Through a New Delivery System: The Emergence and State of Legal Paraprofessionalism*, 71 COLUMBIA LAW REVIEW 1153, 1170.

[2]*See* Jennings Bailey, Jr., *Practice by Non-Lawyers Before the United States Patent Office*, 15 FEDERAL BAR JOURNAL 211 (1955). This material was originally published in the *Federal Bar Journal*, vol. 15 (Summer 1955). It is reprinted here with permission of the Federal Bar Association.

**EXHIBIT 1.1
Roots of the
Paralegal
Profession**

Law Clerk-Apprentice
Administrative Agencies
Legal Secretary
Legal Services Organizations

**National Association
of Legal Secretaries**
A national
organization that
represents the
interests of legal
secretaries.

The **National Association of Legal Secretaries (NALS)** helped develop the role of the nonlawyer. Many legal secretaries became "super secretaries," handling more varied tasks. NALS became a forum for sharing ideas of what responsibilities legal secretaries could grow to perform.

In this way, nonlawyer personnel had a significant impact on the economics of the law firm. It was only a matter of time before the legal profession was looking to hire laypersons, formally trained in various areas of the law, to improve the bottom-line economics of the law firm by handling standardized matters for the attorney.

LEGAL SERVICES ORGANIZATIONS

Legal assistants also developed through the emergence of legal service programs for the poor.

In 1963 the federal government decreed that low-cost legal services be made available to everyone. It also created a national organization, administered by the Office of Economic Opportunity to see that the need for legal services was met.

Upon opening their doors, legal services offices were besieged with requests for help from those who had never been able to afford the cost of legal advice. The staffs, composed of mainly attorneys, were kept extremely busy trying to fulfill this need.

Although there was more work than could be handled by the original staffs, the requests for legal services continued to grow. However, the budgets of these organizations were fixed, so more attorneys could not be hired and legal services organizations could not expand to meet these requests. Alternative solutions were sought.

Once again because much of the attorney's work was routine and did not involve independent problem-solving requiring a particular skill and training in the law, it was determined that it could be handled by a nonlawyer under the supervision of an attorney. Hiring laypersons was the most economical way for legal service organizations to serve as many individuals as possible.[3]

THE DEVELOPMENT OF THE ROLE OF THE PARALEGAL

A number of events contributed to the development of the paralegal position into the thriving profession it now is. The paralegal profession is estimated to be one of the fastest growing careers around.

[3]*See* Carolyn M. Farren, *The Legal Assistant Career, A History,* LEGAL ASSISTANTS UPDATE '81 (American Bar Association) 121. Reprinted by permission. Copyright © 1981 American Bar Association.

PARALEGALS IN THE SPOTLIGHT

Paralegals increasingly try their wings in roles less traditional than that of the legal assistant employed in the law firm. Aida Garcia is one such paralegal—and Aida Garcia's work is making a big difference.

Garcia is the sole paralegal/administrator of Los Angeles County's Legal Aid program for battered wives and children. She assists in obtaining temporary restraining orders (TROs) to prevent the abusing party from having contact with those he or she batters. Garcia meets personally with each claimant seeking a TRO. She explains the procedures in processing requests and reviews the claimant's documents for accuracy. Once Garcia has helped the claimant complete the paperwork, she sends it to the judge for issuance of a TRO that same day.

Garcia also trains, supervises, and evaluates the work of her volunteer staff. Her volunteers usually are law school or paralegal students.

In 1990 Garcia's program helped more than twenty-two hundred individuals. She feels she is really making a difference. "There's nothing that compares to it. . . ."

Source: *Paralegal Assists Battered Wives and Children*, LEGAL ASSISTANT TODAY, Nov.-Dec. 1991. Copyright 1994. James Publishing, Inc. Reprinted with permission from *Legal Assistant Today*. For subscription information, call (714) 755-5450.

However, without the recognition of the American Bar Association, without the development of paralegal schools to provide educational standards, and without the support of paralegal associations, this growth might not have occurred as quickly.

RECOGNITION BY THE AMERICAN BAR ASSOCIATION

Not long after the establishment of this legal service organization, the **American Bar Association (ABA)** began to address the merits of hiring nonlawyer personnel.

The ABA is an organization composed of attorneys from every jurisdiction in the United States. Meeting semiannually, the organization attempts to consider problems that are unique to the legal profession and to offer solutions where possible.

In order to streamline the tasks required of the ABA, it has divided itself into numerous committees. A **standing committee** studies particular issues related to a topic on a regular basis. Its status is permanent in nature. A **special committee** is appointed when a committee is needed to study an issue immediately or to conduct some research or experiments at a specific time. When the work of a special committee is concluded, the committee may be disbanded. However, when the work of a special committee is deemed a necessary part of improving the legal profession and its image, a special committee may become a standing committee.

In the late 1960s the ABA created the Special Committee on the Availability of Legal Services and directed it to evaluate the developing role of the paralegal.

Recognition of the Importance of the Paralegal

In 1968 the **Special Committee on the Availability of Legal Services** issued its report to the ABA, recommending that the legal profession encourage the hiring and training of legal assistants and asking that a separate special

American Bar Association/ABA An organization, composed of attorneys from every jurisdiction in the U.S., that attempts to address problems unique to the legal profession.

ABA Standing Committee A permanent committee of the ABA that studies issues related to a topic and meets on a regular basis.

ABA Special Committee A committee of the ABA that is appointed when there is a need to study an issue immediately, or to conduct some research or experiments at a particular time.

ABA Special Committee on the Availability of Legal Services A special committee established by the ABA in the late 1960s that was directed to evaluate the developing role of the paralegal.

committee be appointed to study this alternative. In addressing this proposal, the Special Committee on the Availability of Legal Services report stated,

> It is now widely recognized that one of the critical problems facing our profession is the inadequacy of the number of lawyers to serve, in the ways in which they have traditionally served, the very greatly expanded requirements of a burgeoning population with expanded needs for legal services in both civil and criminal matters.
>
> • • •
>
> We are convinced that, as other professions are doing, the legal profession can eliminate much of the criticism, can become more efficient and can devote itself to the truly professional legal tasks by permitting skilled assistants to take the responsibility, so long as acting under the supervision of the lawyer, for a very large share of his drudgery.[4]

ABA Special Committee on Lay Assistants for Lawyers A special committee appointed to study the problems unique to the paralegal. (It became the Special Committee on Legal Assistants.)

The recommendation to appoint a special committee to study the problems unique to the paralegal was approved. The next year, the new **Special Committee on Lay Assistants for Lawyers** filed its first report. This proved to be an important first step in ensuring widespread acceptance of the role of the paralegal.

The Special Committee on Legal Assistants

The Special Committee on Lay Assistants for Lawyers was appointed to study the emerging profession of the legal assistant and was directed to consider the following areas:

> (a) The kinds of tasks which may be competently performed by a nonlawyer working under the direction and supervision of a lawyer;
> (b) The nature of the training which may be required and provided to develop competence and proficiency in the performance of such tasks;
> (c) The role, if any, to be played by the legal profession and the bar in providing such training;
> (d) The desirability of recognizing competence and proficiency in such assistants as by academic recognition or other suitable means; and
> (e) All appropriate methods for developing, encouraging and increasing the training and utilization of nonlawyer assistants the better to enable lawyers to discharge their professional responsibilities.[5]

ABA Special Committee on Legal Assistants Formerly the Special Committee on Lay Assistants for Lawyers.

In 1971 the Special Committee on Lay Assistants for Lawyers became the **Special Committee on Legal Assistants.** Two of its greatest responsibilities were to educate attorneys and the public on the use of legal assistants and to ensure that those legal assistants working within the legal profession were properly trained to assume their responsibilities. Therefore, the committee became deeply involved in education.

The committee began studying ways of ensuring adequate training for legal assistants. However, the committee made clear that a formal training program, administered through a university-type setting, was not the only, nor even the most desirable, method of training legal assistants. Despite this, the committee became deeply involved in evaluating training programs for the legal assis-

---

[4]*Report Number 3 of the Special Committee on Availability of Legal Services,* REPORTS OF AMERICAN BAR ASSOCIATION 1968, 529. Reprinted by permission. Copyright © 1969 American Bar Association.
[5]*See Report of the Special Committee on Legal Assistants,* REPORTS OF AMERICAN BAR ASSOCIATION 1971, 710. Reprinted by permission. Copyright © 1972 American Bar Association.

tant. In 1973 it promulgated its first set of rules in order for legal assistant training programs to be approved by the ABA. These rules set this ABA special committee on a course that would force it to devote much of its resources to evaluating and approving training institutions.

The Standing Committee on Legal Assistants

In 1976 the Special Committee on Legal Assistants became the Standing Committee on Legal Assistants. This change in nomenclature reflected a recognition on the part of the ABA that legal assistants had become an integral part of the legal profession and were not likely to soon fade away. A more permanent representative of the paralegal's concerns within the profession would ensure that the paralegal remained a vital force in maintaining an economically sound legal environment.

The standing committee became involved in many worthy projects. Unfortunately, most of its time was soon consumed by the pressing demands of evaluating and approving paralegal training programs. In August 1982 the ABA approved the establishment of an advisory committee to the standing committee to assist in this time-consuming function, thereby freeing the committee to spend more time handling other necessary tasks more in keeping with its original purpose.

Definition of Legal Assistant

One of the tasks of this standing committee involved defining the scope of responsibilities of a legal assistant. The role of legal assistants had developed so quickly that there was little uniformity in the functions that legal assistants performed. Rather, legal assistants were handling a variety of tasks, all designed to assist the attorney by allowing him to rely upon a nonlawyer to handle routinized activities.

This was actually exactly what the special committee had professed to desire. Not wanting to stifle the development of the profession, it had refrained from addressing what the paralegal could or could not do. However, in 1986 the standing committee developed just such a definition.

Almost twenty years after the committee had first been appointed, therefore, the ABA Standing Committee on Legal Assistants promulgated the following definition of a "legal assistant" to give some shape to this developing profession. The definition reads as follows:

> A Legal Assistant is a person, qualified through education, training or work experience, who is employed or retained by a lawyer, law office, governmental agency, or other entity in a capacity or function which involves the performance, under the ultimate direction and supervision of an attorney, of specifically delegated substantive legal work, which work, for the most part, requires a sufficient knowledge of legal concepts that, absent such assistant, the attorney would perform the task.[6]

The ABA made quite clear that a legal assistant works under the direction of an attorney. This attorney is responsible for the work of the legal assistant.

[6]*American Bar Association Standing Committee on Legal Assistants Position Paper On The Question of Legal Assistant Licensure or Certification* (1986) (reprinted in LEGAL ASSISTANT UPDATE, 163). Copyright (c) 1986 American Bar Association.

Moreover, as we will learn throughout the text, the attorney can be brought before the state disciplinary agency to answer to mistakes made by his legal assistant.

Further Recognition by the ABA

On August 12, 1987, the ABA further recognized this new profession by voting to amend its bylaws in order to include legal assistants in an associate capacity.

Guidelines for the Utilization of Legal Assistant Services Guidelines written by the ABA that advise attorneys on using the services of nonlawyer assistants.

In 1991 the ABA's Standing Committee on Legal Assistants developed and proposed **"Guidelines for the Utilization of Legal Assistant Services."** The ABA House of Delegates adopted them later that year, and they are reproduced at the end of this text.

The Guidelines and its accompanying commentary advise attorneys on using the services of nonlawyer assistants in such a way that the attorney does not run afoul of disciplinary rules. Throughout this text the Guidelines will be cited and explained, for the legal assistant likewise has a responsibility to avoid unethical conduct that can result in disciplinary measures.

The ABA continues to study the role of the paralegal in the law office. Throughout 1992–1993, the ABA Commission on Nonlawyer Practice conducted open meetings in seven cities across the nation to address issues pertaining to nonlawyer practice. The meetings sought to ascertain the legal needs of the general public and discuss whether these needs are being met by lawyers and the nonlawyers who work with them.

DEVELOPMENT OF EDUCATIONAL PROGRAMS

Many different kinds of educational programs designed to train the legal assistant developed in response to the perceived needs of the legal profession. Some began as early as the late 1960s, before the ABA had become involved in the profession. By 1971 eleven paralegal training programs existed. Currently, some estimate that more than 500 training programs for legal assistants are in operation.[7]

Educational programs come in a variety of styles. Many community colleges have developed associate degree programs in response to the needs of the legal profession. These programs emphasize basic skills necessary for a legal assistant and also offer students a background in general education courses. Completion of these programs usually entitles one to an associate of arts degree. Most of these colleges have matriculation agreements with several more advanced degree institutions.

Some universities also offer four-year programs, culminating in the award of a bachelor's degree in paralegal studies. These programs emphasize basic paralegal study courses, requiring many hours of study concerning skills endemic to the legal assistant. In addition, basic courses are required of all students. Some students use these programs as a stepping-stone to law school.

Programs are also offered at the post-graduate level. They are available for study after one completes a bachelor's degree and are often offered at a university or proprietary (for-profit) institution. Because students have al-

---

[7]*New Trends in Paralegal Education*, LEGAL ASSISTANT TODAY, Jan.-Feb. 1992. Copyright 1994. James Publishing, Inc. Reprinted with permission from *Legal Assistant Today*. For subscription information, call (714) 755-5450.

ready completed the general education requirements necessary to be awarded a bachelor's degree, the only courses offered teach paralegal skills. Students earn certificates of completion from these programs.

Additionally, many institutions now offer continuing education courses. As the concept of the role of the paralegal expands and as paralegal tasks become more varied, the need for legal assistants to become acquainted with new areas of law grows ever greater. A recent survey conducted by **Legal Assistant Management Association (LAMA)** demonstrated that employers feel that completing continuing legal education courses is a vital part of keeping legal assistants up to date on trends within the legal profession. An impressive seventy-nine percent surveyed indicated that their organizations pay the costs of sending their legal assistants to continuing education courses.

The study also confirms that the number of in-house training programs for paralegals offered through law firms is increasing. The LAMA report suggested that this may be due to the fact that law firms find the continuing education programs currently offered to be somewhat inadequate because legal assistants need additional hands-on training. The report also indicated that this rise in the number of in-house programs may be due to the fact that law firms are growing increasingly sophisticated in their use of legal assistants.

Although schools are not required to obtain approval of their programs from the American Bar Association before admitting students, many do seek it. Debate continues over whether or not ABA approval is necessary.

Currently, the ABA considers programs at the associate degree, bachelor degree, and post-graduate level for the approval process. In order to become approved by the ABA, a program must strive to exceed certain basic requirements set forth describing required faculty, administration, and library resources. At the present, the ABA has no plans to approve continuing education programs, although the organization has expressed a wholehearted endorsement of these programs.

Paralegal education is developing in ways not even imagined when the programs were first adopted. There is an increased awareness of the value of computers to the law office. Consequently more and more paralegal programs offer training in the use of computers, including demonstrating the uses of computerized research. The importance of internship programs is also discussed. An internship serves to provide paralegal students with a practical background.

Increasingly, paralegals with a "specialty" find themselves in demand. Certain areas of the law—such as bankruptcy, environmental law, or elder law—are experiencing rapid growth. Likewise, the need for paralegals specializing in these areas, after they complete their basic educational requirements, is increasing. Many of the proliferating continuing education programs are designed to help meet this need.

Perhaps the most exciting development is the increased use of paralegals in the classroom. Legal assistants are being used to team-teach courses with attorneys. Using this approach, the paralegal student can be made aware of different perspectives in solving legal problems. The lawyer can certainly teach students the law, but the legal assistant can provide information about the practical aspect of her job.

For example, courses in **discovery** may be team-taught. Because the legal assistant is often made a part of the discovery process and is required to sift

Legal Assistant Management Association/LAMA A national organization whose purpose is to address concerns of legal assistant managers specifically, and whose overall goal is to foster the profession of the legal assistant.

Discovery Pre-trial process whereby both parties attempt to gather information about the lawsuit from the opposing side.

through large numbers of documents, the paralegal must understand the practicalities and responsibilities accompanying discovery tasks assigned to him. The attorney is concerned that no mistakes are made in carrying out discovery, that the requested information is produced by opposing counsel, and that appropriate information about his client is being disclosed.

Legal assistants are also being hired to teach certain paralegal courses solo. For example, a legal assistant may be hired to teach legal research or real estate closing skills.

The American Association for Paralegal Education

American Association for Paralegal Education/AAfPE A national organization for paralegal educators, whose goals include promoting high standards for paralegal education.

The **American Association for Paralegal Education (AAfPE)** also had a hand in significantly guiding the development of the paralegal. Established in 1981, AAfPE is a national organization for paralegal educators. As of 1993, 211 schools were institutional members of the organization. Members of the association also include publishers, paralegal associations, faculty members, advisory board members, and other individuals interested in developing and improving the quality of paralegal education.

The goals of AAfPE have been stated as follows:

- To promote high standards for paralegal education.
- To provide a forum for professional improvement for paralegal educators.
- To plan, promote and hold annual conferences and seminars.
- To provide technical assistance and consultation services to institutions, educators and employers.
- To promote research and disseminate information on the paralegal profession and paralegal education.
- To cooperate with the American Bar Association and other institutions and professional associations in developing an approval process for paralegal education programs.
- To promote the goals of the Association through cooperation with other national, regional and local groups and organizations interested in paralegal education.[8]

NATIONAL PARALEGAL ORGANIZATIONS

Initially the only voluntary professional organization that seemed interested in representing the concerns of paralegals was the American Bar Association, an organization comprising solely attorneys. However, there was a general feeling that attorneys would not be able to understand or ultimately express the concerns facing legal assistants. Out of this general discontent arose several national organizations composed solely of paralegals.

The development of these organizations played a large role in the emerging profession of the paralegal. Through these national organizations, legal assistants first found a real outlet for exchanging ideas and learning of issues affecting their roles in law offices. In essence, paralegal organizations allow legal assistants to control their own destinies.

---

[8]AAfPE 1993 MEMBERSHIP DIRECTORY, courtesy of Judith Gibbs, AAfPE President, 1993–94. Reprinted with permission.

Twalla Doupriest, while working as a paralegal, has also been a bankruptcy trustee for the Northern District of Texas U.S. Bankruptcy Court since 1983.

In 1978 Doupriest became the legal secretary of Clifford McMaster, who specialized in bankruptcy work. McMaster's encouragement led Doupriest to complete her paralegal certificate. In 1983 McMaster recommended Doupriest for the bankruptcy trustee panel. Doupriest's specialization in bankruptcy matters certainly helped her to qualify for this work.

Doupriest is one of several trustees appointed on a random basis when a creditor files a bankruptcy petition. As a trustee, Doupriest takes charge of the assets not exempted in the bankruptcy petition. She protects the interests of the creditors.

While many of Doupriest's debtors are individuals, Doupriest also works with bankruptcy petitions of corporations. Doupriest has even handled the bankruptcy affairs of Cullen Davis, a Fort Worth oilman and one-time multimillionaire. Doupriest objected to the court's discharge of Davis's debts and subsequently spent eighteen months investigating his affairs. Her investigation ended when Davis converted his Chapter 7 bankruptcy, seeking discharge of his debts, to a Chapter 11 reorganization of his $850 million debt.

Source: Twalla Doupriest: Bankruptcy Trustee, LEGAL ASSISTANT TODAY, Sept.-Oct. 1989. Copyright 1994. James Publishing, Inc. Reprinted with permission from *Legal Assistant Today*. For subscription information, call (714) 755-5450.

Though they do not account for all paralegals, two of these organizations have grown to represent the largest numbers of paralegals. These organizations are the National Association of Legal Assistants and the National Federation of Paralegal Associations.

The National Association of Legal Assistants

Incorporated in 1975, the **National Association of Legal Assistants (NALA)** soon became an important voice for paralegals.

NALA developed from the former Legal Assistant Section of the National Association of Legal Secretaries. The membership of NALA comprises primarily individuals who each have a vote in the management of the organization. NALA also offers affiliate membership to legal assistant organizations with similar goals and philosophies. More than eighty state and local legal assistant associations are currently affiliated with NALA. Through individual members and these associations, NALA represents more than fifteen thousand legal assistants.

As expressed by NALA, the purposes of the organization are varied and involve furthering the rise of the paralegal profession while providing a voice for its concerns. The goals are as follows:

- Promulgating a Code of Professional Responsibility for legal assistants;
- Establishing a national voluntary certification program;
- Cooperating with schools and colleges offering legal assistant programs;
- Cooperating with local, state and national bar associations in setting standards for legal assistants;
- Promoting the profession of legal assistants, including educating the public for the advancement and improvement of the profession and broadening public understanding of the function of the legal assistant;

National Association of Legal Assistants/ NALA A national organization whose purpose is to further the rise of the paralegal profession while providing a voice for its concerns.

- Informing its members through continuing legal education and providing a forum of exchange where members share experiences, opinions and knowledge with peers.[9]

NALA Code of Ethics A code of ethics adopted by NALA in 1975 for use by legal assistants. Any individual joining NALA is obliged to abide by this code.

NALA proposed and adopted a **Code of Ethics** in 1975. At the time of application to NALA, all members agree to be bound by this code. NALA also provides an annotated ethical code, entitled **"NALA Model Standards and Guidelines for Utilization of Legal Assistants, Annotated"**. The organization is also involved in the development and sponsorship of continuing education programs, which are well-attended by its members.

NALA is also responsible for presenting what is currently the only national certification program in place for paralegals. The voluntary certification program is not a requirement for becoming a legal assistant. However, it has received great recognition in recent years. In addition to its impact, the **Certified Legal Assistant or CLA** program provides a sense of professionalism and standardization within the paralegal sphere. The NALA certification program and its value to the profession are discussed more fully later in this chapter.

NALA Model Standards and Guidelines for Utilization of Legal Assistants, Annotated An annotated ethical code that provides ethical guidelines and annotations to explain from what sources the guidelines derived.

NALA provides many services to its members. It has developed and offers NALA NET, the profession's only on-line information service and bulletin board for legal assistants. It also publishes a quarterly news magazine called *Facts & Findings* and frequent membership newsletters that regularly update members on significant case law, legislative activities, and ethical opinions.

Certified Legal Assistant/CLA A designation given to a legal assistant who successfully completes a voluntary certification examination that is administered by the National Association of Legal Assistants/NALA.

Of particular interest is NALA's Ethics Committee. The committee primarily is engaged when an ethics violation is charged against a member. It will also discuss ethical questions with members, but cannot advise members or guide members as an authority on ethical conduct. The committee may discuss a problem with members and provide any background information on the issue, but the legal assistant must also turn to the state's bar or supreme court for authority.

The National Federation of Paralegal Associations

National Federation of Paralegal Associations/NFPA A national organization for paralegals and paralegal associations.

The **National Federation of Paralegal Associations (NFPA)** was organized in 1974. In that year the Subcommittee on Representation of Citizens' Interests of the U.S. Senate Committee on the Judiciary became involved in determining whether regulation of the emerging paralegal profession should be undertaken by the federal government. In order to represent the interests of the paralegal, it was quickly recognized that a new national representative body would have to be formed. To provide this body, several local organizations joined together to become NFPA.

NFPA became involved in the Senate hearings of 1974 and again presented testimony in 1975 before the ABA concerning the issue of certification of paralegals. The NFPA has remained active in providing a voice for legal assistants and their organizations since that time. Currently NFPA has a membership of more than seventeen thousand.

The purposes of NFPA, as advanced by the organization, are as follows:

- To advance, foster and promote the paralegal profession;
- To monitor and participate in developments in the paralegal profession;

[9]*NFPA/NALA Focus: Two Perspectives*, LEGAL ASSISTANT UPDATE, 81 at 82. Reprinted by permission. Copyright (c) 1983 American Bar Association.

- To maintain a nationwide communications network among paralegal associations and other members of the legal community;

- To advance the educational standards of the paralegal profession; and

- To participate in, carry on and conduct research seminars, experiments, investigations, studies or other work relative to the paralegal profession.[10]

NFPA's membership comprises primarily paralegal associations. Many regional and local organizations have memberships to NFPA. When a legal assistant joins a regional paralegal association that is a member of NFPA, the legal assistant may also receive a membership in NFPA. For example, when a legal assistant joins the Illinois Paralegal Association (IPA), the IPA member also automatically becomes a member of NFPA because IPA is one of those organizations that has joined the national association. NFPA also allows individuals to join its organization.

Like NALA, NFPA developed its own code of professional responsibility, which NFPA expects its members to follow. The **Model Code of Ethics and Professional Responsibility** was overwhelmingly adopted by the NFPA membership at its annual meeting in 1993 and is an expansion of its earlier code, the **Affirmation of Professional Responsibility.**

Model Code of Ethics and Professional Responsibility A code of ethics adopted by NFPA at its annual meeting in May 1993.

Affirmation of Professional Responsibility The name of the first code of ethics written by NFPA.

ISSUES AFFECTING THE FUTURE OF THE PARALEGAL

The future of the paralegal role appears bright. It seems the legal profession is finally beginning to recognize the advantages of hiring nonlawyers.

For instance, a recent ethics opinion of the Advisory Committee on Professional Ethics of New Jersey (state bar ethics opinions are discussed more fully in chapter 2) has this to say about paralegals:

> It cannot be gainsaid that the utilization of paralegals has become, over the last 10 years, accepted, acceptable, important and, indeed, necessary to the efficient practice of law. Lawyers, law firms and, more importantly, clients benefit greatly by their work. Those people who perform paraprofessionally are educated to do so. They are trained and truly professional. They are diligent and carry on their functions in a dignified, proper, professional manner. They understand ethical inhibitions and prohibitions. Lawyers assign them work expecting them to respect confidences which they obtain and to comport themselves in the best traditions of those who serve the legal area. Opinion 647, 1991.[11]

More important, however, is the recognition accorded paralegals by the **U.S. Supreme Court.** In a landmark decision that allowed attorneys to collect fees from opposing counsel for paralegal work rendered in completing a client's representation, the Court recognized the importance of the paralegal, expressly stating that the legal assistant is able to assist attorneys in making the delivery of legal services more cost-effective. See *Missouri v. Jenkins,* 491

U.S. Supreme Court The highest court in the United States.

---

[10]*Id.* at 84. Reprinted by permission. Copyright (c) 1983 American Bar Association.
[11]Reprinted with permission.

PARALEGALS IN THE SPOTLIGHT

In 1987 Arleen Keegan was elected as judge of the probate court in Litchfield, Connecticut. What's so unusual about this? In a day and age when most judges are attorneys, Judge Keegan is a legal assistant.

After ten years at home with her family, Keegan decided to return to school, taking classes to complete an associate degree in paralegal studies. While completing classes, she began working as a clerk of the probate court. When election time rolled around, Keegan's boss, the probate judge, decided not to run for reelection. Fearing she might lose her job once she had a different "boss," Keegan threw her hat into this political ring. (In Connecticut, a law degree is not required before one can become a probate judge.)

Keegan won the election. She claims that the work she is now doing is much the same as the work of the paralegal. Her work includes researching, interviewing people, ensuring that real estate records are properly maintained, and checking on background information.

A Litchfield attorney practicing before Judge Keegan claims a certain advantage attaches in having a nonlawyer judge. This nonlawyer is able to bring to the issues before her a special sensitivity of which attorney judges just aren't always capable.

Source: Terry Howard, *A Legal Assistant is Elected Probate Judge*, LEGAL ASSISTANT TODAY, Mar.-Apr. 1985. Copyright 1994. James Publishing, Inc. Reprinted with permission from *Legal Assistant Today*. For subscription information, call (714) 755-5450.

U.S. 274, 287, 109 S. Ct. 2463, 2471, 105 L.Ed 2d 229 (1989), discussed more fully and excerpted in chapter 7, "Financial Aspects."

Paralegals are doing more than earning respect while holding traditional jobs in law firms. As the Spotlight features demonstrate, opportunities for paralegals are expanding at a great pace. As the profession becomes more widely recognized, the opportunities will grow ever greater.

Paralegals are working for the government, in corporations, for the court system, and within public service agencies.

Within a law firm, their responsibilities are expanding. Paralegals have been given opportunities managing conflict of interest matters for their firms (See chapter 6, "Conflict of Interest"). Legal assistants also work as office managers and within law firm marketing departments. A number of legal assistants have found the satisfaction in their jobs greatly increased by accepting responsibilities supervising their fellow paralegals, working as Legal Assistant Managers.

Interesting and vitally important developments concerning the viability of the profession dominate the news. These issues include the development of freelance paralegal firms and regulation of paralegals. Each paralegal has a responsibility to understand these issues.

THE FREELANCE PARALEGAL

Freelance Paralegal
A paralegal who works independently of attorneys, yet provides legal services to law firms.

More and more paralegals establish paralegal firms. Servicing a number of attorneys who hire the paralegal firm on a temporary basis to assist in completing work on a certain case, the independent paralegal firm offers unique challenges. Paralegals who work independently of attorneys, yet provide legal services to law firms, are known as **freelance paralegals.**

A solo practitioner may have no support staff to help him handle his busy practice. When a case is proceeding to trial, he may become overwhelmed by the large number of documents generated through discovery. At that point, he may decide it is prudent to obtain some temporary help with the case; he therefore may decide to hire a freelance paralegal to assist him with discovery.

Freelance paralegal firms provide an excellent way for an experienced legal assistant to establish her own business. A freelance paralegal firm can also offer new challenges to a seasoned professional.

The fate of freelance paralegals working independently of law firms was recently called into question by an ethics advisory opinion filed in the state of New Jersey. This advisory opinion, Opinion No. 24, disallowed the use of the services of freelance paralegals. The New Jersey Supreme Court, however, rejected that opinion and issued a decision allowing the use of freelance paralegals. See *In re Opinion No. 24*, 128 N.J. 114, 607 A. 2d 962 (1992), excerpted at the end of this chapter.

The endorsement of freelance paralegals contained in *In re Opinion No. 24* has paved the way for the further development of freelance paralegal firms. The use of freelance paralegals is certainly a trend worth following.

Discovery
Examination of and authorization to practice as a paralegal given by a nongovernmental authority.

REGULATION OF LEGAL ASSISTANTS

Until this time, the relatively young profession of the legal assistant has developed without the constraints of regulation. Remember that paralegals developed as a means of reducing legal costs, thereby making legal services available to greater numbers of individuals. Many believed that premature restraints on entry into the profession would discourage individuals from seeking employment as paralegals and thereby hinder the movement seeking to open the legal world to individuals of modest means.

The value of various kinds of regulation has been debated. The kinds of regulation proposed include certification, broad-based licensing schemes, and limited licensure legislation.

Certification

Certification is one method of regulating paralegal activity. The American Bar Association has defined **certification** as the examination of nonlawyers and subsequent authorization to practice as a paralegal given by a *nongovernmental* authority.[12]

Currently, the only national certification program is that administered by NALA. In order to become certified by NALA, one must sit for one of the semiannual exams that NALA administers. As with any significant regulatory examination, preexamination "prep" courses are offered. Passing this examination allows one to use the designation Certified Legal Assistant, abbreviated CLA.[13] For example, if Lorna Legal Assistant has passed the certification exam, she may use the designations "Lorna Legal Assistant, Certified Legal Assistant" or "Lorna Legal Assistant, CLA." Although this program is not compulsory, many have found it useful to have the CLA certification.

Certification
Examination of and authorization to practice as a paralegal given by a nongovernmental authority.

[12]*American Bar Association Standing Committee on Legal Assistants, Position Paper On The Question Of Legal Assistant Licensure Or Certification* (1986), (reprinted in LEGAL ASSISTANTS UPDATE, 164). Reprinted with permission. Copyright (c) 1986 American Bar Association.
[13]Used with permission.

Specialty Certification An additional certification that a Certified Legal Assistant/CLA may undertake in one of several specialty areas. One receives the designation CLAS when one has successfully completed the specialty certification exam.

The actual examination requires two days' commitment. The applicant is examined in communications, ethics, human relations, interviewing techniques, judgment and analytical ability, legal research, and legal terminology. Additionally, the applicant selects four substantive areas of the law in which to be tested. The substantive law areas from which applicants may choose are general law (involving the American Legal System), bankruptcy, corporate, estate planning and probate, contracts, litigation, real estate, criminal, and administrative law.

Recently NALA instituted a second type of certification program, called **Specialty Certification.** One who has already become a CLA may take an additional examination in one of several specialty areas. Upon passing the exam, one may use the designation **CLAS, or Certified Legal Assistant Specialist.**[14]

Not everybody in the paralegal field believes certification programs are necessary. While some believe requiring all paralegals to take and pass a certification examination would ensure that all paralegals meet certain standards of competency, others vehemently disagree. Some believe certification would foreclose avenues of development for the legal assistant.

EXERCISE 1.1

Should legal assistants be required to take and pass a certification exam before being allowed to work for attorneys? Discuss the advantages and disadvantages of certification.

Who should administer such an exam? What material do you feel should be included? Should the exam be modeled after the bar examinations that lawyers are required to endure?

General Licensing

Certified Legal Assistant Specialist/CLAS Designation given to one who obtains a specialty certification.

General Licensing Examination of and authorization to practice as a paralegal given by a governmental body.

Licensing programs have also been proposed for the legal assistant. If such licensing schemes were adopted, legal assistants would be required to take and pass a state-administered examination, ultimately receiving a license, before working as a legal assistant employed by an attorney.

Licensing schemes may appear to resemble certification programs. After all, to obtain a license to practice as a paralegal, one would need to take and pass an examination, not unlike that required under a certification scheme. According to the American Bar Association, however, licensing systems are administered by a *governmental* body.[15]

Opponents of legal assistant licensing argue that such licensing schemes would unduly restrict entry into the profession. Moreover, it is argued that licensing would limit the activities of the licensed paralegal.

On the other hand, many believe that licensing of legal assistants is a necessary part of being considered a *professional.* If nurses must become licensed by a state agency in order to offer their services to doctors, the argument continues, then so should legal assistants in order to offer their services to lawyers.

[14]Used with permission.

[15]*American Bar Association Standing Committee on Legal Assistants, Position Paper On The Question Of Legal Assistant Licensure Or Certification* (1986), (reprinted in Legal Assistants Update, 164). Reprinted with permission. Copyright (c) 1986 American Bar Association.

Limited Licensure

Increasingly the general public has called upon the legislature to propose and support bills allowing nonlawyers to provide some legal services directly to the public. These bills would create a status of **limited licensure** for those nonlawyers who chose to comply with the requirements of the legislation. Generally, one who had been "licensed" pursuant to the legislation would be subsequently bestowed the title **legal technician.** This is perhaps the one type of regulation discussed most frequently.

The bills usually provide that stringent requirements be met before allowing a nonlawyer to "practice law." For instance, recent proposals in several states would require those seeking status as a legal technician to take and pass a rigorous examination in a particular area of law. Upon passing this examination, the legal technician would then be licensed to provide legal services in only that particular area of the law. An individual who had passed the **family law** examination, therefore, would be allowed to prepare simple divorce and adoption papers without the supervision of a lawyer.

An example of the kinds of restrictions put upon these licensing schemes was discussed in a decision of the Nevada Supreme Court. The court was analyzing a suit brought by the state bar against Georgiana and Glen Greenwell, doing business as Greenwell Paralegal Center. The suit alleged that the Greenwells had engaged in the unauthorized practice of law. The Nevada court concluded,

> Based upon the serious issues raised by this appeal, we have ordered the State Bar of Nevada to investigate the alleged unavailability of legal services for low and middle-income Nevadans. The State Bar has been specifically instructed to consider the opinions of the directors of the various legal services agencies of the state as well as the directors of the various pro bono programs. The Bar has also been instructed to formulate rules concerning such conditions, if any, that would allow nonlawyers to provide specific simple legal services. The permitted services are to be specifically defined by the rules, and the activities of non-lawyers are not to exceed the specific definitions. Further, the State Bar has been given authority to train and certify non-lawyers who wish to provide simple legal services. *Greenwell v. State Bar of Nevada*, 108 Nev. 602, 836 P. 2d 70 (1992).

Currently, limited licensure legislation has been introduced in thirty state legislatures. Even so, opposition to such bills has generally kept the proposals from becoming law. According to the American Bar Association, only the state of Washington currently allows nonlawyers to provide limited services that are traditionally considered to belong in the attorney's domain. However, Washington has limited this licensing to the area of real estate matters.

Proposals in California and Illinois have just narrowly missed becoming adopted as laws, disappointing such groups as HALT (Help Abolish Legal Tyranny) that have fought steadfastly for the introduction of such proposals. In Illinois, Sen. Emil Jones introduced Senate Bill 776, entitled "Legal Technician Licensing Act," in April of 1991. The bill eventually made its way to the full Senate for a second reading. However, the bill never received the required third reading under Illinois law and thus died in session.[16]

Limited Licensure
Legislation that allows nonlawyers to provide limited legal services directly to the public.

Independent Paralegal/Legal Technician A nonlawyer who has been licensed pursuant to limited licensure legislation and can therefore provide legal services directly to the public.

Family Law A body of law concerned with domestic issues, such as divorce and adoption.

---

[16]For further discussion, *see* NALA FACTS AND FINDINGS, Sept. 1992.

FOCUS ON ALICE PENNY

Alice Penny began her career as a legal secretary. However, Penny's work soon began to encompass more and more paralegal duties. She decided to complete formal paralegal studies, graduating from Meredith College Legal Assistant Program in 1980. Penny was richly rewarded for her hard work. She is nationally renowned and the charter member of Paralegal Services of North Carolina, Inc., a successful company that provides paralegal services to attorneys from all over the country, encompassing tasks such as corporate filings and document preparation.

Penny is a past national chairperson and current director of Professional Legal Assistants, a national paralegal association. Historically she has been extremely active in paralegal associations and was a founding member of her regional associations—the Raleigh-Wake Paralegal Association and the North Carolina Paralegal Association.

Penny believes paralegals can trace their roots back to legal secretaries. "One day," Penny said, "attorneys looked around and saw that the federal government was effectively using nonlawyers to handle routine matters. Private attorneys then began to look for ways to effectively use their nonlawyer staff." Penny points out that the National Association of Legal Assistants evolved from the National Association of Legal Secretaries. Currently, approximately eight thousand of the twenty thousand members of NALS are legal assistants.

"It is so very important for us to remember our history. History gives us perspective," Penny instructs. "Every paralegal today benefits from the struggles endured by pioneering paralegals who helped to develop the profession. Those struggles served to strengthen the profession and put paralegals in their current position. Experience is a dear teacher and your experiences are your history."

As should be evident, Penny plays a prominent role in the world of paralegals. She believes two things most contributed to public recognition of legal assistants: (1) the emphasis which lawyers place on education for paralegals and the consequent development of a strong awareness of paralegal skills and legal ethics, and (2) acceptance of paralegals by bar associations, particularly the American Bar Association.

Under the guidance and tutelage of individuals such as Alice, the paralegal profession is sure to continue to win wide respect from attorneys and consumers of legal services.

Paralegals must remember their roots. We have to know where we come from but we should not let our history preclude us from having wings to soar toward our future.

A report on the services provided by legal technicians is currently before the Florida Supreme Court. The report makes four recommendations on the delivery of legal services by nonlawyers, one of which is to allow registered nonlawyers to provide legal services directly to the public.

In Appendix E you will find excerpts from recently proposed legislation. As of this writing, none of the introduced bills have been passed. However, in both jurisdictions, there are rumblings that some form of both bills will soon become law. With the passage of these bills, paralegals will, most probably be granted limited licensure. The proposed areas include real estate closings, simple bankruptcies, and simple will drafting.

TIPS FOR PARALEGALS

- ■ Know the history of your profession.
- ■ Join professional associations at your local/regional/national level.
- ■ Become familiar with the various types of legal assistant educational programs/training courses available.
- ■ Keep abreast of the issues that will affect your future as a legal assistant.

CLOSING EXERCISE

List all the arguments you can think of supporting and opposing proposed certification, general licensure, limited licensure schemes. Do you think any of these forms of regulation should be put into effect? Be prepared to debate and defend your answers.

Next, check with your state and local paralegal associations or your state legislator and learn whether there is regulation legislation pending in your jurisdiction.

CHAPTER SUMMARY

■ The paralegal profession developed from the law clerk-apprentice, administrative agency practice, the legal secretary, and legal services organizations. Recognition by the American Bar Association, the development of educational programs, and the advent of national paralegal organizations all contributed to the development and establishment of a strong role for the paralegal in the legal community.

■ The American Bar Association (ABA), an august body representing legal professionals all over the country, recognized and acknowledged that the assistance of a nonlawyer could greatly improve and expand the delivery of legal services to larger segments of the population. The ABA's stamp of approval sounded out to the legal community that the help of nonlawyers could be a valuable contribution to law office practice.

■ National paralegal associations such as NALA, NFPA, and PLA represent the concerns of paralegals around the country. It is through such organizations that legal assistants find an outlet for exchanging ideas and learning about issues that affect their role in the law office.

■ The legal profession is beginning to recognize the advantages of hiring nonlawyers. Issues such as the development of the freelance paralegal and the regulation of legal assistants will affect the role of the paralegal in the future. The profession continues to debate the merits of certification, limited licensure, and general or broad-based licensing.

KEY TERMS

ABA special committee
ABA Special Committee
  on Lay Assistants for
  Lawyers

ABA Special Committee
  on Legal Assistants
ABA Special Committee
  on the Availability of
  Legal Services

ABA standing committee
administrative agency
Affirmation of
  Professional
  Responsibility

American Association for	Guidelines for the	NALA Code of Ethics
Paralegal	Utilization of Legal	NALA Model Standards
Education/AAfPE	Assistant Services	and Guidelines for
American Bar	independent	Utilization of Legal
Association/ABA	paralegal/legal	Assistants
certification	technician	National Association of
Certified Legal	lawyer/attorney	Legal
Assistant/CLA	Legal Assistant	Assistants/NALA
Certified Legal Assistant	Management	National Association of
Specialist/CLAS	Association/LAMA	Legal Secretaries
discovery	legal profession	National Federation of
family law	legal secretary	Paralegal
Federal Administrative	limited licensure	Association/NFPA
Procedures Act	Model Code of Ethics and	paralegal/legal assistant
freelance legal paralegal	Professional	specialty certification
general licensing	Responsibility	U.S. Supreme Court

CASE

In re Opinion No. 24 of the Committee on the Unauthorized Practice of Law

Supreme Court of New Jersey, 1992.
128 N.J. 114, 607 A.2d 962

GARIBALDI, J.

The New Jersey Supreme Court Committee on the Unauthorized Practice of Law (the "Committee") concluded in Advisory Opinion No. 24, 126 *N.J.L.J.* 1306, 1338 (1990), that "paralegals functioning outside of the supervision of an attorney-employer are engaged in the unauthorized practice of law." Petitioners are several independent paralegals whom attorneys do not employ but retain on a temporary basis. They ask the Court to disapprove the Advisory Opinion.

Like paralegals employed by attorneys, independent paralegals retained by attorneys do not offer their services directly to the public. Nonetheless, the Committee determined that independent paralegals are engaged in the unauthorized practice of law because they are performing legal services without adequate attorney supervision. We agree with the Committee that the resolution of the issue turns on whether independent paralegals are adequately supervised by attorneys. We disagree with the Committee, however, that the evidence supports a categorical ban on all independent paralegals in New Jersey.

I

The Committee received inquiries from various sources regarding whether independent paralegals were engaged in the unauthorized practice of law. Pursuant to its advisory-opinion powers under *Rule* 1:22-2, the Committee solicited written comments and information from interested persons and organizations.

In response, the Committee received thirty-seven letters from a wide variety of sources. Additionally, the State Bar Association's Subcommittee on Legal Assistants ("Legal Assistant Subcommittee"), the National Association of Legal Assistants ("NALA"), and the National Federation of Paralegal Associates ("NFPA") provided the Committee with information on regulation, education, certification, and the ethical responsibilities of paralegals.

The Committee characterized the information that it received in two ways: first, the material expressed positive views on the value of the work performed by paralegals; second, all of the materials expressly or implicitly recognized that the work of paralegals must be performed under attorney supervision. None distinguished between paralegals employed by law firms and those functioning as independent contractors offering services to attorneys. Several recurring themes played throughout the submissions:

1. One need not be a full- or part-time employee of a single attorney to be under the direct supervision of an attorney and independent paralegals in particular work under the direct supervision of attorneys.

2. Independent paralegals provide necessary services for sole practitioners and small law firms who cannot afford to employ paralegals on a full-time basis.

3. Independent paralegals confer an invaluable benefit on the public in the form of reduced legal fees.

4. Independent paralegals maintain high standards of competence and professionalism.

5. Rather than exacting a *per se* prohibition, the Committee should consider regulations or standards or other alternative forms of guidance, such as licensure and certification.

6. A blanket prohibition on independent paralegals would work a disservice to the paralegals and the general public.

After receiving those submissions, the Committee held a hearing at which four independent paralegals, three employed paralegals, and three attorneys testified. All the independent paralegals testifying before the Committee were well qualified. One independent paralegal noted that as an NALA member she is bound by both the *ABA Model Code of Professional Responsibility* and the ABA *Model Rules of Professional Conduct*. The independent paralegals stated that although they had worked with many attorneys during their careers, they had worked solely for those attorneys and only under their direct supervision.

The independent paralegals gave several reasons for being retained by attorneys. First, attorneys may be understaffed at any time and may need to devote additional resources to one case. Second, attorneys may need paralegal assistance but be unable to afford a full-time paralegal. Third, attorneys may hire independent paralegals who have expertise in a given field.

Client contact varied for each independent paralegal. Some see the attorney's client in the attorney's office, while others meet outside of the office. One paralegal testified that she carefully ensures that clients understand that she is not an attorney and that she cannot, as a paralegal, answer legal questions.

The independent paralegals correspond with clients on behalf of attorneys, using the attorney's or law firm's letterhead, which is usually kept in the paralegal's office. Although the paralegals noted that the attorneys generally receive copies of any correspondence, one paralegal testified that she did not provide copies of all correspondence to the attorneys. Another paralegal stated that some attorneys authorized her to send out letters without their prior review. All the paralegals pointed out that they use computer technology, which facilitates rapid transmission of letters and other written material to their supervising attorneys to review, correct, and return.

Three paralegals who were full-time employees of law firms also testified before the Committee. Each paralegal represented a paralegal organization, such as NFPA or NALA. They explained that many independent paralegals are members of those organizations and that both organizations have developed guidelines and standards for their paralegal members. In addition, NALA conducts a certification examination that takes over two days and requires extensive knowledge of a variety of legal matters.

All three employed paralegals expressed support for independent paralegals who work under the direct supervision of an attorney and who do not provide services directly to the public.

Two attorneys appeared before the Committee. One testified that as long as attorneys supervise independent paralegals, that those paralegals do not work full-time for one attorney or firm does not matter. The second attorney, a sole practitioner, testified that independent paralegals provide many benefits to both small firms and the general public alike. The Committee, he suggested, should focus on others, known as "legal technicians" or "forms practitioners," who offer their services directly to the public, rather than on independent paralegals who do not offer their services directly to the public but who are retained by attorneys.

II

After the hearing, the Committee issued Advisory Opinion 24, 26 *N.J.L.J.* 1306 (1990), in which it compared the amount of supervision attorneys exercise over employed paralegals and retained paralegals. It concluded that attorneys do not adequately supervise retained paralegals. *Id.* at 1338. The Committee linked the absence of adequate attorney supervision to several different factors.

First, the Committee raised the concern that attorneys retaining independent paralegals do not carefully select those with sufficient training and experience because the short-term working relationship does not allow the attorney enough time to discover their levels of expertise. *Id.* at 1337. In contrast, the Committee presumed that employed paralegals undergo an interview process with an attorney, and the attorney's ongoing relationship with those paralegals allows him or her to determine whether they are qualified for the job. *Ibid.*

Second, the Committee believed that attorneys are unable to undertake reasonable efforts to insure that the conduct of independent paralegals is compatible with the attorney's professional obligations pursuant to *Rule* 5.3 of the *Model Rules of Professional Conduct* ("RPC 5.3"). *Ibid.* The Committee reasoned that an attorney who hires an independent paralegal could not satisfy *RPC* 5.3(c)(3), which requires an attorney to make "reasonable investigations" into a paralegal's misconduct. *Ibid.* That conclusion was based on the Committee's perception that the relationship between an attorney and an independent paralegal is more distant than the one between an attorney and a full-time employed paralegal. *Ibid.*

Third, the Committee maintained that the relationship between attorneys and independent paralegals would cause significant conflicts of interest because the independent paralegal could work for numerous law firms and the attorney might not be able to monitor any conflict that might arise. *Id.* at 1338.

Fourth, the Committee concluded that attorneys not sufficiently skilled in a particular area of the law who charge a fee for the work done by the paralegal violate attorney-ethics considerations by assisting in the unauthorized practice of law. *Ibid.; see also RPC* 5.5(b) (a lawyer shall not assist a person who is not a member of the bar in the performance of activity that constitutes the unauthorized practice of law). The Committee observed that attorneys cannot supervise an independent paralegal who is working in a field that is unfamiliar to the attorney. *Ibid.* It suggested as an alternative that sole practitioners could seek assistance in substantive legal matters from specialist attorneys or law firms rather than from independent paralegals. *Ibid.*

Fifth, and finally, the Committee was troubled by correspondence and communication between attorneys and independent paralegals. The Committee was distressed to learn that paralegals had sent out letters on firm stationary (sic) without prior review by the attorney, creating potential for misunderstanding by the general public. *Ibid.*

The Committee summarized its findings as follows:

> When the paralegal is employed by the attorney, the nature of the employment relationship makes it possible for the attorney to make the decisions as to which matters are appropriate for handling by the paralegal and which

matters require direct hands-on work by the attorney. When the attorney and the paralegal are separated both by distance and the independent nature of the paralegal's relationship with the attorney, the opportunity for the exercise of that most important judgment by the attorney becomes increasingly difficult.

This is not to say that there are not matters that could be handled by an independent paralegal with appropriate supervision by the attorney contracting with the paralegal. The problem is that the decisions as to what work may be done by the paralegal should be the attorney's to make but the distance between attorney and paralegal mandated by the independent relationship may result in the making of those decisions by the paralegal or by default.

It is the view of the Committee, moreover, that the paralegal practicing in an independent paralegal organization, removed from the attorney both by distance and relationship, presents far too little opportunity for the direct supervision necessary to justify handling those legal issues that might be delegated. Without supervision, the work of the paralegal clearly constitutes the unauthorized practice of law. We found, from the testimony and materials presented to our Committee, that the opportunity for supervision of the independent paralegal diminishes to the point where much of the work of the independent paralegal, is, in fact, unsupervised. That being the case, the independent practice by the paralegal must involve the unauthorized practice of law. The fact that some of the work might actually be directly supervised cannot justify the allowance of a system which permits the independent paralegal to work free of attorney supervision and control for such a large part of the time and for such a large part of the work. [*Ibid.*]

Based on those findings, the Committee concluded that attorneys are currently unable to supervise adequately the performance of independent paralegals, and that by performing legal services without such adequate supervision those paralegals are engaging in the unauthorized practice of law. *Ibid.*

We granted petitioners' request for review, — *N.J.* — (1991), and the Chairperson of the Committee granted their motion to stay the enforcement of Opinion No. 24.

III

No satisfactory, all-inclusive definition of what constitutes the practice of law has ever been devised. None will be attempted here. That has been left, and wisely so, to the courts when parties present them with concrete factual situations. See Milton Lasher, *The Unauthorized Practice of Law*, 72 *N.J.L.J.* 341 (1949) ("What is now considered the practice of law is something which may be described more readily than defined.").

Essentially, the Court decides what constitutes the practice of law on a case-by-case basis. *See, e.g., New Jersey State Bar Ass'n v. New Jersey Ass'n of Realtor Bds.*, 93 *N.J.* 470, 461 A.2d 1112 (1983) (permitting real-estate brokers to prepare certain residential-sales and lease agreements, subject to right of attorney review); *In re Education Law Center*, 86 *N.J.* 124, 429 A.2d 1051 (1981) (exempting non-profit corporations from practice-of-law violations); *Auerbacher v. Wood*, 142 *N.J.Eq.* 484, 59 A.2d 863 (E. & A.1948) (holding that services of industrial-relations consultant do not constitute practice of law).

• • •

There is no question that paralegals' work constitutes the practice of law. *N.J.S.A.* 2A:170–78 and 79 deem unauthorized the practice of law by a nonlawyer and make such practice a disorderly-persons offense. However, *N.J.S.A.* 2A:170–81(f) excepts paralegals from being penalized for engaging in tasks that constitute legal practice if their supervising attorney assumes direct responsibility for the work that the paralegals perform. *N.J.S.A.* 2A:170–81(f) states:

> Any person or corporation furnishing to any person lawfully engaged in the practice of law such information or such clerical assistance in and about his professional work as, except for the provisions of this article, may be lawful, but the lawyer receiving such information or service shall at all times maintain full professional and direct responsibility to his client for the information and service so rendered.

Consequently, paralegals who are supervised by attorneys do not engage in the unauthorized practice of law.

IV

Availability of legal services to the public at an affordable cost is a goal to which the Court is committed. The use of paralegals represents a means of achieving that goal while maintaining the quality of legal services. Paralegals enable attorneys to render legal services more economically and efficiently. During the last twenty years the employment of paralegals has greatly expanded, and within the last ten years the number of independent paralegals has increased.

Independent paralegals work either at a "paralegal firm" or freelance. Most are employed by sole practitioners or smaller firms who cannot afford the services of a full-time paralegal. Like large law firms, small firms find that using paralegals helps them provide effective and economical services to their clients. Requiring paralegals to be full-time employees of law firms would thus deny attorneys not associated with large law firms the very valuable services of paralegals.

The United States Supreme Court, in upholding an award of legal fees based on the market value of paralegal services, stated that the use of paralegal services whenever possible "encourages cost-effective legal services * * * by reducing the spiraling cost of * * * litigation." *Missouri v. Jenkins*, 491 U.S. 274, 288, 109 S.Ct. 2463, 2471, 105 L.Ed.2d 229, 243 (1989) (quoting *Cameo Convalescent Center, Inc. v. Senn*, 738 F.2d 836, 846 (7th Cir.1984), *cert. denied*, 469 U.S. 1106, 105 S.Ct. 780, 83 L.Ed.2d 775 (1985)).

> The Court further noted:
> It has frequently been recognized in the lower courts that paralegals are capable of carrying out many tasks, under the supervision of an attorney, that might otherwise be performed by a lawyer and billed at a higher rate. Such work might include locating and interviewing witnesses; assistance with depositions, interrogatories, and document production; compilation of statistical and financial data, checking legal citations, and drafting correspondence. Much such work lies in a gray area of tasks that might appropriately be performed either by an attorney or a paralegal. To the extent that fee applicants under § 1988 are not permitted to bill for the work of paralegals at market rates, it would not be surprising to see a greater amount of such work performed by attorneys themselves, thus increasing the overall cost of litigation. [*Id.* at 288 n. 10, 109 S.Ct. at 2471–72 n. 10, 105 L.Ed.2d at 243 n. 10.]

New Jersey's Advisory Committee on Professional Ethics also has recognized the value of paralegals to the legal profession:

> It cannot be gainsaid that the utilization of paralegals has become, over the last 10 years, accepted, acceptable, important and indeed,

necessary to the efficient practice of law. Lawyers, law firms and, more importantly, clients benefit greatly by their work. Those people who perform paraprofessionally are educated to do so. They are trained and truly professional. They are diligent and carry on their functions in a dignified, proper, professional manner. [ACPE Op. 647, 126 *N.J.L.J.* 1525, 1526 (1990).]

The New Jersey State Bar Association also specifically recognizes the important role of the paralegal. On September 15, 1989, its Board of Trustees voted to allow associate membership for paralegals and legal assistants.

We also note that the American Bar Association ("ABA") has long given latitude to attorneys to employ non-lawyers for a variety of tasks. For example, Ethical Consideration 3-6 of the ABA *Model Code of Professional Responsibility* provides as follows:

A lawyer often delegates tasks to clerks, secretaries, and other lay persons. Such delegation is proper if the lawyer maintains a direct relationship with his/her client, supervises the delegated work, and has complete professional responsibility for the work product. This delegation enables a lawyer to render legal services more economically and efficiently.

The ABA has further stated, in Formal Opinion 316, that "we do not limit the kind of assistance that a lawyer can acquire *in any way* to persons who are admitted to the Bar, so long as the non-lawyers do not do things that lawyers may not do or do the things that [only] lawyers[] may do." (emphasis added).

V

No judicial, legislative, or other rule-making body excludes independent paralegals from its definition of a paralegal. For example, the ABA defines a paralegal as follows:

A person qualified through education, training or work experience; is employed or *retained* by a lawyer, law office, government agency, or other entity; works under the *ultimate* direction and supervision of an attorney; performs specifically delegated legal work, which, for the most part, requires a sufficient knowledge of legal concepts; and performs such duties that, absent such an assistant, the attorney would perform such tasks. (emphasis added).

The ABA definition expands the role of a legal assistant to include independent paralegals, recog-

nizing that attorneys can and do retain the services of legal assistants who work outside the law office.

New Jersey's ethics Rules also recognize independent paralegals. This Court has adopted the ABA's *Model Rules of Professional Conduct* to govern the conduct of New Jersey State Bar members. *R.* 1:14 (adopting the ABA *Model Rules* "as amended and supplemented by the Supreme Court"). The central provision governing the attorney's use of lay employees is *RPC* 5.3:

With respect to a non-lawyer employed *or retained by* or associated with a lawyer:

(a) Every lawyer or organization authorized by the Court rules to practice law in this jurisdiction shall adopt and maintain reasonable efforts to ensure that the conduct of non-lawyers *retained* or employed by the lawyer, law firm or organization is compatible with the professional obligations of the lawyer.

(b) a lawyer having direct supervisory authority over the nonlawyer shall make reasonable efforts to ensure that the person's conduct is compatible with the professional obligations of the lawyer; and (c) a lawyer shall be responsible for conduct of such a person that would be a violation of the Rules of Professional Conduct if engaged in by a lawyer if:

(1) the lawyer orders or ratifies the conduct involved;

(2) the lawyer has direct supervisory authority over the person and knows of the conduct at a time when its consequences can be avoided or mitigated but fails to take reasonable remedial action; or

(3) the lawyer has failed to make reasonable investigation of circumstances that would disclose past instances of conduct by the nonlawyer incompatible with the professional obligations of a lawyer, which evidence a propensity for such conduct. (emphasis added).

The emphasized language indicates that *RPC* 5.3 applies to independent retained paralegals and not just to employed paralegals.

Moreover, the comment following *RPC* 5.3 does not distinguish between employees and independent contractors, stating as follows:

Lawyers generally employ assistants in their practice. * * * Such assistants, *whether employees* *or independent contractors*, act for the lawyer in rendition of the lawyer's professional services. (emphasis added).

Finally, *Rule* 4:42–9(b) implicitly recognizes that attorneys use paralegals by permitting awards of counsel fees to include costs of paraprofessional services. That Rule's definition of "legal assistant" is almost identical to that of the ABA's. The Rule, however, requires only that the paralegal operate under the direction and supervision of the attorney. It does not distinguish between an employed or retained paralegal.

VI

[4] Under both federal law and New Jersey law, and under both the ABA and New Jersey ethics Rules, attorneys may delegate legal tasks to paralegals if they maintain direct relationships with their clients, supervise the paralegal's work and remain responsible for the work product.

[5–7] Neither case law nor statutes distinguish paralegals employed by an attorney or law firm from independent paralegals retained by an attorney or a law firm. Nor do we. Rather, the important inquiry is whether the paralegal, whether employed or retained, is working directly for the attorney, under that attorney's supervision. Safeguards against the unauthorized practice of law exist through that supervision. Realistically, a paralegal can engage in the unauthorized practice of law whether he or she is an independent paralegal or employed in a law firm. Likewise, regardless of the paralegal's status, an attorney who does not properly supervise a paralegal is in violation of the ethical Rules. Although fulfilling the ethical requirements of *RPC* 5.3 is primarily the attorney's obligation and responsibility, a paralegal is not relieved from an independent obligation to refrain from illegal conduct and to work directly under the supervision of the attorney. A paralegal who recognizes that the attorney is not directly supervising his or her work or that such supervision is illusory because the attorney knows nothing about the field in which the paralegal is working must understand that he or she is engaged in the unauthorized practice of law. In such a situation an independent paralegal must withdraw from representation of the client. The key is supervision, and that supervision must occur regardless of whether the paralegal is employed by the attorney or retained by the attorney.

We were impressed by the professionalism of the paralegals who testified before the Committee. They all understood the need for direct attorney supervision and were sensitive to potential conflict-of-interest problems. Additionally, they all recognized that as the paralegal profession continues to grow, the need to define clearly the limits of the profession's responsibilities increases.

Those who testified voiced many of the same concerns expressed by the Committee. Indeed, Opinion No. 24 crystallized issues that both the legal profession and paralegals recognize should be addressed. The Committee enumerated five factors that are of vital importance to the profession and that confront every paralegal and every prospective employer:

(1) There have been no standards or guidelines set down by any body with regulatory authority to control and regulate the activities of independent paralegals.

(2) At least one New Jersey college provides an ABA-approved paralegal program and provides a certificate of completion to successful candidates. A bachelor of arts degree is a prerequisite to obtaining the certificate. Those requirements are applicable only to matriculating students and it is clear that no law or regulation imposes the requirement of obtaining such a certificate on students who propose to practice.

(3) Neither the state of New Jersey, any bar association, nor any organization or affiliation of paralegals or legal assistants provides for a licensing procedure or any other procedure to regulate and control the identity, training and conduct of those who engage in the work.

(4) While the ABA definition states that a legal assistant should be "qualified through education, training or work experience" which serves as a guideline for its members in the use of paralegal assistance, that requirement is not imposed or binding upon a person who desires to engage in independent paralegal practice.

(5) There is no paralegal association or organization that imposes any uniform mechanism of standards of ethics, disciplinary proceedings, and rules and regulations to oversee the activities of paralegals. Those who function as paralegals, therefore, do so pursuant to standards and rules either of their own devising or of the devising of the variety of different groups or organizations, none of which have the power to impose adherence to standards

or to control or discipline those who do not adhere to standards. [Op. No. 24, *supra*, 126 *N.J.L.J.* at 1337.]

Following the introduction of *RPC* 5.3, the Practicing Law Institute correctly noted:

[M]any firms will not be prepared to shoulder [the responsibility of supervising paralegals] within their existing procedures. Accordingly, effective measures will have to be undertaken to ensure compliance. These will include not only procedures and controls, but also communication, training and education of staff employees in the responsibilities inherent in relevant Model Rules. [PLI Order no. A4-A289 (November 1, 1989).]

Although we agree that those concerns must be addressed, we emphasize that they apply equally to employed paralegals and to independent paralegals.

Although the ABA requires that paralegals be qualified through work, education, or training, the State currently requires neither certification nor licensure for paralegals. No regulatory body exists to prevent unqualified persons from working as paralegals. However, the same is true with regard to employed paralegals.

No rule requires that either employed paralegals or independent paralegals belong to any paraprofessional organization. Thus, only those paralegals who are members of such organizations are subject to regulation. Again, the problem is not with independent paralegals but with the absence of any binding regulations or guidelines.

The same holds true with regard to ethical issues. As with other laypersons, paralegals are not subject to any ethics rules governing the practice of law. The ethical prohibitions against paralegals, *RPC* 5.3, therefore focus on the attorney's conduct. However, the language of *RPC* 5.3 applies to attorneys who both employ and retain paralegals.

Underlying many of the Committee's concerns is its belief that the attorney will not be able to comply with *RPC* 5.3 due to the lack of physical proximity to the retained paralegal. That "physical distance" led the Committee to conclude that for an attorney to maintain direct supervisory authority over an independent paralegal who often will not work in the same office as the attorney is too difficult.

We recognize that distance between the independent paralegal and the attorney may create less opportunity for efficient, significant, rigorous supervision. Nonetheless, the site at which the paralegal performs services should not be the determinative

factor. In large law firms that have satellite offices, an employed paralegal frequently has less face-to-face contact with the supervising attorney than would a retained paralegal.

Moreover, in this age of rapidly-expanding instant communications (including fax tele-transmissions, word processing, computer networks, cellular telephone service and other computer-modem communications), out-of-office paralegals can communicate frequently with their supervising attorneys. Indeed, as technology progresses, there will be more communication between employers and employees located at different sites, even different states. That arrangement will be helpful to both the paralegal and the attorney. Parents and disabled people, particularly, may prefer to work from their homes. Sole practitioners and small law firms will be able to obtain the services of paralegals otherwise available only to large firms.

Moreover, nothing in the record before the Committee suggested that attorneys have found it difficult to supervise independent paralegals. Indeed, the paralegals testified that the use of word processing made an attorney's quick review of their work possible. Most of the independent contractors who testified worked under the supervision of attorneys with whom they had regular communication.

Although a paralegal's unsupervised work does constitute the unauthorized practice of law, that issue is not unique to independent paralegals. Rather, we emphasize again, it is the lack of educational and regulatory standards to govern their practice is at the heart of the problem.

• • •

Although we have not incorporated use of paralegals into New Jersey Court Rules, the Advisory Committee on Professional Ethics has considered the practice of paralegals on four prior occasions, most recently in Opinion No. 647, 126 *N.J.L.J.* 1525 (1990). In that opinion the Advisory Committee on Professional Ethics held that paralegals working under the direct supervision of an attorney may carry business cards so long as the name of the attorney or firm appears on the card and the card is authorized by the attorney or law firm.

Giving to them the ability of clearly identifying themselves and for whom they work can only better serve their employers and clients. The business card, as is true in every area where business cards are used, serves to define the status of the person presenting that card and has the desired effect of eliminating confusion.

Other states, bar associations, and paralegal organizations have also begun to regulate paralegals and attorneys' use of them. A significant number of state courts have incorporated into their court rules or ethics opinions rules for the use of legal assistants. Kentucky has promulgated a Paralegal Code of Ethics, which sets forth certain exclusions to the unauthorized practice of law:

For purposes of this rule, the unauthorized practice of law shall not include any service rendered involving legal knowledge or advice, whether representation, counsel or advocacy, in or out of court, rendered in respect to the acts, duties, obligations, liabilities or business relations of the one requiring services where:

A. The client understands that the paralegal is not a lawyer;

B. The lawyer supervises the paralegal in the performance of his duties; and

C. The lawyer remains fully responsible for such representation, including all actions taken or not taken in connection therewith by the paralegal to the same extent as if such representation had been furnished entirely by the lawyer and all such actions had been taken or not taken directly by the attorney. Paralegal Code, Ky.S.Ct.R. 3.700, Sub-Rule 2.

Several states' bar associations have also promulgated guidelines to regulate the paralegal profession. For example, the Colorado Bar Association has issued a set of guidelines under which a lawyer may permit a paralegal to assist in all aspects of the lawyer's representation of a client, provided that:

1. the status of the [paralegal] is disclosed at the outset of any professional relationship with a client, other attorneys, courts or administrative agencies or members of the general public;

2. the lawyer establishes the attorney-client relationship, is available to the client and maintains control of all client matters;

3. the lawyer reviews the [paralegal's] work product and supervises the performance of duties assigned to the [paralegal];

4. the lawyer remains responsible for the services performed by the [paralegal] to the same extent as if such services had been furnished entirely by the lawyer and such actions were those of the lawyer;

5. the services performed by the [paralegal] supplement, merge with and become part of the attorney's work product;

6. the services performed by the [paralegal] do not require the exercise of unsupervised legal judgment; and

7. the lawyer instructs the [paralegal] concerning standards of client confidentiality.

The guidelines also provide:

1. A [paralegal] may author and sign correspondence on the lawyer's letterhead, provided the [paralegal] status is indicated and the correspondence does not contain legal opinions or give legal advice.

2. A [paralegal] may have a business card with the firm name appearing on it so long as the status of the legal assistant is disclosed. However, the name of the [paralegal] may not appear on the letterhead of the firm.

3. A [paralegal] may conduct client interviews and maintain general contact with the client once the attorney-client relationship has been established, so long as the client is aware of the status and duties of the [paralegal], and the client contact is authorized by the attorney.

The Colorado Bar Association has also promulgated a set of ethical requirements for the attorney who hires paralegals:

1. A lawyer shall ascertain the paralegal's abilities, limitations and training, and must limit the paralegal's duties and responsibilities to those that can be competently performed in view of those abilities, limitations and training.

2. A lawyer shall educate and train [paralegals] with respect to the ethical standards which apply to the lawyer.

3. A lawyer is responsible for monitoring and supervising the conduct of [paralegals] to prevent the violation of the ethical standards which apply to the lawyer, and the lawyer is responsible for assuring that [paralegals] do not do anything which the lawyer could not do.

4. A lawyer shall continuously monitor and supervise the work of [paralegals] in order to assure that the services rendered by the [paralegals] are performed competently and in a professional manner.

5. A lawyer is responsible for assuring that the [paralegal] does not engage in the unauthorized practice of law.

6. A lawyer shall assume responsibility for the improper conduct of [paralegals] and must take appropriate action to prevent recurrence of improper behavior or activities.

7. [Paralegals] who deal directly with lawyers' clients must be identified to those clients as non-lawyers, and the lawyer is responsible for obtaining the understanding of the clients with respect to the role of and the limitations which apply to those assistants.

The Michigan, Missouri, and New York Bar Associations have adopted similar requirements.

Additionally, two of the largest paralegal associations have proposed standards for paralegals. NALA has developed an examination procedure for certifying paralegals and has developed ethics guidelines for their work, and NFPA has developed a detailed list of "Paralegal Responsibilities" and maintains a repository of the latest state-by-state statutory and case developments regulating the use of paralegals.

VII

Regulation and guidelines represent the proper course of action to address the problems that the work practices of all paralegals may create. Although the paralegal is directly accountable for engaging in the unauthorized practice of law and also has an obligation to avoid conduct that otherwise violates the Rules of Professional Conduct, the attorney is ultimately accountable. Therefore, with great care, the attorney should ensure that the legal assistant is informed of and abides by the provisions of the Rules of Professional Conduct.

Although an attorney must directly supervise a paralegal, no rational basis exists for the disparate way in which the Committee's opinion treats employed and independent paralegals. The testimony overwhelmingly indicates that the independent paralegals were subject to direct supervision by attorneys and were sensitive to potential conflicts of interest. We conclude that given the appropriate instructions and supervision, paralegals, whether as employees or independent contractors, are valuable and necessary members of an attorney's team in the effective and efficient practice of law.

Subsequent to the issuance of the Committee's decision, the State Bar Association forwarded a reso-lution to this Court requesting the establishment of a standing committee on paralegal education and regulation. We agree that such a committee is necessary, and will shortly establish it to study the practice of paralegals and make recommendations. The committee may consider guidelines from other states, bar associations, and paralegal associations in formulating regulations for New Jersey paralegals. Any such regulations or guidelines should encourage the use of paralegals while providing both attorneys and paralegals with a set of principles that together with the Rules of Professional Conduct can guide their practices. The guidelines drafted will not be static but subject to modification as new issues arise.

We modify Opinion No. 24 in accordance with this opinion.

For modification—Chief Justice WILENTZ and Justices CLIFFORD, HANDLER, POLLOCK, GARIBALDI and STEIN—6.

Opposed—None.

Questions

1. Compare the conclusions reached by the Supreme Court Committee on Unauthorized Practice of Law with those reached by the New Jersey Supreme Court. Which do you find more compelling?

2. Look at the discussion of the value of legal assistants that appears in Section IV. What does the court conclude is the value of legal assistants?

3. What kinds of functions does the court note that paralegals may perform?

4. The Court seems to note that there is little reason to analyze differently the activities of traditional paralegals employed by attorneys and the activities of independent paralegals. Instead, the court concludes that the important inquiry to be considered is whether the attorney has adequately supervised the paralegal. Do you agree with this conclusion? Why or why not?

5. Re-read the five factors of vital importance to legal assistants that were enumerated by the committee. At this point in your career, can you appreciate how these factors might affect you? How do you think they might influence the direction of your career?

6. What problems does the court think regulation can fix? Do you agree?

OVERVIEW OF LEGAL ETHICS

CHAPTER OBJECTIVES

After reading this chapter, you should
be able to:

■ Know that codes of ethics exist for
attorneys and for paralegals.

■ Evaluate the importance of the specific
ethics rules and how they affect the
interests of the client.

■ Recognize the consequences of violating
those rules of ethics.

As legal assistants become increasingly important to the economical
and efficient operation of the law firm, they are entrusted with
greater responsibilities toward clients. Legal assistants become privy
to client confidences that cannot be revealed. They are asked to speak with
clients, yet avoid giving legal advice. In fact, they may have more contact with
clients than the attorney who supervises them.

Of utmost concern to the legal community, however, is protecting those
clients. To ensure that protection, ethics rules have developed. These rules
regulate the conduct of attorneys and of the nonlawyers whom they employ.
Therefore, it is critical for paralegals to be exposed to the principles of legal
ethics as developed through various codes of ethics.

The American Bar Association has developed guidelines (discussed more
fully in this chapter) to assist attorneys in monitoring the behavior of their
legal assistants. The first guideline clearly states that it is the obligation of the
attorney to make sure the conduct of a legal assistant conforms to the
attorney's ethical obligations.

> Guideline 1: A lawyer is responsible for all of the professional actions of a
> legal assistant performing legal assistant services at the lawyer's direction
> and should take reasonable measures to ensure that the legal assistant's
> conduct is consistent with the lawyer's obligations under the ABA Model
> Rules of Professional Conduct. Guideline 1, ABA Model Guidelines for the
> Utilization of Legal Assistant Services.

This chapter will discuss this guideline and how it affects the conduct of
the legal assistant. The first part of this chapter is devoted to a discussion of
the various ethics codes that outline appropriate behavior for a paralegal. The
second half of the chapter addresses the consequences of violating these
codes.

OPENING EXERCISE

Renee is a **solo practitioner** who practices law in Las Vegas, Nevada. As Renee's
practice grows, she realizes she could benefit from the help of a legal assistant. After

Solo Practitioner A sole attorney who owns and manages a law firm.

interviewing several candidates, Renee decides to hire David, a civil engineer who recently enrolled in evening law classes, hoping to earn his law degree in a few years. Renee assures David that he will have time during the day to complete his schoolwork.

As times passes, Renee's reputation as a capable litigator grows. Her caseload has correspondingly grown as a result of this. With increasing frequency, her presence is required in the courtroom so she begins delegating much of the office work to David. David, already extremely busy with his current responsibilities in the office and with his homework, finds himself struggling to keep on top of all of his work.

As a result of Renee's and David's busy schedules, some problems develop. Phone calls are not promptly returned, and correspondence apprising clients of the status of their cases is not sent out. Last week an escrow account executive of the Great Desert Bank of America called to speak with Renee about some directions that were sent out on her (unsigned) stationery, relative to three accounts. David was responsible for handling this matter. The account executive does not understand the directions that were given.

Do you see potential problems with the way Renee is running her law practice? What are some things that might happen as a result of her maintaining such a busy schedule without getting more help? Do you think David could be affected in any way? How?

PRINCIPLES OF LEGAL ETHICS

From the time that we were small children, our parents or those who raised us attempted to instill in us a sense of right and wrong. Our formative years were spent learning to treat other people the way we wanted to be treated—with decency. In essence, we were learning our morals, our ethics.

Ethics The principles of conduct governing an individual or a group.

Ethics is generally defined as "the principles of conduct governing an individual or a group."[1] The word ethics is often considered to be related to the concept of morals and moral choices. **Moral** is defined as "of or relating to principles of right and wrong in behavior."[2]

Moral Of or relating to principles of right and wrong in behavior.

Our personal ethics and moral code guide our conduct. We make decisions each day about how to treat people, how to get along with others, and how to handle problems. **Legal ethics** serve the same function. They guide our behavior toward clients and shape our legal environment. They are a code of conduct self-imposed by the legal profession.

Legal Ethics A code of conduct self-imposed by the legal profession which guides our behavior toward clients and shapes our legal environment.

Because we have strong personal ethics, we may feel it is unnecessary to study legal ethics. After all, at this point in our lives, could there be anything more to learn? You will discover throughout this text, however, that *legal ethics can differ substantially from personal ethics.* A paralegal may feel that it is morally right to reveal a client confidence in order to help the client in nonlegal matters. However, based on what our legal ethics obligations tell us, revealing such a confidence may not be acceptable action. A paralegal's personal ethics may tell her to help her fellow man and woman when they are down on their

---

[1] MERRIAM-WEBSTER'S COLLEGIATE DICTIONARY 398 (10th ed. 1993). By permission. From Merriam-Webster's Collegiate® Dictionary ©1993 by Merriam-Webster Inc., publisher of the Merriam-Webster® dictionaries.
[2] *Id.* at 756.

luck so she may decide to loan money to a client to buy food for his children. Yet this loan may violate conflict of interest rules outlined in the attorney's code of ethics. This conflict is what makes the study of legal ethics so difficult.

The American Bar Association's Center for Professional Responsibility, in the *Annotated Model Rules of Professional Conduct* (2d ed., 1992), notes:

> A lawyer's first professional obligation is to obey the rule of professional ethics of the jurisdiction in which the lawyer is licensed to practice. *Id.* at 580.

This standard applies to the legal assistant helping an attorney. It is therefore imperative that the legal assistant understand her ethical obligations and the sources from which they derive.

No single regulatory body is responsible for monitoring paralegal conduct, nor does one set of ethical rules govern the conduct of all legal assistants. Therefore it is important that the paralegal understand the various codes of ethics designed to influence the paralegal's ethical choices and to guide the legal assistant's ethical behavior toward clients. These codes and guidelines are discussed more fully below.

ATTORNEY CODES OF ETHICS

The first, and perhaps most important, source of ethical rules for the legal assistant is the supervising attorney's **Code of Ethics.** This should always be the first source consulted when the legal assistant faces an ethical dilemma. Each state has developed such a code to which every attorney practicing in that jurisdiction must adhere.

Each state has its own code of ethics because each state is responsible for policing the legal profession and those who want to practice law within that jurisdiction. As the U.S. Supreme Court has stated:

> We recognize that the States have a compelling interest in the practice of professions within their boundaries, and that as part of their power to protect the public health, safety and other valid interests they have broad power to establish standards for licensing practitioners and regulating the practice of professions. *Goldfarb v. Virginia State Bar,* 421 U.S. 773, 793, 95 S. Ct. 2004, 2016, 44 L. Ed. 2d 572 (1975).

This includes establishing standards for attorneys.

Each state's code of ethics is designed to regulate the legal profession. These codes are usually developed and enforced through the highest court in that state.

Each state's code of ethics generally places an obligation upon attorneys to ensure that the conduct of their nonlawyer support staff adheres to the state code of ethics for attorneys. Failing to adequately supervise support staff to ensure that the code of ethics is not violated can lead to serious sanctions being levied against the attorney and to malpractice charges being filed against the legal assistant. For those reasons, the attorney's code of ethics may be the best, most developed guide for discerning the paralegal's ethical obligations. The attorney's code of ethics, therefore, is our starting place throughout this text. It should also be the legal assistant's starting place when faced with an ethical dilemma in the work environment. The paralegal should also consult with supervising attorneys or with the firm's **ethics committee.**

Attorney's Code of Ethics The ethical rules which guide the behavior of attorneys engaged in the practice of law in a particular jurisdiction.

Ethics Committee A committee formed within a law firm by that firm for the purpose of making and enforcing ethical policy decisions based on the rules of ethics.

It should be noted, however, that the disciplinary code in place in one state may not be the same code in place in an adjoining state. Yet, while the codes can and do vary from state to state, their substance is basically the same. This is most likely due to the fact that, when preparing a code of ethics, most states look to the codes of ethics developed by the American Bar Association (ABA) and generally adopt these codes, sometimes with little variation. For that reason, this text relies upon the ABA's codes of ethics to explain ethical obligations.

You should be aware, however, that the code of ethics in place in your state may differ somewhat from the rules developed by the ABA that are discussed in this text. Again, the substance of the rules in place in each state is generally the same and is discussed in general terms throughout these pages. Nonetheless, this textbook should be read in conjunction with your state's disciplinary code. It is a good idea to read any assignments in this book with your state code nearby.

Over the years the ABA has developed several different ethics codes. The following section traces the development of these codes and discusses the features that are part of the two codes still relied upon in most states.

EXERCISE 2.1 | If your instructor has not already supplied you with a copy of the attorney's ethics code in place in your state, visit your local law library or call your state bar association and obtain a copy.

Historical Development of American Bar Association Codes of Ethics

While today we realize the necessity of having in place legal ethics codes, the imposition of the first disciplinary rules upon attorneys did not occur until the early part of this century. Until that time lawyers, as "officers of the court," were not subjected to any disciplinary authority.[3]

Gradually each state began to develop rules to guide the attorney's behavior. Later the states developed codes of ethics. Through the codes of ethics, attorneys were bound to adhere to a minimal standard of conduct toward their clients. The first state to enact a code of ethics was Alabama.[4]

Individual states' adoption of various codes would lead to a haphazard approach to providing attorneys with codes by which to guide their behavior. For this reason, in 1908 the American Bar Association developed a uniform document outlining acceptable professional behavior for attorneys. This document, entitled **Canons of Professional Ethics,** was adopted by the ABA during its first annual meeting.[5] The Canons were designed to serve as "a general guide." The Canons were often quaintly written and used language that is not usually used in statutes.

The Canons were not law simply because the ABA cannot make law in the way the legislature or courts can. However, when faced with ethical problems, courts often cited one or more of the Canons as *evidence* of the law. The ABA Ethics Committee would also issue ethics "opinions" on various questions.

Canons of Professional Ethics
A uniform document developed by the American Bar Association in 1908 that provided general rules to guide acceptable professional behavior for attorneys.

[3]*See* Ronald D. Rotunda, *The Lawyer's Duty to Report Another Lawyer's Unethical Violations in the Wake of Himmel,* 1988 U. ILL. L. REV. 977. Reprinted by permission.
[4]*See* ABA Comm. on Ethics and Professional Responsibility, Informal Op. 1420 (1978).
[5]Canons of Professional Ethics (1908), Preamble; reprinted in T. MORGAN AND R. ROTUNDA, SELECTED STANDARDS ON PROFESSIONAL RESPONSIBILITY (1989).

These opinions were interpretations of the various Canons, and courts still cite these ABA Opinions as evidence of the law.

Disciplinary authorities often complained that vaguely worded Canons were hard to enforce. In addition, attorneys subject to the rules wanted to be governed by "bright" lines rather than vague ones. So, in 1969 the ABA membership adopted a new set of rules that eventually came to be called the *Model Code of Professional Responsibility.*

Throughout this text, you will see the *Model Code of Professional Responsibility* referred to as the *Code* or the *Model Code.* Unlike the earlier Canons, the *Code* was written in statutory language, with specific requirements called "Disciplinary Rules" or DRs that provided minimum standards below which an attorney's conduct could not fall. An attorney subjects himself to discipline if he violates a Disciplinary Rule in a jurisdiction where the court has promulgated the *Code* as positive law. (The Disciplinary Rules are discussed more fully later in this chapter.) The ABA urged the state and federal courts to adopt the *Model Code* (or a nonuniform version of the *Model Code*) into law.

The *Code* was in place for a number of years. During that time the Disciplinary Rules were interpreted by the courts and changes in the attorney's ethical obligations were noted. For example, for a number of years attorney advertising was prohibited. However, beginning in 1977 a series of U.S. Supreme Court decisions relaxed advertising restrictions. (After all, as we will see in chapter 8, a prohibition of advertising by attorneys violates the free speech rights of attorneys.)

In response to these changes, and to provide a more workable disciplinary model, the American Bar Association's *Model Rules of Professional Conduct* were adopted in 1983 ("*Model Rules*"). More than half the states have adopted some variation of the *Model Rules.*[6]

The American Bar Association's *Model Code of Professional Responsibility*

The second code of ethics adopted by the ABA, the **Model Code of Professional Responsibility,** was adopted by many states when it was originally written and presented in 1969. Several states still retain variations of the *Code.* For that reason you must be familiar with sections of the *Code.* Moreover, although the *Code* has now been replaced in most states by the *Model Rules of Professional Conduct* (discussed below), the *Code* also provides guidance in interpreting the newer provisions of the *Model Rules.* Therefore, applicable provisions of the *Model Code* are often addressed throughout this text.

The *Model Code* was written to provide more than a mere outline of the obligations of attorneys. For this reason the *Code* is divided into Canons, Ethical Considerations, and Disciplinary Rules.

The **Disciplinary Rules of the Model Code (DRs)** are the statements by which attorneys are obliged to conform their conduct. Disciplinary Rules state the "minimum level of conduct below which no attorney can fall without being subject to disciplinary action."[7]

To aid the attorney in achieving the guides that are set forth is the Disciplinary Rules, the *Code* provides **Ethical Considerations** (ECs). The

ABA Model Code of Professional Responsibility (Code of Professional Responsibility) The second code of ethics that was adopted by the American Bar Association. It was adopted in 1969.

Disciplinary Rules (DRs) Statements set forth within the *Code of Professional Responsibility* that establish the minimum level of conduct below which no attorney can fall without being subject to disciplinary action.

Ethical Considerations (ECs) Aspirational statements set forth within the *Code of Professional Responsibility* that explain the disciplinary rules.

---

[6]The authors gratefully acknowledge Professor Ronald Rotunda's extensive contribution to this discussion.
[7]RONALD D. ROTUNDA, PROFESSIONAL RESPONSIBILITY, BLACK LETTER SERIES, Glossary (1992), citing MODEL CODE OF PROFESSIONAL RESPONSIBILITY, Preliminary Statement.

Ethical Considerations are aspirational statements. While not mandatory in nature, they explain the rules, providing behavioral guidelines to which attorneys should aspire. A number of Ethical Considerations are provided to explain each Disciplinary Rule. The Ethical Considerations explain each set of Disciplinary Rules and demonstrate what kind of conduct attorneys should strive to achieve in order to maintain their disciplinary obligations, and thus avoid violating the Disciplinary Rules.

The Disciplinary Rules and their corresponding Ethical Considerations are grouped together and organized under headings labeled **Canons.** The Canons express, in general terms, the concepts to be presented and discussed within that grouping of Disciplinary Rules and Ethical Considerations. It should be noted that more than one Disciplinary Rule may be included within that Canon.

Canons Statements under which the DRs and ECs are grouped, that express the ethical concepts to be presented and discussed within the *Code of Professional Responsibility.*

The American Bar Association's *Model Rules of Professional Conduct*

Most states currently rely upon the American Bar Association's *Model Rules of Professional Conduct* (abbreviated throughout this text as "the *Model Rules*"). The *Model Rules*, which do away with aspirational statements of ethical conduct, are arranged quite differently from the *Model Code.*

Each of the *Model Rules* begins by setting forth a Rule of Ethics by which attorneys must abide. Following each Rule is a set of Comments which is intended to interpret and explain the meaning of the particular Rule. Notes follow the Comments. Providing comparisons and references to the *Model Code* sections, the Notes are supplementary and are not intended to affect the application of the Rules.

Because the Rules have been adopted by a majority of the jurisdictions, their content is explained fully, where applicable, throughout this text.

American Bar Association's (ABA's) Model Rules of Professional Conduct (Model Rules) An ethics code adopted by a majority of jurisdictions within the U.S.

DISCIPLINARY AGENCIES, CASE LAW, AND ETHICS ADVISORY OPINIONS

Just as with other laws and rules, the attorney's codes of ethics are subject to interpretation by state and federal courts. Ethical problems arise. Facts surrounding that problem are then presented to a tribunal which determines how the code of ethics should be applied. Analysis and interpretation of the codes helps to explain their meaning. Cases and advisory opinions present that analysis.

The process by which these cases and opinions come about is important to note. The legal profession is **self-policing.** This means that attorneys are responsible for enforcing the codes of ethics. When a client complains of an attorney's conduct, or when members of the legal profession are made aware of ethical violations, the attorney is usually reported to a state attorney disciplinary agency, to which the state supreme court has delegated authority (some states have lay members on the hearing panels of their disciplinary agencies).

The state agency may go by any one of a number of names; for our purposes, however, we shall refer to this body as the **state disciplinary agency.**

Although procedures vary from state to state, the state disciplinary agency generally has the responsibility for investigating the attorney's conduct and

Self-Policing A form of control which is self-imposed by a profession to help ensure that professional standards are maintained and to ensure that the interests of the public are protected.

State Disciplinary Agency The state agency that processes complaints against members of the legal profession concerning an attorney's conduct.

determining whether any ethical violations, based upon the state's code of ethics, have occurred. If the state agency charges an attorney with a violation of ethics rules, the attorney is accordingly disciplined if found to have violated the ethics rules.

Occasionally, decisions of the state disciplinary agency are appealed to the state's highest court. Remember that the state court usually regulates the practice of law. That court reviews the facts that led to the investigation of the attorney by the disciplinary agency. Then, interpreting the code of ethics of that state, the court applies the code to the facts of the case and determines whether that conduct warrants the punishment which the state disciplinary agency deemed warranted. The findings of the court may then be presented in a written opinion.

These opinions have precedential value in that jurisdiction and may be persuasive to a court in another state which is attempting to decide similar issues arising because of a similar code of ethics. They may be used to discipline another attorney who has engaged in similar conduct. Most important, for our purposes at least, is the fact that these opinions interpret sections of the *Model Code* and the *Model Rules* and explain to those who are bound by them exactly what kind of behavior runs afoul of the ethical rules. For that reason, throughout this text, case opinions will be presented, discussed, and excerpted.

Some opinions discuss issues which are jurisdiction-specific, meaning that the state applies facts to an ethical rule which is unique to that jurisdiction. Other opinions are more general in nature, and their discussion provides guidance for those practicing in any number of jurisdictions. These opinions, while **binding** in the jurisdiction in which they were rendered, are **persuasive authority** for others. Always remember, therefore, to compare your jurisdiction's rule with that discussed in any reprinted opinions found in this text.

Members of the legal profession may also have the benefit of access to state and local bar **ethics advisory opinions.** Every state bar has an advisory committee that accepts questions from attorneys contemplating certain behavior that may run afoul of ethics rules. Attorneys who write to the state bar ethics committees seek advice in dealing with certain ethical dilemmas. Many smaller bar associations, whose influence is more regional in nature, also accept ethical questions. For example, the Chicago Bar Association, a local association, offers advice to attorneys who practice law in the city of Chicago. The Illinois State Bar Association offers advice to attorneys from all corners of the state of Illinois.

The state bar responds to these queries by presenting a state ethics advisory opinion. Usually the question presented to the committee is set forth first. Next, while perhaps citing to authority, the state committee will explain why it feels that certain conduct may or may not violate the state code of ethics. These opinions are then usually collected and published for use by others who need assistance in interpreting ethics rules.

Additionally, the American Bar Association presents both Formal and Informal Ethics Opinions which are also advisory in nature. These opinions likewise address a question concerning an ethics problem and explain the correct approach for handling the situation. These opinions are published in looseleaf form and may be available to review in your local law library.

Binding authority Sources of law that must be taken into account by legal professionals in any given jurisdiction.

Persuasive Authority Sources of law that might be considered but are not binding.

Ethics Advisory Opinion An opinion issued by a state bar's advisory committee that addresses a question from an attorney relating to ethics.

State ethics opinions are never binding in nature for they are not a decision or judgment of a court. Rather, they merely provide the studied opinion of the peers of that attorney who is seeking guidance. The opinions of the American Bar Association are also never binding but are merely persuasive. However, attorneys (and courts) often find the ethics advisory opinions helpful. For that reason, state bar ethics opinions or ABA opinions are occasionally addressed throughout the text.

EXERCISE 2.2

Visit your local law library and find a copy of an ethics advisory opinion from your state. Also, find either a Formal or an Informal Ethics Opinion presented by the ABA. Bring your opinions to class and discuss how the state bar or the ABA handled that query. Then compare the format of the opinion with the cases you find excerpted at the end of each of these chapters.

If your local library does not have a copy of these, write to the American Bar Association to obtain a copy.

APPLICATION OF ATTORNEY'S CODES OF ETHICS TO LEGAL ASSISTANTS

The attorney's code of ethics is applied to both the attorney and the legal assistant. This is because the attorney is obliged to ensure that his nonlawyer employees adhere to the attorney's ethical obligations. This obligation is placed upon the attorney both by the ethical codes and through the doctrine of *respondeat superior*.

By the Codes of Ethics

Both the *Model Code* and the *Model Rules* place an obligation upon the attorney to ensure that the attorney's nonlawyer employees adhere to those codes. For that reason, where the legal assistant fails to adhere to the ethical obligations of the state code of ethics, it is the *attorney* who is disciplined, not the nonlawyer assistant. Occasionally, though, the nonlawyer assistant's behavior proves so egregious that she is held responsible under state criminal statutes or under negligence theories. Alternatively, the law firm may terminate the employment of the errant legal assistant. Inasmuch as the nonlawyer employee is not licensed, however, the state bar association has no direct control over the person.

The *Model Rules* place this obligation on lawyers to supervise the conduct of nonlawyers in **Model Rule 5.3**, which provides:

> With respect to a nonlawyer employed or retained by or associated with a lawyer:
> (a) A partner in a law firm shall make reasonable efforts to ensure that the firm has in effect measures giving reasonable assurance that the person's conduct is compatible with the professional obligations of the lawyer;
> (b) A lawyer having direct supervisory authority over the nonlawyer shall make reasonable efforts to ensure that the person's conduct is compatible with the professional obligations of the lawyer; and

Model Rule 5.3 The most important of the Model Rules of Professional Conduct as ethics relate to nonlawyers. This rule, more than any other, encourages both attorneys and the nonlawyers who work for them to strictly adhere to the attorney's code of ethics as it makes an attorney responsible for the nonlawyer in his employ.

(c) A lawyer shall be responsible for conduct of such a person that would be a violation of the rules of professional conduct if engaged in by a lawyer if:

(1) The lawyer orders or, with the knowledge of the specific conduct, ratifies the conduct involved, or

(2) The lawyer is a partner in the law firm in which the person is employed, or has direct supervisory authority over the person, and knows of the conduct at a time when the consequences can be avoided or mitigated but fails to take reasonable remedial action.

Moreover, it is professional misconduct for a lawyer to allow a paralegal to violate an ethics rule. The attorney can be disciplined for a nonlawyer's unethical conduct. Model Rule 8.4 states in part:

It is professional misconduct for a lawyer to:

(a) violate or attempt to violate the rules of professional conduct, knowingly assist or induce another to do so, or do so *through the acts of another* . . . . (emphasis added)

The *Model Code* also places an obligation upon the attorney to ensure that nonlawyer employees adhere to the provisions found in the attorney's code of ethics. Unlike the *Model Rules,* however, the *Model Code* does not detail this obligation in merely one provision. Rather, this obligation is made apparent throughout the *Code* in separate provisions. Disciplinary Rule 4-101(D) is one example of a *Code* section which places ethical obligations of attorneys upon legal assistants. It provides:

(D) A lawyer shall exercise reasonable care to prevent his employees, associates, and others whose services are utilized by him from disclosing or using confidences or secrets of the client . . . .

The corresponding Ethical Consideration reveals, in part:

It is a matter of common knowledge that the normal operation of a law office exposes confidential professional information to non-lawyer employees of the office, particularly secretaries and those having access to the files; and this obligates a lawyer to exercise care in selecting and training his employees so that the sanctity of all confidences and secrets of his clients may be preserved . . . . *Model Code of Professional Responsibility,* EC 4-2.

Can you find other provisions in the *Code* which refer to the lawyer's obligation toward nonlawyer assistants?

From a reading of the *Model Code's* DR 4-101(D) and from Model Rule 5.3, it should be obvious that the rules are not applied solely to attorneys supervising legal assistants. The term *legal assistant* is not used. The rules hold attorneys responsible for their actions in supervising *nonlawyers.* Therefore, an attorney's duty to supervise also applies to employees assuming other supporting roles, such as legal secretaries or private investigators.

Not every instance of unethical conduct by a legal assistant will create disciplinary problems for the supervising attorney. It is important to note that Rule 5.3 says a lawyer shall make "reasonable efforts to ensure that the firm has in effect measures giving reasonable assurance that the person's conduct is compatible with the professional obligations of the lawyer." However, what constitutes "reasonable efforts" depends on the circumstances of the situation.

Under Rule 5.3, an attorney is not required to provide a guarantee that the nonlawyer will never participate in conduct that is not compatible with the professional obligation of a lawyer. However, an attorney is expected to take precautionary measures to prevent ethical violations.[8]

You will also recall that the specific language of Model Rule 5.3 is such that a lawyer is responsible for the conduct of those he supervises if he "orders or with knowledge of the specific conduct ratifies the conduct involved."

Therefore, in not every instance involving errors made by nonlawyers will the attorney be automatically liable. According to Hazard & Hodes,

> An attorney who supervises a nonlawyer associate is not required to guarantee that the associate will never engage in 'incompatible' conduct, for that would be tantamount to vicarious liability. On the other hand, to take no precautionary steps at all is a violation of Rule 5.3 whether or not the nonlegal associate misbehaves.[9]

By this comment we see that the legal ethics rules do not *automatically* make attorneys liable. A sufficient degree of responsibility has to be found.

This means that the attorney, upon hiring nonlawyer personnel, should at a minimum instruct them as to what is proper ethical conduct. The attorney should also inquire as to what training the employee has had in legal ethics. The attorney should also take care to closely supervise the conduct of the nonlawyer. Additionally, when the nonlawyer starts work at a new law firm, the nonlawyer should inquire about any specific guidelines the supervising attorney may wish to discuss.

In many cases, the courts have made very clear that they intend to hold attorneys to a standard whereby attorneys must take precautionary measures to prevent the commission of a violation on the part of those in their employ.

A review of an opinion applying this rule to the actions of the legal assistant may help to explain the consequences that result from a legal assistant's failure to abide by ethical dictates. Just as lying is not accepted in society generally, any form of misrepresentation to a client would be considered a serious ethical violation. *Matter of Martinez* involved a situation where a legal assistant made serious misrepresentations to a client and to others with whom he was dealing on the client's behalf. 107 N.M. 171, 754 P.2d 842 (1988).

An attorney, Mr. Eloy F. Martinez, employed a legal assistant, John Felix. Felix maintained an office separate from that of the attorney. When Rosalba Ortiz contacted Felix, seeking legal assistance in pursuing a claim against Allstate Insurance, Felix told her that he had seven years' experience in the legal field. He also told her that he worked for attorney Martinez and he (Felix) would handle her personal injury case for one-third of whatever amount was recovered. At no time did Felix apprise her of the fact that he was not a lawyer.

When the client first met with Felix, the legal assistant, she had been offered $800.00 by Allstate as a settlement for the property damage of her claim. Felix told Ortiz, the client, to accept this settlement. She did so. Felix then told

---

[8]GEOFFREY C. HAZARD, JR., AND W. WILLIAM HODES, THE LAW OF LAWYERING, vol. 2, (2d ed., 1991). Reprinted from *The Law of Lawyering*, by Geoffrey C. Hazard, Jr., and W. William Hodes, with the permission of Prentice Hall Law & Business.
[9]*Id.* at 785.

Allstate that he was representing the client. The insurance company issued the check to the client *and to John Felix, the attorney for Ortiz.*

Martinez gave Felix permission to cash the check, despite the fact that he realized that the check was written out incorrectly. Felix then took $350.00 out of the $800.00 settlement check and turned the balance over to Ortiz.

Martinez then wrote to Allstate and advised the company that he and Felix would be representing Ortiz. He then set up an appointment for Felix to meet with the claims representative and settle the remainder of the claim. Felix subsequently negotiated a settlement of $5,500.00 for Ortiz on the remainder of the claims without the client's knowledge or approval. Allstate made the checks payable to Ortiz and Martinez. When Ortiz saw the checks, however, she became alarmed because she had never before heard the name of Martinez.

The court held Martinez responsible for the actions of his legal assistant in misrepresenting that he was a lawyer. At page 843 of the opinion the court specifically stated:

> We do . . . . find that Martinez employed Felix as a legal assistant and failed to make reasonable efforts to ensure that the conduct of Felix comported with his own professional obligations . . . . Furthermore, the actions of Felix in making misrepresentations to Ortiz and to Allstate are imputed to Martinez. . . . Martinez has, therefore, engaged in conduct involving misrepresentation and deceit . . . not only through his own failure to clarify the status of Felix in his communications with Allstate, but also by virtue of his responsibility for the dishonest conduct of Felix.

The court also considered other allegedly unethical conduct of Martinez that was brought to its attention. The court found that Martinez had engaged in further wrongful behavior. These circumstances all contributed to the court's decision to indefinitely suspend Martinez from the practice of law in the State of New Mexico.

EXERCISE 2.3

Jack and Ervileen "Ervie" Smidgen are law partners who are also husband and wife. The name of their law firm is "Smidgen and Associates, P.C." Jack and Ervie have a nationally renowned legal practice. Jack's strength lies in his comprehension of the technical aspects of the cases they accept. Ervie excels at litigating, and so she handles issues that end up in court.

One day, as Ervie is preparing for trial in a multimillion dollar case, she is handed a file by Bob, a junior partner of the law firm. Bob handles the defense of white-collar criminals who are charged with violations of environmental codes, and he is extremely selective in the cases that he accepts.

The file Bob has handed Ervie involves a criminal matter. It seems that the brother-in-law of one of the clients that Bob successfully represented last year has been convicted of illegal gambling. The brother-in-law's name is Karl. The former client wants Bob to represent Karl on appeal. Bob tells Ervie that he cannot, in good conscience, represent Karl. He has met Karl and does not trust the way he looks or the story he tells. In the flurry of activity surrounding the final preparation of her case, Ervie tells Bob:

"We can take up this matter later, at lunch, after I select a jury this morning. I will tell Jack to meet us, and we will resolve this."

Bob is called away that afternoon to take an emergency case that has come up along the coast. Ervie's impaneling of jurors takes two days instead of merely a morning. They both forget about the file.

In the meantime, Ziggy, the firm's newest paralegal, finds the file. He assumes that the case has been accepted and decides he will make a name for himself with the firm and begins to regularly correspond with Karl without the knowledge of any of the attorneys. Ziggy then researches the issues on appeal and mails a rough draft of an appellate brief to Karl on June 19th. The brief is due to be filed on August 6th, and the appellate court has marked "no further extensions" on the draft order that was filed with the extension motion.

On the morning of August 1st, Bob receives a call from Karl's brother-in-law, the one who had referred him. He thanks Bob for the effort expended on the brief and says he is calling to check on the status of the case.

Discuss any potential problems. Suggest any precautionary measures that could have been taken to avoid problems such as this one. What should Ervie and Bob do? Who can be held responsible for this activity?

Assume now that Ervie is not a private attorney but is a supervising attorney at the U.S. Occupational Safety and Health Agency. One of her responsibilities is to engage groups of top-notch environmental investigators who are hired by the government on an "as-needed" basis. The owner of one of the investigative services with whom Ervie contracts is George Moons. His company is called "Special Environmental Protection Systems, Inc." (SEPS).

One of the investigators employed by SEPS, Richard Waltech, exchanges words with Andrew, Production Manager of the company that he is spot checking. Their words become heated, and Waltech decides that chemicals are being released into the plant through faulty ventilation. He takes the only copy of the production schedule from Andy's desk to prevent further problems. Andy's company sues Waltech individually, Moons individually, Special Environmental Protection Systems, Inc., Smidgen individually and the U.S. Occupational Safety and Health Agency.

Do you think Andy should prevail? Against which parties, if any? On what basis?

Through the Doctrine of *Respondeat Superior*

Respondeat Superior
A legal doctrine whereby one party becomes responsible for the actions of another party.

Agency A relationship in which one person acts for another or represents another by the latter's authority.

Agent A person authorized to act for another.

Authority The power or right to act or make decisions.

Principal That party within an agency relationship who permits or directs an agent to act for his or her benefit.

Equally important in applying the ethics rules to nonlawyers is the doctrine of *respondeat superior*. Unlike an investigation into the attorney's ethical conduct for disciplinary reasons, a suit filed under the theory of *respondeat superior* would be *civil* rather than *disciplinary* in nature, and its remedy would not be discipline but rather damages.

Respondeat superior is a doctrine whereby one party becomes responsible or liable for the actions of another party. It is based upon the premise that the party who is deemed liable has directed another to act on her behalf. The doctrine is part of the law of **agency.**

In other words, where one's **agent** is given **authority** to act on behalf of a **principal,** an agency situation may arise such that the principal may be held liable for the actions of his agents. Generally, the principal is the party responsible for directing the actions of his subordinates. The agent is the party who takes direction from a principal. A supervising attorney can be likened to a *principal* and the legal assistant supervised by the attorney assumes the role of an *agent*.

Different kinds of authority may be found to exist. The first type of authority is actual authority, arising when an agent is specifically directed to do something by a principal. The next type is apparent authority and is said to exist where a third person can be reasonably expected to have understood that a particular person has authority to enter into negotiations and make representations that he is acting on behalf of the principal. There is implied authority, which is authority arising out of or from the circumstances of actual authority. Finally, there is ratified authority, said to arise when a principal ratifies the actions of her agent after the fact; that is, the principal agrees to be bound by the actions of the agent, regardless of the result, in spite of the fact that the principal did not direct the actions.

Should an agent do something wrong while he is carrying out the authority to act given to him by the principal, the principal may be found liable for the agent's actions. The exception to the application of agency principles occurs where the agent is acting "outside the scope of his employment." If the agent does something wrong or negligent at a time when he is *not* working or when he is doing something clearly not related to his job description, then it is unlikely that the principal can be held liable for that action.

The relationship between an attorney and a legal assistant is clearly an agency relationship. Therefore, the misconduct of the legal assistant may be attributed to the attorney because of agency principles. However, there is an exception where the paralegal is acting "outside the scope of her employment." For example, then, if a paralegal or an investigator or another nonlawyer employee of the law office is shopping in a store for personal items on a weekend and intentionally provokes a fistfight with a stranger, the law firm would not be responsible for the nonlawyer's actions. This is true even if the victim knows that the nonlawyer works for the firm, and even if the nonlawyer is on his way home from the office when the incident occurs. In order for an argument to be made that the attorney is responsible for the nonlawyer's actions, the nonlawyer's activity must be related to his employment by the attorney.

The attorney will not be held liable for the actions of every nonlawyer employee whom she may have occasion to hire. It is the amount of control over the employee that is relevant for purposes of asserting an agency theory. Presumably, where an attorney has hired a legal assistant as a regular employee, then the attorney would have sufficient control such that the attorney will be responsible for that nonlawyer's actions. However, it is unclear whether an attorney would be considered liable for the actions of a freelance paralegal with whom he contracts to complete work on an infrequent basis.

One case discussed whether an attorney would have the required degree of control necessary to hold him liable for the actions of a **process server** with whom he had contracted to serve summons on a party. *Bockian v. Esanu Katsky Korins & Siger,* 124 Misc.2d 607, 476 N.Y.S.2d 1009 (1984).

> **Process Server** A person authorized by law to serve process papers on defendants.

In *Bockian,* the issue involved was whether the attorney who hired a process server could be held responsible for his actions. The process server, named John Doe in the complaint, was alleged to have engaged in harassing conduct. When he went to the business where he believed he could find the person he wanted to serve with summons, Mr. Perelman, he was told that Perelman was out of the country and could not be reached. John Doe's response was to continuously ring the doorbell at the business. He also solicited the help of a delivery person in an attempt to gain access to the office. Further, John Doe taped a sign to the building of the business that proclaimed that Perelman, the person he was seeking to serve, had "venereal herpes." He then proceeded to threaten to post similar signs all over New York City. Finally, it was alleged that the process server assaulted the plaintiff, an employee of Perelman, when she tried to take a picture of him.

The plaintiff sued numerous parties, including the attorney who had hired the process server. While the court could not find a cognizable cause of action stated in the complaint, the court's holding revealed that the attorney's degree of control over the actions of the process server was insufficient to support a finding of liability.

> Nor can an attorney be held vicariously liable for the alleged malfeasance of a process server who arrives at a litigant's business address to serve process at an allegedly inconvenient time. An attorney does not generally retain a sufficient degree of control over an independent process server's performance of his duties as would be necessary to render the process server an agent or employee of the attorney. *Bockian*, 476 N.Y.S.2d at 1012–1013.

EXERCISE 2.4   Research the law in your jurisdiction regarding the doctrine of *respondeat superior*. If you are using the West Digest System, you will need to look under the term "Master-Servant." Try to find cases involving attorneys and their support staff. How does your jurisdiction address this issue?

GUIDELINES FOR THE UTILIZATION OF LEGAL ASSISTANTS

An additional tool for monitoring the ethical conduct of the nonlawyer is found in state and ABA guidelines outlining the acceptable use of legal assistant services. In addition to the attorneys' codes of ethics, these guidelines also provide guidance to paralegals in determining how to shape one's conduct.

As the use of nonlawyers in the law office grows more frequent, more and more attorneys have become conscious of their ethical responsibility to supervise nonlawyer conduct. To assist the attorney in discharging this obligation, many states and, most recently, the ABA have developed guidelines that explain to attorneys how to ethically make use of the services of legal assistants.

As of 1993, seventeen state bars had implemented guidelines to assist lawyers in ethically using the services of nonlawyers. Included among these states are Florida, Michigan, Iowa, Illinois, and Rhode Island. The purpose of such guidelines has been explained as providing "lawyers with a reliable basis for delegating responsibility for performing a portion of the lawyer's tasks to legal assistants." *See* ABA Model Guidelines for the Utilization of Legal Assistant Services, Preamble.

Likewise, in 1991, the American Bar Association published a set of guidelines entitled "ABA Model Guidelines for the Utilization of Legal Assistant Services." These guidelines are presented throughout this text to explain where a particular ethical obligation of the attorney has been made applicable to the legal assistant. The purpose of presenting such guidelines at this time is to "encourage lawyers to utilize legal assistant services effectively and promote the growth of the legal assistant profession. *Id.* After all, legal assistants serve to strengthen the legal profession.

The "ABA Model Guidelines for the Utilization of Legal Assistant Services" is reproduced in Appendix A.

PARALEGAL CODES OF ETHICS

As noted in the previous chapter, several organizations have developed codes of ethics specifically meant for the paralegal. Both the National Association for Legal Assistants (NALA) and the National Federation of Paralegal Associations (NFPA) have such codes. These codes are particularly important for legal assistants because they were drafted by their peers and are specifically meant to be used by legal assistants.

Once a state court adopts a state code of ethics, that code is binding on attorneys practicing law in that state. The codes that various paralegal associations have drafted are not binding because neither the state courts nor the state legislatures have adopted them. They are, of course, useful guidelines and may be persuasive to a court in deciding how to evaluate a paralegal's actions, but they are not law. For this reason, the nonlawyer should consult and abide by the attorney's ethics rules for the jurisdiction in which he is working.

National Association of Legal Assistants

In chapter 1, "An Introductory History of Paralegals," the history of NALA was traced. As was noted, this well-known and important organization has developed a Code of Ethics and Professional Responsibility. The Introduction to the Code provides an overview of its purpose and imparts clear meaning to the value of being a professional paralegal. The Introduction reads as follows:

> It is the responsibility of every legal assistant to adhere strictly to the accepted standards of legal ethics and to live by general principles of proper conduct. The performance of the duties of the legal assistant shall be governed by specific canons and defined herein in order that justice will be served and the goals of the profession attained. The canons of ethics set forth hereafter are adopted by the National Association of Legal Assistants, Inc., as a general guide and the enumeration of these rules does not mean there are not others of equal importance although not specifically mentioned.[10]

The Code is then divided into twelve Canons that provide the legal assistant with a general framework to be used as a guide while working in a law firm, agency, or corporation. The Canons are structured in a fashion similar to that used in the *Model Rules* and the *Model Code*.

These Canons provide ethical parameters for any person who is not a lawyer, yet who wishes to work in a legal setting. They establish general guidelines that are meant to foster professionalism and are designed for an audience that is striving to demonstrate its capacity to grow professionally. They encourage the legal assistant to "strive for perfection through education in order to better assist the legal profession in fulfilling its duty of making legal services available to clients and the public."[11]

Additionally, NALA provides an annotated ethical code, entitled "NALA Model Standards and Guidelines for Utilization of Legal Assistants, Annotated," that provides ethical guidelines and then annotations to explain from what sources the guidelines derive. The annotations are updated on a regular

---

[10]NALA Code of Ethics and Professional Responsibility (1994). Reprinted with permission.
[11]Canon 10, NALA Code of Ethics and Professional Responsibility (1994). Reprinted with permission.

basis to provide the most recent authorities to those intending to rely upon it. The Annotated Code differs from the earlier version of the NALA Code of Ethics in its structure and in that it provides a more workable guideline for the legal assistant.

The Annotated Code first defines the term legal assistant and then provides minimum qualifications that legal assistants should strive to meet. It then addresses guidelines to which it is recommended that legal assistants conform their conduct. After each guideline, the Annotated Code provides a discussion of various cases that have given rise to the proposed guideline.

As noted by NALA in this Code, the purpose of providing an annotated version of the ethical code is to assist state bar associations that are contemplating drafting guidelines for attorneys on the use of legal assistants. "The purpose of the Guidelines is not to place limitations or restrictions on the legal profession. Rather, the Guidelines are intended to outline for the legal profession an acceptable course of conduct.[12] By providing references to caselaw, readers can easily find law designed to explain what the guidelines mean and how best to implement them.

The full text of both the NALA Code of Ethics and Professional Responsibility and the NALA Model Standards and Guidelines for Utilization of Legal Assistants, Annotated, is provided in the appendix to this book.

National Federation of Paralegal Associations

Also addressed in the first chapter of this text is the National Federation of Paralegal Associations, commonly known to the legal community as NFPA. Likewise dedicated to ensuring the professional conduct of its members, NFPA also provides a code of ethics known as the Model Code of Ethics and Professional Responsibility. Historically NFPA's code has been both inspirational and instructive. For example, NFPA's Model Code of Ethics and Professional Responsibility provides:

> It is essential that each paralegal strive for personal and professional excellence and encourage the professional development of other paralegals as well as those entering the profession. Participation in professional associations intended to advance the quality and standards of the legal profession is of particular importance. Paralegals should possess integrity, professional skill, and dedication to the improvement of the legal system and should strive to expand the paralegal role in the delivery of legal services.[13]

NFPA then sets forth eight "Canons" which address various legal ethical concerns such as conflicts of interest, unauthorized practice of law, confidentiality, and billing procedures.

NFPA's Code of Ethics is provided in an appendix at the back of this book.

EXERCISE 2.5   Check with your local paralegal organization and learn whether it is a member of a state or regional alliance. What ethical code is in place for members of this organization?

---

[12]Comment, NALA Model Standards and Guidelines. Reprinted with permission.
[13]NFPA Model Code of Ethics and Professional Responsibility (1993). Reprinted with permission.

VIOLATIONS OF ETHICS RULES

Rules and codes have a specific function in our society—they serve to create order in a sometimes chaotic world. Legal ethics codes serve a similar role. The purpose of ethics codes is to ensure that attorneys and their nonlawyer support staff treat *all* of their clients in the *same* ethical manner.

Just as violating a law may result in sanctions such as jail terms or fines, violations of ethics codes may result in serious sanctions being imposed upon the attorney. Consequences affecting the legal assistant are a little trickier matter, as no body exists with the power and authority to directly discipline the paralegal. One very serious result which might affect a paralegal, however, is the possibility of a legal malpractice suit.

Discipline for a lawyer means that her license to practice law is affected. In contrast, the courts do not discipline legal assistants because they are not licensed. There is no license to take away. However, lawyers can be disciplined for not engaging in adequate supervision of nonlawyer employees. See e.g., *Attorney Grievance Commission of Maryland v. Goldberg,* 292 Md. 650, 441 A.2d 338 (1982). In addition, paralegals can be subject to lawsuits, or their law firms may terminate their employment. (If a jurisdiction were to decide to license legal assistants, however, then.that jurisdiction might also set up a system of discipline.) The full consequences of violating ethics rules are discussed below.

CONSEQUENCES RESULTING TO ATTORNEYS

In a number of cases, in addition to those cited earlier in this chapter, charges against the attorney have been filed where a legal assistant's conduct, or the conduct of a nonlawyer employee, is directly intertwined with the attorney's misconduct. However, only the attorney will be disciplined by the state attorney disciplinary committee. For this reason it is imperative that a paralegal be familiar with the consequences of his ethical errors that might affect his supervising attorney. We therefore begin this discussion with a look at disciplinary actions ordered against attorneys for ethical violations.

Disciplinary Actions for Ethical Violations

A number of sanctions may be imposed on an attorney for a violation of ethics rules. These sanctions include:

1. **Disbarment,**
2. **Suspension, or**
3. **Reprimand/Censure.**

Each jurisdiction has its own particular method of handling complaints filed against attorneys. Each jurisdiction may employ these sanctions or variations of these sanctions against attorneys found guilty of violating ethical codes. However, the following excerpt is representative of the circumstances in which these sanctions are employed.

Disbarment is generally appropriate when a lawyer knowingly engages in conduct that is a violation of a duty owed to the profession with the intent

Disbarment A sanction imposed on an attorney that takes away the attorney's license to practice law.

Suspension A sanction imposed on an attorney that results in a revocation of an attorney's license to practice law for a certain period of time.

Reprimand/Censure A sanction imposed on an attorney that officially (either publicly or privately, depending on the decision by the agency) denounces the actions of the attorney.

to obtain a benefit for the lawyer or another, and causes serious or potentially serious injury to a client, the public, or the legal system. . . . *Suspension* is generally appropriate when a lawyer knowingly engages in conduct that is a violation of a duty owed to the profession and causes injury or potential injury to a client, the public or the legal system. . . . *Reprimand* is generally appropriate when a lawyer negligently engages in conduct that is in violation of a duty owed to the profession, and causes injury or potential injury to a client, the public or the legal system. See *Louisiana State Bar v. Edwins*, 540 So.2d 294, 302 (La. 1989).

Throughout this text you will see cases discussed or excerpted in which the conduct of the attorney or of one of his nonlawyer employees results in one of these sanctions (or some variation of these sanctions) being imposed on the attorney. Try to determine why the courts decided that either disbarment, suspension, or a reprimand was necessary.

As has been previously noted, attorneys often are disciplined because of errors of their nonlawyer employees. Some common types of complaints brought against an attorney that result in disciplinary charges where the misconduct of a paralegal is involved are:

■ Aiding in the unauthorized practice of law;
■ Failing to adequately protect confidential information;
■ Failing to adequately supervise the conduct of the paralegal;
■ Improperly handling a client's funds.

A look at some cases may help to explain this point.

In *Matter of Galbasini*, 786 P.2d 971 (1990), the Supreme Court of Arizona examined the conduct of Galbasini, an attorney, and determined that a six-month suspension from the practice of law was warranted. The court found, first, that the attorney had failed to properly supervise nonlawyer employees assisting the lawyer in debt-collection proceedings. Second, Galbasini had allowed the nonlawyer employees to solicit clients for him. (After reading chapter 8, "Advertising and Solicitation," you will note that solicitation of clients by lawyers or their nonlawyer employees is generally not permitted.)

Galbasini had engaged an employment management firm with expertise in managing accounts and receivables to train and manage his legal assistants in handling debt collections and credit work. The management firm was to have been responsible for all management functions related to Galbasini's nonlawyer employees. The management firm also was to have been responsible for supervising all of the law firm's operations. The attorney was to have maintained overall control of the management company's employees and his own employees.

In reality, the attorney's supervision of his nonlawyer employees was minimal. As time passed, Galbasini grew concerned about his relationship with the management company. Eventually he requested an informal ethics opinion from his State Bar Advisory Committee. Before the Committee replied, however, he ended his arrangement with the management company.

Unfortunately, it was too late. The company used a document called an "Engagement Agreement" as a contract between itself and its clients. Galbasini had wrongly believed that the agreement was used only for individuals who were currently existing clients of the law firm. Instead, this document was used to solicit new clients for the management company and led the new clients to believe that the management company was hiring the law firm's office. The attorney said he did not know about the use of his name for the purpose of solicitation.

The Supreme Court of Arizona stated that the attorney should have seen the potential for abuse of his name and title. The court further said, "[H]aving provided no supervision whatever to guide the actions of the nonlawyer employees of RMJ [the management company], respondent [Galbasini] cannot now claim that he should not be held liable for the misconduct of the nonlawyer employees." *Galbasini* at 975. The court held that if a lawyer disregards his professional responsibilities by allowing nonlawyers to operate a law office in his name, he cannot complain when held responsible for the nonlawyer's misdeeds. *Galbasini* at 977. This, coupled with the fact that Galbasini did not communicate with his clients, in spite of the fact that he claimed that his nonlawyers did not communicate information about his clients to him, resulted in his six-month suspension.

In *Louisiana State Bar Association v. Edwins*, an attorney was accused of aiding in the unauthorized practice of law by a legal assistant, negligently entrusting a legal matter to a legal assistant, and improperly handling a client's money by turning the money over to a legal assistant. 540 So.2d 294 (La. 1989). The ethics committee of his state initiated charges and, ultimately, the attorney was disbarred.

Edwins involved an attorney and a freelance paralegal who entered into an agreement where the freelance paralegal agreed to become Edwins's paralegal, investigator, and client relations and point person in New Iberia. The paralegal maintained a small office in New Iberia (a small town in Louisiana) and employed his daughter as his secretary. He called his service "Prepaid Legal Services, Inc." Edwins maintained a separate office in Baton Rouge and used his paralegal's office as a satellite law office. The Prepaid Legal Services, Inc., sign was taken down. The attorney's law firm's sign was put up. The attorney paid part of the satellite office's expenses.

A personal injury victim went into the paralegal's office in New Iberia to inquire about securing representation in a case. The client later testified that the paralegal had held himself out as an attorney, although the paralegal testified that he had not told the client he was an attorney but rather that he had agreed to investigate the client's case and present it. The paralegal further testified that the client could have had a mistaken impression about his nonlawyer status because he had "represented" the client in an earlier welfare assistance hearing.

The legal assistant prepared the pleadings, motions, answers to discovery, and memoranda in the present case and then signed Edwins's name, clearly violating laws prohibiting the unauthorized practice of law. The paralegal eventually negotiated a $9,000.00 settlement check, which the client and his wife testified they had not received. The legal assistant deposited the settlement check into an account over which only he had control. Again, the paralegal's conduct was clearly unethical. It would appear that, in this instance, the legal assistant had misappropriated client funds.

The Supreme Court of Louisiana concluded that disbarment was the appropriate remedy for the attorney. In doing so, the court noted:

In the present case, the lawyer did not knowingly convert or misappropriate the client's property to his own use, but he certainly knew or should have known that the client's funds would be commingled with that of the non-lawyer and should have foreseen the danger that they would be misapplied to improper charges and expenses. *Edwins*, 540 So.2d at 303.

Edwins magnifies the importance of a paralegal informing a client that he is a paralegal and not an attorney. *Edwins* also demonstrates the importance of behaving in an ethical and professional manner. Remember that the first step to being treated professionally is to act that way. Your professional decorum today will establish how you and legal assistants after you are treated by clients and the public tomorrow.

Attorney Disqualification

Attorney Disqualification A consequence that can result when the attorney discovers that a conflict of interest exists. The attorney is removed from representation of the client.

An additional consequence can result where the attorney discovers that a conflict of interest exists. Usually the attorney will know if a conflict of interest exists before accepting the representation. However, in some instances the opposing counsel may uncover the conflict and may move the court to have the attorney removed from the case. **Attorney disqualification** and, in some instances, disqualification of the entire law firm from representing the client may be the result.

Where this occurs, extreme harm can result. Not only has the law firm expended a great deal of time and energy in representing the client that cannot now be utilized, but the client must now try to find a new lawyer to handle his affairs. This consequence is discussed more fully in chapter 6, "Conflicts of Interest."

Attorney Malpractice

Civilly Liable Responsibility for damages in a civil case where it is determined that the offending party has caused the other party to sustain a loss.

Throughout this text you will have an opportunity to see that violations of ethical rules invariably harm the client's interests. Violations of a state code of ethics are redressed through action undertaken *by the attorney's peers* in a state disciplinary proceeding.

But the attorney may also be held **civilly liable** by the **client** for his ethical mistake. A client who has seen an attorney's error of judgment hurt her interests may elect to sue the attorney for his **legal malpractice,** not unlike the patient who seeks redress from a doctor who performs medical malpractice.

Client A person who employs or retains an attorney for advice and representation on legal matters.

In an action undertaken by the state disciplinary agency for a violation of ethics rules, the attorney faces the possibility of a suspension of his privilege to practice law. After all, the practice of law is a privilege conferred upon an individual by the state and that privilege may be taken away at any time for misconduct. The attorney may lose his livelihood. Legal malpractice actions differ in that, while the privilege to practice law remains intact, the attorney may face financial ruin. In a legal malpractice action, the attorney is sued for money damages, which can be substantial.

Attorney/Legal Malpractice The failure of a lawyer to use such skill, prudence, and diligence as lawyers of ordinary skill and capacity commonly possess and exercise.

Attorneys can avoid a suspension of their privilege to practice law arising from ethical violations by adhering carefully to the code of ethics in place in their state. In this way, the attorney protects his livelihood. To prevent against being financially ruined because of legal malpractice actions arising from a violation of ethics obligations, the attorney can likewise adopt careful and competent practices. He can also purchase a professional malpractice liability insurance policy.

Most professionals purchase a form of insurance to protect their offices and their personal assets from liability claims in lawsuits. In many jurisdictions attorneys are required to purchase malpractice insurance. Generally, the policies state that coverage extends only to mistakes occurring in particular areas of the law. Therefore, prudent attorneys take out policies covering those areas of the law in which they practice. For example, an attorney who handles small personal injury claims may not have a policy that covers work completed in the area of wills and trusts. If the attorney then drafts a will that has an error and is sued, his assets will not be protected.

CONSEQUENCES RESULTING TO PARALEGALS

Under both the codes of ethics and the doctrine of *respondeat superior*, the attorney is held primarily liable for the errors of nonlawyer employees. However, this does not mean the legal assistant escapes responsibility for her conduct.

It is true that there is currently no disciplinary body for paralegals akin to those bodies monitoring attorney conduct. While NALA and NFPA and many local organizations have ethical codes in place, they do not have the authority to discipline legal assistants for violations. They are not designed to serve this regulatory function. Instead, their role is informational and educational.

This is not to imply, however, that the paralegal does not personally face consequences for violations of ethics rules. As is discussed below, the legal assistant should take care to avoid violating ethical rules.

Paralegal Discipline

What happens to the paralegal who violates the rules of ethics? Where a paralegal engages in misconduct that results in discipline being administered to his supervising attorney, the paralegal himself faces consequences perhaps not before contemplated.

Should the supervising attorney find herself suspended from the practice of law or disbarred, the paralegal's work becomes unnecessary. Therefore, the legal assistant will find herself without a job, without an income. Furthermore, after engaging in unethical conduct, finding a new job may not be an easy task. What attorney would risk hiring a legal assistant who was responsible for the suspension or disbarment of her previous employer?

Egregious misconduct of a legal assistant may also cause harm to the client, whose interests the legal professional has an obligation to protect. Turning over privileged documents during discovery may cause the legal assistant to give opposing counsel an advantage that cannot be overcome. Commingling trust fund account money may result in the loss of client funds. The paralegal will then have to live with the knowledge that her actions resulted in the loss of a client's cause of action or the loss of much needed client funds. Although the legal assistant may avoid discipline for her actions, she cannot avoid the guilt that accompanies violations of ethical rules. She will always have to face herself in the mirror each morning.

In very serious cases, the legal assistant who breaches her ethical obligations toward clients may find herself in violation of state law. Obviously, serious criminal conduct will result from the violation of some ethical principles. For example, a legal assistant involved in misappropriating funds from the client's account—a violation of the ethical rule—may also be found to have violated state or federal laws prohibiting embezzlement. (Of course, the attorney may also be found to have violated ethical principles for failing to adequately supervise his nonlawyer employee to prevent the misappropriation.)

Almost every state has a criminal statute prohibiting any person except a lawyer from practicing law. These laws are known as "Unauthorized Practice of Law" statutes (and are discussed fully in chapter 3). To engage in the unauthorized practice of law may result in the nonlawyer being charged with a misdemeanor violation.

What cannot be emphasized enough is that the misconduct of the legal assistant endangers more than a particular client or a supervising attorney or even the paralegal himself. As with any other group of professionals, egregious misconduct of one paralegal reflects upon every other paralegal. An attorney who has been harmed by a legal assistant who joins a firm solely to profit from insider information (see chapter 5) or who embezzles thousands of dollars from clients (see chapter 7) may become reluctant to rely upon the services of other nonlawyers not liable to formal discipline for a violation of a code of ethics. Alternatively, strict adherence to ethical principles may help to further the growth of the profession.

A final consequence of violating ethical rules is that the legal assistant may later be refused the privilege to practice law in that state. Many legal assistants enter the profession because they have an interest in the law. Working as a legal assistant often serves to fan that interest, and the legal assistant may decide to pursue her interest in the law further by attending law school and earning a license to practice law.

However, before conferring a law degree, many states require that a check into the petitioner's character reveal no flaws. The fitness check includes scrutiny by the state into crimes of which the individual may have been found guilty. If an individual has previously been found guilty of engaging in the unauthorized practice of law, for example, the state may refuse to grant a law license, despite the fact that all other requirements to obtain that license may have been met. This is because the individual has previously shown a disregard for the laws that she is expected to uphold. See e.g. *In re Demos*, 579 A.2d 668 (D.C. App. 1990).

Paralegal Malpractice

Just as attorneys may be found civilly liable for any errors that harm a client's interests, so can the paralegal.

Paralegal Malpractice
Professional misconduct or unreasonable lack of skill attributed to a paralegal.

If a legal assistant makes an ethical error that harms the client's interests, the legal assistant may be sued in a civil action for legal malpractice and may find herself liable for substantial damages. In other words, the paralegal may have to defend herself against charges of **paralegal malpractice.**

It is unlikely that a client could sue solely the legal assistant and prevail where the error is not egregious and where the lawyer has carefully monitored

PARALEGALS IN THE SPOTLIGHT

For four years, Sharon Lynn Lapin attended Lincoln School of Law in Sacramento, California, finally graduating and receiving her law degree in 1990. In February of 1992 she passed the California bar exam. However, the California State Court has denied Sharon Lapin a law license.

Why? All the requirements to receive the license appear to have been met. Yet Lapin had been deemed "morally unfit" to practice law by the State Bar of California because she had previously signed a civil settlement to resolve unauthorized practice of law charges filed against her.

Lapin owned a freelance paralegal business known as "Pacific Legal and Business Services." Through this business, Lapin assisted her "clients" by filling out forms for them to help them get through an imposing legal system. Lapin sought a law license so she could expand her forms service, offering legal advice when necessary, acting as an attorney, but maintaining a policy of offering low-cost help in legal matters to those who needed it.

After she had taken the bar exam, the Nevada City District Attorney's office filed unauthorized practice of law (UPL) charges against Lapin. To resolve the matter, Lapin signed a settlement agreement and agreed to pay a $1,500.00 fine. She has asserted that, if the UPL charges had been left unresolved, her application to the California bar would have been impaired. However, because she signed this agreement, she was declared "morally unfit," and this has had the effect of shutting down her freelance paralegal business.

Lapin appealed the denial of her law license to the State Bar Court. In 1993 she reached a settlement with the California State Bar, agreeing to pay restitution to former clients. In exchange, the California bar will reconsider her application.

Source: *News & Trends: Independent Paralegal Battles Bar Association for Right to be an Attorney,* LEGAL ASSISTANT TODAY, Jan./Feb. 1993; *see Former Paralegal Settles in Case Against State Bar,* LEGAL ASSISTANT TODAY, Sept./Oct. 1993, at 16. Copyright 1994. James Publishing, Inc. Reprinted with permission from *Legal Assistant Today.* For subscription information, call 714–755–5450.

the conduct of the legal assistant. Keep in mind that the attorney is ultimately liable for the actions of nonlawyer employees and must therefore carefully supervise their conduct. As long as the attorney has undertaken supervision of the legal assistant, the responsibility for any *honest errors* would likely fall upon the supervising attorney.

However, this does not mean a client could not file a lawsuit and name the legal assistant as one of the parties liable for the error. The paralegal may still be held responsible. The fact that the paralegal was ordered to do it by the lawyer often does not excuse the paralegal from liability. See *Restatement of the Law of Agency.* This means the legal assistant could incur substantial legal costs defending his name. See *Busch v. Flangas,* 108 Nev. 821, 837 P.2d 438 (1992), wherein the Supreme Court of Nevada found that a law clerk can be subject to legal malpractice claims if he attempts to provide legal services; but cf. *Palmer v. Westmeyer,* 48 Ohio App. 3d 296, 549 N.E. 2d 1202 (1988), wherein a court of appeals in Ohio found that a person who was a paralegal and notary public was not an attorney, and thus could not be sued for legal malpractice.

Most paralegals will not engage in such serious misconduct. Mistakes do sometimes occur, however, no matter how hard we may work to prevent them. For this reason, many law firms carry malpractice insurance policies that provide coverage for their nonlawyer employees. It is a good idea, when starting a new job, to make sure you are covered for any potential lawsuits filed against you.

Law firm insurance coverage for mistakes of nonlawyers is not always perceived as adequate, and paralegals may elect to purchase errors and omissions policies on their own.

Errors and Omissions Insurance

Just as members of other professions purchase insurance policies, so do paralegals. As their responsibilities increase, their potential for liability increases exponentially. While legal assistants are usually covered under the law firm's insurance policy, many law firms do not carry what their legal assistants consider to be adequate paralegal protection. As a result, there is a keen interest on the part of the legal assistant to make sure he is adequately insured. This is done through **errors and omissions insurance policies.**

Errors and Omissions Insurance
An insurance policy that is meant to address those professional errors or omissions that result in harm to a client.

If a paralegal has agreed to do something that is in her capacity to do and that she completed but, while completing the work she made a mistake, she is fair game for a lawsuit. Likewise, if she has agreed to do something but she fails to do it, she may also face a lawsuit. If such a consequence results, an errors and omissions policy would protect her assets.

Some insurance carriers provide extensive coverage. They offer policies for the traditional legal assistant who works in a law firm, the independent legal assistant who may have a business selling legal forms and who deals mostly with the pubic, and the freelance paralegal who contracts with a variety of attorneys to complete work.

While these types of policies all have limits on the amounts they pay out on each claim, they are fairly generous in terms of the aggregate amounts of liability coverage they offer. They are purchased the same way any other insurance policy is purchased. Also, just as with other insurance policies, they are tailored to the needs of the individual.

Not every insurance company has become involved in offering this type of insurance, however, and it may be difficult to find such coverage. One of the best ways to find errors and omissions insurance is through your local paralegal organization. For example, the National Federation of Paralegal Associations provides a professional liability insurance package with Meridien General Agency, for the Scottsdale Insurance Company. This policy provides coverage if you are a named party in a lawsuit and you need to hire an attorney. It also provides insurance against potential problems such as slander or libel or false arrest.

According to Deanna Shimko-Herman, a paralegal and Vice-President, Policy, of NFPA:

> The realization of the need for insurance corresponds with members of the paralegal profession saying that they want more responsibility and that greater responsibility provides greater job satisfaction . . . . We need to cover the gaps that law firm insurance does not provide so that we can ask for greater responsibility . . . . There is a percolating realization that particularly experienced paralegals are concerned with liability because of their increased responsibility.[14]

---

[14]Telephone Interview with Deanna Shimko-Herman, Vice-President, Policy, National Federation of Paralegal Associations (Spring 1992).

It is indisputable that paralegals are investing in insurance in the event of liability and claims. This can only serve to enhance professionalism and send out the message to the legal community and the public that it is not only a shrewd economic decision to engage the services of a legal assistant, it is a safe one.

Anna Biselli recently began working as a paralegal in a small law firm in Boston. She was assigned to her first case last week, a complex personal injury matter, and was told she would be working with Angelo Poppos, a more experienced legal assistant. In essence, Angelo would serve as a mentor to Anna.

Anna was thrilled to begin working and she jumped right in, tackling a variety of projects. She was also excited to be working with Angelo. She knew he could teach her a lot about the practical aspects of working as a legal assistant.

One morning, after struggling with discovery requests, Anna decided to seek out Angelo and ask for his help. On entering Angelo's office, she overheard his telephone conversation with their client. "Don't worry, Mrs. Maxwell. All of the documents were filed with the court last week. No need to worry about court deadlines."

After Angelo hung up the phone, Anna watched him gather several papers as he threw on his coat. "I have to run down to the courthouse to file these papers. No time to wait for the attorney to look at these. I just hope we haven't missed any deadlines for filing," Angelo yelled over his shoulder as he raced out the door. Anna knew Angelo had just made a terrible mistake. Not only had he lied to the client, he was not engaging in the unauthorized practice of law. She just did not know what she should do at this point—if she should do anything—to fix the situation.

Do you think Anna should do anything about what she has just witnessed? Should she talk with the supervising attorney? Why or why not? If Anna and Angelo's supervising attorney were to discover Angelo's mistake, what do you think he should do? Do you think Angelo should be disciplined for his error? How?

EXERCISE 2.6

PARALEGAL LIABILITY FOR FREELANCE WORK

The issue of the liability of a freelance paralegal is the one most frequently addressed by the courts. Clearly the freelance legal assistant is the most exposed to liability risks, as the freelance legal assistant does not work under the auspices of a law firm and is not, therefore, protected by a law firm's insurance policy. Most of the cases that address freelance liability involve charges against the layperson for engaging in the unauthorized practice of law.

When a freelance legal assistant contracts with an attorney to provide paralegal services, the first question usually asked is whether that legal assistant will be covered by the law firm's umbrella policy against claims of malpractice. The first piece of business transacted, therefore, usually involves the freelance paralegal and the supervising attorney signing an agreement that the paralegal is so covered.

However, that policy may not provide protection adequate for the legal assistant's tastes. The freelance paralegal may feel it is necessary to carry her own insurance policy.

For the most part, insurance companies are very careful about the policies they provide to freelance paralegals. Policies automatically exclude protection for the unauthorized practice of law. This means that, if a case goes to legal judgment and it is determined that the paralegal was engaging in the unauthorized practice of law, the company will not have to pay the claim.

Freelance legal assistants may purchase a policy if the insurance company considers them a business enterprise. One such business, Paralegal Services, Inc., in Raleigh, North Carolina, is a nationwide information and attorney servicing company. It was able to purchase an insurance policy as a business. The fact that it was a *paralegal* business is incidental.

EXERCISE 2.7 | Check with your state department of insurance to find out whether any insurance agencies provide insurance coverage to paralegals in your state. Next, locate an insurance agency that provides coverage. If you find one that does not currently provide coverage but seems interested, suggest that a representative of the agency call the department of insurance in your state. Sometimes all that is required by law is that an insurance company provide amendments to existing policies from other states that include the law of the state.

PARALEGAL LIABILITY FOR THE ACTIONS OF THE LAW FIRM

Can a paralegal be held responsible if a law firm or a supervising lawyer violates the state code of ethics?

It is unlikely that a legal assistant would be considered liable for any injury that would occur solely from a lawyer's misconduct. Remember that the legal assistant is an agent of the supervising attorney. It is a basic premise of agency law that an agent cannot be held responsible for the conduct of her principal because the agent has *no control* over the principal or her actions. In the same way, the legal assistant has no control over the supervising attorney's actions. Nor may the legal assistant even be aware of the supervising attorney's conduct.

In 1994, the appellate court of Illinois addressed this precise issue. Justice Egan, of the Illinois court, found that paralegals should *not* be held liable for the actions of their supervising attorneys. *In re Estate of Divine* (May 6, 1994 No. 1-92-3636). This case is excerpted at the end of this chapter.[15]

Nevertheless, where the attorney directs the legal assistant to complete a project that involves the violation of an ethical principle and the legal assistant willingly complies, the legal assistant may be civilly sued for malpractice. Such a situation recently came before the Illinois Supreme Court.

In *Superior Bank FSB v. Golding*, 152 Ill.2d 480, 178 Ill.Dec. 720, 605 N.E.2d 514 (1992), the Illinois Supreme Court was faced with a situation where a bank was suing a law firm, Lord, Bissel & Brook, *and its employee, Elizabeth Williams, a notary public,* seeking damages for misrepresentation and negligence. Although the Illinois Supreme Court directly addressed the issue of whether the statute of limitations had run in an action where the parties were attempting to sue for legal malpractice, the context in which that suit arose is what is of interest here.

A partnership, Gash Associates, applied to Superior Bank FSB for a $2.5 million loan. Before granting the loan, the Bank required the partnership to obtain a legal opinion from their lawyers, Lord, Bissel & Brook, regarding the

---

[15]The authors wish to thank Stephanie Williams for her assistance in locating this case.

effect of the loan on the partnership and on the individual partners and the authenticity of certain documents supplied to the bank and signatures on those documents. Additionally, the Bank required personal guaranties from each of the partners on the loan. One of the partners of Gash Associates, William Horwitz, executed a guaranty that was notarized by the law firm's notary public, Elizabeth Williams.

The partnership later defaulted on the loan, and the bank foreclosed on the properties that had secured the mortgage loan. However, money recouped from sale of the properties could not cover the amount of the loan, and the bank received a deficiency judgment for the remaining amount of the money owed. The bank then filed an action against the partnership to recoup this deficiency. The answer filed by Horwitz alleged that he had never executed the guaranty which was witnessed by the notary public.

The bank, therefore, added the law firm and the notary public as defendants to the complaint. In the second count, the bank alleged that Lord, Bissel & Brook and Elizabeth Williams were negligent in their notarization of the signature.

While the court did not address the merits of the suit against the law firm and its notary public, it did hold that the complaints were timely filed and allowed the parties to proceed to litigation on the merits of the complaint. Therefore, the court allowed the parties to litigate whether Elizabeth Williams was guilty of negligence and misrepresentation for her part in attesting to the signature. Regardless of whether the courts later find Williams negligent or not, she is still faced with the prospect of defending herself in several years of litigation, certainly a costly undertaking.

The potential finding of negligence which Elizabeth Williams faces is especially noteworthy for paralegals. Legal assistants are often asked by their law firms to assume the responsibilities of a notary public. The possibility of facing such a lawsuit is, therefore, very real for the paralegal.

PARALEGAL LIABILITY FOR THE ACTIONS OF CORPORATIONS

Attorneys have long been held to have standing to enjoin nonlawyers who engage in activities allegedly harmful to the legal profession. See e.g., *Touchy v. Houston Legal Foundation*, 432 S.W.2d 690 (Tex. 1968); *West Virginia State Bar v. Earley*, 144 W.Va. 504, 109 S.E.2d 420 (1959). Can attorneys also intervene and hold legal assistants responsible for the conduct of the corporation that employs the legal assistant? Alternatively, can paralegals engaged in questionably ethical conduct escape liability for their actions by hiding behind a corporate entity?

In at least one instance, *Kentucky Bar Association v. Legal Alternatives, Inc.*, a paralegal who was personally employed by a corporation to handle bankruptcy petitions lost his job when a complaint was filed against his employer, a corporation doing business under the name Legal Alternatives, Inc. 792 S.W.2d 368 (Ky. 1990).

It is unclear whether the paralegal was merely an employee of the corporation or the owner. This is not to suggest that the paralegal was not engaged in wrongful conduct. He was. He was engaging in the unauthorized practice of law. However, this case is an extreme example. An unauthorized practice of law complaint had been filed against Legal Alternatives, Inc., of

FOCUS ON ESTEBAN SANTANA

In 1988 Esteban Santana was named one of the "rising stars" of the paralegal profession by the editors of *Legal Assistant Today* magazine.

A relatively young legal assistant, Santana received an Associate's Degree in Paralegal Studies from MacCormac Junior College in 1987 and worked as a paralegal in a small law firm for several years. He is currently employed as a supervisor of the research staff at the Cook County Law Library in Chicago, Illinois, while he is completing his Master's Degree in Criminal Justice.

Santana has had a great deal of contact with other legal assistants. He has met other paralegals through his many educational courses and through his work experiences. Additionally, many paralegal classes utilize the law library, and Santana is always ready to lend a hand to the students.

Everything starts with ethics. Every nonlawyer needs to take the initiative to find out what the ethical rules are and to follow those rules—even if it means making a copy of the rules and carrying them around.

Santana is aware that ethical codes for paralegals exist. He advises that the attorney's code of ethics is the most important code the legal assistant can follow. "The paralegal's responsibilities all derive from the supervising attorney's code of ethics. Real problems result for the attorney, the paralegal, and the client where the nonlawyer reveals a client confidence or engages in the unauthorized practice of law."

Santana is aware that there are times when legal assistants have committed ethical violations. "It is inevitable that a professional working in a professional field is going to make a mistake," Santana notes. For example, Santana has heard of instances where legal assistants completed legal documents without any supervision by an attorney, and the attorneys made no attempt to review the documents before they were filed. However, although the unauthorized practice of law is a serious ethical violation (and may even violate the law), Santana has not seen that any consequences resulted to the legal assistants or the supervising attorneys.

Santana feels that the importance of legal ethics cannot be stressed enough because everything—every responsibility of the nonlawyer—starts with ethics. Santana advises nonlawyers who are choosing a paralegal studies program to choose a school that emphasizes the role that legal ethics plays in the paralegal profession. The school's curriculum should emphasize where to find the rules of ethics, which rules of ethics are most important, and how to read and integrate them into their professional lives.

The legal assistant employed in a law firm, public service agency, or corporate environment should always consult the attorney or office manager whenever an ethics question arises, according to Santana. Furthermore, every legal assistant should make an effort to *know* the codes of ethics, even if this means making a copy of the ethics rules and carrying them around with her. Failing to do this can be costly to the client, the supervising attorney, and the legal assistant.

Knowing that ethical violations can seriously harm clients, Santana thinks both the attorney and the paralegal should face serious consequences when an ethical problem occurs. Santana says, "Losing a job is not enough of a sanction when the nonlawyer violates a code of ethics. It's really not such a bad idea to have a paralegal disciplinary agency, a 'PDC,' to which paralegals would be held accountable for violations." One final point Santana makes is that the legal assistant should abide by the codes of ethics established by most paralegal associations to help foster the positive perception by both the legal profession and the public that the paralegal profession *is* a profession.

"Rising stars" such as Santana know that, in order to keep the paralegal profession vital, it is important to know and understand the rules of ethics.

Portland, Oregon, based on its advertisements offering to assist in preparing documents needed in completing bankruptcy filings. A cease and desist order was issued to make the company stop its activity. After another complaint was filed against the corporation that also alleged that the organization was engaging in the unauthorized practice of law, Legal Alternatives was ordered to show cause why it should not be held in contempt. The company never filed a response. The Supreme Court of Kentucky held that the respondent would be ordered to cease and desist its unauthorized practice and levied a $5,000.00 fine and court costs against the person who owned and operated the company.

This case exemplifies the principle that the courts will not permit a layperson to hide behind the veil of a corporate identity when the instigator of the wrongdoing is an identifiable person. This legal capacity to "pierce the corporate veil" is a general principle of corporate law.

Tips for Paralegals

- Familiarize yourself with your supervising attorney's code of ethics.

- Obtain a copy of the attorney ethics rules for your jurisdiction, and consult them if you have any questions pertaining to legal ethics.

- Protect your employment and the livelihoods of people with whom you work by becoming aware that violation of any provision of the attorney's code of ethics could result in the attorney being reprimanded; suspended or disbarred from the practice of law; or sued for malpractice.

- Remember: Ethical violations can result in damage to clients.

CLOSING EXERCISE

Karen L. Zollar is a freelance real estate paralegal who also has a real estate broker's license. Karen's overriding concern, no matter what kind of work she is doing, is that she have a great reputation wherever she goes for being hardworking and doing whatever she needs to do to get the job done.

Recently Karen contracted with Tommy Kathey, a real estate lawyer, to handle the paperwork for a real estate closing on an expensive and much sought-after piece of commercial real estate, pending the divorce of the sellers, Leona and Steve Citizen. Unfortunately for all parties concerned, Leona's and Steve's divorce is very messy and it does not look like there will be a resolution any time soon.

Because Karen has been working with both Leona and Steve very closely to resolve the real estate sale, Leona begins to confide to Karen that she really wishes she could resolve the divorce issue soon because Steve is a very underhanded individual and she does not like being married to such a person. In fact, Leona continues, Steve had bragged about the fact that he had managed to secure the property from its original owner by making up a story about traffic patterns from a nearby shopping mall, a story into which the previous owner was too naive to check.

Steve also begins to consult Karen about his personal problems. He asks Karen whether anything can be done to expedite the divorce proceedings. He asks Karen to check into the matter and get back to him.

Karen knows Steve and Leona's personal problems are mushrooming, and she has to do something or the real estate transaction will fall through. At the same time, Karen has a sinking feeling that Steve and Leona have placed her in a bad position in terms of her ethical responsibilities.

Karen begins to wonder about what Leona has told her. If the story is true, Steve has acquired the property through fraudulent means. Yet Karen does not know if this would affect the subsequent sale of the property and if she can ethically become involved in such a transaction. She comes to you, a fellow paralegal, for advice. Where would you tell her to look for answers? What sources should she consult?

Suppose Karen decides to consult Tommy Kathey, the attorney with whom she has contracted, about these problems. Tommy advises Karen to do everything she can to smooth the way for the divorce proceedings. This means that, if Karen has to look up the law on divorce in that state and advise Steve about his options, she should by all means do so. Karen is dumbfounded, however, because she knows that to do so would mean she was violating the state's statute prohibiting the unauthorized practice of law.

Should Karen advise Steve? What possible results could Karen face if she decides to follow Tommy's advice? What potential problems could Tommy face? What results could Karen face if she decides to ignore Tommy's advice?

CHAPTER SUMMARY

■ Attorneys and legal assistants both have codes of ethics. The ethics rules for attorneys are mandatory and are imposed by the jurisdiction in which the lawyer practices. As such, an attorney's adherence to the rules is tied in with licensing. Violations of the rules by attorneys can result in the loss of a license to practice law. The codes of ethics for legal assistants, however, are not mandatory. They are guidelines but, as paralegals are not currently licensed, the paralegal codes can never be applied to prohibit a legal assistant from working in the field. Nevertheless, it is imperative that the nonlawyer who works for a lawyer be versed in the attorney rules. That is because the attorney is ultimately responsible for the acts of those whom she supervises (even if they are not attorneys) and can be subject to discipline (even disbarment) for the acts of those supervisees.

■ It is critical to the interests of the client that a legal assistant comprehend the importance as well as the nuances of the ethics rules. Each one of the rules has been developed over the course of many years, and after much trial and error, to secure the interests of the public. In short, there is a reason every one of the rules exists, and the legal assistant, as a professional committed to the interests of the public, should make it his business to recognize the rules' importance.

■ Paralegals must recognize that there are serious consequences of violations of ethics rules. Attorneys who violate the rules may suffer consequences at two levels. At one level, attorneys may be subject to discipline by their state attorney disciplinary board. This could result in suspension from practicing or even disbarment. At another level, acts that are violations of the rules may also result in civil and/or criminal liability. Paralegals who work for attorneys cannot be disciplined for violating either the paralegal or attorney codes of ethics. However, as was previously mentioned, when paralegals violate the attorney ethics rules, the attorney (as supervisor) can be disciplined. Moreover, though the paralegal cannot be disciplined by the jurisdiction's attorney disciplinary body, the paralegal may incur civil or criminal liability if the violation also violates the law.

KEY TERMS

ABA Model Code of
    Professional
    Responsibility (Code
    of Professional
    Responsibility)
agency
agent
American Bar
    Association's (ABA's)
    Model Rules of
    Professional Conduct
    (Model Rules)
attorney disqualification
attorney/legal malpractice
attorney's code of ethics

authority
binding authority
Canons
Canons of Professional
    Ethics
civilly liable
client
disbarment
Disciplinary Rules (DRs)
errors and omissions
    insurance
Ethical Considerations
    (ECs)
ethics
ethics advisory opinion

ethics committee
legal ethics
Model Rule 5.3
moral
paralegal malpractice
persuasive authority
principal
process server
reprimand/censure
respondeat superior
self-policing
solo practitioner
state disciplinary agency
suspension

CASE

In re Estate of Divine/Lyster et.al. v. Giancola,

Illinois Appellate Court, 1 Dist., 1994.
____ Ill. App. 3d ____ ,
____ Ill. Dec. ____ , N.E.2d ____ .
No. 1-92-3636

PRESIDING JUSTICE EGAN delivered the opinion of the court:

The petitioners, who are family members and legatees of the deceased Richard Divine (Richard), filed a petition for a citation of recovery against Patricia Giancola, alleging that Giancola wrongly obtained possession of money which was properly part of Richard's estate. Giancola claimed the funds as the surviving joint tenant of two joint bank accounts. After a hearing, the trial judge granted Giancola's motion to dismiss the petition. He held that Giancola was not a fiduciary to Richard as a matter of law and that the petitioners had failed to maintain their burden of proving undue influence over Richard on the part of Giancola. The petitioners maintain that Giancola was a fiduciary to Richard as a matter of law and that it was her burden to prove that the funds she received from Richard were not

the result of a breach of a fiduciary obligation or of undue influence.

Beginning in approximately 1979, Giancola was employed in Chicago by attorney Samuel Poznanovich as a part-time secretary in his law office. Eventually, she became his full-time secretary. Giancola received a paralegal certificate from Roosevelt University in 1980, and took an H & R Block tax course in 1970. Poznanovich employed one other secretary in addition to Giancola.

In 1981, Richard and his wife, Lila, came to Poznanovich's office for income tax services. The Divines did not have any children and both were retired. Giancola estimated that they were in their "early seventies" in 1981. Giancola interviewed the Divines, took tax information from them such as W-2 forms and copies of their previous tax returns, and introduced them to Poznanovich. After this initial meeting, Poznanovich prepared the Divines' tax returns every year until 1986. Each year, Giancola would interview the Divines and gather their tax information. She never prepared their taxes, but simply gathered information for Poznanovich's use. In 1985, Poznanovich also represented Richard in a personal injury case. Giancola was not involved in that case. Additionally, Richard called Poznanovich occasionally for legal advice on other matters. Before 1986, Giancola and Poznanovich saw the Divines only at the law office, although, according to Poznanovich, the relationship became "more and more friendly" each year.

In December 1986, Lila died. Richard called Giancola at the office to tell her about Lila's death. Giancola stated that Richard had "depended on Lila for just about everything" and was very lonely without Lila. Also, he was "unable to do for himself." Giancola went to visit Richard in his apartment on Coles Avenue "within a day or two" of Lila's death. Richard was afraid to leave the apartment alone and could not walk long distances because "his legs were bad." Richard's relatives and Poznanovich also testified that Richard had physical problems with his legs. Giancola stated that for "the most part," Richard was confined to his apartment. After Giancola's first visit, Richard frequently called her and she visited his apartment once or twice a week. Richard asked her to assist him in getting his groceries and other necessities. Richard gave Giancola money for the groceries and supplies. She testified that he did not give her a "fee" for her services, but admitted that sometimes he gave her "something for [her]self." He did his own cooking while living in the Coles Avenue apartment.

Giancola believed that the neighborhood around Coles Avenue was too dangerous for Richard, and she did not like going there to visit him. She suggested that he move to a safer area; she also mentioned to Poznanovich that Richard's neighborhood was unsafe. Poznanovich's office is located in a building he and his sister own. There are four residential apartments in that building which are rented by Poznanovich and his sister. Giancola occasionally takes the rent checks from tenants for Poznanovich. When an apartment became vacant in Poznanovich's building, Giancola told Richard it "would be easier" if he moved into that apartment. She did not know that Richard's relatives wanted him to move to Michigan City, Indiana.

* * *

Richard then told Poznanovich that he wanted to live in Poznanovich's building. Richard moved into the building in June or July, 1987. Giancola and Poznanovich helped him move. He paid rent of $300 per month to Poznanovich, sometimes giving Giancola his rent check. Richard did not socialize with other people and usually did not leave the apartment. Poznanovich testified that in 1987 Richard was not capable of living alone in an apartment without some assistance, although he did his own cleaning. According to Poznanovich, Richard "needed [to be] taken care of." Giancola continued to buy his groceries and supplies, apparently during weekday working hours. She testified that Richard continued to give her money for the groceries and to occasionally give her "something for [her]self." Poznanovich testified that in 1987 Richard trusted Giancola and "she took care of him." Giancola considered herself Richard's friend.

Sometime after Richard moved, Poznanovich shut off the gas to his stove, although the rent included all utilities. Giancola could not remember exactly when the gas was stopped, and Poznanovich was not asked when he turned off the stove. Poznanovich testified that Richard had forgotten a pan on the stove and started a small fire. Therefore, he believed it was dangerous for Richard to have a working stove. Giancola explained that Richard "let a pan burn." When asked if Richard was "getting forgetful" at the time the stove was turned off, Giancola testified that she "guessed so." After the stove was disconnected, Giancola began cooking Richard's meals and bringing him hot food. Without the stove, "it was impossible" for Richard to cook his own food.

* * *

In June, 1990, Poznanovich petitioned the court to be appointed Richard's guardian, alleging that at that time Richard was "suffering from organic brain syndrome and dementia [and was] mentally disoriented most of the time."

* * *

In addition to getting his supplies and cooking his meals, Giancola cashed checks for Richard and made bank deposits for him. She wrote out the checks for all his bills. She explained that she would write the checks, he would sign them, and she would mail them. All these transactions involved only Richard's personal checking account. Richard would discuss "personal problems" with Giancola, but did not talk to her about legal matters.

* * *

In November, 1987, Richard called Poznanovich and asked him to come to his apartment. In the apartment, Richard told Poznanovich that he wanted to "put his affairs in order." First, he handed two bank account passbooks to Poznanovich and said "I want this for my sweetheart." Richard told Poznanovich that his "sweetheart" was Giancola, and that he wanted her to have the two accounts. These two accounts were separate from Richard's personal checking account which Giancola used for his finances. Richard told Poznanovich he did not want to leave the accounts to Giancola in his will because he wanted her "to have them now." Richard explained: "As far as I'm concerned, if it were not for her, I would be dead now." Poznanovich suggested that the accounts be made joint accounts, like the accounts Richard had shared with Lila. When Poznanovich assured Richard that a joint tenancy would allow Giancola to have the money immediately, Richard told Poznanovich to change the two accounts to joint accounts. Giancola was not present during this discussion. Poznanovich testified that he did not receive any direct or indirect financial benefit from this transaction.

Next, Richard asked Poznanovich to draft a will for him. The will made Poznanovich executor of the estate and gave $3000 each to Giancola and Poznanovich. Poznanovich testified: "I had a problem with [Richard] inserting me as a beneficiary under the will, *** [and] we agreed that if I were to remain in the will as a beneficiary, I would waive my executor's fee, which I did." The will made one other specific bequest of $2000, then left one half of the residuary estate to the petitioners and one half to four other family members. After his death, the value of Richard's estate, in addition to the joint accounts, was approximately $150,000.

Poznanovich obtained two signature cards from the bank and had the accounts changed to joint accounts. On November 14, 1987, he asked Giancola to sign these signature cards. Neither Richard nor Poznanovich ever discussed the accounts with Giancola before presenting her with the cards. They also did not discuss the transactions with any members of Richard's family. Poznanovich testified that Giancola was not "in any way aware of the fact" that Richard was giving her joint tenancy of the accounts before November 14. Giancola understood that she was becoming a joint tenant with Richard when she signed the cards on November 14. Immediately after signing the cards, she discussed them with Richard. She did not discuss the joint accounts with any members of his family. She asked Richard if he understood what the cards "meant" and he told her that he understood. Based on her conversation with Richard, Giancola was certain that he knew the nature of a joint tenancy. He never told her the accounts were made joint accounts for his convenience or to make it easier for her to pay his bills. Giancola did not make deposits of either her own money or Richard's money into these accounts, and did not withdraw any money from the accounts until after Richard's death.

On June 19, 1990, Giancola found Richard "semiconscious" in his apartment. She called an ambulance, and Richard was hospitalized. After approximately one week in the hospital, Giancola "had [Richard] transferred to a nursing home." In August, 1990, Richard died at the nursing home. Poznanovich was then appointed executor of Richard's estate.

After Richard's death, Giancola withdrew all the money from the joint accounts. The petitioners [relatives of Richard] allege that Giancola received $165,958.60 from these accounts.

The petitioners filed a petition for a citation to recover assets against Giancola. The original petition is not in the record, but an amended petition refers only to recovery from Giancola, and requests only the return of the $165,958.60. There is no allegation that Poznanovich improperly received estate funds. Further, the petition does not mention the $3000 will bequests to Giancola and Poznanovich, and does not allege that Poznanovich should be ordered to return money to the estate. It asserts that Giancola was a fiduciary to Richard, that she obtained the $165,958.60 through "undue influence and fraud," and that Richard "lacked the mental capacity to understand the consequences of his actions."

At the hearing, the petitioners urged the judge to place the burden of proving the transaction was proper on Giancola. They supported this argument with their contention that Giancola and Poznanovich, as legal professionals, owed Richard a fiduciary duty as a matter of law. The judge repeatedly stated that Poznanovich's actions were not relevant to the question of Giancola's liability to the estate, and placed the burden of proving that the transaction was improper on the petitioners. He then explained: "I don't see from the evidence a legal fiduciary relationship between Giancola and [Richard.]." Also, he explicitly found that Giancola did not exert any undue influence on Richard, especially at the time the accounts were made joint. Finally, he explained that "[t]here [was not] any testimony here, medically that he was incompetent at the time this transaction took place." For these reasons, he denied the petition.

At the hearing in the trial court and in this court the petitioners argued that the actions of Poznanovich and Giancola are inextricably intertwined and that because Giancola was a paralegal and an employee of the lawyer, Poznanovich, who was a fiduciary as a matter of law, so also is Giancola a fiduciary as a matter of law. They also repeatedly assert that Poznanovich gained financially from the transactions which benefitted Giancola. Nonetheless, they never requested that Poznanovich or Giancola return the $3000 bequests and they do not challenge the validity of the will. Additionally, they have never made Poznanovich a party to these proceedings. Essentially, the petitioners argue that Poznanovich's questionable action of drafting a will which gave him a gift and his status as an attorney should be imputed to Giancola and that she should be liable because of his actions.

Under certain circumstances, one person will be charged with liability for the actions of or knowledge given to another person. For example, actions by one partner will be imputed to another partner. (*Couri v. Couri* (1983), 95 Ill. 2d 91, 447 N.E.2d 334.) Also, an employer will be held liable for certain actions of his employee. (*Towns v. Yellow Cab Co.* (1978), 73 Ill. 2d 113, 382 N.E.2d 1217.) There is no case law holding an employee liable for the acts of his employer, however, and the petitioners cite no law to support their position that Giancola should be accountable for Poznanovich's actions. Unfortunately, there also is no case law in Illinois involving the narrower question of a paralegal's fiduciary duty to his employer's client, making this a case of first impression. In fact, we have found no reported case in the United States involving a paralegal's fiduciary responsibility, as a paralegal, to his attorney's client.

Moreover, there is very little case law from Illinois or any jurisdiction generally discussing paralegals. Two cases address the somewhat analogous issue of a paralegal's possible liability for legal malpractice. A divided Nevada Supreme Court, in *Busch v. Flangas* (1992), 108 Nev. 821, 837 P.2d 438, held that an attorney's law clerk or paralegal who attempts to provide legal services can be liable for malpractice to the client. On the other hand, the *Busch* dissent argued that a law clerk or paralegal, as an employee of an attorney, owes no duty to the attorney's client, but is liable only to the attorney. (*Busch*, 837 P.2d at 441 (Springer, J., dissenting).) The Court of Appeals of Ohio, without extensive discussion, determined that a paralegal could not be sued for legal malpractice because she was not an attorney. *Palmer v. Westmeyer* (1988), 48 Ohio App. 3d 296, 549 N.E.2d 1202, 1209.

On the other hand, the idea that an attorney is liable, in malpractice or as an ethical violation, for his paralegal's acts is well-supported in Illinois. Illinois Supreme Court Rule 5.3 places the responsibility for unethical acts by non-lawyer employees on the employing attorney. (137 Ill. 2d R. 5.3; see also Scott R. Stevenson, *Using Paralegals in the Law*, 62 Ill. B.J. 432 (Apr. 1974).) Similarly, in *Glover Bottled Gas Corp. v. Circle M. Beverage Barn, Inc.* (1987), 129 A.D. 2d 678, 514 N.Y.S.2d 440, 441, a New York court held that paralegals are not governed by the Code of Professional Responsibility, but that their employing attorneys are in violation of the Code when they fail to supervise the paralegals properly. The Supreme Court of New Jersey echoed this idea when it held that paralegals who are properly supervised by attorneys are not liable for the unauthorized practice of law. (*In re Opinion Number 24* (1992), 128 N.J. 114, 607 A.2d 962, 966.) The New Jersey court noted that

any supervising attorney who does not properly supervise the paralegals working for him is in violation of the Code of Professional Responsibility. (*Opinion 24*, 607 A.2d at 969.) Finally, in Michigan, paralegals are generally treated as extensions of their supervising attorneys for ethical and malpractice purposes. Vicky Voisin, *Ethical Standards for Legal Assistants*, 70 Mich. B.J. 1178 (Nov. 1991); see generally Symposium, *Legal Assistants in Michigan*, 70 Mich. B.J. 1131-86 (Nov. 1991).

Several Illinois cases support the idea that a (sic) paralegals are an extension of their employing attorney. For example, the presence of an attorney's employee, such as a secretary or law clerk, does not destroy the attorney-client privilege for material disclosed to the attorney in the employee's presence. (*In re Estate of Busse* (1947), 332 Ill. App. 258, 75 N.E.2d 36; M. Graham, Cleary & Graham's Handbook of Illinois Evidence § 505.5, at 274-75 (5th ed. 1990); see, *e.g.*, *Samaritan Foundation v. Superior Court*. (Ct. App. Ariz. 1992), 173 Ariz. 426, 844 P.2d 593, *vacated in part on other grounds*, (S. Ct. 1994), 176 Ariz. 497, 862 P.2d 870 (specifically holding that the presence of a paralegal does not destroy the privilege).) Also, in the majority of Illinois cases discussing paralegals, which involve disputed attorney fee petitions, the courts have held that an attorney may recover reasonable fees for time properly spent by his paralegal. (See, *e.g.*, *In re Petition for Fees* (1983), 117 Ill. App. 3d 744, 747, 453 N.E.2d 949.) Several fees cases stress, however, that compensable time must be spent "under the direction and control of a licensed attorney." See *In re Marriage of Ahmad* (1990), 198 Ill. App. 3d 15, 23, 555 N.E.2d 439.

Based on these cases, we refuse to treat Poznanovich and Giancola as a unit for purposes of Giancola's liability. It is clear that Poznanovich, as a licensed attorney and as an employer, could be held liable for Giancola's actions. Nonetheless, holding Giancola liable as if she were an attorney is not consistent with general *respondeat superior* law or with the decisions discussed above treating paralegals as subordinate employees of attorneys. The theme running through all these cases is that paralegals do not independently practice law, but simply serve as assistants to lawyers. They are not equal or autonomous partners. Thus, while supervisors properly are held liable for paralegals' actions, the subordinate paralegals should not be liable for the actions of these supervisors. Therefore, we refuse to find that Giancola owed Richard a fiduciary duty simply because she worked for Richard's attorney, and we refuse to hold that paralegals are fiduciaries to their employers' clients as a matter of law.

We wish to make our position clear that the trial court and this court must take the case as it has been presented to us. Contrary to the petitioners' statement in oral argument before us, the petitioners did not argue in the trial court that the evidence established a fiduciary relationship between Giancola and Richard even in the absence of her role as a paralegal and employee of Poznanovich.

• • •

We also wish to make it clear that we are not saying that the evidence shows that Poznanovich did anything improper. We have discussed his "actions" only in the general sense to illustrate that, while he was a fiduciary to Richard as a matter of law and if he had been the recipient of the joint account funds, the burden of proof would have been on him to show that the transaction was proper, his fiduciary obligations may not be imposed upon Giancola. Nor are we saying that an improper transfer may never be shown under circumstances like those present in this case. If the petitioners had offered evidence from which it could be inferred that collusion existed between Poznanovich and Giancola or that Poznanovich gained financially in any way from the transfer, our holding would be different. But neither the trial judge nor this court may decide a case on speculation, guess, conjecture or suspicion.

For these reasons, the judgment of the circuit court is affirmed.

Judgment affirmed.

McNAMARA, J., and RAKOWSKI, J., concur.

Questions

1. What does the court conclude about the paralegal's liability for the actions of his or her supervising attorney? Why does the court make this decision?

2. What kinds of cases does the court look at before reaching its decision?

3. How does the court use the doctrine of *respondeat superior* to support its holding?

4. Do you agree with the court's decision?

THE UNAUTHORIZED PRACTICE OF LAW

CHAPTER OBJECTIVES

After reading this chapter, you should
be able to:

■ Define the practice of law.

■ Understand what behavior in the law office
amounts to the practice of law.

■ Understand the limited situations in which
nonlawyers may represent others in court
proceedings.

■ Recognize that practice of law limitations in
administrative agencies may be more

flexible than those guiding paralegal
conduct in the law office.

■ Identify the difference between activities of
typing services and the unauthorized
practice of law.

■ Recognize that nonlawyers may assist in
handling real estate closings.

■ Note that legal assistants should always
disclose their status as nonlawyers.

"There is no question that a paralegal's work constitutes the practice of law[,]" says the supreme court of New Jersey. *In re Opinion No. 24,* 128 N.J. 114, 607 A.2d 962, 966 (1992). However, the practice of law is a responsibility reserved for attorneys. To the extent that a paralegal does work that is traditionally reserved for attorneys, the paralegal's work is allowed because the legal assistant adheres to certain safeguards, including working under the supervision of an attorney. When a paralegal neglects to heed those safeguards or ignores those boundaries, she crosses that almost invisible line into the unauthorized practice of law. When this happens, the legal assistant faces serious consequences.

While Guideline 2 of the ABA Model Guidelines for the Utilization of Legal Assistant Services allows for the delegation of tasks to nonlawyers, Guideline 3 makes clear that certain tasks may not be undertaken by the legal assistant without infringing upon the boundaries of the "practice of law." (Please see chapter 2 for a discussion of the Model Guidelines for the Utilization of Legal Assistant Services.) These rules together provide a foundation for determining what is the practice of law. They read as follows:

Guideline 2: Provided the lawyer maintains responsibility for the work product, a lawyer may delegate to a legal assistant any task normally performed by the lawyer except those tasks proscribed to one not licensed as a lawyer by statute, court rule, administrative rule or regulation, controlling authority, the ABA Model Rules of Professional Conduct, or these Guidelines. Guideline 2, ABA Model Guidelines for the Utilization of Legal Assistant Services.

Guideline 3: A lawyer may not delegate to a legal assistant:
    (a) Responsibility for establishing an attorney-client relationship.
    (b) Responsibility for establishing the amount of a fee to be charged for
        a legal service.

(c) Responsibility for a legal opinion rendered to a client. Guideline 3, ABA Model Guidelines for the Utilization of Legal Assistant Services.

This chapter expands on these guidelines and is designed to show the paralegal how to avoid the unauthorized practice of law by (1) defining "the practice of law" and (2) showing what behavior is forbidden under the practice of law statutes. After study of these principles, the legal assistant should better understand her ethical responsibilities in this area.

OPENING EXERCISE

For months now, a terribly overworked Rupa Cordero has been asking the partners at her law firm to assign her a paralegal. The partners at Hajib, Baxton, Ltd., however, believe a third-year associate like Rupa should be able to handle her own work.

Rupa thought she had reached the point where she could not handle any more cases. That's when she was assigned to handle the representation of John, a horribly injured plaintiff. John was bringing a medical malpractice action against American Hospitals, and the case was proving to present some complicated issues.

In preparing her case, Rupa moved through the mounds of medical documents slowly. Finally, while working late one evening to prepare for a deposition to be taken the next morning, she decided to call Nurse LaShonna Hayward, a neighbor of hers, for her help in understanding certain medical terminology. Rupa knew LaShonna had just completed a paralegal training program and that she was eager to use her medical knowledge in a less physically demanding way. "She should be able and willing to help me understand this case!" Rupa muttered to herself.

LaShonna was extremely flattered to be asked for her help, and she offered advice that proved extremely useful to evaluating the defendant's position. Rupa quickly realized that LaShonna could be a valuable assistant and began to rely upon her expertise quite regularly.

A few months later, after a particularly hectic morning, Rupa realized her secretary had scheduled a witness interview and a deposition at the same time. Thinking quickly, Rupa asked her secretary to call LaShonna and request that she take the deposition. "She'll be talking to American Hospital's medical expert; LaShonna will probably know better than I what is going on!"

LaShonna was more than happy to oblige Rupa. At the deposition, she entered her name as co-counsel, took the deposition of opposing counsel's expert, and discovered a major inconsistency in the expert's testimony.

Should this kind of representation be permitted? Is Nurse LaShonna more qualified than Rupa with respect to protecting the public in medical malpractice actions? Should LaShonna be enjoined from participating in any legal action? Do you think Rupa should be disciplined for her conduct?

HISTORICAL ANALYSIS OF THE UNAUTHORIZED PRACTICE OF LAW

Long ago, it was common for nonlawyers to represent others in legal proceedings.

> The first lawyers were personal friends of the litigant, brought into court by him so that he might "take 'counsel' with them" before pleading. *Turner v.*

American Bar Association, 407 F. Supp. 451 (W.D. Wis. 1975), citing 1 F. Pollock & F. Maitland, The History of English Law 211 (2d ed. 1909). Similarly, the first "attorneys" were personal agents, often lacking any professional training, who were appointed by those litigants who had secured royal permission to carry on their affairs through a representative, rather than personally. *Id.,* at 212–213. *Faretta v. California* 422 U.S. 806, 820, n. 16, 95 S. Ct. 2525, 2534, n. 16, 45 L.Ed.2d 562 (1975).

Today, however, the idea of allowing nonlawyers to appear in court on behalf of friends is usually vehemently opposed. What has changed since earlier times? Why are nonlawyers no longer allowed to represent others? Why is the practice of law now restricted to attorneys?

Law and legal terminology were already extensively developed by the beginning of the thirteenth century. They took the form of treatises and casebooks, which were collections of cases that had been tried before the Inns of Court. At that time, there were no restrictions on who could practice before the courts.

Unauthorized Practice of Law The practice of nonlawyers engaging in activities that only lawyers are licensed and sanctioned to perform.

However, later in that century, in 1292, the court of King Edward I developed the phrase the **"unauthorized practice of law."** During King Edward's reign, a statute was enacted which called for John de Metingham, who was Chief Justice of the Court of Common Pleas, and other justices to select attorneys for the service of the people. They were to have been "the best and the most apt for their learning and skill." Only those chosen and no others "were to be permitted to practice." Hence, unqualified persons were to be excluded from the practice of law.

Later, the reign of Henry IV prompted the expansion of standards for attorneys. In addition to their quick learning ability, attorneys were to be selected based upon their goodness and virtuosity, and were to be sworn to serve in their offices. All others were to be "put out." By the middle of the fifteenth century, those who did not meet the qualifications were disqualified from appearing before the court.

These principles were relaxed, however, in England's colonies in the New World. In an untamed America, there was no cohesion to the population. There was no legal profession per se, so people who were glib of tongue or shrewd in business were hired by others to appear for them in courts composed of other laypersons.

Blackstone's Commentaries Historical commentaries written by Sir William Blackstone, a noted historian who had great influence on England's and America's jurisprudence.

This all changed when, at the close of the eighteenth century, *Blackstone's Commentaries* were published in England. Presumably, Blackstone's work included the laws that limited the practice of law to attorneys. One thousand sets of *Blackstone's Commentaries* were sent to America. Not long after, only those with extensive legal study who could meet the established standards were admitted to the American bar.[1]

Today, American courts continue to look with disfavor on nonlawyers representing others. Many states have even developed unauthorized practice of law statutes that make it a criminal misdemeanor for nonlawyers to engage in the practice of law. The purpose of these statutes is to protect the public from unqualified representation.

---

[1] F. TROWBRIDGE VOM BAUR, *An Historical Sketch of the Unauthorized Practice of Law,* STUDENT LAWYER JOURNAL (1958). Reprinted with permission of the author.

It is imperative, therefore, for nonlawyers—especially paralegals—to recognize what behavior amounts to the practice of law.

THE PRACTICE OF LAW

While the practice of law by nonlawyers has long been frowned upon, it is still not always clear what conduct constitutes this behavior. The **practice of law** remains a nebulous concept.

Many jurisdictions have been reluctant to set forth an all-encompassing definition of the practice of law. For example, the New Jersey Supreme Court has noted,

> The practice of law is not subject to precise definition. It is not confined to litigation but often encompasses "legal activities in many non-litigious fields which entail specialized knowledge and ability." Therefore, the line between permissible business and professional activities and the unauthorized practice of law is often blurred. *In re Opinion No. 24*, 128 N.J. 114, 607 A.2d 962, 966 (1992), quoting *In re Application of the New Jersey Society of Certified Public Accountants*, 102 N.J. 231, 507 A.2d 711 (1986).

And it has been noted in Michigan,

> We are still of the mind that any attempt to formulate a lasting, all encompassing definition of "practice of law" is doomed to failure for the reason that under our system of jurisprudence such practice must necessarily change with the everchanging business and social order. *State Bar v. Cramer*, 399 Mich. 116, 249 N.W.2d 1, 7 (1976), citing *Grand Rapids Bar Assn. v. Denkema*, 209 Mich. 56, 64, 287 N.W. 377, 380 (1939).

Yet definitions do exist that provide guidance as to what constitutes the practice of law. Before addressing these definitions, it is useful to note what is clearly *not* relevant in determining the existence of the practice of law.

Courts have made it clear that certain activities routinely engaged in by nonlawyers do not fall within the definition of the practice of law. Legal assistants are allowed to engage in the completion of legal documents by filling in blanks on pre-prepared forms. The clerical activities of a **scrivener,** therefore, are *not* the unauthorized practice of law. See e.g. *Florida Bar v. Brumbraugh*, 355 So.2d 1186 (Fla. 1978).

It is not necessary to have compensation or to collect fees in order to engage in "the practice of law." Although some have implied that activities completed without an exchange of money do not rise to the level of the practice of law, courts have rejected this view. "[t]he practice of law does not necessarily involve charging or receiving a fee for services performed.... A gratuitous service by a licensed doctor or lawyer is none the less professional." *Darby v. Mississippi State Board of Bar Admissions*, 185 So.2d 684, 687 (Miss. 1966). However, some courts have noted that whether a fee is charged may be relevant in determining whether a party has engaged in the practice of law in that "[a] charge for services usually reflects the parties' judgment of the value of those services." *Cardinal v. Merrill Lynch Realty/Burnet*, 433 N.W.2d 864, 869 (Minn. 1988).

Practice of Law An activity involving the exercise of independent legal judgment such as advising clients and representing clients in court.

Scrivener One who copies; one who prepares written instruments or documents.

It is not necessary for an individual who is not a lawyer to imply or to state that he is a lawyer, for courts to find that the practice of law exists. "It is only by preventing such conduct [nonlawyers rendering legal services to the public] that the general public will be protected from laymen dabbling into areas in which they are incompetent." *Duncan v. Gordon*, 476 So.2d 896, 899 (La. App. 1985). Thus, though defendant never held herself out to be a lawyer, she can still be considered to have engaged in the practice of law.

Regardless of these factors, the essence of the practice of law is the exercise of **independent legal judgment** to influence the conduct of a third party.

Independent Legal Judgment That judgment which is exercised by those educated in the law. It is the application of a general body of law to a specific factual situation.

... [I]f the giving of such advice and performance of such services affect important rights of a person under the law, and if the reasonable protection of the rights and property of those advised and served requires that the persons giving such advice possess legal skill and a knowledge of the law greater than that possessed by the average citizen, then the giving of such advice and the performance of such services by one for another as a course of conduct constitute the practice of law. *State v. Sperry*, 140 So.2d 587, 591 (Fla. 1962).

The *Model Code of Professional Responsibility* addresses professional judgment of a lawyer. It provides:

... The essence of the professional judgment of the lawyer is his educated ability to relate the general body and philosophy of law to a specific legal problem of a client; and thus, the public interest will be better served if only lawyers are permitted to act in matters involving professional judgment. Where this professional judgment is not involved, non-lawyers, such as court clerks, police officers, abstracters, and many governmental employees, may engage in occupations that require a special knowledge of law in certain areas. But the services of a lawyer are essential in the public interest whenever the exercise of professional legal judgment is required. *Model Code of Professional Responsibility* EC 3-6 (1986).

Using all of the foregoing concepts, some courts have attempted to boil down these principles into working definitions of the practice of law. For instance:

The "practice of law" is hereby defined to be and is the appearance as an advocate in a representative capacity or the drawing of papers, pleadings or documents or the performance of any act in such capacity in connection with proceedings pending or prospective before any court of record, commissioner, referee or any body, board, committee or commission constituted by law or having authority to settle controversies. *State of Missouri v. Carroll*, 817 S.W.2d 289, 290 (1991), quoting § 484.020.1 RS Mo. 1986.

The "practice of law" does not lend itself easily to precise definition. However, it is generally acknowledged to include not only the doing or performing of services in the courts of justice, throughout the various stages thereof, but in a larger sense includes legal advice and counsel and the preparation of legal instruments by which legal rights and obligations are established. *Washington State Bar Association v. Great Western Union Federal Savings and Loan Association*, 91 Wash. 2d 48, 586 P.2d 870, 875 (1978).

For the purpose of this case, we hold that the practice of law includes the drafting or selection of documents and the giving of advice in regard there to any time an informed or trained discretion must be exercised in the selection or drafting of a document to meet the needs of the persons being served. The knowledge of the customer's needs obviously cannot be had by one who has no knowledge of the relevant law. One must know what questions to ask. Accordingly, any exercise of an intelligent choice, or an informed discretion in advising another of his legal rights and duties, will bring the activity within the practice of the profession. *Oregon State Bar v. Security Escrows, Inc.*, 233 Or. 80, 377 P.2d 334, 349 (1962).

Essentially, therefore, the practice of law embraces those activities which involve exercising independent legal judgment: advising clients, representing them in court or before other tribunals, and drafting and signing papers for them. Exercising legal judgment is a function reserved for attorneys, so it follows that the legal assistant must avoid these activities in order to comply with unauthorized practice of law statutes.

Of course, there are exceptions to these general principles. You will note these exceptions discussed throughout this chapter.

Now that you understand the general principles that define the limits of the practice of law, you need to understand how to apply these principles. The following discussion on The "Practice of Law" in the Law Office indicates how to use the practice of law definitions to guide your behavior.

Do you think nonlawyers should be allowed to engage in the practice of law? Do you think, as do many commentators, that the organized bar associations and the courts, composed primarily of attorneys, are seeking to create a monopoly? What arguments can you think of to support practice of law restrictions? What arguments can you think of to oppose practice of law definitions? Be prepared to debate and defend your answers. | **EXERCISE 3.1**

THE "PRACTICE OF LAW" IN THE LAW OFFICE

How do these definitions of the practice of law affect what the legal assistant working in the law office under the supervision of an attorney, can ethically do within the scope of his employment?

It is acceptable for lawyers to employ nonlawyer personnel to assist in the delivery of legal services. In fact, the U.S. Supreme Court even encouraged lawyers to do so. See *Missouri v. Jenkins*, 491 U.S. 274, 109 S. Ct. 2463, 105 L.Ed. 2d 229 (1989). To accomplish more efficient operation of the law office, attorneys therefore delegate tasks to their nonlawyer assistants.[2] Yet attorneys must take care not to delegate any responsibility which might be considered the "practice of law."

Activities that might involve the "practice of law," and that therefore may not be delegated, are varied. It is important to keep in mind that as soon as an activity starts to involve the paralegal's use of independent legal judgment, the activity becomes the practice of law. But where are those lines drawn?

---

[2]*See* ABA Model Guidelines for the Utilization of Legal Assistants, Guideline 2; ABA MODEL CODE OF PROFESSIONAL RESPONSIBILITY EC 3-6 (1986).

One unauthorized practice of law case which received national attention unfolded in the State of Louisiana. A legal assistant by the name of Jerome Papania independently helped people work through their legal problems and charged only a relatively small fee. For example, Jerome helped one couple prepare a will for $50.00. He helped another couple file bankruptcy papers for $90.00. Many of his customers were pleased with his work and noted that, if Papania had not been available to handle these matters, they could not have afforded any legal help.

When the authorities learned of the type of work Papania was doing, however, they sent seven sheriff's deputies to raid his home. The deputies confiscated all of his files and records, labeled these things contraband, and charged him with the unauthorized practice of law, a state offense.

A segment about Papania appeared on "20/20," an American Broadcasting Company (ABC) national news-magazine show, on September 7, 1990. When interviewed on television, Papania indicated that his clients knew he was not a lawyer. Papania thought people in his community did not necessarily like using a nonlawyer to obtain access to the legal system. He said they needed his help because they could not afford the costs of attorneys. In fact, the thrust of the entire interview was that the average consumer of legal services cannot afford them.

"20/20" also interviewed an attorney who had served on a committee in California to study the role of nonlawyers. He admitted that most people in the country must have serious trouble and then must make great sacrifices to be able to afford to hire a lawyer. He acknowledged that there is a role for nonlawyers, but he noted that that role is not yet well-defined.

Consider how the perception of that role has changed since this segment was broadcast on TV.

Source: 20/20: Cutting the Fees (ABC television broadcast, Sept. 7, 1990). Reprinted by permission.

Take a careful look at the following topic areas to derive an understanding of the lines of demarcation between the authorized and the unauthorized practice of law.

Initial Client Interview The client's first meeting with a legal professional during which the legal professional attempts to elicit information regarding the nature of the legal problem.

INITIAL CLIENT INTERVIEW

Sometimes attorneys delegate the responsibility for handling the **initial client interview** to the paralegal. (But see, Mich. Op. RI-128 (4-21-92).) During such an interview, the legal assistant attempts to elicit from the potential client the nature of the legal problem, and gather as much detail as possible. The paralegal would also attempt to discover what the client expects the attorney to accomplish, should an **attorney-client relationship** be established.

Attorney-Client-Relationship The relationship between retained counsel and her client which encompasses privileges of communications, legal advice, and representation. This is considered a fiduciary relationship.

Once the information is gathered from a potential client, the legal assistant will usually transcribe her notes about the client's problem for use by the attorney. The attorney then uses the notes to determine which avenues of research will have to be explored and what procedural tactics must be employed.

Asking questions of the potential client does not involve exercising independent judgment. Often, in fact, the law firm may have a list of established questions and areas that the legal assistant should explore, so the legal assistant need not even prepare questions.

However, the paralegal does become involved in the practice of law should she attempt to establish the attorney-client relationship or establish a fee schedule during the initial client interview. After reviewing the paralegal's notes, the attorney may decide that the client's problem is not worth pursuing in court, as there is no cognizable legal claim. The judgment involves applying existing law to the particular facts of the client's case. The attorney, therefore, is responsible for establishing the attorney-client relationship. Likewise, after evaluating the client's case, it is the attorney who can establish a fee schedule.

Moreover, the *ABA's Model Code* clearly states that a *lawyer has an obligation to maintain a direct relationship with the client.*[3] For this reason, the ABA Model Guidelines for the Utilization of Legal Assistants conclude that the paralegal must not become involved in establishing the attorney-client relationship. Consequently, it is the attorney who must contract with the client. The attorney cannot delegate this responsibility to the legal assistant.

Likewise, the legal assistant must refrain from establishing the fee arrangement between the client and the attorney. Again, should the legal assistant be delegated this responsibility, the paralegal and not the attorney would be maintaining a direct relationship with the client. This is simply never acceptable.

ADVISING THE CLIENT

After the attorney-client relationship is established, the legal assistant must continue to carefully avoid behavior that might be considered the practice of law. As the definitions cited previously in this chapter indicate, the paralegal must avoid exercising independent legal judgment. Therefore, the paralegal should not give the client legal advice.

This means that the legal assistant may not independently research an issue, apply the uncovered law to the facts at hand, form a legal conclusion, and relay legal advice to the client based upon this conclusion. This is the practice of law and is reserved for the attorney. Of course, should the attorney render a legal judgment resolving a problem facing the client and then ask the legal assistant to relay her legal advice to the client, the legal assistant may do so. This is not the practice of law since, in this case, the paralegal has not exercised independent legal judgment in carrying out her responsibilities. However, the paralegal must not expound upon the lawyer's advice.

DRAFTING PAPERS AND PLEADINGS

Can the legal assistant prepare court documents or **pleadings** or other client documents? The definitions of the practice of law previously cited state that *independent* preparation of papers for court is the practice of law because, in essence, the legal assistant would be representing the client independently of the attorney.

Pleadings Formal allegations by parties of their claims and defenses.

On the other hand, preparation of papers *for the attorney's review and signature* presents a different situation.

Much of the work of the litigation legal assistant involves drafting papers and pleadings on behalf of the client. Likewise, the attorney may ask a paralegal to draft real estate closing documents or a preliminary copy of a will. One of the ways paralegals can best help the attorney, in fact, is by preparing a rough draft of these papers. The preliminary work may ethically be delegated to a nonlawyer assistant. The *attorney* must review this work,

---

[3]*See* ABA MODEL CODE OF PROFESSIONAL RESPONSIBILITY EC 3-6 (1986).

however, and then must sign the papers before they can be filed with the court or otherwise acted upon. By reviewing and signing the papers, the attorney is acknowledging the work product as his own, completed as part of his representation of the client.[4]

However, should a legal assistant accept responsibility for preparing papers on behalf of a client, and then file those papers in court without the review or signature of his supervising attorney, the paralegal would be involved in the practice of law. After all, the legal assistant had obviously exercised independent legal judgment in completing his delegated assignments.

DISCOVERY

Once the pleadings have been filed, unless the parties have agreed to settle their case out of court, discovery begins. Legal assistants working in a litigation environment often find that they play a major role in this process.

Discovery Pre-trial process whereby both parties attempt to gather information about the lawsuit from the opposing side.

Discovery is the process whereby both parties attempt to gather information from the opposing side. Discovery may involve many techniques, including taking depositions of the opposing party or its witnesses, or it may be completed through the use of interrogatories.

Interrogatory A series of written questions asked of opposing parties.

An **interrogatory** is a series of written questions asked of opposing parties. The party served with a set of interrogatories is expected to answer those questions in writing, swearing to the truthfulness of the responses given, and return them to the opposing counsel within a statutorily specified period of time. Often the attorney and the legal assistant will take it upon themselves to answer the questions, while obviously working with the client, of course, in order to make sure privileged information is not revealed. After that, the interrogatories would be sent to the client, for the client's review, to ensure the accuracy of the answers. Interrogatories are designed to serve a very important function. They help the attorney anticipate evidence that the opposing counsel will present at trial, and they assist the attorney in formulating her theory of the case.

Deposition Pre-trial discovery device whereby one party poses questions to the opposing party.

A **deposition** is another discovery device whereby questions are asked of the opposing party or her witnesses. However, interrogatories are written questions, while, depositions are questions asked orally of the opposing side. Depositions occur before a trial is scheduled to begin. Although a court reporter or stenographer is present to record the answers given during the deposition, depositions are taken outside of the courtroom, out of the presence of the judge. The witness is under oath. During the deposition, objections to questions may be made, and a judge may rule on the objection at a later date, should a ruling be deemed necessary. Depositions serve the same function as do interrogatories. They help the attorney to anticipate evidence that will be presented by opposing counsel and to prepare his theory of the case. However, depositions also give the attorney the opportunity to observe the behavior of the witness as he is responding to the questions. By observing the deponent's nonverbal communication, the attorney can evaluate the truthfulness of the witness's statements. Legal assistants are often called on to abstract deposition testimony in preparation for trial.

[4]*See* FEDERAL RULE OF CIVIL PROCEDURE, No. 11.

Depositions and interrogatories are key components of the litigation process. They are designed to reveal the truth, and the paralegal often plays a significant role in completing the discovery process before trial begins.

The legal assistant may be asked to assist in the preparation of a list of interrogatories designed to be served on the opposing party. Attorneys may instruct their nonlawyer assistants that they need a set of interrogatories designed to inquire about a certain facet of the client's problem or the client's relationship with the opposing party. (There are form books with sets of tailor-made questions for different types of cases, ie., slip and fall, tortious interference with property, breach of contract.) As long as the interrogatories are later reviewed by the attorney, it is fine for nonlawyers to assist in this process. It does not necessarily involve the exercise of independent legal judgment because the attorney retains control over the product and directs its completion. Just as with preparing a rough draft of a pleading, the legal assistant is merely drawing up a preliminary statement for the attorney to adopt as his own work.

Likewise, the legal assistant may be asked to assist in preparing responses to interrogatories served on her client by opposing counsel. Again, as long as this is done under the supervision of the lawyer, with the lawyer's assistance and review, this is an activity in which it is ethically proper for the nonlawyer to engage.

The same is true where the nonlawyer is asked to prepare questions to be asked by his supervising attorney at a deposition. This situation is similar to a legal assistant preparing interrogatories. Again, as long as the attorney directs the work and reviews it, this is acceptable behavior.

Legal assistants must take care to understand the limits of their responsibilities so they do not mistakenly engage in the unauthorized practice of law.

In what discovery activities can the legal assistant ethically engage? Conversely, what activities must the legal assistant avoid during discovery?

First, where the attorney fails to supervise or review the paralegal's drafting of interrogatories, responses to interrogatories, or questions for depositions, the nonlawyer should avoid the work. By failing to participate in the process, the attorney is abdicating the exercise of independent legal judgment to the paralegal. The paralegal is then engaging in the unauthorized practice of law, and the attorney is assisting in the unauthorized practice of law.

Second, the legal assistant may not appear on behalf of a client at a deposition. Depositions may only be taken by an attorney. Nonlawyers are never allowed to present questions to the party being deposed or advise a client as to appropriate answers to questions. That is because legal assistants are not permitted to exercise the independent legal judgment required in so doing. Also, if nonlawyers were permitted to depose parties at depositions or advise clients at depositions, it might give the appearance (to both the party being deposed and the client with whom the nonlawyer has attended the deposition) that the nonlawyer is representing the client.

The opening exercise of this chapter presents an interesting situation. Sometimes the nonlawyer may be in a stronger position to understand information and to discover testimony discrepancies. Regardless of this simple fact, the nonlawyer is not allowed to make such appearances. See Pennsylvania Bar Ass'n. Op. 91-137 (10/18/91); Ethics Opinions 87-127 Philadelphia 1987; *Bilodeau v. Antal*, 123 N.H. 39, 455 A.2d 1037 (1983).

TRIAL PREPARATION

Trial Preparation
Documents prepared for litigation including written memoranda and discovery.

Once discovery is completed and it appears certain that the case will proceed to trial, the nonlawyer may be asked to assist the attorney with **trial preparation.** The nonlawyer may be asked to assist with a variety of tasks. One task might be to prepare trial notebooks that contain copies of pertinent pleadings, court opinions on similar legal issues, even the opening or closing arguments. Other tasks might include contacting and helping to prepare witnesses who are scheduled to testify. (Often the witnesses are instructed as to proper courtroom behavior.) Yet another task is to prepare questions to be posed during *voir dire* at the start of a jury trial.

Assisting the attorney with this work does not involve practicing law because the paralegal is not asked to exercise independent legal judgment. He acts at the behest of the attorney who is representing the client, and his work is reviewed by the attorney who has ultimate responsibility for the product.

As we will discuss in the next segment of this chapter, though the nonlawyer may certainly assist the lawyer in preparing for trial and may even be present during the trial to help the lawyer keep abreast of the direction of the litigation, he cannot independently appear in court on behalf of a client in any manner involving the independent exercise of legal judgment.

EXERCISE 3.2

Using the above principles, analyze the following situations.

A. When Alphonse Attorney is asked to fly out of town to speak at a national conference concerning "Labor Relations and the Government Employee," he asks Peggy Paralegal to write a list of interrogatories that he can serve upon opposing counsel when he returns. If Peggy writes the interrogatories, will she be "practicing law"? Why or why not? If Peggy has the interrogatories served upon opposing counsel before Alphonse returns, does your answer change?

B. He knows he only has a few hours before the filing deadline, but Peter Paralegal cannot find Alice Attorney to review the Plaintiffs' Response to Defendant's Motion. Peter knows that filing this response is extremely important to the case. How should Peter resolve the situation?

C. Pauline Paralegal has been assigned to handle all initial interviews with new worker's compensation clients. During an interview with a new client yesterday, she was asked some rather pointed questions concerning whether or not a penalty against the opposing side can be sought in this claimant's case in addition to the regular worker's compensation award. The claimant also asked how much additional attorney's fees it would cost to appeal the circuit court's ruling. What should Pauline say in response to these questions?

COURT APPEARANCES, CRIMINAL PROCEEDINGS, AND LAY REPRESENTATION

You will recall from our discussion at the beginning of this chapter that all of the definitions of the practice of law emphasize one point: nonlawyers may

Do	Don't
Conduct the initial client interview.	Establish the attorney-client relationship.
	Establish fee arrangements.
Relay the attorney's legal advice to the client.	Give independent legal advice to the client.
Prepare pleadings and court documents for the review and signature of the attorney.	Prepare and sign pleadings or other court documents independent of an attorney.
Prepare interrogatories, answer interrogatories, and prepare questions to be asked at depositions as long as such work is supervised and reviewed by an attorney.	Prepare interrogatories, answers to interrogatories, or questions to be asked at depositions independent of an attorney.
	Ask questions of witnesses at depositions.
Assist in trial preparation.	Represent the client in court (except for limited situations, as discussed in this chapter.)

**EXHIBIT 3.1
Do's and Don't's
to Avoid Engaging
in the Practice of
Law**

not represent clients in court proceedings. However, there are exceptions to this general rule against **court appearances.** For example, nonlawyers may, in certain circumstances, be allowed to represent clients before certain administrative agencies.

Court Appearances
Appearing in court
on behalf of a client.

Perhaps the most interesting exception to the court appearances prohibition is the practice currently allowed in the courts of Illinois. In 1964 the Illinois Appellate Court ruled that nonlawyers may appear in court, on behalf of an attorney, to handle routine motions. *People v. Alexander*, 53 Ill.App.3d 299, 202 N.E.2d 841 (1964).

In *People v. Alexander*, a law student, employed in a law firm as a law clerk, stepped up to the bench when the case was called and helped opposing counsel prepare an order for the court. In other words, the law student "appeared" on behalf of the client. Although the trial court found that he had engaged in the unauthorized practice of law and held him in contempt of court, the appellate court reversed. In so holding, the Illinois Appellate Court stated:

> The preparation of an order, in the instant case, with the collaboration of opposing counsel was a ministerial act for the benefit of the court and a mere recordation of what had transpired. We cannot hold that this conduct of defendant constituted the unauthorized practice of law. *Alexander*, 53 Ill. App. 3d 299, 202 N.E.2d at 843.

The court then noted the definition of the practice of law and, relying upon this definition, analyzed the defendant's appearance in the courtroom:

> Since this statement relates to the appearance and management of proceedings in court on behalf of a client, we do not believe it can be applied to a situation where a clerk hired by a law firm presents information to the court on behalf of his employer.
>
> We agree with the trial judge that clerks should not be permitted to make motions or participate in other proceedings which can be considered as "managing" the litigation. However, if apprising the court of an employer's engagement or inability to be present constitutes the making of a motion, we

must hold that clerks may make such motions for continuances without being guilty of the unauthorized practice of law. Certainly with the large volume of cases appearing on the trial calls these days, it is imperative that this practice be allowed.

. . .

We cannot add to the heavy burden of lawyers who in addition to responding to trial calls must answer pre-trial calls and motion calls—all held in the morning—by insisting that a lawyer must personally appear to present to a court a motion for a continuance on grounds of engagement or inability to appear because of illness or other unexpected circumstances. To reduce the backlog, trial lawyers should be kept busy actually trying lawsuits and not answering court calls. *Alexander,* 53 Ill.App.3d 299, 202 N.E.2d at 843–44.

Status Call A court call in which the parties in a legal matter report to the court what activities have been undertaken to further the litigation.

What kinds of motions are routine matters and are therefore permitted? Illinois courts allow nonlawyers to answer **status calls** (informing the court of what activities have been undertaken to further the litigation). Nonlawyers also appear in court to request continuances in particular matters, though generally, the propriety of these appearances is left to each judge's discretion.

Some judges permit nonlawyers to request **continuances.** It is not uncommon, therefore, to see paralegals—or even legal secretaries—appear in Illinois courts to handle routine motions or court business.

Continuance The adjournment or postponement of a session, hearing, trial, or other proceeding, to another place or time.

Others view the fact that a nonlawyer may be authorized to set court dates as constituting the exercise of independent legal judgment, and hence, the unauthorized practice of law. Judges are cautious in this instance, because they too must avoid assisting in the unauthorized practice of law.

It is, of course, *imperative* that nonlawyers who appear in courts on behalf of attorneys identify their status as nonlawyers at the beginning of courtroom proceedings.

A few other states have adopted similar rules regarding court appearances by nonlawyers, but most states do not permit court appearances by nonlawyers on routine matters. Check the rules governing your jurisdiction to see whether this practice is allowed.

CRIMINAL REPRESENTATION

While most states do not permit nonlawyers to handle routine court motions, exceptions to the general prohibition on courtroom work arise in some criminal courts. One exception is in the area of criminal representation.

Many criminal defendants have attempted to persuade the judiciary that the Sixth Amendment to the U.S. Constitution grants citizens the right to be represented by laypersons in criminal proceedings. The Sixth Amendment reads, in part,

In all criminal prosecutions, the accused shall enjoy the right . . . to have the Assistance of Counsel for his defence.

Criminal defendants have argued that the word "counsel" does not mean advice from an attorney but may be advice from any source, including any nonlawyer. Despite the fact that the language of the Sixth Amendment seems open-ended, courts have universally interpreted "counsel" to mean "licensed attorney." One court that addressed this matter wrote:

This adjuration [contained in the Sixth Amendment] necessitates "the guiding hand of counsel at every step in the proceedings against him", including "the giving of effective aid in the preparation and trial of the case." It is clear that these demands are not satisfied when the accused is "represented" by a layman masquerading as a qualified attorney; it is unthinkable that so precious a right, or so grave a responsibility, can be entrusted to one who has not been admitted to the practice of law, no matter how intelligent or well educated he may be. This is particularly so where, as here, the accused is on trial for an offense upon conviction of which his very life could become forfeit. *Harrison v. United States,* 128 U.S.App.D.C. 245, 387 F.2d 203, 212 (1967) *rev'd on other grounds,* 392 U.S. 219, 88 S.Ct. 2008, 20 L.Ed.2d 1047 (1968).

The carefully considered and often cited *Turner v. American Bar Association,* 407 F.Supp. 451 (1975), presents perhaps the most comprehensive analysis of this issue. In fact, *Turner* was a consolidation of eight cases, all filed by individuals who, though relying upon the ambiguous language of the Sixth Amendment, were denied the right to be represented by laypersons or denied the right to be allowed to represent others.

Virtually every member of the federal judiciary was named a defendant in these lawsuits. The parties alleged that a conspiracy existed among federal courts to confine the practice of law to licensed attorneys. It was alleged that this conspiracy created a monopoly of the practice of law and had the effect of restraining individual rights of plaintiffs. The court characterized the parties' request as seeking to have " ... this Court elevate to the status of a constitutional right their desire to have an unlicensed layman assist them and perform functions in Court ordinarily performed by licensed attorneys." *Turner,* 407 F.Supp. at 477.

The court employed a rigorous analysis of the meaning of the Sixth Amendment. It concluded that the "counsel" referred to in the Sixth Amendment meant "licensed attorney." To justify its interpretation of the meaning of this amendment, the court relied on an examination of both British and American legal history and concluded, "[t]his Court cannot find even a suggestion in the history of the Common Law after its primeval inception or in the history of the American lawyer that the word 'counsel', as used in the Sixth Amendment, was meant to include a layman off the street without qualification as to either training or character." *Turner,* 407 F.Supp. at 474.

This does not mean nonlawyers can never appear in court to handle criminal matters. As with most rules, exceptions to this principle concerning lay representation do exist. For example, the right of an individual to represent himself has been recognized by the Supreme Court to exist in the language of the Sixth Amendment. See *Faretta v. California,* 422 U.S. 806, 95 S.Ct. 2525, 45 L.Ed.2d 562 (1975). A caveat to this rule exists, however, in that the court may require the accused to accept the assistance of "stand-by counsel." See *United States v. Gigax,* 605 F.2d 507 (10th Cir. 1979).

Further, several courts have indicated that, in their discretion, judges may elect to allow lay representation of a criminal defendant. Courts have premised this rule's justification on the "inherent power lodged in a Federal Judge to govern and control the conduct of the trial before him." *Turner,* 407 F.Supp. at 478.

The state of Montana, however, recently limited the rights of laypersons to represent defendants in criminal proceedings on a *regular and recurring basis.* The court limited appearance by lay parties to "'casual, non-recurring, non-pay basis as a means of assisting a party pro se'" before a *justice or magistrate court. Sparks v. Johnson,* 252 Mont. 39, 826 P.2d 928, 930 (1992), quoting *State ex rel. Frieson v. Isner,* 285 S.E.2d 641, 655 (1981). The court further noted, "The salutary purpose of the statute may not thus be perverted to encourage the growth of a class of 'justice court lawyers,' unfettered by the rules that bind licensed attorneys and without training in law and ethics." *Sparks,* 826 P.2d at 930–31, quoting *Bump v. Barnett,* 235 Iowa 308, 16 N.W.2d 579, 582–583 (1944).

Additionally, courts may allow lay representation of prison inmates.

Writ of Habeas Corpus A petition (writ) designed to bring a party before the court in order to test the legality of his or her detention or imprisonment.

For example, the state of Missouri, after looking to an analogous situation in Arizona, decided that nonlawyers should be allowed to prepare habeas petitions for prisoners. Upon noting that the statute allows for a **writ of habeas corpus** to be signed by a party "for whose relief it is intended or *by some person on his behalf,*" the court allowed such a writ to be filed by a nonattorney (emphasis in original). The court noted that this was a necessary means to securing prisoners' rights:

> It is a practical realization that one confined to a cell, without ready access to a lawyer, often must depend on his family or friends to have "his body brought before the court" (i.e. "habeus corpus") to determine the legality of his incarceration. *State of Missouri v. Carroll,* 817 S.W.2d 289, 291 (1991), quoting *Hackin v. State,* 102 Ariz. 218, 427 P.2d 910, 911, *appeal dismissed,* 389 U.S. 143, 88 S.Ct. 325, 19 L.Ed.2d 347 (1967).

Moreover, some state legislatures have adopted statutes allowing inmates to represent fellow inmates in disciplinary actions and, sometimes, post-conviction proceedings. (For such an example, see *State of Arizona v. Melendez,* 172 Ariz. 68, 834 P.2d 154 (1992), which also discussed the subsequent problems arising out of just such a statute. (See chapter 5, "Confidentiality," for further discussion of this case).)

Despite these exceptions, the overwhelming majority of criminal defense work rests in the hands of attorneys. According to the courts, this practice is a firmly entrenched principle because of the interpretation of the language of the Sixth Amendment. It is wise, therefore, for the legal assistant to avoid even attempting to represent parties in criminal proceedings.

EXERCISE 3.3 | Consider the justifications advanced for excluding or including nonlawyers from the practice of law. Should lay representation be allowed in criminal proceedings?

ADMINISTRATIVE AGENCY REPRESENTATION

Understanding what constitutes the "practice of law" is difficult. One of the most difficult areas to understand is administrative agency representation. Congress vested administrative agencies with the authority to adjudicate matters brought before them. In other words, when Congress created administrative agencies, it determined that if a person files a complaint with the agency, the agency must do all it can to resolve the matter, even proceeding to a trial of the issues. However, Congress did not explicitly limit appearances before agencies to licensed attorneys. Consequently, courts are consistently being called upon to review whether a nonlawyer may represent another party in an action before an administrative agency.

In some instances, reviewing courts have ruled that such representation is permissible (if agency rules allow it). However, not all agencies allow such representation. It is vitally important, therefore, that any nonlawyer who contemplates representing people before administrative agencies understand the applicable rules and regulations that are described below.

STATE ADMINISTRATIVE AGENCIES

Networks of administrative agencies have developed at both the state and federal levels. State agencies are designed to handle claims arising under state law; federal agencies handle cases contesting claims arising under federal law.

What confuses this issue is that many state agencies work with complementary federal agencies handling similar kinds of issues. For example, a state department of human rights may handle cases involving violations of basic state civil rights statutes, while the federal equivalent—the Equal Employment Opportunity Commission—would handle similar issues involving violations of federal civil rights.

Despite the fact that certain state and federal agencies may handle similar cases, the state administrative system has developed and adheres to a separate set of administrative practice rules from those of the federal system.

Federal and state governments are considered to be two separate entities with two separate bodies of law. The state agency is guided by state laws. So, although the federal agency may be designed to resolve a similar issue, the federal practice rules and laws may differ significantly from the state's rules.

Many state agencies have specific rules that, despite state unauthorized practice of law statutes, authorize nonlawyers to represent laypersons before certain administrative agencies.

One such statute in Rhode Island authorizes employee assistants of the Department of Worker's Compensation to assist injured employees in hearings before that department. The validity of this statute was addressed in *Unauthorized Practice of Law Committee v. State of Rhode Island, Department of Workers' Compensation* 543 A.2d 662 (R.I. 1988).

The Rhode Island General Assembly had created an employee assistants office. These assistants were to aid employees at informal benefits hearings. They were also to be available to help the employee prepare for the hearing and be present with them during the hearing. The position's description called for someone to provide technical and routine advice and/or information. Although this is generally the work of lawyers, in this case the statute indicated that it was not necessary that the assistant be a lawyer.

The purpose of this enactment, as provided by the Rhode Island General Assembly, was that employee assistants were to be used to "provide advice and assistance to employees under the workers' compensation act and particularly to assist employees in preparing for and assisting at informal conferences under § 28-33-1.1." 543 A.2d at 663.

These provisions were challenged by the members of the Rhode Island Bar because they involved activities believed to be the practice of law by nonlawyers. The Unauthorized Practice of Law Committee, therefore, contested these provisions in court.

The Rhode Island Supreme Court noted that it was not within the power of the legislature to grant anyone the right to practice law unless it was in accordance with the state's supreme court. However, the court recognized that the General Assembly had allowed many things that might fall under the definition of practicing law to be done by nonlawyers. Some of these things included work being done by bank employees, certified public accountants, and interstate commerce practitioners.

Despite this, the court noted, "[t]he plain fact of the matter is that each of these exceptions enacted by the Legislature constituted a response to a public need." 543 A.2d at 665. The court recognized a similar public need in this instance. For this reason, the court held that, although the grant of authorization was experimental, employee assistants were authorized to carry out the functions given to them.

Rhode Island is not the only state in which such a broad authorization of authority has been granted to laypersons. The states of Colorado and Ohio have confronted this issue and have painted very broad strokes of responsibility for nonlawyers working in administrative agencies.

The Ohio Supreme Court, in *Henize v. Giles,* 22 Ohio St. 3d 213, 490 N.E.2d 585 (1986), held that nonlawyer representatives who appeared before the Ohio Bureau of Employment Services and the Unemployment Compensation Board of Review agencies were not engaged in the unauthorized practice of law.

The court noted that claimants were traditionally joined by friends, coworkers, or family in presentation of their claims. Moreover, legal aid societies were known to have provided legal assistants for free, to assist the worker in the presentation of a claim.

Additionally the court noted that, while it possessed the authority to regulate the practice of law and to protect the public, it should not exercise this authority so rigidly that it is at the expense of the public good. It stated:

> In facing their well-equipped adversaries, claimants are crippled by inadequate resources, an inadequate understanding of the variables determining their claims, and a lack of experience in the procedures for defending benefit entitlements ... Legal services attorneys are generally unavailable because their services are limited to clients at or below the poverty level, and their limited resources are already strained by heavy caseloads and inadequate funding. *Henize,* 22 Ohio St. 3d 213, 490 N.E.2d at 590, n. 10.

Lay Representation
Representation of a party's interests by a nonlawyer.

The court then went on to narrowly hold that **lay representation** of parties in preparing and presenting a claimant's case was permissible to facilitate the hearing process.

Similarly, the Unauthorized Practice of Law Committee in Colorado petitioned the Colorado Supreme Court to address the issue of whether nonlawyers practicing in an administrative agency were practicing law. Specifically, in *Unauthorized Practice of Law Committee v. Employers Unity,* the Unauthorized Practice of Law Committee of Colorado asked the state supreme court to issue an injunction to prevent the nonlawyers from engaging in the practice of law before an administrative agency. 716 P.2d 460 (Colo. 1986).

The named parties, all nonlawyers, gave advice to employers and employees concerning claims for unemployment compensation. They prepared and filed documents and pleadings. They appeared before referees at hearings of the Division of Employment and Training of the Colorado Department of Labor. They elicited testimony at the hearing from employees, members of management, claimants and witnesses, and they presented closing argument to referees, often referring to sections of the Colorado Revised Statutes.

The court held that it granted permission to laypersons to represent people at hearings even though it believed this conduct constituted the practice of law.

It noted that Colorado had historically granted this permission in limited circumstances where the monetary amount in issue was very small and there were few disputed legal principles.

What does this all mean for the legal assistant interested in becoming involved in practice before an administrative agency? Paralegals should remember that such practice is allowed, but only in certain states and only before certain agencies. It is best to check the agency's rules and state legislation before attempting to undertake representation of any clients.

The issue of lay representation before administrative agencies may be especially crucial for those legal assistants who are employed in corporations. Increasingly, paralegals are employed by corporate entities, either in legal departments or in other positions which might take advantage of their analytical and organizational skills. Grievances involving the corporation are often resolved before an administrative tribunal, and the legal assistant is often asked to assist in handling such complaints.

The paralegal in this instance must take special care to look beyond the rules of an administrative agency. Because a corporation is a legal entity and is not a human being, the rules regarding corporate representation before administrative agencies are different.

A corporation *must* be represented by an attorney in any court proceeding. Nobody except an attorney, therefore, may represent the corporation in any capacity. Not even the president of the corporation is allowed to appear in court on behalf of the corporation (unless the president is an attorney), because the president is not representing herself. Rather, she is representing the corporation.

Reed v. Labor and Indus. Relations Com'n., 789 S.W.2d 19 (Mo. banc 1990) involved a layperson employee (Kalajian), who worked for a corporation as "unemployment compensation manager." In this position, she filed an appeal on behalf of the organization from a decision by the Missouri Division of Employment Security to the Labor and Industrial Relations Commission. The Missouri Supreme Court held that, by filing this appeal, Kalajian was engaging in the unauthorized practice of law. It noted that, "[i]t is axiomatic that a corporation must act through an attorney in all legal matters." *Reed*, 789 S.W.2d at 23.

The applicable regulation stated that any individual may appear for herself in any hearing. The court noted, however:

The regulation recognizes that individuals and partnerships may appear for themselves but, because they are an artificial entity, corporations or associations must be represented by an attorney. However the Commission may have interpreted the statutes or regulation in the past, the Court now holds that allowing a non-attorney corporate employee to file an application for review with the Commission is the unauthorized practice of law. *Reed*, 789 S.W.2d at 23.

This, of course, is not the rule in every jurisdiction.

Rules regarding the representation of corporations hold true in both state and federal agencies. The next section discusses more fully rules regarding federal administrative practice by nonlawyers.

EXERCISE 3.4

Fran is an employee of Shop-Mart. In her capacity as Human Resources Director, she has regularly been requested to answer requests from employees about unemployment compensation claims to which they believe they are entitled.

In fact, Fran's supervisors have asked her to draft letters to those employees requesting information about unemployment claims. Should Fran participate in this activity? Does it constitute the practice of law?

Fran has also been asked to appear before the unemployment compensation agency, on behalf of Shop-Mart, to provide an independent hearing officer with facts and information to resolve unemployment claims. Should Fran participate in this activity? Why or why not?

FEDERAL AGENCIES

In many instances, federal legislation allows a nonlawyer to appear before a federal agency. See, for example, the *Administrative Procedure Act*, 5 U.S.C.A. § 555 (1994), which authorizes federal agencies to permit nonlawyers to practice before certain administrative agencies.

This practice can set up quite a conflict between the federal regulations and the state unauthorized practice statute. The conflict is often resolved through application of a doctrine known as **preemption.**

Preemption A doctrine which provides that the legislature, and sometimes the courts, determine that certain matters are so important to the nation as a whole that federal law governing that subject will take precedence over any state laws covering that subject. The doctrine is derived from the Supremacy Clause of the U.S. Constitution.

Preemption is a doctrine (derived from the Supremacy Clause of the U.S. Constitution) which provides that the legislature, and sometimes the courts, determines that certain matters are so important to the nation as a whole that federal law governing that subject will take precedence over any state laws covering that same subject. If legislation of the federal government does not address a particular subject, therefore, a state is free to enforce its own regulations. Conversely, if the federal government addresses the issue with the intention that federal law will take precedence over state law—in other words, *preempts* the area—a state may *not* enforce its own regulations.

Patent Practice

Preemption has been applied in the situation of nonlawyer practice before federal administrative agencies. Therefore, courts have been called upon to determine whether federal regulations that allow nonlawyer practice before federal administrative agencies supercede, or preempt, state unauthorized practice of law statutes that forbid the practice. One such area in which the preemption doctrine has been applied is in the U.S. Patent Office.

The U.S. Supreme Court has ruled that the preparation and prosecution of patent applications for others constitutes the practice of law. At the same time, under regulations of the U.S. Patent Office, persons who are not attorneys have been authorized to practice before that office. (See *Sperry v. Florida*, discussed below.) This has resulted in some confusion in the state arena.

In *Sperry v. Florida*, 373 U.S. 379, 83 S.Ct. 1322, 10 L.Ed. 2d 428 (1963), the State of Florida could not prohibit a nonattorney, licensed patent agent from engaging in patent practice before the federal Patent Office. The U.S. Supreme Court applied the Supremacy Clause of the U.S. Constitution, saying that the federal law allowing such practice took precedent over state law which disallowed it. In other words, the federal regulations allowing nonlawyer practice before the Patent Office preempted any state law forbidding the unauthorized practice of law.

To be admitted to practice before the patent office, nonlawyers must meet certain requirements. They must be of good moral character, and they must possess certain legal and scientific skills and qualifications. See *Sperry* at 384–85, 83 S.Ct. at 1325–26. Once it is determined that the nonlawyer meets these qualifications, he can be admitted to practice before the Patent Office.

Admission to the Patent Office allows one to practice before *only* the Patent Office. A person registered before the Patent Office, therefore, is not given license to appear before any other agency or to give general patent advice in her law office. Should the nonlawyer appear before a state administrative agency, then the state would be free to apply that state's unauthorized practice of law statute to regulate the nonlawyer's behavior.

The critical thing to remember is that the layperson must be admitted to practice before the U.S. Patent Office to be engaged in patent practice.

Lizzie is an electronics engineer whose Uncle Ira, she tells us, has invented many things. The problem, according to Lizzie, is that somebody always files papers to secure a patent before her uncle can get around to filing his own. This enrages Lizzie, who has decided she wants to help people protect their inventions. She wants to know how to go about qualifying to do this. Please research the issue, and then write a memo providing the answer to this question.

EXERCISE 3.5

Immigration Practice

Another area of federal administrative agency practice that has grown quite controversial in recent years is immigration. Immigration matters are handled through the Office of Immigration and Naturalization Services (INS).

On June 9, 1992 the General Counsel of the INS issued an opinion that concluded that nonlawyers may not represent individuals in that agency's proceedings. The question presented to the INS for review was as follows: "[I]s a visa consultant who is not a licensed attorney or an authorized representative ... authorized by federal immigration regulations and state laws to represent the Service?" (The opinion defines "visa consultant" as "a person who provides advice or services and/or prepares legal instruments for persons in connection with the immigration laws...." The opinion further notes that visa consultants may be known as "immigration consultants, notarios, travel agents, passport agents," and so forth.)

In deciding that federal regulations do not permit nonlawyers to undertake representation of others before the INS, the opinion noted, "[w]hether or not representation by such a person in violation of federal immigration regulations also violates state laws can only be determined by applying the statutes and regulations that govern the practice of law in each particular state." In other words, because the federal regulations of the INS do not govern this question, the INS regulations do not preempt state regulations in the area of immigration. The opinion continued, "the Service is neither obliged nor in a position to take any action or position regarding whether these persons are engaging in [UPL] in any given state." Memorandum Co 292.2, June 9, 1992, reprinted in Interpreter Releases vol. 69, No. 25, Appendix III, p. 823, July 6, 1992.

In all situations where federal regulations allow nonlawyers to assume responsibilities that are forbidden to them under state law, the nonlawyer must be *admitted* to practice before that agency. Without this admission, the layperson who attempts to practice in the agency leaves herself open to state sanctions. Therefore, before embarking on a career representing others before a federal agency, check its rules.

Some states have enacted legislation relating to unauthorized practice of law rules and immigration agency practice. For example, the State of Virginia has focused much effort on these considerations.[5]

> **REMEMBER:** Investigate the regulations of the agency before which you wish to appear.

EXERCISE 3.6

Contact the state bar in your area and investigate the possibilities that may exist for nonlawyers to participate in administrative agency practice. In the event that your state does not permit nonlawyer agency representation in administrative agencies, you may still be able to contribute to the needs of the clients through some pro bono legal programs.

TYPING SERVICES
AND "DO-IT-YOURSELF" KITS

In a number of areas, legal assistants have developed businesses in which they provide what are purported to be typing services to the public. These businesses are designed to assist the general public in adequately completing complicated legal documents by helping the lay public "fill in the blanks" (or type information in the blank spaces) on pre-printed forms.

Do-It-Yourself/Typing Services Businesses designed to assist the general public in adequately completing complicated legal documents by helping the law public type information in blank spaces on pre-printed forms.

Although these services help to enlarge access to the court system, the paralegal who engages in this kind of work often steps beyond the limits of the practice of law definitions. Eventually, the legal assistant may find himself in a great deal of trouble with the law—the very forum in which he is assisting others.

Paralegals attempt to offer **"do-it-yourself" services** to the public in several basic areas. These services include **typing services** for members of the public who are securing divorces, discharging debts through bankruptcy, and establishing wills and other probate documents.

---

[5]Courtesy of Susan Spielberg, Assistant Bar Counsel, Virginia State Bar.

As you read the following section, keep in mind the comments presented in a recent advisory opinion from the chairman of the Committee on Unauthorized Practice of Law in Kentucky, Richard Underwood:

> ... Generally, courts have concluded that if a divorce or probate kit is accompanied with personal contacts or advice on how to proceed or how to fill in the prescribed forms, the practice of law exists, and is not permitted.[6]

Typing services developed in response to a perceived need for legal services by low- and middle-income families. Many believe that there are low- and middle-income families who simply cannot afford the services of an attorney to help them resolve even simple legal problems. For example, when debts amount to such an overwhelming sum that a debtor must seek the protection of the bankruptcy courts, it is difficult for some to understand how a debtor will find money to retain an attorney. Also, they argue, consider the situation of spouses seeking to dissolve a marriage with few assets. Their financial picture is precarious enough without having to find money to pay for attorney's fees.

In response to this need, some enterprising individuals formed businesses designed to offer help in completing legal forms for a small fee. In *Florida Bar v. Brumbaugh,* the court was faced with a situation in which a woman was offering such assistance. 355 So.2d 1186 (Fla. 1978). The Florida Bar charged that Brumbaugh was engaging in the unauthorized practice of law. The Supreme Court of Florida analyzed the facts and concluded that it was difficult to define just what constitutes the practice of law. The court stated that a set definition of what constitutes the practice of law that would be all-encompassing could never be determined because it would have to be altered according to the ever-changing times. 355 So.2d at 1191–92.

In reviewing the findings of the referee, the *Brumbaugh* court decided that the sale of sample legal forms was authorized. However, when people are given the forms and provided with instructions on how to fill out or use them, the service provider can get into trouble. The primary goal to be achieved by this decision was to protect the public from uneducated advice and assistance in resolving legal matters.

Brumbaugh was charged by the Florida Bar with engaging in the unauthorized practice of law. Specifically, she was charged with preparing legal documents for her customers in uncontested dissolution of marriage cases and with advising her customers as to procedures and costs involved in obtaining the dissolution. Her fee was $50.00. The referee determined that Brumbaugh was operating under the guise of "secretarial" or "typing" services, preparing all the papers that she felt would need to be filed in a particular case. Brumbaugh also gave detailed instructions as to how the suit should be filed, how parties should be served, and how the trial should be conducted.

The court determined that having a typing services business did not constitute engaging in the practice of law. It is when typing services are accompanied by legal advice that problems arise. *Brumbaugh* was an important decision defining the extent of the responsibilities that a nonlawyer operating a typing service can provide to the public. From *Brumbaugh,* it is clear that nonlawyers operating a typing service may sell uncompleted legal forms to the public. However, when the nonlawyer begins to offer advice such as how

---

[6]Reprinted by permission.

HIGHLIGHT   Judge Wapner and the Unauthorized Practice of Law

E ven Judge Wapner addressed the issue of typing services and whether they are legal.

In an episode of *The People's Court* entitled "How To Get A Polish Divorce," Judge Wapner confronted this problem. The plaintiff, a Polish emigré, had secured D & B Services to help him obtain a quick Mexican divorce from his wife, who, it was alleged, still resided in Poland.

The plaintiff told Judge Wapner that he had seen an advertisement in the newspaper which claimed that D & B Services could obtain an international divorce. He called the service and the parties then entered into a contract whereby D & B would secure plaintiff's divorce in exchange for a fee. The plaintiff had, in essence, paid the "typing service" $400.00 to secure the quick Mexican divorce.

When Judge Wapner began to ask the defendants' rendition of the facts, they told Judge Wapner that no employee of D & B Services was a member of the California Bar. In essence, D & B was run entirely by nonlawyers. In fact, the defendants asserted, "we are not lawyers; were are paralegals." The defendants also claimed that the company only provided typing services and was solely involved in helping parties complete the paperwork involved in such things as securing divorces.

Judge Wapner then asked one defendant: "How can you get a divorce if you are not a lawyer?" What followed was a long line of questioning by Judge Wapner concerning the kinds of advice the plaintiff alleged that the defendants had given him.

Judge Wapner ruled in favor of the plaintiff. He awarded him the $400.00 that plaintiff paid to the firm and also assessed $400.00 in punitive damages against the defendants. In rendering the decision, Judge Wapner told the defendants that legal advice had been given to the plaintiff, and that it is improper for anyone except a lawyer to give such advice. Judge Wapner then informed the defendants that they could only act as scriveners and record the answers provided by the customers on legal forms.

Source: *How to Get a Polish Divorce*, THE PEOPLE'S COURT, Ralph Edwards Productions in association with Stu Billett Productions, © 1984 Ralph Edwards Productions (TPC 605). Adaptation of "The People's Court" courtesy of Ralph Edwards Productions.

Divorce Kits
Generally, copies of legal documents necessary for securing a divorce, with instructions for filing in court.

to complete those forms, then the nonlawyer has clearly begun to exercise independent legal judgment, the essence of practicing law.

Many of the same issues arose again, a few years later, when Rosemary Furman began operating her own typing service to assist in completing family law legal forms. This time, however, the issue of **divorce kits** landed a woman in jail and, ultimately, created a national furor. Furman, who was not a member of the Florida Bar and was not licensed to practice law in any state, began operating a "typing service" in which she sold legal forms to the public, helping her clients complete these forms for later filings. An examination of her activities will help to reveal how problems with typing services are analyzed.

In 1979, the Florida Bar petitioned the Florida Supreme Court and alleged that Furman had engaged in the unauthorized practice of law. *The Florida Bar v. Furman*, 376 So.2d 378 (Fla. 1979). It was alleged that Furman gave legal advice and rendered legal services regarding adoptions and dissolutions of marriages. The Bar also alleged that Furman had solicited information from customers and prepared legal pleadings for them. The Bar claimed that this violated Florida law and that, because Furman had advertised her services, she had held herself out to the public as having legal expertise in Florida family law.

The court appointed a referee who received evidence in this case. Relying upon the precedent established in *Brumbaugh,* the referee found Furman guilty of the unauthorized practice of law and permanently enjoined her from further engaging in this practice.

Despite being prohibited by court order from further operating her business of selling do-it-yourself kits, Furman continued to offer legal services, often supplying customers with improper advice. Once again, the Florida Bar took Furman to court.

Furman's real problem with the legal authorities began when she was charged with violating the previous order. This time the Florida Supreme Court held Furman in **contempt of court** for ignoring its previous order. *The Florida Bar v. Furman,* 451 So.2d 808 (Fla. 1984).

In finding Furman in contempt, the court first set forth its holding from the previous *Brumbaugh* case:

Contempt of Court
Willfull disobedience of orders of the court.

> [Respondent] must not, in conjunction with her business, engage in advising clients as to the various remedies available to them, or otherwise assist them in preparing those forms necessary for a dissolution proceeding.... Our specific holding with regard to the dissolution of marriage also applies to other unauthorized legal assistance such as the preparation of wills or real estate transaction documents. While [respondent] may legally sell forms in these areas, and type up instruments which have been completed by clients, she must not engage in personal legal assistance in conjunction with her business activities, including the correction of errors and omissions. *Furman,* 451 So.2d at 812, quoting *Furman, 376* So.2d at 381.

Furman had disregarded this order. According to the court,

> Furman admitted that she did not abide by the dictates of *Brumbaugh.* She says that it is impossible for her to operate her "do-it-yourself divorce kit" business in compliance with this court's ruling in that case. *Furman,* 451 So.2d at 812, quoting *Furman, 376* So.2d at 381.

The Florida Supreme Court did not take this lightly. It very carefully studied the findings of the referee and found no error. It noted that the findings were based on a case-by-case analysis that was uncontradicted by evidence. Among these findings were:

> J. Ms. Furman prepared pleadings that went beyond just transposing information from an intake sheet to a form. She articulated that information in a fashion which raised justiciable issues regarding child custody, child support, division of property.
> K. Ms. Furman explained legal remedies and options to litigating parties which affected the procedural and substantive legal rights, duties, and privileges of those parties.
> L. Ms. Furman construed and interpreted the legal effects of Section 61.13, Florida Statutes, pertaining to shared parental responsibility.
> M. Ms. Furman gave advice on how to construct and prepare a financial picture that would result in increased monetary benefits or decreased monetary obligations as the case may be for the one seeking her advice, without regard for the truth, in some instances.
> N. Ms. Furman, as part of her comprehensive legal assistance, gave advice and direction on how and where to file documents with instructions on how to technically prepare and litigate the case in Court.

O. Ms. Furman was available to her customers to correct erroneous or legally deficient pleadings that she had prepared, and to remedy problems experienced by her customers during the dissolution hearing which otherwise frustrated a conclusion thereto.

P. Ms. Furman professed to her customers to have knowledge of the weight and credibility that judges attach and give to legal documents and crucial legal information and evidence.

Q. Ms. Furman participated in oral dialogues with her customers regarding such issues as money for the support of children, safety of children from abusing parents, the placement of children with the most deserving parent, available remedies and options for litigating parties, her interpretation and understanding of legal documents and pertinent statutes, the financial status of husbands and wives as they bore on their need or ability to receive or pay, the ability of her customers to comply with financial Court-ordered obligations, the importance of Court orders and complications therewith, and corrective procedures for defective dissolution proceedings.

R. Ms. Furman, in each case, was paid a monetary fee ranging up to $100.00. *Furman*, 451 So.2d at 813–14.

As previously noted, the result of Furman's unwillingness or inability to adhere to the court's first ruling enjoining her practice was that she was held in contempt of court. The referee recommended that she serve a sentence of two four-month terms in the state prison. The court, though, was not as harsh. It sentenced her to the county jail for 120 days, suspended 90 days, and assessed all legal fees against her.

These cases are very significant. Beyond being one of the first, complete, well-reasoned analyses of typing services and the unauthorized practice of law, Furman's problems are illustrative of the activities undertaken by many nonlawyers who begin typing services.

Note the referee's specific findings. Each individual finding might have been enough to uphold Furman's conviction for contempt. These findings aptly demonstrate conduct that should be avoided by nonlawyers.

Additionally, Furman's problems spawned a statewide study concerning whether the legal needs of the Florida public were being met.

> Devising means for providing effective legal services to the indigent and poor is a continuing problem. . . . In spite of laudable efforts by the bar, however, this record suggests that even more attention needs to be given to this subject.
>
> Therefore, we direct The Florida Bar to begin immediately a study to determine better ways and means of providing legal services to the indigent. *Furman*, 376 So.2d at 382.

Furman's case is cited repeatedly by courts all over the country as a leading statement on what constitutes the practice of law. Despite this notoriety, or perhaps because of it, Furman has become a "folk hero" of sorts to some of those who seek to open legal processes to nonlawyers.

EXERCISE 3.7

Ralph recently graduated from Pinewood County Community College's Paralegal Studies Program. The program is two years long and exposes its students to many different kinds of legal forms and theories. One of the specialties of the program's director, Lee Krowski, is Family Law. For this reason, it is the best class and, when most of the students graduate, they get jobs in this area.

Ralph has decided to set up an office for filling out dissolution of marriage forms. From a recent inheritance, he will pay the overhead of hiring secretaries and renting space.

Please discuss potential problems Ralph faces.

Unauthorized practice of law issues also arise where nonlawyers operate typing services to assist in preparing **bankruptcy** petitions. Cases that have analyzed these situations build upon the principles discussed in *Furman*.

Bankruptcy The inability to pay debts as they are due.

In their eagerness to help people manage their debts, nonlawyers who prepare bankruptcy documents often make the same mistakes Furman made. For instance, look at the activities of Tom Kavanaugh, acting as San Diego Paralegal Services, who was punished for engaging in the practice of law:

> Kavanaugh held himself out to be qualified to give advice concerning bankruptcies. He interviewed debtor and solicited information from her, from which he selected and prepared bankruptcy schedules. He advised Anderson of her legal rights vis-a-vis secured collateral and of the differences between a Chapter 13 filing and one under Chapter 7. He further (incorrectly) advised her regarding the necessity to file amendments to her schedules to accurately reflect an increased tax refund. It also appears that he selected her exemptions. All of these acts require the exercise of legal judgment beyond the knowledge and capacity of the lay person. *In re Anderson*, 79 B.R. 482, 485 (Bkrtcy. S.D. Cal. 1987).

In re Bachmann, 113 B.R. 769 (Bkrtcy. S.D. Fla. 1990), another bankruptcy case, is especially important to consider, for it developed specific guidelines to which all typing services should adhere. *Bachmann* examined the activities of a typing service that prepared bankruptcy forms for debtors. According to the court, the typing service, Capitol Business Services, was operated by a nonlawyer, Paul C. Meyer. Meyer offered advice and counseling to debtors concerning the preparation of bankruptcy petitions, schedules, and statements, advice that requires "legal judgment requiring legal knowledge, trainings, skill and ability beyond that possessed by the average lay person." *Bachmann*, 113 B.R. at 773. Additionally, Meyer drafted and prepared bankruptcy documents.

However, the court went beyond simply discussing an appropriate discipline for Meyer. It offered guidelines to be strictly followed by all legal assistants aiding indigent debtors. Meyer's activities, performed on a regular basis for a fee, constituted the unauthorized practice of law.

The guidelines state:

> "Typing services", including Mr. Meyer, may type bankruptcy forms for their clients, provided they only copy the written information furnished by his clients. They may not advise clients as to the various remedies and procedures available in the Bankruptcy system. Mr. Meyer and representatives of typing services may not make inquiries nor answer questions as to the completion of particular bankruptcy forms or schedules nor advise how to best fill out bankruptcy forms or complete schedules. They may legally sell bankruptcy forms and any printed material purporting to explain bankruptcy practice and procedure to the public. Under no circumstance may they engage in personal legal assistance in conjunction with typing service business activities, including the correction of errors and omissions.

Exhibit 3.2
Bachmann
Guidelines·for
Typing Services

Nonlawyers may/should:

Type legal forms, copying the information supplied by the clients.

Sell business forms and materials explaining legal processes.

Tape record information taken orally from clients.

However, nonlawyers should not:

Make inquiries.

Answer questions.

Correct errors in information.

Advise as to remedies and procedures.

A problem arises when information is taken orally. Under these circumstances, we are faced with determining what was actually said.

From Mr. Meyer's testimony, it is clear that his memory is not good in that area and the memory or notes of a typing service representative are not sufficient. There were numerous questions asked about what was said that Mr. Meyer just did not remember. Accordingly, it is suggested that typing services may take information from clients orally provided that they record the conversations and preserve the tapes. These tapes must be available at the first meeting of creditors. There is no reason why Mr. Meyer or others cannot charge additional compensation for the cost of using and storing the tapes. The small charge will be more than offset by the precision of the record. *Bachmann,* 113 B.R. at 774.

Since their inception, the *Bachmann* guidelines have been applied in other cases. For instance, the principles of *Bachmann* were violated by Wyoming Document Center and Big Sky Investments in *In re Herren,* 138 B.R. 989 (Bkrtcy. D. Wyo. 1992). Noting that *Bachmann* prohibits typing services from making inquiries of the client to assist in completing bankruptcy forms or advising how to best fill out those forms, the court found that defendants had rendered legal advice, "complete with statutory reference."

Remember, the *Bachmann* guidelines are especially noteworthy since they are applicable to any legal assistant offering *any* kind of typing service. Consideration of these guidelines should not be confined to analyzing the activities of those offering help with bankruptcy petitions.

EXERCISE 3.8

Lauren has just experienced a particularly difficult financial period. Her widowed mother, who has no medical insurance, was hospitalized last month for a serious illness, and Lauren has assumed the responsibility for paying the rather substantial medical bills. However, last week Lauren was laid off from her employment after her company recorded several millions of dollars of losses due to poor investments.

Reading the newspaper one evening, Lauren noticed an advertisement proclaiming, "Solve Your Financial Problems. Low Cost, Easy Bankruptcies. Let Me Help You Complete Your Bankruptcy Forms. Call Julie Cooley." Lauren decided that maybe bankruptcy was the answer and placed a call to Cooley, the woman from the advertisement, for help with filing a bankruptcy petition.

Cooley met Lauren the next day. She told Lauren she was not a lawyer but a legal assistant and, as such, she could do everything that an attorney could do except directly represent clients. Then Cooley pulled out a book of bankruptcy forms and asked Lauren what kind of bankruptcy she was looking to file. When Lauren responded that she did not know there were different kinds from which she could choose, Cooley explained the differences between Chapter 7, Chapter 11, and Chapter 13 bankruptcies. Lauren chose to file a Chapter 7 bankruptcy petition, and Cooley immediately began to ask her questions to complete the form. Cooley typed as Lauren spoke.

When it came time to discuss the exemptions Lauren could claim, Lauren became very confused. Cooley informed Lauren that she did not really seem to understand how to determine what property should be exempted. When Lauren asked for clarification, Cooley proceeded to (incorrectly) explain the process of filing exemptions. Cooley then advised Lauren that she might exempt her home.

Finally Cooley finished typing Lauren's forms. Cooley reminded Lauren that she had merely typed the documents for her and then asked for her fee, noting that if Lauren had sought the advice of an attorney, she would have been charged a substantially larger sum of money.

Apply the guidelines set forth in *Bachmann*. In what activities did Cooley engage that violated these rules? How can she adjust her practice so as to comply with these guidelines? Would your answer change if you knew that Cooley worked under the supervision and at the direction of an attorney?

The guidelines discussed in *Bachmann* are applicable in examining nonlawyers working within the **probate process.** In other words, laypersons cannot advise clients, represent them in court, or prepare their legal documents. Therefore, "[d]rafting a will for another person, advising another person how to draft a will or supervising its execution are activities which constitute the practice of law." *Brammer v. Taylor*, 175 W.Va. 728, 338 S.E.2d 207, 212 (1985).

Probate Process A process by which a will is proved to be valid or invalid.

Although nonlawyers may not address the specific problems of a particular client and offer advice in an attempt to solve that problem, they may be allowed, in some instances, to market generalized legal advice to the lay public. As *Bachmann* suggests, nonlawyers may sell general materials explaining legal documents.

Most often, offering general legal advice is accomplished through the publication and sale of a book or other self-help materials. For example, the publication of a book entitled "How To Avoid Probate!", which contained probate forms and general instructions for completing those forms, has been found to *not* constitute the practice of law. Although the trial court issued an injunction to stop distribution of the book, the appellate court reversed, adopting Justice Stephens's well-reasoned dissent from the trial court's opinion.

> Dacey's book is sold to the public at large. There is no personal contact or relationship with a particular individual. Nor does there exist that relation of confidence and trust so necessary to the status of attorney and client. This is the essence of legal practice—the representation and the advising of a particular person in a particular situation. *New York County Lawyers Ass'n v. Dacey*, 28 A.D.2d 161, 283 N.Y.S.2d 984, 998 (1967), J. Stephens dissenting, *rev'd* 21 N.Y.2d 694, 287 N.Y.S.2d 422, 234 N.E.2d 459 (1967).

However, a recent decision from Texas indicates that such practice may not be condoned in that jurisdiction. The preparation and sale of a will manual that included instructions on how to prepare a will and fill-in-the-blank forms was recently held to constitute the unauthorized practice of law.

The Texas court of appeals rejected the defendant's encouragement to "accept the new age of legal self-help clinics." *Fadia v. Unauthorized Practice of*

Law Committee, 830 S.W.2d 162, 164 (Tex. App. 1992). Concluding that Fadia's manual, entitled "You and Your Will: A Do-It-Yourself Manual," went beyond offering simple layman's advice, the court determined that Fadia purported to advise purchasers of the manual how to draft a will. According to the court, such advice is legal advice. Ultimately, the court noted, "The selling of legal advice is the practice of law. Fadia sold his for $24.95." *Fadia,* 830 S.W.2d at 165. The court then held that Fadia could no longer sell his will manual.

It is difficult to reconcile *Fadia* with *Dacey.* In fact, *Fadia* is difficult to reconcile with modern-day practices. Consider the fact that many bookstores today sell form books that instruct readers about how to complete a will or draft a small-claims complaint. Law librarians often instruct library patrons on how to find a book and then how to use the book. This ambiguity just emphasizes the need for legal assistants to stay apprised of changes or variations in how the practice of law is interpreted.

EXERCISE 3.9

Kay Guten's husband passed away in April. This past May, Kay went into the law offices of Rosario N. Juanez, who specializes in Wills, Trusts and Probate, for help in probating her husband's estate. While sitting in the reception room, weeping, Kay was noticed by Griffin Landrum, Juanez's legal assistant. Landrum asked Kay whether there was anything he could do to help her. He was on his way out the door but, when she asked some general questions about how wills are drafted and how property is disposed of when someone dies, he told her he could give her something to look at until Ms. Juanez was able to meet with her.

Landrum went into his office and took the first book he could find dealing with wills. It was a text he had used in his paralegal studies classes.

Landrum earmarked several pages he believed might be pertinent. He handed the book to Kay and told her he would return in an hour but that he felt certain Ms. Juanez would have met with her by that time. He asked that she return the book to Ms. Juanez.

Has Landrum engaged in any activity that might be considered the practice of law? If so, do you think his employer should be held accountable for his actions?

REAL ESTATE

Real estate is another area in which laypersons are actively involved. Many nonlawyers assist in drafting real estate documents. If the legal assistant is working under the supervision of an attorney, this activity is acceptable and appreciated. However, what happens when a nonlawyer attempts to handle such work independently of an attorney, much as a typing service does?

Just as they have with bankruptcy services and divorce kits, courts have generally determined that, if services are not limited to activities of a clerical nature, the person who is engaging in them is engaged in the unauthorized practice of law. This has taken place in every facet of real estate transactions including preparation of deeds, notes, bills of sale, title certificates, real estate and mortgage closings, and most recently, eviction services.

The legal profession is beginning to witness the relaxation of this rule, however. For example, despite the previously discussed, predetermined limits of "the practice of law," nonlawyers in Washington state are allowed, in some instances, to handle **real estate closings** independently of an attorney. The state of Washington's "Practice Rule 12" (Rule), entitled "Limited Practice Rule for Closing Officers" and in force since 1983, established a system akin to the limited licensure schemes addressed in chapter 1.

Real Estate Closings The final steps in a transaction for the sale of real estate.

The Rule authorizes certain lay persons to select, prepare and complete legal documents that relate to real estate closings and personal property transactions. It prescribes the conditions and limitations upon such activities. It establishes a board whose function is to regulate the activities of closing officers and, where necessary, to institute disciplinary measures for ethical violations. The Rule also imposes certification requirements, including passing an examination, and mandates that closing officers fulfill continuing education requirements to maintain their certification.

Legal assistants who work under the supervision of attorneys are also involved in real estate closings. As noted above, under the supervision of an attorney, the legal assistant may prepare closing forms for the signature of the attorney. However, the legal assistant may also be allowed, in certain jurisdictions, to participate in the real estate closing session.

This means the legal assistant may accompany the client to the real estate closing. At this conference, the paralegal assists the client who must sign various forms that have been prepared long before the closing date, to complete the sale of the property. The lawyer is not present but is available by phone if a problem arises and her assistance is necessary to complete the transaction. An important caveat attaches to the practice of sending legal assistants to handle closings. Although the paralegal may be allowed, in certain jurisdictions, to attend this session, *the paralegal may not give legal advice nor may he enter into any negotiations on behalf of the client.*

Those jurisdictions that keep legal assistants from handling real estate closings have indicated, generally, that limits upon layperson activity are necessary because even the simplest of conveyances may involve legal issues that are simply too complicated for a layperson to be expected to solve. Complex issues of taxation, estate planning, future interests, water rights, equitable conversion, covenants, and easements are just a few of the areas that may spill over into what may appear, at first blush, to be a "simple closing."

Consult the statutes in your jurisdiction under the professions and occupations section. See if you can find how your state regulates nonlawyers handling real estate closings. In your state, are nonlawyers prohibited from representing clients at the closing?

EXERCISE 3.10

DISCLOSURE OF NONLAWYER STATUS

It is important to discuss one practical aspect of the paralegal's attempts to avoid prosecution for the unauthorized practice of law. Regardless of the capacity in which the legal assistant provides services—whether she is working as a litigation paralegal or in real estate—when she first meets the parties, it is imperative that she **disclose** her **nonlawyer status.** She should similarly make her nonlawyer status clear to all people, be they clients, court personnel, or other attorneys.

Disclosure of Nonlawyer Status A rule whereby nonlawyers should always clearly identify themselves as such.

This rule of disclosure is made clear in many of the legal assistant guidelines that have been set forth in states such as Illinois, Michigan, and Rhode Island. Additionally, this rule is part of NALA's guidelines and is discussed in the ABA's Model Guidelines.

In section V of the NALA Model Standards and Guidelines for Utilization of Legal Assistants, Annotated, it is revealed:

Legal assistants should:
1. Disclose their status as legal assistants at the outset of any professional relationship with a client, other attorneys, a court or administrative agency or personnel thereof, or members of the general public; .... [7]

Likewise, the ABA Model Guidelines for Legal Assistant Services make clear in Guideline 4:

It is the lawyer's responsibility to take reasonable measures to ensure that clients, courts, and other lawyers are aware that a legal assistant, whose services are utilized by the lawyer in performing legal services, is not licensed to practice law.[8]

As you begin your career, it will become clear that you will come into contact with many people while performing your duties. Legal assistants are often given responsibility for meeting with clients and conducting the initial client interview. At other times, legal assistants may be asked to contact opposing counsel concerning a discovery matter or to file papers with the court.

This sort of third-party contact is a typical part of any paralegal's day, whether she is involved in real estate, corporate matters, or litigation. Despite a paralegal's scrupulous adherence to all of the previously discussed rules, she still risks running afoul of unauthorized practice of law rules should she fail to reveal her nonlawyer status to these individuals.

Why is that? Because clients, witnesses, and opposing counsel might become confused by the paralegal's role in the case. Then, clients might ask legal assistants for legal advice, or the opposing attorney may call and ask that the woman who has been handling the discovery matters draft a letter to the judge informing him that the case has been settled out-of-court.

When a paralegal fails to announce her nonlawyer status, she places herself in an awkward position. The paralegal may not have engaged in the unauthorized practice of law, but by creating that appearance, others may believe she has done so and attempt to report her or even her supervisor as having violated the rules.

For example, if Paul Paralegal does not reveal to Chloe Client that he is not licensed to practice law, Chloe Client may discover such information long after her representation is established and long after she has already made assumptions about her relationship with Paul. Upon reflection, Chloe may believe Paul has helped her so much that his work was similar to that completed by an attorney. However, after Paul's employer loses Chloe's case, she may conclude the loss was due to the fact that a nonlawyer handled matters that should only have been handled by an attorney. Despite the fact that Paul

[7] NALA Model Standards and Guidelines for Utilization of Legal Assistants Annotated, §V, © 1984, revised 1991 National Association of Legal Assistants, Inc. Reprinted by permission.
[8] Guideline 4, ABA Model Guidelines for the Utilization of Legal Assistant Services, ©1991 American Bar Association. Reprinted by permission.

scrupulously followed the rules as set forth in this chapter, his behavior may be reported to the state's attorney who might initiate an investigation of Paul's activities as a violation of the unauthorized practice of law statutes. Paul's employer may likewise be reported to his state attorney disciplinary commission.

A legal assistant, therefore, must take care to reveal her nonlawyer status whenever she is asked to identify herself. This extends beyond face-to-face meetings and telephone conversations. As will be further discussed in chapter 8, the nonlawyer should be sure to include his title, usually "paralegal" or "legal assistant," on any papers identifying him, including business cards, law firm stationery, or when signing correspondence.

CONSEQUENCES OF VIOLATING PRACTICE OF LAW RULES

Because the legal profession views acts constituting the unauthorized practice of law to be potentially dangerous to the public, violations of the practice of law rules warrant serious sanctions. The legal assistant is technically the one who has engaged in the unauthorized practice of law. However, the attorney will be found culpable for aiding in this practice.

THE CONSEQUENCES FOR THE ATTORNEY

Both the *Model Code of Professional Responsibility* and the *Model Rules of Professional Conduct* forbid an attorney to aid in the unauthorized practice of law.

Disciplinary Rule 3-101(A) of the ABA *Model Code of Professional Responsibility* provides: "A lawyer shall not aid a non-lawyer in the unauthorized practice of law." The accompanying ethical consideration allows delegation of work to laypersons including secretaries and clerks. However, it is imperative that the attorney maintain supervision over nonlawyer employees and responsibility for the delegated work product. Specifically, the Ethical Considerations provide:

> A lawyer often delegates tasks to clerks, secretaries, and other lay persons. Such delegation is proper if the lawyer maintains a direct relationship with his client, supervises the delegated work, and has complete professional responsibility for the work product. This delegation enables a lawyer to render legal service more economically and efficiently. *ABA Model Code of Professional Responsibility* EC 3-6 (1986).

To avoid the possibility of being disciplined for violation of ethical rules, therefore, attorneys must actively regulate the activities of the paralegals to whom they pass along work responsibilities.

Failing to provide the necessary supervision can have disastrous consequences for an attorney. Depending on the degree to which the attorney neglects to supervise the legal assistant and thus fosters the unauthorized practice of law, the attorney may be sanctioned with anything from a simple reprimand to disbarment.

A reprimand—public or private—is often the sanction imposed on the attorney who assists in the unauthorized practice of law through *negligence* in supervising staff. This sanction is usually reserved for those who cause injury to the client through their negligence. A more serious punishment—a suspension, or removal of the attorney from the practice of law for a period of time—may be imposed when attorneys *knowingly* engage in conduct that violates the ethical obligation to avoid aiding the unauthorized practice of law.

The most serious punishment is disbarment, or permanent removal of the attorney from the roll of attorneys licensed to practice law in that state. This is usually recommended to the state court of last resort by the attorney disciplinary agency if an attorney *knowingly engages in assisting* in the unauthorized practice of law. Often, the state disciplinary agency must find that the activity which is considered to have constituted the unauthorized practice of law must have conferred a benefit on the attorney and caused injury or have the potential to cause injury to the client. See *Louisiana State Bar v. Edwins* for a general discussion of these principles.

This is not to suggest that the attorney even needs to be aware of the paralegal's unauthorized activity before that attorney can be disciplined for it. She does not. When a client is injured, courts seek redress on behalf of the client who has sustained those injuries. More often than not, however, under these circumstances, when attorneys are aware of the activity, they are disciplined for having condoned it.

For example, in *In the Matter of Silber*, 100 N.J. 517, 497 A.2d 1249 (1985), the conduct of an attorney who had aided in the unauthorized practice of law was found to be serious enough to warrant a reprimand. Attorney Silber was busy with a client and instructed his law clerk, who was not licensed to practice law, to accompany another client to a court call. Although Silber had told the law clerk, outside the presence of the client, that she was to call him as soon as he was required to appear at the call, the clerk instead informed the client that she would be representing the client at the calendar call.

The law clerk proceeded to negotiate with opposing counsel and represented the client in court, questioned witnesses, and argued before the judge. Silber had never authorized this conduct, but when he realized what had happened, he took steps to cover up the fact that the law clerk had engaged in the unauthorized practice of law. The court therefore found that, because Silber had not taken any action to inform the court of the illegal action, he had aided in the unauthorized practice of law, violating DR 3-101(A), and therefore should be reprimanded.

EXERCISE 3.11

Assume that Toyoko Eguchi, an attorney, has been working closely with her legal assistant, Soo, for several years. Because she has taken on several new, important clients, Eguchi has become very busy as of late. Desiring to somewhat ease her boss's workload, Soo begins signing Eguchi's name to pleadings without Eguchi's knowledge.

Should Eguchi be disciplined for Soo's actions?

Now assume that Eguchi asks Soo to appear at a deposition for her. What discipline do you think is most appropriate for Eguchi?

SANCTIONS AGAINST THE NONLAWYER

The nonlawyer is likewise subject to disciplinary action for violating unauthorized practice of law statutes. Although the state disciplinary agency cannot discipline the nonlawyer, other kinds of sanctions may be levied against the legal assistant.

As we saw in "The People's Court," when a nonlawyer offers to provide services for another, the parties may attempt to secure their individual rights through a contract for services. In this contract the nonlawyer usually agrees to provide some service for a particular fee. Often, upon finding that the nonlawyer engaged in the unauthorized practice of law, the courts will declare the contract between the parties to be a nullity. When declared a nullity, it is as if the contract never existed. Therefore the nonlawyer is forced to forego any fee for services already rendered.

In *Duncan v. Gordon,* 476 So.2d 896 (La. App. 1985), just such an event occurred. When he was nineteen years old, Frederick Duncan was involved in an automobile accident in which he sustained injuries to his back. Rosa Gordon, a nonlawyer, began advising Duncan of the steps he should undertake to secure his claims for damages. Soon Gordon began taking a greater role in this potential settlement. Eventually the two entered into a written fifty percent contingent fee agreement. The contract stated that Gordon was to represent Duncan in any settlement discussions with the insurance company. She soon settled Duncan's claim for $3000.00; pursuant to the contract, she divided the check in half, giving Duncan only $1500.00 less his medical expenses and the transportation expenses she had incurred driving Duncan to his doctor visits. Ultimately, Duncan received only $604.50 out of the entire settlement check. Gordon received the remainder of the money, minus a small sum paid for medical services rendered.

Because he was dissatisfied with the amount of money he had received, Duncan sought to have the contract declared illegal and against the public policy of the state. The court did just that, declaring, "[a]ny contracts made by a non-lawyer to render services in violation of this provision [LSA-R.S. 37:213, the unauthorized practice of law provision in Louisiana] are for an unlawful cause. Consequently, they are against public policy and absolutely null." *Duncan,* 476 So.2d at 897.

Courts have also ordered the nonlawyer to pay court costs of the proceedings in which they are declared to be practicing law. For instance, when Isabel Rodriguez, d/b/a ABC General Services, was permanently enjoined from further engaging in what the court deemed was the practice of law, she was also assessed costs in the amount of $525.32. *The Florida Bar v. Rodriguez, d/b/a ABC General Services,* 509 So.2d 1111 (Fla. 1987).

Injunction/Enjoin A prohibitive, equitable remedy, issued by a court, to forbid someone to do an act that he or she is threatening to do, or restrain him or her from continuing the act.

In rendering decisions that find the nonlawyer guilty of the unauthorized practice of law, courts frequently **enjoin** the nonlawyer from practicing law any further. Should this **injunction** order be violated, the nonlawyer may be held in contempt of court and face stiff penalties including a prison sentence.

Recall *Furman* from earlier in this chapter. In 1979 Rosemary Furman was enjoined from practicing law any further. *The Florida Bar v. Furman,* 376 So.2d 378 (Fla. 1979). Despite this injunction, Furman continued to operate her alleged "typing service," assisting individuals in completing legal documents.

In 1984 Furman found herself before the court again, for violating the injunctive order. Because she had disregarded the prior order, she was held in contempt of the court order and was sentenced to 120 days in the county jail. (The court suspended 90 days of this sentence and stated that if Furman did not practice law for the next two years, the suspended 90-day sentence would be deemed satisfied.) See *Florida Bar v. Furman*, 451 So.2d 808 (Fla. 1984).

Legal assistants who work under the supervision of an attorney must concern themselves with an additional potential sanction: They may lose their jobs. Even worse, they may lose the right to become attorneys at law.

Many nonlawyers working within the legal profession decide they should consider attending law school. Clearly, they enjoy applying the law to factual situations, and perhaps they tire of running up against the limits set by unauthorized practice statutes, so they seek to obtain the right to legally practice law.

However, if a nonlawyer has ever been brought before a court to answer to unauthorized practice charges, he may find that states are reluctant to grant a law license. For instance, Paul Demos had been held in contempt of court while working as a law clerk for his father's law firm when he participated in a deposition and was found guilty of the unauthorized practice of law. The court stated: "The sum of several events in the State of New Mexico [including unauthorized practice of law charges] casts serious doubt upon the applicant's character." *In re Demos*, 579 A.2d 668 (D.C. App. 1990). Demos was then denied admission to the D.C. bar.

THE CHANGING NATURE OF NONLAWYER PRACTICE

Undeniably, the paralegal profession has undergone tremendous change over the past few decades. Substantial changes continue in the extent to which nonlawyers are permitted to handle matters that were traditionally handled exclusively by lawyers. These changes are seen in the responsibilities that freelance paralegals have become entitled to handle, as well as in the tremendous amount of time and effort the American Bar Association has expended in studying nonlawyer practice. This is seen in the following materials.

THE FREELANCE PARALEGAL

Many paralegals have turned to freelance paralegal work in search of new challenges and broader horizons. The role played by freelance paralegals has been considered by the courts of at least one state, New Jersey.

Many people do not make a distinction between the "independent" and the "freelance" paralegal. Yet, you will recall from chapter 1, however, that many working in the legal profession believe the terms are distinct, with "freelance" meaning contracts with an attorney and "independent" meaning works directly with the public.

In the discussion that follows regarding an opinion by the New Jersey Supreme Court, the court used the words interchangeably. However, it is important to note that though the court referred to "independent" paralegals or those paralegals who work under the direction of an attorney, generally they do not.

In Opinion No. 24 the New Jersey Committee on the Unauthorized Practice of Law, which had appointed a committee to study the problem, dissected the relationship shared by the independent paralegal and the attorney. After much analysis, the committee concluded that the freelance paralegal "is always engaged in the unauthorized practice of law."

This conclusion was reached after the committee's analysis revealed that the necessary attorney supervision over the nonlawyer employee was wanting where a freelance paralegal was retained.

The committee tested several factors in reaching its decision. Among these, it was noted that many independent paralegals are hired by attorneys to provide an expertise that the attorney lacks in a particular area of law. In other words, the supervision required by the attorney in this situation becomes "illusory" and, instead, the paralegal becomes a "substitute" for another attorney.

Although many witnesses before the committee argued that the need to provide low-cost legal services could be met through the use of freelance paralegals, the committee soundly rejected this argument. The committee noted that persons not subject to uniform standards, not subject to training should not be allowed to provide legal services and, thus, practice law. It stated: ". . . by performing legal services without such adequate supervision those paralegals are engaging in the unauthorized practice of law." *See In re Opinion No. 24*, 128 N.J. 114, 607 A.2d 962, 966 (1992). The committee reasoned that there were enough attorneys and legal service programs to fill the need for legal services.

Opinion No. 24 was appealed to the New Jersey Supreme Court by a group calling themselves "Independent Paralegals and/or Legal Assistants Doing Business in the State of New Jersey." *In re Opinion No. 24*, 128 N.J. 114, 607 A.2d 962 (1992). Amicus briefs were submitted by a variety of paralegal associations. After a lengthy, thorough discussion of the issues raised by Opinion No. 24, the New Jersey Supreme Court determined that independent paralegals were not practicing law, as long as they received adequate supervision by an attorney, and thereupon reversed the decision reached in Opinion No. 24.

The court began by discussing the difficulty inherent in attempting to define the practice of law. Noting that there "is no question that a paralegal's work constitutes the practice of law[,]" the court explained that what prevents paralegals from being disciplined under unauthorized practice statutes is the fact that their work is supervised by an attorney. The court further recognized that paralegals are increasingly becoming valued members of the legal profession.

> Independent paralegals work either at a "paralegal firm" or freelance. Most are employed by sole practitioners or smaller firms who cannot afford the services of a full-time paralegal. Like large law firms, small firms find that using paralegals helps them provide effective and economical service to their clients. Requiring paralegals to be full-time employees of law firms would thus deny attorneys not associated with large law firms the very valuable services of paralegals." *In re Opinion No. 24*, 607 A.2d at 967.

Recognizing that the important issue in this case is not the status of the paralegal but rather whether he is working under an attorney's supervision, the court went on to decree that a paralegal who is aware that the attorney's supervision is merely "illusory" is required to withdraw from any work product for that particular client.

The overriding problem, as declared by the court, was *the lack of a regulatory body for paralegals*. Regulation would ensure that unqualified persons were not employed as paralegals and would possibly play a role in preventing conflicts of interest.

In re Opinion No. 24 was truly a sweeping endorsement of the paralegal profession. Although its impact has not yet been fully appreciated, it is sure to have a profound effect upon the future of this career.

THE AMERICAN BAR ASSOCIATION COMMISSION ON NONLAWYER PRACTICE

In December of 1992, continuing through October 1993, the **American Bar Association Commission on Nonlawyer Practice** conducted a number of public regional hearings on the topic of nonlawyers providing legal service to the public. Specifically, during the hearings, the Commission related that it was created to determine implications of nonlawyer practice for society, the client and the legal profession.

The hearings took place in major metropolitan cities. The cities included Orlando, Florida; San Antonio, Texas; Boston, Massachusetts; Sacramento, California; Chicago, Illinois; New York, New York; and Phoenix, Arizona. The hearing sites were selected to represent geographic locations. The Commission sought testimony from lawyers, nonlawyers either working under a lawyer's supervision or working independently, members of the judiciary, and consumers (individuals, interest groups, and business entities).

The Commission made clear that it was directed to "determine the best way to provide the highest quality legal services to all current and potential consumers of legal services."[9]

The predecessor Working Group on Nonlawyer Practice stated in its closing report: "The legal profession now finds itself at a crossroads traversed in recent decades by the medical profession when the allied (medical) professions were successfully established as separate and distinct disciplines [from physicians]."[10]

Former counsel to the American Bar Association Commisssion on Nonlawyer Practice, Mr. David Brent, has this to say about the public hearings:

> The hearings enabled the Commission to receive a broad cross-section of information about this sensitive subject.[11]

Regulatory Body An organization designed to oversee/regulate the conduct of its members.

American Bar Association Commission on Nonlawyer Practice A commission created to determine implications of nonlawyer legal practice for society, the client, and the legal profession.

---

[9] American Bar Association Press Release entitled "ABA Commission Seeks Testimony On Delivery Of Legal Services By Nonlawyers."

[10] *Id.*

[11] Interview with Mr. David Brent.

FOCUS ON INGRID-JOY WARRICK

In 1990 Ingrid-Joy Warrick and Jacqueline Wall, two paralegals educated and working in Chicago, started a legal self-help business named FormFillers of Illinois, Inc.

FormFillers sells more than a dozen self-help legal packages, addressing areas

The general public is more sophisticated than legal professionals imagine. Many people know exactly what they want done. They just don't know how to go about getting it done. That's where a service like that provided by FormFillers comes into play.

such as "uncontested divorces" and "co-habitation agreements," to assist *pro se* litigants complete the forms required to be filed in the Cook County, Illinois, court system. They are currently working on form packets for the federal courts.

FormFillers also provides a Document Completion Service that operates much like a typical typing service.

Because Warrick is aware that the unauthorized practice of law exists, FormFillers has implemented measures designed to protect itself. All of the packages are written and reviewed by hired attorneys. A supportive network of attorneys is in place so that questions can be asked of them by paralegals employed by FormFillers. Employees are instructed to accept only

clients who understand their legal rights and know the remedy they seek. If a client is unsure about the remedy he seeks, he is immediately referred to an attorney.

Throughout her career, Warrick has seen paralegals stepping over the limits of the practice of law. Mainly she believes violations are caused by the nonlawyer's ignorance. "There's always the renegade who assumes that he or she knows everything, but, in actuality, they just don't know enough," cautions Warrick.

Warrick strongly supports educational requirements for paralegals to show them how to refrain from engaging in the practice of law. In fact, she advises future paralegals to enroll in an educational program that instructs students "how to think" and how to analyze a situation for potential problems.

Nonetheless, the founder of FormFillers believes nonlawyers are capable of handling a wide variety of legal problems, although she is quick to point out that nonlawyers offering legal services should be held to the same standards as attorneys. For example, nonlawyers should be able to handle real estate closings or simple bankruptcies. Warrick notes that such practice will not infringe upon the market of "mom and pop" law firms who are not interested in financing their practice with, say, $75.00 divorces. Also, says Warrick, "Many of those who use the FormFillers packets would simply never seek out personal legal service because they are afraid that it would be cost-prohibitive."

Warrick is one professional who clearly believes nonlawyers can play a role in assisting *pro se* litigants through the legal system. FormFillers has some very satisfied customers to prove it.

TIPS FOR PARALEGALS

■ Make it your policy to explain your nonlawyer status to all parties at your first meeting with clients, opposing counsel, prospective witnesses, etc.

■ Understand your limitations when conducting the initial client interview: You may not establish an attorney-client relationship or a fee arrangement.

■ Talk to your supervising attorney about the feasibility of drawing up a form with questions to be asked during the initial client interview.

■ Relay the attorney's legal advice to the client but do not give independent legal advice.

■ Whenever you prepare pleadings, court documents, interrogatories, answers to interrogatories, and deposition questions, take them to your supervising attorney for his review and signature.

■ Feel free to assist in trial preparation, but do not represent the client in court.

■ Before appearing in an administrative agency proceeding or in court on behalf of another, research the law to determine whether you are permitted to appear on behalf of clients, in court on routine matters, or before administrative agencies.

■ Before appearing in an administrative proceeding or in court on behalf of another, attend a few sessions where other nonlawyers appear in that courtroom to learn the judge's policies when nonlawyers appear before her.

■ If you call your business a "typing service" or prepare things such as "divorce kits," limit your activities to taking information from the client.

■ If you call your business a "typing service" or you prepare things such as "divorce kits," consider preparing a list of questions to be asked of prospective clients to make sure that handling their business will not involve the exercise of independent legal judgment.

CLOSING EXERCISE

Anne is an experienced paralegal who lives in Charlotte, N.C. She has worked for the same attorney, Mr. K., for twenty-two years. As their working relationship developed, Mr. K. grew to trust Anne's skills and professionalism. Anne therefore was asked to prepare pleadings, real estate closing documents, answers to interrogatories, and bankruptcy petitions for Mr. K.'s review and signature. She has also helped to prepare for trial and has even attended trials with Mr. K., sitting at counsel's table.

Last year, Mr. K. discovered he was ill. Nonetheless, because he was able to help so many people in his practice, he decided to keep the law office open.

As Mr. K. grew weaker, Anne began shouldering more of the responsibilities for managing the law office and clients' affairs. On one particularly hectic afternoon, Anne realized that the following activities were scheduled for the next day:

8:00 Mr. K. Deposition of Expert witness in Barbery case.

10:00 Mr. K. Meet with Am Trust client to advise as to strategies to consider for trial.

12:00 Mr. K. Attend pre-trial conference for Zisker trial.

2:00 Mr. K. Court appearance: Advise court of status of Mau case.

3:00 Mr. K. Initial client interview with Mr. Hareen.

4:00 Mr. K. Answer interrogatories for Patterson case.

6:00 Mr. K. Research bankruptcy issue.

On that next day, however, Mr. K. grew so sick that he needed to see his doctor. Medical tests were conducted and consumed the entire day. Trusting Anne's knowledge of the ethics rules, Mr. K. told her to handle as many of his scheduled activities as she could without violating the practice of law rules. Discuss what responsibilities Anne can and cannot assume.

Unfortunately, Mr. K. suddenly and unexpectedly passed away six months later. Unsure of her future direction, Anne began to consider her options. She knew her small home town had blossomed into one of the largest cities in the Carolinas, and there were a number of people now living in the city who were of limited means and could not afford legal services.

Anne sought to remedy what she believed were social and economic inequities. She decided to open a typing service and provide legal assistance to all who sought her help. This assistance took several forms. One was a packet of information regarding separations and divorces. Anne copied forms used by the attorney for whom she worked, along with copies of uniform state statutes and rules that had been used by Mr. K. She prepared "simple" joint wills and mutual wills with the requisite number of lines for witnesses' signatures. She wrote a pamphlet entitled "Bankruptcy Court for the Layperson." She advertised in the *Charlotte Observer* as someone who "is well-versed in real estate closing details and specializes in sale-by-owner house closings."

Last week Anne received a letter from the state bar regulatory agency. She has been told she must stop what she is doing: rendering her brand of legal assistance. She may no longer provide her services. The state bar's committee on the unauthorized practice of law has deemed Anne's services to be the unauthorized practice of law. If she resists the request to stop her work she could, among other potential consequences, be cited for contempt or put in jail.

Please address all issues. Should any sanctions be levied against Anne? If so, what sanctions are appropriate? On what do you base your conclusions?

CHAPTER SUMMARY

■ The practice of law is the exercise of legal judgment to influence the conduct of a third party. It involves giving legal advice, appearing as an advocate in a courtroom or other tribunal, and drafting and signing papers for clients without the review of an attorney.

■ Actions that constitute engaging in the practice of law include, but are not limited to: establishing the attorney-client relationship or fee arrangement; giving independent legal advice to the client; preparing and signing pleadings or other court documents, interrogatories, answers, or questions to be asked at depositions independent of an attorney's authorization; asking questions of witnesses at depositions; and, generally, representing the client in court.

■ In some jurisdictions a nonlawyer is permitted to appear before the court in very limited and specific instances. Additionally, some states might allow representation of prison inmates by nonlawyers or the representation of criminal defendants on a nonrecurring, nonpay basis before a justice or magistrate court.

■ Many federal agencies have specific rules that, despite state unauthorized practice of law statutes, authorize nonlawyers to appear before them to represent the interests of laypersons.

■ Typing services are businesses that are designed to assist the general public in completing complicated legal documents by helping to type information related by the client in the blank spaces of preprinted legal forms. The typing service must not give any legal advice. Remember, the unauthorized practice of law involves exercising independent legal judgment.

■ In some jurisdictions, nonlawyers may appear at real estate closings but may not give legal advice or enter into negotiations on behalf of the client. In these jurisdictions, the attorney must be available by telephone, should any questions or problems arise. In jurisdictions such as Washington, restrictions on nonlawyers assisting in real estate transactions are growing more relaxed. In the state of Washington, nonlawyers are allowed to represent individuals in real estate transactions independently of an attorney.

■ Legal assistants must always disclose their nonlawyer status to clients, opposing counsel, prospective witnesses, and other parties with whom the legal assistant might come into contact during the course of assisting in a client's representation. It is a good policy to disclose nonlawyer status upon first meeting these individuals.

KEY TERMS

American Bar Association
  Commission on
  Nonlawyer Practice
attorney-client
  relationship
bankruptcy
Blackstone's
  Commentaries
contempt of court
continuances
court appearances
deposition

disclosure of nonlawyer
  status
discovery
divorce kits
do-it-yourself/typing
  services
independent legal
  judgment
initial client interview
injunction/enjoin
interrogatory
lay representation

pleadings
practice of law
preemption
probate process
real estate closings
regulatory body
scrivener
status call
trial preparation
unauthorized practice of
  law
writ of habeas corpus

CASE

Louisiana State Bar Association v. Edwins.

Supreme Court of Louisiana, 1989, 540 So.2d 294.

DENNIS, Justice.

This is an attorney disciplinary proceeding in which the bar association seeks to disbar the respondent attorney, Rallie C. Edwins.

The respondent, who was admitted to practice in 1958, is charged with violating (1) Disciplinary Rule 3-101(A), Code of Professional Responsibility of the

State Bar, by aiding and abetting an unlicensed person to practice law in Louisiana, (2) Disciplinary Rule 3-102 by sharing legal fees with a non-lawyer, (3) Disciplinary Rule 6-101(A)(3) by neglecting a legal matter entrusted to him, and (4) Disciplinary Rule 9-102 by failing to place his client's funds in a separate trust account, by failing to notify his client promptly of receipt of the funds, by failing to maintain complete records of his client's funds, by failing to render appropriate accounts to his client regarding them, and by failing to promptly pay or deliver to his client the funds he was entitled to receive.

We find that the respondent committed three of the alleged violations, viz., (1), (3) and (4), and impose a sanction of disbarment.

1. Whether Respondent Aided A Non-Lawyer in the Unauthorized Practice of Law

Facts

Prior to 1982, Rob Robertson, operated a free lance paralegal service in New Iberia under the name of Prepaid Legal Services, Inc. He maintained a small one paralegal office for himself in which he employed his daughter as secretary. Sometime in 1982, Robertson entered a relationship with Edwins, a Baton Rouge attorney, whereby Robertson became Edwins' paralegal, investigator and client-relations representative in the New Iberia area. Edwins employed Robertson on an hourly basis to investigate, screen and evaluate the claims of prospective clients, do legal research, maintain client relations and perform other services. Under the arrangement, Edwins continued to maintain his law office in Baton Rouge but also used the New Iberia office as a branch law office. The Prepaid Legal Services, Inc. sign was taken down and replaced with the sign of Edwins' law firm. Edwins paid part of the office expenses, including rent, secretary and utilities.

In December, 1982, William Livingston conferred with Robertson about personal injuries he had received in an automobile accident. Livingston testified that Robertson told him he was an attorney and agreed to handle his case for a contingent fee. According to Livingston, Robertson agreed to take the case for 30% of recovery before trial and 40% of recovery in court. Sometime after the attorney-client contract had been entered Robertson disclosed to Livingston that Edwins would act as his attorney and that Robertson was Edwins's associate. Livingston did not meet Edwins until after the suit was filed.

Livingston's case was settled in March, 1984. He testified that before Robertson called him and told him to come get his money that he had had no conversations or correspondence with either Robertson or Edwins about the settlement. He said he went to Robertson's office that same day and Robertson gave him $1,000 in cash with the explanation that the rest of the settlement proceeds had been used to pay expenses. He said that Robertson did not tell him the total amount for which his case had been settled, the amount of the attorney's fees he had been charged or the description or the amounts of the expense items deducted from his recovery. Livingston admitted that he may have signed a release but testified that he was not certain because he could not read or write.

Although Robertson failed to testify categorically that he did not hold himself out to be a lawyer to Livingston he did say that he did not tell Livingston he was an attorney, but agreed to investigate the case and present it to Edwins if it appeared to have merit. He added later in his testimony that Livingston could have gotten the impression that he was an attorney because, at Edwins' request, he represented Livingston at a welfare assistance hearing. Robertson admitted that subsequent to the initial interview he represented Edwins in entering an employment contract with Livingston. Further, he testified that his daughter prepared pleadings, motions and legal memoranda in the New Iberia office for Livingston's case. Robertson acknowledged that he signed Edwins' name as attorney to the pleadings and motions, signed for Edwins as notary on an affidavit and filed these legal instruments in court. Robertson also answered and signed for Edwins the interrogatories connected with Livingston's personal injury action. Robertson testified that at this time Edwins was in a hospital in Memphis but that he had dictated the pleadings, motions and memoranda to Robertson's daughter over the telephone. After Edwins left the hospital, Robertson said, he was confined to his Baton Rouge apartment, but the two continued to converse by telephone.

Robertson testified that Edwins negotiated the settlement with the adverse party and mailed him the $9,000 settlement check. He said that when he received the check it contained what purported to be Livingston's endorsement. Livingston and his wife, Theresa Livingston, testified that neither of them had signed the check and that they had never even seen it. Robertson deposited the check in an account over which he had exclusive control and disbursed the funds with his own checks. He was unable to produce any of the cancelled checks to verify his distribution of the funds, however. Nevertheless, he denied that he had received any part of the attorney's fee in the case.

Edwins testified that he never told anyone that Robertson was an attorney or shared legal fees with him. His testimony was ambivalent in other respects, however. Edwins testified in general terms that he had been in the hospital for extensive periods, but he did not corroborate Robertson's testimony regarding Edwins' Memphis hospital and Baton Rouge apartment confinements. Despite his representation by competent counsel during a full hearing he testified and presented documentary evidence only to his confinement in the Baton Rouge Our Lady of the Lake Hospital from September 29, 1984 to October 3, 1984. This evidence was clearly irrelevant to the question of whether Edwins performed legal services for Livingston in absentia from a hospital between December, 1982 and the settlement of Livingston's case in April, 1984.

Although Edwins testified several times that he explained the proposed settlement to Livingston, he could not recall when, where or how the explanation had occurred. Toward the end of his testimony, he admitted that he could remember talking to Livingston's wife and daughter but that Livingston himself had not been told prior to settlement that he would receive only $1,000.

Edwins first testified that he did not authorize Robertson to sign his name to pleadings and that when he learned of Robertson's actions in this regard he put ads in the newspaper announcing the closing of his New Iberia office. A few moments later Edwins admitted, however, that he had authorized Robertson, and perhaps others, to sign his name to pleadings when he was in the hospital. Moreover, he conceded that Livingston's file was kept in the New Iberia office, not in his Baton Rouge office, and no one ever indicated that the file or any part thereof had ever been transported to him to facilitate his performance of legal services while confined to a hospital.

Regarding the disbursement of the settlement funds, Edwins admitted that he received them from the adverse party but that he did not place them in a client's trust account, keep records of such funds, notify Livingston of his receipt of them, deliver any portion of them to Livingston, or render an accounting of such funds to Livingston. Instead, Edwins testified, he endorsed the settlement check and mailed it to Robertson with instructions to handle it however he saw fit. He said he saw no need in accounting to Livingston because Edwins' and Robertson's expenses had exceeded the recovery.

Cooper, the attorney for the adverse party in Livingston's case, testified that he had discussions with both Edwins and Robertson, but that he discussed settlement primarily with Edwins. He said that an adjuster for his client informed him that Robertson initially held himself out as a lawyer but afterwards confessed that he was a "free lance paralegal operating under the Supreme Court ruling." He said that neither Edwins nor Robertson indicated to him that Robertson was an attorney.

. . .

The prohibition against the practice of law by a layman is grounded in the need of the public for integrity and competence of those who undertake to render legal services. EC 3-1. Competent professional judgment is the product of a trained familiarity with law and legal processes, a disciplined, analytical approach to legal problems, and a firm ethical commitment. EC 3-2. A non-lawyer who undertakes to handle legal matters is not governed as to integrity or legal competence by the same rules that govern the conduct of a lawyer. The Disciplinary Rules protect the public in that they prohibit a lawyer from seeking employment by improper overtures, from acting in cases of divided loyalties, and from submitting to the control of others in the exercise of his judgment. EC 3-3. It is neither necessary nor desirable to attempt the formulation of a single, specific definition of what constitutes the practice of law. Functionally, the practice of law relates to the rendition of services for others that call for the professional judgment of a lawyer. The essence of the professional judgment of the lawyer is his educated ability to relate the general body and philosophy of law to a specific legal problem of a client; and thus, the public interest will be better served if only lawyers are permitted to act in matters involving professional judgment. EC 3-5. A lawyer often delegates tasks to clerks, secretaries, and other lay persons. Such delegation is proper if the lawyer maintains a direct relationship with his client, supervises the delegated work, and has complete professional responsibility for the work product. EC 3-6. Since a lawyer should not aid or encourage a layman to practice law, he should not practice law in association with a layman or otherwise share legal fees with a layman. EC 3-8.

Commentators and ABA Opinions in the field have added enlightenment: The condemnation of the unauthorized practice of law is designed to protect the public from legal services by persons unskilled in the law. The prohibition of lay intermediaries is intended to insure the loyalty of the lawyer to the client unimpaired by intervening and possibly conflicting interests. Cheatham, Availability of Legal Services: The Responsibility of the Individual Lawyer and of the Organized Bar, 12 UCLA Rev. 438, 439 (1965). A lawyer can employ lay secretaries, lay investigators, lay detectives, lay researchers, accountants, lay scriveners, nonlawyer draftsmen or nonlawyer researchers. In fact, he may employ nonlawyers to do any task for him except counsel clients about law matters, engage directly in the practice of law, appear in court or appear in formal proceedings as part of the judicial process, so long as it is he who takes the work and vouches for it to the client and becomes responsible to the client. ABA Comm. on Professional Ethics, Op. 316 (1967). A lawyer cannot delegate his professional responsibility to a law student employed in his office. He may avail himself of the assistance of the student in many of the fields of the lawyer's work, "[b]ut the student is not permitted, until he is admitted to the

Bar, to perform the professional functions of a lawyer, such as conducting court trails, giving professional advice to clients or drawing legal documents for them. The student in all his work must act as agent for the lawyer employing him, who must supervise his work and be responsible for his good conduct." ABA Comm. on Professional Ethics, Op. 85 (1932).

Our courts have expressed or quoted with approval from several general definitions of the practice of law. For example, the court of appeal in *Meunier v. Bernich* drew on several sources:

"[T]he practice of law in this country ... embraces the preparation of pleadings and other papers incident to actions and special proceedings and the management of such actions and proceedings on behalf of clients before judges and courts, and, in addition, conveyancing, the preparation of legal instruments of all kinds, and in general, all advice to clients and all action taken for them connected with the law."

170 So. at 571, quoting from Ballentine's Law Dictionary; and from *In Re Duncan*, 83 S.C. 186, 65 S.E. 210, 211, 24 LRA (N.S.) 750, 18 Ann.Cas. 657 (1909), *Boykin v. Hopkins*, 174 Ga. 511, 162 S.E. 796, 799 (1932); and *People v. Title Guarantee & Trust Co.*, 180 App.Div. 648, 168 N.Y.S. 278, 280 (1917), to similar effect. See also *Duncan v. Gordon*, 476 So.2d 896 (La.App.2d Cir.1985); Model Code of Professional Responsibility EC 3-5 (1988).

In defining the practice of law for purposes of interpreting DR 3-101(A), this court may consider as persuasive, but not binding, pertinent legislative expressions. La. R.S. 37:213 provides, under pain of criminal punishment, that it is unlawful for a non-lawyer to practice law, hold himself out as an attorney, or advertise that he alone or jointly has an office for the practice of law. La. R.S. 37:212 defines the practice of law for this purpose as including the appearance as an advocate, the drawing of papers, pleadings or documents, the performance of any act in connection with pending or prospective proceedings before any court of record; as well as the following, if done for consideration: the advising or counseling of another as to secular law, the drawing or procuring of a paper, document or instrument affecting or relating to secular rights in behalf of another, and the doing of any act, in behalf of another, tending to obtain or secure for the other the prevention or redress of a wrong or the enforcement or establishment of a right.

Upon considering whether an attorney has aided a paralegal or other non-lawyer assistant in the unauthorized practice of law, we conclude, in the light of the foregoing persuasive precepts, that a lawyer may delegate various tasks to paralegals, clerks, secretaries and other non-lawyers; that he or she may not, however, delegate to any such person the lawyer's role of appearing in court in behalf of a client or of giving legal advice to a client; that he or she must supervise closely any such person to whom he or she delegates other tasks, including the preparation of a draft of a legal document or the conduct of legal research; and that the lawyer must not under any circumstance delegate to such person the exercise of the lawyer's professional judgment in behalf of the client or even allow it to be influenced by the non-lawyer's assistance. See also ABA/BNA Lawyers' Manual on Professional Conduct 21:8203 (1984); Model Code of Professional Responsibility EC 3-6 (1988).

Application of Precepts

. . .

(1) Edwins and Robertson did not testify truthfully with respect to Edwins' hospitalization during the evaluation of Livingston's claim, the rendition of legal advice to file suit, and the preparation and filing of the petition, the motions and the legal memoranda. Edwins' general or irrelevant testimony not only fails to confirm, but casts grave doubt upon, Robertson's testimony that Edwins was in a Memphis hospital at these times. Even if Edwins had been in a hospital because of a serious illness, as Robertson claimed, it is highly unlikely in the absence of any further corroborating evidence, that he performed the legal services attributed to him over the telephone, without having interviewed Livingston, with no investigative file, with no law books, and with only the telephonic assistance of Robertson's daughter, who insofar as the record shows was not a legal secretary. The evidence as a whole strongly suggests an ongoing relationship in which Edwins allowed Robertson to perform legal tasks without supervision and to exercise professional judgment properly reserved only for attorneys, rather than an isolated instance in which an attorney was forced to render emergency legal service from a hospital bed.

(2) For the foregoing reasons, we are convinced that Livingston testified truthfully when he said that Robertson held himself out to be a lawyer, entered an employment and contingent fee contract with him, did not reveal to him that Robertson was not a lawyer until sometime after employment commenced, and did not arrange for Livingston to meet

Edwins or receive any advice from him until after the suit had been filed. The record contains independent confirmation that Robertson habitually posed as a lawyer, viz., his sharing an office with a lawyer, partially financed by the lawyer, with the lawyer's sign on the door; his representation to an adjuster that he was a lawyer; his letterhead proclaiming, "Now you can have a lawyer too ... through Prepaid Legal Services, Rob Robertson." Because of the internal consistency and straightforward manner of Livingston's testimony, as well as the foregoing reasons, we believe Livingston's claim that the settlement was presented to him as a fait accompli, that he was given no prior advice regarding the settlement, and that no meaningful explanation of the distribution of his recovery was given him. Indeed, the record plainly indicates that the settlement was effected without his knowing and voluntary consent.

(3) Consequently, the evidence is clear and convincing, and we find it highly probable that, Robertson, and not Edwins, performed the functions and exercised the professional judgment of a lawyer in evaluating Livingston's claim, advising him as to the merits of his case, entering a contract to perform legal services, and preparing a suit, motions, and written legal argument. Further, we are convinced that Edwins improperly delegated the exercise of his professional judgment to Robertson with respect to the rendition of legal counsel to Livingston as to the advisability of settlement. Finally, it is very clear that Edwins wrongfully allowed Robertson to handle and distribute the client's money without close supervision and without any check by the lawyer upon the non-lawyer's judgment in this regard.

. . .

5. Sanctions

The Disciplinary Rules include ethical standards that are not fundamental to the professional relationship but which define certain standards of conduct. These standards concern duties owed to the profession for the benefit of the public, such as the rule prohibiting the assistance of unauthorized practice. ABA Standards for Imposing Lawyer Sanctions 7.0

. . .

The respondent attorney in the present case, in our opinion, knowingly assisted the non-lawyer, Robertson, to engage in the unauthorized practice of law. Even if Edwins was unaware that Robertson had held himself out as an attorney, we are convinced that he knowingly allowed Robertson to perform the functions of a lawyer in advising prospective clients as to their claims, entering employment contracts with them, preparing and filing lawsuits, motions and briefs for them, counseling them on the advisability of the settlement of their cases, and receiving, distributing and accounting for their settlement funds. Moreover, in all of these respects Edwins delegated the exercise of his professional judgment to Robertson, adopting the non-lawyer's decisions as his own with little or no supervision by the attorney.

We are convinced further that Edwins assisted Robertson in the unauthorized practice of law with the intent to obtain a benefit for himself and the non-lawyer. Edwins allowed Robertson to hold his paralegal office out to the public as the attorney's branch law office and paid part of the expenses of its operation. Edwins clearly intended to profit and did profit from the attorney fees that were generated by the unauthorized services performed by Robertson. Likewise, the arrangement intentionally benefited Robertson by enabling Edwins to compensate Robertson for his work in connection with cases that Edwins may not have been able to handle without the unauthorized legal assistance of Robertson.

Edwins' assistance of Robertson's unauthorized practice caused serious injury to his clients, namely Livingston and his wife. Edwins settled Livingston's personal injury case for $9,000, and because of his relationship with Robertson he turned the entire proceeds over to the non-lawyer for the performance of the attorney's professional duties and the exercise of the lawyer's professional judgment. Consequently, Livingston received only $1,000 of his $9,000 recovery. Edwins and Robertson attempted to show at the disciplinary hearing that legitimate expenses of some $8,000 were deducted from the settlement funds. We are not convinced, however, that any of these expenses were owed by Livingston.

. . .

In summary, as general propositions, therefore, before applying the aggravating and mitigating circumstances, disbarment is the prima facie appropriate sanction for the respondent's aiding unauthorized practice violation, and suspension is the proper sanction at first view for his failure to preserve his clients' property.

. . .

Edwins has not introduced any credible evidence which would serve as a mitigating factor.

We conclude that disbarment is appropriate in this case. The absence of mitigating factors, the presence of substantial aggravating circumstances including prior disciplinary suspensions, and the finding of serious violations that presumptively require disbarment and suspension, militate against reducing the degree of sanction below disbarment.

Decree

It is ordered, adjudged and decreed that the name of Rallie C. Edwins, respondent herein, be stricken from the rolls of attorneys and his license to practice law in the State of Louisiana be revoked effective on the date of the finality of this judgment. Respondent will bear all costs of this proceeding.

ATTORNEY DISBARRED.

Questions

1. What do you think the court found most offensive about Edwins's degree of involvement with Robertson?

2. What did the court offer as reasons for the prohibition against the practice of law by laypersons?

3. Provide two of the definitions of the practice of law that are given by the court.

4. What kinds of things did the court state could be delegated to nonlawyers? What kinds of things did the court state could not be delegated?

5. In what ways did the court find that Robertson engaged in the unauthorized practice of law?

4

THE DUTY OF DILIGENCE

CHAPTER OBJECTIVES

After reading this chapter, you should
be able to:

- Know your obligations under the duties of diligence and promptness and how to implement those obligations to protect the interests of the client.

- Understand the special rules of ethics for litigation paralegals that limit the duty of zealous representation.

- Recognize the boundaries of diligent or zealous representation.

One of the reasons being a legal assistant is so exciting is because the position provides countless opportunities. As we have just seen in chapter 3, legal assistants are being given substantial responsibility for advancing the client's interests.

No matter in which area of law the paralegal works, he assists the attorney in representing the client. This assistance may take a variety of forms. The legal assistant may be asked to draft a preliminary will for the attorney's review or pleadings to be filed in court on behalf of the client. In some jurisdictions the legal assistant may appear in court to handle routine motions. There are limits to any kind of representation in which the paralegal assists, however. Rules regarding such things as *ex parte* communications and disclosure of adverse authority will affect how fervently the paralegal can assist in representing the client.

Independently of an attorney, nonlawyers may also represent clients before some administrative agencies. The rules governing such agencies may be designed to control the nonlawyer's zeal in representing his client. However, even where the nonlawyer is not working directly under an attorney or at a law firm, it is always a good rule of thumb for the nonlawyer to adhere to the attorney's code of ethics and to recognize any limitations these codes may set forth before making decisions about how to handle the client's representation.

As we have noted before, the attorney's code of ethics is our starting point in this discussion. For that reason this chapter will set forth and discuss the ethical rules regarding diligent representation of the client (otherwise known as "zealous representation") and the limits on such representation. It will also address how these rules affect the paralegal's work.

OPENING EXERCISE

J. W. was a paralegal working in a small law firm located in a small community. His supervising attorney, Paul, was generally regarded as the most respected citizen in the area. In fact, Paul had just been appointed to serve out the previous mayor's unfinished term because he was known to be so honest and upstanding. For this reason, people came from miles around to secure Paul's legal services, and his thriving law practice grew busier and busier.

In turn, J. W.'s workload grew heavier and heavier. Although he was spending more and more hours at the firm, he found he could not keep up. Instead he began to put several matters to the side and concentrated his attention only on the work he could handle. Because Paul's responsibilities as mayor kept him away from the office for several hours a day, J. W. believed he would be able to get to the matters he had set aside before Paul discovered the projects had not been completed earlier.

Do you see any problems with J. W. putting matters to the side for awhile? If so, what kinds of problems do you think might result? What do you think J. W.'s responsibilities are in this situation?

THE RULE OF ZEALOUS REPRESENTATION

After watching several movies and television shows depicting legal battles, we quickly learn that the lawyer's responsibility is to be a fierce advocate of his client's interests. In other words, the attorney must represent his client with **zeal.** When we think of the **zealous representation** of a client, therefore, we picture a lawyer conducting a brutal cross-examination of an opposing witness or delivering a fiery argument to a jury.

Zeal Enthusiastic or extremely committed devotion to a particular cause.

In truth, courtroom drama is the last stop in a long progression of work on any given case. Representation begins the minute an attorney accepts a client's case. At that time the duties of loyalty, confidentiality, and zealous representation kick in, and the law office must take steps to adhere to these duties. (For a thorough analysis of these obligations, see chapter 6, "Conflicts of Interest.")

Zealous representation The application of the meaning of the word "zeal" to the representation of one's client.

The idea of zealously representing a client extends beyond the courtroom and into every facet of the attorney's relationship with the client. Every real estate closing document or memorandum of law that is drafted on behalf of the client is part of the representation of the client. Every telephone call that is made to verify information given by a client is part of the representation.

Likewise, the concept of zealously representing the client can be extended to the legal assistant. Although most jurisdictions may not allow the legal assistant to go into the courtroom on behalf of a client, any of the work with which the legal assistant can assist the attorney is part of the client's representation.

So what does it mean to zealously represent a client? Ideally, zealous representation is that representation which is characterized by an ardent or fervent demonstration of commitment to the client. However, the "zeal" in zealous representation must be kept in check.

The language of the *Model Code* required that "a lawyer should represent a client zealously within the bounds of the law." See Canon 7, *Model Code of Professional Responsibility.* Therefore the lawyer is constrained in her zealous representation of the client. No matter how fervently she may wish to pursue her client's objectives, the attorney's representation of the client must not exceed the bounds of the law. The paralegal also could be found to have an obligation to zealously assist in the representation of a client within the bounds of the law. This means that the legal assistant, too, must not violate the law or an ethical rule in the interest of helping the client.

It is not easy, however, to define zeal. The drafters of the *Model Rules* were aware of this dilemma. Moreover, the drafters were reluctant to use the word zeal because zealous representation is often confused with overzealous representation, and lawyers are cautioned against having too much zeal in representing a client (zealotry could lead an attorney to go outside the bounds of the law).[1] While the drafters appreciated the spirit of the *Code* and acknowledged that the lawyer should be a zealous advocate of the client's interests, they believed the rule needed to be modified. Because of this, in part, the drafters of the rules changed the standard of representing a client with "zealousness" to representing a client with "reasonable diligence and promptness."

REASONABLE DILIGENCE AND PROMPTNESS

Ignoring the words but not the spirit of zealous representation, the *Model Rules* place an obligation upon the attorney to represent a client with diligence and promptness. The lawyer, therefore, has an obligation of **diligent representation.** Model Rule 1.3 provides:

Diligent representation
Conscientious, attentive, persistent attention to a client's cause.

> A lawyer shall act with reasonable diligence and promptness in representing a client.

But what does this standard mean? What kind of diligence is reasonable? Likewise, what is reasonable promptness? To answer these questions, the Comment explains this Rule:

> A lawyer should pursue a matter on behalf of a client despite opposition, obstruction or personal inconvenience to the lawyer, and may take whatever lawful and ethical measures are required to vindicate a client's cause or endeavor. A lawyer should act with commitment and dedication to the interests of the client and with zeal in advocacy upon the client's behalf. However, a lawyer is not bound to press for every advantage that might be realized for a client. A lawyer has professional discretion in determining the means by which a matter should be pursued. See Rule 1.2. A lawyer's workload should be controlled so that each matter can be handled adequately. *Model Rules of Professional Conduct* Rule 1.3 cmt. (1993).

Therefore, the attorney who agrees to represent a particular client must be committed to the client and must protect that client's interests, no matter what obstacles stand in the way. This does not mean, however, that the lawyer must pursue every possible strategy or tactic in order to win the client's case.

There are boundaries to diligent representation. The attorney *cannot* violate any laws of that state or any ethics rules in the interest of advancing his client's position. For example, the attorney should not suggest, in an attempt to advance his client's interests, that the client pursue criminal or fraudulent behavior. This would violate an ethical obligation of the attorney. (See Rule 1.2.) Neither can the attorney falsify documents on behalf of the client. This would break the law (and, of course, Model Rule 3.4(a)). Therefore, no matter

---

[1]*See* Geoffrey Hazard, Jr., & W. William Hodes, The Law of Lawyering § 1,3:101 (2d ed. 1993). Reprinted from *The Law of Lawyering,* by Geoffrey C. Hazard, Jr., and W. William Hodes, with the permission of Prentice Hall Law & Business.

INTERPLAY:
The Relationship between Rule 1.3 and Other Model Rules

Basically, Rule 1.3 presses the attorney or law office to take every measure that is necessary in advocating a client's cause, as long as those measures are ethical and legal. Based upon this precept, it again becomes important to know the interrelationship between Rule 1.3 and other rules. For example, Hazard and Hodes, *Law of Lawyering* notes: "Zealous representation of a client will not excuse the filing of a frivolous pleadings (Rule 3.1), lying to a court (Rule 3.3), concealing evidence (Rule 3.4), or making extrajudicial statements designed to disrupt a trial (Rule 3.6)."[2] Thus we see that there are interrelationships between Rule 1.3 and other Rules.

---

how strongly a client may wish to, for example, lower his tax liability, the attorney cannot prepare and sign a false tax return. Constraints of this kind serve to limit the attorney's role as an advocate of the client.

The attorney also must act reasonably promptly in handling the client's case. This means the attorney should not take on more work than she can handle. Any work for a potential client that might interfere with completing on a timely basis a particular piece of work for a client whose case has already been accepted should therefore be declined. The Comments also suggest that the attorney should not procrastinate. Unreasonably delaying the client's work can cause needless worry for the client. Matters should be handled as expeditiously as possible.

As they relate to nonlawyers, the rules of ethics regarding prompt and diligent representation operate in much the same way as they do for lawyers. For example, there are boundaries to the diligence that should be exercised by nonlawyers in the law office. Nonlawyers must not engage in any activity that is violative of the laws or ethical rules of the jurisdiction in which they work. Yet, just as it holds true with lawyers, working competently and diligently on a client's case is not only expected of law office staff who work under the lawyers—it is required. (For a complete discussion of this concept, see chapter 2, "Overview of Legal Ethics.")

Generally, diligence and competence are not difficult to attain because most law offices and agencies recognize the value of caring for each case and of averting potential problems. The focus of the office centers on being prompt and diligent.

Problems can arise, however, where the lawyer or legal assistant is unaware of time limitations and their imminent expiration and procrastinates. Therefore, the next sections discuss related problems of statutes of limitation and procrastination.

STATUTES OF LIMITATION AND FILING DATES

Nonlawyers working in a law office are often given responsibility for keeping track of statutes of limitations and other filing dates.

[2]Geoffrey C. Hazard, Jr., and W. William Hodes, THE LAW OF LAWYERING (2nd ed. 1993). Reprinted from *The Law of Lawyering,* by Geoffrey C. Hazard, Jr., and W. William Hodes, with the permission of Prentice Hall Law & Business.

Statutes of limitations A statute that defines the time period within which a lawsuit or other legal action must be brought or be forever barred.

Laws regarding **statutes of limitations** or limitations of actions define the time period in which a lawsuit must be brought or be forever barred. State legislatures enact these laws or, in some states, **common law doctrine** has established these time periods. The length of time of a statute of limitations depends on the kind of action that is being pursued.

Common law doctrine Law made by judges in the absence of controlling statutory law.

Generally, a **cause of action** accrues on the date that one suffers an injury. So, for example, a cause of action would accrue on the day an accident occurs or a **contract** is broken. Once a cause of action accrues, the statute of limitations begins to run from that date. The injured party then must file a lawsuit in court or agree to settle before the time period for filing that kind of lawsuit runs out.

Cause of action The facts that give a person a right to judicial relief.

For example, suppose that Altovese Attorney is consulted by Carlita Client about the possibility of bringing a lawsuit because of a car accident that she had with a flatbed truck driven by Donna Driver, an employee of Petrified Paper and Pulp Co. Carlita tells Altovese that the accident left her with a fractured clavicle and jaw, and she would like to sue both Donna and Petrified Paper and Pulp to recover her damages.

Contract A legally binding agreement that creates an obligation to do or not to do a particular thing.

Altovese then asks Carlita when the wreck occurred. Carlita tells her it took place three and one-half years ago. If the statute of limitations for bringing a personal injury case is three years, Carlita cannot bring a claim against Petrified and Donna. If the statute of limitations is four years, then Carlita has sufficient time to file her claim, as the statute of limitations has not run.

Statutes of limitation are important because they indicate the time limitation for commencing a lawsuit. The legal professional working in a litigation setting must know other, equally important dates.

After a complaint is filed, the defendant has an opportunity to respond to the allegations raised in the complaint. Quite often, this response must be filed within a period of time that is often statutorily determined. As the litigation commences, it is likely that various motions will be filed. The court will usually establish a briefing schedule, which sets filing deadlines for the parties who intend to file motions and responses to motions. Missing a filing deadline can have serious consequences.

Keeping track of statutes of limitation and filing dates is of particular concern to legal assistants because very often the paralegal is called upon to monitor case dates. Some larger law firms employ nonlawyers whose primary role is to monitor the dates. If this becomes your responsibility you will want to use a **tickler system** to monitor important dates.

Tickler system A reminder system that helps office staff remember important deadlines.

You might wonder what would be the consequences of violating the statute of limitations. Of course, one unfortunate consequence would be that the client would not be adequately compensated for any damages she sustained because, without a lawsuit, there can be no judgment.

Another consequence would be that missing a statutory deadline or, as it is otherwise called, "blowing a term," could result in a legal malpractice action for negligence. Simply put, the lawyer (who is ultimately responsible for the case) can be sued if the client's case is not filed. The nonlawyer may also face serious professional consequences. Legal assistants may also find that they can be sued for **negligence.**

Negligence The failure to do what a reasonable person would have done under the same circumstances.

As discussed in chapter 2, professional liability policies are being sold to legal assistants because of this type of problem. This is not to suggest that paralegals should necessarily purchase professional liability policies. That decision is best left to the individual. However, the market demand for such policies demonstrates that liability is a concern of many legal assistants and that the potential exists for liability. (Please consult study aids for specific case study information and published opinions.)

Of course, a final consequence of failing to bring an action within the statute of limitations period might be loss of employment. An attorney confronted by a client whose claim has been lost because a statute of limitations has run may simply decide to terminate the nonlawyer's employment, especially if this is not the first time such a situation has occurred.

Go to the nearest law library and research the various statutes of limitations in your jurisdiction. How long does a party have to file a personal injury case? How long for a contract dispute? | **EXERCISE 4.1**

PROCRASTINATION

One of the greatest problems for legal professionals is the tendency to procrastinate. It is easy to see how it might be tempting to procrastinate. For example, a particularly difficult or novel issue might come up and the attorney or paralegal may feel overwhelmed with the work he already has. Therefore, the legal professional sets the big issue to the side in order to handle simpler matters that can be accomplished with less effort.

The legal assistant's problem with procrastination may often result from an unwillingness to ask for direction. Because he feels that the attorney is also overwhelmed with work, the paralegal may put the problem to the side instead of seeking help from the attorney for whom he is working. Ultimately the problem will have to be addressed. However, because the paralegal has procrastinated, chances are that the case will not get the degree of time and work that must be expended on the case in order to do an adequate job.

Procrastination can be a serious problem in the law. As we saw above, procrastination may lead to statutes of limitations being missed. If a statute of limitations or a filing deadline is missed, a client can find herself without any recourse for a serious injury that she suffered. Furthermore, as the comments suggest, procrastinating can lead to needless worry for the client who wants her affairs handled with dispatch. For these reasons, it is critically important that sufficient time be scheduled to devote to any given legal problem.

How does one determine what will be a sufficient amount of time to devote to a problem? Where does one go to find out how much time should be devoted to a client's case? What is the correct barometer?

The best place for a legal assistant to start is with the supervising paralegal or attorney. Keep in mind that the operations of a law practice require the simultaneous scheduling of many matters. When a case is assigned, the person to whom it is assigned has no way of comprehending all of the goings-on in the firm. Remember, too, financial factors are often considered in a firm's decision to accept a case. The persons managing the firm probably have an idea of how much time will be required to complete any matter.

EXERCISE 4.2   Eadie was assigned to research an issue involving a worker's compensation claim. Because Eadie disliked legal research, she considered putting the matter aside for awhile and instead handling what she considered the more exciting work of abstracting depositions. Eadie recognized that she had not yet been asked to review these depositions, but she knew the work would need to get done eventually.

Should Eadie put the research to the side? What problems do you think could result from Eadie handling her work assignments in this manner? What could Eadie do to avoid having this problem in the future?

WHAT IF THE PARALEGAL HAS NO EXPERIENCE IN A LAW OFFICE SETTING OR LACKS EXPERIENCE IN A PARTICULAR AREA OF THE LAW?

As a legal professional, the paralegal should be diligent in assisting the attorney's representation of the client. To be diligent, it is extremely important that she maintain competence. However, the paralegal who has no prior experience in a legal setting may find it difficult to understand just what constitutes competence.

Competency in the law is not inherently known; it is acquired. The place and the means for acquiring competency are often found right in the law office—from other legal assistants and even from the lawyers themselves. Additionally, seminars where the paralegal can receive formal instruction and converse with other, more experienced professionals are often a great resource.

If the legal assistant does not feel competent in a particular area of the law, he must discuss this problem with his supervising attorney. The attorney might have more knowledge about the particular area of law or might have resources already in place to assist in offering some guidance. All that may be necessary is some additional supervision from the attorney. Therefore, if you feel that you lack the experience to handle a particular issue, you should talk about the matter with your supervising attorney.

Rules regarding procrastination and statutes of limitation help to define diligence in the representation of a client. Remember, however, that the lawyer's representation of clients must be diligent or zealous within the bounds of the law. This means the lawyer, and nonlawyer assistant, must be cognizant of laws or other ethics rules that would affect how zealously they can represent a client.

Litigation paralegal A legal assistant who specializes in assisting attorneys in matters that involve litigation.

Because it is often the **litigation paralegal** who must confront the boundaries of diligent representation, the focus of the chapter now shifts to discuss two ethics rules especially applicable to litigators. Two of the most important rules involve the duty of candor toward the tribunal and the duty to refrain from engaging in *ex parte* communications.

THE DUTY OF CANDOR

Candor Honesty.

Litigator An attorney who settles disputes or seeks relief in a court of law.

Each legal professional has an obligation to be honest with the court. This is known as the "duty of **candor**" and is discussed in *Model Rules of Professional Conduct* Rule 3.3 (1993).

What does this rule mean for the **litigator?** Although a lawyer may wish to do everything she can to advance the client's cause, the lawyer's representa-

 **Example of the Limits of Diligent Representation**

A n example of how a legal professional's diligent or zealous representation of a client is limited may help to explain the concept of this chapter.

Consider the situation of Lou Legal Assistant. Lou was a paralegal in a small law firm that concentrated on sports law matters. As a legal assistant, Lou has an obligation to diligently assist his supervising lawyer in representing the client. Having been a professional bowler at one time, Lou found his work terribly interesting and devoted a substantial amount of time and energy to it.

One day Faye, a professional golfer competing on the FPGA circuit, came into the office. She was involved in a contract dispute with her agent and she wanted to hire the firm to represent her in an upcoming sports arbitration case. Faye's case was assigned to Lou's supervising attorney, Mary, and Lou was soon asked to begin researching a new area of contract law.

Lou had followed Faye's career for a long time, and he was thrilled to be able to help with her case. Lou was a hard worker, giving up even his lunch hours to devote to Faye's case. He conducted some extra research to determine whether any special procedural rules applied in sports arbitration cases. He asked Mary if he could attend an upcoming seminar on sports arbitration.

Lou's work on this particular case is certainly helping to demonstrate his diligence as a legal assistant. By taking these extra steps, Lou has made sure, to the best of his abilities, that Faye's case is being competently handled by the law office.

Suppose, however, that in his enthusiasm and commitment to the case, Lou steps beyond the bounds of diligent representation.

Lou began to feel that all that might be needed to resolve Faye's problem was a little extra communication between the parties. Lou felt that Faye's requests were not unreasonable; her agent probably just needed to have them explained to her a little more clearly. Lou decided to call Faye's agent and talk about the misunderstanding.

Once Lou places such a call, he has stepped beyond the boundaries of diligent, competent representation. When Lou talks to the agent directly, about substantive issues, he has become involved in an *ex parte* communication with an adverse party. *Ex parte* communications with adverse parties are forbidden by the ethics rules because of the danger that someone like Lou could take advantage of a party. (See *ex parte* communications, this chapter.)

---

tion of the client cannot be so single-mindedly zealous that she ultimately places falsehoods before the court. As the comments to the rule suggest, the duty of candor "qualifies" the lawyer's advocacy of the client's interests.

This rule is important for the paralegal and lawyer alike. As we have previously discussed, legal assistants may ethically engage in a number of activities in the courtroom to assist the lawyer in litigating a case. When a nonlawyer appears in court, he must take care to adhere to the attorney's rules of professional conduct that are made applicable to nonlawyers. This means that, when in the courtroom, the nonlawyer must be honest with the court.

However, even if the legal assistant never steps foot in a courtroom, the duty of candor is an important rule to remember. The paralegal often assists in preparing cases for trial. This means the legal assistant will have opportunities to uncover the truth, whether or not that truth is favorable to the client. All information that is discovered by the legal assistant must be turned over to the attorney in order that he can ensure that the court has in its possession all relevant and truthful information bearing upon the case.

As the next section illustrates, this is a particularly important rule for the paralegal handling research matters for an attorney.

REVEALING ADVERSE AUTHORITY

Memorandum of law A document that addresses a particular legal issue or certain facts in a legal matter. It may be written for interoffice use or for use as a persuasive document.

Briefs Written statements that summarize case or other law, and which are often used by attorneys and courts in lieu of use of the entire law. These may be used interoffice, in trials, or on appeal.

Pre-trial hearings Proceedings that occur before the trial which are held to resolve definite issues of fact or of law.

Adverse authority Authority which is controlling in any given jurisdiction, and which is directly adverse to the client's position.

When an attorney is litigating a client's case, she must do a number of things before even getting to trial. For instance, she may be called on to draft a supporting **memorandum of law** to substantiate or deny the claims made in pre-trial motions. She will need to prepare legal arguments present to the court in **briefs** or during **pre-trial hearings.** Therefore, she will need to complete legal research to find her answers.

Needless to say, legal research may make a substantial contribution to preparing a strong legal argument. On the other hand, sometimes research can uncover law that reaches the opposite conclusion from that which the client is seeking. The law may therefore be potentially damaging to the client's position. In other words, sometimes research can uncover **adverse authority.** Despite the importance of this law, however, opposing counsel may fail to uncover this adverse authority.

At this point the attorney may be relieved. However, once the attorney knows such law exists, he has an obligation to disclose the existence of the law to the court. To fail to do so would be dishonest and, therefore, would violate Rule 3.3. See *Model Rules of Professional Conduct* Rule 3.3(a)(3) (1994).

This does not mean, however, that the attorney is required to present to the court a "disinterested exposition of law." See *Model Rules of Professional Conduct* Rule 3.3 cmt. (1994). What information *must* the attorney reveal? The *Model Rules* state that the attorney should disclose any cases or statutes that are (1) controlling in that jurisdiction (in other words, binding upon the court) and (2) directly adverse to the client's position, when such authority has not been disclosed by opposing counsel. See Model Rule 3.3(a)(3); see also *Model Code of Professional Responsibility* DR 7-106 (B)(1) (1986).

Revealing adverse authority helps to ensure that the court has all relevant law before it; it must have all of the law that it should rely on in order to make an informed, correct decision. This is the basis of our system of justice. Attorneys must reveal directly adverse legal information because they are, after all, "officers of the court." As such, they have an obligation to be forthcoming with the court and an interest in seeing that justice is served.

So, the lawyer must disclose to the court any adverse legal authority from a controlling jurisdiction of which he is aware. Often, however, it may be the legal assistant who does the legal research for the attorney. What is the *paralegal's* responsibility when his research uncovers authority directly adverse to the client's position? Must the legal assistant reveal the adverse authority? If so, to whom?

Suppose, for example, a paralegal is researching a real estate tax assessment problem for a client. The client's position is that it is not necessary to exhaust administrative remedies before filing a complaint with the trial court. The legal assistant's research uncovers a case decided earlier in that jurisdiction that discusses a nearly identical factual situation but concludes that an individual *cannot* file a complaint in court before exhausting administrative remedies. This previous case is a directly adverse authority from a controlling jurisdiction. What should the legal assistant do?

As we discussed earlier, Rule 5.3 tells the attorney to ensure that nonlawyers adhere to the attorney's code of ethics. *Model Rules of Professional Conduct* Rule 5.3 (1994). Therefore, the paralegal should remember that, although the rules say it is the lawyer who has a duty to be honest with the court, the paralegal should likewise be forthcoming with his discovery.

The legal assistant's discovery of any adverse authority from a controlling jurisdiction should be revealed to the supervising attorney. The attorney can then make the final decision about whether that authority is from a controlling jurisdiction, whether it is "directly adverse," and, therefore, whether it should be revealed to a court and how it should be revealed. (The caveat to this rule is that a legal assistant should directly inform an administrative agency if the nonlawyer is representing a client before that tribunal.)

Failing to reveal the existence of such information would be dishonest and would violate the code of ethics. The paralegal's discovery of adverse authority, then, should be taken directly to the attorney.

EXERCISE 4.3

Arlene is a legal assistant who has been working with Dennis, her supervising attorney, for a number of years. Dennis has recently agreed to represent Mrs. Peabody in her lawsuit against Carthing Conglomerate, a major corporation.

Mrs. Peabody is a widow whose husband died years before and left her with no children. Because she was alone in the world, Mrs. Peabody showered grandmotherly attention on all of the office staff. For example, Mrs. Peabody baked cookies every week to bring into the office. She offered to mend a tear in Dennis's coat after he caught it in a door on the way to a deposition. She was always willing to lend an ear when Arlene wanted to discuss her boyfriend troubles.

Because she was so fond of Mrs. Peabody, Arlene expended extra effort on her case. One day, however, Arlene's thorough research uncovered an authority that was directly adverse to Mrs. Peabody's position.

Arlene considered whether she should tell Dennis of the existence of this authority. She knew it was the honest thing to do, but if Dennis were aware of the case, he would be obligated to inform the court, and Mrs. Peabody's position would be virtually destroyed. If she did not tell, however, she felt that nobody would be the wiser.

What should Arlene do? Why? If you were in Arlene's shoes, what would you do? Why?

REVEALING NONLAWYER STATUS TO THE COURT

Occasionally the nonlawyer appears before the court for the lawyer. As we saw in chapter 3, in some jurisdictions nonlawyers are allowed to appear before a judge to handle "routine" motions. Some administrative agencies also allow nonlawyers to appear before their tribunals on behalf of clients.

In these instances it is especially important that the nonlawyer remember the rules regarding the duty of candor. Just as attorneys do, legal assistants have an obligation, when appearing before a judge, to avoid misrepresentations.

In maintaining candor and honesty toward the court or administrative agency, the nonlawyer is required to advise the court of his nonlawyer status. Adhering to this rule is critical. Not only is failing to advise the court of nonlawyer status dishonest in that the legal assistant may appear to be representing himself as an attorney, but it may ultimately lead to the charges of unauthorized practice of law.

For example, in some jurisdictions a local rule may state that nonlawyers may appear in court to answer a routine motion, just as many attorneys do. If the judge is not apprised of the nonlawyer's status, however, she could assume that the nonlawyer is actually an attorney. Seeking more information from the parties before her in order to facilitate an expeditious settlement of the matter, the judge could begin to ask questions of the parties—parties whom the judge believes to be attorneys. The nonlawyer's involvement in the motion can quickly shift from handling routine matters to resolving substantive legal issues. When this happens, the nonlawyer has begun practicing law.

EXERCISE 4.4   Do you agree that nonlawyers should identify themselves as such in court? Why or why not?

EX PARTE COMMUNICATIONS

Ex parte communications
Communications in which a lawyer talks to or otherwise communicates with an individual involved in the litigation proceedings and where opposing counsel is not present.

In addition to the duty of candor, other rules play a role in limiting the zealousness of a legal professional's representation of a client. Some of the most important rules are those concerning *ex parte* **communications.**

Black's Law Dictionary defines *ex parte* as that which is "[o]n one side only; by or for one party; done for, in behalf of, or on the application of, one party only."[3] Basically, an *ex parte* communication forbids a lawyer from talking to, or otherwise communicating with, certain individuals involved in the litigation proceedings unless opposing counsel is present. This means the lawyer cannot speak to adverse parties, judges, or jurors unless opposing counsel is present.

The rules concerning *ex parte* contacts especially apply to nonlawyers who assist the attorney. Several cases have held that attorneys cannot escape their obligation to avoid *ex parte* communications by delegating the communication to a nonlawyer employee. See e.g., *In re Burrows*, 291 Or. 135, 629 P.2d 820, 22 ALR4th 906 (1981). Therefore, the attorney cannot tell the legal assistant to initiate an *ex parte* communication with an adverse party, a judge, or a jury member. If the attorney does this, the attorney will be held responsible for that *ex parte* contact just as if he himself had done the communicating. Furthermore, even if the legal assistant attempts to communicate on an *ex parte* basis *of his own volition,* the attorney will still be held responsible.

With this in mind, we now turn to a discussion of particular kinds of *ex parte* communications.

ADVERSE PARTIES

Adverse party
Opposing party in a legal matter.

Lawyers, and their nonlawyer employees, must refrain from communicating on an *ex parte* basis with **adverse parties** who are represented by an attorney. Rule 4.2, which is substantially similar to DR 7-104 (A)(1), states:

---

[3]BLACK'S LAW DICTIONARY 576 (6th ed. 1990). Reprinted with permission from *Black's Law Dictionary,* 6th ed. 1990 (Copyright, West Publishing Co.).

In representing a client, a lawyer shall not communicate about the subject of the representation with a party the lawyer knows to be represented by another lawyer in the matter, unless the lawyer has the consent of the other lawyer or is authorized by law to do so. *Model Rules of Professional Conduct* Rule 4.2 (1994).

Therefore, the attorney or legal assistant cannot seek out the adverse party to discuss any aspect of the litigation unless the adverse party's attorney is present. However, if the legal assistant were to run into the adverse party, they need not completely ignore each other. Rather, they can discuss anything not related in any manner to the case.

An example may help to clarify this rule. Suppose that Allison Attorney represents Craig Client in his lawsuit against Darla Defendant. Darla is represented in this matter by Oliver Opposing Counsel. The rules forbid Allison from speaking to Darla about the litigation unless Oliver is present. However, if Allison were to run into Darla on the bus, they can certainly exchange pleasantries or even idle gossip, even though Oliver may not be there. What they cannot do is discuss the pending lawsuit.

The purpose of the rule is to keep the lawyer from taking advantage of a party. The party whose attorney is not present may be unfairly swayed by her opponent's attorney's arguments, entreaties, or rhetoric. Because this party does not have her own attorney present, she may agree to do something that is not in her best interest.

JUDGES AND JURORS

The ethics rules also forbid *ex parte* contacts of a different type. As a general rule, attorneys and their nonlawyer employees may not engage in *ex parte* communications about a pending case with judges or with members of the jury. Model Rule 3.5 addresses this issue:

3.5 Impartiality and Decorum of the Tribunal
    A lawyer shall not:
        (a) seek to influence a judge, juror, prospective juror or other official by means prohibited by law;
        (b) communicate *ex parte* with such a person except as permitted by law; or
        (c) engage in conduct intended to disrupt a tribunal. *Model Rules of Professional Conduct* Rule 3.5 (1994).

Although this rule is found in the attorney's code of ethics, it is equally applicable to the nonlawyer employee working under the supervision of the lawyer. As previously noted, the lawyer cannot avoid his responsibility under Rule 3.5 by delegating *ex parte* communications with the judge or jury member to the nonlawyer.

The first issue to address is *ex parte* communications with *judges*. Occasionally it may be tempting to seek out a judge to explain what happened in the courtroom or to explain an argument that the judge did not seem to understand. This is true for both the attorney and the paralegal. However, they both have an obligation to not seek out the judge to explain matters unless opposing counsel is also present. As you can imagine, the reason for this rule is to protect the judge from becoming biased toward one side.

FOCUS ON REBECCA BIKE

Rebecca Bike holds what many would consider to be a dream job. She is the legal assistant manager at Vinson & Elkins, a large international law firm, based in Houston, Texas, where she manages 130 legal assistants and 30 project assistants. In November of 1994 Rebecca also became the President of the Legal Assistant Management Association (LAMA). Through her experiences, Rebecca has advised and assisted a great many legal assistants. She therefore offers a unique perspective.

When considering the nonlawyer's obligation to diligently represent the client, she says the paralegal needs to first remember that he or she is an agent of the attorney. Therefore, she notes, "Where the attorney has an obligation to diligently represent the client, the paralegal has a corresponding obligation to diligently assist the attorney's representation of that client." Rebecca further explains that the paralegal needs to keep in mind that she works under the supervision of a lawyer and that her assistance is limited by such things as unauthorized practice of law rules.

The paralegal needs to first remember that he or she is an agent of the attorney. Where the attorney has an obligation to diligently represent the client, the paralegal has a corresponding obligation to diligently assist the attorney's representation of that client.

Rebecca is pleased to note that she has never worked with a legal assistant who was tempted to overstep the boundaries of diligent representation. She is certain that if she were ever approached by a legal assistant who was considering, for example, destroying an incriminating document to help the client, Rebecca would first advise her of the constraints placed on her by the ethical rules. If that didn't persuade the legal assistant, says Rebecca, "I would take steps to terminate her employment."

Turning to specific problems she has witnessed firsthand, Rebecca knows that procrastination can be a special problem for some legal professionals. The first step for handling such a problem, Rebecca believes, is to enroll in a time management class. More often than not, however, problems arise because the paralegal has too much work to get done in a limited time frame. When this happens, Rebecca advises that the legal assistant go to the attorney for guidance about which project should be completed first. According to Rebecca, the legal assistant needs to tell the attorney, "I can't get it all done. Please prioritize for me."

Problems can also arise because the legal assistant just is not aware of how much time should be devoted to a particular matter. Rebecca notes that the first source to consider when you are unsure of this is your supervising attorney. Ask his or her advice.

"There were occasions when I was given assignments and realized later that I needed more information. If I had not gone back to my supervising attorney, I would have wasted a great deal of time. Ultimately, my supervising attorney was grateful that I had asked for his guidance." Another good source to consider is other legal assistants in the firm; ask them how long it takes them to do a particular task.

Rebecca is also quick to point out that handling filing deadlines can be an important part of the paralegal's responsibility to diligently assist the attorney. She knows that legal assistants or legal secretaries are often put in charge of handling these deadlines. The legal assistant who must track filing dates might consider meeting with the attorney once a week to discuss filing deadlines, scheduling orders, and other due dates.

Rebecca has worked with a large number of legal assistants, and she is aware of the very valuable contribution legal assistants can make to the operation of a law firm. However, she strongly cautions all paralegals to remember the limits placed on them in diligently assisting the attorney to represent the client.

For example, a judge may indicate in court that the attorney and his office employees should have devoted more time to research a particular issue. After the court adjourns, the legal assistant, feeling that the attorney had not adequately explained the amount of work which had been done, may want to tell the judge that the research was completed, but it just did not reveal any new cases. If the legal assistant seeks out the judge after court to do this when the other parties are not present, however, the paralegal would be engaging in a forbidden *ex parte* communication.

It is equally important for the lawyer and the legal assistant to avoid communications about a case with *jury members*. This does not mean the legal professional should blatantly shrug off any overtures of conversation with a juror. General social decorum does not create problems, and it is unprofessional to act in a rude manner. The better course is for the legal assistant to avoid altogether those situations where contact with jurors would be inevitable. Thus, the nonlawyer should avoid riding in an elevator with the jury or sitting at a courthouse cafeteria table during the court recesses. If a juror specifically addresses a legal assistant in the corridor, the paralegal should perhaps nod politely and go on about his business. Should the juror press the matter, the legal assistant should say nothing and immediately report the incident to his supervising attorney.

TIPS FOR PARALEGALS

- Avoid self-defeating habits such as procrastination.

- If procrastination is your problem, enroll in a time management or other, related self-improvement course.

- If at all possible, avoid excessive workloads.

- Bring foreseeable problems with the amount of your workload to the attention of your supervising attorney as soon as possible.

- Pay close attention to statutes of limitations, briefing schedules, and all important dates relative to cases your office has on the docket.

- Consider implementing a system of reporting impending filing deadlines on a regular schedule.

- Reveal to your supervising attorney any adverse authority discovered during research assignments.

- Make it a policy to reveal your nonlawyer status to the court, potential clients, opposing counsel, and potential witnesses at a first meeting.

- Do not engage in *ex parte* communications with adverse parties, the judge, or jury members.

CLOSING EXERCISE

Betty, a paralegal at McInerney & Waters, had just been given responsibility for working with Peggy, the attorney handling the new class action lawsuit against Jethro Kanker, a crusty old farmer who had discovered a rich vein of ore on his property several years ago. Kanker had been a cantankerous fellow before but, after discovering his fortune, he had become insufferably self-centered. In fact, he had been quoted in recent news articles as saying that he did not care what environmental damage he caused, as long as he was able to continue to mine his ore and make his fortune.

McInerney & Waters' clients alleged that Kanker's mining operations were causing toxic products to be introduced into the local water supply, causing many of the children of the community to become violently ill. For various reasons, Betty wanted McInerney & Waters' clients to win this suit and to win it big. Not only was winning this case personally important to Betty, but it could be particularly profitable to the firm in terms of client referrals and money.

So, Betty began spending longer and longer hours at the law firm. It had recently become clear to Peggy, however, that there were problems with the case. The judge had denied the motion in limine that Peggy had helped the attorney to draft and had ordered that certain evidence could not be introduced at trial. Depositions of important opposing witnesses had uncovered no significant information to be used at trial. Documents received during discovery had contradicted statements made by their clients.

Betty was heartbroken. If ever clients deserved to win a case, it was this one. She vowed she would do everything she could to see that they did win. She considered what steps she could take.

Review the actions Betty proposes to take. Which of these, if any, would you recommend that Betty implement? Why? What is wrong with the other options?

A. Betty should call the judge and offer to send him copies of recent magazine articles that had outlined problems Kanker had caused in the community.

B. Betty should put to the side the matters she had been assigned to complete for other clients and instead spend all her time handling matters in the Jethro Kanker case.

C. Betty should begin to forego her regular lunch hour and instead devote that time to completing research for the Jethro Kanker case.

D. Betty should hide from Peggy the fact that she recently uncovered a case that appeared to be directly adverse to the position of McInerney's clients.

E. Betty should agree to master computerized research techniques so that she can conduct legal research for the Jethro Kanker case more quickly.

F. Betty knows Kanker is a member of her health club. She should wait for him in the weight room one day and confront him about his unethical practices, hoping that he will see the light and agree to settle.

CHAPTER SUMMARY

■ It is a lawyer's duty to diligently and promptly represent the client's interest, and it is a paralegal's duty to diligently and promptly assist the lawyer in that representation. This means the nonlawyer should not procrastinate when given the responsibility for handling a client matter. Moreover, the legal assistant should be consciously aware of filing deadlines, such as statutes of limitations and briefing schedules.

■ There are boundaries to diligent representation. Although the attorney must diligently represent the client's interests and the legal assistant must diligently assist the attorney, there must never be a compromise of the law or the ethics of the attorney. The best job that *can* possibly be done, should be done. However, there are limits placed upon that representation.

■ Rules such as the duty of candor and the rule prohibiting *ex parte* communications also limit the attorney's diligent representation of the client and the nonlawyer's diligent assistance to the attorney. The duty of candor means that the legal professional must not be so single-mindedly devoted to the client's cause that she ultimately places falsehoods before the court. The rule prohibiting *ex parte* communications means that the lawyer and the legal assistant are prohibited from talking to the judge, the jury, and the adverse party unless opposing counsel is present.

adverse authority	contract	negligence
adverse party	diligent representation	pre-trial hearings
briefs	*ex parte* communications	statutes of limitations
candor	litigation paralegal	tickler system
cause of action	litigator	zeal
common law doctrine	memorandum of law	zealous representation

CASE

In re Conduct of Burrows

Supreme Court of Oregon, 1981.
291 Or. 135, 629 P.2d 820.

PER CURIAM.

Robert M. Burrows, District Attorney, and William D. Hostetler, Deputy District Attorney of Josephine County are accused by the Oregon State Bar of unethical conduct in the criminal proceedings against one Steven McAllister.

On June 13, 1976, at about 10:30 p. m. two people armed with a rifle robbed the "Why Not" market in Grants Pass, Josephine County, Oregon. The robbers fled the scene and were not apprehended.

On December 8, 1976, a 15 year old Grants Pass high school student claimed she was forcibly raped on that date by Steven McAllister.[1] There was evidence that the victim and other female students skipped school, voluntarily entered McAllister's place of residence and smoked marijuana shortly before the alleged rape. On December 10, 1976, the victim took a polygraph examination which indicated that she had told the truth when she said that she had been forcibly raped. McAllister, who was 26

or 27 years of age, was arrested on December 13, 1976, on an information charging him with first degree rape, filed by Hostetler as Deputy District Attorney. McAllister was arraigned on the following day and Brian J. Hawkins, an attorney in Grants Pass, was appointed to represent him.

Hostetler told Hawkins that he had some doubts about proving a first degree rape case because of his reservations about the victim's credibility as to force and resistance. Hostetler had visited with Burrows about the case and Burrows thought that there was room to negotiate. Hawkins took the position that the first degree rape information should be dismissed and McAllister should be charged with a lesser crime. Hawkins would then be willing to negotiate the lesser charge.

On December 23, 1976, a lengthy preliminary hearing was held in the District Court of Josephine County on the first degree rape information. Hawkins, as attorney for McAllister, was given the opportunity to cross examine the alleged victim and the state's other witnesses. The District Court found that there was probable cause to believe that McAllister had committed the crime of first degree rape and "bound him over" to the Circuit Court. McAllister was released from custody on a conditional release.

On February 17, 1977, the grand jury of Josephine County indicted McAllister for the June 13, 1976, armed robbery of the "Why Not" market. On the

---

[1]For the most part our recital of the facts is condensed from the opinion of the Disciplinary Review Board.

following day McAllister was arrested and placed in jail when he could not raise the $25,000 security amount. At the time of his arrest McAllister made a partial confession of his participation in the armed robbery. He admitted that he had driven the get-a-way car, but claimed that he was not inside the market at the time of the holdup.

Five days later, on February 22, 1977, McAllister told Josephine County Deputy Sheriff Dickson and Oregon State Trooper Assmus that he wanted to talk to Hostetler. McAllister wanted to make a "deal" wherein he would be released from custody to engage in undercover work on the local drug scene in exchange for a reduction or dismissal of the pending rape and robbery charges.

The police officers arranged the requested meeting at Hostetler's office. At the beginning of the meeting McAllister waived his *Miranda* rights. Hostetler informed McAllister that the rape case would not be discussed because McAllister was represented by an attorney in that case. Hostetler made no promises to McAllister. It was agreed that McAllister would be required to take a polygraph test to determine his knowledge of the drug traffic as a condition to his release to engage in undercover work. At the end of the meeting the police officers, in Hostetler's presence, told McAllister that he should not inform his attorney, Hawkins, of the proposed undercover work. Nothing was done or said by Hostetler to countermand the police officers' statement.

On February 23, 1977, McAllister was arraigned in the Circuit Court on the robbery charge. The state was represented at the arraignment by Deputy District Attorney Seitz. Hawkins was appointed to represent McAllister on the robbery charge in addition to the rape charge.

Late in the afternoon of February 25, 1977, Trooper Assmus told Hostetler that McAllister had successfully "passed" the polygraph examination and that the police urgently wanted McAllister released from custody that night. The truth was that at that time no examination had been given, and the police wanted McAllister released so that he could help them catch a criminal who had escaped from custody earlier in the day. Hostetler referred the request from the police to Burrows.

Burrows contacted the circuit judge in his chambers on an *ex parte* basis, without the knowledge of Hawkins, and had McAllister's security amount reduced from $25,000 to $2,500. McAllister, with the help of a relative, posted the required security and was released. At this point, both Burrows and Hostetler thought that McAllister had passed a

polygraph examination as to his knowledge of the local drug scene. Burrows specifically told the police officers to inform Hawkins of McAllister's release from jail and the agreement to work undercover. The police officers deliberately failed to inform Hawkins of the undercover work on the grounds that Hawkins could not be "trusted." It was the police officers' opinion that the undercover work and McAllister's safety would be "jeopardized" if they followed Burrows' instructions and told Hawkins. McAllister agreed that his attorney, Hawkins, should not be told about the undercover police work.

• • •

On August 11, 1977, Hawkins filed a complaint in letter form with the Oregon State Bar, complaining about the conduct of Burrows and Hostetler in the McAllister cases. The Oregon State Bar filed individual amended complaints against both Burrows and Hostetler, accusing each of unethical conduct in violation of the established standards of professional conduct.

The amended complaints against Burrows and Hostetler contained five separate causes of complaint. . . .

The trial of Burrows and Hostetler was held jointly before the Trial Board of the Oregon State Bar. The Trial Board found both Burrows and Hostetler not guilty of all causes of complaint except the second cause. It found both of the Accused guilty of the second cause—failure to notify Hawkins that the district attorney's office and the police had repeated contacts and a course of dealing with McAllister, and that they concealed the same from Hawkins.

The Disciplinary Review Board in effect considered the first and second causes of complaint together and then found both Burrows and Hostetler guilty in that they "violated DR 7-104(A)(1) by communicating, or causing others to communicate, with McAllister without obtaining Hawkins' consent." The Board of Review recommended "that each of the Accused be publicly reprimanded." It found both of the Accused not guilty of the third, fourth, and fifth causes of complaint.

The disciplinary rule under which Burrows and Hostetler were found guilty is as follows:

"DR 7-104 Communicating With One of Adverse Interest.

"(A) During the course of his representation of a client a lawyer shall not:

"(1) Communicate or cause another to communicate on the subject of the representation with a party he knows to be represented by a lawyer in that matter unless he has the prior consent of the lawyer representing such other party or is authorized by law to do so. " * * * "

. . .

In regard to the second cause of complaint, Burrows and Hostetler contend that the communications with McAllister did not relate to the rape or robbery but to the separate subject matter of undercover drug activities. They further contend that Burrows on February 25, 1977, clearly, distinctly, and explicitly instructed the police officers to inform Hawkins as to what had taken place and the fact that McAllister was going to engage in undercover work for the police. It is Hostetler's contention that after February 25 he had no further contact with McAllister or the undercover police work.[3]

The opinion of the Disciplinary Review Board as to the charges of violating DR 7-104(A)(1) is as follows:

"We believe that the Accused place an unreasonably narrow interpretation on the words 'subject of the representation,' as used in DR 7-104(A)(1). A criminal charge has two basic elements, guilt and sanction. It had to be obvious to the Accused that McAllister was seeking favorable treatment in the disposition of the pending charges, such as the dropping or reducing of certain charges and leniency with respect to the District Attorney's recommended sentencing. It is entirely possible, if not probable, that an accused needs competent legal counsel representation during the evolution of an agreement for leniency in exchange for cooperation with law enforcement agencies. McAllister was likely as concerned about the ultimate sentence that would be imposed or the charges that might be reduced or dropped as he was about the probabilities of a conviction. For all we know, if Hawkins had been involved in the February 22 and 25, 1977 discussions, an even better arrangement could have been struck in McAllister's behalf. It is quite clear that McAllister was laboring under some interpretations of his 'agreement' which were quite different than those held by the police or the Accused. This type of misunder-

standing would likely be avoided, or less likely to occur, if both sides were represented by competent counsel at all important stages. In short, we think that where it was clear that McAllister's undercover drug activities were likely to, or at least were expected to, impact the pending criminal charges, the subject matter of the communications necessarily involved the pending criminal charges.

"Further, we are not aware of any rule of law or principle which enables an attorney to excuse his failure to obtain an opposing attorney's consent by delegating the task to nonlawyers who, albeit deceptively, failed to follow through with their instructions. It would be difficult to hypothecate a set of circumstances which better illustrate the folly and danger of a principle of ethics which would permit a lawyer to excuse his misfeasance or nonfeasance by delegating to, and then later blaming, a non-lawyer. The overzealous and at times deceptive conduct of one or more of the police officers involved in this episode aptly illustrate the point.

"In any event, by the time the police officers were instructed to 'inform Hawkins,' two proscribed meetings had been held and the die was practically cast. Hawkins merely would have been presented with a *fait accompli*.

"In our opinion, both attorneys violated DR 7-104(A)(1) by communicating, or causing others to communicate, with McAllister without obtaining Hawkins' consent."

We agree with the Disciplinary Review Board and find both Burrows and Hostetler violated DR 7-104(A)(1) by communicating, or causing others to communicate, with McAllister without Hawkins' consent. We also find that Hostetler acted to conceal the communications by his failure to countermand the police officers' suggestion to McAllister that he not tell Hawkins. These violations are within the allegations of the second cause of complaint.

. . .

In regard to the third cause of complaint, the Oregon State Bar contends that Burrows' *ex parte* application to the circuit judge to obtain a reduction in the security amount for McAllister was to the merits of the cause and a violation of DR 7-110(B):

"In an adversary proceeding, a lawyer shall not communicate, or cause another to communicate, as to the merits of the cause with a judge or an official before whom a proceeding is pending * * *."

---

[3]Hostetler also argues: "The law has long permitted a defendant to waive counsel on a new subject matter even though he has counsel on another matter. See, e.g., *State v. Atteberry*, 39 Or.App. 141, 591 P.2d 409 (1979); *State v. Shoemaker*, 41 Or.App. 357, 597 P.2d 1305 (1979); * * *." The Oregon State Bar correctly points out that this argument confuses the law of suppression of evidence with the ethical duties of attorneys.

The Bar argues that the words "on the merits" refer to the content of the communication by counsel to the judge and not to a phase of the proceedings. It further argues that the evils of *ex parte* contact are that (1) the judge may be improperly influenced, and (2) the judge may be inaccurately informed. We agree.

The reduction of the security amount so that McAllister could be released from jail was an essential step in the plan to have McAllister engage in undercover work on the local drug scene. Although the agreement or understanding on the undercover work was indefinite, McAllister expected that he would receive favorable treatment by way of dismissal of charges or reductions of sentences. The District Attorney's office was interested in having McAllister do the undercover work in hope that he might furnish information on the local drug traffic. When Burrows contacted the circuit judge he was talking to the judge who, in the normal course of events, would in the future pass sentence on McAllister. Burrows told the judge that McAllister was being released to do undercover work for the police and innocently misinformed him that McAllister had "passed" a polygraph examination. Burrows' *ex parte* contact with the judge involved more than a reduction of the security amount. It also included information which the judge could use down the road in passing sentence upon McAllister. The fact that, by hindsight, it appears that Burrows' communications with the judge were favorable to McAllister is immaterial. In the context of this case we find the *ex parte* contact was "on the merits" of the proceedings. We find that Burrows is guilty of the third charge in violating DR 7-110(B).

. . .

Questions

1. The Disciplinary Review Board was reviewing the actions of attorneys who had delegated responsibility to police officers. Look at the language used by the Disciplinary Review Board. Do you think this opinion would apply to the activities that attorneys could delegate to paralegals? Why or why not?

2. Why does the Disciplinary Review Board conclude that McAllister's attorney should have been present during these communications? Do you agree with these conclusions?

3. Look at the court's discussion of the evils of *ex parte* communications with judges. Do you think this discussion could be applied to legal assistants who attempt to have an *ex parte* communication with a judge? Why or why not?

CONFIDENTIALITY

CHAPTER OBJECTIVES

After reading this chapter, you should
be able to:

- Understand the ethical obligations of
  confidentiality.
- Distinguish the attorney-client privilege
  from the ethical rule of confidentiality.

- Recognize exceptions to the attorney-client
  privilege and to confidentiality.
- Employ measures in your everyday work
  routine to ensure that client confidences are
  protected.

C onfidentiality. The mere mention of the word conjures up images of
   intriguing secrets.

We all know how difficult it may be sometimes to keep a secret. It is a good
rule of thumb, however, for both the attorney and the nonlawyer employee to
avoid altogether speaking with third parties about any representation of
clients, for an inartful reference about a client may reveal more than intended.
As we will see throughout this chapter, it is vital that both the attorney and
legal assistant preserve the secrets of the client.

Confidentiality is more than a good rule to which the law office should
adhere, though. It is an obligation to the client. Confidentiality obligations are
placed upon the attorney and her nonlawyer employees by way of the rules of
ethics. In addition to the *Model Code* and the *Model Rules*, Guideline 6 of the
American Bar Association Model Guidelines for the Utilization of Legal
Assistant Services states,

> It is the responsibility of a lawyer to take reasonable measures to ensure that
> all client confidences are preserved by a legal assistant.

To help you understand what this obligation means, this chapter will first
discuss the kinds of communication that attorneys are ethically required to
keep confidential. As we see from Guideline 6, these rules have been extended
to the attorney's nonlawyer employees. The second half of this chapter is
therefore devoted to discussing this application and what it means to law
office practice.

OPENING EXERCISE

Upon walking into an initial client conference, Kristen, a legal assistant at a
prominent family law firm in Washington, D.C., was pleasantly surprised to see
Alexandra Busse in the room. Busse was a major Hollywood personality and Kristen
was a big fan.

Busse began the initial interview by asking that anything which they discussed
be kept confidential, as adverse publicity could harm her career. She then explained

that she was seeking representation to help her end her marriage of fifteen years. Although the relationship she and her husband shared was generally a loving one, they had recently had a terrible disagreement. After they had argued for more than an hour, Busse got up to leave the room but instead tripped and fell, giving herself a nasty black eye. This injury held up production of the movie in which Busse was supposed to star, causing her to lose the role for which she had been slated.

Busse had decided the marriage was costing her more than it was worth and concluded that it was time to end it. She therefore sought the services of this group of prominent divorce lawyers.

Kristen was saddened by the story Busse related. She couldn't help thinking that perhaps Busse was ending this relationship prematurely. The conference worried Kristen all day long.

After work, Kristen was to meet her boyfriend, Jim, for dinner. When she arrived at the restaurant, she found that she was still troubled by the meeting. "Maybe I'll talk to Jim about this. If I don't mention any names, it should be okay. After all, Jim is an engineer. How could talking to him possibly hurt Ms. Busse?" Kristen reasoned.

Therefore, in general terms, without mentioning any names, Kristen related some of Busse's story to Jim. Unbeknown to them, a tabloid reporter who knew Busse was in town was seated at the next table. Catching Kristen's name, the reporter did some quick research and learned of Kristen's place of employment. He pieced together several facts.

The next day the headline on the tabloid announced, "Alexandra Busse divorcing wife-beating husband!"

Do you think Kristen has behaved unethically? Assume that Busse had not asked that their discussion be kept confidential. Does your answer change? Should a legal assistant always be prevented from discussing a client's case with third parties? Why or why not?

THE GENERAL RULE
OF CONFIDENTIALITY:
AN ETHICAL OBLIGATION

Preserving the confidences of the client is one of the lawyer's most serious ethical obligations. Therefore, as the exercise demonstrates, our natural inclination to talk about our experiences must be tempered. All too easily, a simple slip of the tongue can seriously harm the client whose interests the law office has a responsibility to protect.

Keeping client information confidential is not merely an obligation of the attorney but, as we shall discuss at length in this chapter, it has also become an obligation of the attorney's nonlawyer support staff. Regularly the nonlawyer learns secrets about the client that the client shares with his attorney. The client shares the information about himself because he believes it will help his attorney understand why the client has sought legal help. Much of the information the client shares is factored into the legal strategy the attorney will employ. For this reason, the legal assistant as well as the attorney must take steps to protect confidential communications from being disclosed.

Disclosure of confidential information happens frequently, though most often inadvertently. Inadvertent disclosure may occur in the preparation of discovery matters, in conversations with peers at a cocktail party, or even when drafting documents. So, despite the best of intentions, communications may be revealed.

Preventing disclosure of information, no matter how it occurs, requires that the legal assistant study and understand the complicated rules of confidentiality.

THE PURPOSE OF THE RULE OF CONFIDENTIALITY

It has been said that the purpose of the confidentiality rules is, in brief, to encourage the client consulting an attorney to be open and honest. In turn, this allows the attorney to provide the best representation possible.

Confidentiality rules encourage the client to be open and honest with his attorney, providing the attorney with all of the background that is necessary to represent the client as effectively as possible. The Ethical Considerations of the *Model Code* explain the purpose behind the rules:

> Both the fiduciary relationship existing between lawyer and client and the proper functioning of the legal system require the preservation by the lawyer of confidences and secrets of one who has employed or sought to employ him. A client must feel free to discuss whatever he wishes with his lawyer and a lawyer must be equally free to obtain information beyond that volunteered by his client. A lawyer should be fully informed of all the facts of the matter he is handling in order for his client to obtain the full advantage of our legal system. . . . The observance of the ethical obligation of a lawyer to hold inviolate the confidences and secrets of his client not only facilitates the full development of facts essential to proper representation of the client but also encourages laymen to seek early legal assistance." *Model Code of Professional Responsibility* EC 4-1.

The confidentiality rule appears to be straightforward, as it is based on the theory that attorneys and their nonlawyer employees should preserve the confidences of their clients. However, it can be difficult to determine what exactly is a confidence.

The idea of attorneys being forced to keep the confidences of those who have sought their advice has always generated significant debate, however. Some believe attorneys hide behind the confidentiality rules to escape a *moral* duty to reveal the unsavory conduct of their clients. Others consider that the attorney-client relationship is sacred and that no shared information should ever be revealed.

What do you think about your corresponding obligation to maintain confidences? How comfortable are you with protecting client's secrets? Do you think a broad rule of confidentiality protection is justified? Be prepared to debate and defend your answers. | **EXERCISE 5.1**

WHAT IS THE RULE OF CONFIDENTIALITY?

The ethical rules of confidentiality require that the attorney (and his nonlawyer support staff) refrain from revealing *any* information about the client.

Ethical Conforming to the standards imposed by the ethical codes in place in the state in which attorney practices law.

Confidentiality The ethical rule imposed upon an attorney or any legal professional to keep the legal professional from revealing any information about the client.

Attorney-Client Privilege A legal doctrine that prohibits an attorney who represents a client from testifying in open court and revealing the secrets of the client.

Work Product Doctrine A legal doctrine that protects documents prepared in anticipation of litigation from being disclosed to the adversary.

Evidentiary Rules Rules designed to protect from disclosure what might otherwise become evidence during court proceedings.

According to the ethical rule of confidentiality, with limited exception, the attorney is prevented from revealing information about the client to anybody, at any time, in any situation. It is an **ethical** obligation of the attorney, imposed upon her by the ethical codes in place in the state in which she practices law.

In addition to the specific rule of **confidentiality,** two related rules exist to protect secret information of the client from being revealed. They are commonly known as the **attorney-client privilege** and the **work product doctrine.** However, these rules apply only in limited situations.

These are **evidentiary rules.** In other words, they are designed to protect from disclosure what might otherwise become "evidence" during court proceedings. The attorney-client privilege prohibits the attorney from testifying in open court and revealing the secrets of the client. The work product doctrine protects documents prepared in anticipation of litigation from being disclosed to the adversary. (Both rules are discussed in full later in this chapter.) Unlike the confidentiality rule that appears only in state ethical codes, the work product doctrine and the attorney-client privilege are codified in the *Federal Rules of Evidence* and, frequently, in state statutes.

What is the relationship between the ethical rule of confidentiality and the two evidentiary rules—attorney-client privilege and work product doctrine? In short, the evidentiary rules are "subsets" of sorts of the ethical rule of confidentiality.

As just noted, the work product doctrine and the attorney-client privilege protect secrets of the client from being disclosed during litigation proceedings. However, the ethical rule of confidentiality protects information about the client from being disclosed at any time. Therefore, the ethical rule of confidentiality provides much greater protection.

Anything protected by the attorney-client privilege or work product doctrine is *necessarily* protected by confidentiality. The reverse is not true. Therefore, not everything that is protected by confidentiality is protected by the work product doctrine or the attorney-client privilege.

The relationship between the attorney-client privilege and the confidentiality rules has been explained by the drafters of the *Model Rules:*

> The principle of confidentiality is given effect in two related bodies of law, the attorney-client privilege (which includes the work product doctrine) in the law of evidence and the rule of confidentiality established in professional ethics. The attorney-client privilege applies in judicial and other proceedings in which a lawyer may be called as a witness or otherwise required to produce evidence concerning a client. The rule of client-lawyer confidentiality applies in situations other than those where evidence is sought from the lawyer through compulsion of law. The confidentiality rule applies not merely to matters communicated in confidence by the client but also to all information relating to the representation, whatever its source. . . ." *Model Rules of Professional Conduct* Rule 1.6, Cmt (1994).

THE ATTORNEY-CLIENT PRIVILEGE

It is important to begin our study of confidentiality with a review of the attorney-client privilege and the work product doctrine. This is because, as you have just seen, the ethical obligation to maintain client confidentiality builds upon the attorney-client privilege and the work product doctrine.

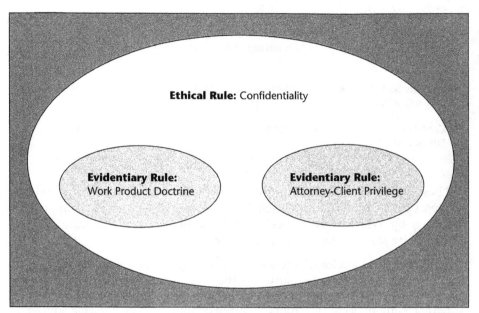

EXHIBIT 5.1
The Relationship
Between the
Ethical Rule of
Confidentiality
and the
Evidentiary Rules

Life has taught us that people often enjoy certain special privileges. We have come to recognize that the word **privilege** means that special rights are given to someone because, in some way, they are special.

As defined by *Merriam-Webster's Collegiate Dictionary*, "privilege" means "a right or immunity granted as a peculiar benefit, advantage or favor."[1] In *Black's Law Dictionary*, "privilege" is defined as:

> A particular and peculiar benefit or advantage enjoyed by a person, company or class, beyond the common advantages of other citizens.[2]

In the law, privileges may exempt certain parties from having an obligation to do something. Often this includes someone's privilege to not have to reveal information or to not have to communicate certain information. The law has specifically defined **privileged communications.** They are "Those statements made by certain persons within a protracted relationship such as husband-wife, attorney-client, priest-penitent and the like which the law protects from forced disclosure on the witness stand at the option of the witness, client, penitent, spouse."[3]

For our purposes, privileges prevent the disclosure of information revealed in confidence to certain parties. The attorney-client privilege is one such privilege. Proposed Federal Rule 503 of the **Federal Rules of Evidence** is a good summary of what is the law in many states.

It is widely recognized that the attorney-client privilege is composed of several components. All of the components must be in place before the privilege can be said to "attach" to a particular communication.

Privilege A particular and peculiar benefit or advantage enjoyed by a person or corporation, beyond the common advantages of other citizens.

Privileged Communications Those statements, made by certain persons within a relationship, that the law protects from forced disclosure.

Federal Rules of Evidence Rules that govern the admissibility of evidence at trial in federal courts and before U.S. Magistrates.

---

[1] MERRIAM-WEBSTER'S COLLEGIATE DICTIONARY 928 (10TH ed. 1993). BY PERMISSION. FROM MERRIAM-WEBSTER'S COLLEGIATE® DICTIONARY © 1993 BY MERRIAM-WEBSTER, INC., PUBLISHER OF THE MERRIAM-WEBSTER® DICTIONARIES.

[2] BLACK'S LAW DICTIONARY 1197 (6th ed. 1990). Reprinted with permission from *Black's Law Dictionary*, 6th ed. 1990 (Copyright, West Publishing Company).

[3] *Id.* at 1198.

EXHIBIT 5.2
What Kind of
Information is
Protected?

- ■ Attorney-Client Privilege: Evidentiary Rule — ■ Prevents the attorney from testifying during court proceedings as to secrets of the client.

- ■ Work Product Doctrine: Evidentiary Rule — ■ Protects documents prepared in anticipation of litigation from being disclosed to adversaries.

- ■ Confidentiality: Ethical Rule — ■ Protects all information from being revealed at any time.

These components were set forth many years ago in a treatise on evidence written by renowned evidence scholar Professor Wigmore. The components espoused by Wigmore have been widely accepted and frequently cited as authority by lawyers and courts. They are as follows:

> (1) Where legal advice of any kind is sought (2) from a professional legal adviser in his capacity as such, (3) the communications relating to that purpose, (4) made in confidence (5) by the client, (6) are at his instance permanently protected (7) from disclosure by himself or by the legal adviser, (8) except the protection be waived. 8 Wigmore, Evidence §2292 (McNaughton rev. 1961).[4]

A discussion of each of these elements will help to explain the rule.

(1) Where Legal Advice of Any Kind Is Sought

Legal Advice Advice that is given exclusively by those licensed to practice law, about legal matters, to clients.

The first element requires that **legal advice** be sought. It is not adequate that the client sought out the attorney for assistance with financial planning matters or tax preparation. In those instances, the privilege will not attach.

One of the original limitations of the privilege was that it only attached where legal representation was sought for purposes of litigation. Therefore, unless the representation actually resulted in litigation, nothing was protected by the attorney-client privilege.

This is no longer the rule. Today, whenever an attorney's advice is sought, and the purpose of the relationship is legal in nature, the privilege will automatically attach to the communication to protect the matters discussed. Therefore, a client seeking an attorney for assistance in structuring an estate or for tax advice will also have the benefit of the attorney-client protection. The advice need not result in litigation. The client may not even agree to retain the attorney. The privilege still attaches.

(2) From a Professional Legal Adviser in His Capacity as Such

The second element requires that the client must seek legal advice from one who is qualified to give legal advice: namely, a lawyer licensed to practice in that particular jurisdiction.

However, as we will discuss more fully later in this chapter, the privilege is extended to those nonlawyers who assist the attorney. This is because modern law office practice encourages attorneys to use the assistance of nonlawyers to

---

[4]JOHN HENRY WIGMORE, EVIDENCE IN TRIALS AT COMMON LAW (revised by John T. McNaughton 1961). Copyright ©1961 by John T. McNaughton. Published by Little, Brown and Company.

| HIGHLIGHT | What Are Privileged Communications? |

If a communication is considered to be privileged that means a certain party cannot reveal the communication in court. However, in order to find that a privilege protects a communication, a special relationship between the parties must exist.

For example, a privilege may protect confidences of a client from being revealed by the attorney. The relationship that exists in this case is attorney-client, and the privilege is therefore known as the attorney-client privilege. Although this may be the most commonly recognized privilege, other kinds of relationships also give rise to privileges. A look at a few cases may illustrate how different kinds of privileges protect confidences.

In *People v. Reyes*, 144 Misc. 2d 805, 545 N.Y.S.2d 653 (1989), the defendant's conversation with a priest was held to be a privileged communication. At issue in the case, then, was the clergyman-penitent privilege.

The defendant, Edwin Reyes, allegedly committed a crime and then went to nearby St. Mary's Church and asked to speak with a priest. Father Schmidt was thereupon summoned to the church to speak with Reyes. During his conversation with Father Schmidt, the defendant told the priest that he "had done something very bad" and related that he had made 10 or 12 people lie down on the floor and then he had fired a shot. At that point, Father Schmidt advised Reyes to go to the police but Reyes refused to do so and instead said that he wanted to pray. Father Schmidt later went to the police and told them about Reyes, who was still at St. Mary's. Reyes was subsequently arrested.

The court held that the conversation between Father Schmidt and Reyes was a communication protected by the clergyman-penitent privilege because, when Reyes sought out a priest, he had been

seeking "spiritual advice" and because he had intended their conversation to be confidential. Father Schmidt's testimony, therefore, should not have been presented to the grand jury.

United States v. Marashi, 913 F.2d 724 (9th Cir. 1990), discussed the application of the husband-wife privilege, also known as the spousal privilege. Generally, the husband-wife privilege works to bar testimony about private communications made between spouses during the course of the marriage.

When Sharon Smith Marashi ("Sharon") discovered that her husband, Dr. Marashi, was having an affair with his secretary (and had even, in fact, flown to Europe with her) Sharon immediately filed for divorce. Apparently, the husband of the secretary, Sherrie Danzig, likewise filed for divorce. However, "[f]iling for divorce was not enough for [Sharon] Smith and [Steve] Danzig. They met several times to discuss how to get even with their unfaithful spouses." Eventually, Sharon and Danzig decided to contact the IRS and report Sharon's husband, Dr. Marashi, for income tax evasion.

During his trial, Dr. Marashi attempted to prevent Sharon's testimony from being heard by invoking the husband-spouse privilege. While the court recognized the validity and viability of the spousal privilege, the court noted that the privilege would not prevent Sharon's testimony *in this case*. As the communication was made before a third party, the court could not find that one set of information was meant to be *confidential*. The court recognized that the second communication (concerning Marashi's instructions to Sharon on how to underreport his income) *was* confidential, but the privilege did not apply because the statements were made in furtherance of joint criminal activity.

---

provide more efficient and economical service. To fail to extend the privilege to nonlawyers would compromise the operation of the law firm and defeat the purpose of the privilege.

(3) The Communication Relating to That Purpose

Wigmore noted that the communication must relate to the reason the client sought the legal advice. This means that, to be protected, the communication must be made in the course of the attorney-client relationship, wherein the attorney is giving counsel or advice. However, as the client should be free to discuss his problems, the privilege is not limited to those comments relevant to the attorney's representation of the client.

(4) Made in Confidence

The fourth requirement is that the communication must be made in confidence. Thus, the communication must be made in a private setting, where it is unlikely that any other individual could overhear the conversation. Moreover, the communication must only be made to those who need to know the information to further the communicant's purpose of receiving legal advice or securing legal representation. Generally this would extend the privilege to any person who was working on this client's representation. Obviously, the attorney should know of the communication. Almost as obvious is the fact that the legal assistant who is assigned to the case should be included within the protection of the privilege.

(5) By the Client

The fifth element merely states that the protection extends to information communicated by the client. Generally, it is acknowledged that the privilege will not include communications *about* the client, gleaned from conversation with another party.

(6) Are at His Instance Permanently Protected

The sixth requirement advises that secrets from the client will be protected *at the client's instance.* This is terribly important language for it demonstrates an important quality of the privilege: the privilege belongs to the *client,* and the attorney must seek permission from the *client* before revealing any information.

(7) From Disclosure by Himself or the Legal Adviser

The seventh component embodies the basic thrust of the entire attorney-client privilege. Confidential information cannot be disclosed by either the client or the attorney.

(8) Except the Protection Be Waived

The eighth component of the privilege is a waiver provision. Waiving the privilege means, in essence, that the client has agreed to disclosure of the information. Seldom are legal rules absolute in their application, and the privilege is no exception. Because of the importance of understanding the waiver rules, the next section is devoted to this discussion.

Waiving the Attorney-Client Privilege

Waiver An express or implied relinquishment of a legal right.

The definition of waiver is simple. A **waiver** is an express or implied relinquishment of a legal right. A privilege can be waived in a number of ways. We have already noted that the privilege belongs to the client. As such, only the client can waive the privilege. Therefore, the privilege is most clearly waived when the client gives permission to the attorney to relate what was said during the confidential consultation or when the client herself speaks out.

Courts have also been willing to infer that the privilege was meant to be waived, despite the fact that the client has not consented to disclosure, when the actions of the client have revealed the information. This is an **implied waiver** because while not expressly saying that the information may be disclosed, the client, through his behavior, has made it necessary to reveal the information. For example, the privilege is said to be waived where the client puts in issue a particular piece of confidential information that goes directly to the claim or defense which the client is asserting. An example may illustrate this point more clearly.

Implied Waiver A waiver that occurs because the client has, through his behavior, made it necessary to reveal the information.

In one case, a husband who was dying of terminal cancer and his wife agreed to divorce before his death. Each retained separate attorneys. They agreed to sign a **separation agreement** drawn up by the husband's attorney and were to meet at a specified time in the husband's attorney's office to sign the agreement. Before her husband arrived, the woman discussed the proposed separation agreement with her husband's attorney. She later discussed the same separation agreement with her own attorney. After her husband's death, she tried to have the separation agreement set aside, claiming she was fraudulently induced into signing the agreement by her husband's attorney.

Separation Agreement A contract between spouses who have separated or who are about to separate, concerning property, child custody, child support, alimony, etc.

The woman argued that her husband's attorney had erroneously advised her that the agreement would only be binding and enforceable after it was approved by the court, and state law dictated that it would take the court ninety days to approve the separation agreement. She claimed that she believed that her husband, whom she knew was suffering from terminal cancer, would not live ninety days. She asserted that this was the only reason she had agreed to sign the separation agreement.

The opposing parties, including her late husband's parents, asserted several defenses to the wife's arguments. Included among their defenses was the theory that the wife could not have relied upon any statements made by her husband's attorney, as she had met with her own attorney several days later and he would have told her the correct law. At trial, to prove their theory, the defendants attempted to **cross-examine** the wife about her conversation with her attorney. The wife asserted that this conversation was protected by the attorney-client privilege.

Defenses Allegations of fact or legal theories offered to offset or defeat claims or demands.

Cross-Examine To question a witness after the direct examination of that witness by the side that initially called the witness.

Upon review of the issue, the Colorado Supreme Court ruled that the client wife had put the communication into issue and thus had impliedly waived the protections of the attorney-client privilege. After all, her entire cause of action was based on her conversations with the attorneys. See *Mountain States Telephone and Telegraph Company v. DiFede*, 780 P.2d 533 (Colo. 1989).

The privilege can also be impliedly waived where the client himself repeats the confidential information to a third party whose input is not needed in completing legal representation. For example, should a client, after consulting a divorce attorney, also talk to his employer about his extramarital relations, the privilege would be considered waived because the employer need not be privy to the information to further the client's legal representation.

Exceptions to the Privilege As distinguished from waiver, exceptions to the privilege exist where the communication is such that it is never found to be within the privilege.

Exceptions to the Attorney-Client Privilege

There are also **exceptions to the privilege.** If a communication falls within one of the exceptions, the attorney or her legal assistant would be required to reveal the information. In other words, the attorney could not protect the communication from disclosure because the privilege is not considered to have ever *attached* to the communication.

Exceptions are quite different from waiver. When asserted, waiver means that, while the communication would under normal circumstances be protected from disclosure, the client has waived the protections of the privilege. However, an *exception* exists where the communication is such that it is never found to be within the privilege.

Therefore, the consent of a client to reveal information is not needed if the information falls within one of the exceptions.

Several exceptions to the privilege exist. For example, the privilege rule usually does not apply when a court asks the attorney to reveal the *identity of a client*. Further, *fee arrangements* between the attorney and client are likewise held to not be confidential.

Crime-Fraud Exception An exception to the attorney-client privilege that arises when a client tells an attorney of an intention to commit a crime or a fraudulent act or seeks advice to assist her in realizing this goal.

An additional exception is the **crime-fraud exception.** If a client tells her attorney of her intention to commit a crime or fraudulent act or seeks advice to assist her in realizing this goal, the attorney may reveal the information to the court because such information cannot be protected by the privilege. This exception is justified as follows:

> In order that the rule [of privilege] may apply there must be both professional confidence and professional employment, but if the client has a criminal object in view . . . one of these elements must necessarily be absent. The client must either conspire with his [counsel] or deceive him. If his criminal object is avowed, the client does not consult his adviser professionally, because it cannot be the [lawyer's] business to further any criminal object. If the client does not avow his object, he reposes no confidence. . . . The [lawyer's] advice is obtained by a fraud. *In re Marriage of Decker,* 153 Ill. 2d 298, 180 Ill. Dec. 17, 606 N.E. 2d 1094, 1101 (1992), quoting *State v. Phelps* 24 Or. App. 329, 332, 545 P.2d 901, 902 (1976).

For an excellent discussion of the attorney-client privilege and the crime-fraud exception, see *In re Marriage of Decker,* 153 Ill. 2d 298, 180 Ill. Dec. 17, 606 N.E.2d 1094 (1992).

THE WORK PRODUCT DOCTRINE

In addition to the attorney-client privilege, the work product doctrine protects the work of the attorney on a client's case from being revealed to a court or other tribunal. It is a slightly different evidentiary rule.

The everyday work of the attorney may require that the lawyer draft internal memoranda for distribution to other members of his litigation team, revealing his courtroom strategy. The lawyer also may forward to the client a letter describing the work that must still be completed in order to be prepared to present a particular theory in the courtroom. To disclose such documents to opposing counsel understandably would have disastrous consequences. For that reason, courts have determined that some protection of these materials was necessary to ensure broad protection of the client's case.

In 1947, in the famous case of *Hickman v. Taylor,* 329 U.S. 495, 67 S.Ct. 385, 91 L.Ed. 451, the court created the work product doctrine. Designed to keep adversarial attorneys from discovering trial preparation of opposing counsel, this doctrine covers only material prepared in anticipation of litigation. Any of the lawyer's ideas on how to conduct a case, known as his **mental impressions,** are considered to be protected by an unqualified privilege.

The only exception to this rule is that **informational materials,** which include factual research materials, can be obtained by opposing counsel where no adequate substitute can be found.

Although the work product rule protects certain documents formulated by an attorney and his staff, an important caveat must be noted. A previously prepared document cannot be protected merely by handing it to an attorney for safekeeping. Many defendants have tried to protect incriminating evidence from disclosure in this way, only to learn that the evidence is not protected.

How the rule works can be seen in the following example. A report written in 1975 may spell out to the vice-president the steps to take when promoting an employee. The report may indicate that women are never to be promoted to a managerial position. When a lawsuit alleging discriminatory hiring practices is brought against the company in 1990, the CEO may not protect the report from being turned over to opposing counsel during discovery simply by handing it to the attorney. It is the work of the *attorney* which is protected from disclosure, after all, and not that of the CEO. Moreover, the document must be prepared in anticipation of litigation in order to be protected by this rule.

As this example shows, the work product doctrine can become especially important when handling discovery matters. In producing documents for opposing counsel, care must be taken to avoid turning over documents protected by this evidentiary rule. Often the paralegal is involved in handling discovery requests. For that reason, it is especially important for the legal assistant to be aware of these rules. Later, this chapter will discuss the application of the work product doctrine to the work of the litigation legal assistant handling discovery requests.

Mental Impressions Any of the ideas of a lawyer on how to conduct a case or her trial strategy.

Informational Materials These materials include factual research materials and can be obtained by opposing counsel where no adequate substitute can be found.

Try applying the attorney-client privilege and the work product doctrine to the following situations. Should the attorney reveal the information?

EXERCISE 5.2

A. Charo Client tells Alan Attorney that, although she had nothing to do with the crime, she knows the location of a kidnapping victim. She asks Alan not to say anything because she does not want to get involved.

B. Alice Attorney learns that her client plans to kidnap his daughter upon their next scheduled parental visit.

C. While divorce proceedings are pending, Carl Client kidnaps his son. His attorney, Anna, asks to withdraw from representation. The court, believing that Anna Attorney has information about the whereabouts of the child, orders Anna to reveal everything she knows.

D. Carlita Client has kidnapped a child from a shopping mall. Two years later, feeling pangs of remorse after the child becomes ill, she consults Anthony Attorney for advice on returning the child.

E. Arthur Attorney has been representing Chen Client for several years and knows that, because Chen was distraught at not being able to have children, Chen's mother kidnapped a baby for her. When the kidnapping is discovered, only Arthur and Chen are implicated in the scheme.

PARALEGALS IN THE SPOTLIGHT

While working as a paralegal at Kentucky's largest law firm, Merrell Williams was exposed to many of the confidential papers of one of the firm's clients, Brown & Williamson Tobacco Corporation. Brown & Williamson manufactures cigarettes, including the brands Kool, Raleigh, and Viceroy.

Presumably, exposure to client documents was part of Williams's responsibilities. However, the law firm did not expect Williams to secretly copy a boxful of those documents.

Williams smoked cigarettes for years and is currently suffering from heart disease. When he read the documents of Brown & Williamson Tobacco Corp., he was convinced that the documents indicated that tobacco companies had engaged in a conspiracy to conceal the dangers of cigarette smoking. Consequently, Williams copied those documents and is considering filing a lawsuit against Brown & Williamson.

The law firm, Wyatt, Tarrant & Combs, and the tobacco company went to court, seeking to secure an injunction to bar Williams from disclosing any of the material Williams had copied. On October 5, 1993, the court awarded the injunction, and Williams is currently barred from revealing any information and, therefore, from filing his lawsuit.

The law firm and tobacco company are also asking Williams to return all of the documents he copied. Williams's attorney says it would be difficult for him to return all of the information because, for four years, Williams's "brain cells absorbed, ordered, collated, and retained" the information contained in the documents... To return this information, Williams would have to cut off his head and return his head in a basket."

Currently, the court is deciding whether the documents are protected by the attorney-client privilege. Williams's attorney contends that the case may be subject to the crime-fraud exception.

Source: *Paralegal fights to use secret tobacco papers,* CHICAGO DAILY LAW BULLETIN, Jan. 3, 1994, at 1, 16. Reprinted by permission.

THE ETHICAL RULES OF CONFIDENTIALITY

The attorney may not often be called to testify against his client. However, the attorney is daily faced with information from clients that must be kept confidential. Confidentiality encourages candor between the attorney and his client, and helps to ensure that the client's interests are protected. The drafters of the *Model Rules* recognized the importance of the confidential aspect of the attorney-client relationship.

The ethical rule of confidentiality embodies both the attorney-client privilege and the work product doctrine. Yet, the confidentiality rules have been extended far beyond the requirements of these evidentiary rules. The ethical rule of confidentiality increases the types of matters that cannot be revealed by a client's attorney. It protects more information than that which is protected by the attorney-client privilege.

The confidentiality rules are ethical obligations of the attorney. Their scope is delineated in attorneys' codes of ethics. The original code of ethics for attorneys was fairly vague about the extent of the confidentiality obligation. In essence, the *Canons* required that attorneys protect the secrets and confidences of a client but did not distinguish the two terms.

The *Model Code,* which was developed in 1969, took steps to provide clearer guidance and defined this obligation in greater detail. Most notably, it created a distinction between confidences and secrets. It also provided somewhat different protections for both. The *Model Rules,* adopted in 1983, created a more expansive definition of confidentiality and now protects the widest array of information from being disclosed.

The *Model Code* and the *Model Rules* allow different information to be revealed in different instances. It is important that you carefully consider the language of the *Rules* or the *Code* governing your jurisdiction.

The Model Code

In DR 4-101, the *Model Code* sets forth the responsibilities of the attorney. The basic rule reads as follows:

> (B) Except when permitted under DR 4-101(C), a lawyer shall not knowingly:
> (1) Reveal a confidence or secret of his client.
> (2) Use a confidence or secret of his client to the disadvantage of the client.
> (3) Use a confidence or secret of his client for the advantage of himself or of a third person, unless the client consents after full disclosure.

Often, we use the terms confidences and secrets interchangeably. According to the *Model Code,* however, these two terms have different meanings that are not to be confused. **Confidence** is defined in DR 4-101(A) to mean information protected by the attorney-client privilege, the evidentiary obligation of the attorney; **secret** means any other information, gained through the professional relationship, that the client has asked be held inviolate or where the disclosure of such information would be embarrassing or detrimental to the client.

The ethical considerations of the *Code* further provide that the privilege extends beyond the termination of the attorney-client relationship. Whether the relationship ends because the attorney is asked to step aside or because the client dies, the attorney remains bound by his ethical obligation to preserve the confidences of the client. See *Model Code of Professional Responsibility* EC 4-6 (1986).

As with most legal principles, exceptions to this rule exist. The exceptions to DR4-101(B) are discussed below in "Exceptions to Confidentiality."

> **Confidence** As used in the *Model Code,* information protected by the attorney-client privilege.

> **Secret** As used in the *Model Code,* any other information, gained through the professional relationship, that the client has asked remain inviolate or which would be embarrassing or detrimental to the client.

The Model Rules

While it seems that the *Code* would protect much of what is related by the client to the attorney, the *Rules* have been said to take an even more expansive approach.

The *Model Rules* require that any information which the attorney has received from the client that relates to that client's representation should be kept confidential. There is little exception built into that rule.

Specifically, Rule 1.6(a), "Confidentiality of Information," states:

> (a) A lawyer shall not reveal information relating to representation of a client unless the client consents after consultation, except for disclosures that are impliedly authorized in order to carry out the representation, and except as stated in paragraph (b). *Model Rules of Professional Conduct* Rule 1.6 (1994).

Exceptions to this rule are discussed below.

The *Model Rules* do not attempt to delineate the kinds of information that may be kept secret, as does the *Code*. Instead, the *Rules* require that any information relating to the client's representation remain between the client and her attorney.

It has been noted that the *Rules* provide a greater degree of protection in terms of confidentiality. Under the *Code,* where the client did not specifically ask that the information be kept secret, if the lawyer was convinced that revealing the information would not harm the client or embarrass him, the attorney could reveal it. Therefore, under the *Code,* the client must specifically request that information be kept confidential in order for it to not be freely revealed.[5]

EXERCISE 5.3   Obtain a copy of your jurisdiction's confidentiality rule. Is it patterned after the *Model Code* or the *Model Rules,* or is your jurisdiction's rule patterned after neither? As you read the following sections, try to determine the scope of your rule.

Exceptions to Confidentiality

There are limited exceptions to the confidentiality rules, however. Both the *Code* and the *Rules* permit attorneys to reveal certain information, in special circumstances, without violating ethical obligations. Many commentators believe that the exceptions created by the *Model Rules* are much more limited than those contained within the *Code,* however; and, again, the *Rules* protect from disclosure a wider variety of information.

We begin, therefore, with the narrow exceptions set forth by the *Rules.* The exceptions to the *Rules,* as provided in Rule 1.6(b), read as follows:

(b) A lawyer may reveal such information to the extent the lawyer reasonably believes necessary:
   (1) to prevent the client from committing a criminal act that the lawyer believes is likely to result in imminent death or substantial bodily harm; or
   (2) to establish a claim or defense on behalf of the lawyer in a controversy between the lawyer and the client, to establish a defense to a criminal charge or civil claim against the lawyer based upon conduct in which the client was involved, or to respond to allegations in any proceeding concerning the lawyer's representation of the client. *Model Rules of Professional Conduct* Rule 1.6(b) (1994).

Before the attorney may reveal communications, she must have a *reasonable belief* that it is necessary to reveal the information. It is simply not enough that the attorney thinks it may be helpful to reveal the information. For example, an attorney is not obligated to report to the police every time a client squeals, "I am so angry with my boss that I could just *kill* him." Unless there is something more such that an event is reasonably likely to occur, the attorney is under no obligation to break his code of silence.

Where an attorney reasonably believes disclosure is necessary in order to prevent a client from committing a criminal act that "the lawyer believes is likely to result in imminent death or substantial bodily harm," the lawyer may disclose the information. *Model Rules of Professional Conduct* Rule 1.6(b) (1994). Therefore, should a client reveal that he plans to kidnap his ex-wife and deprive her of food until she increases her alimony payments to him, the attorney may ethically call the police and inform them of his client's inten-

[5] *See* HAZARD & HODES, THE LAW OF LAWYERING, Section 1.6:201. Reprinted from *The Law of Lawyering,* by Geoffrey C. Hazard, Jr., and W. William Hodes, with the permission of Prentice Hall Law & Business.

tions, if the attorney reasonably believes that the client will carry out the threats. This call will protect the ex-wife from substantial bodily harm and, perhaps, imminent death.

The *Rules* further allow an attorney to reveal information to establish a claim or defense on behalf of the attorney where the dispute involved is one between the client and attorney. For example, in a dispute involving whether certain fees are owed to the attorney by the client, the attorney may reveal information about the representation to the court assisting them in settling the matter. The *Rules* also allow the attorney to speak out to establish a defense for herself to any civil or criminal claim where the client is involved or to respond to allegations in any proceeding concerning the lawyer's representation. Thus, if the client sues the attorney for professional malpractice, the attorney may reveal certain information about the representation in order to mount an effective defense against the allegation. Again, see *Model Rules of Professional Conduct* Rule 1.6(b).

Rule 1.6(a) also allows an attorney to reveal otherwise confidential information where it is necessary in carrying out her representation of the client. The comment to this rule explains this exception.

> A lawyer is impliedly authorized to make disclosures about a client when appropriate in carrying out the representation, except to the extent that the client's instructions or special circumstances limit that authority. In litigation, for example, a lawyer may disclose information by admitting a fact that cannot properly be disputed, or in negotiation by making a disclosure that facilitates a satisfactory conclusion. *Model Rules of Professional Conduct*, Rule 1.6 cmt. (1994).

Other ethical rules discussed within the *Rules of Professional Conduct* also permit the attorney to reveal information relating to the representation without violating any ethical obligations. For example, Rule 3.3, entitled "Candor Toward the Tribunal," says, in essence, that an attorney should refuse to offer proof of a fact that he knows to be false. Where a client may insist on relating a particular story that the attorney knows would result in placing perjury before the court, the attorney (and perhaps the nonlawyer assistant) may have to reveal the confidences of a client. In so doing, she has not violated any confidentiality rules.

The *Model Code* takes a less expansive approach. DR 4-101(C) sets forth the *Code's* exceptions to the confidentiality obligation:

> (C) A lawyer may reveal:
> (1) Confidences or secrets with the consent of the client or clients affected, but only after full disclosure to them.
> (2) Confidences or secrets when permitted under Disciplinary Rules or required by law or court order.
> (3) The intention of his client to commit a crime and the information necessary to prevent the crime.
> (4) Confidences or secrets necessary to establish or collect his fee or to defend himself or his employees or associates against an accusation of wrongful conduct. *Model Code of Professional Responsibility* DR 4-101(C) (1986).

It allows attorneys to reveal information more frequently than do the *Rules*. Like the *Rules*, where other disciplinary rules may require disclosure of confidences, the attorney is free to so disclose. However, the other exceptions do not contain as many limitations. For example, the threat of imminent danger need not be present before the attorney may reveal the intention of his client to commit a crime. Therefore, information about a "white-collar crime," such as embezzlement, that does not result in physical injury to another, may be revealed under the *Code* but not under the *Rules*.

ATTORNEY-CLIENT PRIVILEGE AND RULE OF CONFIDENTIALITY COMPARED

There are several distinctions between the attorney-client privilege and the rule of confidentiality.

The first distinction between the two concepts is when each may come into play. Most often, the attorney-client privilege refers to those situations where the attorney is asked to reveal confidential information to a *court* or other tribunal.

The basis of the attorney-client privilege is the rules of evidence. The rules of evidence guide the conduct of any trial and determine what material is to be allowed as evidence. (However, if a matter is within the attorney-client evidentiary privilege, and the attorney is asked outside of the courtroom to reveal information, the attorney is bound by the evidentiary privilege not to reveal it, even though there is no judge present to order him to keep silent.) The confidentiality rules, however, may be invoked *at any time, in any setting*, and do not merely come into play before a tribunal.

Moreover, the attorney-client privilege only attaches to communications *from a client*. The confidentiality rules provide much broader protection. Confidentiality involves any information *about a client*, regardless of its origin.

To understand the differences that exist between the privilege and the confidentiality rules, let us examine a few illustrations of these principles. Suppose first that Andrew Attorney has been retained to help Clarence Client defend himself against accusations that his corporation is dumping hazardous wastes into a nearby river. During the course of Andrew's meetings with his client, Clarence tells Andrew that manufacturing processes at his company generate three hundred thousand barrels of hazardous waste each year. This waste product is deposited in sealed cylinders that are stored in a landfill located on the east side of his property, near the river. Occasionally, employees had been known to deposit these cylinders on the river banks, to ease crowded conditions in the landfill. Immediately upon discovering that this was going on, however, Clarence halted this practice.

Attorney Andrew has been called to testify before the Environmental Protection Agency as to his knowledge of any wrongdoings by Clarence. Both the attorney-client privilege and the confidentiality rule would prevent Andrew from revealing any information Clarence had revealed to him. Suppose, for a moment, that Andrew is extremely active in several conservation groups that serve to protect the environment. One of these groups asks him to reveal information about Clarence's operations to assist them in cleaning up the river. Both the confidentiality rules and the evidentiary privilege would prevent him from speaking out about his client, despite his personal beliefs and the benefits that might result from disclosure.

Attorney-Client Privilege	Confidentiality Rule
■ Most frequently asserted before a court or other tribunal	■ May be invoked at any time, in any setting
■ Protects information from the client	■ Protects information about the client
■ Must not be revealed to a third party	■ No need to protect against revelation to third party
■ Belongs to the client and may only be waived by the client	■ Confidentiality rule is controlled by both the attorney and the client and information may only be revealed when limited exceptions apply

EXHIBIT 5.3
Distinctions
Between the
Attorney-Client
Privilege and
Confidentiality

Because the confidentiality rule protects any information *about the client*, it provides greater protections to the client. Suppose Andrew had interviewed several other employees of the organization to uncover additional information about the company's storage of hazardous waste. During one of the interviews, he was told that Clarence had once punished an employee who had spoken out about the dumping operations of the company. Andrew would not be allowed to reveal the information, as such would be prohibited by the confidentiality rules.

Another important distinction between the privilege and the rule involves the nature of the communication and disclosure to a third party. The attorney-client privilege requires that information not be revealed to a third party but only to those who need to know to further the client's representation. To assist in preventing inadvertent disclosure to third parties, the privilege must involve communications made in a confidential setting. No such requirement is necessary before the attorney is required to maintain a confidentiality obligation.

Revealing information to a third party has no effect upon the attorney's need to keep the matter confidential. Therefore, the communication can be made in the middle of Candlestick Park, as long as people cannot overhear the conversation, while the attorney and client are watching a baseball game; the attorney would still have an obligation to keep the communication confidential. There is no requirement that the communication be made in a private setting.

One additional important distinction exists between the privilege and confidentiality. The attorney-client privilege belongs to the client and therefore may only be waived by the client. Therefore, the attorney may not independently determine to reveal information to the court that had been received from the client without first receiving the client's permission. However, the confidentiality obligation is ethical. Attorneys are never permitted to disregard their ethical obligations. Generally, this means that the attorney may not reveal confidential information obtained from the client, except when limited exceptions provide an escape from that obligation. The attorney, therefore, controls the ethical obligation of confidentiality.

Despite these distinctions, it is important to remember that anything protected by the privilege is likewise protected by confidentiality rules; it is as if confidentiality has swallowed the privilege intact. The reverse is not true.

EXERCISE 5.4 | Refer back to your answers to the exercise following the discussion of the attorney-client privilege and the work product doctrine. Refer to your jurisdiction's confidentiality rules. Is the information protected by the confidentiality rules?

CONFIDENTIALITY RULES
AND LEGAL ASSISTANTS

Long ago, in a famous treatise on **evidence**, Professor Wigmore recognized,

evidence Any kind of proof offered to establish the existence or non-existence of a fact in dispute.

It has never been questioned that the privilege protects communication to the *attorney's clerks* and his other agents (including stenographers) for rendering his services. The assistance of these agents being indispensable to his work and the communications of the client being often necessarily committed to them by the attorney or by the client himself, the privilege must include all the persons who act as the attorney's agents. 8 Wigmore, Evidence §2301 (McNaughton rev. 1961) (Emphasis in original; footnotes omitted).[6]

Those agents whose work is vital to the competent representation of the client include paralegals and law clerks.

The purpose of the confidentiality rules is to encourage open communication between clients and attorneys so as to enhance the administration of justice. Yet the administration of the judicial system also requires that attorneys hire nonlawyer support staff to assist them in adequately representing clients' interests. Therefore, nonlawyer support staff members are often asked to sit in on client conferences and prepare work that is based upon knowledge of confidential information. The nonlawyer employee, especially the legal assistant, ultimately becomes privy to many confidential materials.

Failing to extend the confidentiality rules to nonlawyers would cause the operation of modern law firms to crumble. Paralegals and other support personnel have necessarily been exposed to this information; therefore, were the attorney-client privilege to not apply to them, the clients' communications would, ultimately, never be protected from discovery.

A discussion of a few cases may help to illustrate concerns raised by the courts when extending the attorney-client privilege to nonlawyers.

One of the earliest decisions to extend the attorney-client privilege to the nonlawyer employee of the attorney is *United States v. Kovel*, 296 F.2d 918 (2d Cir. 1961). In this case the law firm had hired an accountant, Kovel, to help with certain tax matters of a client. That client of the law firm was being investigated by the government for alleged tax violations. Ultimately the accountant was called to testify before a grand jury.

Kovel refused to answer any questions put to him by the grand jury, asserting that the information was protected by the attorney-client privilege. Because Kovel refused to answer the questions put to him and instead asserted the attorney-client privilege, he was brought before Judge Cashin who told him, "There is no privilege—you are entitled to no privilege, as I understand the law."

[6]JOHN HENRY WIGMORE, EVIDENCE IN TRIALS AT COMMON LAW, (revised by John T. McNaughton 1961). Copyright © 1961 by John T. McNaughton. Published by Little, Brown and Company.

The purpose of the confidentiality obligations is to protect the secrets of the client from being disclosed except in certain circumstances. It appears to be a simple concept. However simple it may seem, it creates many problems for those who must adhere to its guidelines. A concept as esoteric as confidentiality often requires illustration to better understand its application. The following is an illustration of the principles previously discussed.

Christophero Cartier was employed by Color Corporation for fifteen years. His responsibilities included maintaining financial records and preparing monthly audits of company purchases.

At the end of last year, Cartier noticed that the purchasing department had recorded an unusually high number of transactions. Wanting to investigate the inventory, Cartier paid a visit to the supply house. As he made his way through boxes that were piled to reach almost to the ceiling, Cartier lost his footing and fell into one of the boxes, causing the entire stack of boxes to fall on him.

The president of Color Corporation, Sheila Begonia, has decided that Color should hire the best plaintiff's injury attorney in town to defend itself against the impending suit. Therefore, she has come to your attorney, Alfred Eitelbaum, seeking representation.

During the meeting, Begonia confides in Eitelbaum that the warehouse was not in compliance with a number of safety standards required by the city building inspector. However, the building inspector had not yet discovered the problems and an inspection visit was not scheduled until next year. By that time, Begonia assured Eitelbaum, the problems would be resolved. At that time, Begonia denies that the inspection problems had anything to do with Cartier's accident, although surely Cartier's attorney might feel otherwise.

Bound by the ethical obligation to keep his client's secrets, Eitelbaum cannot reveal to any other party that the building was not in compliance with local city building codes. Both the *Code* and the *Rules* would forbid disclosure; revealing the information would have a deleterious effect on the client. Color could face stiff penalties for failing to be in compliance; and the possibility exists, under local code, that the warehouse could be closed down, which would severely hamper the work being completed at Color.

Eitelbaum's subsequent investigation and thorough legal work resulted in a minimal damage settlement to Cartier. Color was quite pleased with his work and Begonia proposed at the next directors' meeting that Color pay a retainer fee to Eitelbaum. Therefore, in the event that they had future problems, they could be assured that Eitelbaum would be on hand to quickly resolve them. The board accepted the proposal, and Eitelbaum later accepted a retainer fee.

While Cartier was recuperating in the hospital, he remembered the unusually high number of purchases made by the purchasing department. He called his lawyer and asker her to look into the matter. Upon discovering some discrepancies, Cartier's attorney paid a visit to Eitelbaum, notifying him of the problems in purchasing.

Anything told to Eitelbaum at this point would not be confidential because the information given to Eitelbaum is coming from someone other than his client. Eitelbaum's client, remember, is Color and not Cartier or Cartier's attorney. Therefore, Eitelbaum may reveal the details of his conversation with Cartier's attorney.

Eitelbaum brought Cartier's concerns to Begonia. Begonia confided that Color was purchasing additional engine parts and transfering them to its foreign subsidiaries. Begonia revealed that, because Color can avoid certain additional taxes imposed on direct exports from the manufacturer, Color was able to save money. Begonia revealed that the company felt it was worth risking breaking the tax laws.

Because this information is meant to be confidential, Eitelbaum cannot reveal it to anyone. Eitelbaum should not condone the behavior, however. The problem is that this is an ongoing crime. It has happened in the past and Eitelbaum is obligated to keep this confidential. What the company does in the future, however, is of great concern to Eitelbaum. He must tell the client that the activity is wrong and should be stopped. If the client fails to stop the activity, Eitelbaum's continued silence would assist the commission of a crime.

This crime does not involve death or substantial bodily injury. Under the *Rules*, therefore, Eitelbaum may not have an obligation to reveal this information. If the *Code* is in place in Eitelbaum's jurisdiction, he should reveal the information if the crime continues.

(Continued)

HIGHLIGHT   *(Continued)*

The next month, Begonia called Eitelbaum and asked him to meet in her office that morning. It appeared that a soil sample of some property that Color was attempting to sell had revealed the presence of hazardous wastes. Begonia confided in Eitelaum that, many years ago, Color had been involved in a storage of pesticides and apparently some of the contaminants had leaked into the soil. Begonia confided in Eitelbaum, "Although we appeared to abide by the rules of EPA, it would have cost us a lot more money to follow them too closely. Therefore, we cut some corners here and there. We did it in such a way, however, that nobody would ever know that we had done anything wrong." It appeared, however, that Color's lax storage procedures had wound up contaminating an entire twelve-acre parcel of land.

Eitelbaum must still refrain from disclosing this information. Again, this is a confidence, or secret, of the client and his ethical obligation forbids disclosure.

Seeing so much land contaminated by corporate greed upset Eitelbaum, but he knew that he must proceed to construct a defense for Color. Eitelbaum worked laboriously. Two weeks after their initial meeting concerning the environmental problem, however, Eitelbaum was again summoned to Begonia's office. Begonia confided that Color had another problem. It appeared that the water in a well that had been constructed several years ago but had been forgotten had also revealed signs of contamination. A group of ten-year-old boys had wandered onto the land. Noticing the well, their curiosity caused them to pull up a bucket of water and drink from it. One of the young boys had died soon after from poisoning. Color was not anticipating that a lawsuit would be filed by the boy's family.

Eitelbaum still may not reveal that his client had deliberately caused this contamination. He is still bound by an obligation of confidentiality. No exception applies in this instance, either. This is not a future crime, but rather one that occurred in the past. To require that an attorney reveal information about his clients' past crimes would mean that all defendants who confided to their attorney that they were guilty would be deprived of representation before the judge.

Eitelbaum was deeply distressed by this information but continued to prepare a defense for Color. Once again, Begonia called. The conversation began with Begonia telling Eitelbaum that a developer had called her. He had heard that Color was having problems with the EPA and wanted to know if they would be willing to sell off certain parcels of land held by the company. The developer told Begonia that he wanted the land to build a new shopping mall, the largest on the east side of the state. Only her site was available to accommodate such a large venture. Begonia asked Eitelbaum about the legal ramifications of selling her assets at that time. In an attempt to elevate the selling price of the land, she said she was going to wait on selling for a few months, making it seem as if the company was not interested. Eventually, she confided she would sell the land.

Eitelbaum happened to own a piece of land adjoining Color's property. He decided it would be a good idea to try to buy additional parcels of land before the Color sale was completed. He had a problem, however, because his ex-wife was demanding more money for child support and alimony. Therefore, he needed a partner and decided to call his old friend from grammar school, Greta Greer. When Greta came on the line, Eitelbaum told her all that Begonia had just confided.

It should be clear that Eitelbaum is violating his confidentiality obligation. Eitelbaum is using the secrets of the client to his own advantage. Such action is clearly a violation of both the *Model Code* and the *Rules*. Revealing such information in order to establish his own business may also create a conflict of interest for Eitlebaum. Eitelbaum's venture may put his interests in conflict with those of Color. See Chapter 6, "Conflicts of Interest," for further discussion of this problem.

In reviewing the actions of the judge, the appellate court recognized that the complexities of modern times required the attorney to hire the services of others to assist him in handling the affairs of his client. Then, quoting

Wigmore, the court concluded that the privilege must be extended to include all who work as the agents of the attorney. *Kovel,* 296 F.2d at 921.

The court proceeded to apply this rule to the facts at hand, noting "[w]hat is vital to the privilege is that the communication be made *in confidence* for the purpose of obtaining *legal* advice *from the lawyer." Kovel,* 296 F.2d at 922 (Emphasis in original.) Where these requirements are met, the privilege attaches, even where the nonlawyer employee, such as this accountant or a legal assistant, necessarily becomes privy to the communication because his assistance was needed in providing effective representation.

A recent decision in Arizona expressly applied the attorney-client privilege to legal assistants. See *Samaritan Foundation v. Superior Court,* 173 Ariz. 426 844 P.2d 593 (App. 1992). *Samaritan Foundation* involved a child who was a patient of Phoenix Children's Hospital (part of Good Samaritan Regional Medical Center) who suffered cardiac arrest during surgery at the hospital. The child emerged from the operation neurologically impaired. Not long after the surgery, at the direction of the hospital's legal department, a nurse paralegal interviewed four operating room witnesses. After the interview, each witness signed a form consenting to representation by Samaritan's legal department if a lawsuit were filed against the Medical Center.

The nurse paralegal summarized her interviews with the four witnesses in written form. These documents were kept by the legal department.

At later depositions, the witnesses claimed to recall little of what had occurred during the operation. Samaritan refused to allow the witnesses to refresh their recollections through use of the interview summaries prepared by the nurse paralegal. Samaritan believed that to do so would waive whatever privilege attached to the documents.

One of the issues before the court was, "[d]oes the attorney-client privilege apply when, as here, the conduit of communications is a paralegal?" The court responded that the privilege must apply to this communication. The court's conclusion was based on the fact that it would be unreasonable to require attorneys to do the tasks of paralegals merely to hold intact the attorney-client privilege.

The court began by looking to the Arizona attorney-client statute, section 12-2234, and noted that, while the statute included within the protections of the privilege "[a]n attorney's secretary, stenographer or clerk," it did not specifically mention paralegals. The court rejected the argument that, because of the legislature's failure to specifically mention paralegals, paralegals must not be subject to these protections. The court noted:

> In section 12-2234, our legislature recognized that lawyers often communicate with clients through agents.... We believe that the legislature intended by reference to "secretary, stenographer or clerk" to list a representative, not exclusive, group of agents through whom a lawyer and client might confidentially confer....
>
> The law has recognized in other contexts that an attorney may properly and efficiently act through a paralegal. This Court, for example, has found paralegal services compensable in attorneys' fees awards, reasoning that lawyers should not devote time to tasks more economically assigned to legal assistants, "solely to permit that time to be compensable [in a fee award]." *Continental Townhouses East Unit One Ass'n v. Brockbank,* 152 Ariz. 537, 544, 733 P.2d 1120, 1127 (App. 1986); *accord Missouri v. Jenkins ex rel. Agyei,* 491

U.S. 274, 288 & n. 10, 109 S.Ct. 2463, 2471 & n. 10, 105 L.Ed.2d 229 (1989). Similarly, lawyers should not retain information-gathering tasks more efficiently delegated to paralegals, solely to protect the client's privilege. We hold that a lawyer does not forfeit the attorney-client privilege by receiving otherwise privileged client communications through the conduit of a properly supervised paralegal employee. *Samaritan Foundation v. Superior Court*, 844 P.2d at 599–600. (footnote omitted).

However, the court also noted that it could not create an "automatic 'paralegal-client privilege'." Where legal assistants assume responsibilities in helping the client that are independent of any attorney-client relationship, the court indicated that it did not believe that a paralegal-client privilege *per se* existed. For example, the court stated it would not find certain investigative functions as giving rise to a paralegal-client privilege. Citing *Longs Drug Stores*, the court stated that "[c]ommunications to insurance investigators are not privileged, as they may be used by the investigator's insurance company employer for purposes other than securing legal advice for the insured." *Samaritan Foundation*, 844 P.2d at 600.

The Samaritan Foundation court also briefly addressed the issue of whether the ethical confidentiality rule should be applied to legal assistants. In a footnote, the court stated that confidentiality rules are likewise extended to the nonlawyer because the attorney has been made ethically responsible for the conduct of the nonlawyer. See *Samaritan Foundation*, 844 P.2d at 600, fn 8.

It should be clear, therefore, that the attorney-client privilege has been extended, through caselaw, to the nonlawyer employees of the attorney. However, is the ethical confidentiality rule extended to legal assistants?

The *Model Code* extends the confidentiality rules to nonlawyers in DR 4-101(D). This section reads:

(D) A lawyer shall exercise reasonable care to prevent his employees, associates, and others whose services are utilized by him from disclosing or using confidences or secrets of a client, except that a lawyer may reveal the information allowed by DR 4-101(C) through an employee. *Model Code of Professional Responsibility* DR 4-101(D) (1986).

As the drafters of the *Model Code* noted:

It is a matter of common knowledge that the normal operation of a law office exposes confidential professional information to nonlawyer employees of the office, particularly secretaries and those having access to the files; and this obligates a lawyer to exercise care in selecting and training his employees so that the sanctity of all confidences and secrets of his clients may be preserved. *Model Code of Professional Responsibility* EC 4-2 (1986).

Nothing mandates that a legal assistant adhere to the standards of an attorney. However, nonlawyers are expected to engage in conduct that is compatible with the ethical obligations of the lawyer, and it is the lawyer who will be faced with the consequences of any violation. Model Rule 5.3 requires that the attorney responsible for supervising the legal assistant make reasonable efforts to ensure that her conduct conforms to the ethical obligations of the attorney. Of course, these obligations include the requirement of confidentiality.

What both the *Code* and the *Rule* mean is that the attorney and her law firm must take steps to ensure that her legal assistants will preserve the confi-

---

PARALEGALS IN THE SPOTLIGHT

The problems of legal assistants maintaining client confidences has become especially important to the major international law firm of Skadden, Arps, Slate, Meagher and Flom. In recent years, two of the paralegals employed at Skadden, Arps have pleaded guilty to various charges resulting from misappropriating client secrets and using those secrets to help them make wise decisions trading securities. In other words, the legal assistants became involved in an insider trading scam because of their privileged knowledge.

In October of 1992, Christopher Garvey, a paralegal with Skadden, Arps, pleaded guilty to charges of conspiracy to commit securities fraud. According to prosecutors of the case, Garvey had specifically sought employment as a legal assistant at Skadden, Arps in order to become privy to insider information. Garvey and his boyhood friend Darrin Gleeman had set up an elaborate system, intended to help them avoid detection of their illegal conduct, and had recruited several others into their scheme. In three years, the parties had netted $340,000 from their insider trading scam.

Earlier that year, in March of 1992, another Skadden, Arps legal assistant, Kerry Hurton, pleaded guilty to similar charges. In indictments handed down by a grand jury, it was alleged that Hurton had agreed to supply insider information (in other words, confidential information about clients) to several other individuals. In exchange, Hurton would receive assistance in financing the purchase of her condominium. Hurton also apparently passed the information along to her boyfriend and his cousins.

Although two employees violated ethical rules in highly publicized cases, Skadden, Arps takes significant precautions to protect client information from this sort of abuse. Legal assistants at the firm are advised of their confidentiality obligations during orientation, at which time they are also shown a film about this kind of violation. Employees of Skadden, Arps, including paralegals, are required to sign agreements each year indicating that they understand the firm's policy on using confidential client information to trade securities. Skadden, Arps's policies also include protecting client identity by assigning code names to clients and limiting discussions about clients to only those who need to have access to the information. Nonetheless, Hurton and Garvey were able to abuse the system.

Source: *Mark Dowdy, Skadden Paralegals Indicted for Securities Fraud,* LEGAL ASSISTANT TODAY, Mar.-Apr. 1993. Copyright 1994. James Publishing, Inc. Reprinted with permission from *Legal Assistant Today.* For subscription information, call (714) 755-5450.

---

dences of the client. When hired, for instance, the legal assistant should be reminded of his obligation to keep the confidences of the client.

The application of confidentiality rules to the legal assistant was defined somewhat in *People v. Mitchell,* 86 A.D.2d 976, 448 N.Y.S.2d 332 (1982). In that case, defendant's attorney shared a common waiting room with another attorney. In this waiting room, the defendant made statements to two secretaries and a legal assistant while his attorney was away. The court reasoned the statements were not protected from disclosure, noting:

> Under the circumstances, defendant could not reasonably have expected that the communication would be confidential nor could the communication have been for the purposes of securing legal advice or assistance. *Mitchell,* 448 N.Y.S.2d at 333.

By refusing to apply the privilege or confidentiality rules to the secretaries and paralegals, this court made clear that extension of the confidentiality obligations to nonlawyer support staff would only be done in those circumstances where, had the communication been to a lawyer, it would have been protected.

CONFIDENTIALITY AND LAW OFFICE PRACTICE

When a client visits the office of an attorney to obtain legal advice, the client has initiated a series of communications. These communications may begin with an initial face-to-face meeting. The relationship may develop through letters, telephone calls, faxes, or more in-office visits. In representing this client, notes may be taken by both the attorney and the legal assistant, letters may be drafted, and research memoranda may be prepared.

These communications may range from the mundane to the provocative. Regardless of the substance, however, these communications may all be subject to confidentiality protections. Because the paralegal is often responsible for gathering together confidential information, the legal assistant should scrutinize her daily activities and examine where lapses in confidentiality protection may occur.

INITIAL CLIENT VISIT

Clients often decide to visit an attorney's office before even understanding that a real problem exists or before having decided that the service of a particular attorney should be retained.

During the initial client visit, the lawyer must determine what the problem is, from the perspective of the client. The client, frustrated after grappling with a problem for what may be an extended period of time, may be inclined to reveal a great deal of his side of the story. Whatever information is discussed at the initial client conference falls within the protections of the confidentiality rules.

The legal assistant must make special note of this rule, as often the paralegal may be asked to conduct an initial client interview before the attorney meets with the client. While the paralegal must share whatever information he has uncovered during the interview with the attorney, he must take care to protect the information from others who need not be privy to the client's story.

This is true even if the client is able to settle the problem amicably before much legal work is completed. And this is true *regardless of whether the client actually retains the services of the attorney.*

For example, Catherine Client's neighbor may have warned her that her children's boisterous antics outside his window were disruptive and, should any property damage result from the children's roughhousing, he would sue her. Upon discovering that her neighbor's window had been broken by her children, Catherine may decide to visit Alison Attorney to see if she should worry about this problem. Unless a lawsuit has been filed, however, Alison's services may not be needed.

Often a client may simply need to discuss with a disinterested party the problem she has been experiencing. The attorney may inform the client that legal services are not necessary to resolve an issue. For example, Alison may advise Catherine that she should discuss things with her neighbor and see if they can settle things between themselves. Sometimes an attorney may decide he does not want to represent a particular client. At other times, a client may be "shopping around" for an attorney who will provide the answer she seeks.

As should be evident, therefore not every client contact will lead to the establishment of an attorney-client relationship. For confidentiality purposes, this is irrelevant. Once the client consults with the attorney, a relationship of sorts develops such that the client should be willing to relate his story fully, without fear of revealing incriminating information. To accomplish this objective and to further the attorney-client relationship, the confidentiality rules must protect the communication.

DISCOVERY MATTERS

Discovery is designed to help the parties gather all the information needed to competently prepare a vigorous representation at trial. This includes asking the other side for the information it intends to present at trial. Discovery may include document production, serving interrogatories, or requesting depositions of opposing counsel's witnesses. (See chapter 3, "The Unauthorized Practice of Law," for discussion of the meaning of these terms.)

Legal assistants working in litigation are often called on to handle discovery matters, and discovery is one area where it is quite possible that confidential communications could be revealed.

Moreover, the legal assistant must take care to prevent from being turned over documents not requested by opposing counsel or documents revealing the attorney's mental impressions.

Law firms generate many pieces of written documentation. At a client consultation or after a phone conversation with a client, law firm personnel will take notes, recording what was discussed and advised. Often the attorney will communicate with other members of her firm through different kinds of written documents, including memoranda or letters. Attorneys may ask law clerks or legal assistants to prepare memoranda of law in order to apprise them of the state of the law on a particular point and to apply the facts of their case to that established law. Everything gets written down, however, because internal documents help to provide accuracy and consistency and assure the client that all salient points of her case are being considered.

In preparing for litigation, the litigation paralegal may be asked to supply adversaries with documents. However, these internal documents are not discoverable, as they are protected by the work product rule.

These documents are said to reveal the mental impressions of the attorney (even though they might be prepared by a paralegal). Failing to protect them, therefore, would mean that opposing counsel would discover the other attorney's entire theory of the case and thereby be able to thwart every tactical strike of counsel before it had been presented to the jury or judge.

Likewise, the legal assistant may be asked to answer interrogatories to be turned over to opposing counsel. In preparing responses to these questions, it is imperative that confidential information not be inadvertently revealed. The same concerns as presented for written discovery matters apply in this situation.

What happens if the legal assistant inadvertently discloses confidential information?

When opposing counsel asks to have certain documents produced, it often falls upon the legal assistant to review the discovery request and gather the items needed. However, the legal assistant must scrupulously avoid turning over to opposing counsel any information that is confidential. This requires the legal assistant to review each document, extract the confidential information, and re-copy the document for the adversary.

Occasionally, despite the fact that precautions are taken, confidential information is revealed. Courts are divided as to whether the information loses the protections of the privilege. Remember that the privilege belongs to the client. To waive the privilege, the consent of the client is needed. However, inadvertent disclosure of confidences during discovery is no fault of the client. Rather, because of the attorney's (or his support staff's) actions, opposing counsel has access to the information. Some courts therefore believe that opposing counsel may not use such information.

Practically however, once information is leaked it is virtually impossible to not benefit from the information, using it however subliminally. For that reason, many feel that the privilege has already been destroyed, despite the fact that such disclosure was inadvertent. Therefore, some courts allow opposing counsel to use the information.

Regardless of the approach taken in your jurisdiction, inadvertent disclosure of information results in tremendous headaches for counsel. Either fighting to protect the information or having to deal with the fact that opposing counsel now has the information, the problems become tremendous. For this reason, it is especially crucial that the legal assistant be extra careful to not inadvertently turn over privileged documents. Furthermore, inadvertent disclosure of highly damaging information could result in a malpractice suit against the person making the disclosure.

On the flip side of this coin is the problem of what to do if the opposing counsel has inadvertently disclosed privileged information to you. By all means, immediately consult your supervising attorney if you suspect anything is amiss with the documents generated by discovery.

If documents produced by opposing counsel contain information that was not meant to be disclosed to your client, it is a good idea to refrain from the temptation to study the document. For example, a letter meant only for the eyes of the client might be inadvertently included in the packet sent to opposing counsel. Opposing counsel should refrain from reviewing the document and send it back to the originating attorney.

With the rapid pace of technological advances, many different kinds of threats to confidentiality exist. Fax machines, cellular phones, even computer programs can be fertile ground for abuses of confidential information. Because of this, every member of the law firm must take extra precautions when using this equipment. The nonlawyer must ensure that she faxes to the right number, marks all confidential documents, protects computer screens, uses passwords, and conducts confidential conversations either in person or from the phone in her office. If the law firm or office does not have certain security measures for their computer systems, the legal assistant might want to talk with the office manager about putting greater security measures in place.

Because the legal assistant is privy to confidential information, she may know much more than should be revealed to adversarial parties. When in doubt, however, the legal assistant should always ask the advice of the attorney about what communication is protected.

INTERNAL DOCUMENTS

The work product rule protects from disclosure the *work of the attorney prepared in anticipation of litigation.*

Clients may often generate documents that ultimately contain incriminating information. For example, a corporation may discover that it is being sued for marketing an unsafe product. Its president, upon discovering that some customers have had problems with the product, may consult with the product development team to see if the product may contain hazardous chemicals. The product development team may determine that tests of the product are necessary before the questions posed by the president can be answered. Through a series of memos between the east and west coast plants, the product development team may initiate a study of the product.

As you can see, a number of conversations have taken place. Documents have been generated. However, when the corporation finally consults an attorney, it will be told that all of this work is discoverable, should the corporation be sued because of the unsafe product.

Why? This is because none of the documents were prepared *by the attorney in anticipation of litigation.* Rather, they were prepared in response to the questions of the corporate president. Nor will turning the documents over to the attorney protect them from being discoverable.

By the same token, legal assistants must take care not to accept from the client documents that were previously prepared. To do so would, in essence, result in hiding discoverable materials. Interfering with discovery matters is a grave mistake.

LAW OFFICE DAILY OPERATIONS

As the opening exercise demonstrates, information that is unsettling, upsetting, interesting, or just downright "juicy" may be revealed during the client interview.

It is always tempting to share juicy communications with others, whether we are talking to our mothers, gardeners, or best friends. Attorneys and legal assistants, just as any other professionals, want to discuss their hard days at the office. That is natural. However, no matter how tempting it may be to talk about what a client has told you, it is imperative that this information is not discussed outside of the office. Discussing the confidential affairs of the client can actually harm that client's affairs.

We also may be tempted to reveal information about a client to our coworkers in the office. More likely than not, the legal assistant will be working within close proximity of other paralegals and will be meeting other nonlawyers around the office. It is natural, in establishing relationships, to want to share information concerning the events of the workday.

Remembering that the privilege, and also confidentiality rules, extends only to those who need to know the information, it becomes clear that the legal assistant should not discuss the affairs of the client with those legal assistants who are not assigned to the case. Legal assistants assigned to the bankruptcy department of a large firm would have no need to know the affairs of the wealthy clients embroiled in a bitter divorce. Likewise, family law legal assistants need not know of the assets being disposed of by a large corporate empire fighting for solvency in a reorganization in bankruptcy court. Do not share the information. To do so may destroy the privilege.

Attorneys and legal assistants often socialize with other members of the firm after hours. This sort of networking is often an easy way to establish and solidify working relationships. Because legal assistants may be with other people who are also privy to information revealed at particular client interviews, there may be a natural tendency to discuss what was learned that afternoon. By all means, this temptation should be ignored. Revealing secrets of the client at the neighborhood watering hole may harm the client.

Just as important may be the interoffice precautions that should be undertaken by the paralegal to prevent inadvertent disclosure. To this end, several steps taken by the legal assistant may prevent inadvertent disclosure. For example, when speaking with a client on the telephone, doors should be kept closed. There may be a great deal of movement in a law firm, and those walking past an open door, whether they are clients, attorneys, or messengers, may overhear a secret of the client not meant to be disclosed. Likewise, when speaking with a client, other members of the firm who need not be privy to the information should be asked to step outside of hearing range for a moment.

Clients should never be seated in the legal assistant's office when discussing another client's case with the supervising attorney. Should another client happen to call while a client is seated in the office, the legal assistant should ask if the call can be returned at a later time, when privacy is intact.

TRIAL TESTIMONY

We have seen that, just as the attorney-client privilege prevents the *attorney* from revealing information learned from the client in court, the privilege also has been extended to the *legal assistant.*

Therefore, a paralegal may not testify in court, or before any tribunal, about matters learned from the client. The attorney-client privilege, as applied to the legal assistant, prevents such disclosure by the legal assistant.

Should another attorney, after learning of the paralegal's substantial involvement with the case of that client, subpoena the legal assistant to appear, the paralegal must appear in court on the day and at the time requested. However, when on the witness stand, the legal assistant may assert protection of the information from disclosure by the attorney-client privilege. All rules that attach to the privilege may be applied in this instance, just as they would if an attorney were called to testify as witness. For instance, most statutes allow a judge to order disclosure of the information in limited circumstances. In that case, if the supervising attorney agrees, the information should be disclosed. Before revealing any information, however, the legal assistant should always get approval from the attorney by whom she is being supervised.

THE CORPORATE PARALEGAL

Up to this point, most of this discussion has been directed to the problems of legal assistants employed in law offices. In the last office, new clients enter and exit the law firm on a daily basis. Information is necessarily exchanged in order to facilitate the handling of each client's unique case.

When the paralegal is employed by the corporation, however, an exchange of clients is simply not present. Rather, the legal assistant works for only one client—the corporation.

This does not mean, however, that the corporate paralegal can be lax in adhering to the guidelines proposed by the confidentiality rules. The corporate legal assistant must abide by confidentiality principles with vigor equal to that required by the legal assistant employed by the law office.

The work of the corporate paralegal may involve matters of a more "routine" nature. A corporate legal assistant's responsibilities may be to ensure that a newly proposed trademark does not infringe upon a previously existing and already registered trademark of another organization. A paralegal employed in a corporation also may be involved in drafting documents or reviewing contracts. Nevertheless, the legal assistant must abide by confidentiality obligations. It is important to remember that much of this daily work is handled with an eye toward preventing future litigation. To reveal any information may ultimately harm the corporation, the legal department's "client," should an appearance in court, battling an adversary, be necessary.

Remember likewise that preparing documents and later turning those documents over to an attorney does not protect the documents from disclosure. Therefore, unless the attorney directs that the document be prepared, it is wise to refrain from handling affairs for other departments in the corporation.

Often a corporate legal department is involved in handling litigation matters for the corporation. Whether the dispute involves one disgruntled employee suing the corporation over an alleged discrimination practice or whether the lawsuit involves recovering millions of dollars in costs for cleanup of hazardous waste dumping, the corporate legal assistant may be involved in matters of litigation. In turn, litigation means discovery and trial testimony. Discovery and trial testimony mean that opportunities exist for confidential information to be revealed.

We have seen that discovery is often a matter entrusted to the legal assistant. This is true whether the paralegal is employed by the law firm or the corporation. It is important for both kinds of legal assistants to handle turning over sensitive documents with care. It is equally probable, whether the setting is a law firm or a corporation, that internal documentation, protected from disclosure by confidentiality rules, may be inadvertently turned over during the course of discovery.

FOCUS ON JANIS SHANE

Janis Shane is a legal assistant who has been practicing in law firms for a number of years. Her experiences have been varied. She has been employed in large law firms and smaller firms, handling matters as complicated as taxation or bankruptcy and as time-consuming as litigation. One thing remained constant during her career, however, and that was her awareness of the importance of confidentiality rules.

In her experience, Shane believes legal assistants are most apt to lapse on maintaining client confidentiality at the very beginning of their careers. "After all," Shane advises, "the paralegal has a wonderful new job and he wants everyone to know about what he's doing." As time wears on, and the novelty of the job wears off, though, it is less likely that the paralegal will talk about his clients.

> Confidentiality is one of the most important ethical rules. Paralegals must be aware of this rule in order to protect the client's interests. Fortunately, as tempting as it may be to talk about your cases, I have rarely seen another paralegal violate this ethical obligation.

What is more heartening to note is that, generally, Shane has not seen many legal assistants discussing cases except in a general fashion. Instead of gossiping about the clients and cases, it is much more common, in Shane's opinion, for legal assistants to get together and commiserate about the difficulties they are generally having saying such things as "I spend half my time on the phone trying to get someone at the SEC to talk to me."

Keeping confidences by avoiding gossiping is not difficult. In fact, Shane cannot think of a single occasion where she has overheard a paralegal discuss a case or a client. What is more difficult, in Shane's opinion, is preventing inadvertent disclosure of client information. Most often, this occurs while the legal assistant is generating documents to be turned over during discovery.

Shane offers two pieces of advice to paralegals just beginning their careers who wish to understand how to practically maintain client confidences during discovery. Aware that paralegals are often asked to handle large numbers of documents, especially during discovery matters, Shane advises that paralegals, "implement a system such that all documents which they prepare for a client's case are immediately labelled 'Confidential. Prepared in anticipation of litigation.' Such labelling can always be removed at a later time, should it be determined that there is no need to protect the document as a work product or that it does not meet the requirements of work product material."

Second, if the paralegal has access to a computer and generates documents electronically, each document should be stored in its own subdirectory so it may be immediately defined as work product material.

Essentially, Shane advises, the attorney will decide whether the documents are discoverable or should be protected and, in turn, whether the label should be removed or the document should be saved in an alternate subdirectory. However, by immediately labeling all documents in this manner, there will be no question of the *nature* of the document, and client confidences will be more easily maintained.

Shane is very aware of the importance of protecting the confidences of the client. Throughout her career, she has had many opportunities to learn and implement new systems for protecting client information. Her advice should be closely followed.

TIPS FOR PARALEGALS

■ Do not accept any documents that were prepared by a client at an earlier date, not "in anticipation of litigation," and protect them from discovery. (Such documents are not protected by the work product doctrine.)

■ When speaking with a client, close doors and make sure that no third party is listening to the conversation.

■ When you are socializing with friends from work, stick to topics of conversation that are not work-related. Do not discuss the interesting cases on which you have been working.

■ Protect your computer screen from wandering eyes by turning it away from office doors and windows.

■ If you share an office with another legal assistant, try to schedule a conference room when you know a client is coming in to talk about his case.

■ Avoid speaking on cellular phones about confidential client matters.

■ Doublecheck fax numbers before sending confidential information.

■ When working with document production, take extra precautions to review documents as they come in and label them as "work product" or "confidential" to protect the documents from inadvertent disclosure during discovery.

■ If you are a freelance paralegal, obtain a copy of the confidentiality rule in place in your jurisdiction and stick to that rule.

CLOSING EXERCISE

While the law firm was preparing for an upcoming trial, Susann was asked to sit in on another interview with the client. Susann was one of several legal assistants assigned to assist with this personal injury case.

The attorney overseeing the trial preparation knew he would be calling his rather nervous client to the stand to testify on his own behalf. Because the driver of the car that had hit his client was a well-known politician, he knew all the press and publicity might affect his client's composure while testifying.

A. During the interview, the client reveals to the attorney and Susann information about the criminal action being handled by the state's attorney that also resulted from this accident. He asks that this be kept confidential. Is this protected by the privilege? By confidentiality rules?

B. The attorney asks to be excused for a minute to take a phone call. During that time, the client reveals information to Susann that he asks not be revealed to anyone, not even the attorney. Is the information protected? By what rule? Suppose the information would affect the outcome of the case. What should Susann do?

C. After the attorney has excused himself, the client asks Susann to hold on to certain information for him concerning a report received from a doctor describing earlier injuries that were not caused by the accident. He asks that Susann hold on to the information, to protect it from disclosure. What should Susann do?

D. During the interview, the client reveals information that is protected by the confidentiality rules. Susann finds it extremely interesting and, after the meeting, considers telling another legal assistant in the firm, who has not been assigned to the case, this information. If Susann reveals the information, has she done anything wrong?

E. Opposing counsel discovers that Susann participated in the client interview and decides confidentiality and the privilege do not apply to her. The attorney therefore subpoenas Susann, seeking her testimony in court. When Susann asserts the privilege, the court orders her to reply. What result?

CHAPTER SUMMARY

■ Confidentiality is an ethical obligation of the attorney and legal assistant. Because of the rule of confidentiality, the attorney and legal assistant are prevented from revealing any information about the client to anybody at any time, in any situation. Although both the *Model Code* and the *Model Rules* direct attorneys to protect client confidences, the *Model Rules* take a more expansive approach in protecting confidentiality.

■ The ethical rule of confidentiality embodies the attorney-client privilege and the work product doctrine. The attorney-client privilege prevents the attorney from testifying during court proceedings about the secrets of the client. The work product doctrine protects documents that are prepared in anticipation of litigation from being disclosed to adversaries. Anything protected by these rules is also protected by the ethical rule of confidentiality. They are "subsets" of sorts of confidentiality.

■ There are exceptions to the attorney-client privilege. Nothing in the privilege prevents the attorney or legal assistant from revealing the identity of the client or from revealing fee arrangements. Additionally, the crime-fraud exception means that the attorney may reveal the client's intention to commit a crime without violating the privilege. The *Model Code* and *Model Rules* also provide limited exceptions to the confidentiality rules, such as allowing the legal professional to reveal information to prevent the client from committing a crime or to establish a defense where the lawyer and client become involved in a dispute.

■ The legal assistant should take measures to protect client confidences during his everyday work routine. For example, legal assistants should protect their computer screens from wandering eyes, should doublecheck fax numbers before transmitting a document, and should avoid discussing the client outside of the office. Moreover, the legal assistant working in the area of litigation should take care not to turn over confidences when handling discovery requests.

KEY TERMS

attorney-client privilege	evidentiary rules	privilege
confidence	exceptions to the privilege	privileged
confidentiality	Federal Rules of Evidence	communications
crime-fraud exception	implied waiver	secret
cross-examine	informational materials	separation agreement
defenses	legal advice	waiver
ethical	mental impressions	work product doctrine
evidence		

CASE

The Samaritan Foundation v. Superior Court

Court of Appeals of Arizona, 1992.
173 Ariz. 426, 844 P.2d 593

OPINION

FIDEL, Chief Judge.

In February of 1988, a child suffered a cardiac arrest in surgery and emerged revived but neurologically impaired. This special action arises from discovery disputes in the medical malpractice suit brought by the child and her parents against the hospital and two physicians.

Shortly after surgery, at the direction of the hospital's legal department, a nurse paralegal interviewed four operating room witnesses. The witnesses now claim at depositions to recall little or nothing of the event. Though the paralegal's summaries might refresh the witnesses' recollection, the hospital declines to provide these summaries to the witnesses or release them to plaintiffs' counsel.

Plaintiffs (real parties in interest) moved to compel disclosure. The hospital and its fellow petitioners responded that the summaries are absolutely protected by the attorney-client privilege and immune from discovery under the work product doctrine. The trial court ordered the summaries to be produced for inspection *in camera,* found only portions to be privileged, and ordered the remainder—"the functional equivalent of a witness statement"—disclosed.

In these consolidated special actions, the petitioners allege that the trial court abused its discretion.

• • •

FACTS AND PROCEDURE

Phoenix Children's Hospital ("PCH") is housed within Good Samartian Regional Medical Center, which is owned and operated by Samaritan Health Services ("Samaritan"). PCH and Samaritan share some facilities and personnel, and, according to the affidavit of Samaritan's general counsel, the Samaritan Legal Department advises PCH and its employees "with regard to professional liability incidents and adverse patient occurrences."

In March 1988, anticipating litigation, petitioner Cathey Milam Chester, an attorney employed by Samaritan's Legal Department, directed an investigation of the incident that underlies this case. At Chester's direction, petitioner Elaine Fraiz, a Samaritan nurse paralegal, interviewed various witnesses to surgical and post-surgical events in the operating room and intensive care unit. This special action concerns Fraiz's interviews with four of those witnesses—three nurses and a scrub technician who were present in the operating room during surgery.[1] Each witness signed a form consenting to representation by Samaritan if a claim were filed against her. The form directed the witness not to discuss the event without legal department approval except "1) with health care providers involved with continuing patient care; 2) with Peer Review Committees upon request;[2] and 3) [if required by the employee's participation as] a student ... in a formal SHS teaching program."

Fraiz summarized her interviews of the four witnesses in written memoranda, which were maintained by the legal department. When plaintiffs ultimately deposed the four witnesses, the witnesses claimed to recall little of the surgery and surrounding events. Yet petitioners declined to show them the interview summaries to refresh their recollection, as to do so would have waived whatever privilege might otherwise attach. *See Samaritan Health Servs., Inc. v. Superior Court,* 142 Ariz. 435, 438, 690 P.2d 154, 157 (App.1984).[3]

Plaintiffs' counsel, who had learned of the interview summaries through interrogatories and depositions, sought to depose Chester and Fraiz and subpoenaed documents relating to their investigation. Samaritan moved for a protective order, arguing that Chester and Fraiz knew only what they had learned through investigation and that the attorney-client privilege and work product rule shielded their investigative product from disclosure. As Samaritan was not a party, plaintiffs also moved that defendant PCH be compelled to produce the interview sum-

[1] Plaintiffs sought, and the trial court inspected, Fraiz's summaries of her interviews with two other witnesses, but the trial court limited discovery to portions of Fraiz's summaries of her interviews with the four witnesses whom we discuss.

[2] Petitioners do not claim that the interview summaries were utilized for peer review purposes, and petitioners' counsel made clear to the trial court that they were not invoking a peer review privilege in this case.

[3] In *Samaritan Health Services, Inc. v. Superior Court,* 142 Ariz. 435, 438, 690 P.2d 154, 157 (App.1984), this Court held under comparable circumstances that to allow witnesses to review interview summaries would waive any work product immunity or attorney-client privilege and entitle opposing counsel to review the summaries. The plaintiffs allege, and Samaritan concedes, that after issuance of that decision, the practice of refreshing witnesses' recollection with summaries ceased.

maries, and PCH likewise asserted the attorney-client privilege and work product immunity in response.

The trial court directed Samaritan and PCH to provide copies of the summaries for *in camera* review, but to

> line through on the summaries any and all material which constitutes matters of attorney opinion, attorney theory, attorney interpretation or attorney surmise. Those portions of the summaries which indicate the witnesses statements of what occurred during the operation ... shall be left without lines being drawn through.

The court indicated that it would extract from each summary and provide plaintiffs "the functional equivalent of a witness statement."

Upon receipt of the trial court's order, petitioners brought this consolidated special action and sought a stay, which this Court granted only in part. We directed the trial court to proceed with *in camera* inspection and designate what, if any, summary portions it intended to release. Petitioners' counsel were ordered to file under seal a copy of the summaries with this Court. Release of the designated portions to plaintiffs' counsel was stayed.

The trial court followed our directive, enabling us to review the proposed deletions by the trial court, and the trial court's finding that, without access to its designated portions, plaintiffs would be precluded from proving significant elements of their case. The trial court commented that Samaritan, as soon as an incident is reported, signs up its "employees as 'clients' of the legal department of the hospital, does extensive interviews and summaries and thereby wraps this material in a mantle of peer review, attorney/client privilege and attorney work product." The court concluded that

> a reasonable reading of *Humana Hospital v. Superior Court*, 154 Ariz. 396, 742 P.2d 1382 ([App.] 1987) and *John C. Lincoln Hospital v. Superior Court*, 159 Ariz. 456, 768 P.2d 188 (App.1989) indicates the Court must provide reasonable alternatives.... Where plaintiffs' opportunity to prove [their] case is as effectively blocked as defendants' theories would claim in the fourteen motions before this Court, due process would seem to call for some form of remedy.

I. WORK PRODUCT RULE

Petitioners argue that the trial court abused its discretion because the work product rule immunizes the interview summaries from discovery.[5]

Arizona's work product rule is embodied in Arizona Rule of Civil Procedure 26(b)(3), which provides qualified discovery immunity for material prepared in anticipation of litigation:

> [A] party may obtain discovery of documents ... otherwise discoverable[6] ... and prepared in anticipation of litigation or for trial by or for another party ... or for that other party's representative ... only upon a showing that the party seeking discovery has substantial need of the materials in the preparation of the party's case and that the party is unable without undue hardship to obtain the substantial equivalent of the materials by other means. In ordering discovery of such materials when the required showing has been made, the court shall protect against disclosure of the mental impressions, conclusions, opinions, or legal theories of an attorney or other representative of a party concerning the litigation.

The witness interview summaries that Elaine Fraiz prepared for Samaritan and PCH fall within the general ambit of Rule 26(b)(3). *See Longs Drug Stores v. Howe*, 134 Ariz. 424, 429, 657 P.2d 412, 417 (1983) (finding that summaries of witness interviews concerning an event that creates a substantial risk of legal exposure are documents prepared in anticipation of litigation).

The summaries contain to a limited degree the protected impressions of Ms. Fraiz; however, the trial court followed the approved process of *in camera* inspection and redaction to "protect against disclosure of the mental impressions, conclusions, opinions, or legal theories of an attorney or other representative of a party concerning the litigation...."

The question narrows to whether plaintiffs have shown, as Rule 26(b)(3) requires, substantial need for the redacted summaries and an inability to obtain their equivalent by other means. The trial

---

[5] We preliminarily reject petitioner PCH's argument that it should not be compelled to produce the summaries because they are not in its "possession, custody or control." *See* Ariz.R.Civ.P. 34(a). PCH did not assert before the trial court that it lacked access to the documents. PCH was the client of the Samaritan Legal Department, and a party has control over a document if it has the legal right to obtain the document. *See* 8 Charles A. Wright & Arthur R. Miller, *Federal Practice and Procedure* § 2210, at 621 (1970).

[6] Privileged documents are not "otherwise discoverable." Ariz.R.Civ.P. 26(b)(1). We analyze in Part II whether the interview summaries are protected by the attorney-client privilege. For purposes of work product analysis, however, we assume the summaries are "otherwise discoverable."

court, whose grasp of the evidence surpasses ours, found that without the summaries, plaintiffs would be blocked from proving significant portions of their case.

• • •

We find no abuse of discretion. Because plaintiffs showed substantial need, and because the trial court took proper measures to protect the working impressions of Samaritan's legal staff, we hold that the trial court's order met the requirements of Rule 26(b)(3).

II. ATTORNEY-CLIENT PRIVILEGE

Petitioners and amici argue that, even if work product immunity might yield to plaintiffs' evidentiary needs, the attorney-client privilege absolutely bars disclosure of communications by Samaritan or PCH employees to a member of Samaritan's legal staff. This argument poses several subordinate issues:

(1) Does the attorney-client privilege apply when, as here, the conduit of communications is a paralegal?

• • •

We will discuss each of these issues in turn.

A. COMMUNICATIONS TO A PARALEGAL

Arizona's attorney-client privilege statute provides that

> an attorney shall not, without the consent of his client, be examined as to any communication made by the client to him, or his advice given thereon in the course of professional employment. An attorney's *secretary, stenographer or clerk* shall not, without the consent of his employer, be examined concerning any fact the knowledge of which was acquired in such capacity.

Ariz.Rev.Stat.Ann. ("A.R.S.") § 12-2234 (1982) (emphasis added). Paralegals are not mentioned in the statute.

Plaintiffs argue that paralegals are an omitted and, therefore, unprotected conduit for attorney-client communications. *See Church of Jesus Christ*, 159 Ariz. at 29, 764 P.2d at 764 ("Privilege statutes, which impede the truth-finding function of the courts, are restrictively interpreted."). Although we accept the precept of restrictive construction and will have more to say about it later in this opinion, we find plaintiffs' construction too restrictive in this instance.

In section 12-2234, our legislature recognized that lawyers often communicate with clients through

agents. See Morris K. Udall et al., *Arizona Practice: Law of Evidence* § 74 at 139 (3d ed. 1991); *see also* 8 John H. Wigmore, *Evidence* § 2301, at 583 (John T. McNaughton rev., 1961) (The common law attorney-client privilege traditionally has included a client's communications to the attorney's representative.). We believe that the legislature intended by reference to "secretary, stenographer or clerk" to list a representative, not exclusive, group of agents through whom a lawyer and client might confidentially confer. *See* Udall et al., *supra*, § 74, at 139 ("In recognition of the fact that lawyers have employees who will hear or see confidential communications, at a minimum [section 12-2234] means that such communications do not become unprivileged when revealed to clerical employees hired by the lawyer to assist in furnishing legal advice.").

The law has recognized in other contexts that an attorney may properly and efficiently act through a paralegal. This Court, for example, has found paralegal services compensable in attorneys' fee awards, reasoning that lawyers should not devote time to tasks more economically assigned to legal assistants, "solely to permit that time to be compensable [in a fee award]." *Continental Townhouses East Unit One Ass'n v. Brockbank*, 152 Ariz. 537, 544, 733 P.2d 1120, 1127 (App.1986); *accord Missouri v. Jenkins ex rel. Agyei*, 491 U.S. 274, 288 & n. 10, 109 S.Ct. 2463, 2471 & n. 10, 105 L.Ed.2d 229 (1989). Similarly, lawyers should not retain information-gathering tasks more efficiently delegated to paralegals, solely to protect the client's privilege. We hold that a lawyer does not forfeit the attorney-client privilege by receiving otherwise privileged client communications through the conduit of a properly supervised paralegal employee.[8]

We caution that this holding does not create an automatic "paralegal-client privilege." There may be circumstances in which a nominal paralegal serves an investigative function independent of the attorney-client relationship. *See Longs Drug Stores*, 134 Ariz. at 427–28, 657 P.2d at 415–16 (Communications to insurance investigators are not privileged, as they may be used by the investigator's insurance company employer for purposes other than securing legal advice for the insured.); *Butler v. Doyle*, 112 Ariz. 522, 525, 544 P.2d 204, 207 (1975) (Because

---

[8] An attorney is ethically responsible for the conduct of a nonlawyer employed by, retained by, or associated with the lawyer. 17A A.R.S.Sup.Ct.Rules, Rules of Professional Conduct, Rule 42, ER 5.3 (1988). The Rules of Professional Conduct require the lawyer with direct supervisory control over the nonlawyer to "make reasonable efforts to ensure that the [nonlawyer's] conduct is compatible with the professional obligations of the lawyer." *Id.* Those obligations include client confidentiality. *Id.* ER 5.3 cmt.

insurance carriers may utilize statements received from their insureds for purposes independent of their insureds' legal representation, they are not agents of the attorneys hired to represent their insureds.). Such circumstances, however, are not established here.[9] Ms. Fraiz was an employee of Samaritan's Legal Department, acting solely at its direction, in anticipation of litigation against PCH. Her paralegal status did not strip the communica-

---

[9] Plaintiffs argue that the Fraiz investigation was not done to enable the Samaritan Legal Department to advise Samaritan or PCH. They assert that in matters of this kind, the legal department functions merely as a risk management department and "dispenses no legal advice—it simply marshals and memorializes the facts for use by outside counsel retained in the event litigation does ensue." Citing *State ex rel. Corbin v. Weaver*, 140 Ariz. 123, 680 P.2d 833 (App.1984), plaintiffs urge us to conclude that no attorney-client privilege attaches to this merely investigative, non-advisory process.

This fact-intensive argument was neither the subject of an evidentiary hearing nor the subject of specific trial court findings. Nor did the trial court resolve the issues on this basis. Accordingly, we neither accept nor reject this argument. Rather, we assume for purposes of decision that the Fraiz investigation was undertaken to enable the legal department to advise its corporate client.

tions she received of whatever attorney-client privilege might otherwise attach.

• • •

CONCLUSION

Although the interview summaries are protected by both the work product doctrine and by a qualified attorney-client privilege, plaintiffs have made the requisite showing that their need for disclosure outweighs the corporation's interest in confidentiality. Because the trial court did not abuse its discretion in ordering limited disclosure, the relief that petitioners have requested is denied. CLABORNE, J., concurs.

Questions

1. What authority does the court look to in determining whether there should be "paralegal-client privilege"?

2. Do you agree with the court's justifications for extending the privilege to legal assistants?

3. How does the court justify extending the obligation of client confidentiality to the legal assistant?

4. Do you agree that there should not be an "automatic 'paralegal-client privilege'?" Why or why not?

CONFLICTS OF INTEREST

CHAPTER OBJECTIVES

After reading this chapter, you should
be able to:

- Recognize that the duty of loyalty, the
principle of confidentiality, and the doctrine
of zealous representation within the bounds
of the law serve as the foundation of the
conflict of interest rules.

- Identify different kinds of conflicts of
interest that may affect the lawyer and the
legal assistant.

- Take precautionary measures to avoid
conflicts.

- Understand how conflicts of interest for the
lawyer or legal assistant may result in
disqualification of the attorney or in the
"imputed disqualification" of the entire law
firm.

A s chapter 5 demonstrated, law firms go to great lengths to protect the
confidences of their clients. They likewise expect their nonlawyer
employees to respect this obligation of confidentiality. Paralegals and
attorneys do leave their law firms, however, and difficult questions then arise
as to whether client confidences will remain protected. In response to these
questions, conflict of interest rules developed.

Conflict of interest problems have also evolved from a lawyer's duty of
loyalty to her client. The client's affairs are always to be placed before the
personal affairs and desires of the attorney or legal assistant or even those of
another client. That is because **conflict of interest rules** are designed to protect
the client's interest.

This chapter will focus on analyzing the lawyer's conflict-of-interest rules.
However, as we will see, the law expects these obligations to be upheld as
stringently by the nonlawyer as by the lawyer. For that reason, the attorney
ethics rules regarding conflicts of interest do apply to the legal assistant.

The ABA Model Guidelines for the Utilization of Legal Assistant Services
make clear that attorneys have a responsibility to prevent conflicts of interest
situations from arising out of the conduct of their nonlawyer assistants.
Guideline 7 states:

A lawyer should take reasonable measures to prevent conflicts of interest
resulting from a legal assistant's other employment or interests insofar as
such other employment or interests would present a conflict of interest if it
were that of the lawyer.[1]

What is a conflict of interest? Can conflicts be prevented? What are the
consequences to the lawyer, the law firm, and the client if they are not
prevented?

---

[1] ABA Model Guidelines for the Utilization of Legal Assistant Services, Guideline 7. © 1991 American Bar
Association. Reprinted by permission.

Conflict of Interest Rules Rules designed to prevent lawyers from compromising their client's interests because of information gained through the client-lawyer relationship. They are designed to prevent disharmony and distrust in the client-lawyer relationship.

This chapter defines the different kinds of conflicts of interest that can arise and instructs the legal professional how to prevent conflict of interest problems.

OPENING EXERCISE

Mike Applebee has been a legal assistant at Bifton and James, Ltd., a major downtown law firm, for fifteen years. Because he has a great deal of experience handling copyright and trademark work, he has been asked to assist with a case being brought on behalf of the firm's biggest client, MicroGraphics, Inc. MicroGraphics is suing Digital Data for copyright infringement.

Mike was asked to attend a deposition of the defendant's assistant vice-president that was scheduled to be taken the next day. When Mike arrived at the deposition, he was shocked to discover that the assistant vice-president of Digital Data was Maria Gonzales, a former classmate of his. Maria and Mike had dated for several months in high school.

When the deposition ended and all the attorneys had left the room, Maria asked Mike to join her for lunch so they could catch up on old times. Mike agreed. Later that afternoon, Mike received a bunch of flowers with a note attached that read, "Lunch was fabulous. Looking forward to seeing more of you. Maria."

Do you think Mike has a problem? How should he handle this?

The law firm's other client is Max Fontaine. Mike was assigned to work with Max, a soap opera star. Max was arrested and was standing trial for the murder of his wife, a famous starlet. This case had been discussed in the papers for months now, and the outcome of the trial was eagerly awaited. Max told Mike he sensed that Mike was an understanding soul; Max confided many secrets about his marriage and about the affair he had been having with Felicity English, a young up-and-coming model, at the time of the murder.

Mike has been approached by Lion Literary Publications about writing a novel about Max once the trial is concluded. Should he write the novel? Why or why not? If you think he should write the novel, how much information about the client should he reveal?

CONFLICTS OF INTEREST

Conflicts of Interest Those situations in which a client's interests can be compromised by an attorney because of information gained by the attorney in a client-lawyer relationship with the attorney.

It is inevitable that conflicts arise in our daily lives. They may be simple conflicts between friends, co-workers, or even family members. Generally, societal rules dictate the means by which we settle these conflicts and limit our responses.

Likewise, conflicts arise in legal settings and are often known as **conflicts of interest.** Although legal problems mimic and often are directly the result of the conflicts we face daily, legal conflicts of interest are not resolved through society's rules. Rather, attorneys' codes of ethics, supplemented by statutes and case law, assist us in resolving legal conflicts.

To better understand the concept of conflicts of interest, and to examine measures that can be taken to prevent them from happening, let's take a look at the everyday definition of the word "conflict."

Merriam-Webster's Dictionary defines a conflict as "fight, battle, war; competitive or opposing action of incompatibles."[2] It is very easy to see that it is a conflict, as the term is generally understood, or a desire to avoid a potential conflict that draws people to an attorney in the first place.

Taking the concept of the word conflict a step further, however, if a lawyer or a law firm represents a particular client, a conflict with the interests of that client may develop if: (1) the lawyer or firm then represents a party who is on the other side of the case, (2) the lawyer or firm represents or has represented a party who has diametrically opposing interests to those of the first client, or (3) the attorney has a personal interest that would prevent him from zealously representing the client's interests. Therefore, in a legal setting the word conflict takes on added meaning.

Conflict of interest rules are designed to prevent disharmony or distrust from becoming part of the attorney-client relationship. The rules developed because the lawyer's relationship with his client is special and unique. Conflict of interest rules are based upon three duties owed to the client by the attorney: (1) the duty of loyalty to clients, (2) the duty to protect confidences shared by clients, and (3) the duty to zealously represent client interests. These duties are among the most important things an attorney can ensure for his or her client.

Both the *Model Code* and the *Model Rules* provide guidelines prohibiting attorneys from engaging in specific behavior that could result in a conflict of interest. Many might be tempted to use the confidences of a former client to further the interests of a present client. Others might be tempted to advance their own interests at the expense of the client. However, by providing every lawyer and law office with specific do's and don't's when it comes to serving the interests of clients, the *Rules* and the *Code* remove this temptation.

This chapter sets forth the conflict of interest rules, discusses them in detail, and shows how they are applied to the legal assistant.

CONFLICT OF INTEREST AND THE LEGAL ASSISTANT

Conflict of interest rules likewise extend to the nonlawyer staff of the law firm. Just as the attorney has an obligation to be loyal to the client's interests, so does the legal assistant. Moreover, as we saw in chapter 5, the legal assistant is often made privy to client confidences and secrets. The legal assistant therefore has been found to have a corresponding obligation to protect those confidences. The law recognizes that, because they may become embroiled in matters presenting potential conflict of interest problems, the legal assistant may jeopardize the protection of confidences.

Numerous courts and ethics committees have recognized that the need to protect client confidences and to ensure loyalty to the client requires the application of conflict of interest rules to nonlawyers. For example, look at the following quotes and take note of the courts' ultimate concern that client confidences remain protected:

> Our statutes and public policy recognize the importance of protecting the confidentiality of the attorney-client relationship. The obligation to maintain

---

[2]MERRIAM-WEBSTER'S COLLEGIATE DICTIONARY 242 (10th ed. 1993). By permission. From Merrriam-Webster's Collegiate ® Dictionary © 1993 by Merriam-Webster Inc., publisher of the Merriam-Webster ® dictionaries.

HIGHLIGHT   ## The Foundation of Conflict of Interest Rules

L *oyalty to Client*—Loyalty is a key ingredient of the lawyer-client relationship. When a client hires an attorney, the client has an expectation that the attorney will safeguard his interests. The client believes that, above all else, the attorney will not let any other interests interfere with that client's interests. The law recognizes this dynamic, and labels the relationship shared by an attorney and client a "fiduciary relationship." This means that once the attorney is engaged by the client he assumes certain legal and ethical responsibilities to the client. These include the duty to maintain confidences, the duty to not take selfish advantage of the client, and the duty to not prejudice the client's interests.

Confidentiality—The fiduciary relationship shared by an attorney and client depends on a client's ability to trust the attorney to preserve confidences. This obligation never leaves the attorney, even after the attorney-client relationship ends.

Zealous Representation Within the Bounds of the Law—An attorney is required to represent his client with zeal and dedication. He is acting on the client's behalf and, therefore, the interests of the client come before the interests of all others. Thus, the interests of the client must be vigorously pursued. In serving the client, however, the attorney may be adviser or advocate. Different duties attach to each role. As advocate, he is pressed to advance his client's cause, usually in a courtroom setting. As adviser, the attorney must render objective advice that enables the client to make a reasoned decision about a course of action. In both instances he must act for his client without permitting other interests (his own or any other person's) to impede his representation. Of course, such representation must be accomplished with every deference being given to the laws and rules of ethics.

---

the client's confidences traditionally and properly has been placed on the attorney representing the client. But nonlawyer employees must handle confidential client information if legal services are to be efficient and cost-effective. Although a law firm has the ability to supervise its employees and assure that they protect client confidences, that ability and assurance are tenuous when the nonlawyer leaves the firm's employment. If the nonlawyer finds employment with opposing counsel, there is a heightened risk that confidences of the former employer's clients will be compromised, whether from base motives, an excess of zeal, or simple inadvertence. *In re Complex Asbestos Litigation,* 232 Cal.App.3d 572, 283 Cal.Rptr. 732, 740 (1991) (citations omitted).

And:

If information provided by a client in confidence to an attorney for the purpose of obtaining legal advice could be used against the client because a member of the attorney's non-lawyer support staff left the attorney's employment, it would have a devastating effect both on the free flow of information between client and attorney and on the cost and quality of the legal services rendered by an attorney. Every departing secretary, investigator, or paralegal would be free to impart confidential information to the opposition without effective restraint. The only practical way to assure that this will not happen and to preserve public trust in the scrupulous administration of justice is to subject these "agents" of lawyers to the same disability lawyers have when they leave legal employment with confidential information. *Lackow v. Walter E. Heller & Co. Southeast,* 466 So.2d 1120, 1123 (Fla.App. 3 Dist. 1985).

Both of these quotes indicate that courts will not hesitate to apply conflict of interest rules to nonlawyer employees of the law firm where there exists a real danger that confidences of the client may be jeopardized.

Regardless of how the conflict arises, whether it is because of the activity of a lawyer or a legal assistant, rather severe consequences can result from conflict of interest problems. The following section discusses those consequences. As you read, take note of why tracking potential conflicts is such an important responsibility for the paralegal to remember.

CONSEQUENCES OF VIOLATING CONFLICT OF INTEREST RULES

Before we begin a study of the important conflict of interest rules, it is helpful to understand the consequences of violating the rules.

The conflict of interest rules are found in the attorneys' codes of ethics; therefore the usual disciplinary actions may be levied against the attorney to redress violations of conflicts rules. An attorney might find herself reprimanded, suspended, or disbarred by her local disciplinary agency when she violates conflict of interest rules. Also, an attorney may face a legal malpractice lawsuit to recoup any damages the client suffers that were caused by the conflict.

Additionally, an attorney may be **disqualified** from representing a client when a conflict of interest arises.

Disqualified
Rendered ineligible or unfit to represent a client.

When opposing counsel discovers that a potential conflict exists, he may seek to disqualify the attorney with the perceived conflict. He does this by filing a motion with the court to disqualify the attorney from representing the client. In addressing this motion, courts are aware that they must be cognizant of competing concerns. These concerns were addressed in *Gregori v. Bank of America*, 207 Cal.App.3d 291, 254 Cal.Rptr. 853 (1989).

> Motions to disqualify counsel present competing policy considerations. On the one hand, a court must not hesitate to disqualify an attorney when it is satisfactorily established that he or she wrongfully acquired an unfair advantage that undermines the integrity of the judicial process and will have a continuing effect on the proceedings before the court. On the other hand, it must be kept in mind that disqualification usually imposes a substantial hardship on the disqualified attorney's innocent client, who must bear the monetary and other costs of finding a replacement. A client deprived of the attorney of his choice suffers a particularly heavy penalty where, as appears to be the case here, his attorney is highly skilled in the relevant area of the law.
>
> Additionally, as courts are increasingly aware, motions to disqualify counsel often pose the very threat to the integrity of the judicial process that they purport to prevent. Such motions can be misused to harass opposing counsel, to delay the litigation, or to intimidate an adversary into accepting settlement on terms that would not otherwise be acceptable. In short, it is widely understood by judges that "attorneys now commonly use disqualification motions for purely strategic purposes. . . ." *Gregori*, 254 Cal.Rptr. at 858-59 (citations omitted).

An attorney's disqualification from representing a client may be imputed to his entire law firm. Therefore, the entire law firm may find itself disqualified from representing a client. However, law firms can take protective measures to prevent this imputed disqualification from occurring. (More on imputed disqualification later in this chapter.)

The kinds of conflicts that may arise in the representation of clients are discussed more fully below. Conflicts may involve the simultaneous representation of adverse parties or the lawyer's desire to draft a book concerning his client's case. Conflicts may be a matter of successively representing first the plaintiff and then the defendant in the same matter. Regardless of the nature in which the conflict arises, the attorney or the legal assistant must initially determine whether a conflict of interest exists. If it does, the attorney must ensure that the client's interests are not jeopardized.

INTERPLAY:
The Relationship between Conflict Rules and Other *Model Rules*

A variety of rules, which are discussed throughout this chapter, are designed to prevent conflicts of interest. Before you begin to study the rules, however, it is important for you to note that there is interplay between the conflicts of interest rules contained in the ABA *Model Rules* and other provisions of the *Model Rules*. Some of those other rules include Rule 1.3, which covers diligence on the part of the attorney representing a party. Because a lawyer must diligently represent the interests of the client, any potential conflicts would necessarily affect that duty. Likewise, Rule 1.16, which covers "declining or terminating representation," mandates that an attorney withdraw or disqualify herself if a conflict arises after she has agreed to represent a party. Rule 2.2, which addresses the role of lawyer as intermediary, interacts with conflict of interest rules because there is a potential conflict where the attorney is mediating between conflicting interests.

EXERCISE 6.1

Refer to the concepts of loyalty, confidentiality, and zealous representation within the bounds of the law. Describe how you believe these concepts relate to the nonlawyer who works in the legal setting.

Do you believe these duties should apply to the nonlawyer? Why or why not?

DETERMINING THE EXISTENCE OF A CONFLICT

What, then, is the litmus test for determining whether there is a conflict? To determine whether a conflict exists, the attorney must consider the likelihood that involvement in one matter would interfere with a lawyer's independent judgment on another matter that is **substantially related** to the first matter.

Substantially Related Cases Cases that evolve from the same set of facts or have common elements or parties.

If a lawyer's zealous representation of her client is impeded by the interests of another party, the lawyer's independent legal judgment will be affected. Interference with the lawyer's independent judgment means the lawyer might not be able to consider all the possible courses of action that might be in the client's best interest.

At this point, you will probably note that you have read the phrase "independent legal judgment" before. In chapter 3, "The Unauthorized

Practice of Law," it was said that, because the nonlawyer may not practice law, the nonlawyer may not exercise independent legal judgment on behalf of a client. This means, among other things, that the nonlawyer could not give a client legal advice and could not independently draft legal documents for the client, without the review and signature of the attorney. In the unauthorized practice context, the emphasis, if you will, is on the word *legal*. In a conflict of interest situation, the concern is that the legal judgment exercised be *independent*.

The lawyer must also avoid representing clients whose interests are substantially related. This means the lawyer should avoid representing parties whose cases evolve from the same set of facts or which have common elements or parties. If a lawyer engages in employment that involves representation of a client whose case is a matter substantially related to a matter that the lawyer handled at his former employment, the confidentiality aspect of the attorney-client relationship is presumed to have been violated.

Keep in mind that the confidentiality of communications between an attorney and her client is what is to be protected here. That special relationship is why conflict of interest rules were developed. Therefore, any analysis of a conflict of interest problem must first involve a determination of whether any communication is in need of protection. (See chapter 5, "Confidentiality," for further discussion.)

As previously stated, these conflict of interest rules apply with equal force to the legal assistant. However, the attorney who is assigned to a client's case is in the unique position of being liable to his firm and to his client for problems that arise from such conflicts. The best course for the legal assistant who perceives a potential conflict is to apprise the attorney (or supervising legal assistant) of the problem. Resolution has to come from the attorney or from within the law firm.

When applying this substantially related test, courts and attorney disciplinary agencies look to the facts of each particular case. Any analysis is, then, what we call **fact-sensitive**. In other words, the outcome of each case turns on its particular facts. For this reason, throughout this chapter many different kinds of cases and examples demonstrating these types of conflicts will be discussed.

Fact-Sensitive The outcome of each case turns on its particular facts.

Now that you know how attorneys determine that a conflict exists, you might be wondering just how a *client* learns of the existence of a conflict of interest. Courts have held that it is incumbent upon the attorney to apprise the client of the problem as soon as a potential or an actual conflict becomes apparent. See *Pennwalt Corp. v. Plough, Inc.*, 85 F.R.D. 264 (D. Del. 1980).

EXERCISE 6.2

Paul and Jacquie are 2 top-notch lawyers who specialize in import-export and health care law. Elan consults them about the possibility of retaining Paul and Jacquie to represent her. She wants to import medical equipment used in Europe for the treatment of hair loss.

Paul and Jacquie currently represent Angie in her business dealings for her very successful imported wig and toupee business.

Do you think Elan's and Angie's businesses are substantially related?

What do you think Paul and Jacquie should consider in making this same determination?

SPECIFIC TYPES OF CONFLICTS
OF INTEREST

In order to fully understand the kinds of conflict of interest problems that might arise, it is necessary to review conflict of interest rules individually, studying the *Rules* and *Code* sections from which the issues derive.

Before we begin this analysis, it is important to note that conflicts may arise in different settings. Whether the conflict arises in litigation or nonlitigation settings affects the analysis of the conflict issues.

Conflicts of interest problems arise in both litigation and nonlitigation matters. It is easy to see that an attorney would face difficulties representing both an accused abusive husband and his wife in a trial for battery. Likewise, representing both the corporate honcho drafting a will distributing a million-dollar estate and his designated heirs can create obvious conflicts.

However, differences exist in handling litigation conflicts and nonlitigation conflicts. One important distinction is that litigation conflicts are often more obvious. In a litigation situation, adverse parties are apparent. The plaintiff always sues the defendant. It is easy to see, then, who has opposing interests. The conflicts that can arise in a nonlitigation setting are not so apparent. When analyzing conflict of interest problems arising in your law office, therefore, it is helpful to keep in mind that nonlitigation matters may require more careful scrutiny for potential conflicts.

We now embark on a discussion of specific types of conflicts of interest situations. The *Model Code* and the *Model Rules* are substantially similar regarding conflict of interest rules. The *Model Rules*, however, organize the information concisely and make additions to the *Code*. For that reason, this chapter is organized using the outline of the *Model Rules*. Where applicable, references to the *Model Code* are made.

We therefore will address four conflict of interest provisions found in the *Model Rules*. The first, Model Rule 1.7, specifically addresses the simultaneous representation of adverse clients and interests. Keep in mind that the doctrine of loyalty to the client, the principle of confidentiality, and the concept of zealous representation apply to every one of the conflict of interest problems discussed below.

SIMULTANEOUS REPRESENTATION

What is the simultaneous representation of clients? Simultaneous representation problems arise when an attorney attempts to represent more than one party in a particular legal matter. For example, Alyssa Attorney may seek to represent both Petra Plaintiff and Delores Defendant in the suit P v. D., or Alyssa may attempt to represent Xavier, Yolanda, and Zan in a business incorporation. (See the Highlight for the story on rock star Billy Joel's simultaneous representation problems.)

As a legal assistant, you may be wondering how simultaneous representation problems apply to you. After all, as a legal assistant you do not independently represent any clients and you therefore cannot create a simultaneous representation situation. However, the problems created by simultaneous representation are readily apparent, so it is perhaps easiest to begin a study of conflict of interest rules by examining these problems. You *must* learn and understand complex conflict of interest rules. Other kinds of conflict of interest problems definitely apply to legal assistants and have resulted in the disqualification of entire law firms from representing clients.

Therefore, we begin by looking to Model Rule 1.7:

Rule 1.7
(a) A lawyer shall not represent a client if the representation of that client will be directly adverse to another client, unless:
    (1) the lawyer reasonably believes the representation will not adversely affect the relationship with the other client; and
    (2) each client consents after consultation.
(b) A lawyer shall not represent a client if the representation of that client may be materially limited by the lawyer's responsibilities to another client or to a third person, or by the lawyer's own interests, unless:
    (1) the lawyer reasonably believes the representation will not be adversely affected; and
    (2) the client consents after consultation. When representation of multiple clients in a single matter is undertaken, the consultation shall include explanation of the implications of the common representation and the advantages and risks involved. *Model Rules of Professional Conduct* Rule 1.7 (1994).

The first paragraph, Rule 1.7(a), prohibits a lawyer's representation of parties who are direct opponents in litigation because their interests *will always be* directly adverse to one another. Paragraph (b) cautions a lawyer against representing parties whose interests *might* conflict. These include **co-plaintiffs** or **co-defendants.**

The conflicts of interest set forth in Rule 1.7 do not *automatically* disqualify the attorney from representing the client. You will recall that both (a) and (b) of Model Rule 1.7 provide for "consent after consultation." Consultation means ". . .communication of information reasonably insufficient to permit the client to appreciate the significance of the matter in question."[3] Where the client is informed of the potential for conflicts to arise and, knowing of the potential conflict, consents to the representation, the client is considered to have **waived the conflict of interest** or "cured" the conflict by consent. The best course is for the attorney to obtain the consent in writing.

The test for determining whether a waiver is effective is whether a lawyer who is not interested would conclude that the client should not agree to the representation under the set of circumstances. If a disinterested lawyer would not, then the lawyer who is involved in the circumstances should not ask the client for consent.

Some simultaneous representation provisions in the *Model Code* correspond with those of the *Model Rules.* One instance is seen in DR 5-101 (A) which states, "[e]xcept with the consent of his client after full disclosure, a lawyer shall not accept employment if the exercise of his professional judgment on behalf of the client will be or reasonably may be affected by his own financial, business, property, or personal interests." This Disciplinary Rule also mandates that a lawyer is to "decline proffered employment if the exercise of his independent professional judgment in behalf of a client will be or is likely to

Co-Plaintiffs Parties who, together, bring a legal action against some party(ies).

Co-Defendants More than one defendant being sued in a particular civil case or prosecuted in a criminal case in the same litigation.

Waiving Conflicts of Interest When a client is informed of the potential of conflicts to arise and, knowing of the potential conflict, consents to the representation. Also referred to as being "cured by consent".

[3]MODEL RULES OF PROFESSIONAL CONDUCT, Preamble Scope and Terminology, "Terminology."

HIGHLIGHT   Waiving Conflicts of Interest

H arry H. Schneider, Jr., a partner in the Seattle, Washington firm of Perkins Cole, is chair of the American Bar Association's Standing Committee on Lawyers' Professional Liability. Schneider provides the following checklist of elements that any letter designed to memorialize the client's consent should contain. This list includes among other things:

1. disclosure of the conflict in enough detail to apprise the client of the implications on future representation;

2. signature by each client, evidencing consent;

3. an acknowledgement of the clients' access to, and reliance on, the advice of independent counsel in consenting to the conflict;

4. an unequivocal statement that the firm's undivided loyalty will be exercised solely on behalf of each client in each matter;

5. an indication that the consent letter is being sent to both affected clients.

Source: Harry H. Schneider, Jr., *An Invitation to Malpractice,* ABA JOURNAL, Jan. 1993.

---

be adversely affected by the acceptance of the proffered employment, or if it would be likely to involve him in representing differing interests, except to the extent permitted under DR 5-105 (C)."

DR 5-105(C) permits an attorney to "represent multiple clients if it is obvious that he can adequately represent the interest of each and if each consents to the representation after full disclosure of the possible effect of such representation or the exercise of his independent professional judgment on behalf of each."

Model Rule 1.7, then, has the effect of clarifying both DR 5-105(A) and (C) by including not only client consent but also independent determination that a client's interests would not be adversely affected. See Comparison between the Code and the Rules which appears after Rule 1.7, *Model Rules of Professional Conduct.*

Model Rule 1.7 addresses various kinds of simultaneous representation conflicts of interest. There is the simultaneous representation of adverse clients, simultaneous representation of multiple interests and, finally, simultaneous representation of adverse positions.

EXERCISE 6.3

As a paralegal in a law firm, you will often be called on to conduct the initial client interview. Discuss some of the points mentioned in Rule 1.7 (a) (2) that you might want to tell a client during the consultation.

Simultaneous Representation of Parties The act of engaging in representation of one person against another person also represented by that lawyer.

Simultaneous Representation of Adverse Clients

A lawyer or law firm may not represent one person against another person also represented by that lawyer. Model Rule 1.7 (a) absolutely prohibits this type of **simultaneous representation of parties** with directly adverse interests. Therefore, Antoine Attorney may not represent both Patricia Plaintiff and Debra Defendant in the case of Plaintiff v. Defendant.

Music Rap: The Case Against Allen Grubman

In 1982, Allen J. Grubman was still a little-known music lawyer when he landed one of his biggest clients: Bruce Springsteen. The rocker's longtime manager, Jon Landau, recalls that one of the reasons he hired Grubman was "the word on the street was that Grubman's firm had done such a fantastic job for Billy Joel."

These days, Grubman, 49, is considered the most powerful lawyer in the music business, but Joel is no longer singing his praises. He is suing Grubman for $90 million, alleging fraud and malpractice. Grubman refuses to discuss the case, but in court papers, the lawyer blasts the suit as a "contrived and libelous attempt" to "smear" his firm, Grubman, Indursky, Schindler & Goldstein.

SMALL WORLD.

The case is largely about conflict of interest in the music business, where everybody who is anybody knows everybody else. A clique of lawyers handles most of the deals-often while on retainer to both artists and their labels. In Grubman's case, the suit alleges that, although Joel's recording contract was with CBS Records, neither Grubman nor his firm ever "fully advised" Joel of its representation of CBS or asked him to sign a conflict-of-interest waiver. "Isn't there a risk a lawyer isn't going to be as aggressive for the artist-client because he doesn't want to offend the record company which is hiring him to do other work?" says Joel's lawyer, Leonard M. Marks. Grubman claims the firm didn't represent CBS Records until shortly before Joel fired him.

Is there a conflict inherent in what Grubman does? "Of course there's a conflict of interest there—that's why people want Allen for their attorney," industry executive Irving Azoff says bluntly. "Allen knows everyone in the industry, so he knows who has the money and who doesn't." Grubman represented MCA acts when Azoff headed MCA Records Inc. a few years ago, but that didn't stop Azoff from hiring Grubman to represent MCA in various deals.

Grubman, whose record at Brooklyn Law School was undistinguished, recognizes that clients aren't buying his legal mind. Rather, he is renowned as a relentless bargainer who makes good use of his connections. "The relationships we've created allow us to do great things," says Grubman. He negotiated Michael Jackson's estimated $30 million deal with Sony Music and orchestrated Madonna's $60 million package with Time Warner Inc. His clients include superstars plus top record companies and their executives, such as Sony Music President Tommy Mottola.

"He makes you want to be in business with him." says megaproducer David Geffen.

Grubman started out as a performer. While growing up in Brooklyn, he sang regularly on a television show in Manhattan. Eventually, Grubman decided on a more practical career in entertainment law. The law student worked in the mailroom at William Morris Agency and as a CBS page. After graduating in 1967, he landed a job in a music law firm.

In 1969, Grubman struck out on his own. His firm got lucky in the 1970s by signing obscure disco artists who got hot. Soon it was signing heavyweights.

Grubman credits his rise in part to his forming relationships with "people who became very important." The short list: Mottola, former CBS Records President Walter R. Yetnikoff, and Geffen.

SUCCESS STORY.

Grubman's relationship with Geffen shows how the lawyer nurtures such ties while promoting his own interests. The two met 12 years ago, when Geffen was negotiating a deal for Grubman's client, Hall & Oates, to join Geffen Records. Soon, Geffen wanted out of the deal. He asked Grubman to shop it to another label but agreed to honor the commitment if need be. Grubman signed the group with Arista Records, getting a better deal for the singers and himself. A year later, Geffen hired Grubman as his personal attorney.

If the Joel suit stands up, it could scare away clients for Grubman. A key claim is that Grubman "cast his allegiance" not with Joel, but with his former manager and brother-in-law, Frank Weber. According to the suit, in about 1988, Yetnikoff warned Grubman "something was wrong" with Joel's finances because, despite the millions CBS had paid him, Joel needed to sell his Manhattan apartment so he and his wife, model Christie Brinkley, could build a beachfront home. Grubman allegedly refused to hire an investigator because he feared Weber would fire him. In court papers, Grubman claims the conversation never took place.

Yetnikoff is expected to testify about Grubman and the music business itself. But Yetnikoff may have an ax to grind: There are recurring rumors that Grubman helped do him in at CBS Records. Even so, until the Joel case is resolved, Grubman will be haunted by some of the same people who helped make him an extraordinary success.

Source: Reprinted from: Michele Galen, *Music Rap: The Case Against Allen Grubman,* BUSINESS WEEK, Nov. 2, 1992, 65.

This is directly based on the theory that an attorney is an advocate for a client and must zealously advocate that client's position. Imagine the horror of being an attorney's client and having that attorney know the intimate details of your case at the same time she is agreeing to represent your opponent's position. What would happen to the role of lawyer as advocate? How could you trust your attorney to represent your interests after you have shared confidences with her relative to your case?

It is also improper for an attorney to represent a client in one matter while being adverse to the same client in a different matter—even though the cases are not at all related, and even though there is no chance that any relevant confidences or secrets in one case might be relevant in another. See e.g., *Cinema 5, Ltd v. Cinerama, Inc.*, 528 F.2d 1384 (2d Cir. 1976). Even if there is no breach of confidentiality, the rule protects the client's reasonable expectation in loyalty.

EXERCISE 6.4

Lisa and Flip have no children. They do have a beautiful old Georgian home and a time share. They are talking about getting a divorce. Certain of the assets will probably be contested.

The two each go to see AnnaMarie, a lawyer whom they each know and trust. Can both parties hire AnnaMarie? Discuss any potential problems. What if each knows that AnnaMarie is representing the other?

Do you think your answer would be different if Lisa and Flip's divorce were uncontested?

Simultaneous Representation of Multiple Interests

Different conflicts problems arise when an attorney attempts to represent many clients at the same time, striving to achieve the same goal for all. What of a group of friends, for example, who are interested in setting up a small corporation? What about a husband and wife who are simultaneously represented in a house closing? In these instances an attorney usually does simultaneously represent the interests of multiple clients.

These situations differ from the previous conflict discussed. Litigation is not involved and, instead of serving as an advocate, the attorney acts as a counselor. Most important, the adverse interests of the parties may not be so clearly defined.

This is because, occasionally, although no conflict is apparent at first blush, one may later arise. Suppose, for example, that Henry and Wanda decide to get a divorce. At first, because their separation has been so amicable, they decide to use the same attorney to handle the divorce. However, as time goes by they begin to argue over the details of their property settlement. Small disagreements become conflagrations. Communication between the two completely breaks down. At that point their interests diverge and a conflict may clearly be said to arise.

Governed by Rule 1.7(b), the situation where simultaneous representation of multiple interests is not allowed occurs where the representation of one client would be materially limited by the lawyer's representation of another's interests. Therefore, the attorney is not *automatically* precluded from representing both clients. The question is whether the attorney's independent judgment will be affected in such a way that his representation of the client will be impaired.

Model Rule 1.7(b) also may prohibit an attorney's representation of co-plaintiffs or co-defendants. For example, an attorney should be cautious about defending two teenagers charged with assaulting a woman on the street and robbing her purse. At first it might appear that, because the source of all of the parties' causes of action is the same, no conflict exists. However, this is not always true. See *Model Rules of Professional Conduct* Rule 1.9 cmt. (1994).

Doris, Duke, Gwen, and Rob decide to open a restaurant which they will call "Finger-Lickin' Chicken." They will each hold twenty-five percent of the corporate shares. Doris will be president, Duke will be vice-president, Gwen will be treasurer, and Rob will be secretary.

EXERCISE 6.5

Doris, Duke, Gwen, and Rob decide to open a restaurant which they will call "Finger-Lickin' Chicken." They will each hold twenty-five percent of the corporate shares. Doris will be president, Duke will be vice-president, Gwen will be treasurer, and Rob will be secretary.

Can Martin, a lawyer referred to the four by Gwen, represent all four parties in incorporating? If your answer is Yes, why?

How does this type of representation differ from simultaneous representation of adverse clients?

Simultaneous Representation of Adverse Positions

Conflict of interest rules prohibit an attorney from representing *parties* with adverse interests. However, what happens when the attorney is asked to advocate **adverse positions** on the same legal question?

Suppose a hotly debated issue in a particular jurisdiction is whether the pollution control board or the circuit court should be the appropriate forum for ruling on a recovery of environmental clean-up costs. Two different clients consult with Agatha Attorney about representing them in two different cases. One of the two, Calloway Client, asks Agatha to advocate the position that the circuit court and not the pollution control board should be the appropriate forum to hear such cases. The other, Carter Client, asks Agatha to advocate the position that only the pollution control board can hear such cases.

Adverse Positions Goals, needs, or claims of one person that are different from or opposed to those of another person or group.

The general rule, according to the Comments to Rule 1.7, is that "it is ordinarily not improper to assert such positions in cases pending in different trial courts, but it may be improper to do so in cases pending at the same time in an appellate court." Whether an attorney may present different positions at the same time in the same trial court is still unclear.

For this reason, Agatha may properly consider undertaking representation of both Carter and Calloway at the trial or hearing level if their cases are filed in different courts, but may not properly consider representing both of those parties in the cases are later both pending in appellate court.

What do you think of asserting adverse positions? Do you see how asserting adverse positions can harm a client? Some commentators believe that the comment is vague and not entirely logical. What do you think?

EXERCISE 6.6

Rose is a legal assistant and office manager at the firm Snyder and Burnworth P.C. One evening while she is at work reviewing cases to be assigned to paralegals in the litigation department, Rose sees what she believes is a conflict. An attorney, Sean, has consulted with his client, Irene, regarding a contract she entered into with a company from Canada. However, Sean also represents that same Canadian company on retainer, handling all of their business dealings in the U.S.

Should Rose perceive any potential problems? What would you recommend that Rose do? What would you assess to be her role in this instance? What is the role of Snyder and Burnworth P.C.? Why?

Simultaneous representation is one of the most frequent types of conflict of interest problems that arise. Try the following problem to test your ability to spot a conflict. State what kinds of conflicts you see. You will be called upon to role-play the various parts in the case.

EXERCISE 6.7

Allied Insurance Company has recently run into some difficulties and is looking for a law firm to represent its interests. It seems that, at the last shareholder meeting, several of the shareholders were talking about bringing a shareholder derivative suit against Davis Distributing, who refuses to repay Allied the money Davis borrowed last year.

Allied secures representation by a law firm and later discovers that the firm also boasts as its clients the Allied shareholder group and Davis Distributing. Do you think there might be a problem resulting from the law firm's representation of all the parties? If you perceive a problem, what measures do you think the firm should take to correct the situation?

Allied is also experiencing a problem with a former employee, Cliff Harbaugh. Cliff has decided to sue Allied for employment discrimination and has retained DiStona and Bein, P.C., to represent his interests.

If Allied later decides to retain Judy DiStona and Lewis Bein in an action against Harbaugh for defaming the company throughout the community, is it proper for the law firm to do so? Why or why not? Is there anything that you think the firm might be able to do to prevent any conflict? For example, what if they apprise all parties concerned? Do you believe that notice to the parties operates to prevent any potential problems?

PROHIBITED TRANSACTIONS

Now that you have an understanding of the kinds of problems that result from conflicts of interest, it is important to study the second kind of conflict of interest problem. The second conflict of interest rule addresses types of prohibited transactions and may frequently involve the legal assistant.

The conflict of interest rules frown upon a lawyer entering into certain transactions that might affect her judgment in handling the client's representation. Generally, these transactions have nothing to do with the attorney's representation of other clients. In this respect, they are different from the first type of conflict we discussed.

What kind of transactions could influence the attorney in such a way that the client's interests are jeopardized? Consider a situation where an attorney negotiates to sell the rights to a client's story. The terms of the agreement are that, if the attorney wins the case and the client gets acquitted, the client and attorney would share $80,000. However, if the attorney loses the case and the client is convicted, the attorney and client would share $200,000.

The problems with this kind of conflict should be apparent. The overriding question is whether the lawyer would be able to exercise independent legal judgment in the face of such an agreement. Wouldn't the attorney have more incentive to lose the client's case than to win it? This goes against everything for which the legal profession stands.

This is not the only kind of prohibited transaction set forth in the *Model Rules*. Model Rule 1.8, entitled "Prohibited Transactions," specifically prohibits a number of transactions involving an attorney's interest vis-à-vis her client's interest. The rule provides:

(a) A lawyer shall not enter into a business transaction with a client or knowingly acquire an ownership, possessory, security or other pecuniary interest adverse to a client unless:

  (1) the transaction and terms on which the lawyer acquires the interest are fair and reasonable to the client and are fully disclosed and transmitted in writing to the client in a manner which can be reasonably understood by the client;

  (2) the client is given a reasonable opportunity to seek the advice of independent counsel in the transaction; and

  (3) the client consents in writing thereto.

(b) A lawyer shall not use information relating to representation of a client to the disadvantage of the client unless the client consents after consultation, except as permitted or required by Rule 1.6 or Rule 3.3.

(c) A lawyer shall not prepare an instrument giving the lawyer or a person related to the lawyer as parent, child, sibling, or spouse any substantial gift from a client, including a testamentary gift, except where the client is related to the donee.

(d) Prior to the conclusion of representation of a client, a lawyer shall not make or negotiate an agreement giving the lawyer literary or media rights to a portrayal or account based in substantial part on information relating to the representation.

(e) A lawyer shall not provide financial assistance to a client in connection with pending or contemplated litigation, except that:

  (1) a lawyer may advance court costs and expenses of litigation, the repayment of which may be contingent on the outcome of the matter; and

  (2) a lawyer representing an indigent client may pay court costs and expenses of litigation on behalf of the client.

(f) A lawyer shall not accept compensation for representing a client from one other than the client unless:

  (1) the client consents after consultation;

  (2) there is no interference with the lawyer's independence of professional judgment or with the client-lawyer relationship; and

  (3) information relating to representation of a client is protected as required by rule 1.6.

g) A lawyer who represents two or more clients shall not participate in making an aggregate settlement of the claims of or against the clients, or in a criminal case an aggregated agreement as to guilty or nolo contendere pleas, unless each client consents after consultation, including disclosure of the existence and nature of all the claims or pleas involved and of the participation of each person in the settlement.

(h) A lawyer shall not make an agreement prospectively limiting the lawyer's liability to a client for malpractice unless permitted by law and the client is independently represented in making the agreement, or settle a claim for such liability with an unrepresented client or former client without first advising that person in writing that independent representation is appropriate in connection therewith.

(i) A lawyer related to another lawyer as parent, child, sibling or spouse shall not represent a client in a representation directly adverse to a person who the lawyer knows is represented by the other lawyer except upon consent by the client after consultation regarding the relationship.

(j) A lawyer shall not acquire a proprietary interest in the cause of action or subject matter of litigation the lawyer is conducting for a client, except that the lawyer may:

    (1) acquire a lien granted by law to secure the lawyer's fee or expenses; and

    (2) contract with a client for a reasonable contingent fee in a civil case. *Model Rules of Professional Conduct* Rule 1.8 (1994).

The message is clear: A lawyer may not advance his personal and business interests to the detriment of the client. At the same time, however, where the client has been fully apprised and after the client has consented, transactions between a client and a lawyer that are fair and reasonable to the client will *not* be prohibited. A big part of the equation is always the consideration of whether the lawyer is able to exercise independent legal judgment.

Rule 1.8 discusses situations where the *potential* exists for a conflict to arise. When a situation addressed by Rule 1.8 arises, the attorney is not automatically disqualified from representing the client. Though the attorney should not engage in the activities discussed in Rule 1.8—where certain precautionary measures are taken, such as fully disclosing the potential conflict to the client and securing the client's consent—the attorney may be permitted to undertake the representation.

Just as an attorney may not enter into certain types of transactions with a client, *neither may the paralegal engage in such transactions.* For that reason, it is terribly important for the legal assistant to understand this rule. Sometimes, though, the legal assistant becomes closer to the client than does the attorney. Often, after the attorney has agreed to represent the client, it is the paralegal who conducts additional client interviews. It is the paralegal who tracks down witnesses, does preliminary research, and generates many of the documents in a client's case. It is often the legal assistant's role to serve as a buffer between the attorney and client.

The client might naturally come to feel close to the paralegal and want to reward him for his hard work. The client might want to write the paralegal into her will or offer a business partnership to the paralegal. It therefore becomes the paralegal's responsibility to understand which transactions the rules prohibit and to learn to assess the degree to which involvement with a client is proper. In this way, the paralegal can avoid improper transactions that may jeopardize the client's interests. In other words, the paralegal can learn to avoid conflicts of interest.

However, not every kind of transaction discussed in Rule 1.8 applies to the paralegal. For that reason, several provisions will be addressed in summary fashion at the end of this section.

Prohibited Business Transactions

Model Rule 1.8(a) addresses situations where an attorney enters into business transactions that might conflict with a client's interest or where the attorney acquires an interest that is adverse to a client. The rules frown upon such transactions, but they agree that such transactions are not expressly forbidden as they may be undertaken with client consent. (Of course, because of the general rule that all dealings between the attorney and client must be fair and reasonable to the client, the attorney should cautiously approach any such transaction.)

The first kind of transaction prohibited by the rules involves the situation where the attorney enters into a *business transaction with a client.* There are exceptions to this prohibition, however. The Comments to the Rule tell us that the prohibitions addressed in Rule 1.8(a) do not apply to standard commercial transactions where the client "generally markets" the same products and services to others. Because the client understands the business, it is presumed that the client will not have her interests disadvantaged. For example, the lawyer can buy an apple from her client, the grocer, without going through the hurdles of Rule 1.8. Similarly the lawyer can buy stock from her client, the broker, and pay the same commission as anyone else. In such transactions the lawyer receives no advantage by being the lawyer for the client, so the protections and prohibitions of Rule 1.8 are inapplicable.

Business transactions would be prohibited, however, where a client-attorney relationship exists and the client is assuming a significant risk because of the attorney's presumed superior knowledge. So, for example, courts would frown upon a corporate attorney entering into a business partnership with the neighborhood grocer to start a real estate development corporation.

The other type of prohibited business transaction is where the attorney acquires *business interests which are adverse to the client.* Again, this is not always prohibited. A consideration in determining whether to go ahead with such transactions would be whether the client deals in the same type of business in which the attorney has acquired an interest, and if so would be disadvantaged.

The Comments to the Rule provide an example of a lawyer who has learned that one of her clients is investing in specific real restate. That attorney may not seek to buy property near it if it would adversely affect the client. Additionally, the prudent attorney would get his client's permission to invest in real estate when his investment would affect the client's own real estate investments. However, if the client engages in something like medical services, and the lawyer acquires an interest in a business that provides medical services, the lawyer is considered to not be at an advantage in dealing with the client. Presumably, the lawyer does not have an expertise in medical services.

Remember our friend Arthur Eitelbaum from the previous chapter? Not only were Eitelbaum's actions jeopardizing client confidences but, when we left him, Eitelbaum was also contemplating an arrangement that would have created a conflict of interest situation.

Eitelbaum was planning to attempt to buy property adjoining the property owned by his client, Color Corporation, because he knew that future transactions of the corporation would increase the value of the land.

In advising Color about its business transactions, Eitelbaum may put his own interests before those of Color. Obviously it would be difficult for Eitelbaum to give detached advice to Color. His interest is in increasing the value of his holdings and not in helping Color to make a profit. The activity Eitelbaum was contemplating is clearly unethical and violates Rule 1.8, as it creates a conflict of interest.

This is not to suggest that an attorney is automatically barred from entering into business dealings with his client. The most important consideration in the law is that the attorney is not taking advantage of the client. For this reason, in order for an attorney to escape disqualification because of a conflict, the rule requires:

1. that the interests be *fair and reasonable* to the client and *fully disclosed* to the client, presented in writing in a manner which the client understands;

2. that the client be provided with an opportunity to seek the *advice of independent counsel* in the transaction; and

Consent Agreement or approval.

3. that the client **consent** to the transaction *in writing.*

Where these requirements are met, the law presumes that the transaction need not be prohibited.

Corresponding to Model Rule 1.8(a) is the Model Code's DR 5-104(A). DR 5-104(A) provides: "A lawyer shall not enter into a business transaction with a client if they have differing interests therein and if the client expects the lawyer to exercise his professional judgment therein for the protection of the client, unless the client has consented after full disclosure." This sentiment is echoed in EC 5-3.

Legal assistants also should not become involved in business transactions with clients. However, a legal assistant's involvement in a business transaction with a client is probably not as serious a conflict problem as would result should an attorney enter into a business transaction. This is because, when an attorney is involved, there is a very real danger that her independent legal judgment could be impaired by the transaction. When a legal assistant engages in a business transaction, it is true that *his* independent judgment might be impaired. However, the lawyer, who is impartial, is still there to review the legal assistant's work and to protect the client's interests.

The paralegal may be tempted to engage in such transactions. You must remember, if confronted with such a situation, that the reason for the rule prohibiting such transactions is that the law seeks to protect the interests of the client, and a business transaction between the client and legal assistant may jeopardize those interests. Therefore, entering into a business transaction with a client should be undertaken with caution.

If a legal assistant is provided with the opportunity to engage in a business transaction with a client of the firm, she should first approach her supervising attorney. From that point, the attorney can assess whether the business transaction is fair and reasonable to the client, and the attorney would fully disclose the potential consequences of the transaction to the client. The attorney can present this in writing in a manner which the client understands, and he can see to it that the client is provided with an opportunity to seek the advice of independent counsel in the transaction. Finally, he can assure that the client consents to the transaction in writing. Then once again, just as would result should a lawyer have business dealings with his client, this transaction need not be prohibited.

Let's consider some possible transactions. Comment on whether you believe the legal assistant might have a problem if he engages in these transactions:

- A paralegal buys a car from a client who owns a car dealership.
- A personal injury client of the firm who plans on getting married in four months consults with the firm's paralegal who has a wedding consulting business. The wedding consultation takes place after hours in a coffee shop.
- A paralegal becomes a client of a dentist who is represented by his firm in a malpractice action.

Exploiting Client Information

As has been discussed throughout this text, the interest of the client in a matter is deemed to be the primary concern of the courts. It follows that the interest that the attorney has in the matter is of secondary concern. *Haagen-Dazs Co. v. Perche No! Gelato, Inc.*, 639 F.Supp. 282, 286 (N.D. Cal. 1986).

Yet some attorneys forget this basic principle and seek to exploit the relationship between the client and attorney. In doing so they violate their ethical obligations toward the client, as directed by Rule 1.8(b). After all, it is unseemly and unethical to take advantage of and to benefit personally from disclosing the confidences of a client. A lawyer is absolutely prohibited, therefore, from using information obtained from his client to his advantage. The only exception would be where a client consents.

One relatively recent case illustrates how an attorney's business interests could lead the attorney to take advantage of confidential information of a client. In *Disciplinary Proceedings Against Leaf*, 164 Wis.2d 458, 476 N.W. 2d 13 (1991), an attorney engaged in several businesses with a Dr. Haynes, a licensed divorce mediator. One of the businesses was a counseling business. Leaf referred her clients to Haynes to be provided with "manager, mentor, and motivator services." When Leaf referred the clients to Haynes, she did tell them she was part owner of the counseling business, but failed to fully disclose the conflict of interest and how her interest in her business with Haynes might affect the exercise of her professional judgment for her clients. 476 N.W.2d at 15.

The referee of the hearing concluded that Attorney Leaf had entered into business relationships with clients in situations where her professional judgment was affected by her own financial and business interests. The referee also determined that Leaf had not fully disclosed her business interests to her clients and had not gotten the consent of her clients. Leaf argued that there was no conflict because they would not have to pay the business if the counseling Haynes provided did not yield financial benefits to the clients. Any potential conflict, she asserted, was made obvious to the clients because, when she referred them to Haynes for counseling, she told them she was part owner of the business.

Although the court never specifically mentioned the conflict of interest rule that prevents attorneys from exploiting client information, this case demonstrates such a situation. If the clients had never sought the attorney's services at a time when they were particularly vulnerable, they would have never been referred to Leaf's business. The attorney's business, therefore, received clients because the attorney took advantage of the clients' legal problems.

This conflict of interest problem was just one of numerous violations in which the Supreme Court of Wisconsin believed Leaf had engaged. It ordered her suspension from the practice of law for six months. Among other things, the court said:

> Attorney Leaf apparently fails to comprehend that this falls far short of her professional duty to her clients in the presence of an actual or potential conflict of interest. *Leaf*, 476 N.W.2d at 17.

It is likewise true that the nonlawyer may not exploit client information. This rule derives from the duties of loyalty and confidentiality. As we saw in chapter 5, the nonlawyer cannot reveal the confidences of a client. To do so would obviously jeopardize the client's interest. Moreover, for a legal assistant to use the client's information to his own advantage means that the legal assistant has violated his duty of loyalty to the client. He has put his own interest first, and anything gained from doing so comes at the expense of the client. This is simply unacceptable.

The *Model Code* addresses this problem in DR 4-101 (B) (3), which states: "Except when permitted under DR 4-101 (C), a lawyer shall not knowingly: (3) Use a confidence or secret of his client for the advantage of himself or of a third person, unless the client consents after full disclosure."

EXERCISE 6.8   Discuss what you believe Attorney Leaf did wrong in her client-lawyer relationships. What confidences did she exploit?

Gifts from Clients

Grateful clients often seek to offer a token of their appreciation to the attorney who has handled their case so skillfully.

Rule 1.8(c) speaks to this situation and prohibits the lawyer from drawing up an instrument whose aim is to provide the lawyer with a substantial gift from the client, unless, of course, the gift-giver is a relative of the attorney. For example, attorneys are often called on to draw up wills of the client. A client may ask the attorney to amend her will in order to leave the attorney a substantial bequest. Unless the gift-giver is a relative, however, the attorney should not incorporate her name into the will.

Rather, where the attorney is inclined to accept the gift, the client should consult independent counsel. This provides some assurance that the attorney has not unduly influenced the client and has not coerced her into making the gift. Therefore, when the will is probated, the gift is less likely to be contested.

Moreover, by requiring the client to seek independent legal advice before bequesting a gift, the attorney protects himself against a later lawsuit for fraud and undue coercion. If such a lawsuit were filed and the attorney was found guilty, the attorney would certainly face more than a disciplinary charge. He might also be required to return the gift to the estate and, possibly, be found liable for money damages.

Rule 1.8(c) provides an exception to this general rule where the "gift is not substantial." See *Model Rules of Professional Conduct*, Rule 1.8, cmt (1994). Therefore, if a client wishes to have the attorney draft a will and wants to bequeath to the attorney a novelty paperweight, the *Rules* would presumably permit the drafting of such an instrument, without the client having to seek outside counsel.

Where a gift is offered that does not require the drafting of an instrument, the attorney could most likely accept it. While Rule 1.8(c) does not specifically address the situation, the Comment provides that "[a] lawyer may accept a gift from a client, if the transaction meets general standards of fairness. For example, a simple gift such as a present given at a holiday or as a token of appreciation is permitted." Thus, a box of chocolates offered by a client may be accepted by the attorney.

No Disciplinary Rule in the *Model Code* corresponds to the *Model Rule*. However, Model Rule 1.8(c) does substantially mimic EC 5-5.

The legal assistant should likewise refrain from accepting gifts from the client. As has been previously discussed, the client may see more of the legal assistant than the attorney and so may feel that he should do something to acknowledge the paralegal's help.

The legal assistant should always remember that to accept a gift may create conflict of interest problems for his law firm. The paralegal's acceptance of a substantial gift may affect his duty of loyalty to the client. For example, the legal assistant might work to cause a particular event to occur after the client asks his attorney to draft an instrument that conditions a gift to the legal assistant upon that event. The paralegal could do this even though the event might not be in the best interest of the client.

When would a situation like this occur? Let's look at a hypothetical situation. Suppose a client is pursuing a case to establish the lineage of her champion Golden Labrador. The client may tell the legal assistant that, after her dog has been pronounced of champion lineage *by a judge*, the client will give the legal assistant one of her dog's pedigreed puppies. The legal assistant, eager to have a puppy, may be tempted to expedite her work so that the case can be processed more quickly through the court system. She may decide to cut corners. The legal assistant may consider doing this even though it would be in the best interest of the client to drop the case altogether and not proceed to trial at all. The promise of a puppy may have the effect, therefore, of clouding the legal professional's judgment.

Moreover, the legal assistant would not want to have to defend herself if, for instance, a client's heirs contest a bequest drafted into a will giving the paralegal a substantial gift. Keep in mind, therefore, that a simple gift at holidays or birthdays is acceptable, but excessive gift-giving raises questions of propriety and should be avoided.

What would you say to Chester, a client with an extremely successful shoe manufacturing company who offered you a $500 gift certificate from the nicest department store in town for your two-and-a-half years of outstanding work on a major commercial real estate closing? **EXERCISE 6.9** What would you say to Tom and Audrey Public who offer you an all-expenses-paid vacation to the beach with their family for your outstanding two-and-a-half weeks of work toward closing on their new home?

Literary and Media Rights

Occasionally, cases and clients come along that provide the public with sensationalistic facts. In high-profile trials with high-profile clients, it seems like the public cannot get enough information to satisfy its appetite for news. The media might be drawn to the legal professionals who work on the cases, to solicit them to relate newsworthy facts.

Rule 1.8(d) tells lawyers to avoid negotiating for the literary rights until after the representation of the client is completed. Where the lawyer enters into negotiations for the purchase of the rights before the representation is completed, the lawyer may affect the outcome of the case in such a way as to provide a more sensationalistic ending. Such an ending, after all, provides better material for a book. The attorney may be so caught up in securing an amazing ending that he loses sight of his client's interests. A potential conflict obviously results in such a situation.

Rule 1.8(d) "is substantially similar to DR 5-104(B), but refers to 'literary or media' rights, a more generally inclusive term than 'publication' rights" in the Disciplinary Rule. See Comparison between *Model Code* and *Model Rules*, following Rule 1.8.

The legal assistant should also refrain from engaging in negotiations for literary rights to a client's case until the representation has concluded. A legal assistant's temptation to start writing books in her spare time might be great. However, the paralegal's actions can affect the outcome of a case just as a lawyer's can.

Moreover, you must remember the underpinnings of conflict of interest rules. The underlying reason for the rules includes more than merely zealous representation. It also includes the duties of confidentiality and loyalty.

There is a significant danger that confidential information will be revealed should the legal assistant attempt to write a book discussing the client's case. It is also clear that, just as most other individuals would, the paralegal may be tempted to put her own interests before those of the client when approached by a literary agent and offered a substantial amount of money to write about a client. Potential conflicts can arise unless contracts with literary agents are only entered into after the representation has been ended.

EXERCISE 6.10

Elizabeth is a paralegal for the district attorney's office. She is assisting the district attorney in prosecuting a grisly murder involving the capture of twins who have been charged with the murder.

In her capacity as a legal assistant, Elizabeth has interviewed the families of the victims for impact statements for use in the sentencing hearings, should the twins be convicted. The defendants' cases have been severed for trial. The trials are set to begin in two months.

Elizabeth is approached by a national television station about the possibility of selling what she knows about the case. When the station's agent contacts Elizabeth and senses that she is reluctant, he tells her he believes that the broadcast could save the lives of innocent people who will learn from the show, and that she will earn six figures if she agrees to be interviewed.

Write out, in a step-by-step analysis, the process Elizabeth must go through in getting to a final decision about the offer. Consider the rules and their applicability to Elizabeth as a legal assistant. Please include in your answer any relevant discussion Elizabeth should have with the district attorney.

Then, write out a brief statement you think she should make to the station to either accept or decline the offer.

Would you conclude that the outcome of Elizabeth's decision would be different if she were to be approached five years after the defendants were sentenced and when she changed jobs and was working as a litigation paralegal in a downtown firm?

Loans to a Client

While the reasons people seek the assistance of attorneys vary, people generally seek legal advice because they need help. Often the help they need is related to their personal finances.

Yet Rule 1.8(e) prohibits attorneys from giving loans to clients except in certain limited situations. Few areas of the conflicts rules can be as heartbreaking as this rule. When we see a client suffering so greatly after an injury on the job that she can no longer work, we want to help. The client may need food or medical care. However, as legal professionals you cannot render that type of assistance without risking being disciplined.

The underlying rationale is that the client, indebted to the attorney (or legal assistant), might feel obligated to later pursue a lawsuit despite having a change of heart about wanting to litigate a claim. The attorney then has a personal stake in pursuing the claim because he wants to secure the opportunity to recoup his money.

Exceptions to the rule prohibiting loans to clients are also found in Rule 1.8(e). The lawyer may advance court costs and expenses of litigation to the client, with the expectation of later repayment of these monetary advances. The lawyer, expected to accept cases of indigent clients, may also pay the court costs and expenses of litigation of these indigent clients. Such payments do not amount to loans considered violative of the conflict of interest rules.

Therefore, the attorney can advance the fees required to file a complaint, costs for obtaining transcripts, and expenses incurred while traveling to depositions, expecting repayment contingent upon the outcome of the case, but he may not advance his client living expenses. Where an indigent client is involved, the attorney may assume responsibility for paying these court costs, but an attorney is absolutely prohibited from giving a client money apart from costs incidental to the court case. This even means money for food.

This same rule applies as stringently to legal assistants. Even where the temptation to help is great, the best course is to refer the client to human service agencies that specialize in rendering assistance (i.e., battered spouse shelters, food pantries, county health care facilities). Always remember that, while it may seem morally correct to provide money or assistance to clients for problems that are incidental to their cases, the ethical rules make no exceptions in this area. You will want to do what is better for the client in the long run. That will be to protect the relationship he has with your law firm.

Failing to adhere to this rule against making personal loans to clients could seriously harm the interests of the supervising attorney. Under Rule 5.3, after all, the attorney supervising the legal assistant would be responsible for such a loan. To what advantage would it be to have the client's attorney fighting disciplinary charges just when the client most needs him?

The Model Code's DR 5-103(B) is similar to this provision in the *Model Rules,* but under the *Code,* "the client remained ultimately liable" for expenses. Therefore, the *Code* did not allow the attorney to advance the cost of litigation. Rule 1.8(e)(1) does away with that. The *Code* has absolutely no provision which is similar to Rule 1.8(e)(2).

A recent hurricane swept away the home of Brian and his family three weeks before the holidays. Soon after the hurricane, the die-making factory in which Brian worked laid off his entire unit.

On his way home from work the day he was laid off, Brian was so upset he got into a serious accident with a semi-trailer. Brian suffered rather serious injuries. The police issued a ticket to the driver of the trailer.

EXERCISE 6.11

Brian then retained Michelle, a local attorney, to litigate his claim against the trucking company. Jennifer is Michelle's paralegal and she was asked to meet with Brian to obtain more information.

When Jennifer met with Brian two days later, Brian related his problems. He began to cry as he explained that Santa would not be visiting his family this year. He further explained that he was living in a tent with his pregnant wife and three children, and that they were cooking their meals in a wok over charcoal briquets until they could find more suitable housing.

Jennifer is moved. She envisions her own family's happy holiday celebration and she wants desperately to assist Brian and his family.

What would you recommend?

Relatives of the Attorney or Legal Assistant

What if family members who work in the law end up on opposite sides of a case? As the saying goes, "It's a small world." It is conceivable that if two or more family members work in the law, their paths may cross when they are representing opposing parties. At the same time, because of the attorney's duties of loyalty and zealous representation of the client's interests, she cannot assume any posture that might even appear to compromise her client's interests. Conflicts may therefore result.

Because of the possibility that this might occur, Model Rule 1.8(i) indicates that a lawyer should not represent a client in a matter that is directly adverse to a person whom the lawyer knows is represented by a family member. Therefore, Abigail Attorney cannot represent Clarence Client in a suit where Clarence is suing a party represented by Abigail's husband, Harvey, or her father, sister, cousin, mother-in-law, or any other family member.

In such a situation, the client's interests must be *directly adverse.* This means that if Abigail Attorney is *not* representing Clarence Client in his lawsuit but another member of her law firm *is* representing Clarence, and the opposing party is represented by her husband, no conflict exists under the *Model Rules.*

Where certain precautions are in place, representation by family members of opposing sides may be undertaken. The precautionary measures required by the *Rules* are first, that the client is apprised by the lawyer about the relationship, and then, that the client consents to such representation.

There is no similar provision in the *Model Code.*

Is a possible conflict of interest created when relatives of the *legal assistant* represent parties opposing the law firm's client? What if a paralegal from the law firm and a lawyer representing the adverse client begin dating? Do you see potential problems in this situation? It should be immediately clear that the confidences of the client may be jeopardized in such a situation. As you know, the legal assistant has an obligation to take care to protect client confidences. Even so, when such a relationship exists, the possibility of the opposing attorney being disqualified or the legal assistant creating problems for the firm at which he works is certainly very real. Because of the competing interests involved when considering a motion to disqualify, however, there is an indication that the courts will look beyond the fact that a relationship exists. The courts also consider the nature of the relationship (i.e., was this merely a few dates as opposed to a sustained dating relationship?) and whether client confidences were actually divulged. Keep in mind that, presumably, the courts may conclude that there is a greater possibility that confidences could be revealed during an ongoing relationship.

A situation where a nonlawyer was dating opposing counsel was addressed not too long ago in California. In *Gregori v. Bank of America*, 207 Cal.App.3d 291, 254 Cal.Rptr. 853 (1989), the court addressed the issue of whether this problem required the attorney involved in the relationship to disqualify himself from representing the plaintiff in litigation.

The attorney involved with the nonlawyer, Thomas J. Foley, Jr., was a partner in a law firm representing numerous apple growers in a "lender liability" lawsuit against a bank and an association of apple growers. The law firm representing the directors of the bank was identified in the court opinion as "O'Brien." "Jane Doe" was a secretary at O'Brien who was given substantial responsibility for administering the bank directors' case.

Jane Doe and Foley developed a personal relationship. They met after work for drinks and discussed "personalities involved in litigation." When Jane Doe's employers found out about her relationship with Foley, they told her the date was inappropriate and assumed she would not see Foley socially again. When Jane Doe came in late for work a few months later, she reported that "she had dined with Foley the prior evening and had too much to drink. She told [her employer] that although the case had not been the main topic of conversation, 'certain aspects of the case had been discussed including the lawyers involved, Foley's views on liability, including that the O'Brien law firm clients were 'evil' people who would shortly be put in jail." Once again, Doe was admonished about her relationship. This time she was told she could not have social contact with Foley again. Doe retorted that her time off work was her own time and she would date Foley on her own time if she chose to do so.

Lawyers at O'Brien then told Foley they knew about the dates and asked him to "avoid the appearance of impropriety." Foley assured the lawyers that his social relationship with Jane Doe would stop. However, Foley and Doe continued to have social contact.

Although the court strongly disapproved of Foley's conduct, it refused to disqualify the attorney from continuing in his representation of the apple growers. This conclusion was reached primarily because there were no facts presented that established that confidential information had changed hands. In this situation, where the attorney and secretary had dated only a few times, the court was reluctant to *presume* that confidences had been shared.

> Appellants dispute the trial court's finding that substantive information was not divulged by claiming that the mere fact of the communications between Foley and Jane Doe require the court to *presume* that confidential information passed hands.
>
> · · ·
>
> The relationship between Jane Doe and Foley established by the scant evidence in the record does not create a reasonable probability that important information regarding the lawsuit was divulged. Thus, unlike conflict of interest cases upon which appellants rely, which might otherwise be persuasive, the record in this case does not provide the necessary evidentiary basis for the legal presumption that Foley acquired confidential information useful to his clients. *Gregori*, 254 Cal.Rptr. at 862.

Moreover, the court was reluctant to disqualify Foley merely on the basis of appearance of impropriety.

> The evidence before us does not warrant disqualification. There is no doubt that, as found by the trial court, Foley's acts "were the essence of unprofessionalism and poor judgment." However, it is one thing to say Foley's conduct was unprofessional and showed bad judgment and quite another to say, as the trial court did not, that it warrants disqualification. Resolving conflicts in the testimony and declarations in favor of the prevailing parties, as we must, the record shows only that Foley initiated a social relationship with Jane Doe that consisted of two or three meetings after work. With respect to the substance of their conversations, the record satisfactorily establishes only that in a very general way the two discussed "personalities involved in the litigation." As Shakespeare observed, it is not uncommon for legal adversaries to "strive mightily, but eat and drink as friends." (Shakespeare, *The Taming of the Shrew*, Act I, scene ii.) The impropriety that now appears in this case consists not so much of the fact that Foley initiated and maintained a social relationship with Jane Doe, but that he did so secretly, thereby casting doubt upon his motives. The evidence that the relationship was actually of a more intimate or intense nature than that frequently seen among representatives of competing parties, making it more likely confidential information was disclosed, is based entirely on hearsay declarations. The evidence, taken as a whole, simply does not establish a probability Foley obtained information that could be used advantageously against appellants. Accordingly, on the record before us, we cannot say that denial of the motion to disqualify represents an abuse of discretion. *Gregori*, 254 Cal.Rptr. at 865.

Therefore, not every situation in which a relationship is established will automatically result in disqualification. Whether the legal assistant is related to opposing counsel or is merely dating opposing counsel, the *possibility* of creating a conflict exists. However, it is important to note that a legal assistant's relationship with opposing counsel may not result in an automatic disqualification.

The Michigan Bar has addressed the question where a legal assistant was employed by a legal services organization that represented plaintiffs in claims against the father-in-law and/or husband of the legal assistant. The Michigan Bar noted:

> [This] is not a circumstance which *per se* requires disqualification of the legal services organization from the representation of the clients or termination of the paralegal's employment if the plaintiffs' counsel advises the plaintiffs of the employment of the paralegal and secures the plaintiffs' consent thereto, as well as takes all reasonable steps possible to prevent the paralegal from having access to the file and from having any direct or indirect involvement in the representation of the plaintiffs. CI-1168.[4]

Sometimes a conflict arises and is attributed to the entire law firm, and the firm is disqualified. (See "Imputed Disqualification," this chapter.) In order to avoid disqualification when the legal assistant is somehow related to opposing counsel, therefore, precautionary measures must be taken.

For example, the legal assistant and attorney who are related or who are dating should first take care to never discuss the case between them. More

---

[4]State Bar of Michigan. Reprinted by permission.

important, at the outset of the representation, the attorney and legal assistant should disclose the nature of the relationship to the clients and seek client consent. Revealing the nature of the relationship to the client will also protect against the client later believing that something improper occurred. Finally, the firm should consider restricting the legal assistant's access to client files or, for that matter, to any information about the client's case. Implementing such a protective measure will ensure that the interests of the client cannot be jeopardized by the legal assistant's relationships.

The same principles hold true where a legal assistant who is related to another legal assistant working in the same community finds that they are working on opposite sides of a case. The best course of action is always to first bring the potential problem to the attention of the supervising paralegal or attorney. The firm can then secure client consent.

Additional Types of Prohibited Transactions

Additional types of prohibited transactions result in conflicts of interest. While the legal assistant should certainly be aware of these rules and the problems that derive from them, it is unlikely she will ever be directly involved or instrumental in causing such conflicts. These transactions include third-party payments (Rule 1.8(f)), aggregate settlements (Rule 1.8(g)), agreements limiting malpractice liability (Rule 1.8 (h)), and proprietary interests (Rule 1.8(j)).

ATTORNEY AS WITNESS

The third kind of conflict of interest problem, governed by Rule 3.7, is known as the "lawyer as witness" rule. Rule 3.7 provides:

(a) A lawyer shall not act as advocate at a trial in which the lawyer is likely to be a necessary witness except where:
    (1) the testimony relates to an uncontested issue;
    (2) the testimony relates to the nature and value of legal services rendered in the case; or
    (3) disqualification of the lawyer would work a substantial hardship on the client.
(b) A lawyer may act as advocate in a trial in which another lawyer in the lawyer's law firm is likely to be called as a witness unless precluded from doing so by rule 1.7 or rule 1.9. *Model Rules of Professional Conduct* Rule 3.7 (1994).

During pre-trial and trial proceedings, an attorney is viewed as a client's advocate, a mouthpiece for the client. She is called upon to represent the client in the legal arena. She is skilled in that area of the law and in the rules of evidence. In fact, she establishes credibility as an advocate because of her knowledge of the law.

A witness, however, testifies based on her personal knowledge relating to the case. It is that knowledge upon which her credibility is evaluated by the judge or jury.

Model Rule 3.7 operates to prevent the lawyer who is representing a client in a case from testifying in that case. The attorney cannot therefore assume the role of witness. The rule was developed to safeguard against confusing the trier-of-fact. Should the testimony of the witness (who happens to also be the attorney) be given greater credibility because it is coming from an individual who is accomplished and who has considerable knowledge of the case? Or should the attorney, as advocate, be held in less regard because her testimony as a witness was not credible? For this reason, attorneys are discouraged from appearing as witnesses in a client's case.

It is important to note that, while the rule generally prohibits testimony by an attorney, there are exceptions. Where the attorney will testify to an issue that is not contested (i.e., chain of custody), where her testimony will relate only to the legal services she rendered (fee dispute), or where her disqualification would cause great hardship to the client (solo practitioner works on client's case for five years), she may testify. In these cases, the jury or judge is not likely to naturally confuse the role the attorney is playing as witness with the role she is playing as advocate.

The *Model Code* addresses this dilemma. DR 5-102(A) and (B), and DR 5-101(B)(1) and (2) all apply. For example, DR 5-102(A) prevents an attorney from representing a client where the attorney "learns or it is obvious that he or a lawyer in his firm ought to be called as a witness on behalf of his client." DR 5-102(B) addresses the situation where the "lawyer learns or it is obvious that he or a lawyer in his firm may be called as a witness other than on behalf of his client. . .until it is apparent that his testimony is or may be prejudicial to his client."

How are these rules applied to the legal assistant? The legal assistant is not an advocate in the courtroom for the client. Therefore, the justification prohibiting the practice does not apply where the legal assistant is concerned. There is no danger that the finder of fact (a judge or a jury) will be confused if the legal assistant testifies.

Several state bar ethics opinions have allowed the nonlawyer to testify as a witness without ordering the disqualification of the law firm because of a conflict of interest. Alabama Ethics Opinion RO 87-135 answered the question of whether "a law firm [should] be disqualified from representing a client where its full-time investigator will be called as a witness." The opinion stated that the attorney could allow the nonlawyer to be called to the stand without running the risk of violating a conflict of interest rule. In so holding, the state bar wrote: "The rationale for these rules [prohibiting the attorney as witness] as stated in Ethical Consideration 5-9 is not called into play when a non-lawyer employee is called as a witness. By placing his own employee on the stand, the attorney is not placed in the 'unseemly and ineffective position of arguing his own credibility.' "[5] A similar position was stated in Ohio State Bar Ass'n, Legal Ethics and Professional Comm., Informal Op. 87-7 (1987).

EXERCISE 6.12

Helen is a paralegal at the firm Levitin and Levitin. Helen entered the profession because she was drawn to human drama. That is exactly what she finds in a case involving the Great Lending Savings Bank and Loan.

The Levitin firm represents the savings and loan in a lawsuit that was filed against it by ABC Investment Company. ABC Investment charged that the savings and loan had reneged on an agreement to finance ABC's purchase of future contracts. Levitin and Levitin represented the savings and loan at the time it entered into the multimillion dollar agreement.

---

[5]Reprinted with permission.

Helen is called to testify as to what she heard when she attended the meeting in her capacity as legal assistant during the final negotiations between ABC and the savings and loan.

Do you think Helen should be permitted to testify? Why or why not?

FORMER CLIENTS

The fourth conflict of interest rule relates to the lawyer's and legal assistant's former clients. It addresses situations where a lawyer represents a client in a matter and then later represents the opposing party in another matter. Suppose a lawyer has previously represented Paula Plaintiff in one matter, changes firms, and is requested to represent Darla Defendant in the same matter or one that is very similar to it?

Former client conflicts are the most commonly recognized conflict of interest problems. In fact, much of the literature on conflict of interest issues involves successive representation against former clients. Certainly this situation possesses the greatest potential for a conflict of interest problem for paralegals to arise.

Model Rule 1.9 covers conflict of interest rules arising in matters of subsequent representation. What distinguishes this conflict of interest rule from Rules 1.7 and 1.8 is that Rule 1.9 pertains to situations where *representation of the former client has ended.* This is distinctly different from Rules 1.7 and 1.8, where the representation has yet to occur. Rule 1.9 provides:

Conflict of Interest: Former Client

(a) A lawyer who has formerly represented a client in a matter shall not thereafter represent another person in the same or a substantially related matter in which that person's interests are materially adverse to the interests of the former client unless the former client consents after consultation.

(b) A lawyer shall not knowingly represent a person in the same or a substantially related matter in which a firm with which the lawyer formerly was associated had previously represented a client

   (1) whose interests are materially adverse to that person, and

   (2) about whom the lawyer had acquired information protected by Rules 1.6 and 1.9 (c) that is material to the matter; unless the former client consents after consultation.

(c) A lawyer who has formerly represented a client in a matter or whose present or former firm has formerly represented a client in a matter shall not thereafter:

   (1) use information relating to the representation to the disadvantage of the former client except as Rule 1.6 or Rule 3.3 would permit or require with respect to a client, or when the information has become generally known; or

   (2) reveal information relating to the representation except as Rule 1.6 or Rule 3.3 would permit or require with respect to a client. Model Rules of Professional Conduct Rule 1.9 (1994).

Part (a) of the Rule expressly prohibits an attorney from representing a client where he has formerly represented a party whose interests were adverse. For example, Joe Attorney can represent Cathy Client in her divorce action against her husband Charlie (Cathy v. Charlie) but cannot later represent Charlie in his action against Cathy for increased child support payments. This applies where the interests of both parties are substantially

Former Client A party that previously has been represented by an attorney.

related and directly adverse. (Of course, the client may consent to this representation and thereby waive the conflict.)

Part (b) of the Rule extends this **former clients** prohibition to a lawyer who moves from one law firm to another. For example, Mary Attorney works at the law firm, Dewey, Czezlick & Howe and is assigned to represent Sidney Steamer in a trademark action against Reasonable Upholstery (a huge conglomerate), which is represented by Don, Kable & Associates. If Mary leaves Dewey, and goes to work for Don, she cannot represent Reasonable in an action against Sidney Streamer.

Substantially Related Closely connected. The test is the degree to which the lawyer was previously involved in the client's case.

Rule 1.9 does not prohibit every former client conflict. Rather, it provides several limitations. These are: (1) the representation must be **substantially related** to the former client's representation; (2) the attorney must seek to represent interests that are **materially adverse** to the former client's interests, and (3) the attorney may use general information about a former client without causing a conflict of interest.

Materially Adverse Information acquired by the lawyer in the course of representing a client. It may not subsequently be used or revealed by the lawyer, to the disadvantage of the client.

Substantially related. Both provisions of the rule prohibit an attorney from representing clients in matters that are the same or substantially related. Recall from the beginning of this chapter that the test to determine whether matters are substantially related is the degree to which a lawyer was previously involved in a client's case. The former client must not be disadvantaged in any way by the attorney's representation of another client.

Materially adverse. Both provisions of Rule 1.9 also prohibit representation of interests that are "materially adverse." The Comment to the Rule states: "Information acquired by the lawyer in the course of representing a client may not subsequently be used or revealed by the lawyer to the disadvantage of the client."

General information. This does not mean, however, that *general* information derived from the lawyer-client relationship cannot be used by the attorney. Thus, as the Comment states: "The fact that a lawyer has once served a client does not preclude the lawyer from using generally known information about that client when later representing another client."

The rules regarding the representation of former clients are likewise extended to the legal assistants employed by the law firm. The situation has been addressed by various state bar ethics committees and by several courts. For example:

> Hiring a former employee of an opposing counsel is not, in and of itself, sufficient to warrant disqualification of an attorney or law firm. However, when the former employee possesses confidential attorney-client information, materially related to pending litigation, the situation implicates ". . . considerations of ethics which run to the very integrity of our judicial process." *In re Complex Asbestos Litigation,* 232 Cal.App.3d 572, 283 Cal.Rptr. 732, 744 (1991).

A former-client conflict does not automatically preclude an attorney or the paralegal from representing clients whose interests are adverse to former clients. The rule permits an attorney to secure the consent of the former client after full disclosure of the attorney or legal assistant's former-client conflict. Then, once the attorney has secured that consent, his path is clear for representing the adverse client.

No provision comparable to the Former Clients Rule, Rule 1.9, is found in the *Model Code.* Usually, conflicts of interest problems were handled according to Canon 9, which provides that "a lawyer should avoid even the appearance of impropriety." Also called into play were rules regarding confidentiality.

Rule 1.9 is also viewed as emphasizing that, while a lawyer is of course entitled to change his professional association, he always has a duty to protect the interests of any client with whom he had an attorney-client relationship. This applies with equal force to those attorneys who formerly or successively work for governmental entities (and their legal assistants).

The law does not disregard the interests of the lawyer and the nonlawyer employee in a desire to change employment. However, the law does seek to balance the interests of the client with the attorney's and nonattorney assistant's right to secure employment of their choice, and so it recognizes methods for doing that. For a discussion of this point, see ABA Comm. on Ethics and Professional Responsibility, Informal Op. No. 88-1526 (1988).

EXERCISE 6.13

Tshneka Green decided to open a clothing boutique. Wanting to arrange a partnership agreement, she and her partner sought the advice of an attorney, Louanne Wolf, of the firm, Taylor, Beyer and Wolf. Louanne agreed to help them.

Several years passed and Tshneka's store, "Serendipitous Fashions," grew. She decided to branch into manufacturing and distribution of a clothing line. She called upon Wolf's firm to handle all of their legal needs. Val Beyer's expertise is in the area of commercial litigation, and Paul Taylor's expertise is in taxes. Wolf handles any contract matters that arise.

Then Taylor and Beyer dissolved their partnership with Wolf. Taylor joined a large firm of seventy lawyers, Chatham, Harris and Guzek.

As Tshneka's business grew into an international concern, she decided she needed a larger law firm to represent her interests. She called on Taylor at his new firm and asked if he would be her attorney.

Do you think Taylor has a potential problem here because he previously worked on Tshneka's taxes?

What if Wolf's paralegal, Dorothy, joined Taylor when the firm dissolved but had never been exposed to any information about Tshneka's business?

Do you think any conflicts would result?

IMPUTED DISQUALIFICATION

The rules discussed earlier in this chapter presented a variety of situations in which conflict of interest problems could arise. The final conflict of interest rule we will discuss does not present additional kinds of conflicts to avoid. Rather, Rule 1.10 addresses how the effect of conflict of interest problems can be spread through an entire firm.

The previous conflict of interest rules disqualified individual attorneys. Those rules serve to protect client confidences from being used to the disadvantage of the client and ensure that the attorney's loyalty to the client remains intact.

However, conflict of interest problems often also give rise to questions about whether any member of the lawyer's firm can adequately represent the client's interests. Sometimes a violation of any one of the conflict of interest rules can lead to opposing counsel moving to disqualify the attorney's entire law firm.

PARALEGALS IN THE SPOTLIGHT

In *In re Complex Asbestos Litigation,* a solo practitioner was disqualified from representing asbestos plaintiffs because he had hired a legal assistant who had previously worked for a firm that had represented the defendant corporations. 232 Cal. App.3d 572, 283 Cal.Rptr. 732 (1991).

The problem of legal assistants changing law firms and subsequently representing parties against former clients has become a big issue, especially in California. There the paralegal community was abuzz with news that a legal assistant's actions had resulted in the disqualification of his law firm from a substantial number of cases.

The paralegal, Michael Vogel, had been employed by Brobeck, Phleger & Harrison. The law firm represented corporations being sued for asbestos claims. Vogel's responsiblitites included reviewing discovery matters, extracting critical information, and working on settlement evaluations. Later, Vogel's responsibilities increased and he also attended strategy meetings with the attorneys involved in handling the matter. In October of 1988, however, Vogel was given notice that his employment with Brobeck, Phleger & Harrison was terminated.

Vogel later contacted Jeffrey Harrison, a solo practitioner representing asbestos plaintiffs, about possible employment opportunities. Vogel learned of Harrison's clients and, noticing that Brobeck was representing the defendant in some of the cases, accessed Brobeck's computer files on these plaintiffs. Vogel asserted that this was done as research.

Although Vogel claimed that he had received a waiver from Brobeck to work for Harrison, Brobeck denied having given one, and none had been put into writing.

Vogel's predicament was discussed at length in paralegal journals. An article entitled "In California, It's Better to Stay Put Than To Switch" focused on the fact that Vogel and Harrison had failed to get a written waiver of the conflict and, instead,

had relied upon something as ephemeral as an oral waiver. The article quoted Karen Betzner, the director of professional competence for the California bar in San Francisco, as warning, "What this [opinion] says to lawyers is, 'You are now under a duty to screen your paralegals for conflicts in the same way that you screen your associates.' . . . Law firms already know what to do with associates. You check them, you screen them. . . now you treat your paralegals the same way."[1]

A few months later, Michael Vogel wrote a letter to *Legal Assistant Today* to update his career status. He announced he had been employed for several months as a litigation legal assistant in the products liability department of a firm located in San Francisco. He noted that his case had been appealed to the California appellate courts and all the parties were waiting for the court to hear the case.[2]

Shortly thereafter, the California appellate court heard the case and handed down a lengthy analysis of Vogel's predicament. The court disqualified Harrison, Vogel's former employer, from twenty-one asbestos cases. In essence, this was due to the court's recognition that nonlawyers have the same confidentiality obligations as do attorneys. (See chapter Five, "Confidentiality," for further discussion of this principle.)

The court indicated that such action was necessary because Harrison had made no attempt to screen Vogel to protect client confidences. The court indicated that implementing one of the screening devices (as discussed below) would have protected the firm.

[1] LEGAL ASSISTANT TODAY, *In California, It's Better to Stay Put Than To Switch,* May-Jun. 1990. Copyright 1994. James Publishing, Inc. Reprinted with permission from *Legal Assistant Today.* For subscription information, call (714) 755-5450.

[2] LEGAL ASSISTANT TODAY, *Letters,* Sept. 1990. Copyright 1994. James Publishing, Inc. Reprinted with permission from *Legal Assistant Today.* For subscription information, call (714) 755-5450.

Rule 1.10 addresses the disqualification of an entire law firm. The theory is called "imputed disqualification."

The **imputed disqualification** rule is designed to prevent a lawyer (or a legal assistant) who has access to confidences of the client from moving to another law firm and sharing those confidences with his new partners. Whether the problem involves an attorney or a paralegal, exposure to a client's interest at one job can prevent that person from being able to get another job handling a client whose interests are adverse to the former client. That is because the lawyer or nonlawyer employee who has handled a matter at one firm can be considered "tainted" for purposes of going to work at another firm.

The *Rules* and *Code presume* that confidences have been shared and, therefore, they disqualify the entire firm from representing the adverse party. The courts impute the disqualification of the attorney to the entire firm. Imputed disqualification (also referred to as **vicarious disqualification**) means that the disqualification of the attorney has been transferred or imputed to the entire law firm.

Rule 1.10 provides the following:

(a) While lawyers are associated in a firm, none of them shall knowingly represent a client when any one of them practicing alone would be prohibited from doing so by Rules 1.7, 1.8(c), 1.9 or 2.2.
(b) When a lawyer has terminated an association with a firm, the firm is not prohibited from thereafter representing a person with interests materially adverse to those of a client represented by the formerly associated lawyer and not currently represented by the firm, unless:
   (1) the matter is the same or substantially related to that in which the formerly associated lawyer represented the client; and
   (2) any lawyer remaining in the firm has information protected by Rules 1.6 and 1.9(c) that is material to the matter.
(c) A disqualification prescribed by this rule may be waived by the affected client under the conditions stated in Rule 1.7. *Model Rules of Professional Conduct* Rule 1.10 (1994).

A comparable provision is found in the *Model Code*. In DR 5-105(D), the *Model Code* states that, where a lawyer is required to withdraw from representation of a client, "no partner, or associate, or any other lawyer affiliated with him or his firm, may accept or continue such employment."

Rule 1.10 and DR 5-105(D) operate to permit a law firm to represent a client whose interests are directly adverse to the interests of a client represented by an attorney who was formerly associated with the law firm. It prohibits the firm from representing a client where the matter is the same or substantially related to a matter in which the attorney formerly represented the client and where any other lawyer in the firm has information that is protected by Rules 1.6 and 1.9(c).

The imputed disqualification principles of Rule 1.10(a) apply only when the lawyers are currently associated with a *firm*. The determination of whether an association of attorneys is a "firm" appears to be based on the particular facts of the situation.

Rules regarding imputed disqualification have likewise been applied to legal assistants who change firms. Take, for example, the problems of the paralegal detailed in *Glover Bottled Gas Corp. v. Circle M. Beverage Barn, Inc.*, 129 A.D.2d 678, 514 N.Y.S.2d 440 (1987). A paralegal had been employed by attorneys representing a particular plaintiff. The legal assistant changed firms and became employed by attorneys for the defendant in the same case. Because the plaintiff had worked on litigation pending between the parties at both firms and had interviewed the plaintiff's manager regarding the facts of the case at the first firm, the defendant's attorneys were disqualified from the representation.

Imputed Disqualification
Disqualification of an attorney has been transferred to the entire law firm such that all lawyers in that firm are disqualified from representing the client. Also known as "vicarious disqualification."

However in a case which might appear to be very similar, *Esquire Care, Inc. v. Maguire*, 532 So.2d 740 (Fla. App. 2 Dist. 1988), the court held that a plaintiff's firm did not have to remove or "disqualify" itself from a case where, during litigation, it hired the former secretary for the defendant's attorney. The court, citing *Lackow* (quoted at the beginning of this chapter) noted: "While we accept the premise in *Lackow* that ethical considerations applicable to attorneys might also extend to support personnel, we cannot agree that so strong a presumption arises that potentially damaging confidences are in danger of revelation, as would arise if an attorney left one employer for another." *Esquire Care*, 532 So.2d at 742. The court rejected a notion that would permit disqualification on the basis that the secretary had had mere access to information. The secretary's change of employment was found to not be "disadvantageous to her former employer's client."

An ethics opinion from the New Jersey Advisory Committee on Professional Ethics addressed imputed disqualification in the case of a paralegal who previously worked for an adversary. The opinion reads in pertinent part as follows:

> The inquiring law firm wishes to hire a paralegal to assist one of its partners in the prosecution of breast implant and medical malpractice actions on behalf of plaintiffs. The paralegal, who parenthetically has a nursing background, has been employed since December 1990 by another law firm with a heavy concentration of work in joint medical defense of defendants in asbestos litigation. She has spent the vast majority of her time in that area. The law firm that employs the paralegal does medical defense work only. The firm does not represent the defendants on liability issues, which are handled by other law firms. This arrangement was allowed in a single medical defense. The defendants' answers are filed by the liability firms and contain crossclaims for indemnification and counterclaims. Presumably, no member of the firm would have access to any liability information on medical issues.
>
> The law firm that employs the paralegal and inquiring firm are presently adversaries in many asbestos cases. The other firm has claimed that the paralegal was directly involved in the selection and evaluation of defense experts in cases being prosecuted by the inquiring firm, and has supervised preparation of confidential evaluations of medical issues used by the other firm's clients in settlement negotiations with the inquiring firm.
>
> . . .
>
> The inquiring firm asks whether it may hire the paralegal under the circumstances outlined above. Opinion 665 of the Advisory Committee on Professional Ethics.[6]

The Bar analyzed the inquiry by citing to, among other sources, N.J. Bar Opinion 654, 129 N.J.L.J. 514 (1991), and *Dewey v. R. J. Reynolds Tobacco Co.*, 109 N.J. 201, 536 A.2d 243 (1988). Although the New Jersey Bar noted that decisions in New Jersey had cautioned that lawyers' movement between firms should require strict monitoring procedures, the New Jersey Bar concluded,

> This inquiry involves a paralegal, not a lawyer. While there is a distinction, we believe that the firm should nevertheless be extraordinarily mindful of, and careful about, any exchange of confidential information received during the course of prior employment.

---

[6]Reprinted by permission.

> ## INTERPLAY:
> ## The Relationships among Conflict of Interest Rules
>
> Again we see the interrelation between other ethics rules and this Rule. Model Rule 1.10 specifically refers to Rules 1.7 (which is the general conflict of interest rule), 1.8(c) (which addresses gifts from clients), 1.9 (which addresses the attendant conflicts in representing an interest of a present client that is adverse to a former client).
>
> The imputation principle is also considered in Model Rules 1.11 and 1.12. Model Rule 1.11 addresses successive government and private employment. It additionally specifically addresses imputed disqualification in those contexts. Model Rule 1.12 addresses imputed disqualification in the context of former members of the judiciary.

WAIVING DISQUALIFICATION

As has been noted throughout this chapter, the existence of a potential conflict does not *automatically* lead to disqualification of an attorney from the representation of a client. Where the client consents to continuing the representation, after full disclosure by the attorney of the existence of a conflict, the courts may allow such representation. In such a case, the client is considered to have *waived* the conflict.

Likewise, a client's waiver may also work to prevent the imputed disqualification of the entire firm. Rule 1.10(c) states, "A disqualification prescribed by this rule may be waived by the affected client under the conditions stated in Rule 1.7." Therefore, if the attorney reasonably believes that his representation of a particular client will *not* be adversely affected by his relationship with another client and where there is client consent after full disclosure, the imputed disqualification is waived.

Christine represents Jim in a personal injury action against Peggy Sue. Peggy Sue hires Christine to sue Jim on a residential real estate claim.

    Determine whether there is a conflict. If one exists, state what kind of conflict it is. Could Christine be disqualified? Please cite to the applicable provision in the *Model Code* or *Model Rules.*

    If you have determined that Christine can be disqualified, can that disqualification be avoided? How?

EXERCISE 6.14

AVOIDING IMPUTED DISQUALIFICATION
THROUGH USE OF SCREENING DEVICES

We have seen that, when a conflict of interest arises, it is often in everybody's best interest for the attorney to disqualify himself from representing a client. Even if an attorney disqualifies himself, however, his firm might still face imputed disqualification as a result of the attorney's prior contact with the client.

You might conclude that disqualification is a widespread problem. It is not. The law recognizes that if law firms were repeatedly subject to imputed disqualification because of their lawyers' former clients gained at previous employment, the mobility of legal professionals would be seriously restricted.

This is true for both attorneys and the legal assistants whom they employ. In a recent ABA Informal Opinion, it was recognized that it is important for nonlawyers to have mobility in employment opportunity.[7]

As a method of preventing imputed disqualification, protective or screening devices have been developed. These screening devices are actually defenses that are used to prevent an attorney from "tainting" his entire firm. A screening device allows the firm to continue its representation of the client. The *Model Rules* do not expressly allow for the use of a screening device to prevent imputed disqualification. Nonetheless, when ruling on motions to disqualify, many courts have required such a system to be in place before allowing the law firm's representation to continue.

The "Chinese Wall" and the "Cone of Silence" are two such devices. They are discussed more fully below.

The Chinese Wall

Attorneys and nonattorney support staff who have worked closely with a client's case at one firm are considered to be tainted when they go to a firm that handles substantially related matters. One measure used to prevent disqualification is to have the firm build what is termed a Chinese wall around the tainted attorney; that is, the tainted attorney is precluded from having anything to do with the matter at issue. Chinese walls are screening devices. The idea behind them

> is to build a Wall around the tainted attorney in order to prevent access to him by other attorneys. Discussions with the tainted attorney regarding the subject at issue are forbidden. Files may have to be segregated so that no member of the firm can benefit from the tainted attorney's information. Fees may have to be separated so that the tainted attorney can not benefit from the conflicting representation.[8]

When Chinese walls are constructed, the courts analyze potential conflicts of interest in the following way:

> [T]he particular attorneys who will be working on the later adverse representation are permitted to prove that they were not privy to any of the former clients' confidences...[by proving that] the tainted attorneys are in effect sealed off from the ongoing litigation.[9]

Courts also look to determine whether the walls were timely erected. See *Papanicolaou v. Chase Manhattan Bank, N.A.,* 720 F. Supp. 1080 (S.D.N.Y. 1989); *E Z Paintr Corp. v. Padco, Inc.,* 746 F.2d 1459 (Fed. Cir. 1984).

Though the concept of these walls is abstract, just picture the following scenario:

Assume that an attorney or a legal assistant handled incorporation matters while working in the corporate department of a midsized law firm. One of the cases worked on was the incorporation of ACME Rockets. The attorney or

---

[7]*See* ABA Comm. on Ethics and Professional Responsibility, Informal Op. 88-1526.
[8]*Conflicts of Interests,* 3 GEORGETOWN JOURNAL OF LEGAL ETHICS, 165, 173 (1989). Reprinted with the permission of the publisher, © 1989 The *Georgetown Journal of Legal Ethics* & Georgetown University.
[9]Id.

legal assistant then goes to work at a law firm which represents a company with interests adverse to those of ACME.

The new firm at which the attorney or legal assistant works is very large, and its corporate department is composed of three divisions. The new firm's divisions are (1) incorporation, (2) municipal bonds and business taxes, and (3) business contracts. The attorney or legal assistant, because of her prior experience, has been assigned to the new firm's incorporation division. ACME's competitor is involved in a dispute with ACME over a business contract, which is handled by the third division.

It is reasonable to expect that the new firm should not be disqualified. Though it may be argued that a conflict or a potential conflict exists at the time the attorney or legal assistant is hired, the firm can easily seal off the attorney or legal assistant and prevent ACME's confidences from being shared with other members of the firm undertaking the representation. It will build imaginary walls around the person and preclude the possibility that that person can say anything or act in any way, even inadvertently, that might disadvantage the interests of his or her former employer firm's client.

Chinese walls are erected in any number of ways. Common methods of erecting a Chinese wall include:

- The attorney would have no access to information regarding the matter and would receive no paperwork relative to it.

- The attorney would promise not to discuss the former client's case with other members of the law firm now undertaking representation of that case, and those working on the case would promise not to discuss the matter with the "walled" attorney.

- Files would be coded in such a way that the attorney could not inadvertently review a file detailing the former client's case, and the coding system would be clearly communicated to all members of the firm.

- The attorney would be physically removed from the area in which work on the client's case is being undertaken.

The Cone of Silence

In addition to the erection of Chinese walls, there is also a screening device known as the "Cone of Silence". The cone of silence means that a lawyer switches firms but simply agrees not to share the confidences of former clients with those in the new firm in which he works. There is no burden on the firm to take measures. Rather, it is incumbent upon the attorney to maintain silence.

The cone of silence is not a favored approach by the courts because it does not serve to protect client confidences as vigorously as a Chinese wall. For a discussion of the cone of silence, see *Nemours Foundation v. Gilbane, Aetna, Federal Insurance Co.*, 632 F.Supp. 418 (D. Del. 1986). The question of whether this case will have any real influence is still up in the air. It may not be wise to rely on this approach for protection.

Please discuss the pro's and con's of each screening device discussed above. Which do you think is more practical? | **EXERCISE 6.15**

SCREENING THE LEGAL ASSISTANT

Increasingly, courts and state disciplinary agencies are aware that legal assistants must be screened in the same manner as would any attorney.

In re Complex Asbestos Litigation addressed the issue of implementing screening devices when legal assistants change law firms and become involved in litigation that would affect former clients. 232 Cal.App.3d 572, 283 Cal.Rptr. 732 (1991). Again, protection of client confidences was the overriding factor the court considered in determining that there is a definite need to consider screening nonlawyer employees. While reading the following selection, see if you can recognize the concerns that have been discussed throughout this chapter and that have been applied to both attorneys and legal assistants.

> The most likely means of rebutting the presumption is to implement a procedure, before the employee is hired, which effectively screens the employee from any involvement with the litigation, a procedure one court aptly described as a "cone of silence." Whether a potential employee will require a cone of silence should be determined as a matter of routine during the hiring process. It is reasonable to ask potential employees about the nature of their prior legal work; prudence alone would dictate such inquiries. Here, Harrison's first conversation with Vogel revealed a potential problem—Vogel's work for Brobeck on asbestos litigation settlements.
>
> The leading treatise on legal malpractice also discusses screening procedures and case law. We find several points to be persuasive when adapted to the context of employee conflicts. "Screening is a prophylactic, affirmative measure to avoid both the reality and appearance of impropriety. It is *a* means, but not *the* means, of rebutting the presumption of shared confidences." Two objectives must be achieved. First, screening should be implemented before undertaking the challenged representation or hiring the tainted individual. Screening must take place at the outset to prevent any confidences from being disclosed. Second, the tainted individual should be precluded from any involvement in or communication about the challenged representation. To avoid inadvertent disclosures and to establish an evidentiary record, a memorandum should be circulated warning the legal staff to isolate the individual from communications on the matter and to prevent access to the relevant files.
>
> The need for such a rule is manifest. We agree with the observations made by the *Williams* court: "[Nonlawyer] personnel are widely used by lawyers to assist in rendering legal services. Paralegals, investigators, and secretaries must have ready access to client confidences in order to assist their attorney employers. If information provided by a client in confidence to an attorney for the purpose of obtaining legal advice could be used against the client because a member of the attorney's [nonlawyer] support staff left the attorney's employment, it would have a devastating effect both on the free flow of information between client and attorney and on the cost and quality of the legal services rendered by an attorney." Further, no regulatory or ethical rules, comparable to those governing attorneys, restrain all of the many types of nonlawyer employees of attorneys. The restraint on such employees' disclosing confidential attorney-client information must be the employing attorney's admonishment against revealing the information. *In re Complex Asbestos Litigation*, 283 Cal.Rptr. at 745 (citations omitted).

In re Complex Asbestos Litigation discusses some of the preventative screening measures attorneys can implement when hiring a legal assistant who presents a potential conflict of interest. Other measures can also be implemented.

In 1985 the Kentucky ethics committee addressed this question: "If a paralegal leaves a law firm (the 'former firm') and is hired by another law firm (the 'hiring firm'), which is the opposing counsel in several cases, does the hiring firm have a conflict of interest?" Kentucky Bar Association Ethics Opinion No. 308, 9/85. The Kentucky bar responded "Yes."

In reaching this conclusion, the advisory opinion laid down the following guidelines for preventing such conflicts from arising. The Kentucky Bar noted:

> Despite the foregoing, lawyers have duties regarding the employment of paralegals which can provide a basis for disqualification in the present case. DR 4-101(D) requires a lawyer to exercise reasonable care to prevent employees from disclosing or using confidences or secrets of a client.... [T]hese rules require that the formal (sic) firm: (1) instruct the paralegal not to disclose the client's confidences and secrets after leaving the firm; (2) inform the hiring firm that the paralegal has been so instructed; (3) request that the paralegal not be permitted to work on or discuss the case; (4) request that the hiring firm instruct the paralegal not to disclose confidences or secrets of the former firm's clients; (5) request that the hiring firm inform the former firm if the paralegal discloses confidences or secrets of the former firm's client; (6) request that the hiring firm withdraw from the case if the paralegal discloses confidences or secrets of the former firm's clients; (7)request written assurances from the hiring firm that it will comply with the former firm's requests; (8) advise the clients of the paralegal's change in employment; and (9) move to disqualify the hiring firm if the client so requests. KBA E-308, 9/85.[10]

For these reasons (and because state bar disciplinary rules are recommending it with greater frequency), law firms should institute training systems that incorporate teaching these guidelines to employees at all levels in the firm. If you work in a legal setting, you might want to introduce the Kentucky Bar Association Ethics Opinion to your supervisor.

CONFLICTS CHECKS

Throughout this chapter we have addressed the myriad of problems that conflicts of interest can create. The ultimate concern of these rules is the protection of the client. The ultimate problem that can result is that an entire law firm may be disqualified from representing a client. To safeguard against this, and to ensure that the client's interests are protected, law firms employ various systems or "conflicts checks."

Though conflicts of interest can affect an entire law firm, often the responsibility for monitoring such conflicts lies with nonlawyer personnel. For this reason, it is important that the legal assistant learn methods for monitoring conflicts. Several suggestions for such methods include the following:

1. *Conflicts forms.* Most law firms generate these forms as a precautionary measure against disqualification. The forms are circulated to attorneys

---

[10]Reprinted by permission.

and support personnel when they are hired or whenever they begin to work on new cases. They are usually one or two pages long and ask general questions, such as client names, nature of case, or outcome of the case. The forms are then used by the law firm and the attorneys to track potential conflicts.

2. *Making a list of clients.* It is also prudent for the legal professional to keep track of his own cases. The simplest method of keeping track of the names of all of the clients whose cases you have worked on is to write them down. You might want to keep index cards in a box and keep the names in alphabetical order. You should also include the name of the supervising attorney on the index card so that, should you need additional information about the case or the client in determining the existence of a conflict, you would have a resource. This would be something you would use throughout your professional career, so you would carry it with you if you changed jobs.

3. *Copying title pages of all of the cases on which you work.* One surefire method for collecting names of clients is to copy the case title pages and put them in alphabetical order according to the last name of the first party listed. That way, even if the case on which you worked was a class action, you would have the names of the lead parties or companies that were involved in the suit. At the bottom of the page you would put the name of the supervising attorney.

4. *Computerized systems.* As we will discuss more fully below, with increasing frequency law firms are converting from manual systems to computer systems for monitoring conflicts. However, these systems can be scaled down to meet an individual's need for keeping track of potential clients. Instead of keeping lists on index cards then, keep files on computer disks and save them electronically. Such files are easily transportable.

5. *Software packages.* These systems are addressed in detail in the next segment.

EXERCISE 6.16　　Assume you have been requested by your supervising paralegal to draft a proposal your firm will use in developing conflicts checks for the firm.

Submit a copy of the proposal to your instructor for review.

USING COMPUTER SOFTWARE TO AVOID CONFLICTS

Most of the systems discussed above are manual systems (conflicts forms, index cards, and copying title pages of cases) designed to prevent conflicts of interest problems from interfering with the representation of a client. With increasing frequency, however, law firms are using computerized systems for everything, and one of the areas where this particularly rings true is in the area of conflict of interest. The advent of software packages is steadily changing conflicts check systems. The software has been in existence for nearly two decades and is catching on. It includes information regarding clients' and related parties' matters and offers considerable protection in preventing disqualification.

| HIGHLIGHT | **An Example of Conflicts Checks** |

O ne well-respected law firm located in Chicago, Illinois—Chapman and Cutler—uses its Records Manager, David Smith, as the conflicts manager. Smith provides the attorney or paralegal with a client/matter business intake form or, in the case of a new attorney or paralegal joining the firm, a prior employment questionnaire.

The business intake form lists four factors for the attorney to consider.

1. Is there anything unique or unusual about this matter?

2. Do you see any conflicts or potential conflicts?

3. If a conflict is found, how do you intend to help resolve it?

4. Is this matter confidential and not to be published in the firm's new business report (i.e., confidential information about a corporate merger or acquisition)?

5. The business intake form must be signed by an attorney.

Smith takes all the information he has about the client and, within twenty-four hours of having received the form, he provides a report to the attorney who submitted it. At that point, the attorney who submitted the form is again asked whether there's a conflict and, if there is, the attorney must work with Smith and the firm's practicing standards committee to determine whether there is a solution to the conflict or to decline the representation. In some situations, a possible solution would be to obtain an informed consent from both the new client and the existing or former client. The Committee meets with Smith to review all potential conflicts. The Committee then determines which matters are in need of further review and consideration. Smith's next job then is to build walls around the party who is handling the matter.

*Reprinted by permission of David Smith.

These systems have been promoted by malpractice insurance companies' loss prevention programs for well over a decade. As we previously discussed, most firms use manual systems of building imaginary walls around their personnel. Generally, these walls satisfy the requirements that courts have established for protecting client interests. Now, however, software is taking over the older systems with great success.

Law firms purchase the prepackaged software which is then tailored to meet the needs of the firm. Usually a records manager is the designated receiver of all information about new clients or new matters. From that point, the records manager is responsible for the flow of information regarding the cases.

FOCUS ON. . .MERLE ISGETT

Merle Isgett 1991–1992 and, 1992–1993 President of the National Federation of Paralegal Association and experienced paralegal, knows it is vitally important for legal assistants to avoid even the appearance of a conflict. That is because simply the appearance of a conflict is enough to create problems.

Isgett has been a paralegal for over twenty-seven years, including the last nine years that she has spent in the complex litigation department at the firm Vorys, Sater, Seymour & Pease in Cincinnati, Ohio. Recognizing the importance of legal assistant involvement and organization, she has served two terms as the President of the Cincinnati Paralegal Association and has worked for one-and-one-half years as the Policy Vice President for the National Federation of Paralegal Associations. Throughout 1992 and 1993, she has served as a commissioner on the American Bar Association's Commission on Non-Lawyer Practice. Merle is also the author of the book, available through NFPA, entitled "The Ethical Wall—Its Application to Paralegals."

Isgett's experiences have exposed her to legal assistants from all walks of life, and no one is in a better position to discuss the problems that conflicts of interest pose for legal assistants. During her tenure as an officer of one of the most esteemed paralegal associations in the country, Isgett has learned of a variety of conflict of interest problems and, as a result, has many valuable words of advice to share.

The kind of conflict Isgett believes happens with the greatest frequency is the former client problem. Because the paralegal population is increasingly mobile, she concludes that a legal assistant likely will change employers several times during her legal career. This creates the potential for conflicts of interest to arise.

In fact, Isgett witnessed a situation where a legal assistant had worked on a case for a particular client at one law firm, and later changed firms, thereby creating a former client conflict. The new law firm acted quickly to make sure the paralegal was screened. Isgett relates that one of the steps the firm immediately implemented was to mark files to prevent the paralegal's inadvertent access to information.

To help prevent conflict of interest problems like this one, Isgett advises legal assistants to keep a list of cases on which they have worked. This list can prove invaluable in detecting potential problems when a paralegal changes law firms. Then, when interviewing for a new job, the legal assistant should ask the interviewer, "What kinds of cases will I be working on, and what clients does the firm represent?" Isgett says legal assistants should also be prepared to make the interviewer aware of the cases on which he worked. In this way, the law firm will have the opportunity to recognize potential conflicts and can implement screening measures before disqualifying problems arise.

At times, however, the legal assistant may be the first to recognize a potential conflict. When this happens, Isgett cautions, "The paralegal should go directly to the attorney because that is the person who will need to know. And, if you are new to the firm and feel intimidated by the attorney, take your supervising paralegal with you."

Isgett sums up her philosophy this way: "Avoid *any* appearance of being involved in a conflict of interest by making sure that appropriate information is given to the appropriate individual. While it is not always an easy thing to do, keep in mind that conflict of interest rules were developed to protect the confidentiality of the client's affairs."

Avoid any appearance of being involved in a conflict of interest by making sure that appropriate information is given to the appropriate individual. While it is not always an easy thing to do, keep in mind that conflict of interest rules developed to protect the confidentiality of the client's affairs.

TIPS FOR PARALEGALS

■ Do not enter into business transactions with clients or ever exploit any information you receive from a client.

■ Do not accept gifts from clients.

■ Advise the attorney for whom you work about relatives of yours who work for opposing counsel.

■ Never make or take loans to or from a client.

■ Keep track of former employment and former clients to prevent any potential simultaneous representation of clients problems.

■ Keep the title sheets of cases on which you have worked.

■ Suggest that your supervising attorney invest in software designed to track potential conflicts of interest.

CLOSING EXERCISE

A paid announcement was enclosed in a newsletter that was mailed to all members of the Anytown Paralegal Association last week. The purpose of the announcement was to solicit information from the members. The announcement read:

> Committee which specializes in legal ethics is compiling statistics for the Anytown Bar Association relating to the percentage of problems, arising in law firms, that deal with conflicts of interest.
>
> In the interest of fostering professional growth, you are requested to submit examples of conflicts of interest you have seen to the attached address.
>
> All information will remain confidential and will be used exclusively for the purpose of gathering data

The Anytown Bar Association received hundreds of responses.

You are on the committee that determines how the responses relate to conflicts of interest. Please refer to the four situations listed below and prepare a report to the committee about each situation. You should also provide the committee with recommendations as to how any problems in these situations could be avoided.

A. Priscilla Paralegal, who works for Annette Attorney, is dating Pablo Plaintiff who is represented by Ang Attorney. Pablo sues Annette's client, Dan Defendant. Priscilla is working on the case for Annette.

B. Terry and Maryanne started at a firm six months ago. Each is assigned a different supervising paralegal. Terry's supervising paralegal asked Terry to give him a list of every case she has ever worked on. The supervising paralegal explained to Terry why he needed the list. Maryanne's supervising paralegal failed to determine the names of the cases on which Maryanne had worked. One month ago, the firm was served with a motion to disqualify based on the fact that Maryanne's employment created a conflict of interest.

C. Enrique is a litigation paralegal who worked very closely with Sondra Tolbert when the firm for which he works represented her in a personal injury claim. The period during the pendency of the suit was extremely stressful for Sondra. She greatly appreciated his tremendous work effort. To express her gratitude, Sondra gave Enrique her grandfather's sterling pocket watch.

D. The owner of Frankly Franks Slaughterhouse, Inc., decided to buy the Real Relish & Pickles Co. He contacted his cousins, Hilary and Rachel, about making the purchase with him as co-owners. The three hired the same attorney to handle the incorporation.

CHAPTER SUMMARY

■ Conflict of interest rules are based on three duties the attorney owes to the client: 1) the duty of loyalty to the client, 2) the duty to protect client confidences, and 3) the duty to zealously represent client interests.

■ Conflicts of interest can arise because of different kinds of situations. A conflict of interest can arise when the attorney attempts to simultaneously represent opposing clients or interests. Conflicts of interest may arise when the attorney or legal assistant engages in a prohibited transaction, such as accepting gifts from clients or making loans to clients. A conflict of interest may arise when the attorney must appear as a witness; however, when the legal assistant may be called as a witness, there is some question as to whether this would amount to a conflict of interest. A conflict of interest might also arise when the attorney or legal assistant becomes involved in the successive representation of a former client.

■ In order to avoid conflicts of interest and the imputed disqualification of the law firm, the law firm should employ conflicts checks and screening devices. Both the attorney and the legal assistant are affected by such measures. To discover potential conflicts, conflicts checks should be employed. To this end, many firms use conflicts forms or computerized systems. Once a conflict is discovered, a screening device—such as a Chinese wall or a cone of silence—may be implemented.

■ Just as attorneys may become involved in a conflict of interest, so might legal assistants become involved in a conflict. Such a conflict might result in the attorney or legal assistant being disqualified from the client's case. If a legal assistant causes a conflict of interest, the law firm also might be disqualified from representing a client. This is known as imputed disqualification.

KEY TERMS

adverse positions
co-defendants
conflict of interest rules
conflicts of interest
consent
co-plaintiffs
disqualified

fact-sensitive
former client
imputed disqualification
materially adverse
simultaneous
   representation
   of parties

substantially related
substantially related cases
waiving conflicts of
   interest

CASE

In re Complex Asbestos Litigation.
Court of Appeal, First District, 1991.
232 Cal.App.3d 572, 283 Cal. Rptr. 732.

· · ·

Facts

Michael Vogel worked as a paralegal for the law firm of Brobeck, Phleger & Harrison (Brobeck) from October 28, 1985, to November 30, 1988. Vogel came to Brobeck with experience working for a law firm that represented defendants in asbestos litigation.[3] Brobeck also represented asbestos litigation defendants, including respondents. At Brobeck, Vogel worked exclusively on asbestos litigation.

During most of the period Brobeck employed Vogel, he worked on settlement evaluations. He extracted information from medical reports, discovery responses, and plaintiffs' depositions for entry on "Settlement Evaluation and Authority Request" (SEAR) forms. The SEAR forms were brief summaries of the information and issues used by the defense attorneys and their clients to evaluate each plaintiff's case. The SEAR forms were sent to the clients.

Vogel attended many defense attorney meetings where the attorneys discussed the strengths and weaknesses of cases to reach consensus settlement recommendations for each case. The SEAR forms were the primary informational materials the attorneys used at the meetings. Vogel's responsibility at these meetings was to record the amounts agreed on for settlement recommendations to the clients. Vogel sent the settlement authority requests and SEAR forms to the clients. He also attended meetings and telephone conferences where attorneys discussed the recommendations with clients and settlement authority was granted. Vogel recorded on the SEAR 581 forms the amount of settlement authority granted and distributed the information to the defense attorneys.

The SEAR form information was included in Brobeck's computer record on each asbestos case. The SEAR forms contained the plaintiff's name and family information, capsule summaries of medical reports, the plaintiff's work history, asbestos products identified at the plaintiff's work sites, and any special considerations that might affect the jury's response to the plaintiff's case. The SEAR forms also contained information about any prior settlements and settlement authorizations. Information was added to the forms as it was developed during the course of a case. Vogel, like other Brobeck staff working on asbestos cases, had a computer password that allowed access to the information on any asbestos case in Brobeck's computer system.

Vogel also monitored trial events, received daily reports from the attorneys in trial, and relayed trial reports to the clients. Vogel reviewed plaintiffs' interrogatory answers to get SEAR form data and to assess whether the answers were adequate or further responses were needed.

In 1988, Vogel's duties changed when he was assigned to work for a trial team. With that change, Vogel no longer was involved with the settlement evaluation meetings and reports. Instead, he helped prepare specific cases assigned to the team. Vogel did not work on any cases in which the Harrison firm represented the plaintiffs.

During the time Vogel worked on asbestos cases for Brobeck, that firm and two others represented respondents in asbestos litigation filed in Northern California. Brobeck and the other firms were selected for this work by the Asbestos Claims Facility (ACF), a corporation organized by respondents and others to manage the defense of asbestos litigation on their behalf. The ACF dissolved in October 1988, though Brobeck continued to represent most of the respondents through at least the end of the year.[4] Not long after the ACF's dissolution, Brobeck gave Vogel two weeks' notice of his termination, though his termination date was later extended to the end of November.

Vogel contacted a number of firms about employment, and learned that the Harrison firm was looking for paralegals. The Harrison firm recently had opened a Northern California office and filed a number of asbestos cases against respondents. Sometime in the second half of November 1988, Vogel called Harrison to ask him for a job with his firm.

In that first telephone conversation, Harrison learned that Vogel had worked for Brobeck on asbestos litigation settlements. Harrison testified that he did not then offer Vogel a job for two reasons. First, Harrison did not think he would need a new parale-

---

3. In this opinion we use the term "asbestos litigation" to refer to civil actions for personal injury and wrongful death, allegedly caused by exposure to asbestos products, brought against manufacturers, distributors, and sellers of such products.

4. The exceptions were Eagle-Picher Industries, Inc., which withdrew from the ACF and retained other counsel in February 1988, and Celotex Corporation and Carey Canada, Inc., which were represented by Bjork, Fleer, Lawrence & Harris (Bjork) beginning in December 1988.

gal until February or March of 1989. Second, Harrison was concerned about the appearance of a conflict of interest in his firm's hiring a paralegal from Brobeck. Harrison discussed the conflict problem with other attorneys, and told Vogel that he could be hired only if Vogel got a waiver from the senior asbestos litigation partner at Brobeck.

Vogel testified that he spoke with Stephen Snyder, the Brobeck partner in charge of managing the Northern California asbestos litigation. Vogel claimed he told Snyder of the possible job with the Harrison firm, and that Snyder later told him the clients had approved and that Snyder would provide a written waiver if Vogel wanted. In his testimony, Snyder firmly denied having any such conversations or giving Vogel any conflicts waiver to work for Harrison. The trial court resolved this credibility dispute in favor of Snyder.

While waiting for a job with the Harrison firm, Vogel went to work for Bjork, which represented two of the respondents in asbestos litigation in Northern California. Vogel worked for Bjork during December 1988, organizing boxes of materials transferred from Brobeck to Bjork. While there, Vogel again called Harrison to press him for a job. Vogel told Harrison that Brobeck had approved his working for Harrison, and Harrison offered Vogel a job starting after the holidays. During their conversations, Harrison told Vogel the job involved work on complex, nonasbestos civil matters, and later would involve processing release documents and checks for asbestos litigation settlements. Harrison did not contact Brobeck to confirm Vogel's claim that he made a full disclosure and obtained Brobeck's consent. Nor did Harrison tell Vogel that he needed a waiver from Bjork.

Vogel informed Bjork he was quitting to work for the Harrison firm. Vogel told a partner at Bjork that he wanted experience in areas other than asbestos litigation, and that he would work on securities and real estate development litigation at the Harrison firm. Initially, Vogel's work for the Harrison firm was confined to those two areas.

However, at the end of February 1989, Vogel was asked to finish another paralegal's job of contacting asbestos plaintiffs to complete client questionnaires. The questionnaire answers provided information for discovery requests by the defendants. Vogel contacted Bjork and others to request copies of discovery materials for the Harrison firm. Vogel also assisted when the Harrison firm's asbestos trial teams needed extra help.

In March 1989, Snyder learned from a Brobeck trial attorney that Vogel was involved in asbestos litiga-tion. In a March 31 letter, Snyder asked Harrison if Vogel's duties included asbestos litigation. Harrison responded to Snyder by letter on April 6. In the letter, Harrison stated Vogel told Snyder his work for the Harrison firm would include periodic work on asbestos cases, and that Harrison assumed there was no conflict of interest. Harrison also asked Snyder to provide details of the basis for any claimed conflict. There were no other communications between Brobeck and the Harrison firm concerning Vogel before the disqualification motion was filed.

In June, a Harrison firm attorney asked Vogel to call respondent Fibreboard Corporation to see if it would accept service of a subpoena for its corporate minutes. Vogel called the company and spoke to a person he knew from working for Brobeck. Vogel asked who should be served with the subpoena in place of the company's retired general counsel. Vogel's call prompted renewed concern among respondents' counsel over Vogel's involvement with asbestos litigation for a plaintiffs' firm. On July 31, counsel for three respondents demanded that the Harrison firm disqualify itself from cases against those respondents. Three days later, the motion to disqualify the Harrison firm was filed; it was subsequently joined by all respondents.

The trial court held a total of 21 hearing sessions on the motion, including 16 sessions of testimony.[5] During the hearing, several witnesses testified that Vogel liked to talk, and the record indicates that he would volunteer information in an effort to be helpful.

A critical incident involving Vogel's activities at Brobeck first came to light during the hearing. Brobeck's computer system access log showed that on November 17, 1988, Vogel accessed the computer records for 20 cases$_{584}$ filed by the Harrison firm. On the witness stand, Vogel at first flatly denied having looked at these case records, but when confronted with the access log, he admitted reviewing the

5. We note that a motion to disqualify normally should be decided on the basis of the declarations and documents submitted by the parties. An evidentiary hearing should be held only when the court cannot with confidence decide the issue on the written submissions. Such instances should be rare, as when an important evidentiary gap in the written record must be filled, or a critical question of credibility can be resolved only through live testimony. (See *Dewey v. R. J. Reynolds Tobacco Co.* (1988) 109 N.J. 201, 536 A.2d 243, 253.) Of course, whether to conduct an evidentiary hearing is a matter left to the discretion of the trial court. In light of the broad scope of the disqualification order respondents sought, the sharp conflicts in the testimony, and the unique and difficult issues presented, we cannot criticize the trial court's diligence in conducting such an extensive hearing and providing such a thorough record.

records "to see what kind of cases [the Harrison firm] had filed." At the time, Vogel had no responsibilities for any Harrison firm cases at Brobeck. The date Vogel reviewed those computer records was very close to the time Vogel and Harrison first spoke. The access log documented that Vogel opened each record long enough to view and print copies of all the information on the case in the computer system.

The case information on the computer included the SEAR form data. Many of the 20 cases had been entered on the computer just over a week earlier, though others had been on the computer for weeks or months. The initial computer entries for a case consisted of information taken from the complaint by paralegals trained as part of Brobeck's case intake team. Vogel denied recalling what information for the Harrison firm's cases he saw on the computer, and Brobeck's witness could not tell what specific information was on the computer that day.

Vogel, Harrison, and the other two witnesses from the Harrison firm denied that Vogel ever disclosed any client confidences obtained while he worked for Brobeck. However, Harrison never instructed Vogel not to discuss any confidential information obtained at Brobeck. Vogel did discuss with Harrison firm attorneys his impressions of several Brobeck attorneys. After the disqualification motion was filed, Harrison and his office manager debriefed Vogel, not to obtain any confidences but to discuss his duties at Brobeck in detail and to assess respondents' factual allegations. During the course of the hearing, the Harrison firm terminated Vogel on August 25, 1989.

The trial court found that Vogel's work for Brobeck and the Harrison firm was substantially related, and that there was no express or implied waiver by Brobeck or its clients. The court believed there was a substantial likelihood that the Harrison firm's hiring of Vogel, without first building "an ethical wall" or having a waiver, would affect the outcome in asbestos cases. The court also found that Vogel obtained confidential information when he accessed Brobeck's computer records on the Harrison firm's cases, and that there was a reasonable probability Vogel used that information or disclosed it to other members of the Harrison firm's staff. The court refused to extend the disqualification beyond those cases where there was tangible evidence of interference by Vogel, stating that on the rest of the cases it would require the court to speculate.

The trial court initially disqualified the Harrison firm in all 20 cases Vogel accessed on November 17, 1988, which included 11 cases pending in$_{585}$ Contra Costa County. However, on further consideration,

the trial court restricted its disqualification order to the 9 cases pending in San Francisco. The Harrison firm timely noticed an appeal from the disqualification order, and respondents cross-appealed from the denial of disqualification in the Contra Costa County cases and all asbestos litigation.

. . .

Concerns Raised by Disqualification Motions

Our courts recognize that a motion to disqualify a party's counsel implicates several important interests. These concerns are magnified when, as here, disqualification is sought not just for a single case but for many and, indeed, an entire class of litigation. When faced with disqualifying an attorney for an alleged conflict of interest, courts have considered such interests as the clients' right to counsel of their choice, an attorney's interest in representing a client, the financial burden on the client of replacing disqualified counsel, and any tactical abuse underlying the disqualification proceeding. (*Bell v. 20th Century Ins. Co., supra,* 212 Cal.App.3d at pp. 197–198, 260 Cal.Rptr. 459; *Gregori v. Bank of America, supra,* 207 Cal.App.3d at pp. 300–301, 254 Cal.Rptr. 853; *William H. Raley Co. v. Superior Court* (1983) 149 Cal.App.3d 1042, 1048, 197 Cal.Rptr. 232; but see *River West, Inc. v. Nickel, supra,* 188 Cal.App.3d at pp. 1304–1308, 234 Cal.Rptr. 33.)

An additional concern arises if disqualification rules based on exposure to confidential information are applied broadly and mechanically. In the era of large, multioffice law firms and increased attention to the business aspects of the practice of law, we must consider the ability of attorneys and their employees to change employment for personal reasons or from necessity. To paraphrase Lord Chancellor Eldon's statement in *Bricheno v. Thorp* (1821) Jacob 300, 302 [37 Eng.Reprint 864, 865], as quoted in *Kraus v. Davis* (1970) 6 Cal.App.3d 484, 492, 85 Cal.Rptr. 846: persons going into business for themselves must not carry into it the secrets of their employers; but on the other hand, we think it our duty to take care that they not be prevented from engaging in any business they may obtain fairly and honorably.

Accordingly, judicial scrutiny of disqualification orders is necessary to prevent literalism from possibly overcoming substantial justice to the parties. (*Comden v. Superior Court, supra,* 20 Cal.3d at p. 915, 145 Cal.Rptr. 9, 576 P.2d 971.) However, as the Supreme Court recognized in *Comden,* the issue ultimately involves a conflict between the clients' right to counsel of their choice and the need to maintain ethical standards of professional responsibility. The paramount concern, though, must be the preservation of public trust in the scrupulous administration of justice and the integrity of the bar. The recognized and important right to counsel of one's choosing must yield to considerations of ethics that run to the very integrity of our judicial process. (*Ibid.*)

Confidentiality and the Attorney-Client Relationship

Preserving confidentiality of communications between attorney and client is fundamental to our legal system. The attorney-client privilege is a_{587} hallmark of Anglo-American jurisprudence that furthers the public policy of insuring " 'the right of every person to freely and fully confer and confide in one having knowledge of the law, and skilled in its practice, in order that the former may have adequate advice and a proper defense.' [Citation.]" (*Mitchell v. Superior Court* (1984) 37 Cal.3d 591, 599, 208 Cal.Rptr. 886, 691 P.2d 642.) One of the basic duties of an attorney is "[t]o maintain inviolate the confidence, and at every peril to himself or herself to preserve the secrets, of his or her client." (Bus. & Prof.Code, § 6068, subd. (e).) To protect the confidentiality of the attorney-client relationship, the California Rules of Professional Conduct bar an attorney from accepting "employment adverse to a client or former client where, by reason of the representation of the client or former client, the [attorney] has obtained confidential information material to the employment except with the informed written consent of the client or former client." (Rules Prof. Conduct, rule 3-310(D); *Western Continental Operating Co. v. Natural Gas Corp., supra,* 212 Cal.App.3d at p. 759, 261 Cal.Rptr. 100.)

For these reasons, an attorney will be disqualified from representing a client against a former client when there is a substantial relationship between the two representations. (*Western Continental Operating Co. v. Natural Gas Corp., supra,* 212 Cal.App.3d at pp. 759–760, 261 Cal.Rptr. 100; *River West, Inc. v. Nickel, supra,* 188 Cal.App.3d at pp. 1303–1304, 234 Cal.Rptr. 33.) When a substantial relationship exists, the courts presume the attorney possesses confidential information of the former client material to the present representation. (*Ibid.*)

Confidentiality and the Nonlawyer Employee

The courts have discussed extensively the remedies for the ethical problems created by attorneys changing their employment from a law firm representing one party in litigation to a firm representing an adverse party. Considerably less attention has been given to the problems posed by nonlawyer employees of law firms who do the same. The issue this appeal presents is one of first impression for California courts. While several Courts of Appeal have considered factual situations raising many of the same concerns, as will be discussed below, the decisions in those cases hinged on factors not present here. In short, this case is yet another square peg that does not fit the round holes of attorney disqualification rules. (See, e.g., *Gregori v. Bank of America, supra,* 207 Cal.App.3d at p. 301, 254 Cal.Rptr. 853; *William H. Raley Co. v. Superior court, supra,* 149 Cal.App.3d at pp. 1049–1050, fn. 3, 197 Cal.Rptr. 232.)

Our statutes and public policy recognize the importance of protecting the confidentiality of the attorney-client relationship. (E.g., Bus. & Prof.Code, § 6068, subd. (e); Evid.Code, §§ 915, 917, 951, 952, 954; *Mitchell v._{588} Superior Court, supra,* 37 Cal.3d at pp. 599–600, 208 Cal.Rptr. 886, 691 P.2d 642.) The obligation to maintain the client's confidences traditionally and properly has been placed on the attorney representing the client. But nonlawyer employees must handle confidential client information if legal services are to be efficient and cost-effective. Although a law firm has the ability to supervise its employees and assure that they protect client confidences, that ability and assurance are tenuous when the nonlawyer leaves the firm's employment. If the nonlawyer finds employment with opposing counsel, there is a heightened risk that confidences of the former employer's clients will be compromised, whether from base motives, an excess of zeal, or simple inadvertence.

Under such circumstances, the attorney who traditionally has been responsible for protecting the client's confidences—the former employer—has no effective means of doing so. The public policy of protecting the confidentiality of attorney-client communications must depend upon the attorney or law firm that hires an opposing counsel's employee. Certain requirements must be imposed on attorneys who hire their opposing counsel's employees to assure that attorney-client confidences are protected.

Limits on Protecting Confidentiality

We emphasize that our analysis does not mean that there is or should be any broad duty owed by an attorney to an opposing party to maintain that party's confidences in the absence of a prior attorney-client relationship. The imposition of such a duty would be antithetical to our adversary system and would interfere with the attorney's relationship with his or her own clients. The courts have recognized repeatedly that attorneys owe no duty of care to adversaries in litigation or to those with whom their clients deal at arm's length. (See *Goodman v. Kennedy* (1976) 18 Cal.3d 335, 344, 134 Cal.Rptr. 375, 556 P.2d 737; *Wasmann v. Seidenberg* (1988) 202 Cal.App.3d 752, 755, 248 Cal.Rptr. 744; *Schick v. Lerner* (1987) 193 Cal.App.3d 1321, 1330–1331, 238 Cal.Rptr. 902; *St. Paul Title Co. v. Meier* (1986) 181 Cal.App.3d 948, 951, 266 Cal.Rptr. 538; *Morales v. Field, DeGoff, Huppert & MacGowan* (1979) 99 Cal.App.3d 307, 318, 160 Cal. Rptr. 239.) Instead, we deal here with a prophylactic rule necessary to protect the confidentiality of the attorney-client relationship and the integrity of the judicial system, and with the appropriate scope of the remedy supporting such a rule.

The Harrison firm argues that conflict of interest disqualification rules governing attorneys should not apply to the acts of nonlawyers, citing *Maruman Integrated Circuits, Inc. v. Consortium Co.* (1985) 166 Cal.App.3d 443, 212 Cal.Rptr. 497 and *Cooke v. Superior Court* (1978) 83 Cal.App.3d 582, 147 Cal.Rptr. 915. The courts in both cases refused to₅₈₉ disqualify attorneys who possessed an adverse party's confidences when no attorney-client relationship ever existed between the party and the attorney sought to be disqualified.

. . .

Mere exposure to the confidences of an adversary does not, standing alone, warrant disqualification. Protecting the integrity of judicial proceedings does not require so draconian a rule. Such a rule would nullify a party's right to representation by chosen counsel any time inadvertence or devious design put an adversary's confidences in an attorney's mailbox. Nonetheless, we consider the means and sources of breaches of attorney-client confidentiality to be important considerations.

. . .

Protecting Confidentiality— The Cone of Silence

Hiring a former employee of an opposing counsel is not, in and of itself, sufficient to warrant disqualification of an attorney or law firm. However, when the former employee possesses confidential attorney-client information,[8] materially related to pending litigation, the situation implicates " '. . . considerations of ethics which run to the very integrity of our judicial process.' [Citation.]" (*Comden v. Superior Court, supra*, 20 Cal.3d at p. 915, 145 Cal. Rptr. 9, 576 P.2d 971, fn. omitted.) Under such circumstances, the hiring attorney₅₉₃ must obtain

the informed written consent of the former employer,[9] thereby dispelling any basis for disqualification. (Cf. Rules Prof.Conduct, rule 3-310(D); see Civ.Code, § 3515 ("[One] who consents to an act is not wronged by it.") Failing that, the hiring attorney is subject to disqualification unless the attorney can rebut a presumption that the confidential attorney-client information has been used or disclosed in the new employment.

A law firm that hires a nonlawyer who possesses an adversary's confidences creates a situation, similar to hiring an adversary's attorney, which suggests that confidential information is at risk. We adapt our approach, then, from cases that discuss whether an entire firm is subject to vicarious disqualification because one attorney changed sides. (See, e.g., *Klein v. Superior Court, supra*, 198 Cal.App.3d at pp. 908–914, 244 Cal.Rptr. 226; *Chambers v. Superior Court* (1981) 121 Cal.App.3d 893, 175 Cal.Rptr. 575.) The courts disagree on whether vicarious disqualification should be automatic in attorney conflict of interest cases, or whether a presumption of shared confidences should be rebuttable. (See *Klein, supra*,

---

8. We specifically mean the phrase, "confidential attorney-client information," to correspond to the definition of " 'confidential communication between client and lawyer' " contained in Evidence Code section 952: "information transmitted between a client and his [or her] lawyer in the course of that relationship and in confidence by a means which, so far as the client is aware, discloses the information to no third persons other than those who are present to further the interest of the client in the consultation or those to whom disclosure is reasonably necessary for the transmission of the information or the accomplishment of the purpose for which the lawyer is consulted, and includes a legal opinion formed and the advice given by the lawyer in the course of that relationship." The definition encompasses an attorney's legal opinions, impressions, and conclusions, regardless of whether they have been communicated to the client. (*Benge v. Superior Court* (1982) 131 Cal.App.3d 336, 345, 182 Cal.Rptr. 275; see Cal.Law Revision Com. com., 29B West's Ann.Evid.Code (1991 pocket supp.) § 952, p. 74.)

9. Rule 2-100 of the Rules of Professional Conduct would preclude the hiring attorney from seeking the consent directly from the opposing party. Thus, the consent should be sought from the former employer. The hiring attorney ought to be entitled to rely on a written consent from the former employer. If the opposing party contends the former employer was not authorized to give consent, that is a matter between the former employer and its client.

The hiring attorney, and not the prospective employee, must obtain the consent. The prospective employee is unlikely both to know enough about the new job and to have the legal ethics training necessary to obtain informed consent. Also, an individual under economic pressure to get the new job could be tempted to give less attention to candor and honesty than to securing employment. Harrison should not have delegated this sensitive task to a nonlawyer job seeker. Harrison's reliance on Vogel's word alone for the claimed waiver by Brobeck was unreasonable and a serious lapse in judgment.

198 Cal.App.3d at pp. 910–913, 244 Cal.Rptr. 226.) An inflexible presumption of shared confidences would not be appropriate for nonlawyers, though, whatever its merits when applied to attorneys. There are obvious differences between lawyers and their nonlawyer employees in training, responsibilities, and acquisition and use of confidential information. These differences satisfy us that a rebuttable presumption of shared confidences provides a just balance between protecting confidentiality and the right to chosen counsel.

The most likely means of rebutting the presumption is to implement a procedure, before the employee is hired, which effectively screens the employee from any involvement with the litigation, a procedure one court aptly described as a " 'cone of silence.' " (See *Nemours Foundation v. Gilbane, Aetna, Federal Ins.* (D.Del.1986) 632 F.Supp. 418, 428.) Whether a potential employee will require a cone of silence should be determined as a matter of routine during the hiring process. It is reasonable to ask potential employees about the nature of their prior legal work; prudence alone would dictate such inquiries. Here, Harrison's first conversation with Vogel revealed a potential problem—Vogel's work for Brobeck on asbestos litigation settlements.

The leading treatise on legal malpractice also discusses screening procedures and case law. (1 Mallen & Smith, Legal Malpractice (3d ed. 1989) §§ 13.18–13.19, pp. 792-797.) We find several points to be persuasive when adapted to the context of employee conflicts. "Screening is a prophylactic, affirmative measure to avoid both the reality and appearance of impropriety. It is *a* means, but not *the* means, of rebutting the presumption of shared confidences." (*Id.,* § 13.19, at p. 794, original emphasis, fn. omitted.) Two objectives must be achieved. First, screening should be implemented before undertaking the challenged representation or hiring the tainted individual. Screening must take place at the outset to prevent any confidences from being disclosed. Second, the tainted individual should be precluded from any involvement in or communication about the challenged representation. To avoid inadvertent disclosures and to establish an evidentiary record, a memorandum should be circulated warning the legal staff to isolate the individual from communications on the matter and to prevent access to the relevant files. *Id.,* at pp. 795–796.[10]

The need for such a rule is manifest. We agree with the observations made by the *Williams* court: "[Nonlawyer] personnel are widely used by lawyers to assist in rendering legal services. Paralegals, investigators, and secretaries must have ready access to client confidences in order to assist their attorney employers. If information provided by a client in confidence to an attorney for the purpose of obtaining legal advice could be used against the client because a member of the attorney's [nonlawyer] support staff left the attorney's employment, it would have a devastating effect both on the free flow of information between client and attorney and on the cost and quality of the legal services rendered by an attorney." (*Williams v. Trans World Airlines, Inc., supra,* 588 F.Supp. at p. 1044.) Further, no regulatory or ethical rules, comparable to those governing attorneys, restrain all of the many types of nonlawyer employees of attorneys. The restraint on such employees' disclosing confidential attorney-client information must be the employing attorney's admonishment against revealing the information.[11]

The Substantial Relationship Test and Nonlawyer Employees

We decline to adopt the broader rule urged by respondents and applied by other courts,[12] which treats the nonlawyer employee as an attorney and requires disqualification upon the showing and standards applicable to individual attorneys. Respondents argue that disqualification must follow a showing of a "substantial relationship" between the matters worked on by the nonlawyer at the former and present employers' firms. However, the substantial relationship test is a tool devised for presuming an attorney possesses confidential informa-

10. A further recommendation by the authors is worth noting. To detect conflicts created by employee hiring, a firm's conflict checking system should include the identity of adverse counsel to enable a search for those matters where the prospective employee's former employer is or was adverse. (1 Mallen & Smith, Legal Malpractice, *supra,* § 13.18, at pp. 793–794.)

11. We surmise that a practical, if limited check on the problem may exist. Attorneys are unlikely to hire those who disregard preserving confidences; such persons are a likely to betray new entrustments as old.

12. See, e.g., *Kapco Mfg. Co., Inc. v. C & O Enterprises, Inc.* (N.D.Ill.1985) 637 F.Supp. 1231, 1236–1237 (applying to nonlawyer employee the Seventh Circuit's analysis for disqualification of attorney who changes sides); *Williams v. Trans World Airlines, Inc., supra,* 588 F.Supp. at page 1044 ("The only practical way to assure that [confidences will not be disclosed] and to preserve public trust in the scrupulous administration of justice is to subject these 'agents' of lawyers to the same disability lawyers have when they leave legal employment with confidential information."); *Glover Bottled Gas Corp. v. Circle M. Beverage Barn, Inc.* (1987) 129 A.D.2d 678, 514 N.Y.S.2d 440; *Lackow v. Walter E. Heller & Co. Southeast* (Fla.App.1985) 466 So.2d 1120, 1123; but see *Esquire Care, Inc. v. Maguire* (Fla.App.1988) 532 So.2d 740, 741 (imposing additional step of evidentiary hearing to determine if ethical violation has resulted in one party's obtaining "an unfair advantage over the other which can only be alleviated by removal of the attorney. [Citations.]").

tion material to a representation adverse to a former client. (*Western Continental Operating Co. v. Natural Gas Corp., supra,* 212 Cal.App.3d at pp. 759–760, 261 Cal.Rptr. 100.) The presumption is a rule of necessity because the former client cannot know what confidential information the former attorney acquired and carried into the new adverse representation. (*Ibid.*) The reasons for the presumption, and therefore the test, are not applicable though, when a nonlawyer employee leaves and the attorney remains available to the client. The client and the attorney are then in the best position to know what confidential attorney-client information was available to the former employee.

Respondents' alternative formulation, that a substantial relationship between the type of work done for the former and present employers requires disqualification, presents unnecessary barriers to employment mobility. Such a rule sweeps more widely than needed to protect client confidences. We share the concerns expressed by the American Bar Association's Standing Committee on Ethics and Professional Responsibility: "It is important that nonlawyer employees have as much mobility in employment opportunity as possible consistent with the protection of clients' interests. To so limit employment opportunities that some nonlawyers trained to work with law firms might be required to leave the careers for which they are trained would disserve clients as well as the legal profession. Accordingly, any restrictions on the nonlawyer's employment should be held to the minimum necessary to protect confidentiality of client information." (Imputed Disqualification Arising from Change in Employment by Nonlawyer Employee, ABA Standing Com. on Ethics & Prof. Responsibility, Informal Opn. No. 88-1526 (1988) p. 3.) Respondents' suggested rule could easily result in nonlawyer employees becoming "Typhoid Marys," unemployable by firms practicing in specialized areas of the law where the employees are most skilled and experienced.

Protecting Confidentiality— The Rule for Disqualification

Absent written consent, the proper rule and its application for disqualification based on nonlawyer employee conflicts of interest should be as follows. The party seeking disqualification must show that its present or past attorney's former employee possesses confidential attorney-client information materially related to the proceedings before the court.[13] The party should not be required to disclose the actual information contended to be confidential.

However, the court should be provided with the nature of the information and its material relationship to the proceeding. (See *Elliott v. McFarland Unified School Dist., supra,* 165 Cal.App.3d at p. 572, 211 Cal.Rptr. 802.)

Once this showing has been made, a rebuttable presumption arises that the information has been used or disclosed in the current employment. The presumption is a rule by necessity because the party seeking disqualification will be at a loss to prove what is known by the adversary's attorneys and legal staff. (Cf. *Western Continental Operating Co. v. Natural Gas Corp., supra,* 212 Cal.App.3d at pp. 759–760, 261 Cal.Rptr. 100.) To rebut the presumption, the challenged attorney has the burden of showing that the practical effect of formal screening has been achieved. The showing must satisfy the trial court that the employee has not had and will not have any involvement with the litigation, or any communication with attorneys or coemployees concerning the litigation, that would support a reasonable inference that the information has been used or disclosed. If the challenged attorney fails to make this showing, then the court may disqualify the attorney and law firm.

The Trial Court Properly Exercised Its Discretion

. . .

The Harrison firm's primary contention on appeal is that respondents failed to show that Vogel possessed any specific client confidences. The Harrison firm's repeated invocation of *specific* confidences misses the point and underscores the futility of its factual argument. Vogel admitted reviewing the Harrison firm's cases on Brobeck's computer to see "what kind of cases [the Harrison firm] had filed." The plain inference is that Vogel used his training in asbestos litigation to make a rough analysis of his prospective employer's cases. Vogel acknowledged that because of his experience in looking at SEAR forms, he knew that some cases have more value than others. He also testified that the SEAR forms are used as the basis for evaluating cases. The SEAR form information Vogel obtained about the Harrison firm's cases was part of a system of attorney-client communications.

13. The evidence showing the former employee's possession of such information need not be as dramatic as Vogel's confession in this case. Possession of the information can be shown, for example, by competent evidence of the former employee's job responsibilities or participation in privileged communications. We caution, however, that showing merely potential access to confidences without actual exposure is insufficient. The threat to confidentiality must be real, not hypothetical.

There can be no question that Vogel obtained confidential attorney-client information when he accessed the Harrison firm's case files on Brobeck's computer. Respondents need not show the specific confidences Vogel obtained; such a showing would serve only to exacerbate the damage to the confidentiality of the attorney-client relationship. As discussed above, respondents had to show only the nature of the information and its material relationship to the present proceedings. They have done so.

To blunt the impact of Vogel's misconduct, the Harrison firm argues that the cases on the computer were newly filed and that no evidence showed the computer information to be more than appeared on the face of the complaints, which are public records. The argument is wrong on both points. While many of the cases were entered on the computer little more than a week earlier, others were entered weeks or months before Vogel looked at them. Moreover, the fact that some of the same information may appear in the public domain does not affect the privileged status of the information when it is distilled for an attorney-client communication. (*Mitchell v. Superior Court, supra,* 37 Cal.3d at p. 600, 208 Cal.Rptr. 886, 691 P.2d 642; *In re Jordan* (1974) 12 Cal.3d 575, 580, 116 Cal.Rptr. 371, 526 P.2d 523.) Therefore, there was substantial evidence that Vogel possessed confidential attorney-client information materially related to the cases for which the trial court ordered disqualification.[14]

The Harrison firm also argues that there was no evidence that Vogel disclosed any confidences to any member of the firm, or that any such information was sought from or volunteered by Vogel. Harrison testified that he never asked Vogel to divulge anything other than impressions about three Brobeck attorneys. Harrison and his office manager also testified that Vogel was not involved in case evaluation or trial tactics discussions at the Harrison firm. However, this evidence is not sufficient to rebut the presumption that Vogel used the

confidential material or disclosed it to staff members at the Harrison firm. Moreover, there was substantial evidence to support a reasonable inference that Vogel used or disclosed the confidential information.

Despite Harrison's own concern over an appearance of impropriety, Harrison never told Vogel not to discuss the information Vogel learned at Brobeck and did not consider screening Vogel even after Brobeck first inquired about Vogel's work on asbestos cases. The evidence also amply supports the trial court's observation that Vogel was "a very talkative person, a person who loves to share information." Further, Vogel's willingness to use information acquired at Brobeck, and the Harrison firm's insensitivity to ethical considerations, were demonstrated when Vogel was told to call respondent Fibreboard Corporation and Vogel knew the person to contact there.[15]

The trial court did not apply a presumption of disclosure, which would have been appropriate under the rule we have set forth. The evidence offered by the Harrison firm is manifestly insufficient to rebut the presumption. Beyond that, though, substantial evidence established a reasonable probability that Vogel used or disclosed to the Harrison firm the confidential attorney-client information obtained from Brobeck's computer records. Accordingly, the trial court was well within a sound exercise of discretion in ordering the Harrison firm's disqualification.

. . .

Disqualification in All Asbestos Litigation is Unwarranted

Finally, we consider whether the trial court abused its discretion in not ordering the Harrison firm disqualified from all asbestos litigation before the court. Respondents argue that disqualification should have been extended to all asbestos cases because all are substantially related, or because Vogel's work at Brobeck and the Harrison firm was substantially related—arguments we have considered and rejected. Respondents point to evidence that Vogel was exposed to their counsels' theories,

---

14. We think it important to mention a point not briefed by the parties, though our decision does not turn on it. When Vogel used his computer access, training, and experience at Brobeck to review the information on the Harrison firm's cases, he necessarily formed some impressions, conclusions, and opinions about those cases. It seems to us that such opinions, formed while a Brobeck employee, would constitute confidential attorney-client information belonging to Brobeck. If a Brobeck attorney had directed Vogel to use SEAR form data to prepare a memorandum on "what kind of cases" the Harrison firm filed, no one would dispute that the Harrison firm could not properly obtain that memorandum without Brobeck's consent. We perceive no reason for a different conclusion when such opinions are not recorded and are the result of unauthorized conduct by the employee.

15. We do not address whether this direct contact with a party represented by counsel violated the Rules of Professional Conduct, rule 2-100. We agree with the Harrison firm's contention that this contact would not itself support the trial court's disqualification order. (See *Chronometrics, Inc. v. Sysgen, Inc.* (1980) 110 Cal.App.3d 597, 603, 607, 168 Cal.Rptr. 196 [former Rules Prof.Conduct, rule 7-103].) However, the trial court did not base disqualification on that contact. We consider the contact to be probative of the likelihood that Vogel used or disclosed confidential information during his employment by the Harrison firm.

strategies, and tactics, including assessments of witnesses and settlement values assigned to different types of asbestos cases, as requiring total disqualification. We disagree.

The trial court was satisfied that for the Harrison firm cases Vogel accessed on the computer, there was a reasonable probability that Vogel acquired confidential information that he disclosed or used at the Harrison firm. As to other cases, the court felt it was simply speculative. The record does not show that Vogel possessed and disclosed confidential attorney-client information materially related to all of the Harrison firm's asbestos litigation. On the evidence before the trial court, we cannot say that the court's decision was an abuse of discretion. Indeed, when considered under the standard applicable to our review, the evidence supports a conclusion that a broader disqualification would be unwarranted.

Vogel stopped attending settlement evaluation meetings in mid-1988. These were the principal source of the confidential information to which Vogel was exposed. Vogel did not begin to work for the Harrison firm until January 1989. Initially, Vogel's work and work area were separate and isolated from the Harrison firm's asbestos cases. Vogel first started work on asbestos cases in late February or early March and certainly ceased by the time he was terminated in August. His work for the Harrison firm on asbestos cases apparently was limited and sporadic. Vogel did not participate in any of the Harrison firm's asbestos litigation evaluation and strategy meetings. At the Harrison firm, Vogel processed settlement releases and checks, inventoried and obtained generalized discovery materials, and completed plaintiff questionnaires. These were not the types of duties that required Vogel to use or disclose the broader categories of information respondents contend are confidential.

Undoubtedly, some of the information known by Vogel lost any materiality to the Harrison firm's cases through the passage of time. (Cf. *Johnson v. Superior Court, supra,* 159 Cal.App.3d at p. 579, 205 Cal.Rptr. 605.) The evidence showed that even litigation as subject to routine as asbestos cases nevertheless evolves over time. Moreover, the Harrison firm presented substantial evidence showing that Vogel's use or disclosure of confidential information was not so pervasive as to require disqualification from all asbestos litigation. This conclusion is bol-

stered by the fact that Vogel's termination removed any threat of further disclosures to the Harrison firm.

We have considered the remaining contentions raised by the parties and, in view of the determinations reached above, those contentions do not require further discussion.

Conclusion

We realize the serious consequences of disqualifying attorneys and depriving clients of representation by their chosen counsel. However, we must balance the important right to counsel of one's choice against the competing fundamental interest in preserving confidences of the attorney-client relationship. All attorneys share certain basic obligations of professional conduct, obligations that are essential to the integrity and function of our legal system. Attorneys must respect the confidentiality of attorney-client information and recognize that protecting confidentiality is an imperative to be obeyed in both form and substance. A requisite corollary to these principles is that attorneys must prohibit their employees from violating confidences [603] of former employers as well as confidences of present clients. Until the Legislature or the State Bar choose to disseminate a different standard, attorneys must be held accountable for their employees' conduct, particularly when that conduct poses a clear threat to attorney-client confidentiality and the integrity of our judicial process.

The order of the trial court is affirmed. Each party shall bear its own costs.

WHITE, P. J., and STRANKMAN, J., concur.

Questions

1. Would the court's decision regarding Vogel's employment at the Brobeck firm have been different if Vogel had worked on bankruptcy litigation? Why or why not?

2. What aspects of Vogel's relationship to asbestos cases did the court find problematic?

3. The court stated: "Our courts recognize that a motion to disqualify a party's counsel implicates several important interests." What did the court mean by this statement?

4. What does the court suggest that the "hiring attorney" should do to prevent disqualification problems?

FINANCIAL MATTERS

CHAPTER OBJECTIVES

After reading this chapter, you should
be able to:

- Understand the concept of fee splitting.
- Distinguish the related concepts of fee splitting, bonuses, business enterprises with nonlawyers, and referrals.
- Understand billing practices for paralegal work and recognize the ethical implication of "padding" billable hours.

- Comprehend the importance of not commingling law firm funds with client trust fund accounts.
- Be enthusiastic about pro bono work.

Many professionals forget that the law firm is a business operation with significant financial concerns. Money is required to sustain the firm; it is needed to pay the rent and to pay employee salaries. And the partners are interested in showing a profit.

One key difference between law firms and other businesses, however, is that the law firm is subject to many ethical constraints in its handling of funds. So, while the business is sustained through a constant influx of money generated by the legal services provided, disciplinary codes limit the way in which that money can be handled, shared, and recouped.

For this reason, all of the rules concerning the financial obligations—money matters—of the firm are discussed in this chapter. This chapter covers all financial aspects of the law practice, from sharing legal fees to maintaining client trust fund accounts. Very likely you will find that the rules are straightforward. However, these rules are violated more frequently than any of the other ethical obligations. Money is a great motivator. Unfortunately, it seems to motivate some to engage in unethical practices.

OPENING EXERCISE

Sandra Billings was recently hired as a litigation paralegal at Gilsby, Ganther and Associates, the largest law firm in town. Understandably quite excited, Sandra vowed that she would do the best job she could during her career.

On her first day of work, Sandra's supervising attorney, Barbara Jenkins, explained to Sandra that each hour of her time would be billed to a particular client and she would therefore need to maintain a careful record of the work she completed and the amount of time she spent doing it. She would be required to turn in these records at the end of each week. Sandra assured Barbara that would not be a problem. Then Barbara told Sandra that she would be expected to bill seventeen hundred hours each year. Sandra again assured Barbara that she understood her responsibilities.

Weeks went by, and Sandra found herself enjoying a busy and exciting new career. Although the pace was hectic, Sandra appreciated the challenge. As she became busier, however, Sandra found that she was running into some difficulties with her billing responsibilities.

Toward the end of the year, Sandra realized she had only billed fifteen hundred hours to date and would be required to bill the additional two hundred hours in just three short weeks. She began extending her hours, leaving at midnight and coming in at 7:00 AM. Soon, however, Sandra realized she would not be making her deadline. When her cousin asked her why she was putting in so many hours, Sandra told him about her predicament. Her cousin advised her to just "pad" her hours, billing clients for hours she could not have spent handling their work. Her cousin also advised her to not spend so much time recording how many hours she had spent on a client's case. Instead, her cousin said, at the end of the week she should just estimate what she had done and for whom.

What do you think of Sandra's cousin's suggestion? Should Sandra pad her hours? Do you think it is important to keep careful track of the hours you spend doing work for a client? Should Sandra just estimate the time she has spent on a case? Why or why not?

FEE SPLITTING

Many have repeatedly voiced strong objection to attorneys sharing legal fees with nonlawyer employees. For that reason, both the *Model Code* and the *Model Rules* contain virtually identical rules prohibiting what is known as **fee splitting**. See *Model Code of Professional Responsibility* DR 3-102; *Model Rules of Professional Conduct* Rule 5.4. In other words, nonlawyers may not share legal fees with a lawyer.

Fee Splitting
Sharing legal fees with a nonlawyer. It arises when a particular fee tied to a particular client is paid directly to the nonlawyer as compensation.

It is difficult to determine exactly what is meant by this flat prohibition on fee splitting, also known as "sharing fees." Clearly, attorneys are allowed to compensate nonlawyers for their work and, almost as clearly, the attorney's funds to pay this salary are generated by client fees. This arrangement, however, is not considered to be fee splitting.

So what is fee splitting? Fee splitting situations are generally found to arise where a particular fee, tied to a particular client, is paid directly to the nonlawyer as compensation. A few examples may help to clarify this definition.

Where an attorney tells the nonlawyer she will be compensated at a rate of, for instance, twenty percent of the fees recovered in each case on which she works, this attorney has entered into a fee splitting arrangement. Likewise prohibited is an arrangement where the attorney tells the client that the fee for a particular representation will be payable as follows: the first $500.00 of any court recovery is paid to the attorney, the next $100.00 paid to the legal assistant.

Limited exceptions to the rules exist that allow nonlawyers to receive portions of legal fees in specifically identified situations. These exceptions are set forth in the *Model Code of Professional Responsibility* DR 3–102 (1986) and the *Model Rules of Professional Conduct* Rule 5.4(a) (1994). Also, as discussed later in this chapter, nonlawyers may receive bonuses.

Several rationales have been advanced to justify the rule against fee splitting. The first, and seemingly most frequently asserted, justification is that fee splitting rules protect against nonlawyers engaging in the unauthorized practice of law. Indeed, DR 3–102, the provision against fee splitting, is included in Canon 3, "A Lawyer Should Assist in Preventing the Unauthorized Practice of Law." Although this justification has been criticized, as the relationship between earning a portion of legal fees and engaging in the practice of law might seem tenuous, the rationale is nonetheless often advanced.

For example, in *Committee on Professional Ethics and Conduct of the Iowa State Bar Association v. Lawler*, 342 N.W.2d 486 (Iowa 1984), Lawler, an attorney licensed in Iowa, employed Jack Johnson, a former inmate of a men's reformatory, as a legal assistant. Their agreement was such that Lawler would employ Johnson, and Johnson would refer his former fellow inmates to Lawler. Johnson was not paid a regular fee for his work. Rather, one agreement between Lawler and Johnson indicated that Johnson's compensation was a portion of the legal fees collected by Lawler from a client.

The court refused to allow this kind of agreement, noting,

> A rationale advanced for the prohibition against sharing fees with laypersons, beyond the obvious observation that fee splitting encourages laypersons to practice law, has been stated as follows:
>> [T]he underlying purpose of regulating the practice of law is not so much to protect the public from having to pay fees to unqualified legal advisors as it is to protect the public against the often drastic and farreaching consequences of their inexpert legal advice. (Citation.)
> The net result here was an incentive for Johnson to engage in the unauthorized practice of law under the agreement which provided for splitting of fees from the client between Johnson and respondent [Lawler]." *Lawler*, 342 N.W.2d at 488.

The second justification frequently advanced is that splitting fees allows the nonlawyer to interfere with the exercise of the attorney's independent judgment. In other words, " '[p]rohibited fee-splitting between lawyer and layman ... poses the possibility of control by the lay person, interested in his own profit rather than the client's fate. ...' " *Gassman v. State Bar of California*, 18 Cal.3d 125, 553 P.2d 1147, 1151 (1976), quoting *Emmons, Williams, Mires & Leech v. State Bar*, 86 Cal. Rptr. 367, 372 (1970).

A third reason also advanced in particular circumstances is that the rule against fee sharing discourages attorneys from employing runners to solicit business for them, paying them for their services with a portion of any damages award. As chapter 8 makes clear, attorneys are not allowed to offer anything of value to another person for recommending his services. See *Kentucky Bar Association v. Lorenz*, 752 S.W. 2d 785 (Ky. 1988).

Do you agree with these justifications? Should nonlawyers be allowed to share legal fees with attorneys?

The ABA Model Guidelines for the Utilization of Legal Assistant Services summarize the fee splitting rule and its implications as follows:

> A lawyer may not split legal fees with a legal assistant nor pay a legal assistant for the referral of legal business. A lawyer may compensate a legal assistant based on the quantity and quality of the legal assistant's work and the value of that work to a law practice, but the legal assistant's compensa-

tion may not be contingent, by advance agreement, upon the profitability of the lawyer's practice. Model Guidelines for the Utilization of Legal Assistant Services, Guideline 9.

Clearly, as the ABA Model Guidelines point out, the issue of nonlawyer referrals is related to fee splitting. Additional related issues include distinguishing bonuses from fee splitting and establishing a business enterprise between nonlawyers and lawyers. Read on for further discussion.

NONLAWYER REFERRALS

Nonlawyers employed in a law firm may recommend the services of their supervising attorney to friends who find themselves in need of legal advice. This kind of **nonlawyer referral** is, quite often, the way in which attorneys obtain new clients, and this kind of attorney referral is not unethical.

Why is this practice acceptable? As is explained in Vermont Ethics Opinion 85-9,

> Attorneys need not muzzle their employees or spouses of employees with respect to the work of the firm. An employee's conduct in soliciting clients for the firm would raise substantial ethical concerns if the employee was acting as an agent of or at the behest of the firm; however, absent such an agency relationship, there is no violation for a non-lawyer employee of the firm to recommend the firm's services to other persons.[1]

The issue of attorney referrals by nonlawyer employees becomes a little clouded, however, when the nonlawyer is *paid* for the referral.

As the ABA Model Guidelines point out, this payment is often considered to be unacceptable fee splitting. Payment to the legal assistant for referrals would provide a financial incentive to the nonlawyer to seek out potential lawsuits. This clearly could lead to the unethical solicitation of cases.

As will be discussed in chapter 8, solicitation of clients by attorneys is unethical, and attorneys will be swiftly subjected to discipline where they or their agents attempt to convince an individual in need of legal services to employ that particular attorney.

Nonlawyer Referrals
A situation where nonlawyers employed in a law firm recommend the services of their supervising attorney to friends/people who need legal advice.

BUSINESS ENTERPRISES BETWEEN ATTORNEYS AND NONLAWYERS

Just as the rules say lawyers may not share legal fees with nonlawyers, the rules also forbid the attorney to establish any business with a nonlawyer if any part of that relationship will involve the practice of law. This means the attorney must not form a law practice with a nonattorney. Just as we saw earlier, the justification for this rule is that nonlawyers should not have any control over the lawyer's judgment.

For example, Disciplinary Rule 3-103 states:

> (A) A lawyer shall not form a partnership with a non-lawyer if any of the activities of the partnership consist of the practice of law. *Model Code of Professional Responsibility* DR 3-103 (1986).

---

[1]Vermont Bar Association, Professional Responsibility Committee, Ethics Opinion 85-9. Reprinted by permission.

This Disciplinary Rule is supplemented by the restrictions found in DR 5-107(C). These additional restrictions forbid the lawyer *to practice law* in any organization or professional corporation in which a nonlawyer holds any interest. Where the nonlawyer is a corporate director or officer of the organization, the attorney is likewise forbidden to practice law with that group.

Model Rule 5.4 combines these two disciplinary rules but keeps their content virtually intact.

The Ethical Considerations discuss the reasons for establishing such rules. EC 5-23 makes the justification for such a rule clear:

> A person or organization that pays or furnishes lawyers to represent others possesses a potential power to exert strong pressures against the independent judgment of those lawyers. Some employers may be interested in furthering their own economic, political, or social goals without regard to the professional responsibility of the lawyer to his individual client. Others may be far more concerned with establishment or extension of legal principles than in the immediate protection of the rights of the lawyer's individual client. On some occasions, decisions on priority of work may be made by the employer rather than the lawyer with the result that prosecution of work already undertaken for clients is postponed to their detriment. Similarly, an employer may seek, consciously or unconsciously, to further its own economic interests through the action of the lawyers employed by it. Since a lawyer must always be free to exercise his professional judgment without regard to the interests or motives of a third person, the lawyer who is employed by one to represent another must constantly guard against erosion of his professional freedom. *Model Code of Professional Responsibility* EC 5–23 (1986).

These rules are increasingly attacked as being outdated.

For this reason, the members of the commission responsible for drafting the new *Model Rules of Professional Conduct*, known as the **Kutak Commission**, originally decided to draft Rule 5.4 in such a way as to allow nonlawyers to own a partnership interest in the law firm. As can be imagined, the issue was hotly debated. Realizing that the rule was drafted in a manner such that corporations like Sears, Roebuck and Company could eventually own law firms, the drafters of the *Model Rules* rejected the proposal.

Despite this, many others believed the time had come to expand the possibilities of law firm structure to accommodate the emerging trends within the legal profession. For just such a reason, Washington, D.C., has implemented a rule based upon the rejected proposal of the Kutak Commission. Modifications to the proposed *Model Rule* were made to ensure that conglomerates such as Sears cannot purchase law firms, and the D.C. rule is now in place.

This rule reads as follows:

> (a) (4) Sharing of fees is permitted in a partnership or other form of organization which meets the requirements of Paragraph (b).
>
> (b) A lawyer may practice law in a partnership or other form of organization in which a financial interest is held or managerial authority is exercised by an individual nonlawyer who performs professional services which assist the organization in providing legal services to clients, but only if:
>
>> (1) The partnership or organization has as its sole purpose providing legal services to clients;

Kutak Commission
A commission responsible for drafting the new *Model Rules of Professional Conduct.*

(2) All persons having such managerial authority or holding a financial interest undertake to abide by these Rules of Professional Conduct;

(3) The lawyers who have a financial interest or managerial authority in the partnership or organization undertake to be responsible for the nonlawyer participants to the same extent as if nonlawyer participants were lawyers under Rule 5.1;

(4) The foregoing conditions are set forth in writing.[2]

However, it should be clear that Comments 5 and 6 to the D.C. rule state that the phrase "nonlawyer participants" should not be confused to mean "nonlawyer assistants", which are discussed in Rule 5.3. According to Rule 5.3, nonlawyer assistants are nonlawyers employed or retained by a lawyer. Moreover, the Comments caution that "[n]onlawyer assistants under Rule 5.3" should not have "managerial authority or financial interests in the organization."[3]

Obtain a copy of your jurisdiction's rules. How does your jurisdiction's rule compare to the D.C. rule? Do you favor nonlawyers owning financial interests in law firms? Why or why not?

EXERCISE 7.1

BONUSES

Bonuses paid to nonlawyers are to be distinguished from fee splitting. Sharing legal fees is unacceptable; however, bonuses are an acceptable way for attorneys to compensate nonlawyers. Remember that fee splitting is found to exist when fees paid to the nonlawyer are tied to a particular client. Bonuses, however, may *not* be tied to the receipt of particular fees for a particular case.

For example, a legal assistant employed by a law firm may be paid a year-end bonus as a way of demonstrating a firm's appreciation for that employee's services. As long as this bonus is not tied to a particular client or a particular case, this sort of payment is acceptable.

On the other hand, a paralegal employed by a sole practitioner may expend a great deal of extra effort on a particular case. The attorney may wish to reward that effort by offering to his legal assistant ten percent of the damage award received on behalf of that client, but the rules forbid him to do so.

In the Matter of an Anonymous Member of the South Carolina Bar relates the problems of an attorney who hired several investigators and offered them, as part of their compensation package, a bonus. 295 S.C. 25, 367 S.E.2d 17 (1988). These bonuses were figured at six to eight percent of the legal fees generated on a particular case on which the investigator had worked.

The court held that this arrangement constituted fee splitting, noting, "[t]he bonuses the investigators received were directly related to a percentage of the fees generated in the individual cases they investigated. Clearly, this practice violates the letter and spirit of the *Code's* prohibition on fee splitting between lawyers and non-lawyers." *Anonymous Member of the South Carolina Bar*, 295 S.C. 25, 367 S.E.2d 17 (1988). Ultimately, the attorney received a private reprimand.

Bonuses A form of compensation paid to a nonlawyer that is not tied to the receipt of particular fees for a particular case.

---

[2] District of Columbia Rules of Professional Conduct Rule 5.4.

[3] District of Columbia Rules of Professional Conduct Rule 5.4, cmt.

EXERCISE 7.2

Nikki was a recent MBA graduate who, while in school, had developed a great idea for a new business venture. Nikki had also worked as a legal assistant, so she was aware that a great deal of money changes hands within a legal practice. Therefore, Nikki proposed to start an auditing business that would handle all the bank accounts for the law firm.

To audit bank accounts, Nikki's auditing business would charge a fixed fee. However, the service would not only assume responsibility for reconciling client and firm accounts with bank statements, it would also maintain records of hours spent, by both attorneys and paralegals, working on a particular client's case. Then Nikki's company would bill that client directly, keeping five percent of the client's fees recovered as remuneration and turning the remainder of the money collected over to the law firm.

Knowing how sticky the ethical rules can be, Nikki proposed to hire both an attorney and a legal assistant to serve on the board of directors. In this way, Nikki could make sure she was adhering to all legalities.

Nikki asks you to help her determine the viability of her proposal. Do you think there is anything wrong with Nikki's proposal? If so, what changes could be made to bring it in line with ethical obligations?

BILLING PRACTICES

Billing Practices The procedure by which law firms collect money from clients as compensation for legal services rendered.

Reasonable Fee A legal fee that is clearly not excessive. Whether a fee is reasonable is determined by examining such factors as those set forth in the *Model Rules*.

Billing practices differ from community to community and even from law firm to law firm. Understanding the different kinds of billing procedures helps in determining the source of the firm's income, which is used to keep the firm viable and the firm's staff employed. It also explains the basics behind charging clients for the work of the legal assistant.

When establishing a fee schedule, the overriding consideration is the ethical rule that attorney's fees must be reasonable. If they are not, the attorney is subject to discipline. To assist in determining what is a **reasonable fee,** both the *Code* and the *Rules* list several factors to be considered when establishing fees. For example, see *Model Rules of Professional Conduct* Rule 1.5(a)(1994).

Although the *Model Code* prohibits charging or collecting "illegal or clearly excessive" fees, it later explains that a fee is excessive if another lawyer would not consider it reasonable. See *Model Code of Professional Responsibility* DR 2–106 (1986). Therefore, the *Code* likewise requires attorneys to establish reasonable fees.

The Ethical Considerations to the *Code* explain the justification for this rule. EC 2-17 states:

> A lawyer should not charge more than a reasonable fee, for excessive cost of legal service would deter laymen from utilizing the legal system in protection of their rights. Furthermore, an excessive charge abuses the professional relationship between lawyer and client. . . . *Model Code of Professional Responsibility* EC 2–17 (1986).

Therefore, the attorney is left to determine a fee that is reasonable in light of the factors mentioned. To some extent, the fee that the market will bear will determine what fee can be charged. Whatever the fee, it is always in everyone's best interest to reduce to writing the agreement concerning attorney's fees when entering into a lawyer-client relationship. See e.g., *Model*

Rule 1.5 (b); EC 2-19. In fact, the *Model Rules of Professional Conduct* require that contingent fee agreements be in writing. See Model Rule 1.5 (c).

Attorneys can charge fees in a variety of ways. One method of billing is charging a **fixed fee.** This means that the lawyer charges the same amount to everybody for a particular service rendered. For example, an attorney may bill every client seeking a simple real estate closing $450, regardless of the parties or property involved.

Quite common among those who need legal services on a regular basis is a method of billing called the **retainer.** With a retainer agreement, the client agrees to pay a fixed fee, and the attorney agrees to be available to provide any kind of legal service that client may need. In other words, a retainer is traditionally considered to be an amount fixed by an attorney "to make sure that he will represent and render service to his client in a given matter or matters." *In re Stern*, 92 N.J. 611, 458 A.2d 1279, 1283 (1983).

A **contingent fee** is a common arrangement between clients and attorneys whereby the client agrees to pay the attorney a portion of any recovery. Before any legal work is completed on behalf of the client, the parties enter into an agreement concerning the amount of the attorney's fee. The *Model Rules* require that this contingent fee agreement be reduced to writing.

An example of a contingent fee agreement is one in which the attorney states that her fee will amount to one-third of any recovery of a medical malpractice claim. Should the client agree to this arrangement, the parties would reduce this agreement to writing. If the lawyer's work nets the client a recovery of $30,000, the attorney, by agreement, will receive $10,000 (one-third of $30,000) for her work, regardless of how much time was spent providing legal services.

If the attorney were to settle the case with the hospital's insurance company with just a few phone calls, this fee may seem unreasonably high. The fee is not unreasonable, however, as it must be measured against the risk, assumed by the attorney, that he might receive no payment at all.

Certain kinds of actions are altogether prohibited from being considered on a contingent fee basis. These include criminal actions and divorce agreements. This exemption is justified on public policy grounds. For instance, if the attorney were solely concerned with maximizing a divorce recovery in order to maximize his fee, the attorney might overlook opportunities to save the marriage and keep the family intact.

While the contingent fee agreement is frequently employed, the most common billing arrangement is the **hourly fee.** Attorneys often bill their clients according to the amount of time that was spent preparing their representation. Clients are billed for each fraction of an hour the attorney spends on a case.

Civil or criminal litigation matters may be billed at an hourly rate. Suppose a client enters an attorney's office, seeking to sue a neighbor for erecting a fence over the property line, infringing upon the client's property. This sort of action is generally not billed at a fixed fee; the situation is unique enough that the attorney will not generally know how much effort would go into preparing such a suit. Therefore, the attorney would not know how much money she will be required to charge to cover her expenses. This action would not be billed to the client in terms of a contingent fee, as the client may solely be seeking an equitable remedy, such as having the fence removed. Rather, the attorney would bill the client based upon an hourly rate.

Fixed Fee A uniform or standard fee that a lawyer or a law firm generally charges for performing a particular legal service.

Retainer The client agrees to pay a fixed fee, and the attorney agrees to provide any legal service that he assesses the client may need.

Contingent Fee A common arrangement between clients and attorneys where the client agrees to pay the attorney a portion of any recovery.

Hourly Fee A billing practice whereby attorneys bill their clients by the amount of time spent attending to their representation.

For each hour the attorney spent on this litigation, therefore, the client would pay the firm an agreed-upon amount. Perhaps they have agreed upon a fee of $100.00 for each hour the attorney spends on the client's case. Assuming that the attorney spends 2 hours drafting the complaint, ½ hour traveling to the clerk to file the complaint, and 3 hours attempting to settle the matter with the neighbor's attorney, the client would be billed $550.00 for the attorney's services (5 and ½ hours × $100.00.)

The attorney's hourly fee includes overhead expenses. These expenses are costs incurred by the attorney in representing the client. Each hour spent by the attorney on a particular client means the attorney must keep his office open during that period. The attorney incurs costs during that hour for office rent, electricity, telephone, and support staff wages. When determining an hourly fee, the attorney would take into consideration all of these expenses.

Although each attorney may adopt a different procedure, particularized expenses, which are unique to each client, are usually billed directly to that client and are in excess of any amount charged as the hourly fee. For instance, a particular client's papers may need to be reviewed by a third party before they can be filed with the court. A messenger would be hired to deliver the papers to that third party. The cost of messengering these documents is usually billed back to that client and is a fee added beyond that charged for the hourly rate.

BILLING PARALEGAL TIME

Paralegals perform invaluable tasks for the attorneys who employ them, assisting in providing legal services in the most economical way possible. If these same services were performed by the attorney, the attorney would have no choice but to bill the client for this legal work at the attorney's higher rate. When the work is accomplished by a legal assistant, however, can—and should—the client be billed for these services at the legal assistant's lower fee?

The answer to both questions, most obviously and almost without exception, is a resounding "Yes." Were it otherwise, attorneys would have no incentive to utilize paraprofessionals to assist in supplying legal services.

In fact, most markets support the idea of a paralegal hourly fee, comparable to the hourly fee charged by the attorney. About sixty-seven percent of law firms currently bill clients for paralegal time. See 1993 NALA Utilization and Compensation Survey, Report for the Legal Assistant Profession, p. 31.

In most markets, fees are earned by billing on an hourly basis, so the time a paralegal spends advancing a particular client's representation is billed directly to that client. The paralegal's fee is much lower, understandably, than the fee that would be charged for the attorney's work. The legal assistant works under the direction of the attorney who assumes responsibility for all work product of that employee. The attorney's education, experience, and responsibilities for overseeing the client's representation, therefore, mean that the client will pay more for work done by that attorney.

It should be clear, however, that attorneys taking advantage of the services of legal assistants must disclose to the client that the services for which they are being billed were performed by a nonlawyer employee. Because the ethical rules require that clients be informed concerning matters regarding their representation, it is important that the client know that a paralegal has been employed to handle some of the work.

> The disclosure to the client should state the rate for each attorney and paraprofessional or other non-lawyer who will or may work on the client's matter. If the firm charges for other services, those fees and pass-through costs should also be disclosed.
>
> If requested by the client, the lawyer should also inform the client concerning the qualifications or expertise of the persons who may work on the matter.
>
> It is the Committee's opinion that with proper disclosure it is appropriate for a law firm to bill a client for the professional services of non-lawyers such as law clerks, paralegals, legal assistants or others who perform services for the client under the lawyer's supervision. Such services should be separately itemized in the billing to the client and are normally billed at rates lower than the rates for services of a lawyer. The Committee further believes that it would be a fraudulent misrepresentation to the client that legal services had been rendered by a lawyer if the billing for secretarial, law clerk, paralegal or other non-lawyer services were represented as attorney time. N.M. Advisory Opinion 1990-3.[4]

Keeping in mind that the paralegal can handle matters that would otherwise be handled by the attorney, the cost efficiency of hiring legal assistants becomes clear. Billing at the lower rate of the legal assistant, the client is charged a greatly reduced cost for work which, if done by the attorney, might be prohibitively expensive.

PADDING BILLABLE HOURS

Because the hours the legal assistant spends on a case are billed directly to that client, the paralegal must keep a careful record of everything she does during each of her working hours. Whenever she spends an hour researching an issue or drafting a complaint for a particular client, she must record that hour on her timesheet and note the client for whom the work was completed. Then that hour is billed to the client.

This hour of work is known as a **billable hour.** The more billable hours the paralegal accumulates, the greater the fee the law firm can charge the client. Clearly, the paralegal's work product is tied to the profits of the law firm. Therefore, because the legal assistant wants to maximize her value to the firm, there is an incentive to bill greater and greater numbers of billable hours. In fact, law firms often establish a minimum number of hours that paralegals are expected to bill each year.

The pressure on the legal assistant to accumulate a certain number of billable hours is often great. Sometimes it may even seem to be impossible to reach targeted billable hour requirements. At this point, the nonlawyer may consider "padding" his billable hours.

Padding billable hours means that the legal assistant (or, for that matter, any legal professional) charges hours to a client *even though the legal assistant never spent that time working on the client's case.* For example, the legal assistant may spend two hours researching an issue on damages for a client initiating a

Billable Hour Time billed to the client for work completed on that client's case.

Padding Billable Hours The legal assistant charges hours to a client even though the legal assistant never spent that time working on the client's case.

[4]Reprinted by permission.

HIGHLIGHT   The Debate Concerning Overtime Compensation

It is widely known that the legal assistant's hours at the law firm may be quite long. Are paralegals entitled to overtime pay for all of the extra time they spend at work? Merely asking this question of another legal assistant often generates heated debate.

Robin Oxman was a legal assistant at Hamilton & Samuels in Newport Beach, California. The policy at Hamilton & Samuels is to pay their paralegals high salaries. In return, the firm expects the legal assistants to bill eighteen hundred hours each year. To meet these stringent requirements, the legal assistants had to work extra hours yet were not paid overtime.

When Oxman refused to work one weekend, her employment was terminated. She then applied to the California labor commissioner, seeking $3,500.00 in overtime compensation and $1,958.00 in vacation time. Her request was denied. See Steve Cohn, *California Paralegal Loses Attempt at Overtime Compensation*, LEGAL ASSISTANT TODAY, Jul.-Aug. 1992.

Naturally, the issue of overtime compensation would be controversial. According to a survey conducted by NFPA, only forty-nine percent of paralegals receive overtime compensation. Legal assistants themselves are divided as to whether they *should* receive overtime pay.

Many legal assistants believe that, because they are professionals and because they want their employers to perceive them as professionals, they do not want to receive overtime compensation. In other words, not receiving overtime pay for their work enhances their professional status.

Others argue that federal regulations would seem to require that legal assistants be paid over-

time compensation. Federal law requires that all employees who work overtime be paid an overtime wage unless they fit into one of the exemptions specified in Title 29, CFR, Part 541. These three exemptions are "executive," "administrative," and "professional" and there are clearcut guidelines for determining whether an employee fits into one of these categories. It should be noted that the statutory definitions of these terms are not necessarily the same as their everyday meaning.

To determine if one is entitled to overtime compensation, the Department of Labor looks at an individual's specific job tasks and determines if they fall within one of the exemptions. According to Michael Ginley, Assistant Director of Wage & Hour Division of the Employment Standards Administration of the U.S. Department of Labor in Sacramento, California, most legal assistants do not fall within any of these exemptions and therefore deserve to be paid overtime. For example, in order to fit into the professional exemption, one must exercise independent judgment. As we have seen, however, legal assistants who exercise independent judgment may run afoul of unauthorized practice of law rules.

What do you think? Should paralegals receive overtime pay? What other arguments can you think of in favor of and against receiving overtime?

Source: See NALA 1990-91 Utilization & Compensation Survey; Diane Patrick, *To Be or Not To Be (Exempt)*, LEGAL ASSISTANT TODAY, Sept.-Oct. 1992, 36. Copyright 1994. James Publishing, Inc. Reprinted with permission from *Legal Assistant Today*. For subscription information, call (714) 755-5450.

personal injury claim. Instead of billing the client for *two* hours, the legal assistant may record *three* hours researching the issue on her timesheet, and then the law firm would bill the client for those three hours.

Padding hours sometimes seems like an attractive option, as it inflates the number of billable hours recorded by the nonlawyer and makes the legal assistant appear more valuable to the firm. However, a legal assistant must *never* pad billable hours. To charge hours to the client that were never spent on her case is clearly unethical and dishonest. To do so would be a misrepresentation that could benefit the law firm and the legal assistant only at the expense of the client. Yet legal professionals have an obligation to refrain from making misrepresentations to clients. See *Model Rules of Professional Conduct*

Rule 8.4, made applicable to nonlawyer employees through *Model Rules of Professional Conduct* Rule 5.3 (1994).

Padding hours may seem like an attractive option in the short run, but it can ultimately harm both the paralegal and the client. Should a client discover that the law firm has been charging him for time that was never spent on his case, he would be understandably quite upset. At the least, the firm faces the loss of favorable relations with the client. However, the loss to the law firm may be more substantial. For instance, the client may initiate proceedings to obtain restitution from the law firm and may inform others in the community of the law firms' unethical practices.

What about the related issue of *estimating* the amount of time spent on a client's case? What happens when the legal assistant fails to record her hours as she completes her work? Failing to record the amount of hours spent handling certain matters for a client contemporaneously with completion of the work can result in an inaccurate record and, thus, inaccurate billing. This situation is akin to padding hours. One client may be billed for work that was never completed on her behalf. Reconstructing the time spent on a particular project at a later date, while perhaps not as serious as padding hours, should therefore likewise be avoided.

AWARDING PARALEGAL FEES TO THE PREVAILING PARTY

A **fee shifting statute** generally directs the courts to order the defendants to pay attorney's fees to the plaintiff where the plaintiff has prevailed in an action. Usually in the U.S., unlike the practice in many other countries, each party bears the cost of providing his own legal services. In fact, courts order attorney's fees to be paid to the prevailing party only in limited circumstances and then only when provided for by one of these fee shifting statutes.

Fee Shifting Statute A statute that generally directs the courts to order the defendants to pay attorney's fees of the plaintiff where the plaintiff has prevailed in the action.

Today, several federal statutes provide for the award of attorney's fees. These include statutes such as the Civil Rights Act and the Sherman Anti-Trust Act and Clayton Act. Various state statutes likewise provide for such an award.

When filing a petition seeking such an award for attorney's fees, attorneys recognize that many hours of work have been completed by the paralegal on behalf of that client. According to the Supreme Court, those paralegal fees are as recoverable as attorney's fees.

In 1989 a landmark decision, which recognized the intrinsic value of hiring paralegals, was announced by the U.S. Supreme Court. In *Missouri v. Jenkins*, 491 U.S. 274, 109 S.Ct. 2463, 105 L.Ed. 2d 229 (1989), the Court held that, where a court awards attorney's fees to one party pursuant to a fee shifting statute, it may include an award for paralegal's fees where the prevailing practice in a given community was to bill paralegal time separately at market rates.

The *Jenkins* decision was the result of a lawsuit filed in 1977 against the state of Missouri and other defendants alleging that the defendants had "caused and perpetuated" a system of segregation within the public schools. The district court agreed and ordered defendants to pay more than $460 million to rectify the situation.

Pursuant to the Civil Rights Attorney's Fees Awards Act, 42 U.S.C.A. § 1988, plaintiffs, as prevailing parties, sought to have the court order the defendants to pay their attorneys' fees. Both sides had taken full advantage of the services of legal assistants during the litigation, so the award of paralegal fees was also sought because these fees made up part of the cost of providing legal services. The district court awarded attorney's fees to plaintiffs and calculated an award of fees for legal assistant services at prevailing rates in the Kansas City market. Namely, the district court awarded hourly rates of $35 for law clerks, $40 for paralegals, and $50 for recent law school graduates. One of the issues brought before the Supreme Court was whether this award of fees for the work of nonlawyers was proper.

The Court's analysis began with a look to the meaning of "reasonable attorney's fees" provided for in the statute. In reaching its conclusion that the term must include paralegal fees, the Court reasoned:

> Clearly, a "reasonable attorney's fee" cannot have been meant to compensate only work performed personally by members of the bar. Rather, the term must refer to a reasonable fee for the work product of an attorney. Thus, the fee must take into account the work not only of attorneys, but also of secretaries, messengers, librarians, janitors, and others whose labor contributes to the work product for which an attorney bills her client; and it must also take account of other expenses and profit. The parties have suggested no reason why the work of paralegals should not be similarly compensated, nor can we think of any. *Jenkins*, 491 U.S. at 285, 109 S.Ct. at 2470.

The Court then proceeded to answer the more difficult question of how to calculate the paralegal's fee. First, the Court noted that fees for attorneys are calculated by looking to the prevailing rates in the market for an attorney with similar "skill, expertise, and reputation." The Court then applied this conclusion to its analysis of legal assistant fees:

> In other words, the prevailing "market rate" for attorney time is not independent of the manner in which paralegal time is accounted for. Thus, if the prevailing practice in a given community were to bill paralegal time separately at market rates, fees awarded the attorney at market rates for attorney time would not be fully compensatory if the court refused to compensate hours billed by paralegals or did so only at "cost." Similarly, the fee awarded would be too high if the court accepted separate billing for paralegal hours in a market where that was not the custom. *Jenkins*, 491 U.S. at 287, 109 S.Ct. at 2471.

This analysis, the Court noted, not only makes economic sense by encouraging attorneys to hire paralegals and provide services at lower costs to consumers, but also comports with Congress's intent in enacting the statute to "provide a 'fully compensatory fee.' " See *Jenkins*, 491 U.S. at 287, 109 S.Ct. at 2471. In so noting, the Court also warned that paralegal services of a clerical nature should *not* be billed at a paralegal rate.

> Of course, purely clerical or secretarial tasks should not be billed at a paralegal rate, regardless of who performs them. What the court in *Johnson v. Georgia Highway Express, Inc.*, 488 F.2d 714, 717 (CA5 1974), said in regard to the work of attorneys is applicable by way of analogy to paralegals: "It is appropriate to distinguish between legal work, in the strict sense, and investigation, clerical work, compilation of facts and statistics and other work which can often be accomplished by non-lawyers but which a lawyer may do because he has no other help available. Such non-legal work may command a lesser rate. . . ." *Jenkins*, 491 U.S. at 288, n. 10, 109 S.Ct. at 2471, n 10.

Call several law firms in your area and ask if they bill their clients for paralegal services. If the law firm does bill for legal assistant services, at what rate does it bill? What conclusions can you draw about your legal market and its use of legal assistants?

EXERCISE 7.3

PRACTICAL APPLICATION OF *MISSOURI v. JENKINS*

Missouri v. Jenkins paved the way for courts to freely award paralegal fees. This award is not automatic, however. Rather, when filing a petition seeking such an award, attorneys and their paralegals should take note of the following caveats.

The Court indicated that the award of fees for work done of a clerical nature was improper. This means it is imperative, when seeking an award of fees for paralegal services rendered, that the petition specify the kind of work done by the paralegal for which fees are sought. Without this information, the court cannot award attorney's fees. A vague description of the kinds of paralegal services that were rendered may result in no compensation being awarded for paralegal time.

As noted in *Continental Townhouses East Unit One Ass'n v. Brockbank*, 152 Ariz. 537, 733 P.2d 1120, 1128, 73 A.L.R.4th 921, 936 (1986):

> Clearly, since the legal assistant must perform legal work and be supervised by an attorney, the fee application must contain enough details to demonstrate to the court that these requirements have been met, . . . *Brockbank*, 73 A.L.R.4th at 936.

Likewise, the qualifications of the legal assistant who rendered the legal services should be set forth in the petition. Because a paralegal is defined as "a nonlawyer, qualified through education, training or work experience . . . ," courts often consider the qualifications of the individual doing the work before awarding the attorney's fees.

Moreover, the statute specifies an award for "reasonable" attorney's fees. To that end, the petition should only note fees that are reasonable and that reflect market rates for the kinds of services the legal assistant performed for the client.

For instance, in *In re Continental Illinois Securities Litigation*, 750 F. Supp. 868 (N.D. Ill. 1990), the court refused to award the paralegal fees requested in a petition because they were unreasonable. The law firms had requested fees ranging from $50.00 to $75.00 per hour for the services of their paralegals and law clerks. However, the highest hourly pay received by any of these clerks was $21.50. Noting that the ethical codes generally require that lawyers not charge or collect "an illegal or excessive fee," and that lawyers' fees should be reasonable, the court said the market rate requested for these paralegal services (to be included in the award of attorney's fees) could not be presumed reasonable. "When examination reveals, as it has here, that there is no definable relationship between the cost of the service and the rate petitioners charge for it, any presumption of reasonableness disappears." *Id.* at 891. Therefore, the court downscaled the fees awarded for paralegal services.

Polly Paralegal, a legal assistant with 12 years' experience in litigation matters, has spent a considerable amount of time working on matters for her law firm's client,

EXERCISE 7.4

Despite the ruling in *Missouri v. Jenkins,* an appellate court in Indiana overturned the trial court's conclusion that support staff costs are an element of reasonable attorney's fees and its subsequent award of paralegal fees. See *Johnson v. Naugle,* 557 N.E.2d 1339 (Ind. App. 1990). The court then remanded the case with instructions to the trial court to amend the attorney's fees award.

Naugle was interpreted to mean that paralegal work could not be compensated for when considering a petition for attorney's fees pursuant to a fee shifting statute. After reading this decision, certain attorneys in Indiana started having paralegal fees stricken from the overall attorney's fee awards requested by their opponents. Additionally, when attorney's fees petitions in divorce cases were sent by the wife to the husband for payment, the husband would refuse to pay for any paralegal fees, citing the *Johnson v. Naugle* rule.

"This started affecting some of our [NFPA] members because they were coming close to losing their jobs!" exclaimed Shelly Sutton, NFPA representative from the Indiana Paralegal Association. NFPA and the state legislature soon got to work to remedy the situation.

Representative Donaldson of the Indiana legislature soon became involved. The legislator was called by an attorney who had requested a fee award for a significant amount of legal assistant work; the judge would not award paralegal fees. The attorney asked Representative Donaldson if he could get legislation passed to correct this situation. Representative Donaldson has developed a proposed rule that would limit this decision and is pushing to get it adopted by both the House and the Senate.

Source: *Appeals Court Decides Support Staff Not Part of Attorney's Fees.* LEGAL ASSISTANT TODAY, Jul.-Aug. 1991, 12–13. Copyright 1994. James Publishing, Inc. Reprinted with permission from *Legal Assistant Today.* For subscription information, call (714) 755-5450.

Gertrude, in Gertrude's civil rights lawsuit against BISMO cranes. Gertrude won the suit and Polly's supervising attorney is preparing a petition to recover attorney's fees. Polly's law firm billed Gertrude $35.00 per hour of time that Polly spent working on Gertrude's case.

Should the hours Polly spent on the case be included in the petition for attorney fees? Why or why not? If Polly's supervising attorney decides to include hours Polly spent on the case in the petition, what factors do you think would be important to include?

COMMINGLING FUNDS

When a client seeks out the services of an attorney, it is very likely that money of some sort will change hands. For instance, clients may approach an attorney to seek some sort of redress for a wrong they feel they have suffered. The remedy they are after is money damages. Therefore, when a client retains the services of an attorney, it is quite likely that the representation will conclude with money changing hands.

Clients also often consult an attorney after a loved one has passed on in order to probate the last will and testament. In administering such an estate, the attorney accepts responsibility for distributing estate assets, which are often in the form of money or securities accumulated by the deceased during his lifetime.

Consultation with an attorney may also be commenced when a client is seeking to purchase or sell property or other assets. Checks that are meant to be held in escrow are passed to the attorney.

In all of these situations, the money belongs to the client. It may be held by the attorney, however, for the purpose of keeping it safe. Often, responsibility for maintaining checking accounts and for distributing property is left with the legal assistant or other nonlawyer employee.

On the other hand, the operation of a law firm requires significant outlays of money. To get this money, the attorney charges the client, as discussed above, in exchange for providing legal services. This income is used to pay rent and other office liabilities, including the attorneys' and nonlawyer employees' salaries.

With all this money changing hands, ownership of funds could easily become confused, and money belonging to clients could be used to pay law firm bills. For this reason, both the *Model Code* and the *Model Rules* adopt a simple rule: The attorney should not commingle his funds with those of his clients. See DR 9-102; Model Rule 1.15. Because the legal assistant often has substantial responsibility over safekeeping client property, it is especially important for the nonlawyer to learn and understand the rules against **commingling funds.**

> [C]ommingling is committed when a client's money is intermingled with that of his attorney and its separate identity lost so that it may be used for the attorney's personal expenses or subjected to claims of his creditors. *Black v. State Bar*, 57 Cal.2d 219, 18 Cal.Rptr. 518, 522, 368 P.2d 118, 122 (1962), quoting *Clark v. State Bar*, 39 Cal.2d 161, 168, 246 P.2d 1, 4.

Commingling Funds Intermingling client money with that of the attorney whereby the client's money loses its separate identity.

This commingling rule exists to protect against the danger that commingling will result in the loss of the client's funds. After all, once the funds have been commingled and the identity of the owner is confused, it is much easier to inadvertently spend the funds of the client on the expenses of the law firm.

To keep the money of the client separate from that of the attorney, therefore, the attorney must establish a separate trust account into which only client funds are deposited. From this account, the only withdrawals should be for client purposes. This rule makes sense when it is kept in mind that the attorney's role here, as a fiduciary, is to provide safekeeping for the client's funds. The attorney's function is neither to invest the money at a profit to the client nor to recoup attorney fees out of this money.

The rules concerning commingling are set forth in substantially similar detail in the *Model Code* and the *Model Rules;* both set forth guides to govern the attorney's behavior in safekeeping client property. For example, see *Model Rules of Professional Conduct* Rule 1.15 (1994).

Over time it has become exceedingly clear that, where a lawyer places client property in a safe or in a safe deposit box for safekeeping, the property must be clearly labeled so as not to confuse it with other items of value in that same location. Moreover, it is clear that an attorney generally may open one account into which she may deposit all client funds. However, where a particular client's representation will result in significant and complicated transactions, a separate account, established solely for the purpose of that individual client, may be warranted.

Both the *Code* and the *Rules* provide further guidance to the attorney in keeping intact the separate identity of the client's funds. As a guide for attorneys handling client accounts, DR 9-102 (B) provides:

(B) A lawyer shall:
    (1) Promptly notify a client of the receipt of his funds, securities, or other properties.
    (2) Identify and label securities and properties of a client promptly upon receipt and place them in a safe deposit box or other place of safekeeping as soon as practicable.
    (3) Maintain complete records of all funds, securities, and other properties of a client coming into the possession of the lawyer and render appropriate accounts to his client regarding them.
    (4) Promptly pay or deliver to the client as requested by a client the funds, securities, or other properties in the possession of the lawyer which the client is entitled to receive. *Model Code of Professional Responsibility* DR 9-102(B) (1986).

These rules appear simple to follow, as they provide clear-cut, straightforward standards by which the attorney can conform her conduct. Attorneys are most often disciplined for a violation of the commingling rules. Whether the attorney fails to establish a separate trust account or merely keeps sloppy records of his clients' accounts, attorneys will find that they will be swiftly subjected to disciplinary procedures if they commingle funds.

Courts are particularly strict about commingling rules for, when an attorney commingles funds, a very real danger exists that these client funds may be used to pay the attorney's creditors. When the attorney uses the funds of the client, the attorney has gone beyond commingling and has misappropriated funds.

Misappropriation
Any unauthorized use by the lawyer of client funds entrusted to him, including not only stealing but also unauthorized temporary use for the lawyer's own purpose.

Misappropriation has been defined as "any unauthorized use by the lawyer of client's funds entrusted to him, including not only stealing, but also unauthorized temporary use for the lawyer's own purpose, whether or not he derives any personal gain or benefit therefrom." *In re Wilson*, 81 N.J. 451, 455, n.1, 409 A.2d 1153, 1155, n.1 (1979). No intent on the part of the attorney to deprive the client of the funds is necessary to establish misappropriation, and a single instance of the client's balance falling below the level at which it is supposed to be may be enough to show that the lawyer has misappropriated funds.

APPLICATION TO LEGAL ASSISTANTS

Client Trust Fund Accounts A bank account established for the benefit of the client, to hold the client's money.

Handling these **client trust fund accounts** is often a task delegated to the nonlawyer employee, be that employee the office manager, a legal assistant, or a secretary. Often, because the attorney is busy handling the kind of legal work that cannot be delegated, he turns over such administrative affairs as the accounting of trust fund accounts to his support staff. For this reason, it is vital that nonlawyer employees understand these basic rules concerning trust funds.

As we have seen before, such delegation is proper where the attorney maintains close supervision over the nonlawyer's work. And, while attorneys may not delegate their discretion in handling the client accounts, they may delegate responsibilities to make the exercise of that discretion easier. Whatever responsibilities they delegate, however, attorneys must be sure to closely supervise and direct the work.

Many attorneys have sought to make their legal assistants **signatories** on the client fund account. Therefore, when needed, the attorney may direct the assistant to draw a check on that account. Such practice has generally been approved.

Signatories Someone who can sign on an account.

Likewise, the nonlawyer employee is often asked to keep records of deposits into and withdrawals from the various accounts of the law firm. This includes the trust fund account. This is acceptable, with the caveat that it is the attorney's responsibility to ensure that the accounts are reconciled with the bank balances. Therefore, the attorney must periodically check into the various account balances. While reconciling accounts with bank statements may be delegated to support staff, such as an office manager, the attorney maintains an overall responsibility for those records.

Too often, however, attorneys delegate enormous responsibility to the nonlawyer over the trust accounts, forsaking even their responsibility to exercise discretion over the client funds. A simple and inadvertent accounting mistake by the nonlawyer, however, may be all that is needed to begin inquiry into the practices of both that attorney and the nonlawyer. In turn, the inquiry may ultimately result in discipline for having commingled funds.

DISPUTED FUNDS

What happens when the client disagrees with the attorney over the amount of money that should be paid to the client?

Attorney fees are often paid out of the client's funds received from a settlement. For instance, Alexandra Attorney and her client Clyde may agree to settle a particular personal injury suit for $10,000. Before settlement, the parties may agree that Alexandra would receive, as fees, 30 percent of any recovery, or, in this case, $3,000. The opposing party, who must now pay $10,000, may decide to write this check for $10,000, payable to both Alexandra and Clyde. Alexandra's $3,000 fee is paid directly from this check.

Now, upon receipt of the $10,000 check, Alexandra's firm would deposit it in a client account and promptly notify Clyde of receipt of the check. As agreed, Alexandra may withdraw her $3,000 and deposit that in her firm's account for, by agreement, the $3,000 does not really belong to the client but rather to the attorney.

Suppose, however, that upon notification of receipt of the check, Clyde disagrees with Alexandra that she is entitled to that $3,000. Should Alexandra still withdraw her fee from the client account?

Where any portion of the money owed to the attorney is disputed, the attorney is not allowed to withdraw any of that money. See DR 9-102(A)(2); Model Rule 1.15(c). In other words, the disputed portion must remain in the client account until such time as the dispute over the amount of fees owed is resolved. However, any undisputed portion of the funds should be promptly distributed to the client.

INTEREST ON ACCOUNTS

Another critical factor in managing client accounts is the matter of interest on that account. Generally, attorneys are not required to deposit funds in accounts that will earn their clients interest, as the attorney is merely safekeeping the funds as a fiduciary and not holding them for investment purposes.

However, where large amounts of money will be held for the client for a substantial period of time, the attorney may be required to inquire of the client whether investment of the funds should be undertaken. If client funds were invested so as to earn interest, it is clear that interest earned on the account also becomes property of the client and should not be distributed to anyone except to that client. See ABA Formal Opinion 348 (July 1982).

Interest on Lawyer's Trust Accounts/IOLTA An account into which interest that is earned on client trust accounts is deposited in order to fund programs that serve clients of limited means.

Some states have created **IOLTA (Interest on Lawyer's Trust Accounts)** funds into which such interest must be deposited. The state then uses this money for programs that serve poor clients.

After reading this section, you should have a better understanding of the responsibilities of the attorney and the nonlawyer employee with regard to client trust funds. A failure to heed any one of the rules could result in serious discipline or even, possibly, prison sentences.

CONSEQUENCES OF COMMINGLING FUNDS

Taking into consideration a number of factors, the courts look closely at the misconduct charged of the attorney where commingling issues arise before ordering any disciplinary action. Two things are clear, however: The amount of money claimed to be commingled or misappropriated does not matter, and it does not matter whether the attorney's misappropriation was alleged to have occurred during the practice of law. A review of the following cases helps to illustrate all that is considered by the courts in making determinations of appropriate discipline.

In *In re Vrdolyak,* the Supreme Court of Illinois decided not to impose any sanctions for the actions of the attorney's nonlawyer office manager in commingling and converting client funds. While recognizing that an attorney must not commingle funds and a single act of commingling may result in disbarment, the court concluded that the attorney's connection to the office manager's error "was, at most, tenuous." *Vrdolyak,* 137 Ill.2d 407, 428, 560 N.E.2d 840, 848 (1990).

It appears this decision was based on the fact that the office manager was told by another attorney's secretary that funds received on behalf of a client were meant to pay "for costs" and should therefore be deposited in the firm's operating account. "Furthermore, as respondent [attorney Vrdolyak] was not at all involved in the handling of the case, it does not appear that respondent could have learned of the misplaced funds." *Id.* at 428, 560 N.E.2d at 848.

In another decision where the willful embezzlement of funds was solely the product of the nonlawyer's actions, the attorney was suspended for ninety days. In *In the Matter of Scanlan,* the court noted that the discipline was necessary because the attorney had failed to maintain supervision over the accounts. 144 Ariz. 334, 697 P.2d 1084 (1985). The secretary was sent to jail for her actions.

In 1981 Fred Scanlan, a sole practitioner, employed Rachel Galvez as a replacement secretary and soon thereafter expanded her responsibilities to include acting as secretary, file clerk, purchasing agent, and bookkeeper. Scanlan even made Rachel Galvez a signatory upon the office "operating expenses" account. Unbeknownst to Scanlan, who did not conduct a reference check before hiring her, Rachel Galvez was under indictment for forgery and theft of funds. It appears she had stolen from two of her previous employers.

In addition to a general office account, Scanlan had established an account for one of his clients, Olson Dairy, and a general clients' trust account. Shortly after hiring Galvez, Scanlan confided that he was in need of a personal loan. She offered to loan him $10,000, telling him the money came from proceeds from the recent sale of her home. Instead, Galvez wrote a $10,000 check, drawn upon the Olson Dairy account, and loaned this money to Scanlan.

Thus began a pattern of behavior whereupon Galvez stole money from the accounts and then transferred money from one account to another to hide her actions. Eventually Galvez was caught when Olson Dairy declared bankruptcy and asked the firm to turn over all the money held in trust in its account. Upon reviewing the balances of all the accounts, Scanlan discovered that Galvez had stolen more than $30,000 from the clients.

Scanlan was suspended from the practice of law for ninety days. In ordering the suspension, the court rejected arguments that Scanlan was being disciplined for having been 'duped by Rachel,' stating:

> The 90-day suspension is warranted not because Scanlan was a victim of Galvez, but because Scanlan failed to exercise even minimal care over his various trust accounts. Had Scanlan checked with Galvez's prior employers, most likely the thefts would not have occurred. Had Scanlan dismissed her after discovering the thefts from his operating account, the decimation of the Olson Dairy account would not have been complete. Even after Scanlan discovered this theft, he did not question the source of his $10,000 loan.... He did not audit any of his other accounts, nor did he take adequate precautions to put them beyond Galvez's reach.... [S]uffice it to say that these acts and omissions constituted gross negligence and violated the disciplinary rules governing trust accounts. *In the Matter of Scanlan*, 144 Ariz. 334, 697 P.2d 1084 1087-88 (1985).

In another case, Raul Palomo, an attorney practicing in California, was suspended from the practice of law for one year. Palomo had endorsed a check made payable to the client, without his client's consent, and instructed his office manager to deposit it into the office payroll account. The court found that the attorney's actions amounted to a willful violation of his ethical responsibilities. *Palomo v. State Bar of California*, 36 Cal.3d 785, 205 Cal.Rptr. 834, 685 P.2d 1185 (1984).

Palomo contended that the blame for commingling these funds was properly placed upon human error, attributable to his employee. Therefore, he argued that, at most, he could only be guilty of negligence.

The court responded to these contentions, stating,

> At the outset, petitioner's [Palomo's] contention overlooks his intentional and unauthorized endorsement of Torres' signature on the check. Beyond that, it ignores the fact that attorneys assume a personal obligation of reasonable care to comply with the critically important rules for the safekeeping and disposition of client funds. [Citations.]
>
> Attorneys cannot be held responsible for every detail of office operations. [Citation.] However, where fiduciary violations occur as the result of serious and inexcusable lapses in office procedure, they may be deemed "wilful" for disciplinary purposes, even if there was no deliberate wrongdoing.... "[W]e have repeatedly held that trust account deficiencies are attributable to attorneys—not to their employees." *Palomo*, 205 Cal.Rptr. at 840, 685 P.2d at 1190-91.

PARALEGALS IN THE SPOTLIGHT

Anthony D. D'Aurora was a legal assistant employed at Widett, Slater & Goldman, P.C., in Boston from June 1988 to January 1991. While employed at the firm he was made custodian of the bankruptcy debtor's account, with responsibility for preparing checks for distribution to the bankruptcy trustee. On January 21, 1992, D'Aurora pled guilty to embezzlement of $8,000 from the bankruptcy account.

D'Aurora faced a maximum sentence of five years in prison and a $250,000 fine. On April 15, 1992, D'Aurora was sentenced to two months house detention and one year of probation. Be-cause he had repaid the money he had embezzled from the firm and restitution had left him financially unable to pay a fine, he was ordered to pay a $50 special assessment fee. D'Aurora also informed the U.S. Attorney's Office, who had prosecuted the case, that he was no longer employed at his new law firm and that he had withdrawn from law school.

Source: Sheila Christensen, *Former Paralegal Sentenced in Embezzlement Case*, LEGAL ASSISTANT TODAY, Sept.-Oct. 1992, 27. Copyright 1994. James Publishing, Inc. Reprinted with permission from *Legal Assistant Today*. For subscription information, call (714) 755-5450.

Reviewing these cases reveals several principles regarding the consequences for both attorneys and nonlawyers concerning the actions of nonlawyer employees with respect to commingling or misappropriating client funds. First, where the attorney has no knowledge of the error and has taken reasonable precautions to prevent the mistake from occurring, disciplinary measures taken against the attorney will most likely be slight.

Second, where the attorney's conduct did not assure that the nonlawyer was adequately supervised and where the attorney's actions resulted in some of his discretion over client accounts being delegated to the nonlawyer, the attorney will often be found liable for negligently supervising the conduct of the nonlawyer employee and will face more serious discipline.

Third, where the attorney's actions contributed to the commingling of client funds with office money, the attorney's conduct will be deemed "willful" and the attorney will face extreme disciplinary sanctions. Furthermore, any misappropriation of funds may result in criminal charges being filed against the attorney.

Action taken against the legal assistant or other nonlawyer employee of the firm will also vary, depending upon the "willfulness" of the conduct. Therefore, where the nonlawyer's actions were the result of a mistake, the action taken by the court is likely to be slight. Where the actions of the nonlawyer indicate that he intentionally misappropriated funds, the nonlawyer may face criminal charges, especially for embezzlement. As always, with any mistake of significance, regardless of the intent involved, there is always the potential for the nonlawyer to lose his job. The law firm which hires the individual may not be able to easily absorb the liability for this nonlawyer's mistakes.

These principles hold true whenever an attorney may handle funds for another as a fiduciary. For example, should an attorney run a collection agency apart from his law firm and employ nonlawyers to assist him in its organization, the attorney is likewise required to avoid commingling funds and to promptly turn over collected monies to the client. See *State of Kansas v. Caenen*, 235 Kan. 451, 681 P.2d 639 (1984), where a delay in turning over $30.00 in money collected by nonlawyer employees, despite repeated requests from the client for the money, resulted in suspension for the attorney.

Franco had been employed as a legal assistant with Hughes and Dunthrop for several years. The longer he was there, the more his responsibilities grew and the more was expected of him. | **EXERCISE 7.5**

He had just discovered that his required billables were being significantly raised. All this, and he had just been put in charge of client trust fund accounts.

Being very conscientious, Franco studied the rules and procedures regarding handling client trust fund accounts. He wrote a procedure book to guide him in handling his responsibilities. Only after he had completed this work did he sit down and proceed to reconcile the account balances with the bank statements. He concluded that, at this point, there were no problems with the accounts.

A few weeks later Franco sat down to review the client trust fund accounts again. Something was wrong; another check drawn on the client account had been returned marked "insufficient funds." This was the third check this week. Franco assumed the bank had to be making another mistake.

Upon opening the ledger, Franco realized that his supervising attorney had inadvertently deposited a check from a client settlement into the general office account and not into the client trust fund account. Unfortunately, as yesterday was payday, the balance on the general account was too low to transfer funds into the appropriate account.

Has Franco violated any of his ethical obligations? What do you think he should do now? Is the firm responsible for violating any rules? What discipline do you think should result, if any?

PRO BONO WORK

Attorneys are encouraged to engage in **pro bono work.** In other words, whenever possible, attorneys should render legal services free of charge to those who need them but cannot afford them. For example, Rule 6.1 states,

Pro Bono Work
Work or services performed free of charge.

> A lawyer should render public interest legal service. A lawyer may discharge this responsibility by providing professional services at no fee or a reduced fee to persons of limited means or to public service or charitable groups or organizations, by service in activities for improving the law, the legal system or the legal profession, and by financial support for organizations that provide legal services to persons of limited means. *Model Rules of Professional Conduct* Rule 6.1 (1994).

Therefore, attorneys are encouraged to discharge their responsibilities to the legal community by seeking out such opportunities as noted above, opening doors to legal tribunals on behalf of the disadvantaged. What about the legal assistant's corresponding responsibilities?

The ABA Model Guidelines for the Utilization of Legal Assistant Services state:

> A lawyer who employs a legal assistant should facilitate the legal assistant's participation in appropriate continuing education and pro bono publico activities. ABA Model Guidelines for the Utilization of Legal Assistant Services Guideline 10.

Many legal assistants enter the profession looking to serve the legal community in some way. Just as attorneys have an obligation to provide pro bono services, legal assistants should likewise assume their corresponding obligation, as they are part of the same community and share the same responsibilities for it. However, restrictions on legal assistants in the form of the unauthorized practice of law rules limit the ways in which they can help the disadvantaged.

Legal assistants can help by offering assistance, free of charge, to the attorney who accepts a pro bono case. Many attorneys are more inclined to accept a pro bono case when they know a legal assistant will be providing support and assistance.

Another way for legal assistants to get involved is to offer their services to a legal aid organization. Through the organization, legal assistants can provide needed support to attorneys completing legal work for low-income persons. Legal assistants can also help by providing administrative assistance to the legal aid organization. The legal assistant can help recruit attorneys to handle cases or can work to coordinate the assignment of pro bono cases to volunteer attorneys.

Legal assistants interested in pro bono work would also be well advised to contact their local paralegal organization. Often the paralegal association will have established a particular pro bono program. If a legal assistant simply wishes to volunteer his time, he might look into more traditional volunteer programs, such as literacy training or providing crisis support.

Legal assistants looking for pro bono ideas might consider investing in a copy of NFPA's *Paralegals and Pro Bono*. For excellent sources of ideas for pro bono work, some of which have been summarized here, see Whiteside, "Volunteering Your Paralegal Services," *Legal Assistant Today* (Mar.-Apr. 1993); Whiteside, "A Career of Service," *Legal Assistant Today* (Sept.-Oct. 1992).[5]

In these ways the legal assistant can begin to offer to the community some assistance to help its members through the often labyrinthine legal world. This is true, as well, of the freelance paralegal offering services to any number of attorneys on an independent contractor basis.

[5]Copyright 1994. James Publishing, Inc. Reprinted with permission from *Legal Assistant Today*. For subscription information, call (714) 755-5450.

FOCUS ON KAREN JUDD

Karen Judd has been a certified legal assistant at Reno, O'Byrne & Kepley, P.C., in Champaign, Illinois, for a number of years. Judd has additionally been quite active in developing and supporting the paralegal profession, serving as NALA's president from 1988 through 1990 and on its board of directors for seven years. Her association with NALA has led to her substantial assistance in completing the *amicus* brief filed on behalf of NALA in *Missouri v. Jenkins.*

Judd believes *Jenkins* resolved whatever questions might have remained concerning compensation for legal assistant work pursuant to either state or federal fee shifting statutes. "Where it's the prevailing practice in the legal community to bill paralegal work on an hourly basis, paralegal fees may be awarded," Judd notes. In Judd's opinion, awarding paralegal fees only becomes controversial where attorneys do not bill clients separately for paralegal work yet seek an award of fees from a court pursuant to a fee shifting statute. "Where paralegal work is billed as a part of overhead or where the work which the paralegal is doing is clerical, *Jenkins* holds that lawyers may not request paralegal fee awards."

Moreover, Judd believes *Jenkins* has helped attorneys to recognize the value of their legal assistants. "Billing clients for paralegal time provides the attorney with a means of evaluating the value and benefits of the legal assistant," Judd states. By recording the time a paralegal spends on a case and then billing the client for that time, attorneys will be able to see the substantial amount of effort the legal assistant has devoted to the client. This is time and effort the attorney would have otherwise spent on the case.

As far as overtime compensation is concerned, Judd believes there may be no easy resolution to this issue, at least not until the regulations themselves are changed. In fact, Judd is not even sure that paralegal associations agree on the overtime compensation issue.

Judd believes most major law firms are looking into paying overtime compensation because they are aware of the severe penalties they would face if the Department of Labor found that the firm had violated the federal regulations. The biggest problem, in Judd's opinion, is that whether overtime compensation should be paid is determined on a firm-by-firm, individual-by-individual basis, and each firm utilizes legal assistants differently.

The one area where nonlawyers must be especially careful, in Judd's opinion, is when they are handling client trust fund accounts, because mistakes can easily result in disciplinary action. Judd advises that nonlawyers need to get educated about trust fund accounts and understand their purpose.

Judd concludes with some advice for legal assistants who will work in law firms. "Lawyers might want to take special care in instructing legal assistants about their ethical responsibilities when handling financial matters. We all know that lawyers need to make sure that their nonlawyer employees follow the disciplinary code in place in their jurisdiction. They also need to make sure that their nonlawyer employees *understand* such matters as fee splitting and handling trust fund accounts."

> Because of *Missouri v. Jenkins*, attorneys are coming to realize the value of their legal assistants. Billing for paralegal time provides the attorney with a means of evaluating the value and benefit of the legal assistant.

TIPS FOR PARALEGALS

■ Do not share legal fees with any lawyer, but do feel free to accept a salary and bonuses.

■ You may refer clients to your supervising attorney, as long as you are not asked to do so by your attorney and you do not accept a fee for such referrals.

■ Do not agree to establish a business with a lawyer when any part of the business involves the practice of law.

■ Keep careful note of the hours you spend on a client's case.

■ Make it a policy to stop and make note of the work you have completed at the end of each hour.

■ Never pad your billable hours.

■ Talk with your supervising attorney about implementing a computerized system to help you keep track of billable hours and client trust fund accounts.

■ Maintain a careful ledger system, if you are given responsibility for handling client trust fund accounts.

■ If you are given responsibility for handling client trust fund accounts, draw up a checklist that would show the date of receipt, when the money was deposited, etc., to help you keep track of the receipt of money.

■ Keep separate bank deposit receipts for client trust fund accounts and receipts for law office accounts.

■ Consider enrolling in some kind of accounting course.

■ Call your local paralegal organization to inquire about pro bono opportunities in your community.

CLOSING EXERCISE

After spending several years working as a tax accountant, Andrea became bored and decided to use her fine skills with detail work in a new profession—she would become a legal assistant.

At her first interview with a law firm for a position as a legal assistant, Andrea was asked if she had ever prepared a tax form. Soon began a protracted discussion of her tax experience.

The attorney interviewing Andrea soon realized the potential that Andrea could bring to the firm. Not wanting to let this "gold mine" get away, the attorney proposed the following arrangements to entice Andrea to accept his offer of employment:

A. Andrea could work as a legal assistant, handling everything from probate matters to divorce cases. However, when a client came in to discuss tax matters, the attorney would refer the client to Andrea. Andrea and the attorney would then split the fee received from the client.

B. Andrea would continue to work part-time as an accountant and would assume part-time responsibilities as a legal assistant. Any time she ran across an accounting client who seemed to have problems that would require the services of an attorney, Andrea would refer the client to the attorney. The attorney and Andrea would then split the fee.

C. Same arrangement as in section (b); however, instead of splitting the fee, Andrea would receive a bonus of $150 for each client she referred.

D. Andrea and the attorney would open a business together, teaching nonaccountants to prepare tax forms. Andrea would teach the classes; the attorney would handle attracting students and collecting payments. The tuition and costs would be split between them.

E. Andrea would be hired as a full-time legal assistant. Her responsibilities would include handling all tax matters when probating estates and organizing and maintaining the records for the client trust fund account. Andrea would have ultimate responsibility for reconciling the client accounts with the bank statements.

Which of these arrangements, if any, are acceptable? Why or why not? If the proposed arrangement is not acceptable, can you structure it so that it meets the requirements of the ethical rules?

CHAPTER SUMMARY

■ Fee splitting is the practice of a nonlawyer sharing legal fees with a lawyer. Fee splitting arises when a particular legal fee, tied to a particular client, is paid directly to a nonlawyer as compensation. This practice is strictly prohibited.

■ Fee splitting refers to the practice of lawyer sharing legal fees with a nonlawyer. This practice is related to—but distinguished from—bonuses, business enterprises with nonlawyers, and referrals. Bonuses are compensation paid to nonlawyers that is not tied to any particular case. This is an acceptable form of compensation. Business enterprises between lawyers and nonlawyers that involve the practice of law are also generally not acceptable because such enterprises might compromise the independent legal judgment of the lawyer. Nonlawyer referrals are an acceptable practice. The nonlawyer may recommend the services of her supervising attorney to friends who need legal advice.

■ In many jurisdictions, law firms can bill clients for paralegal time that is spent completing work on a client's case. However, it must be disclosed to the client that a legal assistant has worked on a particular matter for which the client has been billed. The paralegal must keep a careful record of the time he has spent on a case. The legal assistant should never pad those hours, for to do so would mean that the legal assistant was charging hours to a client that she had never spent working on that client's case.

■ The attorney and the legal assistant may never commingle the law firm's funds with those of the client. This means that the firm may not intermingle its funds with those of the client. The rule exists to protect the client's funds from becoming lost. Therefore, to make sure the client's funds are not commingled with those of the law firm, the firm must establish a client trust fund account. Because handling trust fund accounts is often a task delegated to legal assistants, nonlawyers should be particularly familiar with this rule.

■ Nonlawyers are encouraged to engage in pro bono work. This means that nonlawyers should look for opportunities to assist in providing legal services free of charge. By participating in pro bono activities, the legal assistant can actively help to broaden the access of the delivery of legal services.

KEY TERMS

billable hour
billing practices
bonuses
client trust fund accounts
commingling funds
contingent fee
fee shifting statute

fee splitting
fixed fee
hourly fee
interest on lawyer's trust
    accounts/IOLTA
Kutak Commission
misappropriation

nonlawyer referrals
padding billable hours
pro bono work
reasonable fee
retainer
signatories

CASE

Missouri v. Jenkins

Supreme Court of the United States, 1989.
491 U.S. 274, 109 S.Ct. 2463, 105 L.Ed. 2d 229.

BRENNAN, J., delivered the opinion of the Court, in which WHITE, BLACKMUN, STEVENS, and KENNEDY, JJ., joined, and in Parts I and III of which O'CONNOR and SCALIA, JJ., joined. O'CONNOR, J., filed an opinion concurring in part and dissenting in part, in which SCALIA, J., joined and REHNQUIST, C.J., joined in part. REHNQUIST, C.J., filed a dissenting opinion. MARSHALL, J., took no part in the consideration or decision of the case.

———

Justice BRENNAN delivered the opinion of the Court.

This is the attorney's-fee aftermath of major school desegregation litigation in Kansas City, Missouri. We granted certiorari, 488 U.S. ___, 109 S.Ct. 218, 102 L.Ed. 2d 209 (1988), to resolve two questions relating to fees litigation under 42 U.S.C. § 1988. First, does the Eleventh Amendment prohibit enhancement of a fee award against a State to compensate for delay in payment? Second, should the fee award compensate the work of paralegals and law clerks by applying the market rate for their work?

I

This litigation began in 1977 as a suit by the Kansas City Missouri School District (KCMSD), the School Board, and the children of two School Board members, against the State of Missouri and other defendants. The plaintiffs alleged that the State, surrounding school districts, and various federal agencies had caused and perpetuated a system of racial segregation in the schools of the Kansas City metropolitan area. They sought various desegrega-

tion remedies. KCMSD was subsequently realigned as a nominal defendant, and a class of present and future KCMSD students was certified as plaintiffs. After lengthy proceedings, including a trial that lasted 7½ months during 1983 and 1984, the District Court found the State of Missouri and KCMSD liable, while dismissing the suburban school districts and the federal defendants. It ordered various intradistrict remedies, to be paid for by the State and KCMSD, including $260 million in capital improvements and a magnet-school plan costing over $200 million. See *Jenkins v. Missouri*, 807 F.2d 657 (CA8 1986) (en banc), cert. denied, 484 U.S. 816 (1987); *Jenkins v. Missouri*, 855 F.2d 1295 (CA8 1988), cert. granted, 490 U.S. ___, 109 S.Ct. 1930, ___ L.Ed.2d ___ (1989).

The plaintiff class has been represented, since 1979, by Kansas City lawyer Arthur Benson and, since 1982, by the NAACP Legal Defense and Educational Fund, Inc. (LDF). Benson and the LDF requested attorney's fees under the Civil Rights Attorney's Fees Awards Act of 1976, 42 U.S.C. § 1988.[1] Benson and his associates had devoted 10,875 attorney hours to the litigation, as well as 8,108 hours of paralegal and law clerk time. For the LDF the corresponding figures were 10,854 hours for attorneys and 15,517 hours for paralegals and law clerks. Their fee applications deleted from these totals 3,628 attorney hours and 7,046 paralegal hours allocable to unsuccessful claims against the suburban school districts. With additions for post-judgment monitoring and for preparation of the fee application, the District Court awarded Benson a total of approximately $1.7 million and the LDF $2.3 million. App. to Pet. for Cert. A22–A43.

1. Section 1988 provides in relevant part: "In any action or proceeding to enforce a provision of sections 1981, 1982, 1983, 1985, and 1986 of this title, title IX of Public Law 92-318 [20 U.S.C. 1681 et seq.], or title VI of the Civil Rights Act of 1964 [42 U.S.C. 2000d et seq.], the court, in its discretion, may allow the prevailing party, other than the United States, a reasonable attorney's fee as part of the costs."

In calculating the hourly rate for Benson's fees the court noted that the market rate in Kansas City for attorneys of Benson's qualifications was in the range of $125 to $175 per hour, and found that "Mr. Benson's rate would fall at the higher end of this range based upon his expertise in the area of civil rights." *Id.*, at A26. It calculated his fees on the basis of an even higher hourly rate of $200, however, because of three additional factors: the preclusion of other employment, the undesirability of the case, and the delay in payment for Benson's services. *Id.*, at A26–A27. The court also took account of the delay in payment in setting the rates for several of Benson's associates by using current market rates rather than those applicable at the time the services were rendered. *Id.*, at A28–A30. For the same reason, it calculated the fees for the LDF attorneys at current market rates. *Id.*, at A33.

Both Benson and the LDF employed numerous paralegals, law clerks (generally law students working part-time), and recent law graduates in this litigation. The court awarded fees for their work based on Kansas City market rates for those categories. As in the case of the attorneys, it used current rather than historic market rates in order to compensate for the delay in payment. It therefore awarded fees based on hourly rates of $35 for law clerks, $40 for paralegals, and $50 for recent law graduates. *Id.*, at A29–A31, A34. The Court of Appeals affirmed in all respects. 838 F.2d 260 (CA8 1988).

. . .

III

Missouri's second contention is that the District Court erred in compensating the work of law clerks and paralegals (hereinafter collectively "paralegals") at the market rates for their services, rather than at their cost to the attorney. While Missouri agrees that compensation for the cost of these personnel should be included in the fee award, it suggests that an hourly rate of $15—which it argued below corresponded to their salaries, benefits, and overhead—would be appropriate, rather than the market rates of $35 to $50. According to Missouri, § 1988 does not authorize billing paralegals' hours at market rates, and doing so produces a "windfall" for the attorney.[7]

We begin with the statutory language, which provides simply for "a reasonable attorney's fee as part of the costs." 42 U.S.C. § 1988. Clearly, a "reasonable attorney's fee" cannot have been meant to compensate only work performed personally by members of the bar. Rather, the term must refer to a reasonable fee for the work product of an attorney. Thus, the fee must take into account the work not only of attorneys, but also of secretaries, messengers, librarians, janitors, and others whose labor contributes to the work product for which an attorney bills her client; and it must also take account of other expenses and profit. The parties have suggested no reason why the work of paralegals should not be similarly compensated, nor can we think of any. We thus take as our starting point the self-evident proposition that the "reasonable attorney's fee" provided for by statute should compensate the work of paralegals, as well as that of attorneys. The more difficult question is how the work of paralegals is to be valued in calculating the overall attorney's fee.

The statute specifies a "reasonable" fee for the attorney's work product. In determining how other elements of the attorney's fee are to be calculated, we have consistently looked to the marketplace as our guide to what is "reasonable." In *Blum v. Stenson*, 465 U.S. 886, 104 S.Ct. 1541, 79 L.Ed.2d 891 (1984), for example, we rejected an argument that attorney's fees for nonprofit legal service organizations should be based on cost. We said: "The statute and legislative history establish that 'reasonable fees' under § 1988 are to be calculated according to the prevailing market rates in the relevant community. . . ." *Id.*, at 895, 104 S.Ct., at 1547. See also, *e.g.*, *Delaware Valley*, 483 U.S., at 732, 107 S.Ct., at 3090 (O'CONNOR, J., concurring) (controlling question concerning contingency enhancements is "how the market in a community compensates for contingency"); *Rivera*, 477 U.S., at 591, 106 S.Ct. at 2703 (REHNQUIST, J., dissenting) (reasonableness of fee must be determined "in light of both the traditional billing practices in the profession, and the funda-

---

7. The Courts of Appeals have taken a variety of positions on this issue. Most permit separate billing of paralegal time. See, *e.g.*, *Save Our Cumberland Mountains, Inc. v. Hodel*, 263 U.S. App.D.C. 409, 420, n. 7, 826 F.2d 43, 54, n. 7 (1987), vacated in part on other grounds, 273 U.S.App.D.C. 78, 857 F.2d 1516 (1988) (en banc); *Jacobs v. Mancuso*, 825 F.2d 559, 563, and n. 6 (CA1 1987) (collecting cases); *Spanish Action Committee of Chicago v. Chicago*, 811 F.2d 1129, 1138 (CA7 1987); *Ramos v. Lamm*, 713 F.2d 546, 558–559 (CA10 1983); *Richardson v. Byrd*, 709 F.2d 1016, 1023 (CA5), cert. denied *sub nom. Dallas County Commissioners Court v. Richardson*, 464 U.S. 1009, 104 S.Ct. 527, 78 L.Ed.2d 710 (1983). See also *Riverside v. Rivera*, 477 U.S. 561, 566, n. 2, 106 S.Ct. 2686, 2690, n. 2, 91 L.Ed.2d 466 (1986) (noting lower-court approval of hourly rate for law clerks). Some courts, on the other hand, have considered paralegal work "out-of-pocket expense," recoverable only at cost to the attorney. See, *e.g.*, *Northcross v. Board of Education of Memphis City Schools*, 611 F.2d 624, 639 (CA6 1979), cert. denied, 447 U.S. 911, 100 S.Ct. 3000, 64 L.Ed.2d 862 (1980); *Thornberry v. Delta Air Lines, Inc.*, 676 F.2d 1240, 1244 (CA9 1982), vacated, 461 U.S. 952, 103 S.Ct. 2421, 77 L.Ed.2d 1311 (1983). At least one Court of Appeals has refused to permit any recovery of paralegal expense apart from the attorney's hourly fee. *Abrams v. Baylor College of Medicine*, 805 F.2d 528, 535 (CA5 1986).

mental principle that the award of a 'reasonable' attorney's fee under § 1988 means a fee that would have been deemed reasonable if billed to affluent plaintiffs by their own attorneys"). A reasonable attorney's fee under § 1988 is one calculated on the basis of rates and practices prevailing in the relevant market, *i.e.*, "in line with those [rates] prevailing in the community for similar services by lawyers of reasonably comparable skill, experience, and reputation," *Blum, supra,* 465 U.S., at 896, n. 11, 104 S.Ct., at 1547, n. 11, and one that grants the successful civil rights plaintiff a "fully compensatory fee," *Hensley v. Eckerhart,* 461 U.S. 424, 435, 103 S.Ct. 1933, 1940, 76 L.Ed.2d 40 (1983), comparable to what "is traditional with attorneys compensated by a fee-paying client." S.Rep. No. 94-1011, p. 6 (1976), U.S.Code Cong. & Admin.News 1976, pp. 5908, 5913.

If an attorney's fee awarded under § 1988 is to yield the same level of compensation that would be available from the market, the "increasingly widespread custom of separately billing for the services of paralegals and law students who serve as clerks," *Ramos v. Lamm,* 713 F.2d 546, 558 (CA10 1983), must be taken into account. All else being equal, the hourly fee charged by an attorney whose rates include paralegal work in her hourly fee, or who bills separately for the work of paralegals at cost, will be higher than the hourly fee charged by an attorney competing in the same market who bills separately for the work of paralegals at "market rates." In other words, the prevailing "market rate" for attorney time is not independent of the manner in which paralegal time is accounted for.[8] Thus, if the prevailing practice in a given community were to bill paralegal time separately at market rates, fees awarded the attorney at market rates for attorney time would not be fully compensatory if the court refused to compensate hours billed by paralegals or did so only at "cost." Similarly, the fee awarded would be too high if the court accepted separate

billing for paralegal hours in a market where that was not the custom.

We reject the argument that compensation for paralegals at rates above "cost" would yield a "windfall" for the prevailing attorney. Neither petitioners nor anyone else, to our knowledge, have ever suggested that the hourly rate applied to the work of an associate attorney in a law firm creates a windfall for the firm's partners or is otherwise improper under § 1988, merely because it exceeds the cost of the attorney's services. If the fees are consistent with market rates and practices, the "windfall" argument has no more force with regard to paralegals than it does for associates. And it would hardly accord with Congress' intent to provide a "fully compensatory fee" if the prevailing plaintiff's attorney in a civil rights lawsuit were not permitted to bill separately for paralegals, while the defense attorney in the same litigation was able to take advantage of the prevailing practice and obtain market rates for such work. Yet that is precisely the result sought in this case by the State of Missouri, which appears to have paid its own outside counsel for the work of paralegals at the hourly rate of $35. Record 2696, 2699.[9]

Nothing in § 1988 requires that the work of paralegals invariably be billed separately. If it is the practice in the relevant market not to do so, or to bill the work of paralegals only at cost, that is all that § 1988 requires. Where, however, the prevailing practice is to bill paralegal work at market rates, treating civil rights lawyers' fee requests in the same way is

10. It has frequently been recognized in the lower courts that paralegals are capable of carrying out many tasks, under the supervision of an attorney, that might otherwise be performed by a lawyer and billed at a higher rate. Such work might include, for example, factual investigation, including locating and interviewing witnesses; assistance with depositions, interrogatories, and document production; compilation of statistical and financial data; checking legal citations; and drafting correspondence. Much such work lies in a gray area of tasks that might appropriately be performed either by an attorney or a paralegal. To the extent that fee applicants under § 1988 are not permitted to bill for the work of paralegals at market rates, it would not be surprising to see a greater amount of such work performed by attorneys themselves, thus increasing the overall cost of litigation. Of course, purely clerical or secretarial tasks should not be billed at a paralegal rate, regardless of who performs them. What the court in *Johnson v. Georgia Highway Express, Inc.,* 488 F.2d 714, 717 (CA5 1974), said in regard to the work of attorneys is applicable by analogy to paralegals: "It is appropriate to distinguish between legal work, in the strict sense, and investigation, clerical work, compilation of facts and statistics and other work which can often be accomplished by non-lawyers but which a lawyer may do because he has no other help available. Such non-legal work may command a lesser rate. Its dollar value is not enhanced just because a lawyer does it."

8. The attorney who bills separately for paralegal time is merely distributing her costs and profit margin among the hourly fees of other members of her staff, rather than concentrating them in the fee she sets for her own time.

9. A variant of Missouri's "windfall" argument is the following: "If paralegal expense is reimbursed at a rate many times the actual cost, will attorneys next try to bill separately—and at a profit—for such items as secretarial time, paper clips, electricity, and other expenses?" Reply Brief for Petitioners 15–16. The answer to this question is, of course, that attorneys seeking fees under § 1988 would have no basis for requesting separate compensation of such expenses unless this were the prevailing practice in the local community. The safeguard against the billing at a profit of secretarial services and paper clips is the discipline of the market.

not only permitted by § 1988, but also makes economic sense. By encouraging the use of lower-cost paralegals rather than attorneys wherever possible, permitting market-rate billing of paralegal hours "encourages costeffective delivery of legal services and, by reducing the spiraling cost of civil rights litigation, furthers the policies underlying civil rights statutes." *Cameo Convalescent Center, Inc. v. Senn,* 738 F.2d 836, 846 (CA7 1984), cert. denied, 469 U.S. 1106, 105 S.Ct. 780, 83 L.Ed. 2d 775 (1985).[10]

Such separate billing appears to be the practice in most communities today.[11] In the present case, Missouri concedes that "the local market typically bills separately for paralegal services," Tr. of Oral Arg. 14, and the District Court found that the requested hourly rates of $35 for law clerks, $40 for paralegals, and $50 for recent law graduates were the prevailing rates for such services in the Kansas City area. App. to Pet. for Cert. A29, A31, A34. Under these circumstances, the court's decision to award separate compensation at these rates was fully in accord with § 1988.

IV

The courts below correctly granted a fee enhancement to compensate for delay in payment and ap-

11. *Amicus* National Association of Legal Assistants reports that 77 percent of 1,800 legal assistants responding to a survey of the association's membership stated that their law firms charged clients for paralegal work on an hourly billing basis. Brief for National Association of Legal Assistants as *Amicus Curiae* 11.

proved compensation of paralegals and law clerks at market rates. The judgment of the Court of Appeals is therefore

Affirmed.

Questions

1. What reason did the U.S. Supreme Court provide for its conclusion that the work of paralegals should be factored into what constitutes "reasonable attorney's fees"?

2. In its decision, the Court noted that:

> By encouraging the use of lower cost paralegals rather than attorneys wherever possible, permitting market-rate billing of paralegal hours "encourages cost-effective delivery of legal services" and, by reducing the spiraling cost of civil rights litigation, furthers the policies underlying civil rights statutes."

Can you provide an argument for the position that permitting market-rate billing of paralegal hours would encourage cost-effective delivery of legal services across the board?

3. In applying § 1988, the Court determined that reasonable attorney's fees must include the work of nonlawyers. Do you agree or disagree?

ADVERTISING
AND SOLICITATION

CHAPTER OBJECTIVES

After reading this chapter, you should
be able to:

- Understand the U.S. Supreme Court's
  decisions that loosened restrictions on
  attorney advertising.

- Recognize how the attorney's rules affect
  paralegals' advertising practices.

- Appreciate the restrictions placed on
  paralegals who wish to solicit clients on
  behalf of attorneys.

N ot so long ago the idea of attorneys advertising their services to the
public was looked upon with horror. Gradually, with the U.S.
Supreme Court's recognition of attorney's First Amendment rights,
changes were made in how the legal profession marketed legal services.

Today law firms regularly market their services, identifying for the client
what they can accomplish. This may include advertising the employment and
use of nonlawyer support staff such as paralegals, by including the names of
legal assistants on the law firm's letterhead, or by giving the legal assistant
business cards to distribute.

For example, Guideline 5 of the ABA Guidelines for the Utilization of Legal
Assistant Services directs:

A lawyer may identify legal assistants by name and title on the lawyer's
letterhead and on business cards identifying the lawyer's firm. ABA Guidelines for the Utilization of Legal Assistant Services Guideline 5.

As with other ethical obligations, the rules guiding paralegal advertising
derive from the disciplinary rules regulating attorney conduct. Just as important, paralegals are often given responsibility for marketing the services of the
attorneys who employ them. For these two reasons, this chapter will first
discuss in some detail the attorney's rules regarding advertising and how
advertising differs from the related area of solicitation of clients. Finally, this
chapter will apply the attorney's rules to paralegal advertising matters.

OPENING EXERCISE

Several years ago, Nick Abromowitz left the law firm that employed him as a legal
assistant and began a freelance paralegal operation which grew quite successful.

Through word-of-mouth referrals, Nick established a wide-spread list of clients.
His success enabled him to develop more glamorous marketing techniques,
including the distribution of glossy brochures and the placement of colorful
advertisements in legal journals. Nick also had embossed business cards that read:

> **Nick Abromowitz**
> *Paralegal For Hire*
> 355-555-1897

Walking down the street one day, Nick marveled at his phenomenal success and popularity with the attorneys who hired him. Suddenly, without warning, the driver of a car traveling down the street ignored a stop sign and crashed his vehicle into another car. Nick and several other pedestrians rushed to help.

After determining that the occupants of the cars were safe, Nick produced several of his business cards and distributed them. He told all involved that they should give him a call; he knew plenty of attorneys and he would be able to refer them to a good one. By offering referrals, Nick felt he could finally repay the attorneys who had been so good to him and his practice.

Do you think Nick should be allowed to carry these business cards? Should Nick be able to carry a different kind of card? Should he be allowed to distribute the cards in this fashion? Do you feel that the brochures and colorful advertisements are proper? What other problems do you see? Read on for further discussion of this topic.

THE RULES REGARDING ADVERTISING IN THE LEGAL ENVIRONMENT

Within the legal profession, advertising—of any form—is strictly regulated. Any announcement of the attorney meant to attract the attention and business of prospective clients is subjected to strict scrutiny by attorney regulatory commissions and, potentially, by the judicial system.

Because the attorney is ultimately responsible for the conduct of any paralegal she employs, advertising done by the paralegal is also subject to inspection. Law firms often desire to advertise that they employ legal assistants, because they want prospective clients to see that they provide the most economical services available. The firms include paralegal names on letterheads and allow paralegals to distribute business cards. Moreover, the "advertising" of attorney services handled by the paralegal must likewise conform to the requirements set forth for the regulation of attorney conduct. Presenting misleading information or going beyond merely advertising legal services—and, for example, engaging in in-person solicitation of clients—can have dire consequences. Understanding the advertising rules can certainly help the paralegal avoid serious problems.

Attorney Advertising Practice of attorneys announcing firm services in order to attract potential clients.

Generally, the rules governing **attorney advertising** prohibit any communication that is false or misleading. Any further prohibition on advertising has been found to violate the free speech rights of members of the legal community. See, for example, *In re R. M. J.*, 455 U.S. 191 102 S.Ct. 929, 71 L.Ed. 2d 64 (1982); *Bates v. State Bar of Arizona*, 433 U.S. 350, 97 S.Ct. 269, 53 L.Ed. 2d 810 (1977), both discussed below. This rule is perhaps best summarized in the position taken by the drafters of the American Bar Association's *Model Rules of Professional Conduct:*

RULE 7.1 Communications Concerning a Lawyer's Services

A lawyer shall not make a false or misleading communication about the lawyer or the lawyer's services. A communication is false or misleading if it:

(a) contains a material misrepresentation of fact or law, or omits a fact necessary to make the statement considered as a whole not materially misleading;

(b) is likely to create an unjustified expectation about results the lawyer can achieve, or states or implies that the lawyer can achieve results by means that violate the rules of professional conduct or other law; or

(c) compares the lawyer's services with other lawyers' services, unless the comparison can be factually substantiated. *Model Rules of Professional Conduct* Rule 7.1 (1994).

The ABA's *Model Code* provides a more specific rule that was drafted at a time when attorney advertising was frowned upon. While the *Code* prohibits "any form of public communication containing a false, fraudulent, misleading, deceptive, self-laudatory or unfair statement or claim," the *Model Code* limits the information that can be provided in any attorney's advertisement, with the caveat that it must be presented in a "dignified manner." See *Model Code of Professional Responsibility* DR 2-101 (1986). Therefore, a television commercial advertising the services of a personal injury attorney who dresses as Batman, leaps over an ambulance in a single bound, and rushes into a hospital to rescue a potential client from the evils of medical malpractice may be considered to be a violation of the *Code*, as the attorney is not portrayed in a dignified manner.

The organized bar was reluctant to permit attorneys to advertise. It was feared that clients would be unduly coerced at a time when those clients were particularly vulnerable. (See "Historical Restrictions on the Law Office," this chapter.) However, over time, courts have weakened the restrictions placed on attorney advertising, recognizing that, if any harm were to result, the harm caused by a generic advertisement would most likely be minimal.

Solicitation The act of approaching or enticing persons whom one seeks to have as clients, in a direct manner, in order to secure their business.

Yet advertisements have been found to be quite different from the "in-person" solicitation of clients. **Solicitation** is generally considered more dangerous and is much more heavily regulated. This is because there is a greater possibility that the lawyer will take advantage of the prospective client.

Advertising has as its purpose the attraction of potential clients. Solicitation, on the other hand, is considered to be seeking out the representation of clients in a direct, personal manner. Solicitation involves appearing before a prospective client (or contacting her by telephone) and recommending the services of an attorney. Then the attorney asks the individual to retain her services. The solicitation often occurs at an accident scene or in a hospital. Therefore, solicitation may be more commonly known as "ambulance chasing."

> ### ▮HIGHLIGHT   How Do Lawyers Advertise?
>
> ■ Distribute **brochures** describing the law firm and the services it can provide.
>
> ■ Prepare **newsletters** for distribution to the legal community describing legal victories the law firm has recently accomplished and indicating recent developments in the law that may affect the law firm's clientele.
>
> ■ List the law firm's name in the local **telephone directories.**
>
> ■ List the law firm and describe its services in a **legal directory.**
>
> ■ Place **print advertisements** in law journals or newspapers describing the services the law firm can provide, usually targeting a particular client group.
>
> ■ Broadcast advertisements on local **radio** or **television** stations.
>
> **REMEMBER:** No matter how a lawyer chooses to advertise, the advertisement must not prove misleading!

A separate agenda of guidelines therefore exists to address solicitation. With regard to this problem, the ABA's *Model Rules of Professional Conduct* read in part as follows:

RULE 7.3 Direct Contact With Prospective Clients
(a) A lawyer shall not by in-person or live telephone contact solicit professional employment from a prospective client with whom the lawyer has no family or prior professional relationship when a significant motive for the lawyer's doing so is the lawyer's pecuniary gain.
(b) A lawyer shall not solicit professional employment from a prospective client by written or recorded communication or by in-person or telephone contact even when not otherwise prohibited by paragraph (a), if:
   (1) the prospective client has made known to the lawyer a desire not to be solicited by the lawyer; or
   (2) the solicitation involves coercion, duress or harassment. *Model Rules of Professional Conduct* Rule 7.3 (1994).

In other words, "ambulance chasing" is not allowed.

This chapter will trace the emergence of attorney advertising, a previously forbidden activity. You will see that states are allowed to regulate attorney advertising, to prevent such advertising from misleading or deceiving the public. However, all regulation must be *reasonable;* unreasonable restrictions on nondeceptive advertising will be struck down.

HISTORICAL RESTRICTIONS ON THE LAW OFFICE

Until fairly recently, attorneys were not allowed to reach out to prospective clients through advertising. Those few lawyers who dared attempt to inform prospective clients of the availability of legal services or the cost of legal services, whether through the use of newspaper listings or through mailings, were routinely and summarily disciplined.

Some courts and commentators felt it was a matter of "etiquette" for attorneys to refrain from advertising. Others felt that any form of advertising brought a certain disrespect to the noble ranks of the legal profession. Still others felt attorney advertising would pose a significant risk of "overreaching" or coercing individuals who were in a position of desperately needing legal services to protect their rights.

In chapter 1 we talked about the increasing use of paralegals as a means of making low-cost legal services available to a greater portion of society. Before attorney advertising was allowed, one attorney from New York, seeking an injunction against enforcement of advertising bans, argued that prohibiting advertising resulted in an inability of attorneys to get sufficient repetitive legal business, handling routine matters. Without this repeat business, paralegals could not be employed efficiently, since paralegals handle standardized tasks. Presumably, the inability to hire paralegals would keep the cost of consumption of legal services too high for the average consumer. The court was not persuaded by the attorney's argument. See *Person v. Association of the Bar of the City of New York,* 414 F.Supp. 133, 135 (E.D.N.Y. 1975).

For many years, therefore, attorneys did not advertise. However, courts gradually accepted the idea that advertising could help consumers make choices as to where they could go to protect their legal rights. By making available to the public such information as the availability of legal services and an estimation of the cost of the services, more of the American public would become aware of affordable access to the court system.

EXERCISE 8.1 | Are the justifications advanced for banning all advertising in the legal profession valid? Consider the historically unmet need for legal services. Read on for a discussion of how the Supreme Court addressed the question.

THE RELAXATION OF ADVERTISING RESTRICTIONS

In the 1970s the discontent of the legal profession and the public with an overall ban on advertising grew ever more apparent. Soon the U.S. Supreme Court began to heed this sentiment.

Bates v. State Bar of Arizona

In 1977 the U.S. Supreme Court decided *Bates v. State Bar of Arizona,* 433 U.S. 350, 97 S.Ct. 2691, 53 L.Ed.2d 810 (1977). *Bates* was the first opinion to allow advertising by attorneys of routine legal services to the public; it was premised upon the notion that First Amendment rights of free speech would be violated by holding otherwise.

John Bates and Van O'Steen were attorneys licensed in the state of Arizona. The disciplinary rules of that state placed a blanket prohibition on advertising by attorneys, disallowing advertising in newspapers, magazines, in telephone directories, or through radio or television announcements.

The attorneys operated a legal clinic in Arizona that sought to provide affordable legal services to individuals of modest means. Relying on extensive use of paralegals and standardized office procedures, the clinic only accepted routine cases for which costs could be kept low. The nature of their business was such that they depended upon having a relatively substantial volume of clients traveling through their doors. To achieve this end, they determined it would be necessary to place an advertisement in one of the daily newspapers.

The advertisement placed set forth the kinds of cases that could be accepted and the fees for such routine services.

Under the disciplinary rules of Arizona, the attorneys were disciplined. The attorneys appealed this decision, eventually reaching the U.S. Supreme Court. The issue before the Court was narrow; the Court answered only the question of whether attorneys could constitutionally advertise the *price charged* for handling routine legal services. It specifically reserved questions of whether an attorney can tout the quality of his services or whether an attorney and his agents may solicit clients in person or face-to-face.

The Court said that advertising prices of legal services was protected by the First Amendment's guarantees of free speech. As long as the information contained in the advertisement was not misleading or deceptive in any manner, the state could not prohibit it. However, the state could place reasonable restrictions on advertising as to the "time, place and manner" of advertising and the state may regulate advertising so as to ensure that the advertisement is not false or misleading.

In reaching this conclusion, the Court addressed many key arguments that historically had been advanced to justify a prohibition of advertising. First, the Court found that there would be no adverse effect on the legal profession should advertising be allowed. Although advertising opponents argued that "price advertising will bring about commercialization, which will undermine the attorney's sense of dignity and self-worth," the Court believed otherwise.

> In fact, it has been suggested that the failure of lawyers to advertise creates public disillusionment with the profession. The absence of advertising may be seen to reflect the profession's failure to reach out and serve the community: Studies reveal that many persons do not obtain counsel even when they perceive a need because of the feared price of services or because of an inability to locate a competent attorney. *Bates*, 433 U.S. at 370, 97 S.Ct. at 2702. (Footnotes omitted.)

Second, the Court concluded that attorney advertising was not inherently misleading. Legal services are not, in themselves, so unique to each individual as to prevent advertising to the public. Further, while legal services are not fungible, as long as the attorney does the work at the advertised price, the advertisement cannot be misleading. Additionally, because the client can determine generally the kind of service needed, the advertisement will not be misleading.

The Court also found that advertising by attorneys would not improperly serve to encourage litigation and thereby to muddle the administration of justice by making the courts too crowded and by "unsettling" society. "Although advertising might increase the use of the judicial machinery, we cannot accept the notion that it is always better for a person to suffer a wrong silently than to redress it by legal action." *Bates*, 433 U.S. at 376, 97 S.Ct. at 2705. Rather, the Court acknowledged that the rule banning advertisement has the effect of hindering the attorney in fulfilling his or her obligation to assist in making legal services available to the public. The Court rejected the argument that more litigation is necessarily bad, simply accepting that there would be more litigation.

The Court found that advertising would quite likely have the effect of reducing the cost of legal services to the public through creating something akin to price competition. Further, relying on the integrity of the majority of the legal profession, the Court found that advertising would not affect the quality of legal services given nor would it create unreasonable difficulties in policing the profession.

EXERCISE 8.2 | Obtain a copy of *Bates* and read it carefully. Do you agree with the justifications advanced by the Supreme Court? Should attorneys be allowed to advertise?

Attorney Advertising After *Bates*

Bates spawned additional challenges to the advertising rules. With each challenge, regulation became less rigid.

In *In re R. M. J.*, 455 U.S. 191, 102 S.Ct. 929, 71 L.Ed.2d 64 (1982), the U.S. Supreme Court again upheld the exercise of the free speech rights of an attorney who attempted to advertise his services. *In re R. M. J.* served to define the requirements of *Bates* by examining a disciplinary rule enacted in response to this opinion. While *Bates* had come to stand for the proposition that states could regulate attorney advertising to prevent the public from being misled, it had also been made clear that state regulation must be no more extensive than necessary to prevent deception. In essence, the *In re R. M. J.* Court held that the disciplinary rule at issue in *In re R. M. J.* was considered overbroad.

Relying upon *Bates,* the state of Missouri had placed certain restrictions on advertising in an effort to regulate the practice. One of the state's advertising restrictions required that attorneys use only certain terms in their advertisement to describe their practice. R. M. J.'s advertisement had used terms which were not included in this list. For instance, he described his practice in terms of "real estate" when the disciplinary rule required use of the term "property law."

While affirming its earlier holding in *Bates* that the states may place *reasonable* restrictions on advertising, the court held that Missouri's restrictions did not serve to prevent deception of the public. The Court therefore struck down the requirements set forth in Missouri's disciplinary rule.

The Court also ruled that there was nothing inherently misleading in listing in the advertisement the jurisdictions in which one is licensed to practice. It therefore allowed this part of the advertisement to stand, despite the fact that the state disciplinary rule did not allow such wording in advertisements.

The next significant step in relaxing advertising restrictions came in *Zauderer v. Office of Disciplinary Counsel of Supreme Court of Ohio,* 471 U.S. 626, 105 S.Ct. 2265, 85 L.Ed.2d 652 (1985). The Court decreed that advertising geared to specific individuals with specific legal problems, offering legal advice to these individuals, could not be banned if it was not misleading. The Court further held that the state could not prohibit the use of a nondeceptive drawing in an attorney's advertisement.

Zauderer had placed several advertisements, one of which publicized his willingness to help women suffering from injuries caused by an intrauterine device known as the Dalkon Shield. Among other things, this advertisement featured a line drawing of the intrauterine device, and stated that the Dalkon Shield had generated a large amount of lawsuits. Ultimately, the advertisement earned Zauderer 106 clients.

The Court disagreed with arguments that advertising free legal advice was no different than face-to-face solicitation. An advertisement that offered free legal advice within its text to potential clients was "not likely to involve pressure on the potential client for an immediate yes-or-no answer to the offer of representation" as was in-person solicitation. Therefore, advertisements that offer legal advice could not be prohibited. The Court also addressed Ohio's prohibition of drawings in attorney advertisements. Expressly noting that preserving the dignity of the legal profession is not a sufficient justification for banning all nondeceptive illustrations, the Court held that accurate illustrations in drawings could not be prohibited.

However, the Court did allow some discipline of Zauderer to stand. A portion of Zauderer's advertisement read: "If there is no recovery, no legal fees are owed by our clients." Because clients would still be liable for court costs and because the ordinary layman would not understand the difference between "fees" and "costs," the Court found the ad deceptive.

Shapero v. Kentucky Bar Association, 486 U.S. 466, 108 S.Ct. 1916, 100 L.Ed.2d 475 (1988), involved the issue of whether attorneys could constitutionally engage in direct mailings of advertisements, targeted toward potential clients. As long as the letter was not deceptive, the Court held that state regulations could not ban it. **Direct mail,** although addressed to a specific person, is not face-to-face solicitation; rather, it is advertising.

Relying on its reasoning in these previous cases, the U.S. Supreme Court also addressed the issue of what constitutionally may be included in an attorney's **letterhead.** In *Peel v. Attorney Registration and Disciplinary Commission of Illinois*, 496 U.S. 91, 110 S.Ct. 2281, 110 L.Ed.2d 83 (1990), the Court overturned the Illinois Supreme Court and allowed attorney Peel to place in his letterhead, "Certified Civil Trial Specialist-By the National Board of Trial Advocacy." Because this statement was found not to be inherently misleading, the state could not constitutionally ban Peel's actions.

> We may assume that statements of "certification" as a "specialist," even though truthful, may not be understood fully by some readers. However, such statements pose no greater potential of misleading consumers than advertising admission to "Practice before: The United States Supreme Court," *In re R. M. J.,* 455 U.S. 191, 102 S.Ct. 929, 71 L.Ed.2d 64 (1982) of exploiting the audience of a targeted letter, *Shapero v. Kentucky Bar Assn.,* 486 U.S. 466, 108 S.Ct. 1916, 100 L.Ed.2d 475 (1988), or of confusing a reader with an accurate illustration, *Zauderer v. Office of Disciplinary Counsel of Supreme Court of Ohio,* 471 U.S. 626, 105 S.Ct. 2265, 85 L.Ed.2d 652 (1985). In this case, as in those, we conclude that the particular state rule restricting lawyers' advertising is " 'broader than reasonably necessary to prevent the' perceived evil." *Peel,* 496 U.S. 91, 110 S.Ct. at 107, 110 L.Ed.2d 83 (Citations and footnote omitted.)

During this period of weakening advertising restrictions, the Supreme Court also addressed the propriety of attorney solicitation. Because of greater concern over attorneys overreaching clients and unduly influencing the public, the Court has held that the state can subject in-person solicitation of clients to greater regulation.

Ohralik v. Ohio State Bar, 436 U.S. 447, 98 S.Ct. 1912, 56 L.Ed.2d 444 (1978), addressed an attorney's actions attempting to get two young women to retain

Direct Mail A mailing addressed to a specific person and targeted for particular clients.

Letterhead Legal stationery with a printed heading. Generally letterhead indicates the law firm partner names by named partner, other partners, and associates.

his services. Ohralik discovered the two women had been in an accident. Being somewhat acquainted with one of these women, he called her home and discovered she was in the hospital. He asked the woman's parents to retain his services but they responded that the choice of an attorney was her decision. He then went to the hospital to visit the woman. Eventually, Ohralik obtained the woman's consent to hire him. He also obtained the name of the other woman involved in the accident.

He proceeded to visit the other young lady and managed to obtain her oral consent to his representation. Later her mother tried to repudiate this consent. Ohralik continued to press both the mother and the accident victim. Eventually his actions were brought to the attention of the bar.

In discussing whether this activity could be constitutionally banned, the Court noted, "[t]he substantive evils of solicitation have been stated over the years in sweeping terms: stirring up litigation, assertion of fraudulent claims, debasing the legal profession, and potential harm to the solicited client in the form of overreaching, overcharging, underrepresentation, and misrepresentation." *Ohralik*, 98 S.Ct. at 1921. The Court concluded that, in protecting the public, the state had a legitimate and compelling interest and could ban solicitation.

However, in a comparison case, the Court held that a nonprofit organization, proposing litigation as a means of political expression, could solicit clients. In *In re Primus*, 436 U.S. 412, 98 S.Ct. 1893, 56 L.Ed.2d 417 (1978), a lawyer from the American Civil Liberties Union, seeking to persuade a woman to file a lawsuit to redress a violation of her rights after the state had forced her to be sterilized, had done nothing worthy of discipline, and it would be unconstitutional for the state to discipline her.

So widespread has the development of attorney advertising become that the American Bar Association has set up a special Commission on Advertising to serve as a clearinghouse and information resource center concerning what and how an attorney can advertise.

You should re-read the discussion of the *Bates* decision, noting the factors addressed by the Court in determining that advertising would not harm the public or the profession. Likewise, note that many of the same concerns were mentioned in *Ohralik* to justify a ban on solicitation. Do you see the distinction drawn between advertising and solicitation? Isn't advertising a kind of solicitation? Should a distinction be drawn? Should attorneys be allowed to advertise? To solicit clients?

Why do you think the Court distinguished between the activities of nonprofit organizations seeking litigation as a means of political expression and the activity of a private attorney, Ohralik? Obtain copies of *Primus* and *Ohralik*, companion cases decided on the same day. What distinctions are drawn? Are they valid to you?

EXERCISE 8.3

Brett Smith was something of an upstart within the legal profession. Licensed to practice law in the state of Columbia (which had adopted the *Model Rules of Professional Conduct*), Brett was thrilled by the relaxation of advertising restrictions. He decided to start exercising his free speech rights.

He quickly set about letting his community know about his law firm. He began by placing an advertisement in the local newspaper that read:

Involved in an Accident?
Don't know where to turn??
LEGAL SERVICES CHEAP!!
If we don't win your case, you pay us no fee.
Call **Brett Smith & Associates!** We can get desired results!
Hundreds of happy customers.

Brett then printed this advertisement on several hundred sheets of colored paper. He mailed the first 150 announcements to names he randomly chose from the phone book. He carried the remainder down to the grocery store and distributed the announcements to all shoppers as they exited the store.

Howard Lightfeather was one of those shoppers handed a flyer as he left the store with his grocery cart. Approaching his car, he noticed that the vehicle had been severely damaged while he had been in the store. It looked as if someone had hit it with a shopping cart. He returned to Brett and said, "You must be Brett Smith. It looks like I've been involved in an accident and I'd like to retain your services."

Carefully re-read Brett's advertisement. Analyze whether the advertisement would be proper, based on the Supreme Court's decisions.

The state of Columbia has adopted the *Model Rules.* Is anything wrong with the ad under these disciplinary requirements? Suppose the state of *Columbia* had adopted the *Model Code.* Would the advertisement be approved?

Would you change the advertisement? How?

Has Brett engaged in solicitation? Would it be improper for Brett to accept Howard Lightfeather's case? Why or why not?

RESTRICTIONS ON THE PARALEGAL

We have just seen how significantly the Supreme Court has relaxed the restrictions on attorney advertising. Likewise, restrictions on paralegal advertising have weakened. This change is often justified by using the same rationales advanced by the Supreme Court in its landmark advertising decisions.

There is generally no need for the paralegal to reach out directly to the public. Therefore, there is generally no need for the paralegal to advertise his services to the public. However, lawyers often want clients to see that they have adopted the cost-effective practice of hiring paralegals and, for that reason, lawyers may want to advertise that they employ legal assistants. Therefore, concerns such as what information can be placed on law firm letterhead or on business cards may be relevant.

It is also important to note that more and more attorneys are turning over to paralegals the responsibility of placing advertisements. Whether this advertisement is in the form of a listing in a telephone directory, an advertisement in a bar association journal, or development of a brochure for distribution to clients, the paralegal must heed the requirements as set forth by *Bates* and its progeny. In essence, the paralegal must take care not to mislead.

As we have noted throughout the text, with increasing frequency paralegals are working in a freelance capacity, developing their own independent firms. These firms market their services directly to lawyers. Paralegals also may desire, when they are looking for new jobs, to advertise their availability to potential employers. Special advertising concerns attach to this practice.

PARALEGALS IN THE SPOTLIGHT

Beginning with the 1992 edition, the *Martindale-Hubbell Law Directory* allows law firms to list paralegals and their biographies in the law firm listing.

For each jurisdiction in the county, *Marindale-Hubbell* directories provide a list of law firms. The listings traditionally indicate the law firm's name, address and telephone number and the areas of law in which the firm's practice is concentrated. Historically, a *Martindale-Hubbell* listing also includes a short professional biography for each attorney working in the firm. Now those listings may include biographies of the paralegals the firms hire.

Martindale-Hubbell believes that, as clients become more concerned with the cost-effectiveness of legal services, they will be concerned with how the law firm delivers those services. They will be concerned with whether the firm hires paralegals, whose services can reduce the cost of the representation. As legal assistants become more widely utilized, clients will also want to know the backgrounds of the support staff as a way to evaluate the reputation of the firm and the quality of the service it can provide.

At this point, only legal assistants employed by the law firm may be listed. Whether the law firm decides to include the paralegals' biographies is a decision for each individual firm. Independent legal assistants may not be included in listings in *Martindale-Hubbell*, although they may place an advertisement describing the services they can provide.

Source: See *Martindale-Hubbell Includes Paralegal Listings*, LEGAL ASSISTANT TODAY, Mar.-Apr. 1992. Copyright 1994. James Publishing, Inc. Reprinted with permission from *Legal Assistant Today*. For subscription information, call (714) 755-5450.

Martindale-Hubbell Law Directory
Listing of law firms located in each jurisdiction of the country.

What of the nonlawyer who is asked to solicit clients on behalf of her attorney-employer or who simply decides to take such action of her own accord?

All of these concerns are addressed more fully below.

PARALEGALS HANDLING ATTORNEY ADVERTISING

As restrictions on advertising relaxed, attorneys and law firms began implementing various marketing techniques in an effort to inform prospective clients about the services they can provide. Some firms have even developed their own marketing departments. Others hire outside marketing consultants to help them develop colorful, informative, and attractive brochures.

With increasing frequency, paralegals are asked to assume the responsibility of attracting new clients. What happens if the legal assistant makes a mistake in the ad?

Such a situation occurred in Missouri where a legal assistant's mistake ultimately contributed to his employing attorney's suspension. *In the Matter of Kinghorn* recounted the activities of a legal assistant, Donald Erickson, and how they affected his attorney-employer, Edmond Kinghorn. 764 S.W.2d 939 (Mo. banc 1989). Kinghorn's law firm placed listings in the St. Louis yellow pages, once under the heading "Attorney Referral and Information Service" and once under "Attorneys." Unfortunately, Kinghorn's law firm was not in the business of giving any referrals and, therefore, the listing under the former heading was incorrect.

During testimony at a disciplinary hearing, it was revealed that Erickson, Kinghorn's paralegal, had placed the advertisement under the "Attorney Referral" heading. Further, Erickson had signed the order for the advertisements that were sent to the publisher of the telephone directory.

The Court found that this listing was a misleading communication violative of the state's ethics rules. While the Court recognized that the attorney had not placed the ad and could not erase it from the yellow pages, the attorney was obliged to take affirmative steps to prevent callers responding to that ad from being misled. This Kinghorn did not do.

The attorney was also found guilty of charging and collecting an excess fee and for failing to make a timely refund when legal services were terminated. All the violations together led the court to suspend the attorney for an indefinite period, with leave to petition the court for reinstatement after a year.

A legal assistant given any responsibility to handle advertising matters should undertake the task with care. Above all else, the legal assistant must take care to avoid misleading the public as to the services the attorney can provide and the results that attorney can achieve.

PARALEGALS ON LAW FIRM LETTERHEAD

Placing legal assistant names on letterhead is often a desired option for the law firm that relies heavily on the high quality of the nonlawyer's work product. It is a way to publicly acknowledge the services provided by that individual. It also shows its clients that the firm utilizes the services of legal assistants and thereby provides the most economical legal services possible.

Many states have addressed this issue and most agree that paralegal names may be included on the law firm's letterhead. The caveat to this rule is that the paralegal's title must clearly appear as part of the letterhead listing so as not to mislead the public into believing that the paralegal is an attorney capable of providing legal services to the public. You may want to check what the practice is in your state.

The states have usually justified this rule on *Bates* and its progeny. As long as the letterhead itself does not convey information designed to mislead its readers, states have been forbidden the opportunity to further restrict the listing.

ABA Informal Opinion 89-1527 withdraws previous ABA opinions that had prohibited such a listing on the letterhead. Allowing nonlawyer names to be included on law firm letterhead was recognized to follow from the Supreme Court's decision that communication that is not misleading cannot be prohibited. Therefore, as long as the title of the paralegal clearly appears so that the public is not misled into believing that the legal assistant is an attorney, the name of the legal assistant may appear on the letterhead.

Natasha Schmirtov is a legal assistant employed with a solo practitioner, Ferguson McDonough. Recently her employer has agreed to list her name on the law firm's letterhead. Design the letterhead for the firm, making sure you adhere to the rules discussed above.

EXERCISE 8.4

PARALEGALS AND BUSINESS CARDS

Many paralegals have significant contact with the public—through firm clients, court personnel, potential witnesses, or agency employees. Like any professional, paralegals have found the need to carry with them some form of identification to assist them in carrying out the responsibilities assigned to them by the lawyer.

Business Cards A commonly accepted form of identification that indicates the person's name, occupation, business address, and business phone number.

A number of states have addressed the question of whether the nonlawyer employee of a law firm should be allowed to carry **business cards** to be distributed to members of the public. After *Bates,* most states have responded affirmatively to this question and allow the legal assistant to carry and distribute business cards. (It is important to note, however, that some states, such as Iowa, still refuse to allow paralegals to carry business cards.)

In most states, as in the matter of letterheads, the title of the legal assistant must appear on the business card so as to prevent those who receive the card from being misled into believing that the nonlawyer is actually an attorney capable of providing legal services. Because business cards often get passed along to other parties, this becomes especially important. The foundation for this rule is often, again, the *Bates* line of cases.

Many states further regulate the information appearing on the business card, requiring the name of the law firm that employs the paralegal to appear on the card. Ostensibly, this rule is to further prevent the legal assistant from being mistaken for an attorney.

PARALEGAL ADVERTISEMENT

Because paralegals, by definition, work under the direction of an attorney, they do not provide services directly to the public. (See chapter 3, "The Unauthorized Practice of Law.") There exists, therefore, a general prohibition on legal assistants advertising legal services directly to the public. The states, presumably, may regulate and restrict such speech, having a substantial government interest in protecting the public. However, it will be interesting to note how advertising legal services to the public by legal technicians will be handled should one of the many limited licensure laws recently presented in state legislatures ever be adopted.

Legal assistants may seek to advertise their services to *attorneys,* however, because attorneys are the consumers of paralegal services. They may wish to do this for two reasons. First, when looking for a job, the paralegal may wish to place "seeking jobs" advertisements. For example, if the attorney for whom Peggy Paralegal worked decides to retire, she may embark on a job search, looking for a new law firm that could use her services. Peggy may decide to place an ad in a law-related journal to notify prospective employers that she is available.

Second, freelance paralegals may want to advertise their services to attorneys. Because the freelancer is not employed by any one attorney in particular, the need to get out the word that she has certain valuable skills to provide to attorneys is especially acute.

This kind of advertising would presumably, not be governed by the attorney's code of ethics because the legal assistant is not undertaking this activity on behalf of a client under the direction of a lawyer. There is no client, in this instance, to protect. However, the paralegal should take care to never present a misleading advertisement. Not only would such conduct be *morally* inappropriate, but to do so would only damage the paralegal's reputation in a legal culture in which honest communication is important.

Advertising to attorneys may take any number of forms. Most commonly, legal assistants advertise in newspapers or trade journals or place listings in telephone directories. Ideally, the legal assistant should provide her qualifications within the advertisement to assist her consumer, the attorney, in assessing the reliability of her work product. Again, whatever the advertisement says, the legal assistant should take care to avoid including misleading information.

Chapter 3, "The Unauthorized Practice of Law," discussed the issue of paralegals offering their services directly to the public by providing typing services or assembling do-it-yourself kits. Remember that where the service to be provided by the paralegal is *legal* in nature, the legal assistant cannot offer it directly to the public. However, services that do not involve offering legal advice *can* be offered directly to the public by the legal assistant. Therefore, the paralegal may offer such things as typing services or other kinds of routine services that do not involve the practice of law. Where the paralegal engages in such a business, it may be desirable to advertise to the public.

The free speech concerns implicated by *Bates* and the cases in its wake would presumably be at issue in such a situation. In essence, the legal assistant has a First Amendment right to speak out about the services she can provide to the public. The paralegal must make clear, however, that he is a nonlawyer so as to avoid confusion and so as to provide effective communication. The legal assistant also must notify the potential client that no legal services can be provided. In essence, the paralegal must avoid deceptive advertising practices.

In re Bachmann, 113 B.R. 769 (Bkrtcy. S.D. Fla. 1990), discussed advertising considerations. As you will recall from chapter 3, Bachmann was engaged in providing what he called a "typical service." He assisted laypersons in completing bankruptcy forms. It was necessary, therefore, for Bachmann to distribute business cards identifying the services he could provide to the lay public.

Bachmann held that the freelance paralegal is forbidden to use the term "paralegal" on a business card to be distributed to the public. Presumably, "paralegal" indicates that one is capable of providing legal services under the direction of an attorney. The nonlawyer may place on business cards, however, that he is capable of providing non-legal services, such as secretarial, typing, or notary services.

Likewise, advertisements of the legal assistant placed in newspapers may not offer legal services or legal advice to the public. However, *Bachmann* held that freelance paralegals may advertise the availability of pre-prepared legal forms and general information that corresponds to those forms.

Obtain a copy of a local law journal that accepts advertisements for employment. Do you find any advertisements of paralegals? Look for advertisements which indicate that a paralegal is seeking employment with a law firm or corporate legal department. How specific is the advertisement? Does the advertisement appear misleading to you? Can you find an advertisement of an independent paralegal firm? How would you evaluate that advertisement? | **EXERCISE 8.5**

PARALEGAL SOLICITATION

Generally the legal profession is greatly concerned with the problem of solicitation of clients. Particularly relevant is the problem of lay employees of an attorney requesting accident victims to hire a certain attorney (usually his employer) to represent them in litigation. This action is almost uniformly disfavored by the courts.

As shown earlier, *Ohralik* disallowed attorney solicitation of clients. The holding rested on the basic foundation that in-person solicitation presented certain dangers to the public. After an accident, when victims or their survivors are shaken up or otherwise hurt, they are particularly vulnerable to overreaching or coercion to accept representation of an attorney. In reaching this holding, the *Ohralik* court stated, ". . . solicitation by a lawyer's agents or **runners** would present similar problems" of overreaching and undue coercion.

Runners One who solicits business for an attorney from accident victims.

The disciplinary rules also make plain that attorneys should make sure that nonlawyer employees' conduct is compatible with the attorneys' rules of professional conduct. See *Model Rules of Professional Conduct* Rule 5.3 (1994). Since attorneys are forbidden to solicit clients, so should be their lay employees. See Model Rule 8.4. (However, nonlawyer employees are allowed to refer friends and acquaintances to their attorney where they are not asked to do so by the supervising attorney and where they receive no compensation for the referral. See chapter 7.)

Discussion of a sample situation may help make this problem clearer. We thus turn to the facts presented in *Kitsis v. State Bar of California*, 23 Cal.3d 857, 153 Cal.Rptr. 836, 592 P.2d 323 (1979). For a period of three years, an attorney, Kitsis, employed three laypersons to solicit employment for him. One of his employees was a woman by the name of April Turner. Ms. Turner was in possession of a radio which was tuned to such a frequency that she could listen to police dispatch messages. Upon hearing of an accident, Turner would drive to the accident scene and recommend the services of Kitsis. This was done on more than 200 occasions and resulted in as many as 150 clients retaining Kitsis's services.

Turner also visited auto body repair shops and informed the owner and the manager that Kitsis would pay them $50 for each client they referred to him. When the manager of one auto body repair shop referred one couple to Kitsis, he was paid the agreed-upon $50.

Turner would also visit hospital rooms and offer the services of Kitsis to the patient. After seeing some newspaper accounts of patients being solicited at hospitals, Turner inquired of Kitsis if what she was doing was illegal. Kitsis replied that her actions were merely unethical but not illegal. Kitsis's actions

FOCUS ON LUCY EBERSOHL

Lucy Ebersohl has been a paralegal for more than eighteen years and is currently employed at The Stolar Partnership in St. Louis, Missouri, where she supervises other paralegals in litigation. Throughout her paralegal career, Ebersohl has been very active in paralegal associations, including NALA and SLALA (St. Louis Association of Legal Assistants), working for recognition of the role of the legal assistant. She received her NALA certification in 1982 (making her a certified legal assistant) and has recently completed a year serving as the NALA ethics committee chairperson for 1992–1993, where she assists in handling ethics problems current NALA members are confronting. She is also a member of NALA's Committee on Professional Development, a committee position she has held for a number of years.

"It is important for paralegals' names to appear on law firm letterheads and for paralegals to be allowed to carry business cards," Ebersohl acknowledges. Of course, care must be taken to avoid setting forth any misleading communication by plainly identifying the nonlawyer as a paralegal or legal assistant.

Business cards for paralegals is an idea in which Ebersohl wholeheartedly believes. The firm for which she works prints business cards for the paralegals they employ. Ebersohl's card clearly identifies her as a legal assistant and contains the "CLA" designation, although in every other respect the paralegals' business cards are patterned after the cards of the attorney.

The concept of carrying business cards was in place at The Stolar Partnership when Ebersohl began working there several years ago. She finds that the cards prove very useful. "My business card identifies me when I need to interview a witness or when I am speaking with other paralegals," Ebersohl

> **It is so important for paralegal names to appear on law firm letterhead and for paralegals to be allowed to carry business cards. It allows witnesses and clients to get back in touch with an identifiable party.**

advises. "It also helps to have something which I can give to witnesses and clients which identifies the name of a person with whom they can get back in touch, without calling the attorney, to check on the current status of their cases." However, at Ebersohl's first job as a paralegal, her employer did not supply its paralegals with business cards. Lucy eventually requested a business card, but her request was granted after the firm checked into the idea and learned that it would not be an ethical violation.

Today she notes most legal assistants carry business cards (except, she notes, in Iowa, where paralegal business cards are not allowed). If a paralegal feels that carrying and distributing a business card would be helpful to her work, Ebersohl advises that she should discuss the matter over with her supervising attorney and ask that she be provided with a business card. (Note, however, that the card should clearly identify the paralegal's status so as to avoid misleading any parties.)

Because the management of The Stolar Partnership recognized the importance and professionalism signified by a legal assistant's name appearing on the letterhead, it adopted the policy to include the name and job title of the legal assistant on its stationery. It is the firm's and Lucy's belief that it identifies the author of the letter and gives a professional appearance to any correspondence which the legal assistant sends out on behalf of the law firm.

Ebersohl also notes that she is not aware of any legal assistants being asked to solicit clients for their employing attorneys. It is believed all-around that this is just a sleazy, unethical practice.

Quickly reviewing Ebersohl's biography, you can readily perceive that she is an expert on the ethical responsibilities of legal assistants and other nonlawyer employees of the law office. Her advice should be well-noted.

were eventually brought to the attention of the state bar and, because of the egregious nature of his conduct, Kitsis was disbarred. Turner, the nonlawyer, lost her employer, her job, and therefore her income.

Numerous courts have similarly expressed their repugnance for this sort of conduct. However, while this conduct is unethical, pursuant to the attorneys' Code of Ethics, approaching an individual and making a recommendation is not per se illegal for the layperson. Therefore, in addressing these matters, the courts usually confine their discipline to the attorneys. As *Kitsis* has shown, such disciplinary procedures have even led to disbarment, in egregious cases. "Punishment" meted out to the nonlawyer employee is not discussed and, presumably, none would be provided by the disciplinary agency.

However, whenever an attorney-employer is restricted from practicing law, whether she is suspended or disbarred, the nonlawyer employee is likewise injured, as the paralegal's livelihood is stripped away. Moreover, after having been found to have engaged in unethical conduct, the nonlawyer may find it difficult to find another employer who will take a chance on hiring him.

The freelance paralegal who recommends an attorney faces no similar reprisals. May a freelance paralegal, then, recommend the services of an attorney? The legal assistant may give a recommendation, as long as he is not paid for doing so. This is acceptable because the paralegal's advice to hire an attorney is not coming from an interested party. However, if the freelance legal assistant receives some form of payment for recommending an attorney, then the paralegal's advice is not disinterested and should not be allowed.

In summary, the paralegal is advised to avoid solicitation of clients on behalf of an attorney, as solicitation may result in disciplinary proceedings being brought against your employer and the loss of the paralegal's job.

TIPS FOR PARALEGALS

■ Double-check all marketing work done on behalf of your supervising attorney to make sure the advertisement could not be misleading.

■ Make sure the words "paralegal" or "legal assistant" appear after your name on your business card or on the law firm's letterhead.

■ Check that the name of the law firm by which you are employed appears on your business card.

■ If you are designing a business card yourself, obtain the business cards of other legal assistants working in your legal community by calling friends from paralegal school or attending legal assistant association meetings. Use those cards as guides.

■ Limit your marketing efforts to advertising to attorneys.

■ Never agree to solicit clients on behalf of an attorney, if you are asked to do so by any member of your law firm.

CLOSING EXERCISE

Sabrina has been a legal assistant for several years at Molavia & Mohammed, Ltd., a midsized firm. She is well respected at the firm and is often sought out by the attorneys there because of the quality of her work. However, Sabrina and her fellow legal assistants believe their firm's clients do not give the legal assistants enough recognition. When Sabrina calls a client to provide an update on a particular case, the client often responds, "May I speak with the attorney to confirm what you have just told me?" Letters the legal assistants send likewise meet with a call from the client, seeking to confirm the information with an attorney.

There are rumblings among the legal assistant staff that this is the fault of the firm. Sabrina and her friends decide it's time to do something about this. They approach the managing partners and ask that some changes be made.

What can Sabrina and the other legal assistants recommend to Molavia & Mohammed to get out the word about their services? How should these actions be implemented and regulated?

Unfortunately, Molavia & Mohammed decided against implementing Sabrina's suggestions. She and several of her co-paralegals determine therefore, to develop their own legal assistant agency, providing services on a freelance basis. They know they will need to attract clients somehow and have decided to try advertising. What would you recommend to Sabrina and her friends?

CHAPTER SUMMARY

■ Traditionally, attorneys were not allowed to advertise to prospective clients. In 1977, however, the U.S. Supreme Court decided *Bates v. State Bar of Arizona*. In *Bates* the Supreme Court permitted attorneys to advertise routine legal services. To hold otherwise would violate an attorney's First Amendment rights to free speech. *Bates* did allow the states to place reasonable restrictions on attorney advertising, however. Following *Bates*, the U.S. Supreme Court issued a series of decisions that served to loosen restrictions on attorney advertising. The Court nonetheless recognized that in-person solicitation of clients by attorneys was not permitted. Today, of course, attorneys are given almost free reign to advertise their services as long as the advertisements in no way mislead the prospective client.

■ Just as attorneys are permitted to advertise as long as the advertisements are not misleading, so too can legal assistants advertise their services. As long as the paralegal's status as a nonlawyer is clearly indicated, paralegal names may appear on law firm letterheads in most jurisdictions, and legal assistants are allowed to carry business cards in most jurisdictions.

■ Nonlawyers should not engage in the active solicitation of clients on an attorney's behalf. However, where the nonlawyer recommends to a friend or family member the services of his supervising attorney, without being asked to do so and without receiving any kind of compensation for the referral, the legal assistant may make a referral. Likewise, the freelance paralegal may recommend the services of an attorney if the freelance legal assistant is not paid for doing so.

KEY TERMS

attorney advertising	letterhead	runners
business cards	Martindale-Hubbell Law	solicitation
direct mail	Directory	

CASE

In re Bachmann

United States Bankruptcy Court,
S.D. Florida, 1990.
113 B.R. 769.

Memorandum Opinion

A. JAY CRISTOL, Bankruptcy Judge.

On November 15, 1988, the debtors, Christopher Bachmann and Charlene Rae Bachmann, filed a joint bankruptcy petition under Chapter 13 of the United States Bankruptcy Code. During the administration of this case, it was alleged that a typing service in South Florida was abusing the Bankruptcy system.

At the confirmation hearing on December 20, 1988, the Chapter 13 trustee advised the Court that he had examined the Chapter 13 plan and discussed the plan with the debtors at the first meeting of creditors. The trustee advised the debtors that the plan was improperly prepared and could not be recommended for confirmation. The Chapter 13 plan as filed by the debtors was vague, indefinite, contrary to the Code, and only provided for payment of twenty percent of the unsecured indebtedness, notwithstanding available additional income.

The debtors told the Chapter 13 trustee that the debtors knew nothing about Chapter 13 nor did they understand how to prepare or file a plan. The debtors told the trustee that a typing service advised them to file a Chapter 13 petition and prepared the plan for them. The debtors identified Paul C. Meyer of Capital Business Services, Inc. as the typing service.

The Court, sua sponte, entered an "Order to Show Cause Why Paul C. Meyer and Capital Business Services, Inc. Should Not Be Held in Contempt of Court For The Unauthorized Practice of Law" and set a hearing thereon.

. . .

There is little factual dispute. Paul C. Meyer was forthright and candid. He testified that he is the vice president of Capital Business Services, Inc. (hereinafter referred to as Capital). It is not disputed that he is not a licensed attorney-at-law. Mr. Meyer testified that Capital provides services similar to those provided the debtors in this case to individuals who desire to file voluntary petitions for bankruptcy. Captial also sells bankruptcy forms to debtors. Mr. Meyer described the services performed. Based on his testimony and the documentary evidence, it appears that Mr. Meyer d/b/a Capital did

more than merely sell and type the bankruptcy forms. The evidence indicates that Mr. Meyer d/b/a Capital, is or has been engaging in the unauthorized practice of law.

Capital advertised in *The Flyer* and *The Pennysaver*, local community newspapers. The advertisements suggest that Capital provides bankruptcy services. *See* Appendix, Exhibits A, B, C, D. The Bachmanns, suffering financial misfortune, read one of these advertisements. On October 5, 1988, the Bachmanns went to Capital. At Capital, the Bachmanns were given Mr. Meyer's business card which indicates that Mr. Meyers is a trained paralegal. *See* Appendix, Exhibit E. The Court is unaware of any authority allowing a paralegal to practice law, assist in the practice of law, or provide services to clients where the paralegal is not supervised by a licensed attorney at law.

Mr. Meyer d/b/a Capital held himself out, through both newspaper advertisements and his business card, as being qualified to provide legal services as a paralegal to individual debtors who are in need of the relief provided under the Bankruptcy Code. According to Mr. Bachmann's testimony, Mr. Meyer not only selected the bankruptcy Chapter for the debtors, but also prepared the plan and prepared the debtors' petition.

. . .

Persons not licensed as attorneys-at-law are prohibited from practicing law within the State of Florida. Fla. Const. of 1968 art. V. § 15 (1989). The Supreme Court of Florida broadly defines the practice of law. In *State v. Sperry*, 140 So.2d 587, 591 (Fla.1962) the Supreme Court of Florida stated that:

> . . . . if the giving of such advice and performance of such services affects important rights of a person under the law, and if the reasonable protection of the rights and property of those advised and served requires that the persons giving such advice possess legal skill and a knowledge of the law greater than that possessed by the average citizen, then the giving of such advice and the performance of such services by one for another as a course of conduct constitutes the practice of law.

In determining whether a particular act constitutes the practice of law, the Court's concern is the protection of the public. However, any limitation on the free practice of law necessarily affects important constitutional rights. This decision definitely affects Mr. Meyer's constitutional right to pursue a lawful business. This decision also affects Mr. Meyer's First

Amendment right to speak and print what he chooses. However, the Court must balance Mr. Meyer's rights against the public policy of protecting the public from being advised and represented in legal matters by unqualified persons over whom the judicial department can exercise little, if any, control in the matter of infractions of the Code of conduct which, in the public interest, lawyers are bound to observe. *Sperry,* at 595.

. . .

Although Mr. Meyer d/b/a Capital Business Services, Inc. has engaged in the unauthorized practice of law in this case, the Court is satisfied that Mr. Meyer's actions were without intent to violate the law. Therefore, the Court does not determine Mr. Meyer to be in contempt of this Court. Rather it is deemed appropriate to enjoin Mr. Meyer d/b/a Capital Business Services, Inc. from further engaging in the unauthorized practice of law.

. . .

Another problem arises with regard to advertising. Mr. Meyer is enjoined from using the word "paralegal" on his business cards. Mr. Meyers may advertise his business activities of providing secretarial, notary, and/or typing services. Mr. Meyer may also advertise that he sells bankruptcy forms and general printed information with regard to those forms. However, Mr. Meyer may not advertise in any misleading fashion which leads a reasonable lay person to believe that he offers the public legal services, legal advice or legal assistance regarding Bankruptcy.

. . .

The Court in its ruling is sympathetic to the needs of indigent debtors. The Court must also be cognizant of the purpose for which Congress enacted the Bankruptcy Code. This decision is not made to protect the members of the legal profession either in creating or maintaining a monopoly or closed shop. Tragically there are few attorneys-at-law available to represent debtors in this fee range. This opinion is entered specifically to clarify congressional efforts to protect the public from being advised and represented in bankruptcy legal matters by unqualified persons and to protect them from being overcharged. Further, the Court must take into account the rights of the innocent creditors which may be adversely impacted. Therefore, after consideration, it is ORDERED as follows:

1. Paul C. Meyer, d/b/a Capital Business Services, Inc., is permanently enjoined and restrained from engaging in the unauthorized practice of law.

2. Paul C. Meyer d/b/a Capital Business Services, Inc., is enjoined from advertising such as that set forth in Exhibits A, B, C, and D attached hereto.

3. Paul C. Meyer d/b/a Capital Business Services, Inc., is enjoined from using the title paralegal or advertising himself as a paralegal. He may seek dissolution of this portion of the injunction upon presentation of adequate evidence that he is qualified to be a paralegal and is working under the supervision of a licensed attorney.

4. Paul C. Meyer d/b/a Capital Business Services, Inc., is directed to turn over to the trustee herein the sum of $50 as a return of excessive compensation, pursuant to 11 U.S.C. § 329.

DONE and ORDERED.

Portions of these exhibits of newspaper advertisements in this appendix have been deleted.

APPENDIX—EXHIBIT A

LET US HELP WITH YOUR PAPER WORK!
Divorce, Credit Repair, Corporation, Bankruptcy, Immigration. Call 735-7598 (6/30-435-A)

APPENDIX—EXHIBIT B

WE'LL HELP YOU
With divorce, credit repair, corporation, bankruptcy, immigration. Call 735-7598.

APPENDIX—EXHIBIT C

BANKRUPTCY $85
Corporation $35, divorce $4, adoptions $75.
Capital Business Services 735-7598.

APPENDIX—EXHIBIT D

BANKRUPTCY $85-$160
Divorce $45-$149, Adoptions $75-$95, Corporation $35-$149, 735-7598.

APPENDIX—EXHIBIT E ———————————————————————————————

CAPITAL BUSINESS SERVICES, INC.

Paralegal & Financial Services

Paul C. Meyer
Consultant

8370 W. Flagler Street	2300 W. Oakland Park Blvd.
Suite 230	Suite 501
Miami, FL 33164	Ft. Lauderdale, FL 33311
(305) 948-3553 (Dade)	(305) 735-7598 (Broward)

Questions

1. Look at the business card and advertisements in the appendices. How should they be changed to conform to the court's order?

2. What interests is the court balancing in this opinion?

3. Do you agree with the court that Meyer may not use the word paralegal in his business cards? Why or why not?

4. How does removing the word paralegal from his business card keep the advertisement from being misleading?

REPORTING ATTORNEY AND PARALEGAL MISCONDUCT

CHAPTER OBJECTIVES

After reading this chapter, you should
be able to:

- Understand the attorney's obligation to report attorney misconduct.

- Appreciate the different schools of thought regarding whether paralegals should report attorney and paralegal misconduct.

- Consider the options available to a nonlawyer working in a legal environment when she discovers the misconduct of a fellow legal professional.

P articipating in the legal culture can be exciting and rewarding. For most of us, working in the legal field conjures thoughts of an opportunity to utilize our skills to work with and help people—to make good things happen.

However, the lofty and noble goals of the law to better the human condition are sometimes compromised by actions or inactions of attorneys and paralegals that violate the legal professional's ethical obligations. What should lawyers and nonlawyers do to ensure that abuses of trust in the system do not occur? What *must* lawyers and nonlawyers do?

Throughout this text we have examined the law with respect to different legal substantive topic areas. In this chapter we will address types of situations that might arise where there is a duty to report. We will also address some of the consequences that can be met by those in the legal profession for their failure to report. First we will discuss an attorney's obligation to report another attorney. Next we will focus on a legal assistant's obligation to report an attorney. Finally, we will consider what a nonlawyer may do if he believes there is a duty to apprise someone of his peers' misconduct. Remember, these are not generally easy dilemmas to resolve.

OPENING EXERCISE

LaTisha is an Estates and Trusts paralegal who has recently begun working in the law firm of Martin, Foster, and Doe. Frieda Finn and Julian Sample are the two partners to whom LaTisha is assigned. Leslie Wrap is a partner who offices next to Julian but does not supervise LaTisha. LaTisha is assigned to a complex estate planning problem involving a couple of local renown, Eugene and Renee Gold. Consequently LaTisha is spending more hours at the office than she has spent to date. She works most evenings until 9:00 PM and most Saturdays until 4:00 PM. This work schedule is rigorous but has been approved by the office manager at the firm. It is expected to continue for a couple of more months.

Over the course of the last two weeks, LaTisha has noticed the presence of Leslie Wrap at the office. Leslie is there when LaTisha arrives in the morning. She is also there when LaTisha leaves at night. At first, LaTisha believed Wrap's presence was attributable to a rigorous work schedule. For the past few days, however, LaTisha has been paying closer attention to Wrap. Wrap, she has discovered, is spending the evenings at work becoming intoxicated.

Last night LaTisha left the office particularly late, at 10:30 PM. On her way out she stopped at Wrap's office to say goodnight. She saw that Wrap had fallen asleep on the floor, and an empty bottle of whiskey was turned over on the floor next to Wrap.

Is LaTisha obliged to take any action relative to what she has seen? If so, what kind of action would you recommend?

ATTORNEY MISCONDUCT

Unethical Conduct
Conduct that is proscribed by each state's code of legal ethics.

As previously discussed, most states have adopted the *Model Rules of Professional Conduct*. Those rules set out a mandatory duty to report unethical conduct. **Unethical conduct** is that conduct which is proscribed by each state's code of ethics and is the conduct addressed in the other chapters in this text. For this reason we can conclude that most states require that attorneys report unethical conduct of their fellow attorneys. Not every state, however, has a mandatory duty to report. Check your jurisdiction's duty to report rules.

The American Bar Association Comment to Model Rule 8.3 emphasizes the need for self-regulation of the legal profession. This self-regulation, it notes,

> ". . . requires that members of the profession initiate disciplinary investigation when they know of a violation of the Rules of Professional Conduct." *Annotated Model Rules of Professional Conduct*, Rule 8.3, cmt. (1992).

Duty to Report An obligation many codes of ethics place upon attorneys to report to the state disciplinary agency the unethical conduct of another lawyer.

This **duty to report** is not to be taken lightly. In fact, it is something to which each member of a law office or legal department must pay particularly close attention. It does seem distasteful to report the conduct of an attorney and jeopardize that attorney's livelihood. However, as you will learn, the reporting of a suspected violation does not equate with serving as judge and jury. Studies regarding the subject of whether lawyers are willing to report other lawyers indicate that most lawyers will report serious misconduct.[1] Interestingly, the percentage of lawyers who are willing to report incidents of misconduct increases in direct proportion to an increase in size of law firm surveyed.[2]

Model Rule 8.3, which was derived from the *Model Code's* Disciplinary Rule 1-103, requires a lawyer to report professional misconduct of another attorney. Model Rule 8.3 provides the following:

> a) A lawyer having knowledge that another lawyer has committed a violation of the rules of professional conduct that raises a substantial question as to that lawyer's honesty, trustworthiness or fitness as a lawyer in other respects shall inform the appropriate professional authority.

[1] *See* ABA/BNA Law. Manual Prof. Conduct 101:201–203 (1989); *See* also Lynch, *The Lawyer Informer*, 1986 DUKE L. J. 491, 539 (1986).
[2] Note, *The Lawyer's Duty to Report Professional Misconduct*, 20 ARIZ. L. REV. 509, 515–516 (1978).

b) A lawyer having knowledge that a judge has committed a violation of applicable rules of judicial conduct that raises a substantial question as to the judge's fitness for office shall inform the appropriate authority.

c) This Rule does not require disclosure of information otherwise protected by Rule 1.6 or information gained by a lawyer or judge while serving as a member of an approved lawyers assistance program to the extent that such information would be confidential if it were communicated subject to the attorney-client privilege.

WHAT CONSTITUTES THE VIOLATION

The *Annotated Model Rules of Professional Conduct* that is published by the American Bar Association's Center for Professional Responsibility (2d ed. 1992) notes that:

"A lawyer's first professional obligation is to obey the rule of professional ethics of the jurisdiction in which the lawyer is licensed to practice." *Annotated Model Rules of Professional Conduct*, at 580.

One professional obligation we have seen is the duty to report unethical conduct. Before we address the manner by which violations must be reported, we will learn just what violations fall into this category.

The duty to report arises when a lawyer has 1) **non-privileged** 2) knowledge of 3) a violation of the **disciplinary rules** of the jurisdiction in which the attorney is licensed to practice law.

Non-privileged Information that is not protected by the attorney-client privilege.

Just what is meant by the term non-privileged? As we discussed in chapter 5, client confidences which are shared with his attorney are protected from disclosure. The same holds true in the case where an attorney is the client. If an attorney-client seeks the legal advice of an attorney-adviser about whether that attorney-client's conduct was violative of the rules of ethics, that attorney-adviser is bound by the principle of confidentiality and cannot reveal the confidences. The information, for purposes of reporting, is considered privileged. Only information that is non-privileged can be reported by the attorney.

Disciplinary Rules Rules that are set out in the codes of ethics.

The Comment to Rule 8.3 specifically provides that: "A report about misconduct is not required where it would involve violation of Rule 1.6." *Id.* (Remember that Rule 1.6 protects the confidentiality of information that the client shares with his lawyer.) However, it further provides that, ". . . a lawyer should encourage a client to consent to disclosure where prosecution would not substantially prejudice the client's interest." *Id.*

Second, the attorney must have actual knowledge that a violation has occurred. It is not enough that the attorney suspects that a violation has occurred. She must actually know that one has taken place. Suspicion that an attorney has engaged in misconduct is not enough of a foundation for reporting the conduct.

The proof need not be beyond any dispute. The person who is **blowing the whistle** does not need to be certain. He or she only needs to have "knowledge."[3] Knowledge, according to the *Model Rule* definition, means "actual knowledge of the fact in question." Therefore, if an attorney is just suspicious

Blowing the Whistle Reporting misconduct.

---

[3]*See* Ronald D. Rotunda, *The Lawyer's Duty to Report Another Lawyer's Unethical Violation in the Wake of Himmel*, U. ILL L. REV 977, 984 (1988). Reprinted with permission.

that misconduct has occurred, or has heard a rumor to that effect, there is no duty to report the offending attorney. An attorney's actions must raise a "... substantial question about the fitness of the offending lawyer to carry out his professional role."[4]

The attorney who has knowledge of what he or she believes is violative behavior must next determine whether the behavior violates any ethical rules. This, of course, includes criminal conduct. The rules of ethics forbid attorneys to engage in acts involving deceit, misrepresentation, dishonesty, and **moral turpitude.** Therefore, every violation of a rule of law is a violation of the rule of ethics.

Moral turpitude Acts or behavior that gravely violate accepted moral standards of the community.

Nonetheless, what is prohibited behavior is determined on a state-by-state basis. Even at that, the conduct that is reportable changes from state to state. However, most jurisdictions have based their rules on the American Bar Association's *Model Rules of Professional Conduct* and therefore have similar duty to report rules.

Model Rule of Professional Conduct 8.4 is entitled "Misconduct." It is substantially similar to the *Model Code's* DR 9-101 (C) and outlines what is considered to be **attorney misconduct.**

Attorney Misconduct An attorney's violation of the established rules of ethics.

> It is professional misconduct for a lawyer to:
> a) violate or attempt to violate the rules of professional conduct, knowingly assist or induce another to do so, or do so through the acts of another;
> b) commit a criminal act that reflects adversely on the lawyer's honesty, trustworthiness or fitness as a lawyer in other respects;
> c) engage in conduct involving dishonesty, fraud, deceit or misrepresentation;
> d) engage in conduct that is prejudicial to the administration of justice;
> e) state or imply an ability to influence improperly a government agency or official; or
> f) knowingly assist a judge or judicial officer in conduct that is a violation of applicable rules of judicial conduct or other law. *Model Rules of Professional Conduct* Rule 8.4 (1994).

Essentially, Model Rule 8.4 provides a fail-safe or catchall provision such that any conduct that has not been proscribed but which denigrates the legal profession is forbidden.

EXERCISE 9.1

Attorneys Eileen, Ken, Fitz, and Bill are in practice together. Because their practice has been steadily growing, the four discuss the possibility of expanding it and hiring two associates and a legal assistant.

They interview ten people for the associate positions and five people for the paralegal position. They divide the interviewing process so that only two of them will have to miss their billable time and meet with the candidates. During the interviews with the legal assistants, one of the candidates, when asked why she has decided to leave her employer, tells Eileen and Bill that she is afraid to stay at her current job. She says her employer is giving her more and more work but is providing her with no supervision. He tells her to draft pleadings, sign his name to them, and then file them. She is not sure, she says, but she believes this is wrong. He also tells her to do legal research and, when distraught clients call the office, he

---

[4]*HAZARD AND HODES,* The Law of Lawyering 941 (2d ed. 1993). Reprinted from *The Law of Lawyering,* by Geoffrey C. Hazard, Jr., and W. William Hodes, with the permission of Prentice-Hall Law & Business.

has them talk to her about the course of action they should pursue based on her preliminary research. She says she feels terrible about this because she knows that most of the time she is not giving good advice.

Bill and Eileen note that the paralegal's current employer is listed on her resume. What course of action would you recommend they take relative to the interviewee? Should they apprise the legal assistant of her duty to report? What course of action would you recommend they take relative to the paralegal's current employer?

Do you believe that quitting her job should be the legal assistant's most appropriate course of action here? What other options would you recommend?

During another interview Ken and Fitz meet with a person who works for a medium-sized law firm that had an active civil practice but is now disbanding. Ken and Fitz decide to quiz her on some of the rudiments of civil practice. They ask her what she knows about the rules of discovery. She tells them she is very good with the rules of discovery and that her specialty is confidential documents. She relates an incident to them in which, while she was reviewing documents produced by opposing counsel, she came across confidential information that she presumed had been inadvertently disclosed. When she called it to the attention of her supervising attorney, he congratulated her find and suggested that she make several copies for each of the attorneys working on the case and then return the information to the opposing counsel. With this information, her firm was able to successfully secure a large settlement for their client. She says she really felt that she helped the client and that she would work as hard for Ken and Fitz's firm.

Do Ken and Fitz have any duties relative to the attorney regulatory agency of their state? Do they have a duty to apprise the legal assistant that what she did was wrong?

TO WHOM THE VIOLATIONS ARE REPORTED

We have seen that where one attorney has information that another attorney has engaged in misconduct, the attorney who possesses the knowledge is under a mandatory duty in most states to report that other attorney's actions to the appropriate disciplinary agency. Just what that agency is called is left to each jurisdiction to determine. The American Bar Association Comment to Model Rule 8.3 suggests that "A report should be made to the bar disciplinary agency unless some other agency, such as a peer review agency, is more appropriate in the circumstances."

Each state has its own method of resolution and provides agencies or channels through which the report should be made. These agencies have been established by virtue of the authority vested in the highest court of each state.

While reports are most frequently made to state disciplinary agencies, some states, such as Wisconsin, have offered an alternative and provide that misconduct may, if appropriate, be reported to the district attorney. See Wisconsin Ethics Opinion E-85-11 (Undated).[5] Reprinted with permission from Wisconsin Ethics Opinions, published by the State Bar of Wisconsin. The State of Illinois has provided even broader options, suggesting that a report could be made to a number of appropriate tribunals that could include the district attorney's or U.S. Attorney's offices, or Attorney Registration and Disciplinary Commission.

What happens to a lawyer who fails to report an offending lawyer's misconduct? This point has been the subject of debate throughout our legal

---

[5]Reprinted with permission from Wisconsin Ethics Opinions, published by the State Bar of Wisconsin.

history. Various jurisdictions have dealt with this problem. They have imposed sanctions such as reprimanding, suspending, and disbarring attorneys.

Discipline was imposed upon an attorney in the case of *In re Rivers*, 285 S.C. 492, 331 S.E.2d 332 (1984), where the Supreme Court of South Carolina reprimanded a lawyer for a failure to report another lawyer's misconduct. The offending lawyer was found to have engaged in misconduct after he improperly contacted jurors.

In a controversial opinion construing the duty to report, the Illinois Supreme Court in *In re Himmel*, 125 Ill. 2d 531, 127 Ill. Dec. 708, 533 N.E.2d 790 (1988), suspended a non-reporting attorney from engaging in the practice of law. The court found that the attorney, Himmel, had possessed non-privileged knowledge that his client's prior attorney had misappropriated personal injury settlement funds in the amount of $35,000. After he made the discovery, Himmel drafted an agreement whereby the attorney who had misappropriated the $35,000, agreed to pay the client $75,000 in exchange for an agreement. That agreement was to not initiate any criminal, civil, or attorney disciplinary action against the client's former attorney. Himmel's share of the settlement was to have been approximately $25,588.

As a result of his failure to report that the former attorney had converted client funds, Himmel was suspended for one year over his objections that the information he had received from the client had been privileged and that the client had specifically directed him to not take action against the attorney. See also, "A Practical Guide To The Attorney Registration and Disciplinary Commission Of The Supreme Court Of Illinois Including An Overview Of Relevant Supreme Court Rules And A Discussion Of *In Re Himmel* And The Duty To Report Professional Misconduct," James J. Grogan, Chief Legal Counsel, Attorney Registration and Disciplinary Commission 47 (1992). Reprinted by permission.

EXERCISE 9.2

Linda and Yolonda are attorneys who have decided to leave the law firm Dubas and Renard where they are currently employed as associates. They have decided to start their own firm with three of their friends, Michelle, Katie, and Veronica, who all work for the firm Whethers and Associates. Theirs will be a general practice boutique law firm.

The five give notice to their employers and set up shop in an upscale downtown location. Each of the five has agreed to work in her specialty area and handle her own cases from their inception to their completion. Each has agreed to try to not bother the other with questions unless it is absolutely necessary.

Over the course of the next several months, the five attorneys become extremely busy. A series of incidents unfolds. Please discuss how you would handle each of the incidents.

Linda, who is a tax specialist, receives a corporate referral from another attorney, Dennis Mace. Dennis has told Linda that, in exchange for referring this lucrative client to her, he would like her to do his taxes for the year, for free. There is, he has told her, just one catch. That is that Dennis does not want Linda to compute taxes on income that he has earned at his satellite law office in Atlantic City, New Jersey, into his gross income. Dennis alone will sign off on the tax forms and says he will be solely responsible for any repercussions that might occur.

What would you advise and why?

Yolonda is the personal injury specialist in the firm. She has been called on by an insurance agency that wants her to do their insurance defense work. When the company's representative meets with Yolonda, he tells her that the company for which he works has been discovering what they believe are illegal practices on the part of the attorneys who currently represent them. He names the attorneys but does not provide specific information.

Does Yolonda have a duty to report the names of the attorneys to the state attorney disciplinary agency? Why or why not?

Michelle is the firm's family law specialist. Her clients have followed her to the new firm. One of the clients is Arny Goodfellow. Arny's former lawyer had negotiated a divorce settlement for him one year prior to the time that he sought Michelle's advice. As a part of the settlement, Arny's lawyer was to have secured $35,000 from the sale of what had been the marital home. However, when the home was sold, Arny's lawyer did not give Arny one penny. He kept it all for his own use. Arny tells Michelle about this problem. Michelle decides to consider suing the former attorney for the money he owes Arny. Arny does not really feel comfortable with this and would just like bygones to be bygones. He does not want to cause any trouble and specifically tells Michelle he does not want to get the former attorney into any trouble. Besides, he tells Michelle, he has become engaged to another woman and is blissfully happy.

What should Michelle do and why?

Katie is a criminal law specialist who lectures around the country on the doctrine of double jeopardy. She has learned from one of her law clerks that a lawyer from the state prosecutor's office is having an affair with the purported victim in the case.

Does Katie have a duty to report the conduct of the lawyer? Why or why not? To whom would she report it?

Veronica is the firm's international business specialist. She has recently learned that one of the regular customers by whom the law firm is employed has diversified and now owns a house of prostitution on the California/Mexico border.

What kinds of duties does Veronica have relative to what she has learned? What are some of the things she might want to investigate? Why? What if the corporate customer that bought the brothel believed it was buying a glue factory, and the customer has been duped. Does that information alter Veronica's responsibilities?

OBLIGATION OF THE PARALEGAL
TO REPORT ATTORNEY MISCONDUCT

The paralegal must learn that, while he is working for an attorney, many delicate situations may arise. However, for as many delicate situations that arise there are as many methods of dealing with the problems. The paralegal community often hotly debates whether the paralegal has an obligation to report the attorney. Two schools of thought about this matter have evolved.

Some paralegals believe that, just as an attorney has a duty to report another attorney's misconduct, the legal assistant likewise has a duty to report attorney misconduct. Though there have yet to be any published cases to this effect, it can be argued that the rules extend the duty to report to the non-lawyer. Both the *Model Rules of Professional Conduct* (Rule 5.3) and the *Model Code of Professional Responsibility* make supervising attorneys responsible for their non-lawyer personnel. That is, lawyers must ensure that their non-lawyer personnel comply with the ethics rules. Therefore, it is incumbent upon non-lawyer personnel to work to ensure that the ethics rules are adhered to by attorneys with whom they work. Just as the attorney must report ethical violations, the paralegal should report the attorney who engages in ethical violations. Both must adhere to the legal disciplinary rules of the jurisdiction in which they reside.

The function of those who serve in the legal profession, as well as the purpose of the rule requiring reporting, is to protect the client's interest. For this reason, even the nonlawyer individual who works in the law and sees that an attorney is violating his duties to his client should report that misconduct. The paralegal who sits by and watches while an attorney violates his ethical obligations enables the attorney to actually harm the client.

When a paralegal signs on to work as an assistant she is enlisted to adhere to conduct that protects the interests of clients and fosters her employer's reputation for professionalism in the legal community. The task is much more easily completed by adherence to the rules of legal ethics. The rules have a demonstrated track record of working for the benefit of all. They must be the legal assistant's guidepost.

Other paralegals subscribe to the theory that a nonlawyer working for a lawyer has no obligation to report that attorney's misconduct to the local disciplinary agency. This theory is based on the fact that the codes of ethics for paralegals are in no way legally binding on the paralegal and that, therefore, the paralegal cannot be punished for a failure to abide by them. One well-respected paralegal educator has said the following:

> According to the Code, it is clear what the self-regulating monopoly must do. Attorneys are watch dogs for each other. Yet the distinction regarding an employee or paralegal is not a must-do situation because there is no code of ethics for the paralegal, nor are they self-regulated at this time. Instead for them, it is more of a conscience "should do" call.

Regardless of the school of thought to which you subscribe, it is clear that a nonlawyer cannot blindly ignore what is perceived as a violation. For that reason, the legal assistant should carefully consider the following sections.

WHAT CONSTITUTES THE VIOLATION

Just as the attorney has an obligation to report non-privileged knowledge of a violation, the paralegal may have a corresponding duty to report such information. You will recall that the duty to report arises when a lawyer has 1) non-privileged 2) knowledge of 3) a violation of the disciplinary rules of the jurisdiction in which the attorney is licensed to practice law. When the legal assistant finds herself in possession of such information, she must very carefully consider her options: 1) Should she report the attorney's conduct and, if so, to whom; or 2) should she take some other action?

It might seem that ethical dilemmas exist in black and white, but ethics is a gray area. What might seem like appropriate conduct to one person may not be considered appropriate to another person. This is true for lawyers and legal support staff. For example, one paralegal might consider that the fees charged by her firm for routine work are excessive and that, therefore, the firm's conduct is unethical. Another legal assistant might believe that the fees the same firm charges are reasonable and that the firm's conduct is therefore ethical.

Because of the discrepancy in defining what conduct is ethical in the legal profession (just as in every other avenue of life), the legal assistant must not immediately cry wolf when he learns of something he believes is misconduct. He must analyze the conduct, be certain it is not based on mere speculation but has its basis in fact, and then determine what action should be taken.

After all, reporting an attorney with whom the legal assistant works to a disciplinary agency might, at the very least, make for an uncomfortable working environment. At the most extreme level of this problem, a legal assistant might lose her job.

Any analysis of what constitutes a violation must involve a determination of whether a violation of the jurisdiction's code of ethics has occurred. Consider, however, that what looks like it may be a violation may be perfectly and easily explained by the attorney.

An example might be a situation wherein a legal assistant who is in charge of the billing for a law firm has to compile and itemize the hours that a particular attorney spent on a facet of a case. While she is putting together the information she notices that the time sheets seem to indicate that the client is being charged for more hours than the attorney is working in the office on the case. However, what the legal assistant does not know is that the attorney has been taking the case home with him and working nights and weekends. Just because the paralegal did not see the attorney at work for all of the hours indicated on the time sheets does not mean the attorney was padding the time sheets. Perhaps the attorney had been given permission by a supervising attorney to work at home. The moral of this story is that one should not jump to any conclusions about whether the attorney is compromising his ethical principles.

For this reason, a legal assistant must be prudent. He must analyze the conduct. He must be certain it is not based on mere speculation but has its basis in fact. He must study the rules and then determine what action should be taken.

Jorge Canova is a legal assistant at the law firm LaRue, Dimarsico and Price. The firm is extremely large (100 lawyers, 25 legal assistants, and 60 other nonlawyer support persons). Because of its size, the firm cannot easily focus on training every person in all of the ethics rules. The firm has periodically, throughout the seven months Jorge has worked there, conducted seminars in ethics training. Yet he does not feel quite sure about just what conduct is proscribed.

What are your suggestions as to how Jorge should analyze a situation that arises that he might think is an ethical violation? How might he be sure it *is* an ethical problem in the first place? How should Jorge's analysis differ from an attorney's analysis?

EXERCISE 9.3

OPTIONS FOR PARALEGAL ACTION

Once the decision has been made to report the attorney's misconduct, the legal assistant must consider his options. A paralegal's rule of thumb here should be to take some action if he perceives that there might be an ethical dilemma in his workplace. Next the paralegal must trust that once the matter is taken to the attention of another person, it has been addressed. Of course, the legal assistant must never be so unprofessional as to discuss with the firm's clients any suspicions of an attorney's unethical conduct.

> **CAUTIONARY NOTE:** The course of action the paralegal should pursue depends on the individual circumstances of the situation. No two situations are alike.

Option A—Where the paralegal believes the supervising attorney has committed an ethical violation, she should discuss the matter with the **supervising attorney.** This course should be pursued only when the legal assistant feels comfortable and has a close enough relationship with the attorney that she trusts the attorney.

Supervising Attorney The attorney who supervises the legal assistant and other office staff.

Sometimes mistakes occur and the attorney may be unaware of the existence of an ethical violation. By discussing the problem with the attorney a legal assistant might be guiding her to take steps to remedy a matter before it becomes a problem.

At other times, an attorney might already be considering the possibility that a problem may exist, but is unaware that the paralegal is also considering that there might be a problem. In that case, the legal assistant's action might press the attorney to move more quickly in dealing with the matter, thereby protecting the client.

When the paralegal goes to the attorney for an explanation, he should accept the explanation and let the issue rest. It is not the paralegal's responsibility to second-guess the attorney's decisions, nor is it the attorney's responsibility to fully explain to the paralegal every decision made with respect to client representation.

Where the attorney whom the legal assistant believes has committed the ethical violation is not the paralegal's supervising attorney, the legal assistant should still take the matter to the attention of the supervising attorney. The paralegal should then trust that the supervising attorney will take care of the problem.

Option B—The paralegal can go to the supervising paralegal or office manager. One might not be aware of all of the facts surrounding the situation and the supervising paralegal may be in a better position to assess whether there is a problem. Once the matter is reported to the supervising paralegal, the better course is to trust that it will be resolved by that supervisor.

Option C—The final, albeit least palatable, alternative is to report the attorney to the state bar regulatory or disciplinary agency. As discussed in chapter 2, these agencies are responsible for ensuring that attorney conduct meets with the highest of ethical standards and for safeguarding the public from abuses. This approach should only be done in the event that a legal assistant has actual knowledge of an extremely serious ethical violation (and this should provide extra incentive for learning the rules).

> **CAUTIONARY NOTE:** This alternative is the most extreme of the choices. This choice must never be lightly taken. If the paralegal is in any way in error in his analysis, it could cost the attorney her livelihood, her reputation, her law license.

These alternatives should be carefully considered whenever the paralegal believes an attorney has violated an ethical code. However, special problems arise for the paralegal who works for a solo-practitioner. What should the paralegal who works for a solo-practitioner do when he believes the attorney may have engaged in unethical conduct? It is very possible that the solo-practitioner will not employ other nonlawyers. It is also very possible that the paralegal may be uncomfortable approaching the attorney. In this case, however, the paralegal should try to put his apprehension over approaching the attorney to the side. Failing to discuss the situation will only serve to increase tension in the working environment. After all, the paralegal will believe he is working for a supervising attorney who is harming her clients.

If, after weighing all the alternatives, the legal assistant still believes she cannot approach the attorney, she should consider discussing the matter with, perhaps, another paralegal with whom she has gone to school or with whom she attends paralegal association meetings. Discussing the matter with someone who is somewhat experienced with the ethical rules may help the legal assistant focus the issues and find an acceptable course of conduct. Remember, however, that discretion is always terribly important when undertaking to discuss the matter with a third party.

PARTICULARLY SENSITIVE AREAS

As the opening exercise demonstrates, mistakes may be the result of a more serious, underlying problem. This problem might be linked to substance abuse or dependency. Directly approaching an attorney about this problem might encourage her to get help. Most states have programs, typically called **lawyer's assistance programs,** that are specifically designed to assist attorneys in dealing with these types of problems. State bars and attorney regulatory agencies are generally very willing to provide information about these programs to those who inquire. These programs might also be listed in the phone book.

Lawyer's Assistance Programs Programs specifically designed to help lawyers deal with problems linked to substance abuse or dependency.

In the event that the legal assistant is unwilling to directly confront the attorney, it should be understood that most of the lawyer's assistance programs accept anonymous information by phone. These agencies then discreetly contact the attorney. When the paralegal has actual knowledge of the existence of a substance abuse problem, he might consider contacting one of these agencies.

SPECIAL CONCERNS FOR THE FREELANCE PARALEGAL

An interesting dilemma arises where a freelance paralegal is contracted to work on a case which, she believes, should have been referred to another attorney. New Jersey Opinion No. 24, previously discussed, says she should decline the employment. Does she have an obligation to report her belief to the state attorney regulatory agency? She does not. It is a prospective or anticipated violation of the rules against assisting in the unauthorized practice of law.

If the freelance paralegal *knows* of a violation and has an established working relationship with the attorney, she should discuss this dilemma with the attorney with whom she has contracted.

Su Chen is a legal assistant who works for two attorneys, Stuart and Fotios. They have a burgeoning real estate and personal injury practice. They also have an associate who works for them by the name of Trainer.

EXERCISE 9.4

Though the law firm is small, everyone is so busy that no one really has time to pay attention to anyone else's business. Fotios is the one person whom everyone at the firm trusts. He is the "glue" that holds the firm together. Stuart, on the other hand, is a no-nonsense type. He is the "rain-maker" of the firm and is particularly proud of a recent asbestos litigation matter that he has brought into the firm.

One afternoon, after she has returned from filing several documents, Su Chen returns to the office and overhears Trainer on the phone. He keeps saying, "Yes, Margaret, yes, dear." Su Chen knows that the legal assistant who works for opposing counsel on the asbestos litigation matter is named Margaret. Her suspicion that it is the same Margaret, she believes, is confirmed when she hears Trainer say, "Don't worry, the case is almost settled." She also knows that Trainer is married.

Suggest several courses of action Su Chen might pursue if she decides there is an ethical problem.

OBLIGATION OF THE PARALEGAL TO REPORT PARALEGAL MISCONDUCT

What should the nonlawyer do when she believes another nonlawyer in the firm is engaging in unethical conduct? The paralegal deals with attorneys, judges, mortgage companies, other paralegals, and clients. Misconduct of a legal assistant can injure every one of these persons. In the interest of all of these parties, and in the interest of fostering the growth of the paralegal profession, the legal assistant should take some action when he is aware of another paralegal's misconduct.

Just what constitutes paralegal misconduct? You will recall from previous chapters that the rules which guide attorney conduct apply to legal assistants. A legal assistant who violates these rules is then subject to being reported. However, to quote an old adage, "Discretion is the better part of valor." What looks like misconduct might be something else entirely. Therefore, a paralegal should not report his co-worker too hastily or indiscriminately. Examine what you perceive to be misconduct carefully.

The question of to whom the conduct should be reported is not clearly answered. The decision should be made based on the particular circumstances of each case. Keep in mind this rule of thumb: The paralegal should go to the person she most trusts.

SUPERVISING PARALEGAL

A good choice might be a supervising paralegal or even office manager. After all, the supervisor is in the best position to correct the offending legal assistant's behavior. Chances are that they participated, to some extent, in the hiring of the legal assistant or at least are familiar with the work produced by the legal assistant.

For example, if a paralegal's co-worker is sleeping at her desk but is billing the same time to a client's account, the paralegal may want to report that behavior to the supervising paralegal. The supervising paralegal can then take the appropriate action to ensure that the client's interests (and the law firm's reputation) are safeguarded.

SUPERVISING ATTORNEY

Though a supervising paralegal or office manager is the best choice, many firms do not have either. Another option available where it is discovered that a paralegal is violating the rules of ethics is to report the paralegal misconduct first to your supervising attorney.

Remember, both the *Model Rules* and the *Model Code* specifically address responsibilities of an attorney who supervises nonlawyer assistants. This is particularly important because the attorney for whom the paralegal works would likely be held accountable for the actions of the paralegal.

If the paralegal whom you believe has violated ethics rules is employed by another firm or company, you should first report this misconduct to your supervising attorney. It is best to provide your law office with the opportunity to correct the problem. Remember, the actions of that legal assistant may injure your client, and the supervising attorney has the ultimate responsibility for protecting those interests.

An example of this can be seen where a paralegal shares an office with another paralegal. One morning the paralegal overhears her co-worker giving advice to a client about child support payments. The paralegal should notify her attorney because that attorney could be cited by the local bar regulatory agency for assisting in the unauthorized practice of law.

LOCAL PARALEGAL ASSOCIATIONS

An excellent source of knowledgeable and experienced paralegals is the local paralegal association in the area in which the legal assistant works. Because

FOCUS ON . . . LAURIE ROSELLE

Laurie Roselle, a litigation paralegal and coordinator at the law firm of Rogers & Wells in New York, graduated from the Philadelphia Institute for Paralegal Training. Soon after graduation, Roselle founded the Indiana and Manhattan Paralegal Associations. She served as both Association's president and later became president of the National Federation of Paralegal Associations (and was the first person ever to have served in that position for two consecutive terms).

Roselle's work as a legal assistant and her service as paralegal association president have put her in the envious position of having interacted with many professional legal assistants. Through these contacts, she has heard about a variety of sticky situations where paralegals have wondered what action they should take when they believe a supervising attorney has engaged in misconduct.

Roselle believes paralegals who feel they have witnessed misconduct in the workplace must take some action, but should be cautious. Roselle warns, "You shouldn't run around making accusations. You could seriously damage an attorney's reputation and put her livelihood in jeopardy. It's possible that the problem is merely one of miscommunication."

The duty to report is more than a duty to report. It is a duty to know your ethical obligations. Ignorance of ethics rules does not excuse failure to take some action to protect the client.

For the person who believes there is a problem, Roselle believes that it is a good idea to talk to your supervising attorney or your paralegal coordinator (depending upon the structure of your employer).

When you think you have witnessed something unethical, Roselle also advises her paralegals to take dictaphones (with attorney approval, of course) into the meetings they have with attorneys who are giving them instructions. In this way, she believes episodes of miscommunication can be avoided.

However, Roselle is also aware that many legal assistants have wondered about their responsibilities when they think another legal assistant has committed an ethical violation. Because many legal assistants do not understand that ethical guidelines apply to them, Roselle notes, they may make errors in judgment. She says, "There are paralegals who just don't realize that if something goes wrong, the supervising attorney and paralegal will have to pay." For this reason, Roselle again believes it is important to talk about problems with your supervising attorney or paralegal coordinator.

Roselle advises all legal assistants to learn and to understand the code of ethics. Knowing the rules of ethics can protect paralegals and their supervising attorneys. "The duty to report," Roselle says, "is more than just a duty to report. It is a duty to know your ethical obligations."

---

the paralegal profession is dynamic, not static, the flux of problems that arise should be discussed between those who deal with them on a daily basis—paralegals.

For example, associations are very helpful in the case of a real estate closing. In the recent past, the legal assistant was not permitted to engage in a real estate closing to any degree like that in which she can now participate. It seemed that the rules regarding what the paralegal could and could not do changed by the day. Activity proscribed one day could become acceptable the following day. Paralegal associations worked to keep paralegals apprised of the changes and made it possible for paralegals to engage in correct (and legal) conduct.

Associations promote networking and the sharing of information. Very often, legal assistants inform the attorneys for whom they work about the conduct in which other paralegals are permitted to engage.

It is extremely important that suspected misconduct be discussed with these local associations. As the legislatures in more and more jurisdictions debate the questions of whether and how paralegals are to be licensed, these associations take on added importance in terms of their ability to provide a place for exchange of ideas.

TIPS FOR PARALEGALS

When confronted with what you believe is an ethical violation, the most important rule to keep in mind is to *consider the individual circumstances.* (Depending on the circumstances, your responses might be different.)

Reporting Attorney Misconduct

■ Consider speaking with your supervising attorney when you believe you have observed an attorney's violation of the code of ethics.

■ Consider discussing what you perceive as an ethical violation with your supervising paralegal or office manager.

Reporting Paralegal Misconduct

■ Consider discussing what you perceive as an ethical violation with your supervising paralegal or office manager.

■ You might discuss what you perceive to be an ethical violation with your supervising attorney.

■ You could discuss the matter with other members of your local paralegal association.

CLOSING EXERCISE

Paralegals Bridget and Deb are supervised by Sally Bliss, a well-respected attorney. Last week, Bridget and Deb worked on a real estate closing with Sally. The jurisdiction in which they work permits legal assistants to participate in real estate closings. Deb and Bridget prepare the closing package and attend the closing on behalf of Bliss's firm. The buyer's law firm's paralegal, Sandi Jones, is also at the closing.

During the closing Jones decides that the amount her firm's client is paying for the house is too high. Jones scratches out the amount on the documents and subtracts $100 from the closing price. Bridget and Deb cringe as they witness this and are incredulous at what they are seeing! However, they take no action at this time.

You will role-play and put yourself in their shoes. Do Bridget and Deb have a duty to report the paralegal's misconduct? If so, to whom do they report it?

Assume that Bridget and Deb go to Bliss and relate the incident to her. Bliss thanks the two and tells them she will handle the matter. After the two legal assistants leave her office, Bliss decides she will handle this the best way she can and, at the same time, avoid creating "bad blood" between her firm and the other firm. One complicating matter is the fact that Bliss teaches at a local paralegal program and thinks she recognizes the name of the "offending" legal assistant as that of one of her students. Bliss goes directly to Kurtis J. Smythe, a veteran attorney at her law firm, to seek his advice about how to handle this situation.

You will role-play and put yourself in Smythe's shoes. Please itemize the available options.

Assume that two months pass and Deb and Bridget learn that neither Bliss nor Smythe have taken any action. Do the two have an independent duty as legal assistants to report the paralegal's action? To whom would they report it?

CHAPTER SUMMARY

■ The legal profession is self-regulated. This means that in many jurisdictions attorneys have an obligation to report the misconduct of other attorneys. The duty to report arises when a lawyer has 1) non-privileged 2) knowledge 3) of a violation of the disciplinary rules of the jurisdiction in which the attorney is licensed to practice law. Attorneys should report other lawyers' misconduct to the appropriate state disciplinary agency.

■ There are different schools of thought regarding whether paralegals should report attorney misconduct. Some legal assistants believe that, just as an attorney has a duty to report another attorney's misconduct, the paralegal likewise has a duty to report attorney misconduct. This belief derives from the fact that the attorney's code of ethics is applied to legal assistants through Rule 5.3. Other legal assistants believe the nonlawyer has no obligation to report attorney misconduct because the codes of ethics are not binding on paralegals and, therefore, the paralegal cannot be punished for failing to abide by them.

■ The legal assistant who perceives that there may be an ethical violation by either an attorney or another legal assistant should consider what alternatives are available. One option is to take the matter directly to the attention of the paralegal's supervising attorney. Especially when the paralegal believes her supervising attorney has engaged in misconduct, it is important that the legal assistant discuss her concerns with the attorney. After all, what the paralegal perceives as misconduct may simply be a misperception of the situation. The nonlawyer should also consider approaching a supervising paralegal or office manager with his concerns.

KEY TERMS

attorney misconduct	Lawyer's Assistance	non-privileged
blowing the whistle	Programs	supervising attorney
disciplinary rules	moral turpitude	unethical conduct
duty to report		

CASE

In re Himmel

Supreme Court of Illinois
125 Ill.2d 531,
127 Ill.Dec.708,
533 N.E.2d 790.

Justice STAMOS delivered the opinion of the court:

This is a disciplinary proceeding against respondent, James H. Himmel. On January 22, 1986, the Administrator of the Attorney Registration and Disciplinary Commission (the Commission) filed a complaint with the Hearing Board, alleging that respondent violated Rule 1-103(a) of the Code of Professional Responsibility (the Code) (107 Ill.2d R. 1-103(a)) by failing to disclose to the Commission information concerning attorney misconduct. On October 15, 1986, the Hearing Board found that respondent had violated the rule and recommended that respondent be reprimanded. The Administrator filed exceptions with the Review Board. The Review Board issued its report on July 9, 1987, finding that respondent had not violated a disciplinary rule and recommending dismissal of the complaint. We granted the Administrator's petition for leave to file exceptions to the Review Board's report and recommendation. 107 Ill.2d R. 753(e)(6).

We will briefly review the facts, which essentially involve three individuals: respondent, James H. Himmel, licensed to practice law in Illinois on November 6, 1975; his client, Tammy Forsberg, formerly known as Tammy McEathron; and her former attorney, John R. Casey.

The complaint alleges that respondent had knowledge of John Casey's conversion of Forsberg's funds and respondent failed to inform the Commission of this misconduct. The facts are as follows.

In October 1978, Tammy Forsberg was injured in a motorcycle accident. In June 1980, she retained John R. Casey to represent her in any personal injury or property damage claim resulting from the accident. Sometime in 1981, Casey negotiated a settlement of $35,000 on Forsberg's behalf. Pursuant to an agreement between Forsberg and Casey, one-third of any monies received would be paid to Casey as his attorney fee.

In March 1981, Casey received the $35,000 settlement check, endorsed it, and deposited the check into his client trust fund account. Subsequently, Casey converted the funds.

Between 1981 and 1983, Forsberg unsuccessfully attempted to collect her $23,233.34 share of the settlement proceeds. In March 1983, Forsberg retained respondent to collect her money and agreed to pay him one-third of any funds recovered above $23,233.34

Respondent investigated the matter and discovered that Casey had misappropriated the settlement funds. In April 1983, respondent drafted an agreement in which Casey would pay Forsberg $75,000 in settlement of any claim she might have against him for the misappropriated funds. By the terms of the agreement, Forsberg agreed not to initiate any criminal, civil, or attorney disciplinary action against Casey. This agreement was executed on April 11, 1983. Respondent stood to gain $17,000 or more if Casey honored the agreement. In February 1985, respondent filed suit against Casey for breaching the agreement, and a $100,000 judgment was entered against Casey. If Casey had satisfied the judgment, respondent's share would have been approximately $25,588.

The complaint stated that at no time did respondent inform the Commission of Casey's misconduct. According to the Administrator, respondent's first contact with the Commission was in response to the Commission's inquiry regarding the lawsuit against Casey.

In April 1985, the Administrator filed a petition to have Casey suspended from practicing law because of his conversion of client funds and his conduct involving moral turpitude in matters unrelated to Forsberg's claim. Casey was subsequently disbarred on consent on November 5, 1985.

A hearing on the complaint against the present respondent was held before the Hearing Board of the Commission on June 3, 1986. In its report, the Hearing Board noted that the evidence was not in dispute. The evidence supported the allegations in the complaint and provided additional facts as follows.

Before retaining respondent, Forsberg collected $5,000 from Casey. After being retained, respondent made inquiries regarding Casey's conversion, contacting the insurance company that issued the settlement check, its attorney, Forsberg, her mother, her fiance and Casey. Forsberg told respondent that she simply wanted her money back and specifically instructed respondent to take no other action. Because of respondent's efforts, Forsberg collected another $10,400 from Casey. Respondent received no fee in this case.

The Hearing Board found that respondent received unprivileged information that Casey converted Forsberg's funds, and that respondent failed to relate the information to the Commission in violation of Rule 1-103(a) of the Code. The Hearing Board noted, however, that respondent had been practicing law for 11 years, had no prior record of any complaints, obtained as good a result as could be expected in the case, and requested no fee for recovering the $23,233.34. Accordingly, the Hearing Board recommended a private reprimand.

Upon the Administrator's exceptions to the Hearing Board's recommendation, the Review Board reviewed the matter. The Review Board's report stated that the client had contacted the Commission prior to retaining respondent and, therefore, the Commission did have knowledge of the alleged misconduct. Further, the Review Board noted that respondent respected the client's wishes regarding not pursuing a claim with the Commission. Accordingly, the Review Board recommended that the complaint be dismissed.

The Administrator now raises three issues for review: (1) whether the Review Board erred in concluding that respondent's client had informed the Commission of misconduct by her former attorney; (2) whether the Review Board erred in concluding that respondent had not violated Rule 1-103(a); and (3) whether the proven misconduct warrants at least a censure.

As to the first issue, the Administrator contends that the Review Board erred in finding that Forsberg informed the Commission of Casey's misconduct prior to retaining respondent. In support of this contention, the Administrator cites to testimony in the record showing that while Forsberg contacted the Commission and received a complaint form, she did not fill out the form, return it, advise the Commission of the facts, or name whom she wished to complain about. The Administrator further contends that even if Forsberg had reported Casey's misconduct to the Commission, such an action would not have relieved respondent of his duty to report under Rule 1-103(a). Additionally, the Administrator argues that no evidence exists to prove that respondent failed to report because he assumed that Forsberg had already reported the matter.

Respondent argues that the record shows that Forsberg did contact the Commission and was forwarded a complaint form, and that the record is not

clear that Forsberg failed to disclose Casey's name to the Commission. Respondent also argues that Forsberg directed respondent not to pursue the claim against Casey, a claim she had already begun to pursue.

We begin our analysis by examining whether a client's complaint of attorney misconduct to the Commission can be a defense to an attorney's failure to report the same misconduct. Respondent offers no authority for such a defense and our research has disclosed none. Common sense would dictate that if a lawyer has a duty under the Code, the actions of a client would not relieve the attorney of his own duty. Accordingly, while the parties dispute whether or not respondent's client informed the Commission, that question is irrelevant to our inquiry in this case. We have held that the canons of ethics in the Code constitute a safe guide for professional conduct, and attorneys may be disciplined for not observing them. (*In re Yamaguchi* (1987), 118 Ill.2d 417, 427, 113 Ill.Dec. 928, 515 N.E.2d 1235, citing *In re Taylor* (1977), 66 Ill.2d 567, 6 Ill.Dec. 898, 363 N.E.2d 845.) The question is, then, whether or not respondent violated the Code, not whether Forsberg informed the Commission of Casey's misconduct.

As to respondent's argument that he did not report Casey's misconduct because his client directed him not to do so, we again note respondent's failure to suggest any legal support for such a defense. A lawyer, as an officer of the court, is duty-bound to uphold the rules in the Code.

. . .

As to the second issue, the Administrator argues that the Review Board erred in concluding that respondent did not violate Rule 1-103(a). The Administrator urges acceptance of the Hearing Board's finding that respondent had unprivileged knowledge of Casey's conversion of client funds, and that respondent failed to disclose that information to the Commission. The Administrator states that respondent's knowledge of Casey's conversion of client funds was knowledge of illegal conduct involving moral turpitude under *In re Stillo* (1977), 68 Ill.2d 49, 54, 11 Ill.Dec. 289, 368 N.E.2d 897. Further, the Administrator argues that the information respondent received was not privileged under the definition of privileged information articulated by this court in *People v. Adam* (1972), 51 Ill.2d 46, 48, 280 N.E.2d 205, *cert. denied* (1972), 409 U.S. 948, 93 S.Ct. 289, 34 L.Ed.2d 218. Therefore, the Administrator concludes, respondent violated his ethical duty to report misconduct under Rule 1-103(a). According to the Administrator, failure to disclose the information deprived the Commission of evidence of serious misconduct, evidence that would have assisted in the Commission's investigation of Casey.

Respondent contends that the information was privileged information received from his client, Forsberg, and therefore he was under no obligation to disclose the matter to the Commission. Respondent argues that his failure to report Casey's misconduct was motivated by his respect for his client's wishes, not by his desire for financial gain. To support this assertion, respondent notes that his fee agreement with Forsberg was contingent upon her first receiving all the money Casey originally owed her. Further, respondent states that he has received no fee for his representation of Forsberg.

· · ·

Petitioner's belief in a code of silence indicates to us that he is not at present fully rehabilitated or fit to practice law." (*Anglin*, 122 Ill.2d at 539, 120 Ill.Dec. 520, 524 N.E.2d 550.) Thus, if the present respondent's conduct did violate the rule on reporting misconduct, imposition of discipline for such a breach of duty is mandated.

The question whether the information that respondent possessed was protected by the attorney-client privilege, and thus exempt from the reporting rule, requires application of this court's definition of the privilege. We have stated that " '(1) [w]here legal advice of any kind is sought (2) from a professional legal adviser in his capacity as such, (3) the communications relating to that purpose, (4) made in confidence (5) by the client, (6) are at his instance permanently protected (7) from disclosure by himself or by the legal adviser, (8) except the protection be waived.' " (*People v. Adam* (1972), 51 Ill.2d 46, 48, 280 N.E.2d 205 (quoting 8 J. Wigmore, Evidence 2292 (McNaughton rev.ed.1961)), *cert. denied* (1972), 409 U.S. 948, 93 S.Ct. 289, 34 L.Ed.2d 218.) We agree with the Administrator's argument that the communication regarding Casey's conduct does not meet this definition. The record does not suggest that this information was communicated by Forsberg to the respondent in confidence. We have held that information voluntarily disclosed by a client to an attorney, in the presence of third parties who are not agents of the client or attorney, is not privileged information. (*People v. Williams* (1983), 97 Ill.2d 252, 295, 73 Ill.Dec. 360, 454 N.E.2d 220, *cert. denied* (1984), 466 U.S. 981, 104 S.Ct. 2364, 80 L.Ed.2d 836.) In this case, Forsberg discussed the matter with respondent at various times while her mother and her fiance were present. Consequently, unless the mother and fiance were agents of respondent's cli-

ent, the information communicated was not privileged. Moreover, we have also stated that matters intended by a client for disclosure by the client's attorney to third parties, who are not agents of either the client or the attorney, are not privileged. (*People v. Werhollick* (1970), 45 Ill.2d 459, 462, 259 N.E.2d 265.) The record shows that respondent, with Forsberg's consent, discussed Casey's conversion of her funds with the insurance company involved, the insurance company's lawyer, and with Casey himself. Thus, under *Werhollick* and probably *Williams*, the information was not privileged.

Though respondent repeatedly asserts that his failure to report was motivated not by financial gain but by the request of his client, we do not deem such an argument relevant in this case. This court has stated that discipline may be appropriate even if no dishonest motive for the misconduct exists. (*In re Weinberg* (1988), 119 Ill.2d 309, 315, 116 Ill.Dec. 216, 518 N.E.2d 1037; *In re Clayter* (1980), 78 Ill.2d 276, 283, 35 Ill.Dec. 790, 399 N.E.2d 1318.) In addition, we have held that client approval of an attorney's action does not immunize an attorney from disciplinary action. (*In re Thompson* (1963), 30 Ill.2d 560, 569, 198 N.E.2d 337; *People ex rel. Scholes v. Keithley* (1906), 225 Ill. 30, 41, 80 N.E. 50.) We have already dealt with, and dismissed, respondent's assertion that his conduct is acceptable because he was acting pursuant to his client's directions.

· · ·

In his defense, respondent reiterates his arguments that he was not motivated by desire for financial gain. He also states that Forsberg was pleased with his performance on her behalf. According to respondent, his failure to report was a "judgment call" which resulted positively in Forsberg's regaining some of her funds from Casey.

· · ·

We have held that fairness dictates consideration of mitigating factors in disciplinary cases. (*In re Yamaguchi* (1987), 118 Ill.2d 417, 428, 113 Ill.Dec. 928, 515 N.E.2d 1235, citing *In re Neff* (1988), 83 Ill.2d 20, 46 Ill.Dec. 169, 413 N.E.2d 1282.) Therefore, we do consider the fact that Forsberg recovered $10,400 through respondent's services, that respondent has practiced law for 11 years with no record of complaints, and that he requested no fee for minimum collection of Forsberg's funds. However, these considerations do not outweigh the serious nature of respondent's failure to report Casey, the resulting interference with the Commission's investigation of Casey, and respondent's ill-advised choice to settle with Casey rather than report his misconduct.

Accordingly, it is ordered that respondent be suspended from the practice of law for one year.

Respondent suspended.

Questions

1. How do you think the court's holding in *Himmel* could be applied to nonlawyers?

2. What was the most important point from the court's point of view in its decision to impose so severe a penalty on Himmel?

3. How did the court rebut Himmel's argument that the information shared by his client was privileged and that he therefore believed he was under no obligation to disclose it?

4. How did the court rebut Himmel's argument that his failure to report Casey's misconduct was motivated not by financial gain but by the request of his client?

5. Do you agree or disagree with the court's decision here? Give three points in support of your answer.

PROFESSIONAL CONDUCT IN THE LAW OFFICE

CHAPTER OBJECTIVES

After reading this chapter, you should
be able to:

- Understand why it is important to study professional behavior.
- Recognize the three dimensions of professionalism.

- Understand how the three dimensions of professional behavior can be applied in the legal assistant's work environment.

Throughout history, lawyers have garnered respect. In part that is because attorneys are entrusted with matters that are critical to our lives. They handle our divorces; our wills, trusts, and taxes; the affairs of our corporations—and, when we are injured, they help us get compensated so we might be in the position we were before we were injured.

Additionally, lawyers are educated as experts in the law and must demonstrate a minimum degree of competency before they are legally entitled to call themselves attorneys. They belong to a profession.

During the past three decades, paralegals working with those lawyers have also come to be highly respected. Various types of legal assistant educational programs have developed, areas of specialization have grown, and certification as a legal assistant is an option to nonlawyers who wish to possess a nationally recognized credential. National and regional paralegal associations have drafted and adopted directory codes of ethics. Indeed, the "para" of the designation "paralegal" has not impeded the legal community's perception of paralegals as professionals who take their work very seriously.

But, how does the paralegal learn professional behavior? The same way everybody else does—through education, observation, and life experience. Certainly, the first step to learning professional behavior is for the legal assistant to appreciate and understand the rules of ethics, which this text has discussed at length. Additionally, as you may have guessed, professional behavior involves more than adopting a socially acceptable manner in the workplace. Learning what each legal culture considers to be socially acceptable is a continual process. It can be helpful to know some basics.

This chapter is devoted to a general discussion of what constitutes professional behavior and why it is so important for the legal assistant to understand how to achieve it.

OPENING EXERCISE

Carol was very excited. Her supervising attorney told her the firm was going to pay all expenses to send her to a conference in Memphis, Tennessee, that was being sponsored by one of the national legal assistant organizations. Because attending the conference could help her do her job more effectively, Carol would be allowed to attend the conference.

The format of the conference looked great. Paralegals from all over the country would be there, discussing issues of vital importance to the growth of the profession. Carol was especially interested in a seminar entitled, "Professional Conduct for Paralegals." She knew she would learn a great deal and have fun at the same time.

When she arrived at the conference, Carol was thrilled to run into Joan and Loretta, two people with whom she had served on the board of her regional paralegal association. Joan and Loretta told her they were thinking of skipping the "Professional Conduct" seminar and heading off to see Elvis Presley's Graceland. Carol had received all of the printed material that would be distributed at the seminar, and she has never been to Graceland and would really like to see it. What do you advise? What problems do you think could result if Carol does not attend the seminar? What do you think Carol can learn at this seminar?

PROFESSIONAL CONDUCT

Newcomers to a profession need not feel that they have been tossed blindly into the profession without any guidance as to what conduct is or is not professional. As we noted earlier, learning professional behavior is a function of education, life experience, and observation. Good judgment is developed through years of experiencing different kinds of situations.

Professional
Characterized by or conforming to the technical or ethical standards of a profession.

As one progresses through a career and comes into contact with many individuals, the kind of behavior that is considered **professional** becomes clearer.

Professionalism
Professional status, methods, or standards.

This chapter offers advice concerning how to handle common situations you will confront that will test your sense of **professionalism.** First, though, it is important to understand what is professional behavior and why it must be studied. Professionalism means "professional status, methods, or standards."[1]

EXERCISE 10.1

Consider what kinds of life experience, education, and observation you bring into your workplace. Do you believe you could improve the quality of your workplace if you focused on applying these three features there?

WHY STUDY PROFESSIONAL BEHAVIOR?

Civility Politeness.

Many believe that **civility** and old-fashioned good manners are in short supply in today's world, and that this deficit affects lawyers' behavior in the courtroom and their behavior toward their clients.

As one judge has observed,

Today, our talk is coarse and rude, our entertainment is vulgar and violent, our music is hard and loud, our institutions are weakened, our values are

---

[1]MERRIAM-WEBSTER'S COLLEGIATE DICTIONARY 930 (10th ed. 1993). By permission. From Merriam-Webster's Collegiate® Dictionary © 1993 by Merriam-Webster Inc., publisher of the Merriam-Webster® dictionaries.

superficial, egoism has replaced altruism and cynicism pervades. Amid these surroundings none should be surprised that the courtroom is less tranquil. Report on Civility of the Seventh Judicial Circuit, p. 5. Reprinted by permission.

Those calling for reform in the legal community point to examples of **unprofessional** conduct that have served to undermine the public's confidence and trust in their lawyers and legal professionals. They point to instances of lawyers and judges who have been criminally prosecuted for engaging in corrupt conduct.

Unprofessional
Violating the code of a profession or occupation.

One such case is *Castillo v. St. Paul,* 938 F.2d 776(7th Cir. 1991). In *Castillo,* the plaintiff's attorneys had repeatedly interfered with opposing counsel's attempts at discovery. The plaintiff's attorney refused to allow his client to answer certain questions during a deposition, which violated Rule 30(c) of the *Federal Rules of Civil Procedure.* Nonetheless, defendant's counsel, Attorney Y, attempted to pursue questioning. In response to defendant's counsel's attempts to question, the plaintiff's attorney screamed that defense counsel was harassing his client. He also refused to produce certain documents.

To resolve the problems at the deposition, the parties went to the trial judge who found the objections of the plaintiff's attorney to be without merit. The judge then assessed fees and expenses against the attorney and his client in the amount of $6,317.66 and also ordered a second deposition to be scheduled. The trial judge instructed the attorneys to call him if there were more problems with the deposition questions, and he would resolve any problems.

During the second deposition, a new attorney, who was a partner of the plaintiff's original counsel, appeared on behalf of the plaintiff. In direct violation of the judge's orders that had been given to the first attorney, the new attorney for the plaintiff instructed the plaintiff not to answer questions during the deposition. Defense counsel suggested calling the judge to resolve the problem. When the plaintiff's attorney did not immediately respond, defense counsel said that he would place the call. The plaintiff's attorney then told the defense counsel: "I would caution you not to use any telephones in this office unless you are invited to do so, Counsel." Defense counsel responded: "You're telling me I can't use your telephone?" The plaintiff's attorney retorted: "You can write your threatening letters to me. But you step outside this room and touch the telephone and I'll take care of that in the way one does who has **possessory rights.**" The plaintiff's attorney was ultimately cited for contempt.

Possessory Rights
Relating to, founded on, or claiming possession.

A federal court of appeals, after noting the lower court's characterization of counsel's behavior as "the most outrageous example of evasion and obfuscation that I have seen in years," upheld the lower court's decision to cite an attorney for contempt.

Unfortunately, this is just one example of unprofessional conduct among legal professionals. In response to what was perceived as a growing problem in the legal world, various organizations started studying lawyers' professionalism. For example, in April of 1991, after eighteen months of study, the Committee on Civility of the Seventh Judicial Circuit presented a final report that proposed standards of professional conduct for lawyers and judges practicing and working within the Seventh Federal Judicial Circuit.

Perhaps the most interesting recommendation contained in the report is Comment 3 of the Lawyer's Duties to Other Counsel. Comment 3 reads:

We will not encourage or knowingly authorize any person under our control to engage in conduct that would be improper if we were to engage in such conduct.

Those who work under the control or supervision of lawyers include such nonlawyers as investigators, secretaries, and paralegals. By including such a statement in its recommendations, the Seventh Circuit has concluded that professionalism and civil conduct is as much a responsibility for the nonlawyer working in the legal community as it is for the lawyer.

Undoubtedly, the nonlawyer's conduct affects a nonlawyer's relationships with clients, attorneys, and other nonlawyer support staff. It impacts upon the degree of trust and responsibility a nonlawyer is given. Professional conduct, then, ultimately serves to advance the role of the nonlawyer in the legal community, as well as the interests of the clients.

WHAT IS PROFESSIONAL CONDUCT?

When faced with the prospect of defining professional conduct, we may sputter, "Well, I can't think of the definition, but I certainly know it when I see it." It is difficult to define because it may mean different things to different people. However, as we will see shortly, certain characteristics are common to all kinds of professional behavior.

Adhering to a code of ethics is the first step to learning professional behavior. A code of legal ethics, then, is the first source for determining what conduct is professional in a law environment. However, adhering to a Code of Ethics is just a *first step*. Although it is a good beginning, it is not the entire answer. For example, gossiping about your significant other at the water cooler all morning may not violate any rule of the Code of Ethics *per se*, but it certainly would not be considered professional.

What additional sources can we consult to determine what is professional behavior? The dictionary defines words by considering the meanings attributed to certain words, as they are used by members of society, so one additional source we can consult is the dictionary. In the dictionary, "professional" is defined as "characterized by or conforming to the technical or ethical standards of a profession."[2]

By this definition, the conduct considered to be professional conduct in a law office environment would include the character and standards of other legal assistants and legal professionals working in that environment. A paralegal should take care, then, to observe the standards of legal assistants employed in that environment, as well as the standards of legal assistants with whom the paralegal comes in contact through legal assistant organizations or seminars.

Yet another description of professional behavior comes from periodicals which are designed for the legal assistant or the nonlawyer. For example, an article in *Legal Assistant Today* quoted *Basic Business and Professional Speech Communication* by Ted Frank and David Ray. The article stated: "Those people who are viewed as real 'professionals' are people who have developed an important skill: *They are good at getting along with themselves.* They are usually not any more talented, intelligent, knowledgeable or hard-working than the

[2]MERRIAM-WEBSTER'S COLLEGIATE DICTIONARY 930 (10th ed. 1993). By permission. From Merriam-Webster's Collegiate® Dictionary © 1993 by Merriam-Webster Inc., publisher of the Merriam-Webster® dictionaries.

| HIGHLIGHT | The Three Dimensions of Professionalism |

■ Adhere to a Code of Ethics.

■ Adopt the highest standards of conduct of other legal professionals.

■ Respect co-workers.

---

rest of us. What we admire about them is an attitude that displays confidence and makes us feel comfortable and confident about ourselves.' "[3] (emphasis in original)

To summarize the above quotation: A real professional is someone who respects himself and makes his co-workers feel respected, confident, and comfortable.

To recap, then, professional conduct has three dimensions. The first dimension is adherence to a Code of Ethics. The second is that the professional adopts the highest standards of conduct of the legal professionals working around her and in her community. Third, the professional respects herself and shows her co-workers respect. She enables co-workers to feel confident about themselves. Within these three dimensions, however, learn your own judgment when making any decision about professional behavior.

Draft a definition of what you believe is professional conduct. | **EXERCISE 10.2**

ACHIEVING HIGH STANDARDS OF PROFESSIONAL CONDUCT

Paralegals are presented on a daily basis with an opportunity to interact with other legal assistants, with lawyers, and with clients. Routinely, paralegals are given responsibilities that must be completed in order to advance the client's representation. These activities require the paralegal to exhibit professional behavior. It is a responsibility of the paralegal, then, to exercise professional judgment every day. This may seem like an overwhelming responsibility.

In fact, it might be easier than you think. Remember, professionalism is a function of education, observation, and experience. We have all had some experiences that required us to respond professionally. Therefore, we all have some idea of how to behave professionally.

The situations that may arise in our legal careers to test our professional behavior will be unique and require different responses, so this book cannot give pat answers to questions concerning how to behave professionally.

The rest of the chapter, however, will provide you with some typical situations that are resolved by applying the three dimensions of professionalism. Continue reading and test your concept of what is professional behavior.

[3]LEGAL ASSISTANT TODAY, Mar.-Apr. 1992, 135. Copyright 1994. James Publishing, Inc. Reprinted with permission from *Legal Assistant Today*. For subscription information, call (714) 755-5450.

CONDUCT IN THE LAW OFFICE

The paralegal's conduct in the law office certainly affects whether she is perceived as a professional.

It is important to learn professional conduct in this context for, rightly or wrongly, acting unprofessionally may affect whether our work product is perceived as being professionally completed. Consider this: No matter how much effort is put into completing a project, if it is handed to a supervising attorney late and with coffee stains, it will be perceived as substandard. Analogously, we may be intelligent and hardworking, but if we are blemished with some stain—such as a reputation for gossiping or having a snobbish attitude—we will be perceived as substandard professionals.

How can a new paralegal learn these unwritten rules of office etiquette? By consulting the three dimensions of professionalism we mentioned earlier, test your knowledge with this exercise.

Ping Paralegal and Oliver Office Clerk had started work at Gershwin and Associates on the same day, several years ago. Although Gershwin's legal environment was generally conservative, its legal staff was a congenial group of people who got along well with each other and with clients, and Ping and Oliver fit right in with the law firm culture.

The two usually arrived at work about one-half hour before their co-workers. Ping and Oliver would get cups of coffee and settle into one of their offices for about twenty minutes to discuss current events. Many of the members of the law firm would stop in and chat for a while.

Gershwin recently hired Loni Legal Assistant to help Ping handle the discovery matters in a complex litigation, class action suit the firm had filed several months ago. Loni had just moved to this large city on the west coast to join the staff of Gershwin. She was originally from a small town in another part of the country. Loni knew she would have to work hard to adapt to this office climate. However, Loni was uncomfortable with the behavior she had observed to date.

Although she knew that Ping and Oliver arrived at work early, Loni was astonished that they would have the audacity to "coffee-klatsch" in the morning. She also noticed that the office staff all dressed in very formal business attire. She was accustomed to wearing more casual work clothing.

Because Loni was confused about how to fit in, she sought the advice of an image consultant. The consultant gave Loni three choices. Which would you recommend that she adopt?

A. Begin arriving at work several minutes early and stop in to chat with Ping and Oliver for an amount of time with which Loni was comfortable. Adopt the style of dress the firm employs. If Loni is unsure about what kinds of clothing to purchase, perhaps she could ask Ping to go shopping with her.

B. Seek the advice of one of the members of the law firm, asking about how she can better fit into the law firm culture. Specifically mention that Loni felt Ping and Oliver were using exclusionary tactics and not making her feel welcome.

C. Begin taking more of the work load on herself. Send out documents requested in discovery without clearing everything with the supervising attorney so that the attorney will be impressed with Loni's work ethic and will appreciate that she can trust Loni's judgment.

Let's consider Loni's options. When forced to decide on a course of conduct, the first rule to remember is to look to the three dimensions of professionalism. Consider first Alternative "C."

Clearly, there are problems associated with choosing Alternative "C." This alternative violates the first dimension of professional behavior in that it infringes upon the Code of Ethics.

If Loni does not have the supervising attorney review the documents, she may find that she is revealing confidential information to the opposing counsel and is jeopardizing the client's position. If she continues on this course of behavior and fails to receive approval from the supervising attorney before turning over documents and before filing papers with the court, Loni may find herself in violation of unauthorized practice of law rules. She should definitely reject this proposal.

Choice "B" involves discussing the behavior of Loni's co-workers, Ping and Oliver, with another co-worker. This is also not a professional choice.

When we feel excluded, we may feel hurt and we may be inclined to want to discuss the matter. This is a natural response. However, if you must complain about a co-worker, choose someone outside the firm with whom to discuss the situation. Talk instead to your parents, spouse, or best friends who work outside the office. A simple disagreement between co-workers that is discussed among the office staff may create divisions among all the employees and irreparably harm interoffice relations.

Alternative "A" is the most professional solution for Loni in this instance. Remember that one dimension of professionalism is to adopt the highest standards of behavior of others in your legal environment. By adopting the style of dress of Ping, Oliver, and other members of the firm, Loni will be making great strides toward assuming a professional air. Moreover, if she is uncomfortable with a twenty-minute chat before beginning work, stopping by for just several minutes will show that she is not adopting an elitist attitude and is making an effort to get along with her co-workers. On the other hand, while adapting to the highest standards of members of your law firm is important, the paralegal should take care to avoid engaging in any behavior with which she is personally uncomfortable.

INTERACTION WITH CLIENTS

How the paralegal interacts with clients is also a good indicator of the paralegal's sense of professionalism.

The paralegal often has a great deal of client contact and, in interacting with those clients, serves as a representative of the law firm. The law firm has been entrusted to safeguard the client's affairs. It is imperative, then, that the paralegal's conduct reassure the client that she has entrusted her affairs to the right organization. This means it is imperative that the paralegal present a professional demeanor (i.e., do not gossip with the client or dress too casually).

The failure to do so could also hurt the client's representation. Remember that the first dimension of professionalism is adhering to a code of ethics. What client would be inclined to divulge confidential information to an individual who does not appear to respect ethical obligations? In other words, what client would trust an individual who presented a less than professional image? This could certainly affect the law firm's presentation of that client.

How can a legal assistant present a professional demeanor? Not every situation is identical and not every client is identical. You will often be called on to use your best judgment in defining your relationship with any client. Test your sense of professionalism with this hypothetical situation.

Penny Paralegal and her supervising attorney, Abernathy, had both started at Lu, Pahl and Cooke on the same day. As Abernathy's responsibilities grew, so did Penny's.

After a particularly busy week, Abernathy asked Penny to handle a few initial client interviews. Penny got along extremely well with the clients; so well, in fact, that several clients told Abernathy that, although they had been anxious about consulting an attorney, Penny had calmed their fears. A big part of the reason they had chosen Lu, Pahl and Cooke to handle their representation, they said, was because Penny worked there and she was so professional.

Abernathy was very grateful to Penny. He asked her to continue handling initial client interviews.

One day, a new and somewhat intimidating client, Campbell, walked into the office. Campbell owned several thriving businesses in this small town and he had the reputation of being a hard man who pushed his employees to get the most work from them. It was also rumored that Campbell had fired his last attorney because he felt he had not received enough personal attention.

Although she was somewhat nervous, Penny began to ask Campbell some routine questions. After a while, they learned they had both graduated from the same small liberal arts college, Alpha College. Campbell told Penny, "This is amazing! Not many people have even heard of our alma mater. I know I may be biased, but I immediately trust anyone who has graduated from Alpha College." Campbell then became more forthcoming in his answers.

Penny began to relax during this interview. It ended on a positive note, with Campbell indicating his desire to retain the services of Abernathy. A few days later, Campbell called Penny to ask her when he should send in the initial retainer fee. The conversation wound around to other topics (unrelated to Campbell's representation) and Penny found herself talking to Campbell for twenty minutes.

Campbell's calls to Penny began to come on a regular basis. In fact, he stopped calling Abernathy altogether. During one of his calls, Campbell told Penny he had begun to trust her more than Abernathy. One day Campbell sent Penny flowers to thank her for her help in drafting incorporation papers. Finally, Campbell called Penny one day and insisted she take his call, although she was meeting with another client, Connie, in the conference room. Campbell said, "My company is hosting a fund-raising dinner for the new gubernatorial candidate. I would like someone from my law firm to attend but I feel much closer to you than to Abernathy. Therefore, I was wondering if you would not mind attending this function."

What do you think Penny should do?

A. After talking to Campbell, Penny should return to her office. When Connie asks her if anything is wrong, Penny should tell her about Campbell and his affairs.

B. Penny should politely ask Campbell if she can return his call and notify him about whether she would accept his invitation later. When she is finished meeting with Connie, she should then go to Abernathy to discuss the situation with him.

C. Penny should agree to attend the fund-raiser with Campbell and should encourage his attentions. After all, he is a rather wealthy man and anything could happen.

Penny's situation is not a common one for a legal assistant to face. Clients may feel stronger attachments to a paralegal than to an attorney. The legal assistant's role is often considered by some to be that of a buffer between the client and the attorney. Because the legal assistant may come into contact with the client more than the attorney does, the client may come to rely on the paralegal and her relationship with him.

Keeping this premise in mind, consider Penny's options as we apply the three dimensions of professionalism. First, let's look at Alternative "A". The first dimension of professionalism is for the legal assistant to adhere to the Code of Ethics. The Code of Ethics in place in any state and the Code of Ethics of either of the national legal assistant organizations reminds paralegals that they must maintain the confidences of the client. Penny should be very careful, therefore, in discussing with another client her problems with Campbell.

Although Penny may not intend to reveal any confidential information, she could very easily let slip information that would reveal Campbell's identity or his position in the small town. Consequently, she could inadvertently harm the interests of Campbell. Remember that chapter 5 instructed that it is best to not reveal *any* information about a client or a prospective client.

Another important point to remember about discussing a client with another client is that your indiscretion may disquiet the second client. If Penny talks about Campbell and his problems with Connie, Connie may wonder if Penny is going to be speaking to a third client later this morning about Connie's legal problems. This certainly does not engender trust and respect for professional behavior.

For these reasons, it should be clear that option "A" is not the most professional choice.

Should Penny attend the fund-raiser and encourage Campbell's attentions, as Option "C" suggests? This is probably not the most professional choice. It is always wise to maintain a professional distance from the client. Becoming too involved in the client's personal affairs will only have the effect of distracting the legal assistant and keeping her away from her responsibilities in the law firm. If Penny spends more time talking with Campbell about his personal problems, she will be spending less time handling such matters as drafting his incorporation papers. Even if this friendship is purely platonic, this will certainly not benefit the client.

You can also be assured that amorous relationships with clients will be discouraged in most law offices. Why is this? Sexual relations with clients certainly can cloud the legal assistant's judgment. The legal assistant's relationship with a client can also compromise the client's relationship with the entire law firm. (The consequences of sexual relationships between the legal assistant and the client are illustrated in the "Spotlight" feature.)

This leaves Option "B" to consider. The third dimension of professionalism requires us to respect ourselves and our co-workers. Although the paralegal may be a buffer between the lawyer and the client, the paralegal should remember to respect them both and be loyal to them both.

When a client complains about an attorney or makes any kind of disparaging remark about the attorney, it is probably best to just listen to the client's concerns without adding your own complaints about the attorney. If the client has expressed a valid concern, the legal assistant can later bring the concerns to the attorney or to a supervising legal assistant. In this example, there is no indication that Abernathy has done anything wrong. Instead, it merely appears that Campbell has grown closer to Penny than to Abernathy.

Nor does it appear that Abernathy has given Penny any reason to distrust him. It is probably best, therefore, for Penny to discuss with Abernathy her situation with Campbell. Remember, too, that there may be other problems involved here. As a general rule, chapter 6 advises that legal assistants are not to accept gifts from clients. Penny should advise Abernathy of the gift of flowers and seek his advice on how to handle this situation, should more gifts follow. After all, if there is an ethical problem, Abernathy may face serious consequences.

For these reasons, Option "B" is probably the most professional choice to make in this situation. After all, the client has expressed a desire to have a member of his law firm present at the function. Depending on the client, of course, an outright refusal may create friction between the parties operating within the attorney-client relationship. However, once Abernathy is fully apprised of the situation, he and Penny can discuss the best approach to take with this client.

Remember, not every situation is identical. Depending on the characters involved, there may be other choices to make which have not been discussed here. For example, a legal assistant may consider consulting her supervising paralegal if she feels that the attorney, for whatever reason, would not understand her problems with the client.

RELATIONSHIPS WITH ATTORNEYS

The legal assistant's relationship with attorneys likewise affects her professional demeanor.

Attorneys will interact with paralegals in two different capacities. (1) as the paralegal's supervising attorney(s) and (2) as opposing counsel. Certainly, the legal assistant will benefit from being pleasant and courteous with these attorneys. Being on friendly terms with opposing counsel helps to facilitate expeditious settlement of cases. However, in order to maintain professional decorum, there are limits to these kinds of friendships.

Test your awareness of the professionalism that is necessary in relationships with attorneys.

Pedro Paralegal had just started working with Anastasia Attorney at Jefferson, Niarchos and LaSalle, Ltd. Anastasia's legal assistant had just resigned after eleven years with Jefferson, Niarchos and LaSalle, and Pedro was hired to replace him. Despite the fact that his experience was in intellectual property matters and Anastasia handled family law matters almost exclusively, Pedro was hired because he had a strong reputation for being a hardworking, competent paralegal.

Pedro was precisely what Anastasia needed. She had just been assigned a high-profile case representing a professional tennis player whose husband was seeking a divorce on the grounds that the client had been having affairs with several professional ball players. Anastasia knew the case was going to receive a great deal of publicity, and she wanted to be able to devote her full attention to the matter.

Anastasia had also been working on several other matters, including completing a few adoptions and drafting some prenuptial agreements for several of her clients. Pedro would be needed to assist in drafting and to do research in each of these cases. However, because each case was different and Anastasia was taking a different approach in each, Pedro believed he would need to work closely with her. Unfortunately, it seemed to Pedro that Anastasia was often too busy to spend much time with him. He did not believe he would be given the necessary degree of supervision.

Pedro knew he had a strong reputation in this legal community for being a capable, professional legal assistant, and he did not want to jeopardize this reputation. However, his relationship with his supervising attorney was a little troublesome. He discussed the problem with a good friend from his graduating class. Then Pedro sat down and considered his options. What would you suggest that Pedro do to ensure that his reputation in the legal community as a professional legal assistant remain unscathed?

A. Pedro should put in extra time researching and should then prepare the adoption papers to the best of his ability and file them. He should also prepare all the prenuptial agreements and send them to the clients for their review before Anastasia has approved them. After all, Anastasia is extremely busy right now and Pedro would be helping her to get her work done.

B. Pedro should ask for regular meetings with Anastasia. When they meet, he should take a legal pad into the office with him and he should ask for specific directions in completing his work, writing the instructions down word-for-word.

C. Pedro should follow the advice of his friend and form an intimate relationship with Anastasia who would then, Pedro's friend suggests, devote more time to Pedro.

Let's look at Pedro's alternatives. In Option "A," Pedro is considering preparing and filing papers with Anastasia's review and signature. At first glance, Option "A" may appear attractive because Anastasia is so busy. However, Option "A" is clearly not the most professional (or ethically correct) option.

If Pedro were to do as Option "A" suggests, he would most certainly be engaging in the unauthorized practice of law. This clearly violates the code of legal ethics. He may also find that Anastasia, whom he was trying to help, will face discipline for failing to adequately supervise her legal assistant and thereby aiding in the unauthorized practice of law.

Pedro, of course, decided to immediately dismiss Option "C" as an alternative. He knows that, for the legal assistant to achieve what is perceived to be professional behavior, he should keep his relationship with his supervising attorney on a professional level.

Certainly, the paralegal and the supervising attorney can be friends and can share meals; but there are limits to this kind of relationship. Problems result when the friendship is more than platonic.

Because of the long hours and exciting working environment of the law firm, it is often easy for legal assistants to consider becoming involved with a co-worker. Paralegals are best advised to enter into such relationships with caution. An amorous relationship between the attorney and legal assistant can lead to distrust and gossip in the legal environment. It can cause friction among co-workers. Ultimately, it can lead to charges of sexual harassment. In addition, although the personal relationship between the attorney and legal assistant may end, the professional relationship between the two must continue, unless one or the other leaves the firm. This situation often creates unbearable tension for every employee in the law firm.

An article in *Legal Assistant Today* discussed this issue.[4] The author of the article also advised paralegals to enter with caution into personal relationships with co-workers. Noting the following problems, the article listed "seven dangers of office dating." These are:

1. Co-workers become jealous and/or suspicious.
2. When a couple plays, someone always pays.
3. Productivity plunges.
4. It's difficult to separate the professional and the personal.
5. Your office romance can topple your professional image.
6. Your office romance can end.
7. You may spend too much time worrying about it.

All of these dangers certainly affect whether a paralegal's behavior is perceived as professional. Sometimes, however, a legal assistant and co-worker may feel that a personal relationship is worth all the risks. Therefore, author Lowndes also notes that, if a paralegal wants to "navigate the love boat through turbulent office waters," he or she should heed the following advice:

1. Choose a co-worker of equal status.
2. Don't date a married co-worker.
3. Don't date anyone who has financial dealings with your firm.
4. Make sure your romance doesn't cause disturbances.
5. Be discreet.

It is also wise to remember that personal relationships with opposing counsel can harm a professional reputation. As chapter 6 advised, relationships with opposing counsel may result in serious conflict-of-interest problems. In turn, such a conflict of interest may lead to the disqualification of a supervising attorney or law firm.

The most professional alternative in this instance is, therefore, Alternative "B." Anastasia has been doing this work for a long time and has been supervising legal assistants for a while. Pedro should respect this experience and seek out her guidance.

Anastasia's former legal assistant had worked with her for eleven years. The former paralegal probably did not need as much guidance as Pedro might need right now, since Pedro comes from an intellectual property background. Anastasia may just be unaware that Pedro needs help.

Asking for specific directions is always the best way the nonlawyer can protect the client's interests. After writing down the instructions, Pedro can be

---

[4]Leil Lowndes, *Dangerous Office Liaisons*, Legal Assistant Today, Sept.-Oct. 1993, 64+. Copyright 1994. James Publishing, Inc. Reprinted with permission from *Legal Assistant Today*. For subscription information, call (714) 755-5450.

HIGHLIGHT   An Illustration of Seriously Unprofessional Conduct

Sexual harassment takes place in all settings. It is sad to note that professionals engage in such conduct, too. As the following contract illustrates, the legal world is not immune from displays of unprofessional conduct.

An attorney from Ventura, California, had two legal secretary positions available in his office. (For the sake of convenience, he will be referred to as "Al Attorney.") In a written job description, Al Attorney stated that his prospective secretaries must be "loyal, discreet, submissive when appropriate, dominant when appropriate." Though it may be difficult to believe that an attorney would do such a thing, the attorney who drafted the following contract claimed as a defense that he did so to protect himself against being blackmailed.

The contract reads:

STANDARD MENTOR/PROTEGEE CONTRACT

■ [Al Attorney] is the mentor.

■ Protegee is (Name) _____

Address _____

Phone _____

■ [Protegee] agrees to return all keys, credit cards, answering machines, and other property of [Al Attorney] before leaving if she decides to terminate this relationship.

■ Protegee and mentor agree to attempt to maintain the highest degree of mutual respect, concern, honesty, etc.

■ WAIVER AND CONSENT. Mentor and Protegee hereby mutually consent to all words, acts, sexual innuendo, sexual acts, touching, lewd behavior, etc. The exclusive remedy for [unwanted] behavior shall be persuasion or termination of the relationship. This clause does not anticipate any sexual activity but is designed primarily to protect the mentor against sexual blackmail.

■ ACKNOWLEDGEMENT AND DISCLOSURE. [Al Attorney] hereby discloses that [Protegee] was selected primarily on the basis of sexual appeal, polite attitude, pleasant disposition, and generally refined behavior. [Al Attorney] further discloses that he is currently looking for a new girlfriend and that Protegee is a candidate. This does not mean that Protegee must agree to sexual activity, but it is a disclosure of sexual interest.

■ JEALOUS BOYFRIENDS/HUSBANDS. Both parties agree to maintain discretion and confidentially to preclude any unpleasant scenes. By signing this contract, Protegee hereby declares under penalty of perjury that she does not have a jealous husband or boyfriend. This clause is very important and non-negotiable.

■ GOALS. The work items are fully described in the Office Procedure Manual. Here are the nonwork things [Al Attorney] would like Protegee to do. None of them are compulsory.
Sex and Romance would be nice.

If not you, then help me find somebody else.
I need a new apartment.
I need somebody to go to the beach, bladeskate, etc., with me.

A Gentleman's Agreement, HARPER'S MAGAZINE, Apr. 1992, 19–20.
Copyright © 1992 by *Harper's Magazine*. All rights reserved. Reprinted from the April issue by special permission.

assured that he is following Anastasia's directions to the letter. It is important that all paralegals remember this advice. A legal assistant should never feel too intimidated by a supervising lawyer's busy schedule to ask for directions. Remember: You are protecting the client's interests by asking for and writing down specific directions. You should not be afraid to ask questions—even if your supervising attorney appears busy or preoccupied.

The above example constitutes flagrant mis-conduct. However, every person must be sensitive to the existence of more subtle forms of harassment and discrimination (i.e., lewd comments, physical overtures, derogatory comments regarding ethnicity, gender, religion, and special physical challenges).

CONDUCT TOWARD PARALEGALS

Finally, a legal assistant's conduct toward his fellow legal assistants must also be professional.

Adopting professional behavior will not only help your own reputation. Your professional behavior will reflect on other paralegals working in your legal culture. Because the paralegal community is still young and working toward developing widespread acceptance among legal professionals, this is especially important. As had been noted in NALA's publication, *Facts & Findings,* "Legal assistants everywhere will benefit when each of us, individually, conducts ourself in a courteous, trustworthy and professional manner."[5]

How should a paralegal treat fellow paralegals? What steps can a legal assistant take to ensure that legal assistants are recognized for their contribution to the legal profession? Test your sense of professionalism.

Prudence is a supervising paralegal at the law firm, Burnworth and Tolva. Paco and Peggy work under Prudence. They have been assigned to a case involving computer technology, working with Lillian, an attorney who has been with the firm for fifteen years. The main issue in the case involves a question of whether a former employee of the company represented by Burnworth and Tolva infected the company's computer system with a virus and then shared confidential information from the company's computer systems with his new employer.

Peggy is a two-year veteran of the firm and was a computer science major in college. Paco has worked in the torts department at Burnworth for four years and has worked on trade-secret cases before. Penny believes she is best suited to orchestrate the organization of documents for trial, while Paco feels he is better suited to make the determinations about the documents.

The two strongly disagree about document organization. Their disagreements have started to impede their ability to work together. They complain to their co-workers about one another. They cannot communicate with each other about any facet of the upcoming trial and what needs to be done for Lillian.

Two weeks before the trial, Paco decides to go to Prudence, who tells him he should sit down with Peggy, discuss several options, and choose one to resolve their differences. The two take her advice. The following are the options they consider. Which one do you think they should select?

A. Paco and Peggy decide to go to Lillian, the supervising attorney, and tell her they can no longer work together. They will tell Lillian that she will have to decide which one should go.

B. Paco and Peggy decide to make the best of their differences and let the experiences they both bring to the situation work to the advantage of the client.

---

[5]*Legal Assistant Professionalism in the Decade of Confusion,* FACTS & FINDINGS, Nov. 1993, 30–33.

C. Paco and Peggy decide that, since Lillian is so busy, they will call the judge and tell him Lillian's theory of the case. Then they will ask which of the two of them he thinks should have the final say regarding the documents.

Clearly, in the interests of the firm and, of course, the client, Peggy and Paco should work to choose the most professional way to resolve their differences. To do so, they must consider the three dimensions of professionalism. With this in mind, let's consider Peggy and Paco's options.

Seeking out the judge outside of the courtroom and outside of the presence of opposing counsel certainly violates the code of ethics. To do what Peggy and Paco suggest would amount to an *ex parte* communication with the judge. The paralegals propose to discuss the attorney's theory of the case, which would clearly involve communicating about the substantive aspects of the matter before that judge. Option "C" is not the most professional choice.

Although Option "A" may not violate any code of ethics, it is also not the most professional choice to make. Going to the attorney two weeks before trial to advise her that her legal assistants may not be able to complete their assigned work for the pending trial will only create problems. A great deal of work is always involved in any trial, and the attorney cannot afford to lose either of the people she was depending on for help. Losing one paralegal may mean that trial preparation is not as complete as it should have been. This means the paralegals' disagreement will ultimately affect the one person whom they are supposed to be helping—the client.

Option "B" is clearly the most professional choice in this situation. It is in everybody's best interests to agree to resolve their differences and to appreciate their individual strengths. Both Paco and Peggy have a great deal to offer their client. Working together, they can increase the chances that the attorney will present a winning case on behalf of the client. By putting their differences to the side, they are adhering to one of the dimensions of professional behavior: They are learning to respect their co-workers and the experiences those co-workers can bring to the situation.

Attorney Carl hires Velta to work as a legal assistant in his law firm. Velta has worked for many years as a top-notch legal secretary but has decided to try her hand at a new challenge.

Carl has decided to meet with Velta to discuss some of the aspects of her new position.

Are there any aspects of professional conduct in the law office setting of which Velta might not be aware because she has never worked as a legal assistant? Why are these aspects unique to the position of the paralegal?

EXERCISE 10.3

FOCUS ON SHELLEY WIDOFF

Shelley Widoff has been active in legal assistant practice and education for as long as there has been a paralegal profession. Currently, she runs Boston University's degree and certificate paralegal programs, and she is CEO of her own company which provides paralegal services and recruits and places legal assistants. Widoff is also the author of a feature column that appears in *Legal Assistant Today* entitled "On the Docket." As her career has progressed, Widoff has observed many instances of professional, and sometimes unprofessional, behavior by legal assistants and by the supervising attorneys to whom they report.

Never forget that you are a professional working for and reporting to a professional. How the legal assistant behaves in the law office is one aspect of his or her professionalism. A second aspect of your professional status to remember is that, as a legal assistant, you work for the attorney and not for the client.

Widoff agrees that becoming acquainted with the parameters of professional behavior and acting as a professional in the workplace are essential to the continuing evolvement of the status of the paralegal as a professional. "Paralegals work in a professional environment, and any activity they engage in which does not meet standards of professionalism will stick out like a sore thumb." Moreover, Widoff notes, "If the client perceives that a legal assistant is anything other than a complete professional, this will adversely affect a client's confidence in the competence of the particular legal assistant as well as a client's

acceptance of the paralegal as a member of the legal team. It will also impact a client's belief whether or not the paralegal should continue to assist in handling the client's case."

Widoff has carefully studied the issue of professionalism from both academic and practical perspectives. She has concluded that paralegal professionalism has a second component. How the paralegal acts in the law office is one critical aspect of defining what is professional behavior.

The second and equally defining aspect of paralegal professionalism requires that the legal assistant take special care to refrain from invading the province of the attorney. According to Widoff, this means the paralegal must make clear to any client with whom she or he comes into contact that the *lawyer* has the ultimate responsibility for representing the client; the paralegal does not.

Observes Widoff "A paralegal who has developed a rapport with a client may find that over time the client may be inclined to bypass the attorney and to work directly with the paralegal. When that very natural phenomenon occurs the paralegal must always run it by the attorney. Moreover, paralegals cannot and must not exercise independent legal judgment. A paralegal's loyalty has to be to the attorney he or she reports to."

—Continued

FOCUS ON SHELLEY WIDOFF

(Continued)

According to Widoff, "There may come a time when the client seeks your independent judgment on a legal issue which has not been reviewed by the attorney you work for. In such an instance, you must be very supportive of the attorney you report to. You must then inform the client that you are a legal assistant and that you do not have the training and expertise to provide legal judgment calls."

On occasion Widoff has also observed other unprofessional conduct by paralegals. She notes that the most likely problem to occur is what she describes as paralegal "insubordination." According to Widoff, "I have seen a paralegal second-guess an attorney's directives and/or legal judgment calls and, when called on the carpet, the paralegal becomes defensive and insubordinate." Widoff emphasizes that paralegals must learn that they have a responsibility to follow directives given by the person to whom they report.

Widoff offers the following advice to those paralegals who wish to learn professional behavior. "If you work in a law firm, identify the most professional attorney in your office and use that person as a role model with which to conform your behavior."

Widoff believes "freelance" paralegals encounter special problems relating to professionalism because of the ambiguity of their status. A code of paralegal professional responsibility has not yet been proposed or promulgated for them. In the meantime, she says independent paralegals should become familiar with and, when relevant, follow to the extent possible the code of professional responsibility for lawyers practicing in their state, using that code as a guide to what she or he can and should do or not do.

As an aside, Widoff's advice to the independent paralegal is to avoid exaggerating his or her abilities to any attorney who is preparing to hire him or her. "The independent paralegal should always give a fair and reasonable disclosure of his or her ability and experience," emphasizes Widoff. "However, after that and once an assignment is made, the freelancer should feel free to seek assistance from the attorney who has employed you, and you should not feel as though you are expected to know everything and to act as a substitute lawyer."

How far have paralegals come in learning and maintaining professional behavior? According to Widoff there is always room for improvement. A significant problem is that, because the profession is still relatively new, there are not many seasoned paralegals working within any particular office environment. Widoff believes, however, that the paralegal profession is finally coming into its own—there are professional role models available to emulate. Widoff's final advice is to identify whom these paralegals are and look to them for advice.

TIPS FOR PARALEGALS

- Be aware of and strictly adhere to a code of ethics.

- Observe the conduct of other paralegals in your working environment and adopt the highest standards of conduct you observe.

- Attend paralegal association meetings and get involved in working with other paralegals whom you observe to be professional.

- Always choose to respect yourself and your co-workers.

- Dress in a professional manner, and pay strict attention to the dress code of your office.

- Choose to attend seminars that are offered locally in your community and that address issues as diverse as dressing for success and avoiding discrimination in the workplace.

- Avoid using profanity in the law office.

- Never gossip about co-workers or clients.

- Don't date your co-workers or clients.

- Avoid engaging in any conduct that is denigrating to co-workers or clients, including but not limited to: making ethnic, gender, physical or religious slurs, making physical overtures, and commenting on remuneration and pay scales.

CLOSING EXERCISE

Bill is a legal assistant who works for a national law firm. He is known at the firm for his writing ability.

Because of his reputation, Bill is asked by the managing partners of the law firm to put together a "Manual for Professional Conduct." He is told that it is to be general in scope and must appeal to each of the fifteen national offices of the firm.

List some features Bill should include in the manual.

Then use your list to write a simple manual for acting professionally in any law office environment.

Chapter Summary

- It is important to study professional behavior because professional conduct ultimately serves to advance the role of the paralegal in the legal community and to advance the client's interests. The degree of trust and responsibility a nonlawyer is given is affected by the nonlawyer's conduct. Moreover, studies such as that conducted by the Committee on Civility of the Seventh Judicial Circuit recommend to lawyers that they discourage improper conduct among their nonlawyer employees.

- Professional behavior comprises three dimensions. 1) Paralegals should adhere to a Code of Ethics. 2) Paralegals should adopt the highest standards of conduct of other professionals. 3) Paralegals should respect themselves and their co-workers.

- The three dimensions of professionalism can be applied throughout every facet of the paralegal's work routine. First, the legal assistant's conduct in the law office affects whether he is perceived as a professional. How the paralegal interacts with clients is also a good indicator of the paralegal's sense of professionalism. The legal assistant's relationship with attorneys likewise affects her professional demeanor. Finally, a legal assistant's conduct toward his fellow paralegals must also be professional.

KEY TERMS

civility	professional	unprofessional
possessory rights	professionalism	

CASE

Castillo v. St. Paul Fire & Marine Insurance Company

United States Court of Appeals,
Seventh Circuit.
938 F.2d 776.

HARLINGTON WOOD, Jr., Circuit Judge.

Chief Judge Baker labelled the behavior of plaintiff, a doctor, and his counsel "the most outrageous example of evasion and obfuscation that I have seen in years," and "a deliberate frustration of defendants' attempt to secure discovery." He sanctioned the doctor and both of his counsel, holding one in civil contempt. Thereafter Judge Baker dismissed the doctor's case with prejudice saying he was "truly sorry to be brought to this situation" finding it "most distasteful" and "an unfortunate duty." The doctor appeals, represented by attorneys James G. Walker and Dean R. Engelbrecht of James Walker, Ltd. of Bloomington, Illinois, the trial attorneys personally involved who also seek sanction relief in their own behalf. Objected to by the doctor and his counsel on appeal are the sanctions, the contempt and the dismissal. They also launch a counterattack. We affirm Judge Baker in all respects. The doctor and his attorneys' conduct which wasted much district court and attorney time need not waste much more here. The issues will only briefly be examined.

The story begins when doctor Guillermo Castillo, a physician who enjoyed medical staff privileges at Burnham City Hospital in Champaign, Illinois, refused to increase his medical malpractice coverage to the limits required by the medical staff bylaws of the hospital. These new higher limits, a minimum of one million dollars per occurrence and three million dollars aggregate, were imposed to comply with an underwriting requirement of the hospital's malprac-

tice carrier, St. Paul Fire and Marine Insurance Company.[1] The doctor's failure to comply resulted in the suspension of his medical staff privileges at the hospital. The doctor responded by filing this suit alleging violations of the Sherman and Clayton Acts, the Civil Rights Act of 1871, and the Illinois Antitrust Act, seeking declaratory and injunctive relief, damages, and attorney's fees. (footnote omitted) Any possible merit those allegations might have is not directly at issue in this appeal.

. . .

Discovery then began and so did the trouble. In June 1989 each of the defendants, after considerable scheduling difficulties, undertook to depose Dr. Castillo, but did not get very far with it even though it took all day and 281 pages of transcript. The doctor was at this session represented by attorney Dean Engelbrecht, an associate of Walker. The session began by counsel objecting, without prior notice to defendants, to producing certain documents previously requested on the basis that the documents were irrelevant, duplicative, or a violation of physician-patient privilege. The doctor's counsel also made it plain that the requested documents would not be provided because he argued the hospital had itself previously refused to provide the doctor with the same types of documents. Counsel also stated that this was the last and only time the doctor would be made available for a deposition. In spite of this rocky beginning and without the previously requested documents, defendants' counsel proceeded.

After that, from time to time similar objections to questions followed. Sometimes there was a claim the question called for the doctor to speculate or give a legal opinion. If it was deemed irrelevant the doctor was also instructed not to answer in spite of

---

[1]We have some appreciation of the problems doctors have with malpractice insurance and claims, but the conduct in this case was the wrong prescription for any ailment.

Rule 30(c) requiring that evidence objected to shall be taken subject to objections. A number of questions for one reason or another did not get answered. When counsel for defendants tried to pursue a question which the doctor or his lawyer had tried to fence away the doctor's counsel charged harassment. Counsel, among other things, protected the doctor from answering questions about claimed damages, the meaning of letters the doctor had signed, and other questions related to the allegations of the complaint. The objections were on the basis that the doctor was not a lawyer and the letters and complaint, although signed by the doctor, had been composed by his present counsel. The questions called for legal conclusions or violated the privilege, it was claimed. Then followed some discussion about whether the deposition would have to be of the doctor's counsel. The doctor, however, needed little protection by his counsel as he was very adept at evading the questions, giving unresponsive answers and stonewalling.

Judge Baker fully reviewed the deposition objections after defendants filed motions to compel discovery and to require answers from the doctor. He found no merit in the particular objections whether for relevance or privilege or otherwise. Even if some particular question may have had some basis for an objection, that would not cure the overwhelming and continuing abuse of the discovery process by the plaintiff and his counsel throughout much of the deposition.

After reading the deposition, this court fully agrees with Judge Baker. It is plain, as Judge Baker said, that the doctor's counsel was engaged in a "deliberate frustration of defendants' discovery attempts." As a result of that conduct Judge Baker assessed fees and expenses of $6,317.66 divided equally between the doctor and his counsel. That assessment was fully warranted. A district judge has wide discretion in these discovery matters and we will not disturb the rulings absent a clear finding of abuse of discretion, *Brown-Bey v. United States*, 720 F.2d 467, 470-71 (7th Cir.1983), and there was none.

As some of the deposition questions therefore had not been answered, Judge Baker directed that they forthwith be answered without interference from the doctor's counsel. A further effort was made to depose the doctor. This time it was attorney James Walker who appeared with the doctor, but this lawyer substitution did not improve the situation. Attorney Engelbrecht was also present. As Judge Baker later found and as is evident to us from the deposition, the doctor's counsel willfully and contumaciously disobeyed the court's order by interfering

with the questions posed by defendants' counsel, and by directing the doctor not to respond to certain questions already approved by the court. The only issue of any possible consequence was the challenge to the questions allegedly on the basis of attorney-client privilege which, if answered, might waive the privilege. Judge Baker found, however, that few if any of the objections on the basis of privilege had any merit. We fully agree with that assessment. These repetitious obstructive tactics clearly deserved sanctions.

One remarkable incident occurring at this second deposition deserves telling. The deposition this time was being taken in attorney Walker's offices in Bloomington, Illinois. At another impasse, counsel for the hospital suggested that the differences between counsel be resolved by an immediate telephone conference with Judge Baker, a procedure Judge Baker had recommended. Attorney Walker did not immediately respond to the suggestion and hospital counsel therefore indicated he would go ahead and place the call. Then attorney Walker did respond:

> MR. WALKER: I would caution you not to use any telephones in this office unless you are invited to do so, counsel.
>
> MR. STANKO: You're telling me I can't use your telephones?
>
> MR. WALKER: You can write your threatening letters to me. But, you step outside this room and touch the telephone, and I'll take care of that in the way one does who has possessory rights.

When these deposition problems later came before Judge Baker he was not sure whether attorney Walker had actually threatened and intended physical violence or not. Attorney Stanko, the hospital counsel, advised the court that he had felt no fear of physical violence. Be that as it may, that exchange remains an example of professional incivility, a situation of general concern in this circuit and elsewhere.[3]

Judge Baker found that attorney Walker's arguments and statements were capricious and aimed at stymieing the defense efforts to find out through discovery what the doctor's case was about. The court's order which was intended to avoid a repeat of the prior deposition problem had been ignored. The proceedings had been unreasonably and vexatiously prolonged in violation of 28 U.S.C. § 1927. Attorney Walker was also subject to sanctions under

---

[3]Interim Report of the Committee on Civility of the Seventh Federal Judicial Circuit, April 1991.

Rule 16 and Rule 37(b). The doctor's case was thereupon dismissed with prejudice and attorney Walker was found to be in civil contempt. Dismissal of a doctor's case for conduct similar to this is not unknown to us. *Godlove v. Bamberger,* 903 F.2d 1145 (7th Cir.1990), *cert. denied,*—U.S.—, 111 S.Ct. 1123, 113 L.Ed.2d 230 (1991). The contempt, it was provided, could be purged by paying the expenses and fees of the defense. In addition, Judge Baker, after a hearing on a rule to show cause, concluded that attorney Walker's conduct was so unprofessional that it required referral to the other two judges in the district to determine the appropriate discipline, if any, including reprimand, censure, suspension, disbarment, or whatever might be found to be just.

The doctor in return filed a Rule 59 motion to reconsider, reverse, alter or amend the judgment, and also sought Rule 11 sanctions against the hospital, all viewed by Judge Baker as without merit and merely retaliatory for sanctions imposed on the doctor and his counsel. All motions were denied including also a motion by defendants for Rule 11 sanctions against plaintiff and his counsel for certain antitrust allegations in the complaint. Fees and costs totalling $5,085.50 were later allowed to defendants as part of the discovery sanctions.

. . .

We find this unfortunate situation as professionally disagreeable as did Judge Baker. The doctor and his counsel fully deserve the sanctions imposed and leave no alternative but to affirm the district court in all respects.[4] Hopefully we will be spared further cases of this nature which only thwart and disrupt our judicial processes to the detriment of all concerned. Where Judge Baker exercised his discretion he did so carefully and without abuse. It would only have been an abuse of his discretion for him not to have imposed the sanctions.

All this trouble was the doctor's and his counsels' own doing. It almost appears as if for some reasonthey did not want to the case tried. If that be so, at least to that extent, they prevail as it will not be.

AFFIRMED.

Questions

1. Do you think the behavior of attorneys Engelbrecht and Walker was unprofessional? Do you think they were simply doing what the client hired them to do?

2. Were these attorneys serving their client? Did becoming embroiled in this protected litigation work a disservice to their client?

3. In your opinion, should such unprofessional conduct as that described in this case warrant to a disciplinary violation?

4. What kind of discipline do you think this court would order if a paralegal attempted to interfere with discovery by, for example, destroying incriminating documents instead of producing them for the opposing side?

---

[4]This case, by reason of the sanctioned conduct, may cast some shadow over the professional standing of attorneys Walker and Engelbrecht, but that is not the intent of this court. We are judging only this one case, and as unfortunate as it was, this opinion should not be read expansively to generally tarnish the professional reputations of these attorneys, which not knowing differently, we may assume are otherwise good.

ABA Model Guidelines for the Utilization of Legal Assistant Services

PREAMBLE

State courts, bar associations, or bar committees in at least seventeen states have prepared recommendations[1] for the utilization of legal assistant services.[2] While their content varies, their purpose appears uniform: to provide lawyers with a reliable basis for delegating responsibility for performing a portion of the lawyer's tasks to legal assistants. The purpose of preparing model guidelines is not to contradict the guidelines already adopted or to suggest that other guidelines may be more appropriate in a particular jurisdiction. It is the view of the Standing Committee on Legal Assistants of the American Bar Association, however, that a model set of guidelines for the utilization of legal assistant services may assist many states in adopting or revising such guidelines. The Standing Committee is of the view that guidelines will encourage lawyers to utilize legal assistant services effectively and promote the growth of the legal assistant profession.[3] In undertaking this project, the Standing Committee has attempted to

state guidelines that conform with the American Bar Association's Model Rules of Professional Conduct, decided authority, and contemporary practice. Lawyers, of course, are to be first directed by Rule 5.3 of the Model Rules in the utilization of legal assistant services, and nothing contained in these guidelines is intended to be inconsistent with that rule. Specific ethical considerations in particular states, however, may require modification of these guidelines before their adoption. In the commentary after each guideline, we have attempted to identify the basis for the guideline and any issues of which we are aware that the guideline may present; those drafting such guidelines may wish to take them into account.

Guideline 1: A lawyer is responsible for all of the professional actions of a legal assistant performing legal assistant services at the lawyer's direction and should take reasonable measures to ensure that the legal assistant's conduct is consistent with the lawyer's obligations under the ABA Model Rules of Professional Conduct.

Comment to Guideline 1: An attorney who utilizes a legal assistant's services is responsible for determining that the legal assistant is competent to perform the tasks assigned, based on the legal assistant's education, training, and experience, and for ensuring that the legal assistant is familiar with the responsibilities of attorneys and legal assistants under the applicable rules governing professional conduct.[4]

Under principles of agency law and rules governing the conduct of attorneys, lawyers are responsible for the actions and the work product of the nonlawyers they employ. Rule 5.3 of the Model Rules[5]

---

1 An appendix identifies the guidelines, court rules, and recommendations that were reviewed in drafting these Model Guidelines.

2 On February 6, 1986, the ABA Board of Governors approved the following definition of the term "legal assistant":

> A legal assistant is a person, qualified through education, training, or work experience, who is employed or retained by a lawyer, law office, governmental agency, or other entity in a capacity or function which involves the performance, under the ultimate direction and supervision of an attorney, of specifically delegated substantive legal work, which work, for the most part, requires a sufficient knowledge of legal concepts that, absent such assistant, the attorney would perform the task.

In some contexts, the term "paralegal" is used interchangeably with the term legal assistant.

3 While necessarily mentioning legal assistant conduct, lawyers are the intended audience of these Guidelines. The Guidelines, therefore, are addressed to lawyer conduct and not directly to the conduct of the legal assistant. Both the National Association of Legal Assistants (NALA) and the National Federation of Paralegal Associations (NFPA) have adopted guidelines of conduct that are directed to legal assistants. *See* NALA, "Code of Ethics and Professional Responsibility of the National Association of Legal Assistants, Inc." (adopted May 1975, revised November 1979 and September 1988); NFPA, "Affirmation of Responsibility" (adopted 1977, revised 1981).

4 Attorneys, of course, are not liable for violations of the ABA Model Rules of Professional Conduct ("Model Rules") unless the Model Rules have been adopted as the code of professional conduct in a jurisdiction in which the lawyer practices. They are referenced in this model guideline for illustrative purposes; if the guideline is to be adopted, the reference should be modified to the jurisdiction's rules of professional conduct.

5 The Model Rules were first adopted by the ABA House of Delegates in August of 1983. Since that time many states have adopted the Model Rules to govern the professional conduct of lawyers licensed in those states. Since a number of states still utilize a version of the Model Code of Professional Responsibility ("Model Code"), which was adopted by the House of Delegates *(continued)*

requires that partners and supervising attorneys ensure that the conduct of non-lawyer assistants is compatible with the lawyer's professional obligations. Several state guidelines have adopted this language. *E.g.*, Commentary to Illinois Recommendation (A), Kansas Guideline III(a), New Hampshire Rule 35, Sub-Rule 9, and North Carolina Guideline 4. Ethical Consideration 3-6 of the Model Code encouraged lawyers to delegate tasks to legal assistants provided the lawyer maintained a direct relationship with the client, supervised appropriately, and had complete responsibility for the work product. The adoption of Rule 5.3, which incorporates these principles, implicitly reaffirms this encouragement.

Several states have addressed the issue of the lawyer's ultimate responsibility for work performed by subordinates. For example, Colorado Guideline 1.c, Kentucky Supreme Court Rule 3.700, Sub-Rule 2.C, and Michigan Guideline I provide: "The lawyer remains responsible for the actions of the legal assistant to the same extent as if such representation had been furnished entirely by the lawyer and such actions were those of the lawyer." New Mexico Guideline X states "[the] lawyer maintains ultimate responsibility for and has an ongoing duty to actively supervise the legal assistant's work performance, conduct and product." Connecticut Recommendation 2 and Rhode Island Guideline III state specifically that lawyers are liable for malpractice for the mistakes and omissions of their legal assistants.

Finally, the lawyer should ensure that legal assistants supervised by the lawyer are familiar with the rules governing attorney conduct and that they follow those rules. *See* Comment to Model Rule 5.3; Illinois Recommendation (A)(5), New Hampshire Supreme Court Rule 35, Sub-Rule 9, and New Mexico, Statement of Purpose; *see also* NALA's Model Standards and Guidelines for the Utilization of Legal Assistants, guidelines IV, V, and VIII (1985, revised 1990) (hereafter "NALA Guidelines").

The Standing Committee and several of those who have commented upon these Guidelines regard Guideline 1 as a comprehensive statement of general principle governing lawyers who utilize legal assistant services in the practice of law. As such it, in effect, is a part of each of the remaining Guidelines.

Guideline 2: Provided the lawyer maintains responsibility for the work product, a lawyer may delegate to a legal assistant any task normally performed by the lawyer except those tasks proscribed to one not licensed as a lawyer by statute, court rule, administrative rule of regulation, controlling authority, the ABA Model Rules of Professional Conduct, or these Guidelines.

Comment to Guideline 2: The essence of the definition of the term legal assistant adopted by the ABA Board of Governors in 1986 is that, so long as appropriate supervision is maintained, many tasks normally performed by lawyers may be delegated to legal assistants. Of course, Rule 5.5 of the Model Rules, DR 3-101 of the Model Code, and most states specifically prohibit lawyers from assisting or aiding a non-lawyer in the unauthorized practice of law. Thus, while appropriate delegation of tasks to legal assistants is encouraged, the lawyer may not permit the legal assistant to engage in the "practice of law." Neither the Model Rules nor the Model Code define the "practice of law." EC 3-5 under the Model Code gave some guidance by equating the practice of law to the application of the professional judgment of the lawyer in solving clients' legal problems. Further, ABA Opinion 316 (1967) states: "A lawyer can employ lay secretaries, lay investigators, lay detectives, lay researchers, accountants, lay scriveners, nonlawyer draftsmen or nonlawyer researchers. In fact, he may employ nonlawyers to do any task for him except counsel clients about law matters, engage directly in the practice of law, appear in court or appear in formal proceedings as part of the judicial process, so long as it is he who takes the work and vouches for it to the client and becomes responsible for it to the client."

Most state guidelines specify that legal assistants may not appear before courts, administrative tribunals, or other adjudicatory bodies unless their rules authorize such appearances; may not conduct depositions; and may not give legal advice to clients. *E.g.*, Connecticut Recommendation 4; Fla. EC 3-6 (327 So.2d at 16); and Michigan Guideline II. *Also see* NALA Guidelines IV and VI. But it is also important to note that, as some guidelines have recognized, pursuant to federal or state statute legal assistants are permitted to provide direct client representation in certain administrative proceedings. *E.g.*, South Carolina Guideline II. While this does not obviate the attorney's responsibility for the legal assistant's work, it does change the nature of the attorney supervision of the legal assistant. The opportunity to use such legal assistant services has particular benefits to legal services programs and does not violate Guideline 2. *See generally ABA Standards for Providers of Civil Legal Services to the Poor*, Std. 6.3, at 6.17–6.18 (1986).

---

5 in August of 1969, however, these comments will refer to both the Model Rules and the predecessor Model Code (and to the Ethical Considerations and Disciplinary Rules found under the canons in the Model Code).

The Model Rules emphasize the importance of appropriate delegation. The key to appropriate delegation is proper supervision, which includes adequate instruction when assigning projects, monitoring of the project, and review of the completed project. The Supreme Court of Virginia upheld a malpractice verdict against a lawyer based in part on negligent actions of a legal assistant in performing tasks that evidently were properly delegable. *Musselman v. Willoughby Corp.*, 230 Va. 337, 337 S.E.2d 724 (1985). *See also* C. Wolfram, *Modern Legal Ethics* (1986), at 236, 896. All state guidelines refer to the requirement that the lawyer "supervise" legal assistants in the performance of their duties. Lawyers should also take care in hiring and choosing a legal assistant to work on a specific project to ensure that the legal assistant has the education, knowledge, and ability necessary to perform the delegated tasks competently. *See* Connecticut Recommendation 14, Kansas Standards I, II, and III, and New Mexico Guideline VIII. Finally, some states describe appropriate delegation and review in terms of the delegated work losing its identity and becoming "merged" into the work product of the attorney. *See* Florida EC 3-6 (327 So.2d at 16).

Legal assistants often play an important role in improving communication between the attorney and the client. EC 3-6 under the Model Code mentioned three specific kinds of tasks that legal assistants may perform under appropriate lawyer supervision: factual investigation and research, legal research, and the preparation of legal documents. Some states delineate more specific tasks in their guidelines, such as attending client conferences, corresponding with and obtaining information from clients, handling witness execution of documents, preparing transmittal letters, maintaining estate/guardianship trust accounts, etc. *See, e.g.,* Colorado (lists of specialized functions in several areas follow guidelines); Michigan, Comment to Definition of Legal Assistant; New York Specialized Skills of Legal Assistants; Rhode Island Guideline II; and NALA Guideline IX. The two-volume *Working with Legal Assistants,* published by the Standing Committee in 1982, attempted to provide a general description of the types of tasks that may be delegated to legal assistants in various practice areas.

There are tasks that have been specifically prohibited in some states, but that may be delegated in others. For example, legal assistants may not supervise will executions or represent clients at real estate closings in some jurisdictions, but may in others. *Compare* Connecticut Recommendation 7 and Illinois State Bar Association Position Paper on Use of Attorney Assistants in Real Estate Transactions (May 16, 1984), which proscribe legal assistants conducting real estate closings, *with* Georgia "real estate job description," Florida Professional Ethics Committee Advisory Opinion 89-5 (1989), and Missouri, Comment to Guideline I, which permit legal assistants to conduct real estate closings. *Also compare* Connecticut Recommendation 8 (prohibiting attorneys from authorizing legal assistants to supervise will executions) *with* Colorado "estate planning job description," Georgia "estate, trusts, and wills job description," Missouri, Comment to Guideline I, and Rhode Island Guideline II (suggesting that legal assistants may supervise the execution of wills, trusts, and other documents).

Guideline 3: A lawyer may not delegate to a legal assistant:

(a) Responsibility for establishing an attorney-client relationship.

(b) Responsibility for establishing the amount of a fee to be charged for a legal service.

(c) Responsibility for a legal opinion rendered to a client.

Comment to Guideline 3: The Model Rules and most state codes require that lawyers communicate with their clients in order for clients to make well-informed decisions about their representation and resolution of legal issues. Model Rule 1.4. Ethical Consideration 3-6 under the Model Code emphasized that "delegation [of legal tasks to nonlawyers] is proper if the lawyer *maintains a direct relationship with his client,* supervises the delegated work and has complete professional responsibility for the work product." (Emphasis added.) Accordingly, most state guidelines also stress the importance of a direct attorney-client relationship. *See* Colorado Guideline 1, Florida EC 3-6, Illinois Recommendation (A)(1), Iowa EC 3-6(2), and New Mexico Guideline IV. The direct personal relationship between client and lawyer is necessary to the exercise of the lawyer's trained professional judgment.

An essential aspect of the lawyer-client relationship is the agreement to undertake representation and the related fee arrangement. The Model Rules and most states require that fee arrangements be agreed upon early on and be communicated to the client by the lawyer, in some circumstances in writing. Model Rule 1.5 and Comments. Many state guidelines prohibit legal assistants from "setting fees" or "accepting cases." *See, e.g.,* Colorado Guideline 1 and NALA Guideline VI. Connecticut recommends that legal assistants be prohibited from accepting or rejecting cases or setting fees "if these tasks entail any discretion on the part of the paralegals." Connecticut Recommendation 9.

EC 3-5 states: "[T]he essence of the professional judgment of the lawyer is his educated ability to relate the general body and philosophy of law to a specific legal problem of a client; and thus, the public interest will be better served if only lawyers are permitted to act in matters involving professional judgment." Clients are entitled to their lawyers' professional judgment and opinion. Legal assistants may, however, be authorized to communicate legal advice so long as they do not interpret or expand on that advice. Typically, state guidelines phrase this prohibition in terms of legal assistants being forbidden from "giving legal advice" or "counseling clients about legal matters." *See, e.g.,* Colorado Guideline 2, Connecticut Recommendation 6, Florida DR 3-104, Iowa EC 3-6(3), Kansas Guideline I, Kentucky Sub-Rule 2, New Hampshire Rule 35, Sub-Rule 1, Texas Guideline I, and NALA Guideline VI. Some states have more expansive wording that prohibits legal assistants from engaging in any activity that would require the exercise of independent legal judgment. Nevertheless, it is clear that all states, as well as the Model Rules, encourage direct communication between clients and a legal assistant insofar as the legal assistant is performing a task properly delegated by a lawyer. It should be noted that a lawyer who permits a legal assistant to assist in establishing the attorney-client relationship, communicating a fee, or preparing a legal opinion is not delegating responsibility for those matters and, therefore, may be complying with this guideline.

Guideline 4: It is the lawyer's responsibility to take reasonable measures to ensure that clients, courts, and other lawyers are aware that a legal assistant, whose services are utilized by the lawyer in performing legal services, is not licensed to practice law.

Comment to Guideline 4: Since, in most instances, a legal assistant is not licensed as a lawyer, it is important that those with whom the legal assistant deals are aware of that fact. Several state guidelines impose on the lawyer responsibility for instructing a legal assistant whose services are utilized by the lawyer to disclose the legal assistant's status in any dealings with a third party. *See, e.g.,* Michigan Guideline III, part 5, New Hampshire Rule 35, Sub-Rule 8, and NALA Guideline V. While requiring the legal assistant to make such disclosure is one way in which the attorney's responsibility to third parties may be discharged, the Standing Committee is of

the view that it is desirable to emphasize the lawyer's responsibility for the disclosure and leave to the lawyer the discretion to decide whether the lawyer will discharge that responsibility by direct communication with the client, by requiring the legal assistant to make the disclosure, by a written memorandum, or by some other means. Although in most initial engagements by a client it may be prudent for the attorney to discharge this responsibility with a writing, the guideline requires only that the lawyer recognize the responsibility and ensure that it is discharged. Clearly, when a client has been adequately informed of the lawyer's utilization of legal assistant services, it is unnecessary to make additional formalistic disclosures as the client retains the lawyer for other services.

Most state guidelines specifically endorse legal assistants signing correspondence so long as their status as a legal assistant is indicated by an appropriate title. *E.g.,* Colorado Guideline 2; Kansas, Comment to Guideline IX; and North Carolina Guideline 9; *also see* ABA Informal Opinion 1367 (1976). The comment to New Mexico Guideline XI warns against the use of the title "associate" since it may be construed to mean associate-attorney.

Guideline 5: A lawyer may identify legal assistants by name and title on the lawyer's letterhead and on business cards identifying the lawyer's firm.

Comment to Guideline 5: Under Guideline 4, above, an attorney who employs a legal assistant has an obligation to ensure that the status of the legal assistant as a non-lawyer is fully disclosed. The primary purpose of this disclosure is to avoid confusion that might lead someone to believe that the legal assistant is a lawyer. The identification suggested by this guideline is consistent with that objective, while also affording the legal assistant recognition as an important part of the legal services team.

Recent ABA Informal Opinion 1527 (1989) provides that non-lawyer support personnel, including legal assistants, may be listed on a law firm's letterhead and reiterates previous opinions that approve of legal assistants having business cards. *See also* ABA Informal Opinion 1185 (1971). The listing must not be false or misleading and "must make it clear that the support personnel who are listed are not lawyers."

Nearly all state guidelines approve of business cards for legal assistants, but some prescribe the contents and format of the card. *E.g.,* Iowa Guideline 4 and Texas Guideline VIII. All agree the legal assistant's status must be clearly indicated and the card may not be used in a deceptive way. New

Hampshire Supreme Court Rule 7 approves the use of business cards so long as the card is not used for unethical solicitation.

Some states do not permit attorneys to list legal assistants on their letterhead. *E.g.*, Kansas Guideline VIII, Michigan Guideline III, New Hampshire Rule 35, Sub-Rule 7, New Mexico Guideline XI, and North Carolina Guideline 9. Several of these states rely on earlier ABA Informal Opinions 619 (1962), 845 (1965), and 1000 (1977), all of which were expressly withdrawn by ABA Informal Opinion 1527. These earlier opinions interpreted the predecessor Model Code and DR 2-102 (A), which, prior to *Bates v. State Bar of Arizona*, 433 U.S. 350 (1977), had strict limitations on the information that could be listed on letterheads. States which do permit attorneys to list names of legal assistants on their stationery, if the listing is not deceptive and the legal assistant's status is clearly identified, include: Arizona Committee on Rules of Professional Conduct Formal Opinion 3/90 (1990); Connecticut Recommendation 12; Florida Professional Ethics Committee Advisory Opinion 86-4 (1986); Hawaii, Formal Opinion 78-8-19 (1978, as revised 1984); Illinois State Bar Association Advisory Opinion 87-1 (1987); Kentucky Sub-Rule 6; Mississippi State Bar Ethics Committee Opinion No. 93 (1984); Missouri Guideline IV; New York State Bar Association Committee on Professional Ethics Opinion 500 (1978); Oregon, Ethical Opinion No. 349 (1977); and Texas, Ethics Committee Opinion 436 (1983). In light of the United States Supreme Court opinion in *Peel v. Attorney Registration and Disciplinary Commission of Illinois*, _____ U.S. _____, 110 S. Ct. 2281 (1990), it may be that a restriction on letterhead identification of legal assistants that is not deceptive and clearly identifies the legal assistant's status violates the First Amendment rights of the lawyer.

Guideline 6: It is the responsibility of a lawyer to take reasonable measures to ensure that all client confidences are preserved by a legal assistant.

Comment to Guideline 6: A fundamental principle underlying the free exchange of information in a lawyer-client relationship is that the lawyer maintain the confidentiality of information relating to the representation. "It is a matter of common knowledge that the normal operation of a law office exposes confidential professional information to non-lawyer employees of the office. This obligates a lawyer to exercise care in selecting and training his employees so that the sanctity of all confidences and secrets of his clients may be preserved." EC 4-2, Model Code. Rule 5.3 of the Model Rules requires "a lawyer who has direct supervisory authority over the non-

lawyer [to] make reasonable efforts to ensure that the person's conduct is compatible with the professional obligations of the lawyer." The Comment to Rule 5.3 makes it clear that lawyers should give legal assistants "appropriate instruction and supervision concerning the ethical aspects of their employment, particularly regarding the obligation not to disclose information relating to the representation of the client." DR 4-101(D) under the Model Code provides that: "A lawyer shall exercise reasonable care to prevent his employees, associates and others whose services are utilized by him from discharging or using confidences or secrets of a client. . . ."

It is particularly important that the lawyer ensure that the legal assistant understands that *all* information concerning the client, even the mere fact that a person is a client of the firm, may be strictly confidential. Rule 1.6 of the Model Rules expanded the definition of confidential information ". . . not merely to matters communicated in confidence by the client but also to all information relating to the representation, whatever its source."[6] It is therefore the lawyer's obligation to instruct clearly and to take reasonable steps to ensure the legal assistant's preservation of client confidences. Nearly all states that have guidelines for the utilization of legal assistants require the lawyer "to instruct legal assistants concerning client confidences" and "to exercise care to ensure that legal assistants comply" with the Code in this regard. Even if the client consents to divulging information, this information must not be used to the disadvantage of the client. *See, e.g.,* Connecticut Recommendation 3; New Hampshire Rule 35, Sub-Rule 4; NALA Guideline V.

Guideline 7: A lawyer should take reasonable measures to prevent conflicts of interest resulting from a legal assistant's other employment or interests insofar as such other employment or interests

---

6 Rule 1.05 of the Texas Disciplinary Rules of Professional Conduct (1990) provides a different formulation, which is equally expansive:

"Confidential information" includes both "privileged information" and "unprivileged client information." "Privileged information" refers to the information of a client protected by the lawyer-client privilege of Rule 503 of the Texas Rules of Evidence or of Rule 503 of the Texas Rules of Criminal Evidence or by the principles of attorney-client privilege governed by Rule 501 of the Federal Rules of Evidence for United States Courts and Magistrates. "Unprivileged client information" means all information relating to a client or furnished by the client, other than privileged information, acquired by the lawyer during the course of or by reason of the representation of the client.

would present a conflict of interest if it were that of the lawyer.

Comment to Guideline 7: A lawyer must make "reasonable efforts to ensure that [a] legal assistant's conduct is compatible with the professional obligations of the lawyer." Model Rule 5.3. These professional obligations include the duty to exercise independent professional judgment on behalf of a client, "free of compromising influences and loyalties." ABA Model Rules 1.7 through 1.13. Therefore, legal assistants should be instructed to inform the supervising attorney of any interest that could result in a conflict of interest or even give the appearance of a conflict. The guideline intentionally speaks to other employment rather than only past employment, since there are instances where legal assistants are employed by more than one law firm at the same time. The guideline's reference to "other interests" is intended to include personal relationships as well as instances where a legal assistant may have a financial interest (i.e., as stockholder, trust beneficiary or trustee, etc.) that would conflict with the client's in the matter in which the lawyer has been employed.

"Imputed Disqualification Arising from Change in Employment by Non-lawyer Employee," ABA Informal Opinion 1526 (1988), defines the duties of both the present and former employing lawyers and reasons that the restrictions on legal assistants' employment should be kept to "the minimum necessary to protect confidentiality" in order to prevent legal assistants from being forced to leave their careers, which "would disserve clients as well as the legal profession." The Opinion describes the attorney's obligations (1) to caution the legal assistant not to disclose any information and (2) to prevent the legal assistant from working on any matter on which the legal assistant worked for a prior employer or respecting which the employee has confidential information.

If a conflict is discovered, it may be possible to "wall" the legal assistant from the conflict area so that the entire firm need not be disqualified and the legal assistant is effectively screened from information concerning the matter. The American Bar Association has taken the position that what historically has been described as a "Chinese wall" will allow non-lawyer personnel (including legal assistants) who are in possession of confidential client information to accept employment with a law firm opposing the former client so long as the wall is observed and effectively screens the non-lawyer from confidential information. ABA Informal Opinion 1526 (1988). *See also* Tennessee Formal Ethics Opinion 89-F-118 (March 10, 1989). The implication of this Informal

Opinion is that if a wall is not in place, the employer may be disqualified from representing either party to the controversy. One court has so held. *In re: Complex Asbestoses Litigation,* No. 828684 (San Francisco Superior Court, September 19, 1989).

It is not clear that a wall will prevent disqualification in the case of a lawyer employed to work for a law firm representing a client with an adverse interest to a client of the lawyer's former employer. Under Model Rule 1.10, when a lawyer moves to a firm that represents an adverse party in a matter in which the lawyer's former firm was involved, absent a waiver by the client, the new firm's representation may continue only if the newly employed lawyer acquired no protected information and did not work directly on the matter in the former employment. The new Rules of Professional Conduct in Kentucky and Texas (both effective on January 1, 1990) specifically provide for disqualification. Rule 1.10(b) in the District of Columbia, which became effective January 1, 1991, does so as well. The Sixth Circuit, however, has held that the wall will effectively insulate the new firm from disqualification if it prevents the new lawyer-employee from access to information concerning the client with the adverse interest. *Manning v. Waring, Cox, James, Sklar & Allen,* 849 F.2d 222 (6th Cir. 1988). [As a result of the Sixth Circuit opinion, Tennessee revised its formal ethics opinion, which is cited above, and now applies the same rule to lawyers, legal assistants, law clerks, and legal secretaries.] *See generally* NFPA, "The Chinese Wall—Its Application to Paralegals" (1990).

The states that have guidelines that address the legal assistant conflict of interest issue refer to the lawyer's responsibility to ensure against personal, business or social interests of the legal assistant that would conflict with the representation of the client or impinge on the services rendered to the client. *E.g.,* Kansas Guideline X, New Mexico Guideline VI, and North Carolina Guideline 7. Florida Professional Ethics Opinion 86-5 (1986) discusses a legal assistant's move from one firm to another and the obligations of each not to disclose confidences. *See also* Vermont Ethics Opinion 85-8 (1985) (a legal assistant is not bound by the Code of Professional Responsibility and, absent an absolute waiver by the client, the new firm should not represent client if legal assistant possessed confidential information from old firm).

Guideline 8: A lawyer may include a charge for the work performed by a legal assistant in setting a charge for legal services.

Comment to Guideline 8: The U.S. Supreme Court in *Missouri v. Jenkins,* 491 U.S.274 (1989), held that in setting a reasonable attorney's fee under 28 U.S.C. § 1988, a legal fee may include a charge for legal assistant services at "market rates" rather than "actual cost" to the attorneys. This decision should resolve any question concerning the propriety of setting a charge for legal services based on work performed by a legal assistant. Its rationale favors setting a charge based on the "market" rate for such services, rather than their direct cost to the lawyer. This result was recognized by Connecticut Recommendation 11, Illinois Recommendation D, and Texas Guideline V prior to the Supreme Court decision. *See also* Fla. Stat. Ann. § 57.104 (1991 Supp.) (adopted in 1987 and permitting consideration of legal assistant services in computing attorneys' fees) and Fla. Stat. Ann. § 744.108 (1991 Supp.) (adopted in 1989 and permitting recovery of "customary and reasonable charges for work performed by legal assistants" as fees for legal services in guardianship matters).

It is important to note, however, that *Missouri v. Jenkins* does not abrogate the attorney's responsibilities under Model Rule 1.5 to set a reasonable fee for legal services and it follows that those considerations apply to a fee that includes a fee for legal assistant services. Accordingly, the effect of combining a market rate charge for the services of lawyers and legal assistants should, in most instances, result in a lower total cost for the legal service than if the lawyer had performed the service alone.

Guideline 9: A lawyer may not split legal fees with a legal assistant nor pay a legal assistant for the referral of legal business. A lawyer may compensate a legal assistant based on the quantity and quality of the legal assistant's work and the value of that work to a law practice, but the legal assistant's compensation may not be contingent, by advance agreement, upon the profitability of the lawyer's practice.

Comment to Guideline 9: Model Rule 5.4 and DR 3-102(A) and 3-103(A) under the Model Code clearly prohibit fee "splitting" with legal assistants, whether characterized as splitting of contingent fees, "forwarding" fees, or other sharing of legal fees. Virtually all guidelines adopted by state bar associations have continued this prohibition in one form or another.[7] It appears clear that a legal assistant may

not be compensated on a contingent basis for a particular case or paid for "signing up" clients for a legal practice.

Having stated this prohibition, however, the guideline attempts to deal with the practical consideration of how a legal assistant properly may be compensated by an attorney or law firm. The linchpin of the prohibition seems to be the advance agreement of the lawyer to "split" a fee based on a pre-existing contingent arrangement.[8] There is no general prohibition against a lawyer who enjoys a particularly profitable period recognizing the contribution of the legal assistant to that profitability with a discretionary bonus. Likewise, a lawyer engaged in a particularly profitable specialty of legal practice is not prohibited from compensating the legal assistant who aids materially in that practice more handsomely than the compensation generally awarded to legal assistants in that geographic area who work in law practices that are less lucrative. Indeed, any effort to fix a compensation level for legal assistants and prohibit greater compensation would appear to violate the federal antitrust laws. *See, e.g., Goldfarb v. Virginia State Bar,* 421 U.S. 773 (1975).

Guideline 10: A lawyer who employs a legal assistant should facilitate the legal assistant's participation in appropriate continuing education and pro bono publico activities.

Comment to Guideline 10: While Guideline 10 does not appear to have been adopted in the guidelines of any state bar association, the Standing Committee on Legal Assistants believes that its adoption would be appropriate.[9] For many years the Standing Committee on Legal Assistants has advocated that the improvement of formal legal assistant education

---

7 Connecticut Recommendation 10; Illinois Recommendation D; Kansas Guideline VI; Kentucky Supreme Court Rule 3.700, sub-rule 5; Michigan Guideline III, part 2; Missouri Guidline II; New Hampshire Rule 35, Sub-Rules 5 and 6; New Mexico Guideline IX; Rhode Island Guideline VIII and IX; South Carolina Guideline V; Texas Guideline V.

8 In its Rule 5.4, which will become effective on January 1, 1991, the District of Columbia will permit lawyers to form legal service partnerships that include non-lawyer participants. Comments 5 and 6 to that rule, however, state that the term "nonlawyer participants" should not be confused with the term "nonlawyer assistants" and that "[n]onlawyer assistants under Rule 5.3 do not have managerial authority or financial interests in the organization."

9 While no state has apparently adopted a guideline similar to Model Guideline 10, parts 4 and 5 of NALA Guideline VIII suggest similar requirements. Sections III and V of NFPA's "Affirmation of Professional Responsibility" recognize a legal assistant's obligations to "maintain a high level of competence" (which "is achieved through continuing education . . .") and to "serve the public interest." NFPA has also published a guide to assist legal assistant groups in developing public service projects. *See* NFPA, "Pro Bono Publico (For the Good of the People)" (1987).

will generally improve the legal services rendered by lawyers employing legal assistants and provide a more satisfying professional atmosphere in which legal assistants may work. *See, e.g.,* ABA, Board of Governors, Policy on Legal Assistant Licensure and/or Certification, Statement 4 (February 6, 1986); ABA, Standing Committee on Legal Assistants, "Position Paper on the Question of Legal Assistant Licensure or Certification" (December 10, 1985), at 6 and Conclusion 3. Recognition of the employing lawyer's obligation to facilitate the legal assistant's continuing professional education is, therefore, appropriate because of the benefits to both the law practice and the legal assistants and is consistent with the lawyer's own responsibility to maintain professional competence under Model Rule 1.1. *See also* EC 6-2 of the Model Code.

The Standing Committee is of the view that similar benefits will accrue to the lawyer and legal assistant if the legal assistant is included in the pro bono publico legal services that a lawyer has a clear obligation to provide under Model Rule 6.1 and, where appropriate, the legal assistant is encouraged to provide such services independently. The ability of a law firm to provide more pro bono publico services will be enhanced if legal assistants are included. Recognition of the legal assistant's role in such services is consistent with the role of the legal assistant in the contemporary delivery of legal services generally and is consistent with the lawyer's duty to the legal profession under Canon 2 of the Model Code.

**THE STANDING COMMITTEE ON
LEGAL ASSISTANTS OF THE
AMERICAN BAR ASSOCIATION
May 1991**

STATE GUIDELINES

COLORADO	CBA Legal Assistants Committee Proposed Guidelines for the Utilization of Legal Assistants (February, 1986)
CONNECTICUT	Lawyers' Professional Responsibility Obligations Concerning Paralegals (1985)
FLORIDA	In re Petition to Amend Code of Professional Responsibility (Fla. 327 So.2d 15) (February 11, 1976)
GEORGIA	Efficient Utilization of Legal Assistants or Paralegals
ILLINOIS	Recommendations to Attorneys for the Use of Legal Assistants (June 25, 1988)
IOWA	Ethical Guidelines for Legal Assistants in Iowa (March 1988)
KANSAS	Guidelines for the Utilization of Legal Assistants in Kansas (December 2, 1988)
KENTUCKY	Supreme Court Rule 3.700, Provisions Relating to Paralegals (September 4, 1979)
MICHIGAN	Guidelines for the Utilization of Legal Assistant Services (May 28, 1976)
MISSOURI	Practicing with Paralegals—Answers to Frequently Asked Questions and The Missouri Bar Guidelines (April, 1987)
NEW HAMPSHIRE	Supreme Court Rule 35, Guidelines for the Utilization by Lawyers of the Services of Legal Assistants Under the New Hampshire Rules of Professional Conduct (August, 1987)
NEW MEXICO	Guidelines for the Use of Legal Assistant Services (October 1, 1981)
NEW YORK	The Expanding Role of the Legal Assistant in New York State
NORTH CAROLINA	Guidelines for Use of Non-Lawyers in Rendering Legal Services
RHODE ISLAND	Guidelines for Use of Legal Assistants (February 1, 1983)
SOUTH CAROLINA	Guidelines for the Utilization by Lawyers of the Services of Legal Assistants (December 11, 1981)
TEXAS	General Guidelines for the Utilization of the Services of Legal Assistants by Attorneys (July 1, 1981)

OTHER

NATIONAL ASSOCIATION OF LEGAL ASSISTANTS Model Standards and Guidelines for Utilization of Legal Assistants, Annotated (1985, revised 1990)

NFPA MODEL CODE OF ETHICS AND PROFESSIONAL RESPONSIBILITY

PREAMBLE

The National Federation of Paralegal Associations, Inc. ("NFPA") is a professional organization comprised of paralegal associations and individual paralegals throughout the United States. Members of NFPA have varying types of backgrounds, experience, education, and job responsibilities which reflect the diversity of the paralegal profession. NFPA promotes the growth, development and recognition of the paralegal profession as an integral partner in the delivery of legal services.

NFPA recognizes that the creation of guidelines and standards for professional conduct are important for the development and expansion of the paralegal profession. In May 1993, NFPA adopted this Model Code of Ethics and Professional Responsibility ("Model Code") to delineate the principles for ethics and conduct to which every paralegal should aspire. The Model Code expresses NFPA's commitment to increasing the quality and efficiency of legal services and recognizes the profession's responsibilities to the public, the legal community, and colleagues.

Paralegals perform many different functions, and these functions differ greatly among practice areas. In addition, each jurisdiction has its own unique legal authority and practices governing ethical conduct and professional responsibilities.

It is essential that each paralegal strive for personal and professional excellence and encourage the professional development of other paralegals as well as those entering the profession. Participation in professional associations intended to advance the quality and standards of the legal profession is of particular importance. Paralegals should possess integrity, professional skill and dedication to the improvement of the legal system and should strive to expand the paralegal role in the delivery of legal services.

CANON 1.

A PARALEGAL[1] SHALL ACHIEVE AND MAINTAIN A HIGH LEVEL OF COMPETENCE.

EC-1.1   A paralegal shall achieve competency through education, training, and work experience.

EC-1.2   A paralegal shall participate in continuing education to keep informed of current legal, technical and general developments.

EC-1.3   A paralegal shall perform all assignments promptly and efficiently.

CANON 2.

A PARALEGAL SHALL MAINTAIN A HIGH LEVEL OF PERSONAL AND PROFESSIONAL INTEGRITY.

EC-2.1   A paralegal shall not engage in any ex parte[2] communications involving the courts or any other adjudicatory body in an attempt to exert undue influence or to obtain advantage for the benefit of only one party.

EC-2.2   A paralegal shall not communicate, or cause another to communicate, with a party the paralegal knows to be represented by a lawyer in a pending matter without the prior consent of the lawyer representing such other party.

---

1 "Paralegal" is synonymous with **"Legal Assistant"** and is defined as a person qualified through education, training, or work experience to perform substantive legal work that requires knowledge of legal concepts and is customarily, but not exclusively performed by a lawyer. This person may be retained or employed by a lawyer, law office, governmental agency or other entity or may be authorized by administrative, statutory or court authority to perform this work.

2 **"Ex Parte"** denotes actions or communications conducted at the instance and for the benefit of one party only, and without notice to, or contestation by, any person adversely interested.

EC-2.3   A paralegal shall ensure that all timekeeping and billing records prepared by the paralegal are thorough, accurate, and honest.

EC-2.4   A paralegal shall be scrupulous, thorough and honest in the identification and maintenance of all funds, securities, and other assets of a client and shall provide accurate accountings as appropriate.

EC-2.5   A paralegal shall advise the proper authority of any dishonest or fraudulent acts by any person pertaining to the handling of the funds, securities or other assets of a client.

Canon 3.

A PARALEGAL SHALL MAINTAIN A HIGH STANDARD OF PROFESSIONAL CONDUCT.

EC-3.1   A paralegal shall refrain from engaging in any conduct that offends the dignity and decorum of proceedings before a court or other adjudicatory body and shall be respectful of all rules and procedures.

EC-3.2   A paralegal shall advise the proper authority of any action of another legal professional which clearly demonstrates fraud, deceit, dishonesty, or misrepresentation.

EC-3.3   A paralegal shall avoid impropriety and the appearance of impropriety.

Canon 4.

A PARALEGAL SHALL SERVE THE PUBLIC INTEREST BY CONTRIBUTING TO THE DELIVERY OF QUALITY LEGAL SERVICES AND THE IMPROVEMENT OF THE LEGAL SYSTEM.

EC-4.1   A paralegal shall be sensitive to the legal needs of the public and shall promote the development and implementation of programs that address those needs.

EC-4.2   A paralegal shall support bona fide efforts to meet the need for legal services by those unable to pay reasonable or customary fees; for example, participation in pro bono projects and volunteer work.

EC-4.3   A paralegal shall support efforts to improve the legal system and shall assist in making changes.

Canon 5.

A PARALEGAL SHALL PRESERVE ALL CONFIDENTIAL INFORMATION[3] PROVIDED BY THE CLIENT OR ACQUIRED FROM OTHER SOURCES BEFORE, DURING, AND AFTER THE COURSE OF THE PROFESSIONAL RELATIONSHIP.

EC-5.1   A paralegal shall be aware of and abide by all legal authority governing confidential information.

EC-5.2   A paralegal shall not use confidential information to the disadvantage of the client.

EC-5.3   A paralegal shall not use confidential information to the advantage of the paralegal or of a third person.

EC-5.4   A paralegal may reveal confidential information only after full disclosure and with the client's written consent; or, when required by law or court order; or, when necessary to prevent the client from committing an act which could result in death or serious bodily harm.

EC-5.5   A paralegal shall keep those individuals responsible for the legal representation of a client fully informed of any confidential information the paralegal may have pertaining to that client.

EC-5.6   A paralegal shall not engage in any indiscreet communications concerning clients.

3 **"Confidential Information"** denotes information relating to a client, whatever its source, which is not public knowledge nor available to the public. (**"Non-Confidential Information"** would generally include the name of the client and the identity of the matter for which the paralegal provided services.)

Canon 6.

A PARALEGAL'S TITLE SHALL BE FULLY DISCLOSED.[4]

EC-6.1   A paralegal's title shall clearly indicate the individual's status and shall be disclosed in all business and professional communications to avoid misunderstandings and misconceptions about the paralegal's role and responsibilities.

EC-6.2   A paralegal's title shall be included if the paralegal's name appears on business cards, letterhead, brochures, directories, and advertisements.

Canon 7.

A PARALEGAL SHALL NOT ENGAGE IN THE UNAUTHORIZED PRACTICE OF LAW.

EC-7.1   A paralegal shall comply with the applicable legal authority governing the unauthorized practice of law.

Canon 8.

A PARALEGAL SHALL AVOID CONFLICTS OF INTEREST AND SHALL DISCLOSE ANY POSSIBLE CONFLICT TO THE EMPLOYER OR CLIENT, AS WELL AS TO THE PROSPECTIVE EMPLOYERS OR CLIENTS.

EC-8.1   A paralegal shall act within the bounds of the law, solely for the benefit of the client, and shall be free of compromising influences and loyalties. Neither the paralegal's personal or business interest, nor those of other clients or third persons, should compromise the paralegal's professional judgment and loyalty to the client.

EC-8.2   A paralegal shall avoid conflicts of interest which may arise from previous assignments whether for a present or past employer or client.

EC-8.3   A paralegal shall avoid conflicts of interest which may arise from family relationships and from personal and business interests.

EC-8.4   A paralegal shall create and maintain an effective recordkeeping system that identifies clients, matters, and parties with which the paralegal has worked, to be able to determine whether an actual or potential conflict of interest exists.

EC-8.5   A paralegal shall reveal sufficient nonconfidential information about a client or former client to reasonably ascertain if an actual or potential conflict of interest exists.

EC-8.6   A paralegal shall not participate in or conduct work on any matter where a conflict of interest has been identified.

EC-8.7   In matters where a conflict of interest has been identified and the client consents to continued representation, a paralegal shall comply fully with the implementation and maintenance of an Ethical Wall.[5]

---

5 **"Ethical Wall"** refers to the screening method implemented in order to protect a client from a conflict of interest. An Ethical Wall generally includes, but is not limited to, the following elements: (1) prohibit the paralegal from having any connection with the matter; (2) ban discussions with or the transfer of documents to or from the paralegal; (3) restrict access to files; and (4) educate all members of the firm, corporation or entity as to the separation of the paralegal (both organizationally and physically) from the pending matter. For more information regarding the Ethical Wall, see the NFPA publication entitled "The Ethical Wall—Its Application to Paralegals." Source: *National Federation of Paralegal Associations, Inc., Model Code of Ethics and Professional Responsibility* (1993). Reprinted with permission.

---

4 **"Disclose"** denotes communication of information reasonably sufficient to permit identification of the significance of the matter in question.

NALA Model Standards and Guidelines for Utilization of Legal Assistants Annotated

Introduction

The purpose of this annotated version of the National Association of Legal Assistants, Inc. (NALA) Model Standards and Guidelines for the Utilization of Legal Assistants is to provide references to the existing case law and other authorities where the underlying issues have been considered. The authorities cited will serve as a basis upon which conduct of a legal assistant may be analyzed as proper or improper.

The Guidelines represent a statement of how the legal assistant may function in the law office. The Guidelines are not intended to be a comprehensive or exhaustive list of the proper duties of a legal assistant. Rather, they are designed as guides to what may or may not be proper conduct for the legal assistant. In formulating the Guidelines, the reasoning and rules of law in many reported decisions of disciplinary cases and unauthorized practice of law cases have been analyzed and considered. In addition, the provisions of the American Bar Association's Model Code of Professional Responsibility and the Model Rules of Professional Conduct, as well as the ethical promulgations of various state courts and bar associations have been considered in development of the Guidelines.

While the Guidelines may not have universal application, they do form a sound basis for the legal assistant and the supervising attorney to follow in the operation of a law office. The Model will serve as a definitive and well-reasoned guide to those considering voluntary standards and guidelines for legal assistants. If regulation is to be imposed in a given jurisdiction the Model may serve as a comprehensive resource document.

I Preamble

Proper utilization of the services of legal assistants affects the efficient delivery of legal services. Legal assistants and the legal profession should be assured that some measures exist for identifying legal assistants and their role in assisting attorneys in the delivery of legal services. Therefore, the National Association of Legal Assistants, Inc., hereby adopts these Model Standards and Guidelines as an educational document for the benefit of legal assistants and the legal profession.

Comment

The three most frequently raised questions concerning legal assistants are (1) How do you define a legal assistant; (2) Who is qualified to be identified as a legal assistant; and (3) What duties may a legal assistant perform? The definition adopted answers the first question insofar as legal assistants serving attorneys are concerned. The Model sets forth minimum education, training, and experience through standards which will assure that one denominated as a legal assistant has the qualifications to be held out to the public in that capacity. The Guidelines identify those acts which the reported cases hold to be proscribed and give examples of services which the legal assistant may perform under the supervision of an attorney.

The three fundamental issues in the preceding paragraph have been raised in various cases for the past fifty years. In *Ferris v. Snively,* 19 P.2d 942 (Wash. 1933), the Court, stated work performed by a law clerk to be proper and not the unauthorized practice of law required supervision by the employing attorney. The Court stated:

We realize that law clerks have their place in a law office, and we recognize the fact that the nature of their work approaches in a degree that of their employers. The line of demarcation as to where their work begins and where it ends cannot always be drawn with absolute distinction or accuracy. Probably as nearly as it can be fixed, and it is sufficient to say that it is work of a preparatory nature, such as research, investigation of details, the assemblage of data and other necessary information, and such other work as will assist the employing attorney in carrying the matter to a completed product, either by his personal examination and approval thereof or by additional effort on his part. The work must be such, however, as loses its separate identity and becomes either the product, or else merged in the product, of the attorney himself. (19 P.2d at pp. 945–46.) (See Florida EC3-6, infra at, Section IV.)

The NALA Guidelines constitute a statement relating to services performed by non-lawyer employees as approved by court decisions and other sources of authority. The purpose of the Guidelines is not to place limitations or restrictions on the legal profession. Rather, the Guidelines are intended to outline for the legal profession an acceptable course of conduct. By voluntary recognition and utilization of the Model Standards and Guidelines the legal profession will avoid many problems.

II DEFINITION

Legal assistants* are a distinguishable group of persons who assist attorneys in the delivery of legal services. Through formal education, training, and experience, legal assistants have knowledge and expertise regarding the legal system and substantive and procedural law which qualify them to do work of a legal nature under the supervision of an attorney.

COMMENT

This definition has been used to foster a distinction between a legal assistant as one working under the direct supervision of an attorney and a broader class of paralegals who perform tasks of similar nature, but not necessarily under the supervision of an attorney. In applying the standards and guidelines it is important to remember that they in turn were developed to apply to the legal assistant as defined therein.

III STANDARDS

A legal assistant should meet certain minimum qualifications. The following standards may be used to determine an individual's qualifications as a legal assistant:

1. Successful completion of the Certified Legal Assistant certifying ("CLA") examination of the National Association of Legal Assistants, Inc.;

2. Graduation from an ABA approved program of study for legal assistants;

3. Graduation from a course of study for legal assistants which is institutionally accredited but not ABA approved, and which requires not

less than the equivalent of 60 semester hours of classroom study;

4. Graduation from a course of study for legal assistants, other than those set forth in (2) and (3) above, plus not less than six months of in-house training as a legal assistant;

5. A baccalaureate degree in any field, plus not less than six months in-house training as a legal assistant;

6. A minimum of three years of law-related experience under the supervision of an attorney, including at least six months of in-house training as a legal assistant; or

7. Two years of in-house training as a legal assistant.

For purposes of these Standards, "in-house training as a legal assistant" means attorney education of the employee concerning legal assistant duties and these Guidelines. In addition to review and analysis of assignments the legal assistant should receive a reasonable amount of instruction directly related to the duties and obligations of the legal assistant.

COMMENT

The Standards set forth suggested minimum qualifications for a legal assistant. These minimum qualifications as adopted recognize legal related work backgrounds and formal education backgrounds, both of which should provide the legal assistant with a broad base in exposure to and knowledge of the legal profession. This background is necessary to assure the public and the legal profession that the one being identified as a legal assistant is qualified.

The Certified Legal Assistant ("CLA") examination offered by NALA is the only voluntary nationwide certification program for legal assistants. The "CLA" designation is a statement to the legal profession and the public that the legal assistant has met the high levels of knowledge and professionalism required by NALA's certification program. Continuing education requirements, which all certified legal assistants must meet, assure that high standards are maintained. Certification through NALA is available to any legal assistant meeting the educational and experience requirements.

IV GUIDELINES

These guidelines relating to standards of performance and professional responsibility are intended

---

*Within this occupational category some individuals are known as paralegals.

to aid legal assistants and attorneys. The responsibility rests with an attorney who employs legal assistants to educate them with respect to the duties they are assigned and to supervise the manner in which such duties are accomplished.

COMMENT

In general, a legal assistant is allowed to perform any task which is properly delegated and supervised by an attorney, so long as **the attorney is ultimately responsible to the client and assumes complete professional responsibility for the work product.**

The Code of Professional Responsibility of the American Bar Association, EC3-6 states:

ABA Model Rules of Professional Conduct, Rule 5.3 provides:

With respect to a non-lawyer employed or retained by or associated with a lawyer:

(a) a partner in a law firm shall make reasonable efforts to ensure that the firm has in effect measures giving reasonable assurance that the person's conduct is compatible with the professional obligations of the lawyer;

(b) a lawyer having direct supervisory authority over the non-lawyer shall make reasonable efforts to ensure that the person's conduct is compatible with the professional obligations of the lawyer; and

(c) a lawyer shall be responsible for conduct of such a person that would be a violation of the rules of professional conduct if engaged in by a lawyer if:

(1) the lawyer orders or, with the knowledge of the specific conduct ratifies the conduct involved; or

(2) the lawyer is a partner in the law firm in which the person is employed, or has direct supervisory authority over the person, and knows of the conduct at a time when its consequences can be avoided or mitigated but fails to take reasonable remedial action.

The Florida version of EC3-6 provides:

A lawyer or law firm may employ non-lawyers such as secretaries, law clerks, investigators, researchers, legal assistants, accountants, draftsmen, office administrators, and other lay personnel to assist the lawyer in the delivery of legal services. A lawyer often delegates tasks to such persons. Such delegation is proper if a lawyer retains a direct relationship with his client, supervises the delegated work, and has complete professional responsibility for the work product.

The work which is delegated is such that it will assist the employing attorney in carrying the matter to a completed product either by the lawyer's personal examination and approval thereof or by additional effort on the lawyer's part. The delegated work must be such, however, as loses its separate identity and becomes either the product or else merged in the product of the attorney himself.

The Kentucky Paralegal Code defines a legal assistant as:

. . . a person under the supervision and direction of a licensed lawyer, who may apply knowledge of law and legal procedures in rendering direct assistance to lawyers engaged in legal research; design, develop or plan modifications or new procedures, techniques, services, processes or applications; prepare or interpret legal documents and write detailed procedure for practicing in certain fields of law; select, compile and use technical information from such references as digests, encyclopedias or practice manuals; and analyze and follow procedural problems that involve independent decisions.

Kentucky became the first state to adopt a Paralegal Code, which sets forth certain exclusions to the unauthorized practice of law:

For purpose of this rule, the unauthorized practice of law shall not include any service rendered involving legal knowledge or advice, whether representation, counsel or advocacy, in or out of court, rendered in respect to the acts, duties, obligations, liabilities or business relations of the one requiring services where:

A. The client understands that the paralegal is not a lawyer;

B. The lawyer supervises the paralegal in the performance of his duties; and

C. The lawyer remains fully responsible for such representation, including all actions taken or not taken in connection therewith by the paralegal to the same extent as if such representation had been furnished entirely by the lawyer and all such actions had been taken or not taken directly by the attorney. Paralegal Code, Ky. S.Ct. R 3.700, Sub-Rule 2.

While the Kentucky rule is an exception, it does provide a basis for expanding services which may be performed by legal assistants.

There are many interesting and complex issues involving the use of legal assistants. One issue which is not addressed in the Guidelines is whether a legal assistant, as defined herein, may make appearances before administrative agencies. This issue is discussed in Remmer, *Representation of Clients Before Administrative Agencies: Authorized or Unauthorized Practice of Law?*, 15 Valparaiso Univ. L.Rev. 567 (1981). The State Bar of California Standing Committee on Professional Responsibility and Conduct, in opinion 1988-103 (2/8/89) has stated a law firm can delegate authority to a legal assistant employee to file petitions, motions and make other appearances before the Workers' Compensation Appeals Board provided adequate supervision is maintained by the attorney and the client is informed and has consented to the use of the legal assistant in such fashion.

In any discussion of the proper role of a legal assistant attention must be directed to what constitutes the practice of law. The proper delegation of work and duties to legal assistants is further complicated and confused by the lack of adequate definition of the practice of law and the unauthorized practice of law.

In *Davis v. Unauthorized Practice Committee*, 431 S.W.2d 590 (Texas, 1968), the Court found that the defendant was properly enjoined from the unauthorized practice of law. The Court, in defining the "practice of law," stated:

According to the generally understood definition of the practice of law, it embraces the preparation of pleadings and other papers incident to actions of special proceedings, and the management of such actions in proceedings on behalf of clients before judges in courts. However, the practice of law is not confined to cases conducted in court. In fact, the major portion of the practice of any capable lawyer consists of work done outside of the courts. The practice of law involves not only appearance in court in connection with litigation, but also services rendered out of court, and includes the giving of advice or the rendering of any service requiring the use of legal skill or knowledge, such as preparing a will, contract or other instrument, the legal effect of which under the facts and conclusions involved must be carefully determined.

The important distinguishing fact between the defendant in Davies and a legal assistant is that the acts of the legal assistant are performed under the supervision of an attorney.

EC3-5 of the Code of Professional Responsibility states:

It is neither necessary nor desirable to attempt the formulation of a single, specific definition of what constitutes the practice of law. Functionally, the practice of law relates to the rendition of services for others that call for the professional judgment of a lawyer. The essence of the professional judgment of the lawyer is his educated ability to relate the general body and philosophy of law to a specific legal problem of a client; and thus, the public interest will be better served if only lawyers are permitted to act in matters involving professional judgment. Where this professional judgment is not involved, non-lawyers, such as court clerks, police officers, abstracters, and many governmental employees, may engage in occupations that require a special knowledge of law in certain areas. But the services of a lawyer are essential in the public interest whenever the exercise of professional legal judgment is required.

There are many cases relating to the unauthorized practice of law, but the most troublesome ones in attempting to define what would or would not form the unauthorized practice of law for acts performed by a legal assistant are those such as *Crawford v. State Bar of California*, 355 P.2d 490 (Calif. 1960), which states that any act performed in a law office is the practice of law because the clients have sought the attorney to perform the work because of the training and judgment exercised by attorneys.

See also, Annot. "Layman's Assistance to Parties in Divorce Proceedings as Unauthorized Practice of Law," 12 ALR4 656; Annot. "Activities of Law Clerks as Illegal Practice of Law," 13 ALR3 1137; Annot. "Sale of Books or Forms Designed to Enable Layman to Achieve Legal Results Without Assistance of Attorney as Unauthorized Practice of Law," 71 ALR3 1000; Annot. "Nature of Legal Services or Law-Related Services Which May Be Performed for Others By Disbarred or Suspended Attorney," 87 ALR3 272. See also, Karen B. Judd, CLA, "Beyond the Bar: Legal Assistants and the Unauthorized Practice of Law," *Facts and Findings*, Vol. VIII, Issue 6, National Association of Legal Assistants, May-June, 1982.

V

Legal assistants should:

1. Disclose their status as legal assistants at the outset of any professional relationship with a client, other attorneys, a court or administrative agency or personnel thereof, or members of the general public;

2. Preserve the confidences and secrets of all clients; and

3. Understand the attorney's Code of Professional Responsibility and these guidelines in

order to avoid any action which would involve the attorney in a violation of that Code, or give the appearance of professional impropriety.

COMMENT

Routine early disclosure of the legal assistant's status when dealing with persons outside the attorney's office is necessary to assure that there will be no misunderstanding as to the responsibilities and role of the legal assistant. Disclosure may be made in any way that avoids confusion. If the person dealing with the legal assistant already knows of his or her status, further disclosure is unnecessary. If at any time in written or in oral communication the legal assistant becomes aware that the other person may believe the legal assistant is an attorney, it should be made clear that the legal assistant is not an attorney.

The attorney should exercise care that the legal assistant preserves and refrains from using any confidence or secrets of a client, and should instruct the legal assistant not to disclose or use any such confidences or secrets.

DR 4-101(D), ABA Code of Professional Responsibility, provides in part that:

A lawyer shall exercise reasonable care to prevent his employees, associates, and others whose services are utilized by him from disclosing or using confidences or secrets of a client. . . .

This obligation is emphasized in EC4-2:

It is a matter of common knowledge that the normal operation of a law office exposes confidential professional information to non-lawyer employees of the office, particularly secretaries and those having access to the files; and this obligates the lawyer to exercise care in selecting and training his employees to that the sanctity of all confidences and secrets of his clients may be preserved.

The ultimate responsibility for compliance with approved standards of professional conduct rests with the supervising attorney. *In the Matter of Martinez,* 107 N.M. 171, 754 P.2d 842 (N.M. 1988). However, the legal assistant should understand what he may or may not do. The burden rests upon the attorney who employs a legal assistant to educate the latter with respect to the duties which may be assigned and then to supervise the manner in which the legal assistant carries out such duties. However, this does not relieve the legal assistant from an independent obligation to refrain from illegal conduct. Additionally, and notwithstanding that the Code is not binding upon non-lawyers, the very

nature of a legal assistant's employment imposes an obligation not to engage in conduct which would involve the supervising attorney in a violation of the Code. NALA has adopted the ABA Code as a part of its Code of Ethics.

VI

Legal assistants should not:

1. Establish attorney-client relationships; set legal fees, give legal opinions or advice; or represent a client before a court; nor

2. Engage in, encourage, or contribute to any act which could constitute the unauthorized practice of law.

COMMENT

Reported cases of holding which acts can and cannot be performed by a legal assistant are few:

The legal assistant cannot create the attorney-client relationship. *DeVaux v. American Home Assur. Co.,* 444 N.E.2d 355 (Mass., 1983).

The legal assistant cannot make court appearances. The question of what constitutes a court appearance is also somewhat vague. See, for example, *People v. Alexander,* 53 Ill. App.2d 299, 202 N.E.2d 841 (1964), where preparation of a court order and transmitting information to court was not the unauthorized practice of law, and *People v. Belfor,* 611 P.2d 979 (Colo. 1980), where the trial court found that the acts of a disbarred attorney did not constitute an appearance and the Supreme Court of Colorado held that only the Supreme Court could make the determination of what acts constituted an appearance and the unauthorized practice of law.

The following cases have identified certain areas in which an attorney has a duty to act, but it is interesting to note that none of these cases state that it is improper for an attorney to have the initial work performed by a legal assistant. This again points out the importance of adequate supervision by the employing attorney.

Courts have found that attorneys have the duty to check bank statements, preserve a client's property, review and sign all pleadings, insure that all communications are opened and answered, and make inquiry when items of dictation are not received. *Attorney Grievance Commission of Maryland v. Goldberg,* 441 A.2d 338, 292 Md. 650 (1982). See also *Vaughn v. State Bar of California,* 100 Cal. Reptr. 713, 494 P.2d 1257 (1972).

The legal assistant cannot exercise professional legal judgment or give legal advice. In *Louisiana State Bar v. Edwins*, 540 So.2d 294 (La. 1989) the court held a paralegal was engaged in activities constituting the unauthorized practice of law, which included evaluation of claims and giving advice on settlements. The attorney who delegated the exercise of these acts aided in the unauthorized practice of law. See also, *People of the State of Co. v. Gelker*, 770 P.2d 402 (Col. 1989).

Attorneys have the responsibility to supervise the work of associates and clerical staff. *Moore v. State Bar Association*, 41 Cal. Rptr. 161, 396 P.2d 577 (1964); *Attorney Grievance Committee of Maryland v. Goldberg*, supra.

An attorney must exercise sufficient supervision to insure that all monies received are properly deposited and disbursed. *Black v. State Bar of California*, 103 Cal. Rptr. 288, 499 P.2d 968 (1972); *Fitzpatrick v. State Bar of California*, 141 Cal. Rptr. 169, 569 P.2d 763 (1977).

The attorney must insure that his staff is competent and effective to perform the work delegated. In *Re Reinmiller*, 325 P.2d 773 (Oregon, 1958). See also, *State of Kansas v. Barrett*, 483 P.2d 1106 (Kansas, 1971); *Attorney Grievance Committee of Maryland v. Goldberg*, supra.

The attorney must make sufficient background investigation of the prior activities and character and integrity of his employees to insure that legal assistants have not previously been involved in unethical, illegal, or other nefarious schemes which demonstrate such person unfit to be associated with the practice of law. See *In the Matter of Shaw*, 88 N.J. 433, A.2d 678 (1982), wherein the Court announced that while it had no disciplinary jurisdiction over legal assistants, it directed that disciplinary hearings make specific findings of fact concerning paralegals' collaboration in nefarious schemes in order that the court might properly discipline any attorney establishing an office relationship with one who had been implicated previously in unscrupulous schemes.

VII

Legal assistants may perform services for an attorney in the representation of a client, provided:

1. The services performed by the legal assistant do not require the exercise of independent professional legal judgment;

2. The attorney maintains a direct relationship with the client and maintains control of all client matters;

3. The attorney supervises the legal assistant;

4. The attorney remains professionally responsible for all work on behalf of the client, including any actions taken or not taken by the legal assistant in connection therewith; and

5. The services performed supplement, merge with and become the attorney's work product.

COMMENT

EC3-6, ABA Code of Professional Responsibility, recognizes the value of utilizing the services of legal assistants, but provides certain conditions to such employment:

A lawyer often delegates tasks to clerks, secretaries, and other lay persons. Such delegation is proper if the lawyer maintains a direct relationship with his client, supervises the delegated work, and has complete professional responsibility for the work product. This delegation enables a lawyer to render legal services more economically and efficiently.

VIII

In the supervision of a legal assistant, consideration should be given to:

1. Designating work assignments that correspond to the legal assistants' abilities, knowledge, training and experience.

2. Educating and training the legal assistant with respect to professional responsibility, local rules and practices, and firm policies;

3. Monitoring the work and professional conduct of the legal assistant to ensure that the work is substantively correct and timely performed;

4. Providing continuing education for the legal assistant in substantive matters through courses, institutes, workshops, seminars and in-house training; and

5. Encouraging and supporting membership and active participation in professional organizations.

COMMENT

Attorneys are responsible for the actions of their employees in both malpractice and disciplinary proceedings. The attorney cannot delegate work to a legal assistant which involves activities constituting the unauthorized practice of law. See *Louisiana State Bar v. Edwins*, 540 So.2d 294 (La. 1989), and *People of the State of Colorado v. Felker*, 770 P.2d 402 (Col. 1989). In the vast majority of the cases, the courts have not censured attorneys for the particular act delegated to the legal assistant, but rather, have been critical of . . . imposed sanctions against attorneys for failure to adequately supervise the legal assistants. See e.g., *Attorney Grievance Commission of Maryland v. Goldberg, supra.*

The attorney's responsibility for supervision of legal assistants must be more than a willingness to accept responsibility and liability for the legal assistant's work. The attorney must monitor the work product and conduct of the legal assistant to insure that the work performed is substantively correct and competently performed in a professional manner. This duty includes the responsibility to provide continuing legal education for the legal assistant.

Supervision of legal assistants must be offered in both the procedural and substantive legal areas in the law office.

In *Spindell v. State Bar of California*, 118 Cal. Rptr. 480, 530 P.2d 168 (1975), the attorney was suspended from practice because of the improper legal advice given by a secretary. The case illustrates that it is important that both attorneys and legal assistants confirm all telephonic advice by letter.

In all instances where the legal assistant relays information to a client in response to an inquiry from the client, the advice relayed telephonically by the legal assistant should be confirmed in writing by the attorney. This will eliminate claims if the client acts contrary to the advice given. It will establish that the legal advice given is in fact that of the attorney, not the legal assistant, and obviate any confusion resulting from transmission of the advice through the legal assistant.

The *Spindell* case is an example of an attorney's failure to supervise and educate his staff. Not only was the secretary uneducated as to the substantive provisions of the law, but more importantly, she was uneducated as to her duty and authority as an employee of the attorney.

IX

Except as otherwise provided by statute, court rule or decision, administrative rule or regulation, or the attorney's Code of Professional Responsibility; and within the preceding parameters and proscriptions, a legal assistant may perform any function delegated by an attorney, including but not limited to the following:

1. Conduct client interviews and maintain general contact with the client after the establishment of the attorney-client relationship, so long as the client is aware of the status and function of the legal assistant, and the client contact is under the supervision of the attorney.

2. Locate and interview witnesses, so long as the witnesses are aware of the status and function of the legal assistant.

3. Conduct investigations and statistical and documentary research for review by the attorney.

4. Conduct legal research for review by the attorney.

5. Draft legal documents for review by the attorney.

6. Draft correspondence and pleadings for review by and signature of the attorney.

7. Summarize depositions, interogatories, and testimony for review by the attorney.

8. Attend executions of wills, real estate closings, depositions, court or administrative hearings and trials with the attorney.

9. Author and sign letters provided the legal assistant's status is clearly indicated and the correspondence does not contain independent legal opinions or legal advice.

COMMENT

The United States Supreme Court has recognized the variety of tasks being performed by legal assistants and has noted that use of legal assistants encourages cost effective delivery of legal services, *Missouri v. Jenkins*, 491 U.S. 274, 109 S.Ct. 2463, 2471, n.10 (1989). In Jenkins, the court further held that legal assistant time should be included in compensation for attorney fee awards at the prevailing practice in the relevant community to bill legal assistant time.

Except for the specific proscription contained in Section VI, the reported cases, such as *Attorney Grievance Commission of Maryland v. Goldberg*, supra, do not limit the duties which may be performed by a legal assistant under the supervision of the attorney. The Guidelines were developed from generally accepted practices. Each supervising attorney must be aware of the specific rules, decisions and statutes applicable to legal assistants within his jurisdiction.

Source: *National Association of Legal Assistants, Model Standards and Guidelines for Utilization of Legal Assistants* (1984, rev'd 1991). Reprinted by permission.

CODE OF ETHICS AND PROFESSIONAL RESPONSIBILITY OF NATIONAL ASSOCIATION OF LEGAL ASSISTANTS, INC.

PREAMBLE

It is the responsibility of every legal assistant to adhere strictly to the accepted standards of legal ethics and to live by general principles of proper conduct. The performance of the duties of the legal assistant shall be governed by specific canons as defined herein in order that justice will be served and the goals of the profession attained.

The canons of ethics set forth hereafter are adopted by the National Association of Legal Assistants, Inc., as a general guide, and the enumeration of these rules does not mean there are not others of equal importance although not specifically mentioned.

Canon 1

A legal assistant shall not perform any of the duties that lawyers only may perform nor do things that lawyers themselves may not do.

Canon 2

A legal assistant may perform any task delegated and supervised by a lawyer so long as the lawyer is responsible to the client, maintains a direct relationship with the client, and assumes full professional responsibility for the work product.

Canon 3

A legal assistant shall not engage in the practice of law by accepting cases, setting fees, giving legal advice or appearing in court (unless otherwise authorized by court or agency rules).

Canon 4

A legal assistant shall not act in matters involving professional legal judgment as the services of a lawyer are essential in the public interest whenever the exercise of such judgment is required.

Canon 5

A legal assistant must act prudently in determining the extent to which a client may be assisted without the presence of a lawyer.

Canon 6

A legal assistant shall not engage in the unauthorized practice of law and shall assist in preventing the unauthorized practice of law.

Canon 7

A legal assistant must protect the confidences of a client, and it shall be unethical for a legal assistant to violate any statute now in effect or hereafter to be enacted controlling privileged communications.

Canon 8

It is the obligation of the legal assistant to avoid conduct which would cause the lawyer to be unethical or even appear to be unethical, and loyalty to the employer is incumbent upon the legal assistant.

Canon 9

A legal assistant shall work continually to maintain integrity and a high degree of competency throughout the legal profession.

Canon 10

A legal assistant shall strive for perfection through education in order to better assist the legal profession in fulfilling its duty of making legal services available to clients and the public.

Canon 11

A legal assistant shall do all other things incidental, necessary, or expedient for the attainment of the ethics and responsibilities imposed by statute or rule of court.

Canon 12

A legal assistant is governed by the American Bar Association Model Code of Professional Responsibility and the American Bar Association Model Rules of Professional Conduct.

Source: *National Association of Legal Assistants, Code of Ethics and Professional Responsibility of National Association of Legal Assistants, Inc.* (1975 rev'd 1988). Reprinted by permission.

SAMPLE LIMITED LICENSURE LEGISLATION
SENATE BILL NO. 0776 87TH GENERAL ASSEMBLY STATE OF ILLINOIS 1991 AND 1992 INTRODUCED APRIL 11, 1991, BY SENATOR JONES A BILL FOR AN ACT TO LICENSE LEGAL TECHNICIANS.

BE IT ENACTED BY THE PEOPLE OF THE STATE OF ILLINOIS, REPRESENTED IN THE GENERAL ASSEMBLY:

Section 1. Short title. This Act may be cited as the Legal Technician Licensing Act.

Section 5. Definitions. As used in this Act:

"Board" means the Legal Technician Licensing and Disciplinary Board established under this Act.

"Department" means the Department of Professional Regulation.

"Director" means the Director of Professional Regulation.

"Legal assistant" has the same meaning as "paralegal".

"Legal technician" means a person licensed under this Act to serve the general public for compensation without being under the supervision of a licensed attorney.

"Paralegal" means a person qualified through education, training, or work experience to perform substantive legal work that requires knowledge of legal concepts and that is customarily, but not exclusively, performed by an attorney. A paralegal is retained or employed by an attorney, law office, governmental agency, or other entity under the supervisory authority of an attorney; or is authorized by governmental administrative agency or statutory or court authority to perform this work.

"Service as a legal technician" shall include, but not be limited to, the following areas:

(a) administrative law;
(b) real estate law;
(c) bankruptcy law;
(d) family law; and
(e) immigration and naturalization law.

Section 10. Examination.

(a) The Department shall conduct or authorize examinations to ascertain the fitness and qualifications of applicants for licenses and issue licenses to those who are found to be fit and qualified.

(b) There shall be an examination to qualify an applicant to be licensed under this Act which shall consist of a general section and a specialty section, both of which must be passed.

(1) The general section shall consist of definitions, ethics, and basic federal and State legal procedure.

(2) The specialty section shall consist of questions that are specific to the State of Illinois and the specialty area for which the licensure is being applied.

(c) The examination shall be developed, administered, and periodically reviewed for validity and reliability by an independent examining or testing organization.

(d) The examination shall be administered in June and January of each year.

(e) A failed examination or failed section can be retaken a maximum of 2 times. Further re-examination shall not be permitted until 3 years have elapsed and all other requirements have been met. A fee is required for each retaking of the entire or partial examination as determined by the Department.

(f) A statement of successful completion or failure of the qualifying examination shall be issued by the Department to the applicant within 30 days after the examination.

(g) The examination shall be administered under the supervision of the Department at places within this State and at times as the Department may determine. The Director shall give reasonable public notice of the examinations at least 60 days prior to their administration.

Section 15. Legal Technician Licensing and Disciplinary Board. There is created the Legal Technician Licensing and Disciplinary Board to be composed of 7 persons appointed as follows:

(a) Two shall be licensed to practice law in this State and are to be appointed by the Supreme Court; 3 shall be paralegals recommended by the Illinois Paralegal Association at least 2 of whom shall be legal technicians; and 2 shall be public members, one appointed by the Senate and one appointed by the Governor. Neither public member is to be licensed to practice law in this State nor licensed under this Act. One public member must be a consumer activist. The Supreme Court shall appoint 3 paralegals to the Board from those recommended by the Illinois Paralegal Association for an initial term after which the Supreme Court shall fill at least 2 of those seats with currently licensed legal technicians for all subsequent terms.

(b) Terms for all members shall be for 3 years. For initial appointments, 2 members shall be appointed to serve for one year, 2 shall be appointed to serve for 2 years, and the remaining members shall be appointed to serve for 3 years and until their successors are appointed and qualify. Initial terms shall begin on the effective date of this Act. Partial terms over 2 years in length shall be considered as full terms. A member may be reappointed for a successive term, but no member shall serve more than 2 full terms.

(c) The composition of the Board should reasonably reflect representation from the various geographic areas of the State.

(d) In making appointments to the Board, the Supreme Court, Governor, and State shall give due consideration to recommendations by organizations of paralegals and of attorneys in this State, and shall give due notice within 15 days to those organizations of any vacancy in the composition of the Board. Vacancies shall be filed within 60 days. A Board member may be terminated for any cause that in the opinion of the majority of the Board reasonably justifies termination. In the event of a tie vote, the Director shall have the deciding vote.

(e) A vacancy on the Board shall not impair the right of a quorum to exercise all the rights and perform all the duties of the Board. A majority of the Board constitutes a quorum to do business only if at least 2 of the members present are paralegals and one of the members present is a public member.

(f) The members of the Board shall each receive, as compensation, a reasonable sum as determined by the Director for each day actually engaged in the duties of the office, and all legitimate and necessary expenses incurred in attending the meetings of the Board.

(g) Members of the Board, individually or collectively, shall be immune from suit in any action based upon any disciplinary proceedings or other activities performed in good faith as members of the Board.

(h) The Board shall meet quarterly and may meet at other times on the call of a majority of its members or the Director.

(i) The Board shall prescribe the form of the application for a legal technician license.

(j) The Board is authorized to require each applicant for a legal technician license to provide any information reasonably necessary to make a determination of eligibility for licensure under this Act.

Section 20. Powers and duties of the Board.

(a) The Board shall independently exercise its powers, duties, and functions prescribed by law relating to licensing, discipline, and regulation.

(b) The Board shall specify:

(1) guidelines for the professional code of conduct for legal technicians that are not contrary to the ABA Model Code of Professional Responsibility;

(2) those tasks that are presently performed by attorneys but which can be performed by a legal technician; and

(3) disciplinary procedures under this Act.

(c) The Board has the authority to determine reciprocal agreements on licensure with other states.

(d) The Board shall also take disciplinary action as defined in this Act.

(e) The Board, at any time, may seek expert advice and knowledge on any matter relating to the administration, delineation of tasks, or enforcement of this Act and is encouraged to seek such input from State and local paralegal associations.

(f) No rule or standard governing the licensing of legal technicians shall become effective until its adoption by the Board and approval of the Director.

Section 25. License requirement.

(a) Beginning January 1, 1992, no person shall serve the general public as a legal technician without being licensed under this Act. The Department shall issue a license to any natural person who meets all of the following:

(1) Submits an application on the form prescribed by the Department specifying in which fields of service set forth in Section 5 the applicant wishes to serve as a legal technician.

(2) Is at least 18 years of age.

(3) Is a high school graduate or possesses a GED.

(4) Has not been convicted of a felony and is not a disbarred attorney.

(5) Pays the required application fee.

(6) Submits proof to the Board of completion of one of the following:

(A) A bachelor's degree from an ABA approved course in paralegal studies or a program essentially in compliance with ABA standards plus 2 years of paralegal experience limited to the applicant's specialty area and under the supervision of an attorney.

(B) A bachelor's degree from other than an ABA approved course in paralegal studies plus 3 years of paralegal experience limited to the applicant's specialty area and under the supervision of an attorney.

(C) A bachelor's degree in any field, graduation from an ABA approved course, and 2 years of paralegal experience limited to the applicant's specialty area and under the supervision of an attorney.

(D) A bachelor's degree in any field, graduation from a non-ABA approved course, and 3 years of paralegal experience limited to the applicant's specialty area and under the supervision of an attorney.

(E) A bachelor's degree in any field plus 4 years paralegal experience limited to the applicant's specialty area and under the supervision of an attorney.

(F) Graduation from an ABA approved course plus 5 years of paralegal experience limited to the applicant's specialty area and under the supervision of an attorney.

(G) A minimum of 6 years of paralegal experience limited to the applicant's specialty area with or without graduation from a non-ABA approved course and under the supervision of an attorney. For purposes of this subsection, one year of experience is equivalent to 2000 hours of work under the direct supervision of an attorney. The applicant may submit to the Board a request for special consideration with supporting documentation that the Board may find satisfactorily meets the intent of this Act.

(7) Passes the appropriate examination for licensure identified by this Act and administered by the Department.

(c) The license issued by the Department shall authorize the legal technician to serve in the specialty area stated on the face of the license and in accordance with the allowances and limitations as set forth by this Act.

(d) A legal technician practicing under this Act shall display the license for inspection in the legal technician's place of business.

(e) A legal technician license shall not be transferable.

(f) Each licensee shall report any conviction of any crime or any finding of administrative violation, in any jurisdiction, that involves fraud, dishonest dealing, or any other act of moral turpitude, to the Department in writing not later than 30 business days after the conviction or administrative action.

(g) Each self-employed legal technician shall report any action in bankruptcy, voluntary or involuntary, to the Department not later than 7 business days after the action is instituted.

(h) The license issued by the Department shall authorize the licensee to practice only in the fields of practice specified in Section 5. The license shall state on its face which each specialty area in which the licensee is authorized to practice.

(i) If an applicant neglects, fails, refuses to take or fails to pass an examination for licensure under this Act within 3 years after filing his or her application, the fee paid by the applicant shall be forfeited and the application denied. The applicant, however, may thereafter submit a new application for examination accompanied by the required fee and evidence of meeting the requirements in force at the time of the new application.

Section 30. License renewal.

(a) The legal technician license shall be renewed every 2 years.

(b) The legal technician shall submit proof to the Board of 10 hours of continuing legal education during the previous 2 years of which a minimum of 5 hours shall be in the licensee's specialty area.

(c) The legal technician shall submit reverification of insurance to the Board.

(d) The Director shall renew a legal technician's license upon receipt of the completed renewal application, the renewal fee specified by the Board, proof of completion of the required number of hours of continuing legal education, and reverification of insurance.

(e) A license that is not renewed by the end of the 2 year period prescribed by the Director shall automatically refer to inactive status. An inactive license may be reactivated by the filing of a completed reactivation application with the Director, payment of the renewal fee, and payment of a reactivation fee equal to the renewal fee.

(f) A license that is not renewed within 2 years of becoming inactive shall expire.

Section 35. Insurance; bonding; Client Compensation Fund.

(a) Within 30 days after the issuance of a license or its renewal, a legal technician shall:

(1) obtain a surety bond in an amount as established by the Board;

(2) obtain professional liability insurance (as available) in an amount as established by the Board; or

(3) submit evidence of coverage or a statement by the employing attorney that the legal technician is practicing in a law firm, corporation, or agency of government and is covered under the attorney's professional liability insurance.

(b) There is established in the State Treasury the Client Compensation Fund. An amount to be established by the Board shall be included in the fee for both application and renewal of a legal technician license. This amount shall be deposited into the Client Compensation Fund.

(c) If the Client Compensation Fund at any time exceeds a maximum sum to be determined by the Board, collection of the fees for this fund shall be discontinued and the fees shall not be reimposed unless the fund is reduced below the maximum amount by disbursement made in accordance with this Act.

(d) The Client Compensation Fund shall be disbursed by the Board to clients of a legal technician who the Board has determined, after hearing, to have been injured up to the following amounts for each violation:

(1) fees and disbursement to a maximum of $1,000; and

(2) compensatory damages to a maximum of $1,000.

Section 40. Funding.

(a) There is created a fund in the State treasury to be known as the Legal Technician Fund. The purpose of the fund is to provide monies to the Department to employ staff necessary to administer this Act.

(b) With the exception of deposits made to the Client Compensation Fund, all fees, fines, and penalties collected under this Act shall be deposited into the Fund. This Fund is separate from the Client Compensation Fund.

(c) The funds in the Legal Technician Fund and the Client Compensation Fund shall be invested by the Treasurer under the same limitations as other State funds, and the interest earned on the funds shall be retained in each fund and be available as other monies deposited in the respective funds.

Section 45. Practice requirements.

(a) A legal technician shall not represent a client if the representation of a client may be materially limited by the scope of the legal technician's license.

(b) Before undertaking to act on behalf of a client, a legal technician shall advise the client that the legal technician is (i) not an attorney and (ii) is prohibited from acting or advising on a matter that is not within the scope of the legal technician's license.

(c) A legal technician shall not represent a client:

(1) If the representation of the client will be directly adverse to another client unless each client consents in writing after consultation; or

(2) if the representation of that client may be materially limited by the legal technician's responsibilities to another client or to a third person, or by the legal technician's own interests.

When practicing under the supervision of an attorney, a legal technician shall not knowingly represent a person in the same or a substantially related matter in which that legal technician, or law firm or other business entity with which that legal technician was associated, had previously represented a client whose interests are materially adverse to that person and about whom the legal technician had acquired confidential information.

(d) A legal technician shall not use a title or communicate in such a manner that would be likely to mislead the public as to the legal technician's qualifications or occupation. A communication is false or misleading if it:

(1) contains a material misrepresentation of fact or law, or omits a fact necessary to make the statement considered as a whole not materially misleading;

(2) is likely to create an unjustified expectation of the results the legal technician can achieve, or states or implies that the legal technician can achieve results by means that violate the scope of the legal technician's license or the standards of conduct of the profession;

(3) compares the legal technician's services with other legal services, unless the comparison can be factually substantiated; or

(4) contains any paid testimonial about, or paid endorsement of, the legal technician without identifying the fact that payment has been made

or, if the testimonial or endorsement is not made by an actual client, without identifying that fact;

Any advertising of a legal technician's services shall contain the designation "Legal Technician in (Specialty Area)".

(e) A legal technician shall communicate to clients and the public the fact that the legal technician's practice is limited to a particular specialty area or areas of the law, as well as the scope of the legal technician's limited license.

(f) The legal technician shall supply the client with a contract including fees, deadlines, and a statement that the legal technician is not an attorney. The contract shall allow for a 3-day cooling off period.

(g) The legal technician must advise the client of consumer complaint procedures.

Section 50. License revocation or suspension.

(a) A decision by the Board to revoke a license may be appealed by the legal technician to the Director within 30 days of the decision of the Board. The Director, after a review of the case, must issue a decision to the appealing legal technician reversing or upholding the Board's decision within 45 days of receipt of the appeal.

(b) The Director may temporarily suspend the license of a legal technician without a hearing simultaneous to the institution of proceedings for a hearing under this Act if the Director finds that evidence in the Director's possession indicates that a legal technician's continuation in practice would constitute an immediate danger to the public. In the event that the Director temporarily suspends the license of a legal technician without a hearing, a hearing by the Board must be held within 15 days after the suspension has occurred and concluded without appreciable delay.

(c) Whenever the Director is satisfied that substantial justice has not been done either in an examination or in the revocation, suspension, or refusal to issue a license, or other disciplinary action, the Director may order a re-examination or rehearing.

Section 55. Disciplinary action.

(a) The Board may refuse to issue or renew, or may revoke, suspend, or take other disciplinary action as the Board may deem proper, including fines and compensatory damages not to exceed $5,000 per violation, with regard to any license for any one or combination of the following causes:

(1) Any violation or misconduct as defined by the professional code of conduct to be established by the Board.

(2) Fraud in procuring the license.

(3) Making any misrepresentation or false statements, directly or indirectly, to influence, persuade, or induce patronage.

(4) Improper, unprofessional, or dishonorable conduct of a character likely to deceive, defraud, or harm the public.

(5) Conviction in any state or federal court of any crime which is a felony.

(6) Revocation by another state, the District of Columbia, territory, or foreign nation of a license for paralegal services in its jurisdiction if at least one of the grounds for that revocation is the same as or the equivalent of one of the grounds for revocation set forth in this Act.

(7) Gross or repeated malpractice.

(8) Professional incompetence as manifested by poor standards of practice or mental incompetence as declared by a court of competent jurisdiction.

(9) Advertising in a manner that is false or misleading to the public.

(10) Habitual intoxication or addiction to the use of drugs.

(11) Exceeding the authority of the license issued to the paralegal specialist.

(b) Upon a verified written complaint of any person setting forth facts which, if proven, would constitute grounds for discipline, suspension, or revocation of license under this Act, the Board shall investigate the actions of the legal technician.

(c) At least 30 days before the date set for a hearing concerning the written complaint a written notice of the scheduled hearing and a copy of the written complaint must be served on the legal technician. Service may be accomplished by personal delivery or by registered or certified mail to the legal technician's address. The Board shall direct the legal technician to file a written answer to the complaint within 20 days after service. Failure to file an answer may result in the suspension or revocation of the legal technician's license before the scheduled hearing.

(d) The Director shall have the authority to appoint a hearing officer for any action for refusal to issue or renew a license or discipline of a legal technician. The hearing officer shall be neither an attorney nor a paralegal.

(e) At the time and place fixed in the notice, the Board and hearing officer shall proceed to hear the charges of all parties. The hearing officer shall have full authority to chair the hearing.

(f) Within 30 days after the hearing, the hearing officer and the Board shall report their findings and recommendations to the Director. The Director shall issue the order within 10 days after receipt of the report.

(g) The Board may advise the Director that probation be granted or that other disciplinary action be taken, including the limitation of the scope, nature, or extent of the legal technician's practice, or compensation be paid to the client from the Client Compensation Fund. If disciplinary action other than suspension or revocation is taken, the Board may advise the Director to impose reasonable limitations and requirements upon the legal technician to insure compliance with the terms of the probation or the disciplinary action, including, but not limited to, regular reporting by the legal technician to the Director of the legal technician's actions, or limiting the legal technician's practice in a manner that the Director may require.

(h) Each order of revocation, suspension, or other disciplinary action shall contain a brief and concise statement of the grounds upon which the Department's action is based, as well as the specific terms and conditions of the action.

(i) At the expiration of the time allowed for filing a motion for rehearing, the Director may take action recommended by the Board.

(j) Upon suspension, revocation, or the taking of any other disciplinary action, including the limiting of the scope, nature, or extent of the legal technician's practice, deemed proper by the Board with regard to the license, the legal technician shall surrender the license to the Department if ordered to do so by the Director and upon the legal technician's failure to do so, the Department may seize the license.

(k) At any time after suspension, revocation, or the taking of any other disciplinary action with regard to any license, the Director may restore the license, or take any action to reinstate the license to good standing, without examination, upon the written recommendation of the Board.

(l) In all hearings conducted under this Act, information received, pursuant to law, relating to any information acquired by a legal technician in serving any individual in a professional capacity, and necessary to professionally serve that individual, shall be deemed strictly confidential and shall only be made available, either as part of the record of a hearing or otherwise: (i) when the record is required, in its entirety, for purposes of judicial review under this Act; or (ii) upon the express, written consent of the individual served, or in the case of the individual's death or disability, the consent of his or her personal representative.

(m) The physical possession of original documents shall be determined by the hearing officer during the pendency of the complaint procedures.

(n) A legal technician shall have the right to appeal the final decision of the Director under the Administrative Review Law.

(o) Any person who practices or offers to practice as a legal technician in this State without being licensed for that purpose or whose license has been suspended or revoked, or who violates a provision of this Act for which no specific penalty has been provided herein, is guilty of a Class C misdemeanor.

Illegal practice under this Act is declared to be inimical to the public welfare, to constitute a public nuisance, and to cause irreparable harm to the public welfare. The Board, the Attorney General, the State's attorney, or any person may maintain an action in the name of the people of this State and may apply for an injunction in any circuit court to enjoin any person from engaging in unlawful practice.

(p) Any person who has been previously convicted of a violation of any of the provisions of this Act and who subsequently violates any of the provisions of this Act is guilty of a Class 3 felony. In addition, whenever any person is punished as a subsequent offender under this Section, the Director shall proceed to obtain a permanent injunction prohibiting that person from practicing as a legal technician.

(q) Any person filing, or attempting to file as one's own, the diploma or license of another, or a forged affidavit of identification or qualifications, upon conviction, shall be subject to the fine and imprisonment provided by the statutes of this State for the crime of forgery.

Section 60. Exemption. A person who is employed as a paralegal under the direct supervision of a licensed attorney and is not engaged in service directly to the public as a paralegal shall not be required to be licensed under this Act.

. . .

Source: "Office of Senator Emil Jones"

The principal cases are in bold type. Cases cited or discussed in the text are roman type. Cases cited in principal cases and within other quoted materials are not included. References are to pages.

Alexander, People v., 75
Anderson, In re, 89
Anonymous Member of South Carolina Bar, Matter of, 223
Arizona, State of v. Melendez, 78
Attorney Grievance Commission of Maryland v. Goldberg, 45

Bachmann, In re, 89, 90, 261, 266
Bates v. State Bar of Arizona, 250, 252, 254, 256, 259, 260, 265
Bilodeau v. Antal, 73
Black v. State Bar of California, 233
Bockian v. Esanu Katsky Korins & Siger, 41
Brammer v. Taylor, 91
Bump v. Barnett, 78
Busch v. Flangas, 51

Cardinal v. Merrill Lynch Realty/Burnet, Inc., 67
Castillo v. St. Paul Fire & Marine Ins. Co., 291, 307
Cinema 5, Ltd. v. Cinerama, Inc., 176
Committee on Professional Ethics and Conduct of Iowa State Bar Ass'n v. Lawler, 220
Complex Asbestos Litigation, In re, 168, 194, 196, 202, 209
Conduct of Burrows, In re, 120, 125
Continental Illinois Securities Litigation, In re, 231
Continental Townhouses East Unit One Ass'n v. Brockbank, 231

Darby v. Mississippi State Bd. of Bar Admissions, 67
Decker, In re Marriage of, 138
Demos, In re, 50, 98
Dewey v. R.J. Reynolds Tobacco Co., 198
Disciplinary Proceedings Against Leaf, Matter of, 183
Divine, In re Estate of, 54, 59
Duncan v. Gordon, 68, 97

Emmons, Williams, Mires and Leech v. State Bar of Cal., 220
Esquire Care, Inc. v. Maguire, 198
Estate of (see name of party)
EZ Paintr Corp. v. Padco, Inc., 200

Fadia v. Unauthorized Practice of Law Committee, 91
Faretta v. California, 66, 77
Florida Bar v. Brumbaugh, 67, 85, 87

Frieson, State ex rel. v. Isner, 78

Galbasini, Matter of, 46
Gassman v. State Bar, 220
Gigax, United States v., 77
Glover Bottled Gas Corp. v. Circle M. Beverage Barn, Inc., 197
Gregori v. Bank of America, 169, 189

Haagen-Dazs Co., Inc. v. Perche No! Gelato, Inc., 183
Henize v. Giles, 80
Herren, In re, 90
Hickman v. Taylor, 138
Himmel, In re, 274, 285

In re (see name of party)
Isner, State ex rel. Frieson v., 78

Johnson v. Naugle, 232

Kansas, State of v. Caenen, 238
Kentucky Bar Ass'n v. Legal Alternatives, Inc., 55
Kentucky Bar Ass'n v. Lorenz, 220
Kinghorn, Matter of, 258
Kitsis v. State Bar, 262
Kovel, United States v., 146

Lackow v. Walter E. Heller & Co. Southeast, Inc., 168
Louisiana State Bar Ass'n v. Edwins, 46, 47, 48, 104

Marashi, United States v., 135
Marriage of (see name of party)
Martinez, Matter of, 38
Matter of (see name of party)
Missouri v. Jenkins, 13, 69, 224, 229, 232
Missouri, State of v. Carroll, 68
Mitchell, People v., 151
Mountain States Tel. & Tel. Co. v. DiFede, 137

Nemours Foundation v. Gilbane, Aetna, Federal Ins. Co., 201
New York County Lawyers' Ass'n v. Dacey, 92

Ohralik v. Ohio State Bar Ass'n, 255, 256, 262

Opinion No. 24 of Committee on Unauthorized Practice of Law, In re, 15, 20, 64, 99
Oregon State Bar v. Security Escrows, Inc., 69

Palmer v. Westmeyer, 51
Palomo v. State Bar of California, 237
Papanicolaou v. Chase Manhattan Bank, N.A., 200
Peel v. Attorney Registration and Disciplinary Com'n of Illinois, 255
Pennwalt Corp. v. Plough, Inc., 171
People v. (see opposing party)
Person v. Association of Bar of City of New York, 252
Primus, In re, 256

Reed v. Labor and Indus. Relations Com'n, 81
Reyes, People v., 135
Rivers, In re, 274
R. M. J., In re, 250, 254, 255

Samaritan Foundation v. Superior Court In and For County of Maricopa, 149, 161
Scanlan, Matter of, 236, 237
Shapero v. Kentucky Bar Ass'n, 255
Silber, Matter of, 96
Sparks v. Johnson, 78
Sperry v. Florida, 83
State v. (see opposing party)

State ex rel. v. (see opposing party and relator)
Stern, Matter of, 225
Superior Bank FSB v. Golding, 54

The Florida Bar v. Furman, 451 So.2d 808, pp. 87, 98
The Florida Bar v. Furman, 376 So.2d 378, pp. 86, 97
The Florida Bar v. Rodriguez, 97
The Telephone Cases, 3
Touchy v. Houston Legal Foundation, 55
Turner v. American Bar Ass'n, 66, 77

Unauthorized Practice of Law Committee v. State of Rhode Island, Dept. of Workers' Compensation, 79
Unauthorized Practice of Law Committee v. Employers Unity, Inc., 80
United States v. (see opposing party)

Vrdolyak, In re, 236

Washington State Bar Ass'n v. Great Western Union Federal Sav. and Loan Ass'n, 68
West Virginia State Bar v. Earley, 55
Wilson, In re, 234

Zauderer v. Office of Disciplinary Counsel of Supreme Court of Ohio, 254, 255

GLOSSARY

AAfPE American Association for Paralegal Education

ABA American Bar Association

ABA Commission on Nonlawyer Practice A commission created to study and determine the implications of nonlawyer legal practice for society, the lay public, and the legal profession.

ABA Model Code of Professional Responsibility (Model Code) The second code of ethics, adopted by the American Bar Association in 1969. The Model Code serves as a guide to state attempts to draft their own binding codes of ethics.

ABA Model Rules of Professional Conduct (Model Rules) An ethics code drafted by the American Bar Association and adopted by the majority of jurisdictions in the U.S.

ABA Special Committee A committee of the ABA that is appointed when there is a need to study an issue immediately and to conduct some research or experiments at a particular time.

ABA Special Committee on Lay Assistants for Lawyers A special committee appointed early in the development of the role of the paralegal to study the problems unique to the paralegal. This committee eventually became the Special Committee on Legal Assistants.

ABA Special Committee on Legal Assistants Formerly the Special Committee on Lay Assistants for Lawyers.

ABA Special Committee on the Availability of Legal Services A special committee established by the American Bar Association in the late 1960s that was directed to evaluate the developing role of the paralegal.

ABA Standing Committee A permanent committee of the ABA that studies issues related to a particular topic and meets on a regular basis.

*Administrative Agency A governmental body that carries out or administers the law.

Adverse Authority Authority which is controlling in any given jurisdiction, and which is directly adverse to the client's position.

Adverse Party Opposing party in a legal matter.

*Adverse Position Goal, need, or claim of one person that is different from or opposed to that of another person or group.

Affirmation of Professional Responsibility The name of the first code of ethics written by NFPA.

*Agency A relationship in which one person acts for another or represents another by the latter's authority.

*Agent A person authorized to act for another.

American Association for Paralegal Education (AAfPE) A national organization for paralegal educators, whose goals include promoting high standards for paralegal education.

American Bar Association (ABA) An organization composed of attorneys from every jurisdiction in the U.S., that attempts to address problems unique to the legal profession.

Attorney A legal advisor or counselor who is an officer of the court, educated in the law, and licensed by the jurisdiction in which he practices law. See also "lawyer."

Attorney Advertising The practice of attorneys announcing the availability of law firm services in order to attract potential clients.

Attorney-Client Privilege A legal doctrine that prohibits an attorney who represents a client from testifying in open court and revealing the secrets of the client.

Attorney-Client Relationship The relationship between retained counsel and her client which encompasses privileges of communication, legal advice, and legal representation. This is considered a fiduciary relationship.

Attorney Disqualification A consequence that can result when the attorney discovers that a conflict of interest exists. The attorney is removed from representation of the client.

*Attorney Malpractice The failure of a lawyer to use such skill, prudence, and diligence as lawyers of ordinary skill and capacity commonly possess and exercise. If a lawyer is found to have engaged in malpractice, the lawyer is held civilly accountable for his actions. See also "legal malpractice."

Attorney Misconduct An attorney's violation of the established rules of ethics.

Attorney's Code of Ethics The ethical rules which guide the behavior of attorneys engaged in the practice of law in a particular jurisdiction.

*Authority The power or right to act or make decisions.

*Bankruptcy The inability to pay debts as they are due.

Billable Hour A measurement of the time billed to the client for work completed on the client's case.

Billing Practice The procedure by which law firms collect money from clients as compensation for legal services rendered.

Binding Authority Sources of law that must be taken into account by legal professionals in a given jurisdiction.

Blackstone's Commentaries Historical commentaries written by Sir William Blackstone, a noted historian who had great influence on America's and England's jurisprudence.

Blowing the Whistle Reporting misconduct.

Bonus A form of compensation paid to a nonlawyer employee that is not tied to the receipt of particular fees for a particular case.

Brief Written statement that summarizes cases or other kinds of law, and which is often used by attorneys and courts to define the issues in a given legal proceeding. "Briefs" may be used in the office, at trials, at hearings, or on appeal.

Business Card A commonly accepted form of identification that indicates the holder of the business card's name, occupation, business address, and business phone number.

Candor Honesty.

Canons In the *Model Code of Professional Responsibility*, statements under which the Disciplinary Rules and the Ethical Considerations are grouped, that express the ethical concepts to be presented and discussed within the *Model Code*.

Canons of Professional Ethics A uniform document developed by the American Bar Association in 1908 that provided general rules stating acceptable professional behavior for attorneys.

*Cause of Action The facts that give a person a right to judicial relief.

Censure A form of discipline for attorneys. The sanction imposed on an attorney that officially de-

nounces the actions of the attorney. A censure may be public or private. See also "reprimand."

Certification Examination of nonlawyers and authorization to practice as a paralegal given by a nongovernmental authority.

Certified Legal Assistant (CLA) A designation given to a legal assistant who successfully completes a voluntary certification examination that is administered by the National Association for Legal Assistants/NALA.

Certified Legal Assistant Specialist (CLAS) Designation given to a CLA who successfully completes a specialty examination and thereby obtains a specialty certification.

*Civility Politeness.

Civilly Liable Responsibility for damages in a civil case where it is determined that the offending party has caused the other party to sustain a loss.

CLA Certified Legal Assistant

CLAS Certified Legal Assistant Specialist

*Client A person who employs or retains an attorney for advice and representation on legal matters.

Client Trust Fund Account A bank account established for the benefit of the client, to hold the client's money.

*Co-Defendants More than one defendant being sued in a particular civil case or prosecuted in a criminal case in the same litigation.

Commingling Funds The practice of intermingling client money with that of the attorney whereby the client's money loses its separate identity.

*Common Law Doctrine Law made by judges in the absence of controlling statutory law.

Confidence As used in the *Model Code*, information protected by the attorney-client privilege.

Confidentiality The ethical rule that imposes upon the attorney and all legal professionals an obligation to refrain from revealing information about the client's affairs.

Conflict of Interest Rules Rules designed to prevent lawyers from compromising their clients' interests because of information gained through the lawyer-client relationship. They are designed to prevent disharmony and distrust in the attorney-client relationship.

Conflicts of Interest Those situations in which a client's interests can be compromised by an attorney because of information gained by an attorney through the attorney-client relationship.

*Consent   Agreement or approval.

Contempt of Court   Willful disobedience of orders of the court.

Contingent Fee   A common arrangement between clients and attorneys where the client agrees to pay the attorney a portion of any recovery in a particular matter.

*Continuance   The adjournment or postponement of a session, hearing, trial, or other proceeding, to another place or time.

*Contract   A legally binding agreement that creates an obligation to do or not to do a particular thing.

Co-Plaintiff   Parties who together bring a legal action against some party or parties.

Court Appearance   Appearing in court on behalf of a client.

Crime-Fraud Exception   An exception to the attorney-client privilege that arises when a client tells an attorney of the client's intention to commit a crime or a fraudulent act or seeks advice from the attorney to assist the client in realizing this goal.

*Cross-Examine   To question a witness after the direct examination of that witness by the side that initially called the witness.

Cured by Consent   Term used when a client is informed of the potential for a conflict of interest to arise and, knowing of the potential conflict, consents to the representation. See also "waiving conflicts of interest."

*Defenses   Allegations of fact or legal theories offered to offset or defeat claims or demands.

Deposition   Pre-trial discovery device whereby one party poses questions to the opposing party, in the presence of a court reporter.

Diligent Representation   Conscientious, attentive, persistent attention to a client's cause.

Direct Mail   A mailing addressed to a specific person and targeted to reach particular clients.

Disbarment   A sanction imposed on an attorney when he or she violates an ethical rule. This sanction takes away the attorney's license to practice law.

Disciplinary Rules   Rules that are set out in the codes of ethics.

Disciplinary Rules (DRs)   Statements set forth within the *Model Code of Professional Responsibility* that establish the minimum level of conduct below which no attorney can fall without being subject to disciplinary action.

Disclosure of Nonlawyer Status   A rule whereby nonlawyers should always clearly identify themselves as nonlawyers.

Discovery   Pre-trial process whereby both parties attempt to gather information about the lawsuit from the opposing side. Discovery can include, but is not limited to, taking depositions, answering interrogatories, and producing documents.

Disqualified   Rendered ineligible or unfit to represent a client.

Divorce Kits   Generally, copies of legal documents required to be completed and filed in order to secure a divorce, with instructions for filing in court.

Do-It-Yourself Services   Businesses designed to assist the general public in completing complicated legal documents. Such services help the lay public to type information in blank spaces on pre-printed forms. See also "typing services."

DR   Disciplinary Rule

Duty to Report   An obligation many codes of ethics place on attorneys to report to the state disciplinary agency what is perceived to be the misconduct of another lawyer.

EC   Ethical Consideration

Errors and Omissions Insurance   An insurance policy that is meant to address those professional errors or omissions that result in harm to the client.

Ethical   Conforming to the standards imposed by the ethical codes in place in the state in which the attorney practices law.

Ethical Considerations (ECs)   Aspirational statements set forth within the *Model Code of Professional Responsibility* that explain the Disciplinary Rules.

Ethics   The principles of conduct governing an individual or a group.

Ethics Advisory Opinion   An opinion issued by a state bar's advisory committee that addresses a question from an attorney relating to an ethical problem.

Ethics Committee   A committee within a law firm formed by that firm for the purpose of making and enforcing ethical policy decisions based on the rules of ethics.

*Evidence   Any kind of proof offered to establish the existence or nonexistence of a fact in dispute.

Evidentiary Rules   Rules designed to protect from disclosure what might otherwise become evidence during court proceedings.

Exceptions to the Privilege As distinguished from waiver, exceptions to the privilege exist where the communication is such that it is never found to be within the protections of the privilege.

***Ex Parte* Communications** Communications in which a lawyer talks or otherwise communicates with an individual involved in the litigation proceedings and where opposing counsel is not present.

Fact-Sensitive The outcome of each case turns on its particular facts.

Family Law A body of law concerned with domestic issues, such as divorce and adoption.

Federal Administrative Procedures Act A federal law which establishes administrative procedures to guide any person who is handling or involved in matters before any federal administrative agency.

***Federal Rules of Evidence** Rules that govern the admissibility of evidence at trial in federal courts and before U.S. magistrates.

Fee Shifting Statute A statute that generally directs the courts to order defendants to pay the attorney's fees of the plaintiff where the plaintiff has prevailed in the action.

Fee Splitting Sharing legal fees with a nonlawyer. It arises when a particular fee tied to a particular client is paid directly to the nonlawyer as compensation.

Fixed Fee A method of billing a client such that a uniform or standard fee is charged by the lawyer or law firm to the client for performing a particular legal service.

Former Client A party that previously has been represented by an attorney.

Freelance Legal Assistant/Paralegal A paralegal who works independently of attorneys, yet provides legal services to law firms.

General Licensing Examination of nonlawyers and authorization to work as a paralegal given by a governmental body.

Guidelines for the Utilization of Legal Assistant Services Guidelines written by the ABA that advise attorneys on using the services of nonlawyer assistants.

Hourly Fee A billing practice whereby attorneys charge their clients for the amount of time spent attending to their representation.

Implied Waiver A waiver that occurs because the client has, through his behavior, made it necessary to reveal the information which would otherwise be protected by the attorney-client privilege.

Imputed Disqualification A legal consequence that results when disqualification of an attorney from representing a particular client has been transferred to the entire firm such that all lawyers in that firm are disqualified from representing that client. See also "vicarious disqualification."

Independent Legal Judgment That judgment which is exercised by those educated in the law. It is the application of a general body of law to a specific factual situation.

Independent Paralegal A nonlawyer who has been licensed pursuant to limited licensure legislation and can therefore provide legal services directly to the public. See also "legal technician."

Informational Materials Materials that may be excluded from the protection of the work product doctrine. These materials can be obtained from opposing counsel where no adequate substitute can be found and include factual research materials.

Initial Client Interview The client's first meeting with a legal professional during which the legal professional attempts to elicit information regarding the nature of the legal problem.

***Injunction** A prohibitive, equitable remedy, issued by a court, to forbid someone to do an act that he or she is threatening to do, or restrain him or her from continuing the act. An injunction is issued against a party who is then "enjoined" from continuing in that practice.

Interest on Lawyer's Trust Accounts (IOLTA) An account into which interest that is earned on client trust fund accounts is deposited in order to fund programs that serve low-income clients of attorneys.

Interrogatories A pre-trial discovery device. A series of written questions asked of opposing parties.

IOLTA Interest on Lawyer's Trust Accounts

Kutak Commission A commission responsible for drafting the new *Model Rules of Professional Conduct*.

LAMA Legal Assistant Management Association

Lawyer A legal advisor/counselor who is an officer of the court, educated in the law, and licensed by the jurisdiction in which he practices law. See also "attorney."

Lawyer's Assistance Programs Programs specifically designed to help lawyers deal with problems linked to substance abuse or dependency.

Lay Representation Representation of a party's interests by a nonlawyer.

Legal Advice Advice about legal matters that may be given to clients exclusively by those licensed to practice law.

Legal Assistant A nonlawyer, working under the supervision of an attorney, who handles legal tasks but whose work does not involve the exercise of independent legal judgment. See also "paralegal."

Legal Assistant Management Association (LAMA) A national organization whose purpose is to address concerns of legal assistant managers specifically, and whose overall goal is to foster the improvement of the profession of the legal assistant.

Legal Ethics A code of conduct self-imposed by the legal profession which guides the legal professional's behavior toward clients and shapes the legal environment.

*Legal Malpractice The failure of a lawyer to use such skill, prudence, and diligence as lawyers of ordinary skill and capacity commonly possess and exercise. If a lawyer is found to have engaged in malpractice, the lawyer is civilly accountable for his actions. See also "attorney malpractice."

*Legal Profession A vocation or occupation requiring the special education and skill of one trained in the law.

Legal Secretary A nonlawyer working in the law office, who specializes in routine functions like typing, transcribing, and communicating with clients.

Legal Technician A nonlawyer who has been licensed pursuant to limited licensure legislation and can therefore provide legal services directly to the public.

Letterhead Legal stationery with a printed heading. Generally, the letterhead of a law firm indicates the names of the attorneys with that law firm, showing named partners, other partners, and associates.

Limited Licensure Legislation that allows nonlawyers to provide limited legal services directly to the public.

Litigation Paralegal A legal assistant who specializes in assisting in matters that involve litigation.

*Litigator An attorney who settles disputes or seeks relief in a court of law.

Martindale-Hubbell Law Directory Listing of law firms located in each jurisdiction of the country.

Materially Adverse As used in the conflicts of interest rules, information acquired by the lawyer in the course of representing a client. It may not subsequently be used or revealed by the lawyer, to the disadvantage of the client.

Memorandum of Law A written statement that addresses a particular legal issue or certain facts in a legal matter. It may be written for interoffice use or for use as a persuasive document.

Mental Impressions Any of the ideas of a lawyer on how to conduct a case. A lawyer's trial strategy.

Misappropriation Any unauthorized use by the lawyer of client funds entrusted to him. Misappropriation includes not only stealing the funds, but also any unauthorized temporary use of those funds for the lawyer's own purposes.

Model Code ABA *Model Code of Professional Responsibility*

Model Code of Ethics and Responsibility A code of ethics adopted by NFPA at its annual meeting in May 1993.

Model Rule 5.3 In terms·of relating ethics to nonlawyers, this rule is the most important of the *Model Rules of Professional Conduct.* This rule, more than any other, encourages both attorneys and the nonlawyers who work for them to strictly adhere to the attorney's code of ethics as it makes an attorney responsible for the nonlawyer in his or her employ.

Model Rules ABA *Model Rules of Professional Conduct*

Moral Of or relating to principles of right and wrong in behavior.

*Moral Turpitude Acts of behavior that gravely violate accepted moral standards of the community.

NALA National Association of Legal Assistants

NALA Code of Ethics A code of ethics adopted by NALA in 1975 for use by legal assistants. An individual joining NALA is obliged to abide by this code.

NALA Model Standards and Guidelines for the Utilization of Legal Assistants, Annotated An annotated ethical code that provides ethical guidelines and annotations to explain from what sources the guidelines derive.

National Association of Legal Assistants (NALA) A national organization whose purpose is to further the rise of the paralegal profession while providing a voice for its concerns.

National Association of Legal Secretaries (NALS) A national organization that represents the interests of legal secretaries.

National Federation of Paralegal Associations (NFPA) A national organization for paralegals and paralegal associations.

*Negligence   The failure to do what a reasonable person would have done under the same circumstances.

NFPA   National Federation of Paralegal Associations

NFPA Affirmation of Professional Responsibility   The first code of ethics written by NFPA.

NFPA Model Code of Ethics and Professional Responsibility   A code of ethics adopted by NFPA at its annual meeting in May 1993. Members of NFPA should abide by this code.

Nonlawyer Referral   A situation where nonlawyers employed in a law firm recommend the services of their supervising attorney to friends or other people who may need legal advice.

Non-Privileged   Information that is not protected by the attorney-client privilege.

Padding Billable Hours   A practice where the legal professional charges hours to a client even though the legal professional never spent that time working on the client's case.

Paralegal   A nonlawyer, working under the supervision of an attorney, who handles legal tasks but whose work does not involve the exercise of independent legal judgment. See also "legal assistant."

*Paralegal Malpractice   Professional malpractice or unreasonable lack of skill attributed to a paralegal.

Persuasive Authority   Sources of law that might be considered by a legal professional but are not binding (or conclusive) in that jurisdiction.

*Pleadings   Formal allegations by parties of their claims and defenses.

*Possessory Rights   Related to, founded on, or claiming possession.

Practice of Law   An activity involving the exercise of independent legal judgment such as advising clients and representing clients in court proceedings.

Preemption   A doctrine which provides that the legislature, and sometimes the courts, determine that certain matters are so important to the nation as a whole that federal law governing the subject will take precedence over any state laws covering that same subject. The doctrine is derived from the Supremacy Clause of the U.S. Constitution.

Pre-trial hearings   Proceedings that occur before the trial which are held to resolve definite issues of fact or law.

*Principal   That party within an agency relationship who permits or directs an agent to act for his or her benefit.

Privilege   A right or immunity granted as a peculiar benefit, advantage, or favor.

Privileged Communication   Those statements, made by certain persons within a relationship, that the law protects from forced disclosure.

*Probate Process   A process by which a will is proved to be valid or invalid.

*Pro Bono Work   Work or services performed free of charge.

*Process Server   A person authorized by law to serve process papers on defendants.

*Professional   Characterized by or conforming to the technical or ethical standards of a profession.

Professionalism   Professional status, methods, or standards.

*Real Estate Closing   The final steps in a transaction concerning the sale of real property.

Reasonable Fee   A legal fee that is clearly not excessive. Whether a fee is reasonable is determined by examining such factors as those set forth in the *Model Rules*.

Regulatory Body   An organization designed to oversee/regulate the conduct of the members of a particular group.

Reprimand   A form of discipline for attorneys. The sanction imposed on an attorney that officially denounces the actions of the attorney. A reprimand may be public or private. See also "censure."

Respondeat Superior   A legal doctrine whereby one party becomes responsible for the actions of another party.

*Retainer   A method of billing a client for legal services where the client agrees to pay a fixed fee and the attorney agrees to provide any legal service that he assesses the client may need.

*Runner   One who solicits business for an attorney from accident victims.

*Scrivener   One who copies; one who prepares written instruments or documents.

Secret   As used in the *Model Code*, any other information, beyond that protected by the attorney-client relationship, that is gained through the professional relationship and which the client has asked remain inviolate or which would be embarrassing or detrimental to the client if revealed.

Self-Policing   A form of control which is self-imposed by a profession to help ensure that professional standards are maintained and to ensure that the interests of the public are protected.

*Separation Agreement A contract between spouses who have separated or who are about to separate, concerning property, child custody, child support, alimony, etc.

Signatory Someone who can sign on a bank account.

Simultaneous Representation of Parties The act of engaging in representation of one person against another person also represented by the same lawyer.

Solicitation The act of approaching or enticing persons whom one seeks to have as clients, in a direct, in-person manner, in order to secure their representation.

Solo Practitioner A sole attorney who owns and manages a law firm.

Specialty Certification An additional certification that a Certified Legal Assistant (CLA) may undertake in one of several specialty areas. A certified legal assistant receives the designation "CLAS" when he or she has successfully completed the specialty certification examination.

State Disciplinary Agency The state agency that processes complaints against members of the legal profession concerning an attorney's conduct.

Status Call A court call in which parties in a legal matter report to the court what activities have been undertaken to further the litigation.

Statute of Limitation A statute that defines the time period within which a lawsuit or other legal action must be brought or be forever barred.

Substantially Related Closely connected. For purposes of applying the conflicts of interest rules, the test is the degree to which the lawyer was previously involved in the client's case.

Substantially Related Cases Cases that evolve from the same set of facts or have common elements or parties.

Supervising Attorney The attorney who supervises the legal assistant and other office staff.

Suspension [from the practice of law] A sanction imposed on an attorney that results in a revocation of an attorney's license to practice law for a certain period of time.

*Tickler System A reminder system that helps office staff remember important deadlines.

Trial Preparation Documents prepared for litigation including written memoranda and discovery.

Typing Services Businesses designed to assist the general public in completing complicated legal documents. Typing services help the lay public by typing information in blank spaces on pre-printed forms. See also "do-it-yourself services."

Unauthorized Practice of Law The practice of nonlawyers engaging in activities that only lawyers are licensed and sanctioned to perform.

Unethical Conduct Conduct that is proscribed by each state's code of legal ethics.

*Unprofessional Violating the code of a profession or occupation.

U.S. Supreme Court The highest court in the United States.

Vicarious Disqualification A legal consequence that results when disqualification of an attorney from representing a particular client has been transferred to the entire law firm such that all lawyers in that firm are disqualified from representing that client. See also "imputed disqualification."

Waiver An express or implied relinquishment of a legal right.

Waiving Conflicts of Interest Term used when a client is informed of the potential for conflicts to arise and, knowing of the potential conflict, consents to the representation. See also "cured by consent."

*Work Product Doctrine A legal doctrine that protects documents prepared in anticipation of litigation from being disclosed to the adversary.

*Writ of Habeas Corpus A petition (writ) designed to bring a party before the court in order to test the legality of his or her detention or imprisonment.

Zeal Enthusiastic or extremely committed devotion to a particular cause.

Zealous Representation The application of "zeal" to the representation of one's client.

---

*All terms marked with an asterisk are from: WILLIAM P. STATSKY, WEST'S LEGAL THESAURUS AND DICTIONARY, (1985). Reprinted by permission, West Publishing Company.

INDEX

A

Actual authority, 40, 41
Administrative agencies, 3
  representation, 78–79
    for federal agencies, 82–84
    for state agencies, 79–82
Administrative Procedure Act, 82
Adverse authority, 118
  revealing, 118–19
Adverse clients, simultaneous representation of, 174, 176
Adverse parties in *ex parte* communications, 120–21
Adverse positions, simultaneous representation of, 177–78
Affirmation of Professional Responsibility, 13
Agency
  law of, 40
    relationship of attorney and paralegal as relationship of, 41
Agent, 40
American Association for Paralegal Education (AAfPE), 10
American Bar Association (ABA), 5
  Annotated Model Rules of Professional Conduct of, 271
  Center for Professional Responsibility in, 31, 271
  Commission on Nonlawyer Practice in, 8, 100
  definition of paralegal by, 7–8
  development of educational programs for, 8–10
  Disciplinary Rules of the Model Code of, 33, 37
  Formal Ethics Opinions of, 35
  historical development of ethics codes for, 32–33
  Informal Ethics Opinions of, 35
  Model Code of Professional Responsibility of, 33–34, 111
    on confidentiality, 141
    on professional judgment of lawyer, 68
    on unauthorized law practice, 95
  Model Guidelines for the Utilization of Legal Assistant Services, 8, 42
    on advertising, 248
    on confidentiality, 129
    on delegation of tasks to nonlawyers, 64-65

    on disclosure of nonlawyer status, 94
    on prevention of conflicts of interest, 165
    on pro bono work, 239–40
    on responsibility of attorney for paralegal, 29
  Model Rules of Professional Conduct of, 33, 34
    on attorney supervision of nonlawyers, 302-3
    on confidentiality, 141–42
    on diligent representation, 112-13
    on fee splitting, 219, 220-21
    relationship between, and other conflict rules, 170
    on reporting unethical conduct, 270-71
    on supervision of nonlawyers, 36-38
    on unauthorized law practice, 95
    on zealous representation, 111
  recognition of paralegal by, 5–6, 8
  Special Committee on Availability of Legal Services in, 5–6
  Special Committee on Lay Assistants for Lawyers in, 6
  Special Committee on Legal Assistants in, 6–7
  Standing Committee on Legal Assistants in, 7
Apparent authority, 40
Attorney
  business enterprises between nonlawyers and, 221–23
  code of ethics for, 31-34
    application to paralegals, 36-39
    consequences resulting to, for violations of ethics rules, 45–49
  consequences of violating practice of law rules for, 95–96
  definition of, 2
  disqualification of, 48, 169–70
  relationship between paralegal and, 1, 41, 298-304
  relatives of, as conflict of interest, 188–91
  supervising, 281
  as witness, as conflict of interest, 191
Attorney advertising
  definition of, 250
  methods of, 251

  purpose of, 250–51
  restrictions on paralegal, 257–58
    advertisement, 260–61
    on business cards, 259–60
    handling attorney advertising, 258–59
    on law firm letterhead, 259
    solicitation, 261–62, 264
  rules regarding, 249–51
    historical restrictions on law office, 251–52
    relaxation of restrictions, 252–57
Attorney-client privilege
  comparison of, with rule of confidentiality, 144–45
  and confidentiality, 132–38
  definition of, 152
  exceptions to, 137–38
  waiving, 136–37
Attorney-client relationship, 70–71
Attorney malpractice, 48–49
Attorney misconduct, 270–74
  definition of, 272
  obligation of paralegal to report, 275–80
Authority, 40–41
  actual, 40, 41
  adverse, 118-19
  apparent, 40
  binding, 35
  implied, 40–41
  persuasive, 35
  ratified, 41

B

Bankruptcy petitions, 89–90
Bike, Rebecca, 122
Billable hours, 227
  padding, 227–29
Billing practices, 224–26
  awarding paralegal fees to prevailing party, 229–31
  padding billable hours, 227–29
  for paralegal time, 226–27
  practical application of *Missouri* v. *Jenkins* in, 231–32
Binding authority, 35
Blackstone, William, 66
Blackstone's Commentaries, 66
Blowing the whistle, 271–72
Bonuses, 223
Briefs, 118

Business cards, paralegal names on, 259–60
Business enterprises between attorneys and nonlawyers, 221–23
Business transactions, prohibited, and conflict of interest, 180–82

C
Candor
definition of, 116
duty of, 116–18
Canons of Professional Ethics, 32–33, 34
Cause of action, 114
Certification, 15–16
Certified Legal Assistant (CLA) program, 12
Certified Legal Assistant Specialist (CLAS), 16
Chicago Bar Association, 35
Chinese wall, 200–201
Civility, 290
Civilly liable, 48
Civil Rights Act, 229
Civil Rights Attorney's Fee Awards Act, 229–30
Clayton Act, 229
Client, 48
former, as conflict of interest, 193–95
gifts from, as conflict of interest, 184–85
initial interview of, 70–71
initial visit of, and confidentiality, 152–53
loans to, as conflict of interest, 186–87
professionalism in interacting with, 295–98
role of paralegal in advising, 71
simultaneous representation of adverse, 174, 176
zealous representation of, 111–16
Client information, exploitation of, as conflict of interest, 183–84
Client trust fund accounts, 234
interest on, 235–36
paralegal as signatories on, 235
Co-defendants, 173
Code of ethics
attorney, 31–34
paralegal, 43–44
Commingling funds, 232–34
application to paralegals, 234–35
consequences of, 236–39
definition of, 233
disputed funds, 235
interest on accounts, 235–36
Common law doctrine, 114

Communications
ex parte, 120–21, 123
privileged, 133, 135
Computer software, using to avoid conflict of interest, 204–5
Cone of silence, 201
Confidentiality, 129
application of, 147–48
comparison of rules of, with attorney-client privilege, 144–45
and conflict of interest, 168, 171
for corporate paralegal, 156–57
definition of, 132
ethical rules for, 140–44
exceptions to, 142–44
Model Code on, 141
Model Rules on, 141–42
general rule of, 130–31
attorney-client privilege in, 132–38
definition of, 131–32
purpose of, 131
work product doctrine in, 138–39
and law office practice, 152
daily operations in, 155–56
discovery matters in, 153–55
initial client visit in, 152–53
internal documents in, 155
trial testimony in, 156
rules for paralegals in, 146, 148–51
Conflict
definition of, 167
determining existence of, 170–71
Conflict of interest, 166–67, 172
attorney as witness as, 191–92
conflict checks on, 203–5
consequences of violating rules of, 169–71
definition of, 166
and imputed disqualification, 195–203
and paralegals, 167–69
prohibited transactions, 178, 180–82, 191
exploiting client information, 183–84
with former clients, 193–95
gifts from clients, 184–85
literary and media rights, 185–86
loans to a client, 186–87
relatives of attorney or paralegal, 188–91
relationship between other Model Rules and, 170
simultaneous representation, 172–74, 176–78
using computer software to avoid, 204–5
waived, 173

Conflict of interest rules
definition of, 166
foundation of, 168
relationships among, 199
Conflicts forms, 203–4
Consent, 182
Contempt of court, 87
Contingent fee, 225
Continuances, 76
Contract, 114
Co-plaintiffs, 173
Corporate paralegal, 156–57
Corporations, paralegal liability for actions of, 55, 57
Court
appearances at, 75–76
contempt of, 87
revealing nonlawyer status to, 119–20
Crime-fraud exception, 138
Criminal representation, 76–78
Cross-examine, 137

D
Defenses, 137
Deposition, 72–73
Diligence, 110
duty of candor, 116-18
revealing adverse authority, 118-19
revealing nonlawyer status to court, 119-20
ex parte communications, 120
adverse parties, 120-21
judges and jurors, 121, 123
rule of zealous representation, 111–12
on procrastination, 115–16
on reasonable diligence and promptness, 112–13
on statutes of limitation and filing date, 113–15
Diligent representation, 112–13
limits of, 117
Direct mail, advertising by, 255
Disbarment, 45–46
Disciplinary actions, for ethical violations, 45
Disciplinary rules, 271
Disciplinary Rules of the Model Code (DRs), 33, 37
Disclosure of nonlawyer status, 93–95
Discovery, 9–10, 72–73
and confidentiality, 153–55
Disputed funds, 235
Disqualification
of attorney, 48, 169–70
imputed, and conflicts of interest, 195–203
vicarious, 197
waiving, 199

Divorce kit, 86–87
Do-it-yourself services, 84–92
Duty to report, 270

E
Ebersohl, Lucy, 263
Educational programs, development
   of, for paralegals, 8–10
Engagement Agreement, 46–47
Errors and omissions insurance,
   52–53
Ethical, 132
Ethical considerations (ECs), 33–34
Ethical violations, disciplinary actions
   for, 45
Ethics, 30–31
   case law in, 35
   codes of
      for attorney, 31-34
         application to paralegals,
         36-42
      for paralegal, 43-44
   confidentiality in, 130–45
   definition of, 30
   development of code of
      by National Association for Legal
         Assistants (NALA), 12
      by National Federation of Parale-
         gal Associations (NFPA), 13
   disciplinary agencies in, 34–35
   ethics advisory opinions in, 35
   Guidelines for Utilization of Legal
      Assistants on, 42
   rules on confidentiality, 140–44
      exceptions, 142–44
      Model Code on, 141
      Model Rules on, 141–42
   violations of rules on, 45
      consequences resulting to attor-
         neys, 45–49
      consequences resulting to parale-
         gals, 49–53
      paralegal liability for freelance
         work, 53–54
      paralegal liability for actions of
         corporations, 55, 57
      paralegal liability for actions of
         law firm, 54–55
Ethics advisory opinions, 35
Ethics committee, 31
Evidentiary rules, 152
Exceptions to the privilege, 137
Ex parte communications, 120
   adverse parties in, 120–21
   judges and jurors in, 121, 123

F
Fact-sensitive analysis, 171
Facts & Findings, 12

Family law, 17
Federal Administrative Procedures
   Act, 3
Federal agencies, 82–84
   and immigration practice, 83–84
   and patent practice, 82–83
Federal Rules of Evidence, Proposed
   Federal Rule 503 of, 133
Fee
   contingent, 225
   fixed, 225
   hourly, 225–26
   reasonable, 224
Fee splitting, 219–21
   bonuses, 223
   business enterprises between attor-
      neys and nonlawyers, 221–23
   nonlawyer referrals, 221
   statute for, 229
Filing dates, 113–15
Financial issues
   billing practices, 224–32
   commingling funds, 232–39
   fee splitting, 219–24
   pro bono work, 239–40
Fixed fee, 225
Former client
   conflict of interest with, 193–95
   definition of, 194
FormFillers of Illinois, Inc., 101
Freelance paralegal, 14–15, 98–100
   liability for work, 53–54
   special concerns for, 279–80

G
General licensing, 16
Gifts from clients, as conflict of inter-
   est, 184–85

H
Help Abolish Legal Tyranny (HALT),
   17
Historical restrictions on law office,
   251–52
Hourly fee, 225–26

I
Illinois State Bar Association, 35
Immigration and Naturalization Ser-
   vices (INS), 83–84
Immigration practice, 83–84
Implied authority, 41
Implied waiver, 137
Imputed disqualification, 195–203
   avoiding through screening devices,
   199–201
Independent legal judgment, 68,
   170–71
Independent paralegal, 17

Informational materials, 139
Initial client interview, 70–71
Insurance, errors and omissions, 52–53
Interest on client fund accounts, 235–36
Internal documents, and confidential-
   ity, 155
Interrogatory, 72–73
Interest on lawyer's trust accounts
   (IOLTA), 236
Isgett, Merle, 206

J
Judd, Karen, 241
Judges, in *ex parte* communications,
   121
Jury, in *ex parte* communications,
   121–23

K
Kutak Commission, 222–23

L
Law clerk-apprentice, 2–3
Law office
   and confidentiality, 152
      daily operations, 155–56
      discovery matters, 153–55
      initial client visit, 152–53
      internal documents, 155
      trial testimony, 156
   letterhead of, paralegal on, 259
   paralegal liability for actions of,
      54–55
   practice of law in, 69–70
      advising the client, 71
      discovery, 72–73
      drafting papers and pleadings, 71
      initial client interview, 70–71
      trial preparation, 74
   professional conduct in, 294–95
Law rules, consequences of violating
   practice of, 95
   for the attorney, 95–96
   sanctions against the nonlawyer,
      97–98
Lawyers. *See* Attorney
Lawyer assistants. *See* Paralegals
Lawyers assistance programs, 279
Lay representation, 80–82
Legal advice, 134
Legal Assistant Management Associa-
   tion (LAMA), 9
Legal assistants. *See* Paralegals
Legal malpractice, 48–49
Legal profession, 1, 2
Legal secretary, 3–4
Legal services organizations, 4
Legal technician, 17
Letterhead, advertising on, 255

Licensing
general, 16
limited, 17-18
Limited licensure, 17–18
Literary rights, 185–86
Litigation paralegal, 116
Litigator, 116
Loans to client, as conflict of interest, 186-87
Local paralegal associations, 281–83
Loyalty to client, 168

M
Malpractice
attorney, 48–49
paralegal, 50–52
Martindale-Hubbell Law Directory, 258
Materially adverse, 194
Media rights, 185–86
Memorandum of law, 118
Mental impressions, 139
Metingham, John de, 66
Misappropriation, 234
Model Code of Professional Responsibility.
See under American Bar Association
Model Guidelines for the Utilization
of Legal Assistant Services. *See*
under American Bar Association
Model Rules of Professional Conduct.
See under American Bar Association
Moral, 30
Moral turpitude, 272
Multiple interests, simultaneous representation of, 176–77

N
National Association for Legal Assistants (NALA), 11-12, 43
ethics codes of, 12, 49
Model Standards and Guidelines
for Utilization of Legal Assistants, on disclosure of nonlawyer status, 94
national certification program of, 15–16
National Association of Legal Secretaries (NALS), 41
National Federation of Paralegal Associations (NFPA), 12-13, 43, 44
ethics codes of, 49
Model Code of Ethics and Professional Responsibility of, 13, 44
National paralegal organizations, 10–11
National Association of Legal Assistants (NALA), 11–12, 15-16, 43, 49, 94

National Federation of Paralegal
Associations (NFPA), 12–13, 43, 44
Negligence, 114
Nonlawyers. *See also* Paralegals
changing nature of, 98-100
disclosure of status, 93–95
to court, 119–20
referrals of, 221
sanctions against, for violating
practice of law rules, 97–98
Non-privileged information, 271

O
Overtime compensation, debate concerning, 228

P
Paralegals, 1. *See also* Nonlawyers
advertising restrictions on, 257–62, 264
in advising client, 71
application of attorney's codes of
ethics to, 36-39
applications of commingling funds, 234-35
awarding fees to prevailing party, 229–31
billing for time of, 226–27
code of ethics for, 43-44
confidentiality rules for, 146, 148-51
conflict of interest rules for, 167-69
consequences resulting to, for violation of ethics rule, 49–53
corporate, 156–57
court appearances by, 75–76
in criminal representation, 76–78
definition of, 2, 7–8
delegation of initial client interview
to, 70–71
development of role of, 4–13
discipline of, 49–50
in discovery, 72–73
in drafting papers and pleadings, 71–72
freelance, 14–15, 98–100
guidelines for, 29, 42
in handling attorney advertising, 258–59
issues affecting future of, 13–18
litigation, 116
local associations for, 281-83
obligations to report
attorney misconduct, 275–80
paralegal misconduct, 280–83
personal ethics for, 30–31
professionalism toward, 302–3
real estate services offered by, 92–93

regulation of, 15-18
relationship between attorney and, 1, 41, 298-304
relatives of, as conflict of interest, 188-91
responsibilities of, 29
roots of profession, 2-4
screening, 202-3
solicitation by, 261-62, 264
supervising, 281
in trial preparation, 74
typing services offered by, 84–92
liability of
for actions of corporations, 55, 57
for actions of law firm, 54–55
for freelance work, 53–54
malpractice by, 50–52
Paralegal Services of North Carolina, 262
Patent practice, 82–83
Penny, Alice, 18
Persuasive authority, 35
Pleading, 71
drafting, 71–72
Possessory rights, 291
Practice of law, 67–69
in law office, 69–70
advising client, 71
discovery, 72–73
drafting papers and pleadings, 71
initial client interview, 70–71
trial preparation, 74
unauthorized, 86
historical analysis of, 65–66
Preemption, 82
Pre-trial hearings, 118
Principal, 40
Privilege, 133
Privileged communications, 133, 135
Probate process, 91–92
Pro bono work, 239–40
Process server, 41
Procrastination, 115–16
Professional conduct, 290
achieving high standards of, 293
conduct in law office, 294–95
conduct toward paralegals, 302–3
interaction with clients, 295–98
relationships with attorneys, 298–302
definition of, 292
reasons for studying, 290–92
Professionalism, 290
dimensions of, 293
Professional liability policies, 114–15
Prohibited transactions, 180-82
and conflicts of interest, 178–80
Promptness, reasonable diligence and, 112–13

R
Ratified authority, 41
Real estate, 92–93
  closings in, 93
Reasonable fee, 224
Regulatory body, 100
Relatives, of attorney or paralegal, as
  conflict of interest, 188–91
Reprimand/censure, 45
Respondeat superior, doctrine of, 40–42
Retainer, 225
Roselle, Laurie, 282
Runners, 262

S
Santana, Esteban, 56
Screening
  avoiding imputed disqualification
    through use of, 199–201
  of paralegal, 202–3
Scrivener, 67
Secret, 141
Secretary, legal, 3–4
Self-policing, 34
Separation agreement, 137
Sexual harassment, 301
Shane, Janis, 158
Sharing fees. *See* Fee splitting
Sherman Anti-Trust Act, 229
Signatories, paralegal as, on client
  fund account, 235
Simultaneous representation
  of adverse clients, 174, 176
  of adverse positions, 177–78
  as conflict of interest, 172–74,
    176–78
  of multiple interests, 176–77
Sixth Amendment, and criminal rep-
  resentation, 76–77

Solicitation
  definition of, 250
  paralegal, 261–62, 264
  propriety of attorney, 255–56
Solo practitioner, 30
Special committee, 5. *See also under*
  American Bar Association
Specialty certification, 16
Standing committee, 5. *See also under*
  American Bar Association
State administrative agencies, 79–82
State disciplinary agencies, 34–35
State ethics opinions, 36
Status calls, 76
Statutes of limitations, 113–15
Substantially related cases, 170–71,
  194
Supervising attorney, 278, 281
Supervising paralegal, 281
Supremacy Clause of the U.S. Consti-
  tution, and preemption, 82, 83
Suspension, 45

T
Temporary restraining orders (TROs),
  5
Tickler system, 114
Trial preparation, 74
Trial testimony, and confidentiality,
  156
Typing services, 84–92

U
Unauthorized practice of law
  definition of, 66
  historical analysis of, 65–66
Unethical conduct, 270

U.S. Patent office, 83
United States Supreme Court, 13
  on patent practice, 82–83
Unprofessional conduct, 291, 301

V
Vicarious disqualification, 197

W
Waiver
  of attorney-client privilege, 136–37
  of conflict of interest, 173
  definition of, 136
  of disqualification, 199
  implied, 137
Wall, Jacqueline, 101
Warrick, Ingrid-Joy, 101
Widoff, Shelley, 304–5
Witness, attorney as, as conflict of interest, 191–92
Working Group on Nonlawyer Practice, 100
Work product doctrine, 138–39
  and confidentiality, 155
  definition of, 152
Writ of habeas corpus, 78

Z
Zeal, 111
Zealous representation, 168
  definition of, 111
  rule of, 111–16
    on procrastination, 115–16
    on reasonable diligence and
      promptness, 112–13
    on statutes of limitation and fil-
      ing date, 113–15

CPSIA information can be obtained
at www.ICGtesting.com
Printed in the USA
FFHW010610181218
49920467-54540FF

9 780314 041739